Ōoku

THE INNER CHAMBERS

by **Fumi Yoshinaga**

D1300759

VOL. 10

TABLE *of* CONTENTS

CHAPTER FORTY
· *page 5* ·

CHAPTER FORTY-ONE
· *page 52* ·

CHAPTER FORTY-TWO
· *page 119* ·

CHAPTER FORTY-THREE
· *page 185* ·

END NOTES
· *page 252* ·

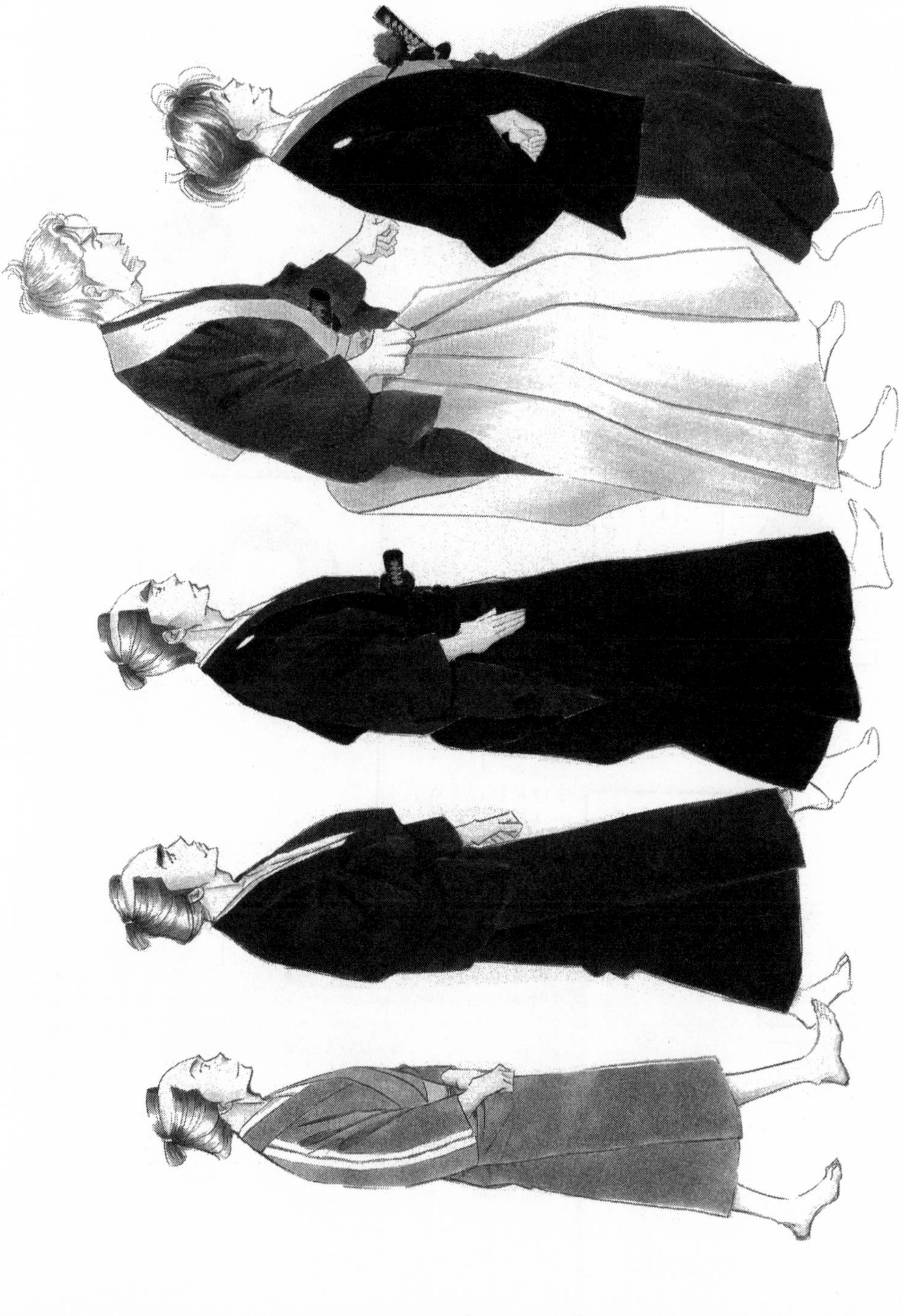

THE INNER CHAMBERS

CAST *of* CHARACTERS

From the birth of the "inverse Inner Chambers" to its zenith, and on to ending the Redface Pox?!

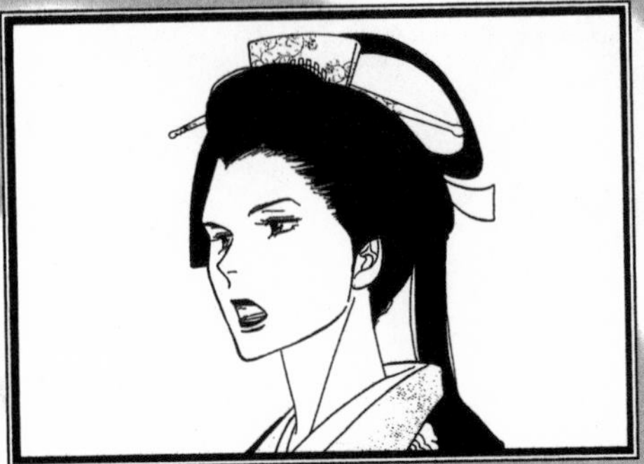

TOKUGAWA IEMITSU (III)

Impersonated her father, Iemitsu, at Lady Kasuga's urging after he died of the Redface Pox. Later became the first female shogun.

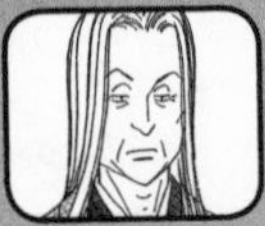

SENIOR CHAMBERLAIN

LADY KASUGA

↓

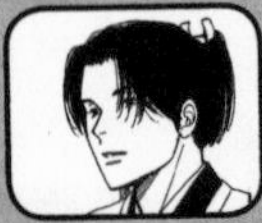

MADE-NOKOJI ARIKOTO

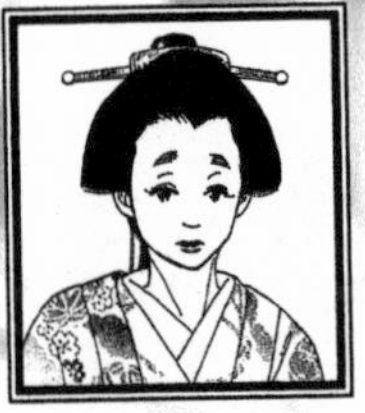

TOKUGAWA IETSUNA (IV)

Iemitsu's eldest daughter, known as "Lord Aye-do-so."

TOKUGAWA TSUNASHIGE

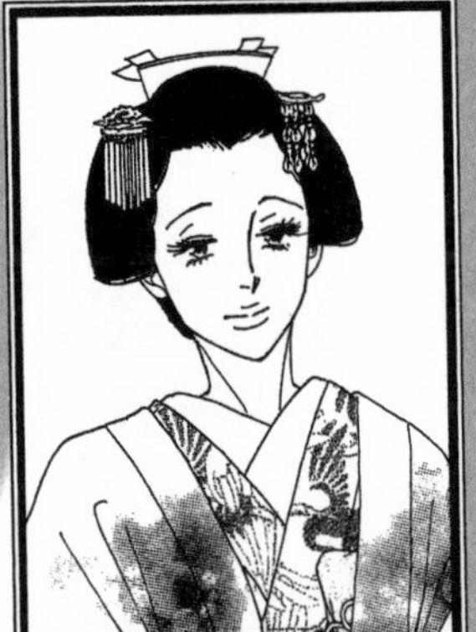

TOKU-GAWA TSUNA-YOSHI (V)

Iemitsu's third daughter. Endowed with both intellect and beauty, she did her best to rule wisely, but became known as "the Dog Shogun" due to unpopular policy mistakes later in her reign. The Ako Ronin incident led to official recognition of female inheritance of domain lord titles.

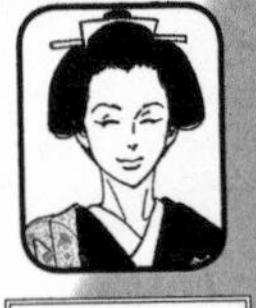

PRIVY COUNCILLOR

YANAGISAWA YOSHIYASU

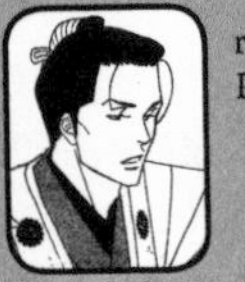

SENIOR CHAMBERLAIN

EMONNOSUKE

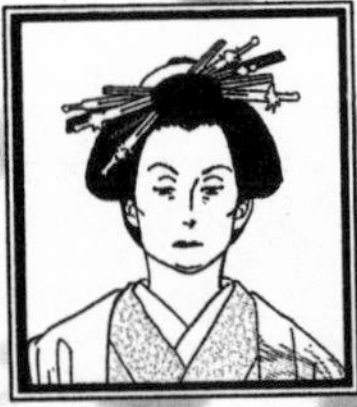

TOKUGAWA IENOBU (VI)

Iemitsu's granddaughter and Tsunayoshi's niece. A ruler of sterling character but poor health, who died soon after assuming office.

PRIVY COUNCILLOR

MANABE AKIFUSA

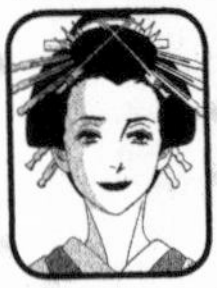

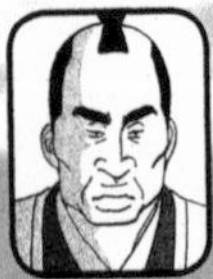

SENIOR CHAMBERLAIN

EJIMA

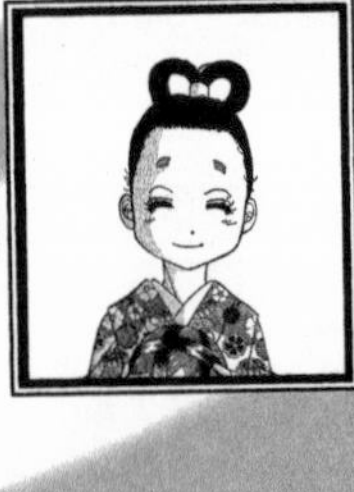

TOKUGAWA IETSUGU (VII)

Ienobu's fourth daughter, she died in childhood.

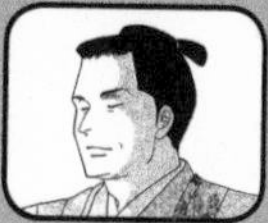

SENIOR CHAMBERLAIN

FUJINAMI

↓

SUGISHITA

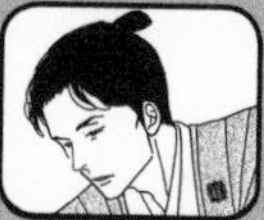

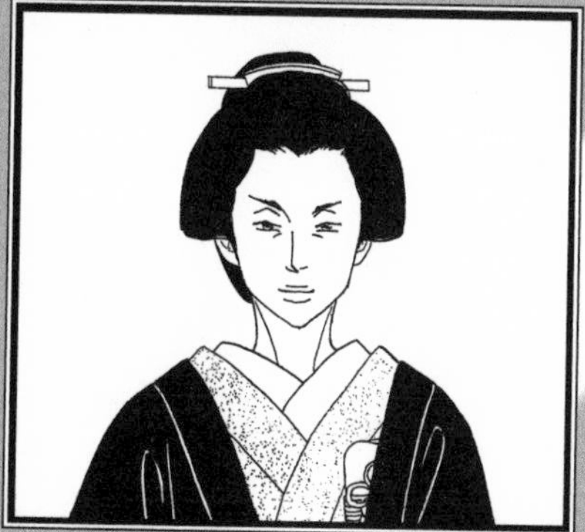

TOKUGAWA YOSHIMUNE (VIII)

Third daughter of Mitsusada, the second head of the Kii branch of the Tokugawa family. Acceded to domain lord and then, upon the death of Ietsugu, to shogun. Imposed and lived by a strict policy of austerity, dismissing large numbers of Inner Chamber courtiers and pursuing policies designed to increase income to the treasury.

PRIVY COUNCILLOR

KANO HISAMICHI

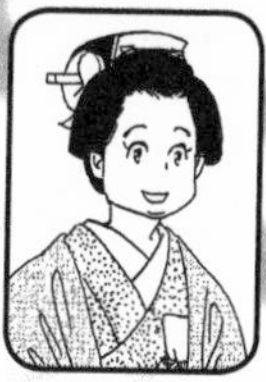

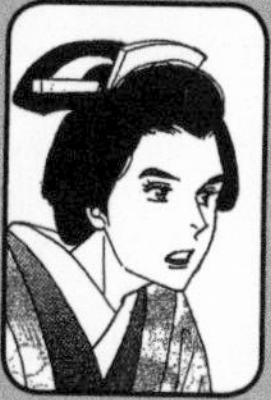

CHAMBERLAIN ↓ SENIOR COUNCILLOR

TANUMA OKITSUGU

Selected to serve Ieshige as Valet of the Chamber, promoted to Chamberlain, then Privy Councillor and later Senior Councillor by Ieharu, by whom she was charged with finding a cure for the Redface Pox.

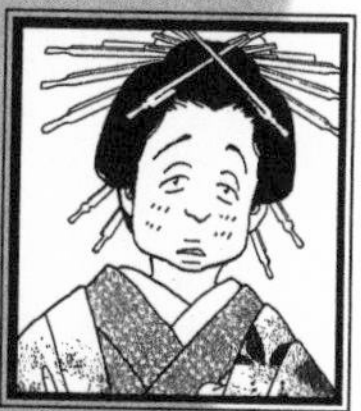

TOKUGAWA IESHIGE (IX)

Yoshimune's eldest daughter. Afflicted with a speech impediment, but not mentally disabled.

MUNETAKE (TAYASU BRANCH)

Yoshimune's second daughter

MATSUDAIRA SADANOBU

Munetake's daughter, she idolizes Yoshimune. Named lord of Shirakawa domain due to Harusada's plotting. Strongly opposes Tanuma Okitsugu.

MUNETADA (HITOTSUBASHI BRANCH)

Yoshimune's third daughter

TOKUGAWA HARUSADA

Munetada's daughter and head of the Hitotsubashi branch of the Tokugawa family. Secretly plotting something, making sure Okitsugu and Sadanobu remain ignorant of her aims…

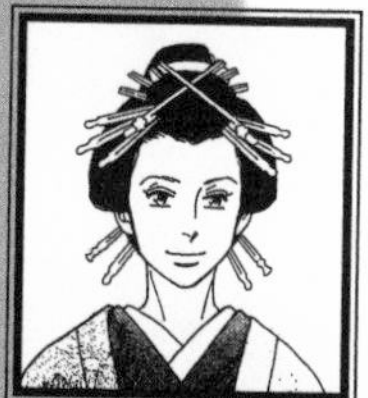

TOKUGAWA IEHARU (X)

Yoshimune's granddaughter. Intelligent and obedient to her mother and grandmother.

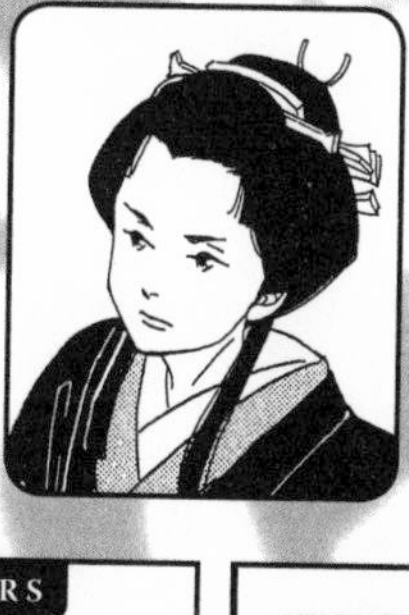

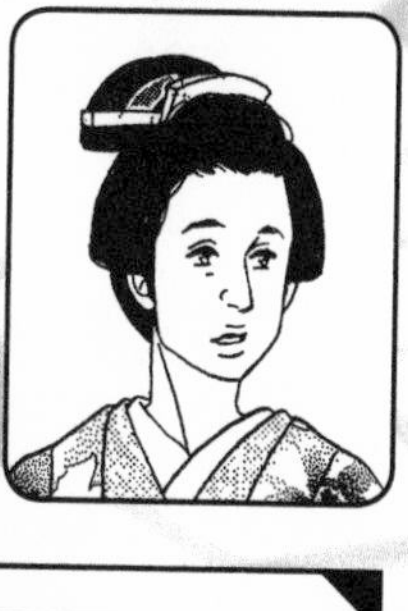

INNER CHAMBER CHARACTERS

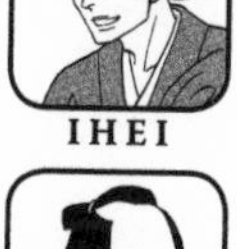

IHEI

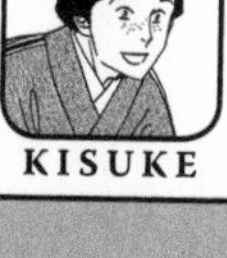

KISUKE

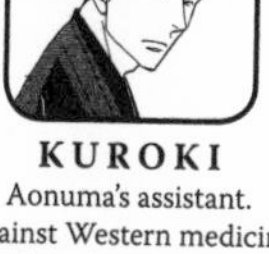

KUROKI

Aonuma's assistant. Against Western medicine at first, due to his own father's quackery, but…

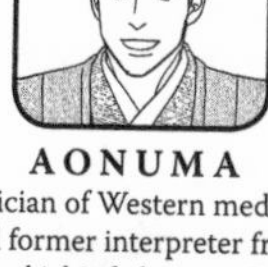

AONUMA

Physician of Western medicine and former interpreter from Nagasaki, his father was Dutch. Called to Inner Chambers to serve as a scribe and lecturer.

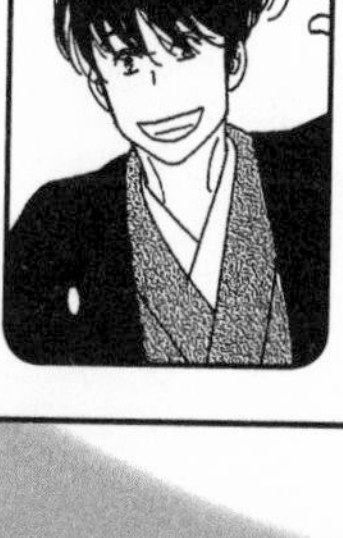

HIRAGA GENNAI

Cross-dressing genius and Renaissance (wo)man. A deep admirer of Okitsugu, and devoted to finding a cure for the Redface Pox.

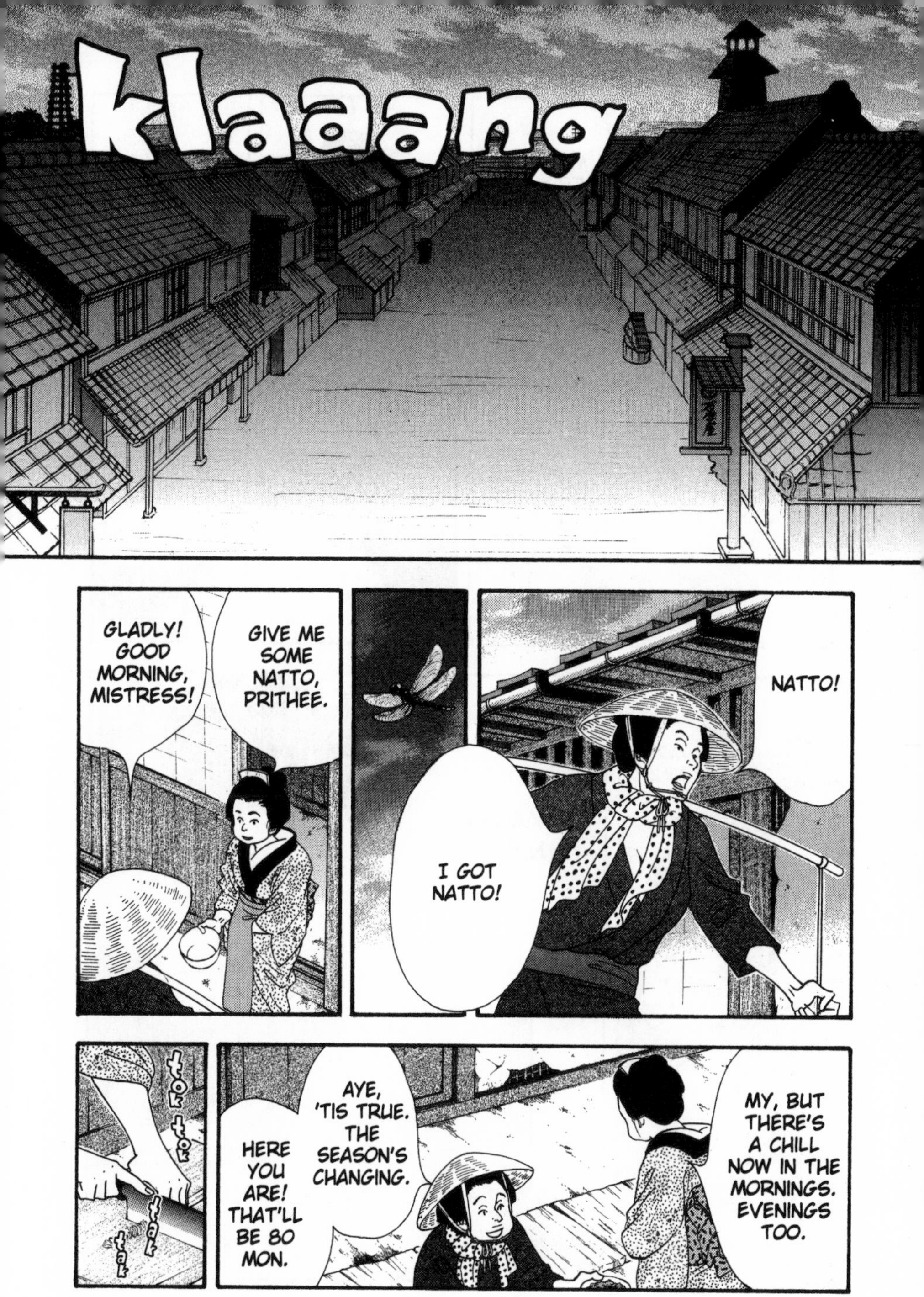
klaaang
NATTO!
I GOT NATTO!
GIVE ME SOME NATTO, PRITHEE.
GLADLY! GOOD MORNING, MISTRESS!
MY, BUT THERE'S A CHILL NOW IN THE MORNINGS. EVENINGS TOO.
AYE, 'TIS TRUE. THE SEASON'S CHANGING.
HERE YOU ARE! THAT'LL BE 80 MON.
tok tok
ttak ttak

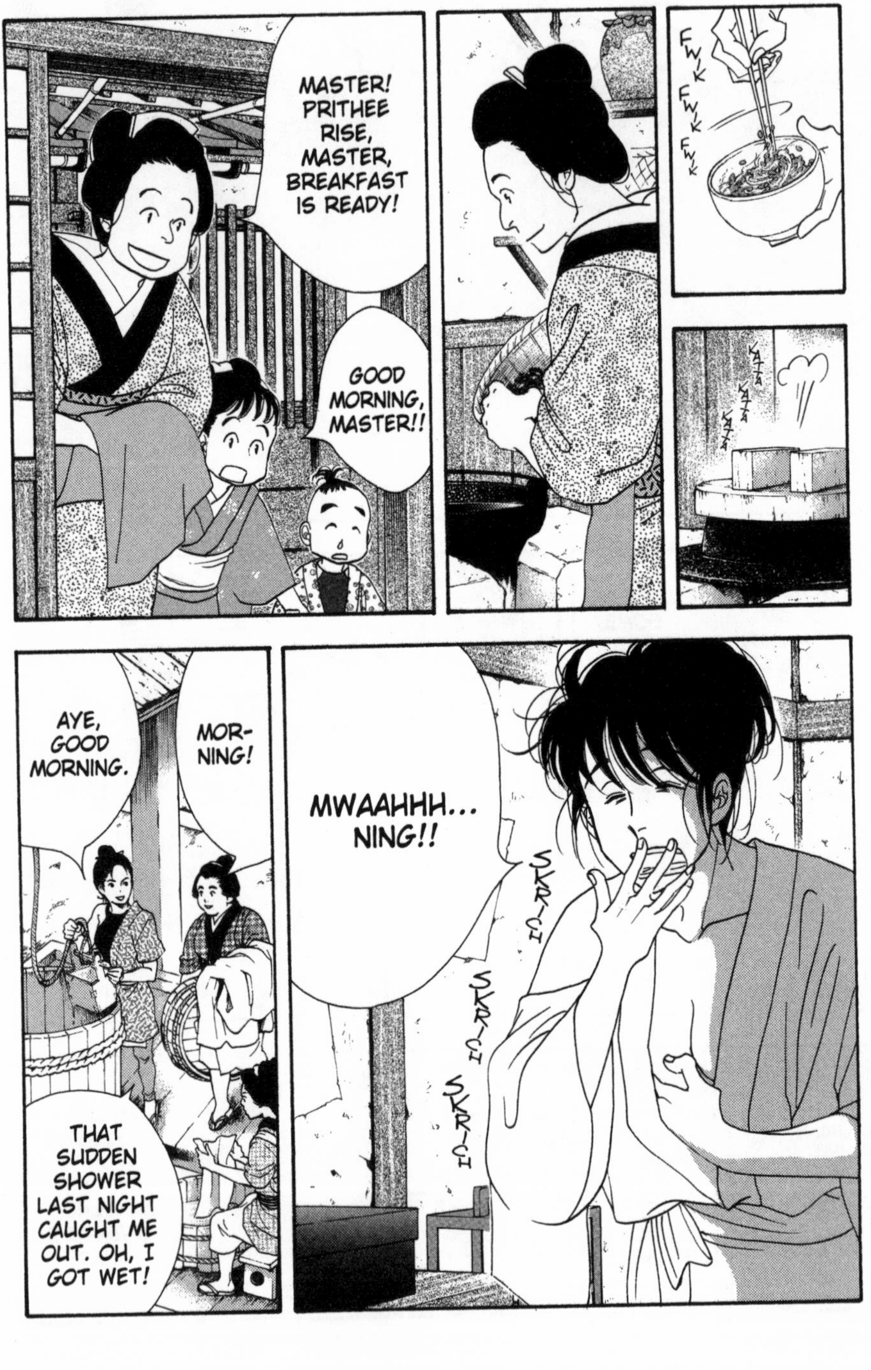
FWIK
FWIK
FWIK
KATA
KATA
KATA
MASTER! PRITHEE RISE, MASTER, BREAKFAST IS READY!
GOOD MORNING, MASTER!!
MWAAHHH... NING!!
SKRICH
SKRICH
SKRICH
MOR-NING!
AYE, GOOD MORNING.
THAT SUDDEN SHOWER LAST NIGHT CAUGHT ME OUT. OH, I GOT WET!

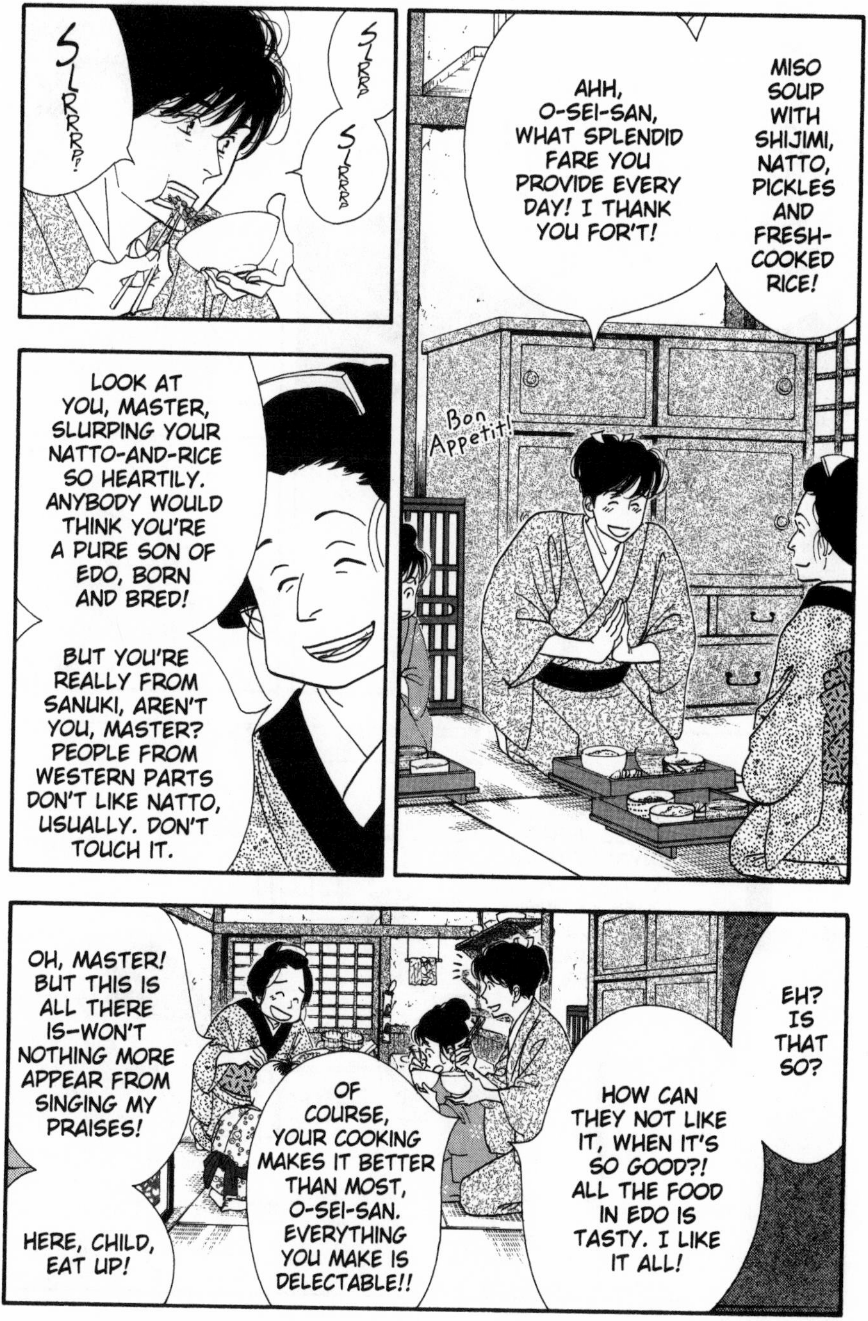

MISO SOUP WITH SHIJIMI, NATTO, PICKLES AND FRESH-COOKED RICE!
AHH, O-SEI-SAN, WHAT SPLENDID FARE YOU PROVIDE EVERY DAY! I THANK YOU FOR'T!
Bon Appetit!
SLRRP SLRRRP
SLRRRP!
LOOK AT YOU, MASTER, SLURPING YOUR NATTO-AND-RICE SO HEARTILY. ANYBODY WOULD THINK YOU'RE A PURE SON OF EDO, BORN AND BRED!
BUT YOU'RE REALLY FROM SANUKI, AREN'T YOU, MASTER? PEOPLE FROM WESTERN PARTS DON'T LIKE NATTO, USUALLY. DON'T TOUCH IT.
EH? IS THAT SO?
HOW CAN THEY NOT LIKE IT, WHEN IT'S SO GOOD?! ALL THE FOOD IN EDO IS TASTY. I LIKE IT ALL!
OF COURSE, YOUR COOKING MAKES IT BETTER THAN MOST, O-SEI-SAN. EVERYTHING YOU MAKE IS DELECTABLE!!
OH, MASTER! BUT THIS IS ALL THERE IS—WON'T NOTHING MORE APPEAR FROM SINGING MY PRAISES!
HERE, CHILD, EAT UP!

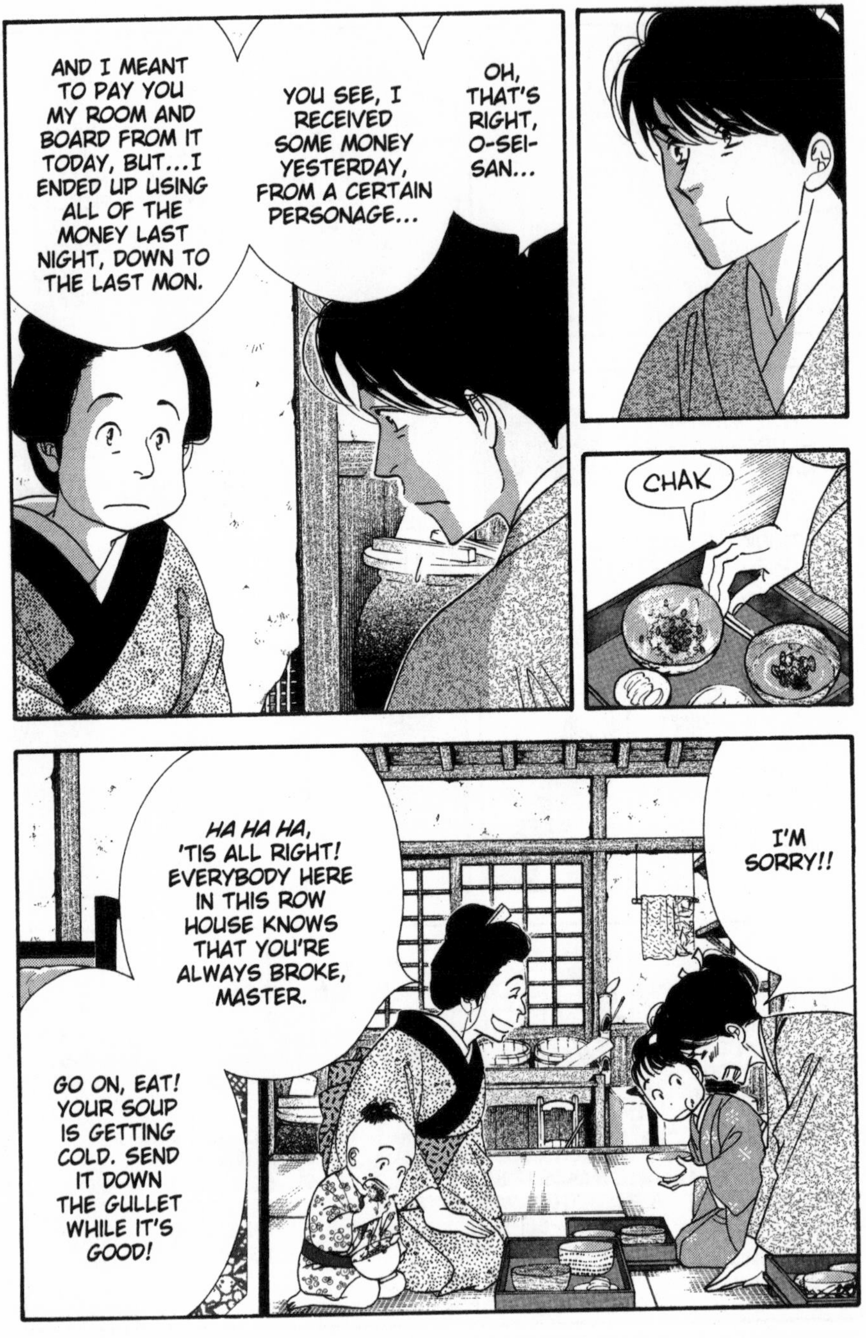
CHAK
OH, THAT'S RIGHT, O-SEI-SAN...
YOU SEE, I RECEIVED SOME MONEY YESTERDAY, FROM A CERTAIN PERSONAGE...
AND I MEANT TO PAY YOU MY ROOM AND BOARD FROM IT TODAY, BUT...I ENDED UP USING ALL OF THE MONEY LAST NIGHT, DOWN TO THE LAST MON.
I'M SORRY!!
HA HA HA, 'TIS ALL RIGHT! EVERYBODY HERE IN THIS ROW HOUSE KNOWS THAT YOU'RE ALWAYS BROKE, MASTER.
GO ON, EAT! YOUR SOUP IS GETTING COLD. SEND IT DOWN THE GULLET WHILE IT'S GOOD!

O-YUUUKIII-CHAN!
Exercise Book
OH, O-TAE-CHAN! WAIT!
KYAK KYAK KYAK KYAK KYAK
MAM, MAFTER, I'M OFF TO FKOOL!!
AYE, OFF THOU GOEST THEN! TAKE HEED!
FARE THEE WELL, O-YUKI-CHAN!
SO SHE'S ALREADY MADE A FRIEND AT SCHOOL! I'M GLAD TO SEE SHE GOES WILLINGLY.
AYE, 'TIS A GOOD SCHOOL, THE ONE SHE GOES TO NOW. THE TEACHER IS KINDLY, AND ABOVE ALL, IT'S SUCH A HELP TO ME.
THEY TAKE O-YUKI DURING THE DAY WHILE I WORK, AND TEACH HER TO READ AND WRITE AND USE THE ABACUS TO BOOT! THOSE SKILLS WILL STAND HER IN GOOD STEAD, NO MATTER WHAT TRADE SHE TAKES UP LATER.
NGAAA
HERE, MIYOKICHI! STAY STILL, WILT THOU?!

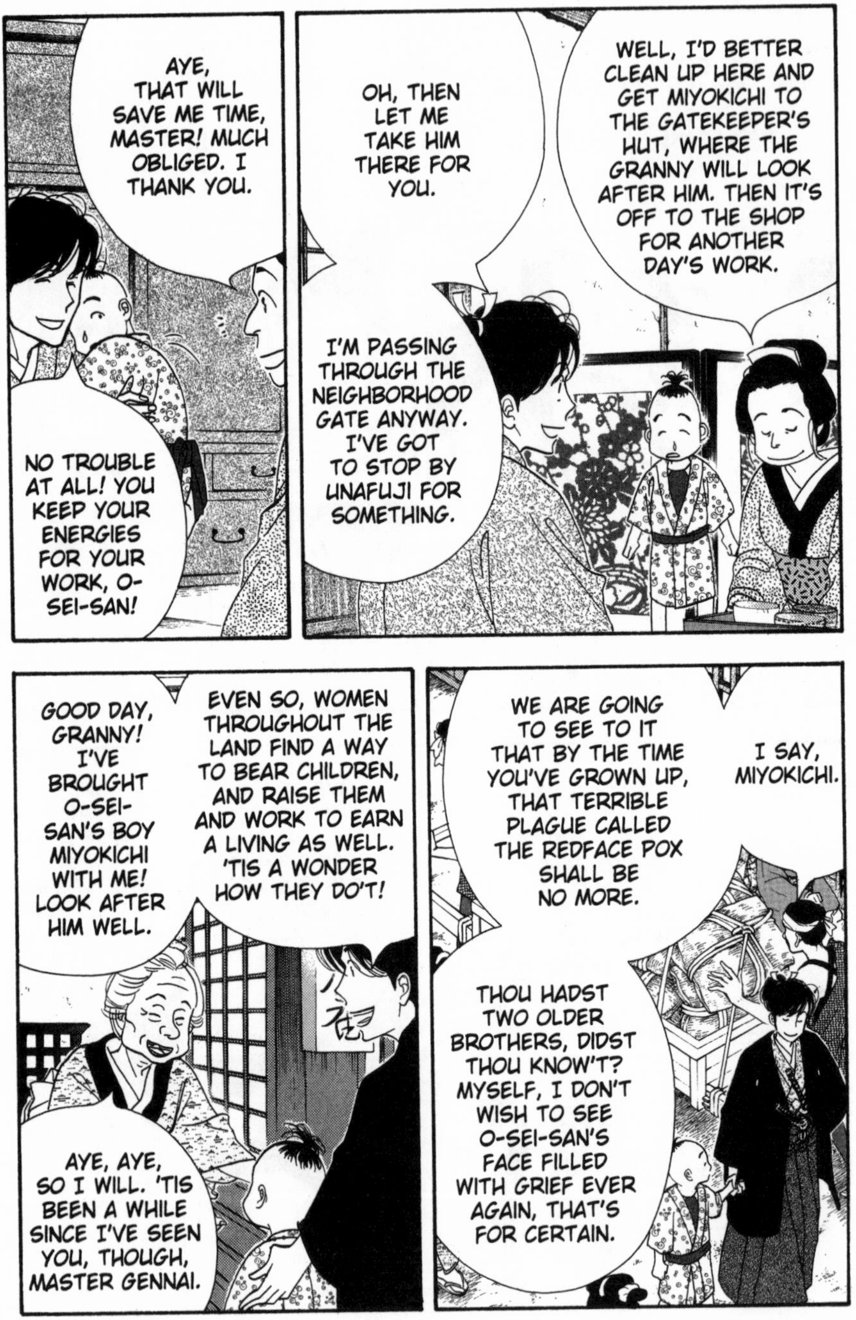
WELL, I'D BETTER CLEAN UP HERE AND GET MIYOKICHI TO THE GATEKEEPER'S HUT, WHERE THE GRANNY WILL LOOK AFTER HIM. THEN IT'S OFF TO THE SHOP FOR ANOTHER DAY'S WORK.
OH, THEN LET ME TAKE HIM THERE FOR YOU.
I'M PASSING THROUGH THE NEIGHBORHOOD GATE ANYWAY. I'VE GOT TO STOP BY UNAFUJI FOR SOMETHING.
AYE, THAT WILL SAVE ME TIME, MASTER! MUCH OBLIGED. I THANK YOU.
NO TROUBLE AT ALL! YOU KEEP YOUR ENERGIES FOR YOUR WORK, O-SEI-SAN!
I SAY, MIYOKICHI.
WE ARE GOING TO SEE TO IT THAT BY THE TIME YOU'VE GROWN UP, THAT TERRIBLE PLAGUE CALLED THE REDFACE POX SHALL BE NO MORE.
THOU HADST TWO OLDER BROTHERS, DIDST THOU KNOW'T? MYSELF, I DON'T WISH TO SEE O-SEI-SAN'S FACE FILLED WITH GRIEF EVER AGAIN, THAT'S FOR CERTAIN.
EVEN SO, WOMEN THROUGHOUT THE LAND FIND A WAY TO BEAR CHILDREN, AND RAISE THEM AND WORK TO EARN A LIVING AS WELL. 'TIS A WONDER HOW THEY DO'T!
GOOD DAY, GRANNY! I'VE BROUGHT O-SEI-SAN'S BOY MIYOKICHI WITH ME! LOOK AFTER HIM WELL.
AYE, AYE, SO I WILL. 'TIS BEEN A WHILE SINCE I'VE SEEN YOU, THOUGH, MASTER GENNAI.

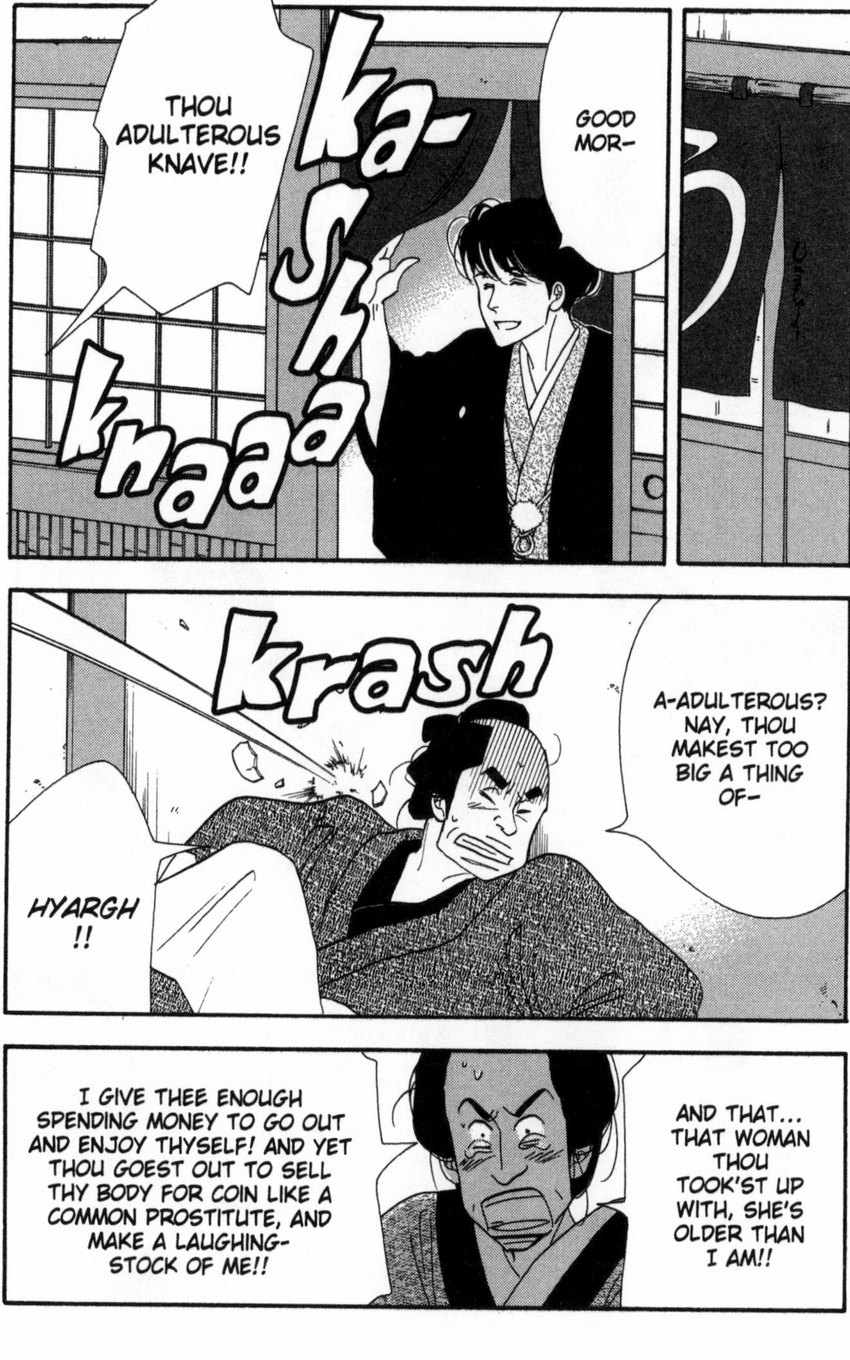
GOOD MOR-
ka-shha
THOU ADULTEROUS KNAVE!!
knaaa
krash
A-ADULTEROUS? NAY, THOU MAKEST TOO BIG A THING OF-
HYARGH !!
AND THAT... THAT WOMAN THOU TOOK'ST UP WITH, SHE'S OLDER THAN I AM!!
I GIVE THEE ENOUGH SPENDING MONEY TO GO OUT AND ENJOY THYSELF! AND YET THOU GOEST OUT TO SELL THY BODY FOR COIN LIKE A COMMON PROSTITUTE, AND MAKE A LAUGHING-STOCK OF ME!!

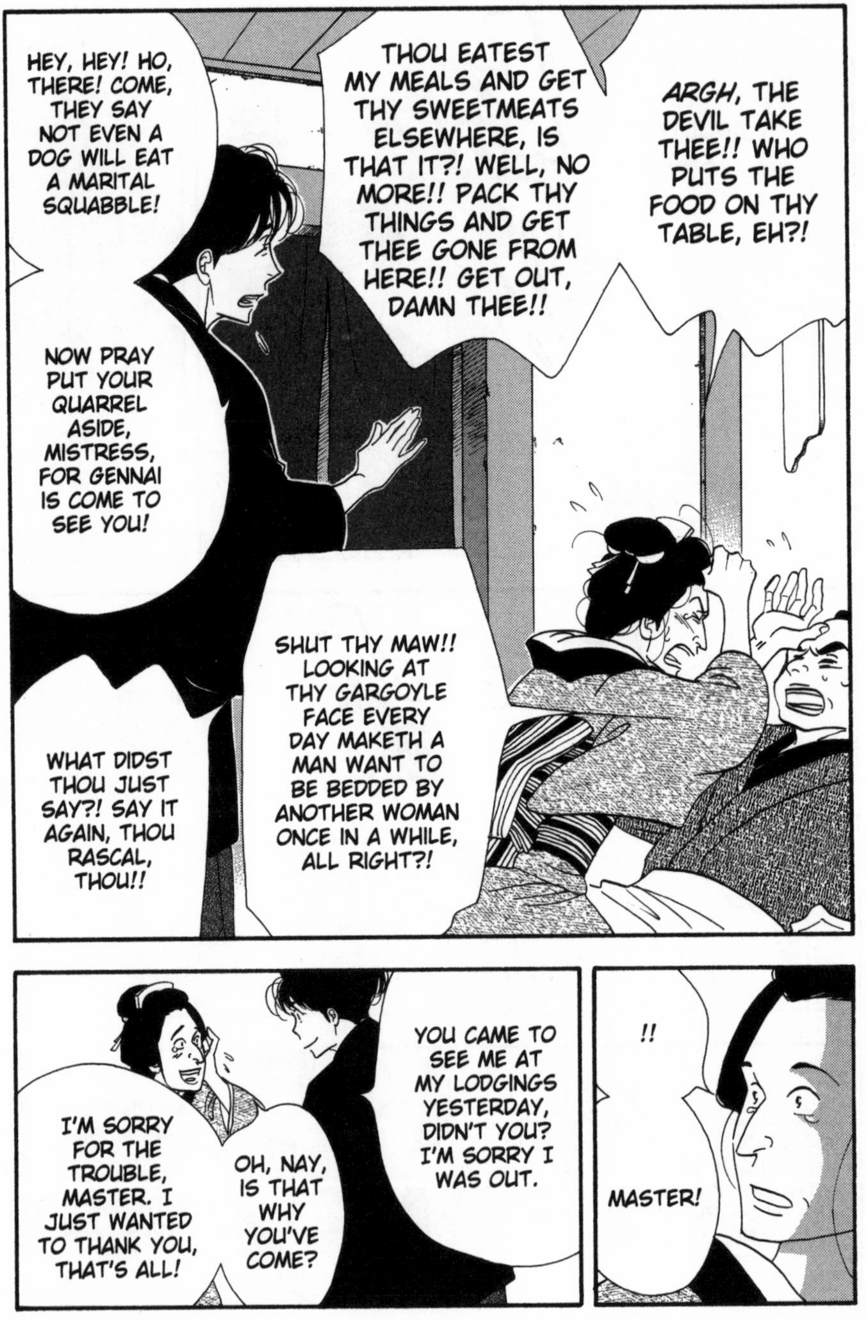
ARGH, THE DEVIL TAKE THEE!! WHO PUTS THE FOOD ON THY TABLE, EH?!
THOU EATEST MY MEALS AND GET THY SWEETMEATS ELSEWHERE, IS THAT IT?! WELL, NO MORE!! PACK THY THINGS AND GET THEE GONE FROM HERE!! GET OUT, DAMN THEE!!
HEY, HEY! HO, THERE! COME, THEY SAY NOT EVEN A DOG WILL EAT A MARITAL SQUABBLE!
SHUT THY MAW!! LOOKING AT THY GARGOYLE FACE EVERY DAY MAKETH A MAN WANT TO BE BEDDED BY ANOTHER WOMAN ONCE IN A WHILE, ALL RIGHT?!
NOW PRAY PUT YOUR QUARREL ASIDE, MISTRESS, FOR GENNAI IS COME TO SEE YOU!
WHAT DIDST THOU JUST SAY?! SAY IT AGAIN, THOU RASCAL, THOU!!
!!
MASTER!
YOU CAME TO SEE ME AT MY LODGINGS YESTERDAY, DIDN'T YOU? I'M SORRY I WAS OUT.
OH, NAY, IS THAT WHY YOU'VE COME?
I'M SORRY FOR THE TROUBLE, MASTER. I JUST WANTED TO THANK YOU, THAT'S ALL!

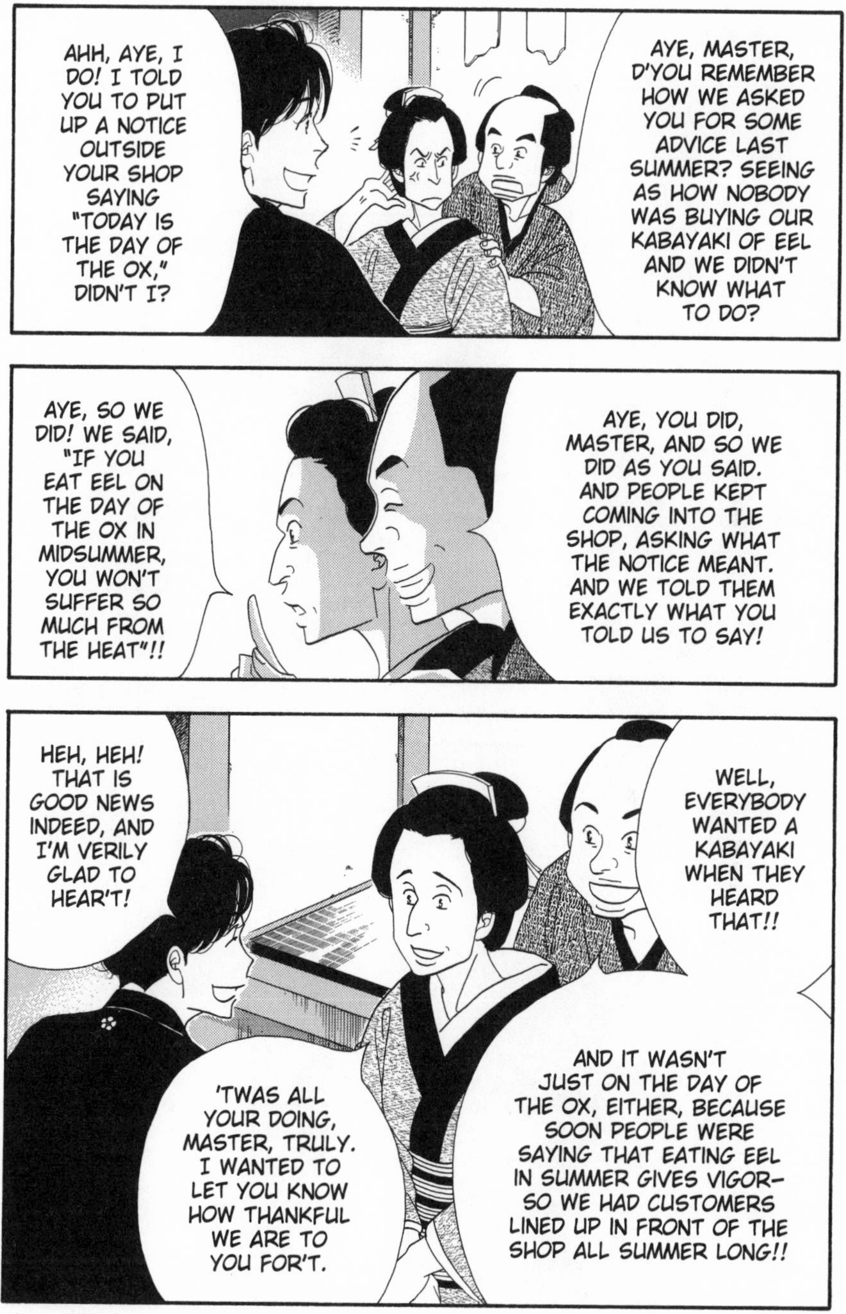
AYE, MASTER, D'YOU REMEMBER HOW WE ASKED YOU FOR SOME ADVICE LAST SUMMER? SEEING AS HOW NOBODY WAS BUYING OUR KABAYAKI OF EEL AND WE DIDN'T KNOW WHAT TO DO?
AHH, AYE, I DO! I TOLD YOU TO PUT UP A NOTICE OUTSIDE YOUR SHOP SAYING "TODAY IS THE DAY OF THE OX," DIDN'T I?
AYE, YOU DID, MASTER, AND SO WE DID AS YOU SAID. AND PEOPLE KEPT COMING INTO THE SHOP, ASKING WHAT THE NOTICE MEANT. AND WE TOLD THEM EXACTLY WHAT YOU TOLD US TO SAY!
AYE, SO WE DID! WE SAID, "IF YOU EAT EEL ON THE DAY OF THE OX IN MIDSUMMER, YOU WON'T SUFFER SO MUCH FROM THE HEAT"!!
WELL, EVERYBODY WANTED A KABAYAKI WHEN THEY HEARD THAT!!
HEH, HEH! THAT IS GOOD NEWS INDEED, AND I'M VERILY GLAD TO HEAR'T!
AND IT WASN'T JUST ON THE DAY OF THE OX, EITHER, BECAUSE SOON PEOPLE WERE SAYING THAT EATING EEL IN SUMMER GIVES VIGOR-SO WE HAD CUSTOMERS LINED UP IN FRONT OF THE SHOP ALL SUMMER LONG!!
'TWAS ALL YOUR DOING, MASTER, TRULY. I WANTED TO LET YOU KNOW HOW THANKFUL WE ARE TO YOU FOR'T.

TISN'T MUCH, BUT PRAY TAKE IT AS A TOKEN OF OUR GRATITUDE...
NAAAYYY!! THIS KIND OF GRATITUDE I DON'T ACCEPT!! THERE'S SOMETHING ELSE I'D LIKE INSTEAD, THOUGH!!
MMM, GENNAI-SAN, WHAT A GOOD SMELL THAT IS!
I HAD SOME OVER THE SUMMER. THEY SAY KABAYAKI OF EEL IS GOOD FOR THE HEALTH IN THE HEAT!
AYE, I'VE HEARD THAT TOO. WELL, SUMMER IS OVER NOW, BUT EEL IS TASTY ANYTIME! I'M TAKING THIS AS A GIFT.
WHERE?
OH, JUST OVER TO EDO CASTLE!

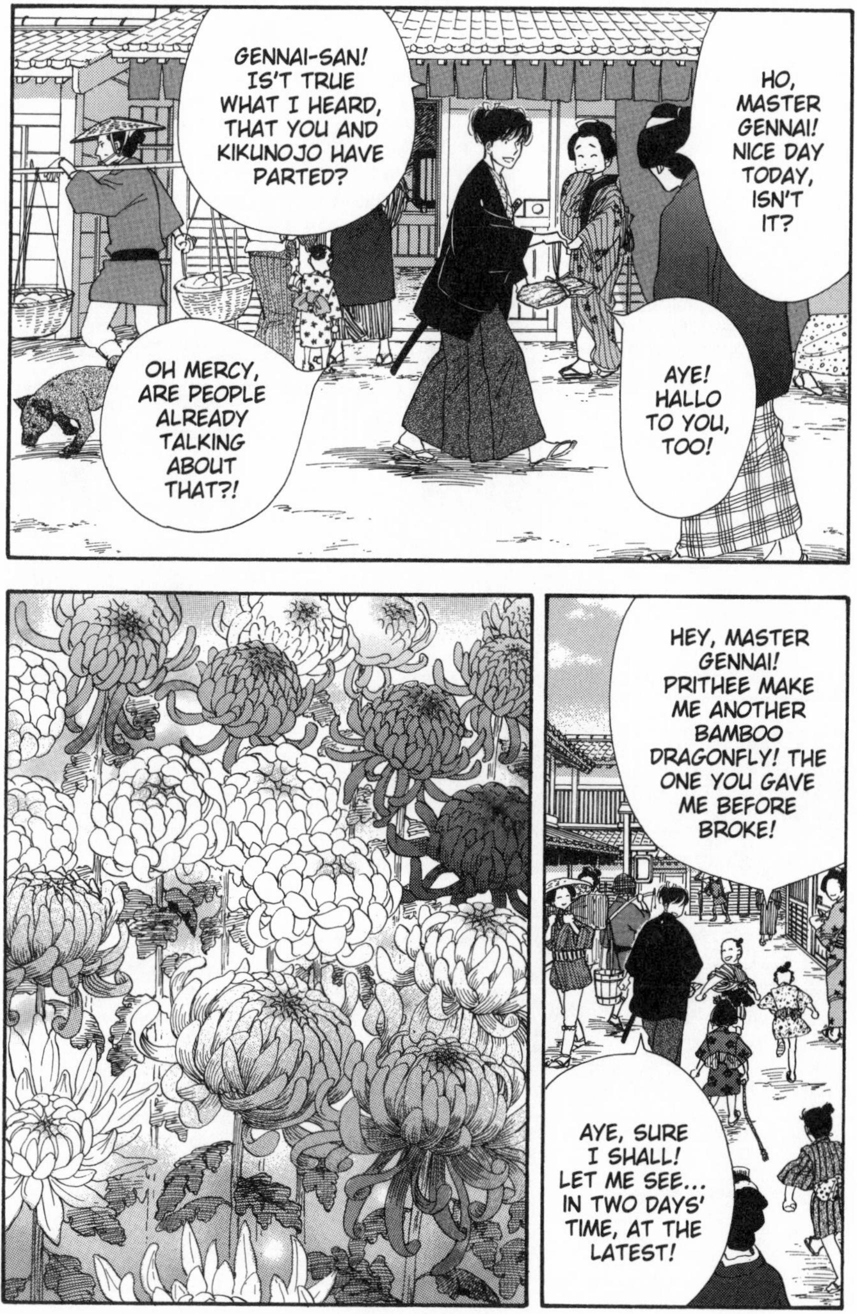
HO, MASTER GENNAI! NICE DAY TODAY, ISN'T IT?
GENNAI-SAN! IS'T TRUE WHAT I HEARD, THAT YOU AND KIKUNOJO HAVE PARTED?
AYE! HALLO TO YOU, TOO!
OH MERCY, ARE PEOPLE ALREADY TALKING ABOUT THAT?!
HEY, MASTER GENNAI! PRITHEE MAKE ME ANOTHER BAMBOO DRAGONFLY! THE ONE YOU GAVE ME BEFORE BROKE!
AYE, SURE I SHALL! LET ME SEE... IN TWO DAYS' TIME, AT THE LATEST!

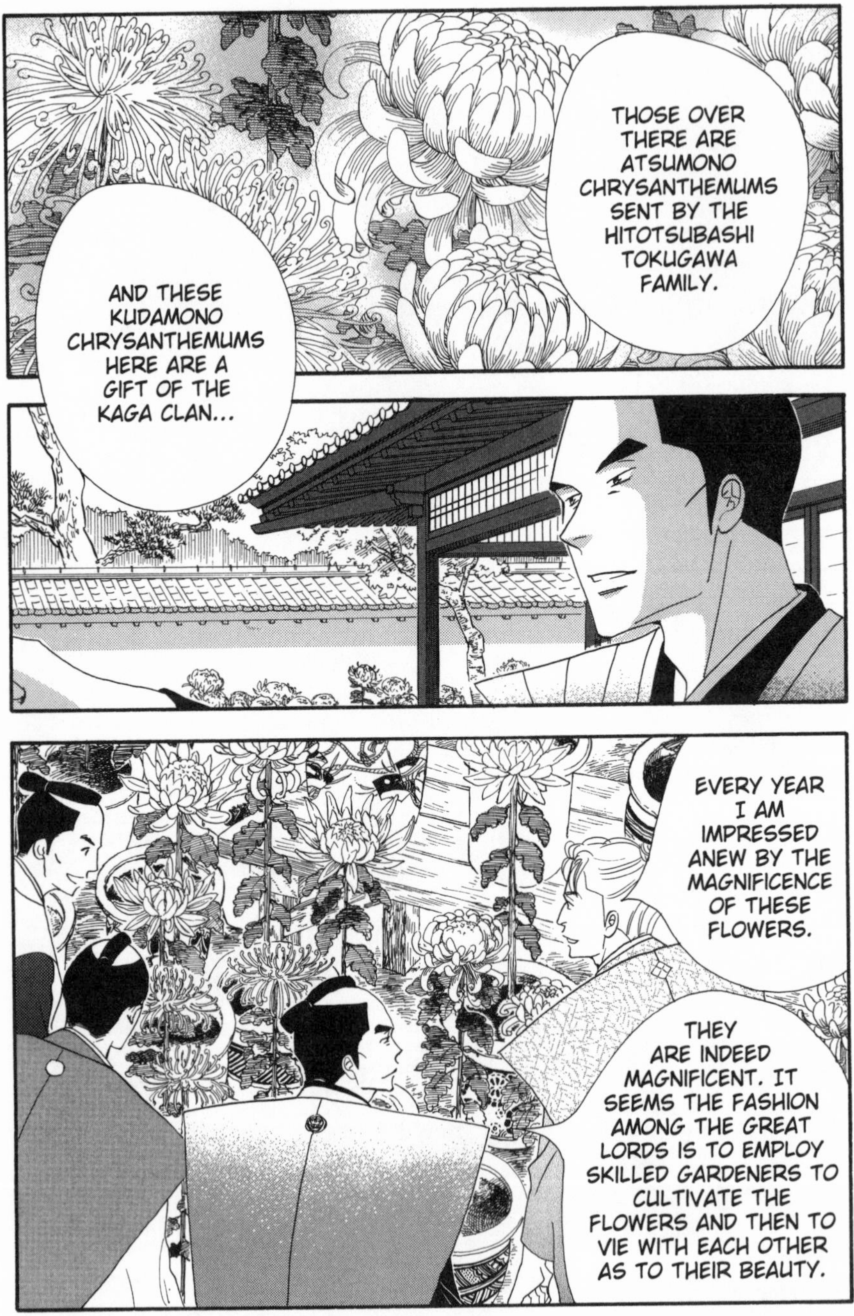
THOSE OVER THERE ARE ATSUMONO CHRYSANTHEMUMS SENT BY THE HITOTSUBASHI TOKUGAWA FAMILY.
AND THESE KUDAMONO CHRYSANTHEMUMS HERE ARE A GIFT OF THE KAGA CLAN...
EVERY YEAR I AM IMPRESSED ANEW BY THE MAGNIFICENCE OF THESE FLOWERS.
THEY ARE INDEED MAGNIFICENT. IT SEEMS THE FASHION AMONG THE GREAT LORDS IS TO EMPLOY SKILLED GARDENERS TO CULTIVATE THE FLOWERS AND THEN TO VIE WITH EACH OTHER AS TO THEIR BEAUTY.

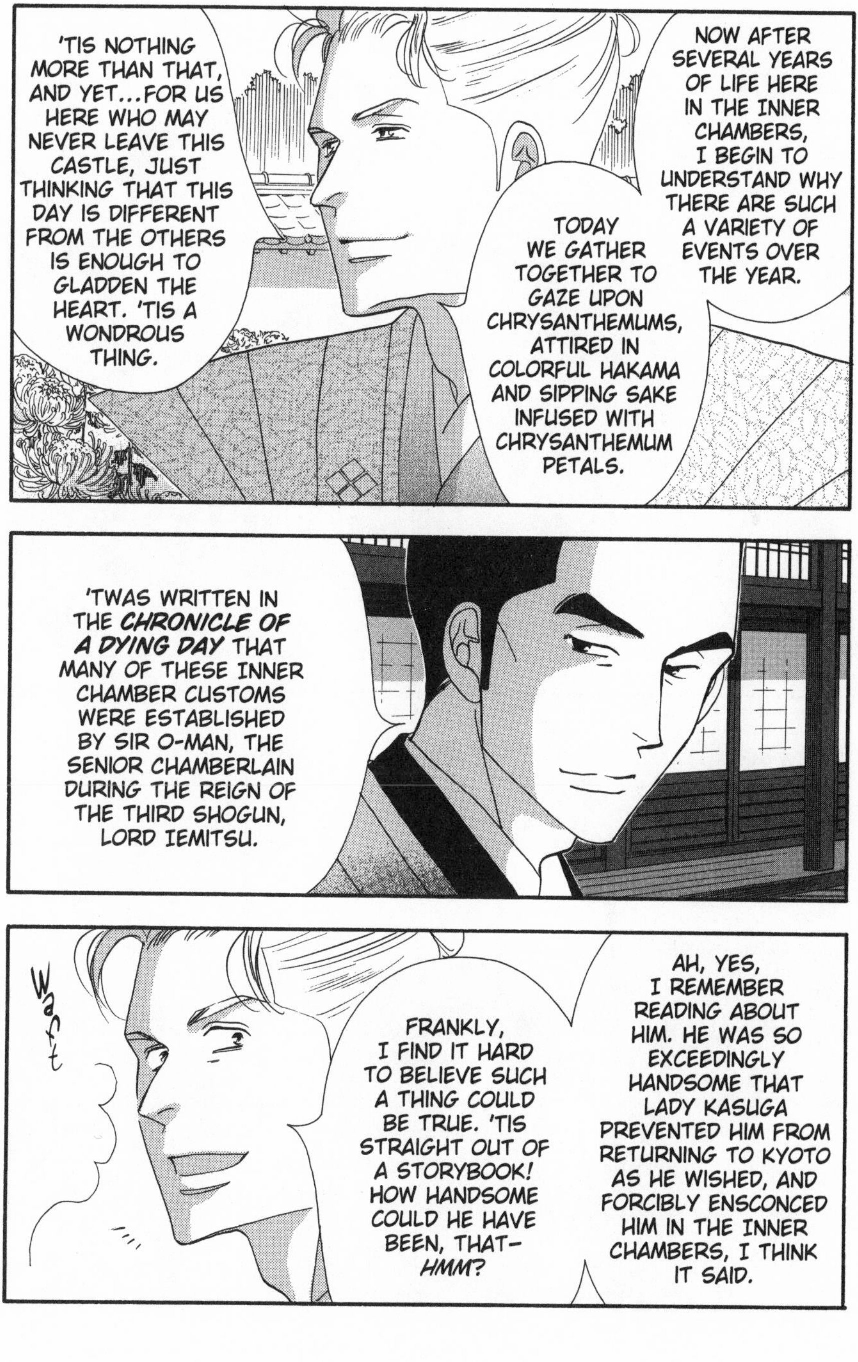
NOW AFTER SEVERAL YEARS OF LIFE HERE IN THE INNER CHAMBERS, I BEGIN TO UNDERSTAND WHY THERE ARE SUCH A VARIETY OF EVENTS OVER THE YEAR.
TODAY WE GATHER TOGETHER TO GAZE UPON CHRYSANTHEMUMS, ATTIRED IN COLORFUL HAKAMA AND SIPPING SAKE INFUSED WITH CHRYSANTHEMUM PETALS.
'TIS NOTHING MORE THAN THAT, AND YET...FOR US HERE WHO MAY NEVER LEAVE THIS CASTLE, JUST THINKING THAT THIS DAY IS DIFFERENT FROM THE OTHERS IS ENOUGH TO GLADDEN THE HEART. 'TIS A WONDROUS THING.
'TWAS WRITTEN IN THE *CHRONICLE OF A DYING DAY* THAT MANY OF THESE INNER CHAMBER CUSTOMS WERE ESTABLISHED BY SIR O-MAN, THE SENIOR CHAMBERLAIN DURING THE REIGN OF THE THIRD SHOGUN, LORD IEMITSU.
AH, YES, I REMEMBER READING ABOUT HIM. HE WAS SO EXCEEDINGLY HANDSOME THAT LADY KASUGA PREVENTED HIM FROM RETURNING TO KYOTO AS HE WISHED, AND FORCIBLY ENSCONCED HIM IN THE INNER CHAMBERS, I THINK IT SAID.
FRANKLY, I FIND IT HARD TO BELIEVE SUCH A THING COULD BE TRUE. 'TIS STRAIGHT OUT OF A STORYBOOK! HOW HANDSOME COULD HE HAVE BEEN, THAT– *HMM*?
Waft

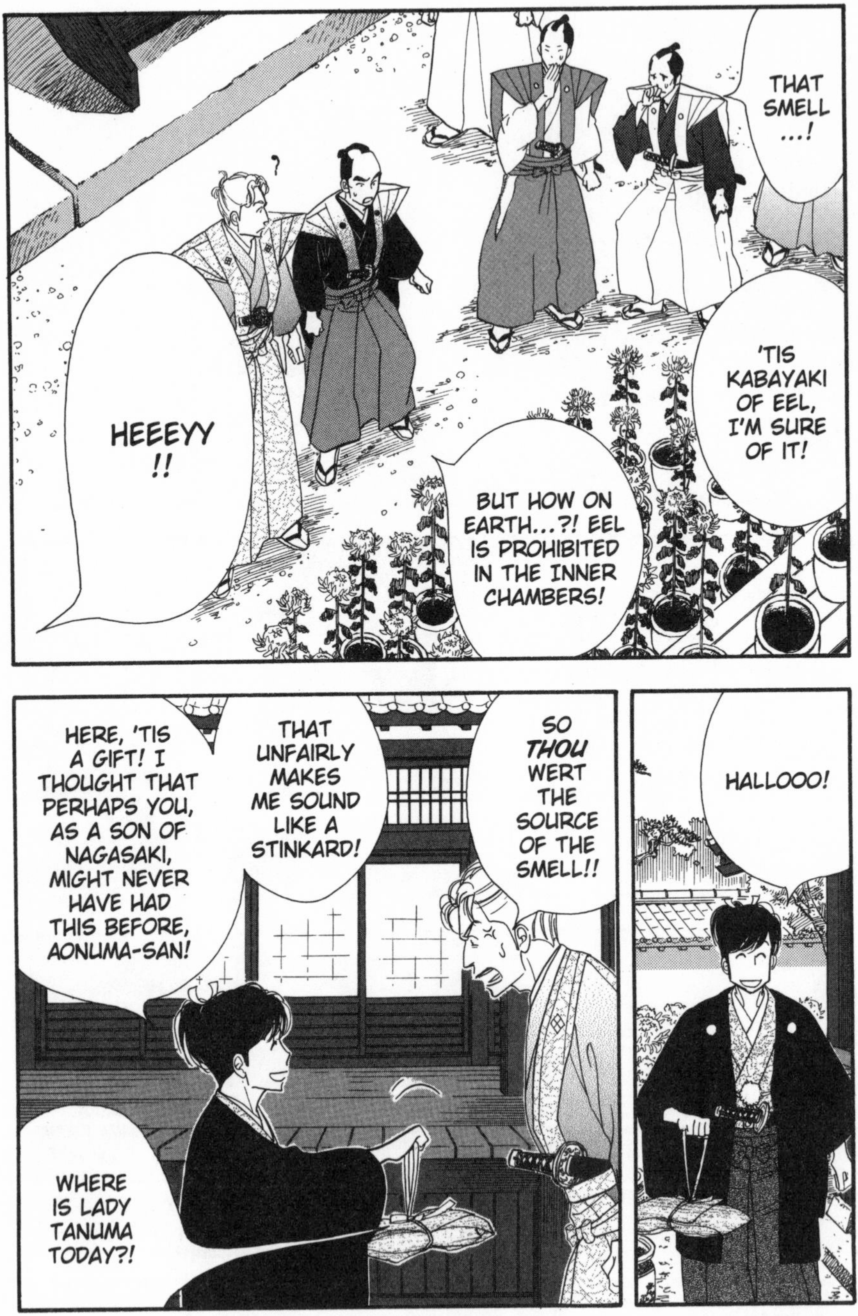
THAT SMELL ...!
'TIS KABAYAKI OF EEL, I'M SURE OF IT!
BUT HOW ON EARTH...?! EEL IS PROHIBITED IN THE INNER CHAMBERS!
HEEEYY !!
HALLOOO!
SO *THOU* WERT THE SOURCE OF THE SMELL!!
THAT UNFAIRLY MAKES ME SOUND LIKE A STINKARD!
HERE, 'TIS A GIFT! I THOUGHT THAT PERHAPS YOU, AS A SON OF NAGASAKI, MIGHT NEVER HAVE HAD THIS BEFORE, AONUMA-SAN!
WHERE IS LADY TANUMA TODAY?!

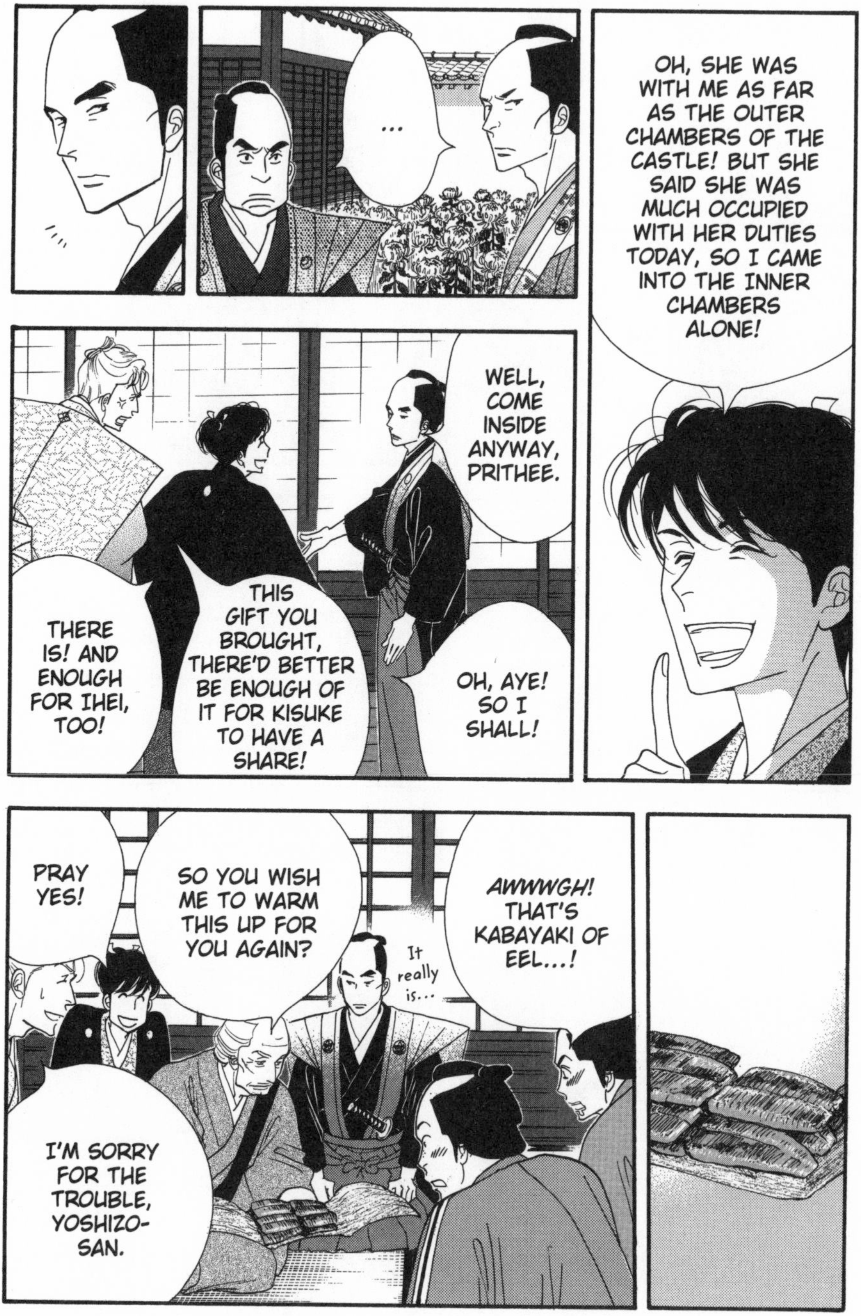
OH, SHE WAS WITH ME AS FAR AS THE OUTER CHAMBERS OF THE CASTLE! BUT SHE SAID SHE WAS MUCH OCCUPIED WITH HER DUTIES TODAY, SO I CAME INTO THE INNER CHAMBERS ALONE!
...
WELL, COME INSIDE ANYWAY, PRITHEE.
OH, AYE! SO I SHALL!
THIS GIFT YOU BROUGHT, THERE'D BETTER BE ENOUGH OF IT FOR KISUKE TO HAVE A SHARE!
THERE IS! AND ENOUGH FOR IHEI, TOO!
AWWWGH! THAT'S KABAYAKI OF EEL...!
It really is...
SO YOU WISH ME TO WARM THIS UP FOR YOU AGAIN?
PRAY YES!
I'M SORRY FOR THE TROUBLE, YOSHIZO-SAN.

ARRANG-ING IT...?

THE RICE FOR THE MIDDAY MEAL IS ON THE FIRE JUST NOW. MAY I TAKE THE LIBERTY OF ARRANGING THE EEL SOMEWHAT DIFFERENTLY?

...

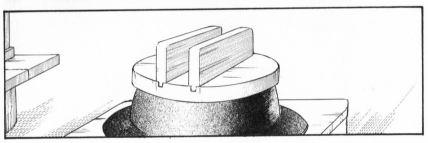

I SHALL SERVE THE EEL, HEATED BY STEAMING, ON TOP OF FRESHLY COOKED RICE. I BEG YOU TO EAT THE TWO THINGS TOGETHER.

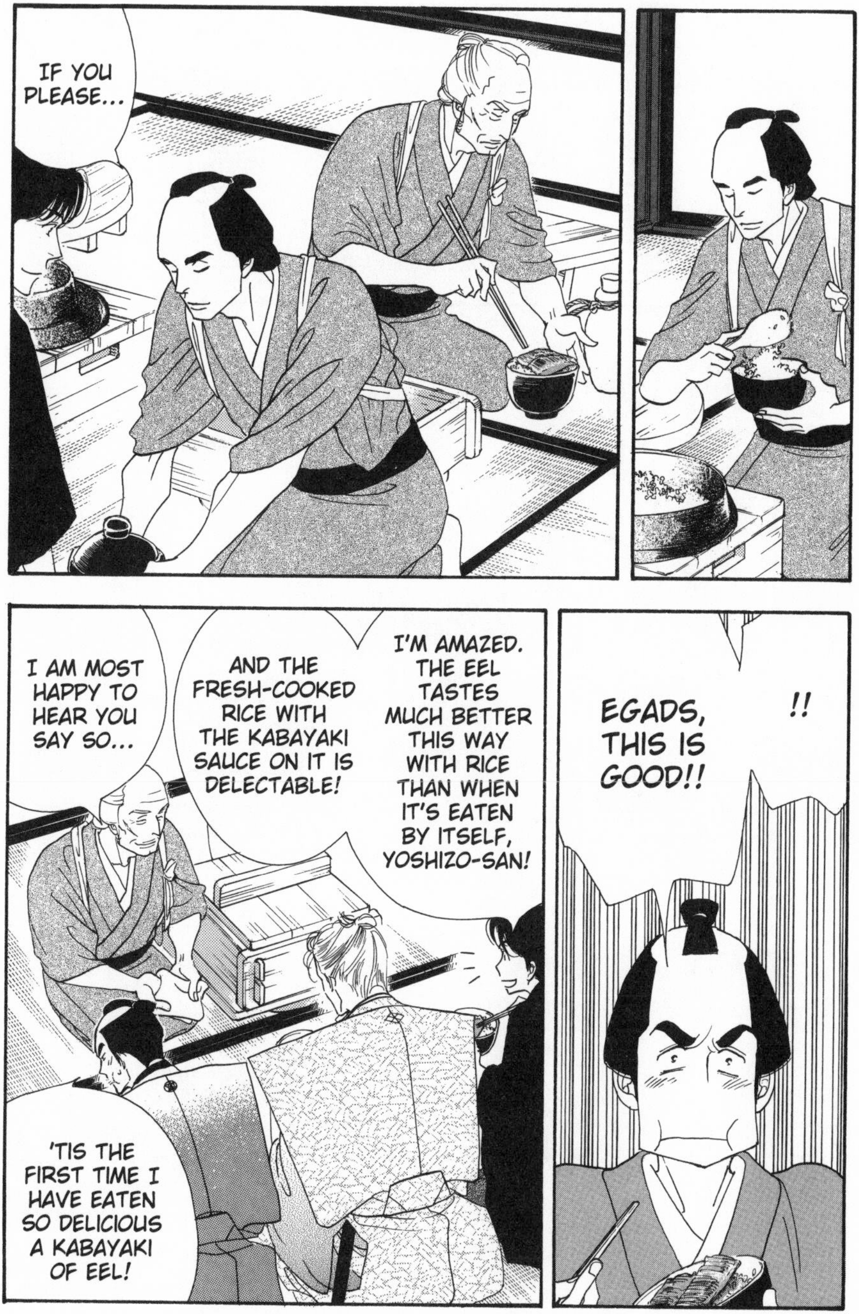
IF YOU PLEASE...
!!
EGADS, THIS IS GOOD!!
I'M AMAZED. THE EEL TASTES MUCH BETTER THIS WAY WITH RICE THAN WHEN IT'S EATEN BY ITSELF, YOSHIZO-SAN!
AND THE FRESH-COOKED RICE WITH THE KABAYAKI SAUCE ON IT IS DELECTABLE!
I AM MOST HAPPY TO HEAR YOU SAY SO...
'TIS THE FIRST TIME I HAVE EATEN SO DELICIOUS A KABAYAKI OF EEL!

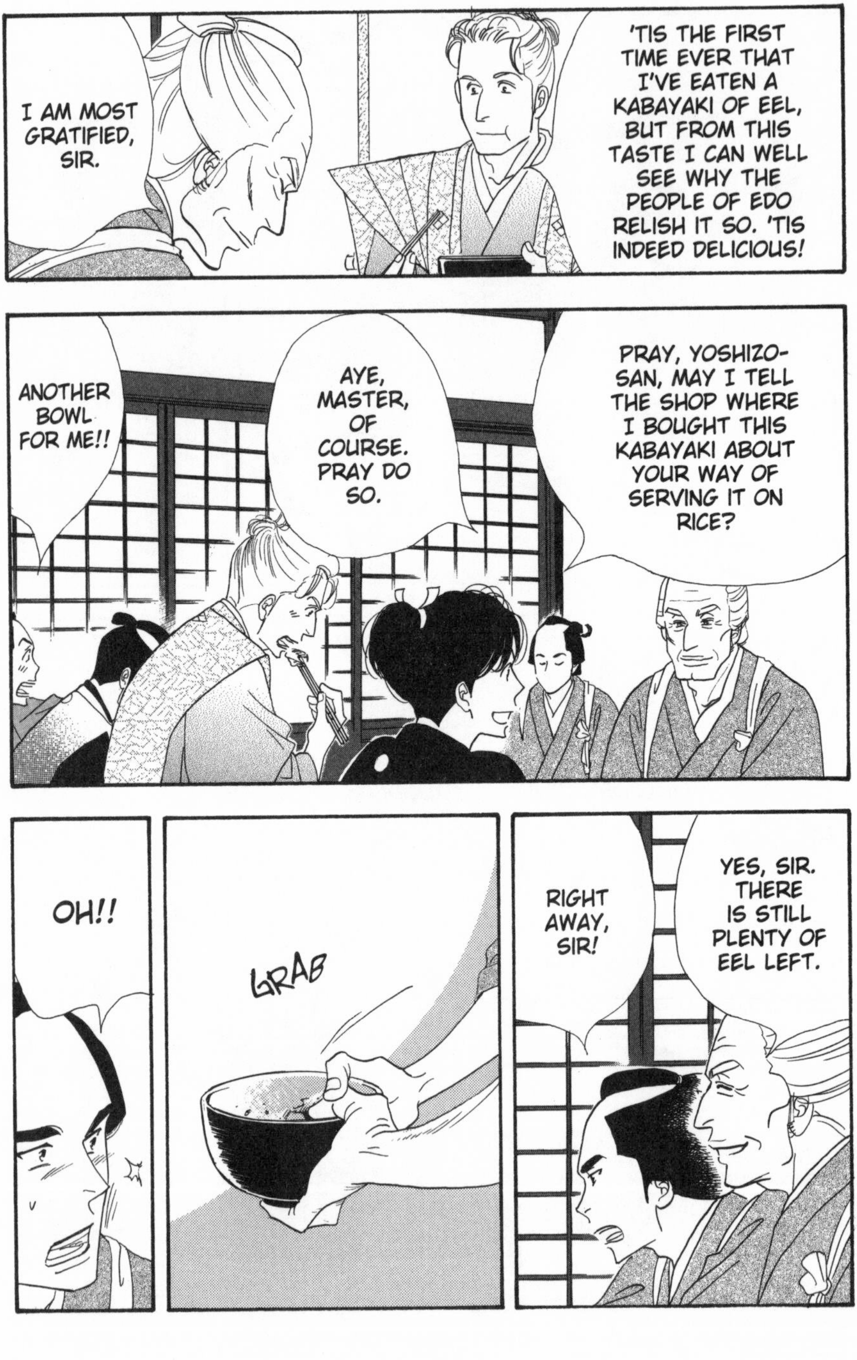
'TIS THE FIRST TIME EVER THAT I'VE EATEN A KABAYAKI OF EEL, BUT FROM THIS TASTE I CAN WELL SEE WHY THE PEOPLE OF EDO RELISH IT SO. 'TIS INDEED DELICIOUS!
I AM MOST GRATIFIED, SIR.
PRAY, YOSHIZO-SAN, MAY I TELL THE SHOP WHERE I BOUGHT THIS KABAYAKI ABOUT YOUR WAY OF SERVING IT ON RICE?
AYE, MASTER, OF COURSE. PRAY DO SO.
ANOTHER BOWL FOR ME!!
YES, SIR. THERE IS STILL PLENTY OF EEL LEFT.
RIGHT AWAY, SIR!
GRAB
OH!!

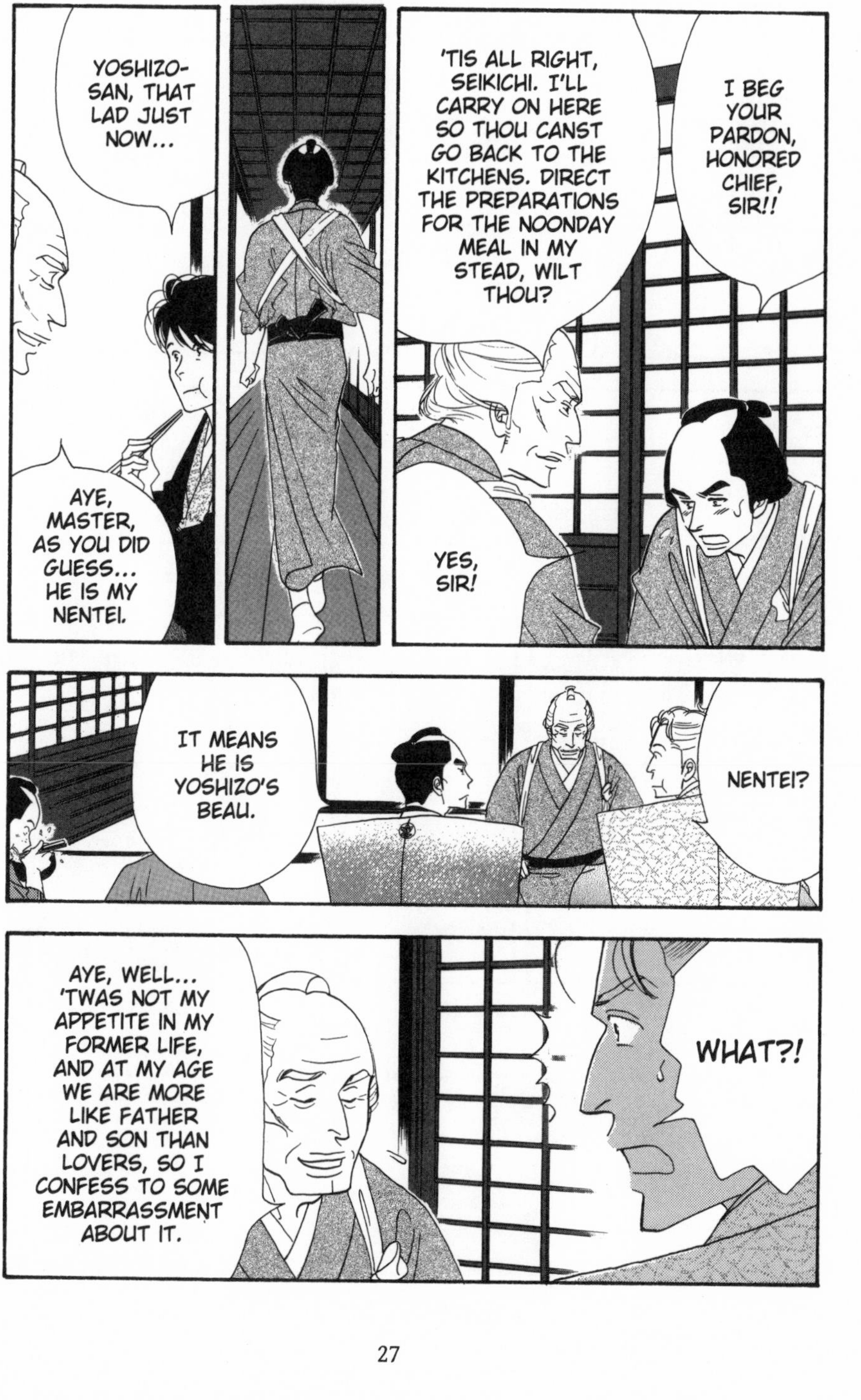
I BEG YOUR PARDON, HONORED CHIEF, SIR!!
'TIS ALL RIGHT, SEIKICHI. I'LL CARRY ON HERE SO THOU CANST GO BACK TO THE KITCHENS. DIRECT THE PREPARATIONS FOR THE NOONDAY MEAL IN MY STEAD, WILT THOU?
YES, SIR!
YOSHIZO-SAN, THAT LAD JUST NOW...
AYE, MASTER, AS YOU DID GUESS... HE IS MY NENTEI.
NENTEI?
IT MEANS HE IS YOSHIZO'S BEAU.
WHAT?!
AYE, WELL... 'TWAS NOT MY APPETITE IN MY FORMER LIFE, AND AT MY AGE WE ARE MORE LIKE FATHER AND SON THAN LOVERS, SO I CONFESS TO SOME EMBARRASSMENT ABOUT IT.

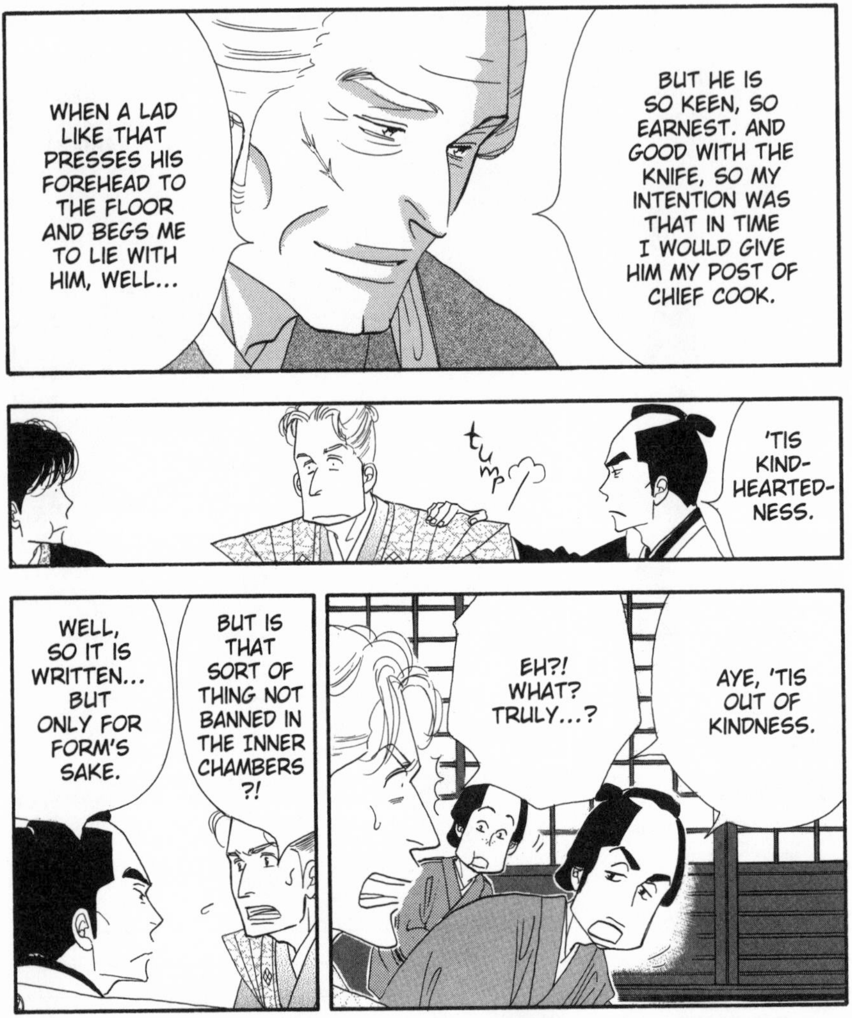
BUT HE IS SO KEEN, SO EARNEST. AND GOOD WITH THE KNIFE, SO MY INTENTION WAS THAT IN TIME I WOULD GIVE HIM MY POST OF CHIEF COOK.
WHEN A LAD LIKE THAT PRESSES HIS FOREHEAD TO THE FLOOR AND BEGS ME TO LIE WITH HIM, WELL...
'TIS KIND-HEARTED-NESS.
tump
AYE, 'TIS OUT OF KINDNESS.
EH?! WHAT? TRULY...?
BUT IS THAT SORT OF THING NOT BANNED IN THE INNER CHAMBERS?!
WELL, SO IT IS WRITTEN... BUT ONLY FOR FORM'S SAKE.
EXACTLY! IT'S WRITTEN TOO THAT THE SHOGUN IS THE ONLY WOMAN ALLOWED TO ENTER THE INNER CHAMBERS, AND HERE'S A WOMAN WHO PASSES FREELY IN AND OUT ALMOST EVERY DAY!
Ha ha ha, true, true!!
What? This master is a woman?!

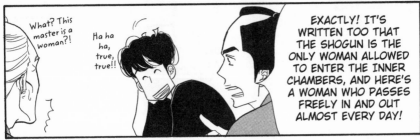

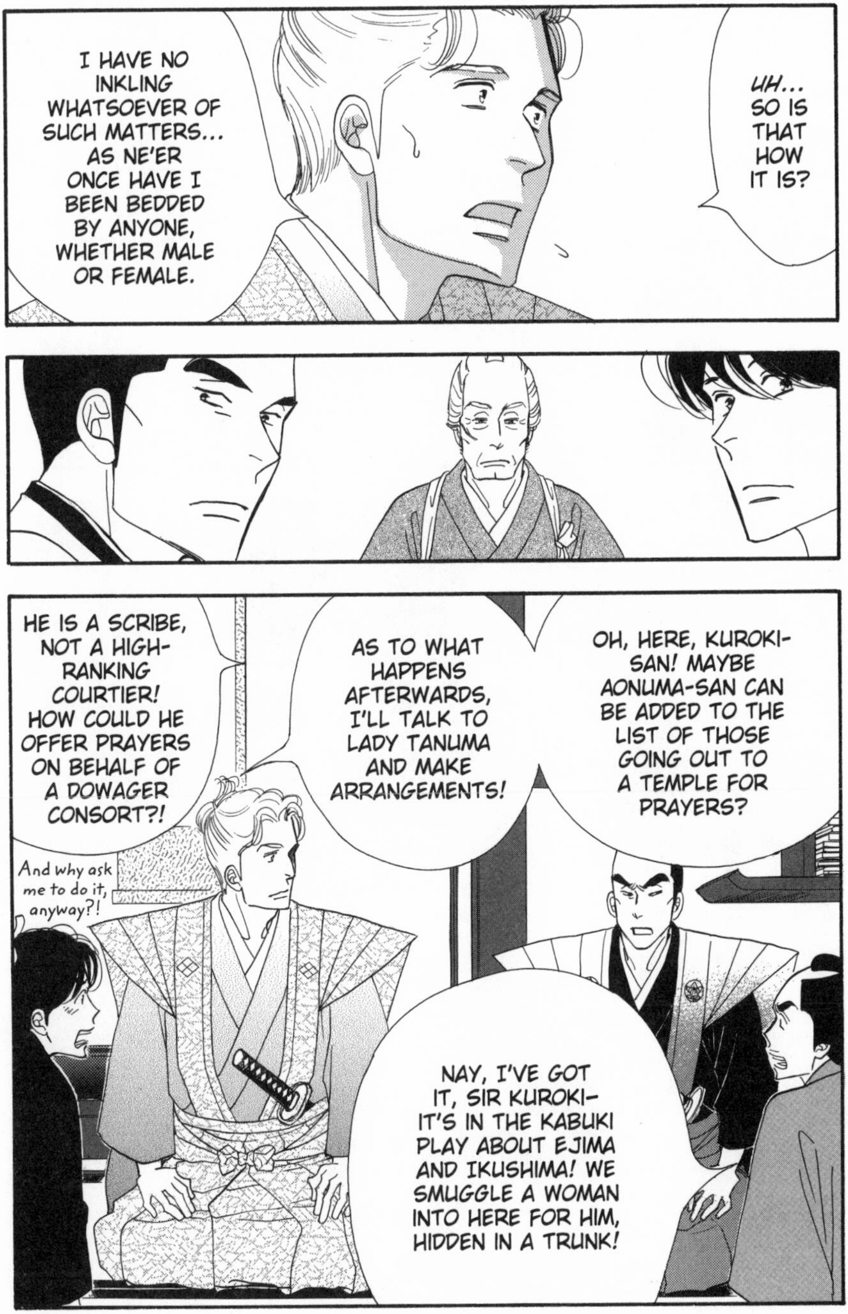
UH... SO IS THAT HOW IT IS?
I HAVE NO INKLING WHATSOEVER OF SUCH MATTERS... AS NE'ER ONCE HAVE I BEEN BEDDED BY ANYONE, WHETHER MALE OR FEMALE.
OH, HERE, KUROKI-SAN! MAYBE AONUMA-SAN CAN BE ADDED TO THE LIST OF THOSE GOING OUT TO A TEMPLE FOR PRAYERS?
AS TO WHAT HAPPENS AFTERWARDS, I'LL TALK TO LADY TANUMA AND MAKE ARRANGEMENTS!
HE IS A SCRIBE, NOT A HIGH-RANKING COURTIER! HOW COULD HE OFFER PRAYERS ON BEHALF OF A DOWAGER CONSORT?!
And why ask me to do it, anyway?!
NAY, I'VE GOT IT, SIR KUROKI-IT'S IN THE KABUKI PLAY ABOUT EJIMA AND IKUSHIMA! WE SMUGGLE A WOMAN INTO HERE FOR HIM, HIDDEN IN A TRUNK!

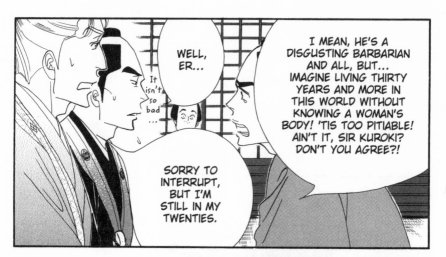

I MEAN, HE'S A DISGUSTING BARBARIAN AND ALL, BUT... IMAGINE LIVING THIRTY YEARS AND MORE IN THIS WORLD WITHOUT KNOWING A WOMAN'S BODY! 'TIS TOO PITIABLE! AIN'T IT, SIR KUROKI? DON'T YOU AGREE?!
WELL, ER...
It isn't so bad...
SORRY TO INTERRUPT, BUT I'M STILL IN MY TWENTIES.
TRULY?!
WE'RE... ABOUT THE SAME AGE, THEN...
THAT'S RIGHT, I KNEW THAT... I'M ASTOUNDED EVERY TIME I HEAR IT, THOUGH.
I'm used to this by now.

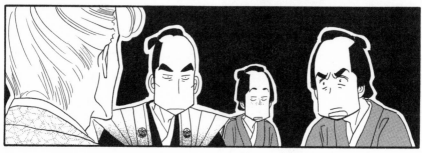

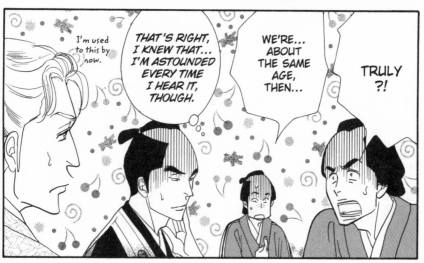

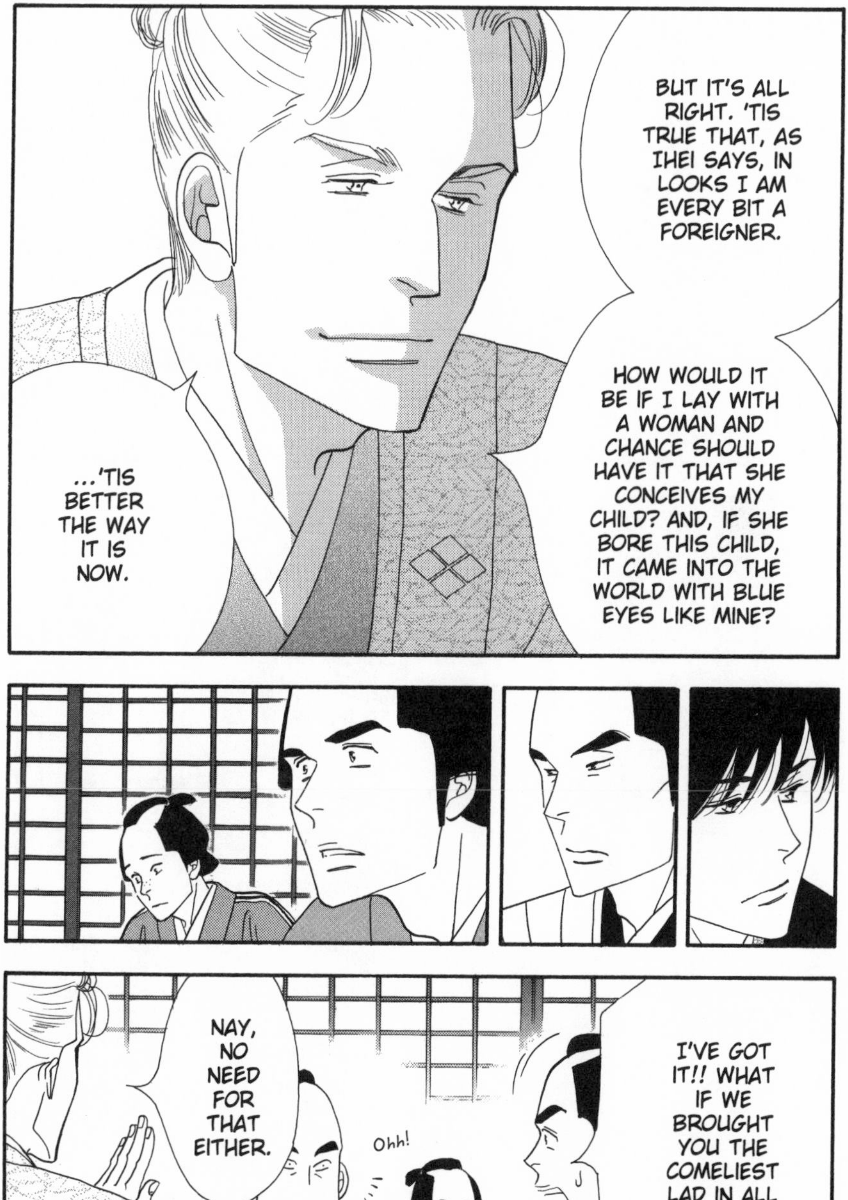
BUT IT'S ALL RIGHT. 'TIS TRUE THAT, AS IHEI SAYS, IN LOOKS I AM EVERY BIT A FOREIGNER.
HOW WOULD IT BE IF I LAY WITH A WOMAN AND CHANCE SHOULD HAVE IT THAT SHE CONCEIVES MY CHILD? AND, IF SHE BORE THIS CHILD, IT CAME INTO THE WORLD WITH BLUE EYES LIKE MINE?
...'TIS BETTER THE WAY IT IS NOW.
I'VE GOT IT!! WHAT IF WE BROUGHT YOU THE COMELIEST LAD IN ALL THE INNER CHAMBERS?!
Ohh!
NAY, NO NEED FOR THAT EITHER.

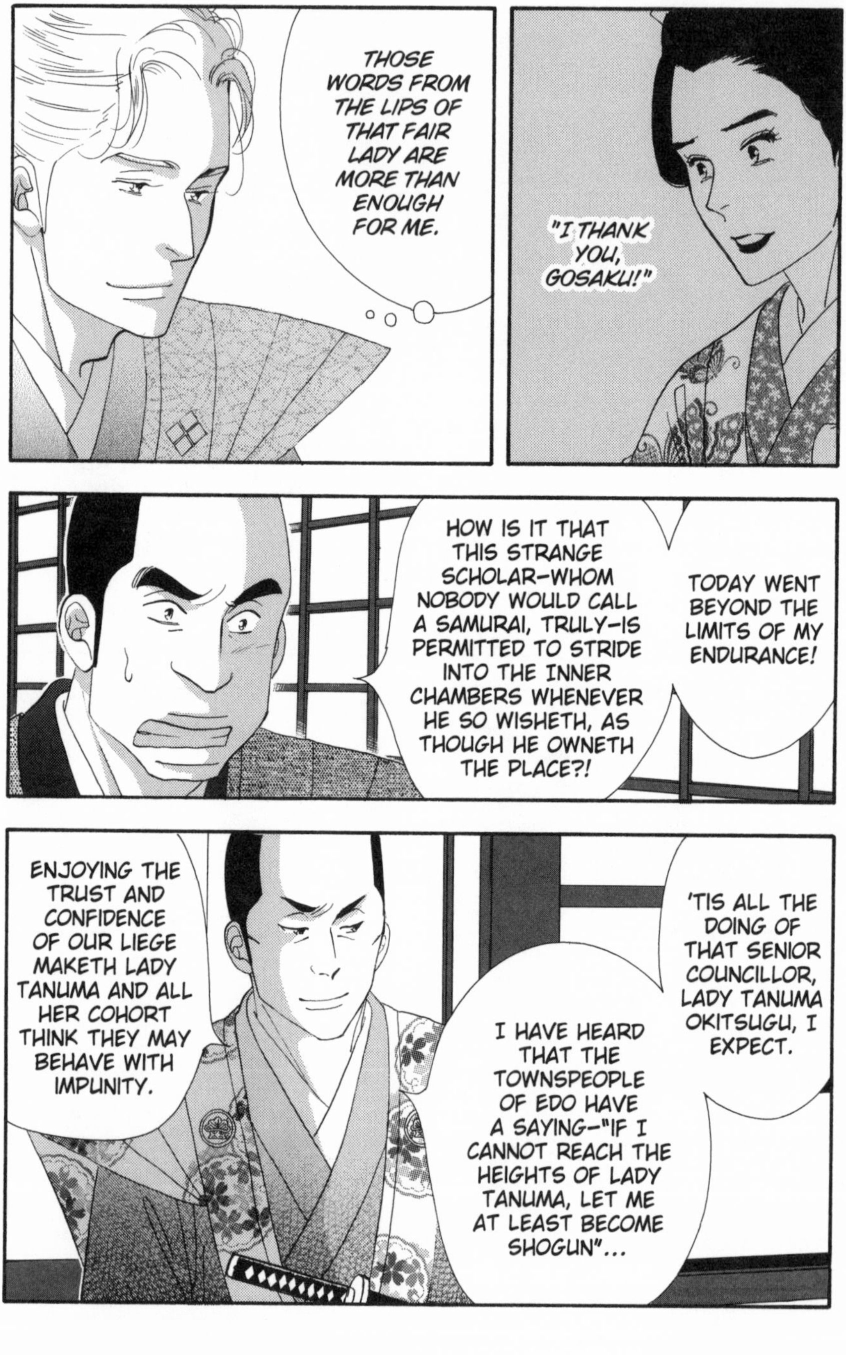
"I THANK YOU, GOSAKU!"
THOSE WORDS FROM THE LIPS OF THAT FAIR LADY ARE MORE THAN ENOUGH FOR ME.
TODAY WENT BEYOND THE LIMITS OF MY ENDURANCE!
HOW IS IT THAT THIS STRANGE SCHOLAR—WHOM NOBODY WOULD CALL A SAMURAI, TRULY—IS PERMITTED TO STRIDE INTO THE INNER CHAMBERS WHENEVER HE SO WISHETH, AS THOUGH HE OWNETH THE PLACE?!
'TIS ALL THE DOING OF THAT SENIOR COUNCILLOR, LADY TANUMA OKITSUGU, I EXPECT.
ENJOYING THE TRUST AND CONFIDENCE OF OUR LIEGE MAKETH LADY TANUMA AND ALL HER COHORT THINK THEY MAY BEHAVE WITH IMPUNITY.
I HAVE HEARD THAT THE TOWNSPEOPLE OF EDO HAVE A SAYING—"IF I CANNOT REACH THE HEIGHTS OF LADY TANUMA, LET ME AT LEAST BECOME SHOGUN"...

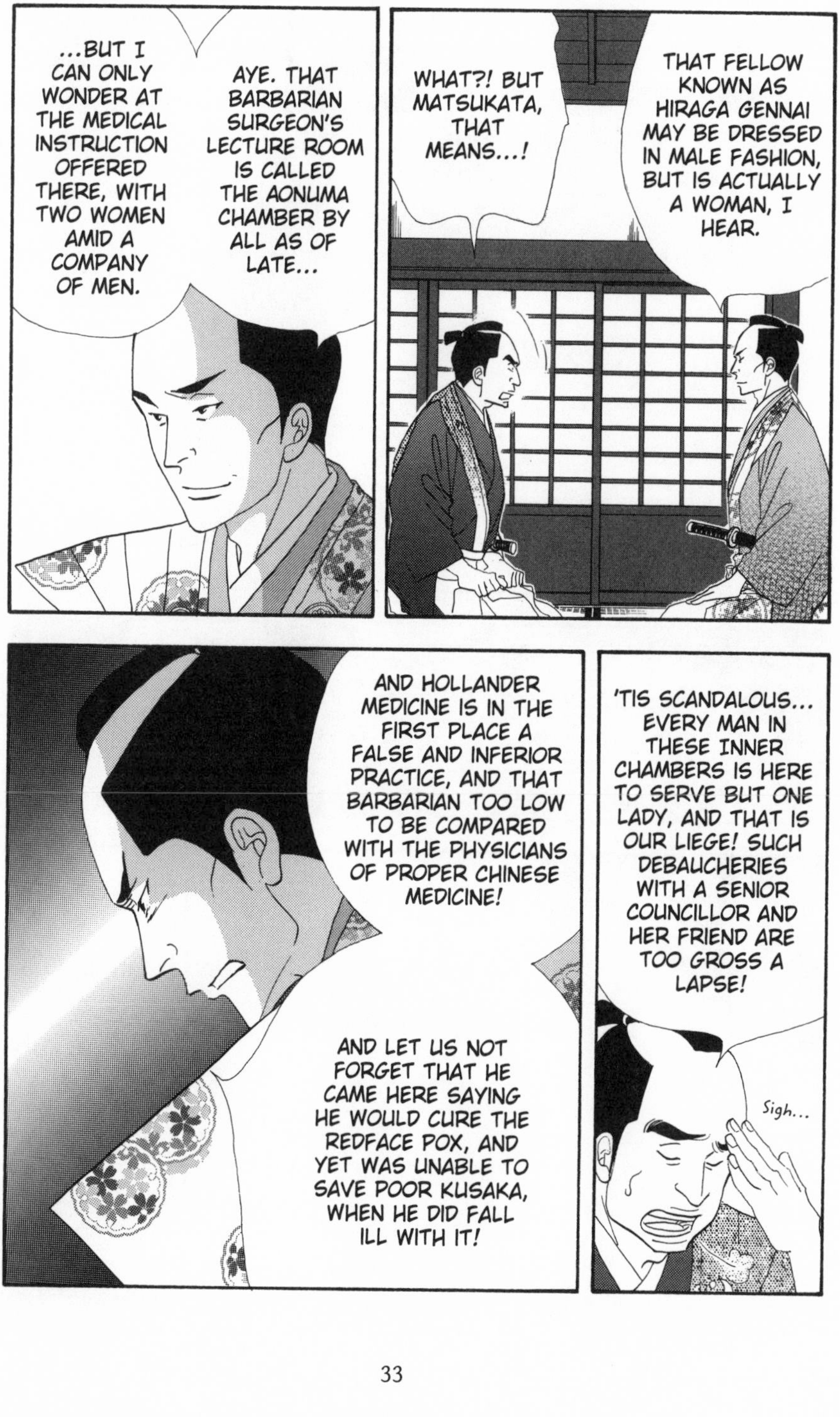
THAT FELLOW KNOWN AS HIRAGA GENNAI MAY BE DRESSED IN MALE FASHION, BUT IS ACTUALLY A WOMAN, I HEAR.
WHAT?! BUT MATSUKATA, THAT MEANS...!
AYE. THAT BARBARIAN SURGEON'S LECTURE ROOM IS CALLED THE AONUMA CHAMBER BY ALL AS OF LATE...
...BUT I CAN ONLY WONDER AT THE MEDICAL INSTRUCTION OFFERED THERE, WITH TWO WOMEN AMID A COMPANY OF MEN.
'TIS SCANDALOUS... EVERY MAN IN THESE INNER CHAMBERS IS HERE TO SERVE BUT ONE LADY, AND THAT IS OUR LIEGE! SUCH DEBAUCHERIES WITH A SENIOR COUNCILLOR AND HER FRIEND ARE TOO GROSS A LAPSE!
Sigh...
AND HOLLANDER MEDICINE IS IN THE FIRST PLACE A FALSE AND INFERIOR PRACTICE, AND THAT BARBARIAN TOO LOW TO BE COMPARED WITH THE PHYSICIANS OF PROPER CHINESE MEDICINE!
AND LET US NOT FORGET THAT HE CAME HERE SAYING HE WOULD CURE THE REDFACE POX, AND YET WAS UNABLE TO SAVE POOR KUSAKA, WHEN HE DID FALL ILL WITH IT!

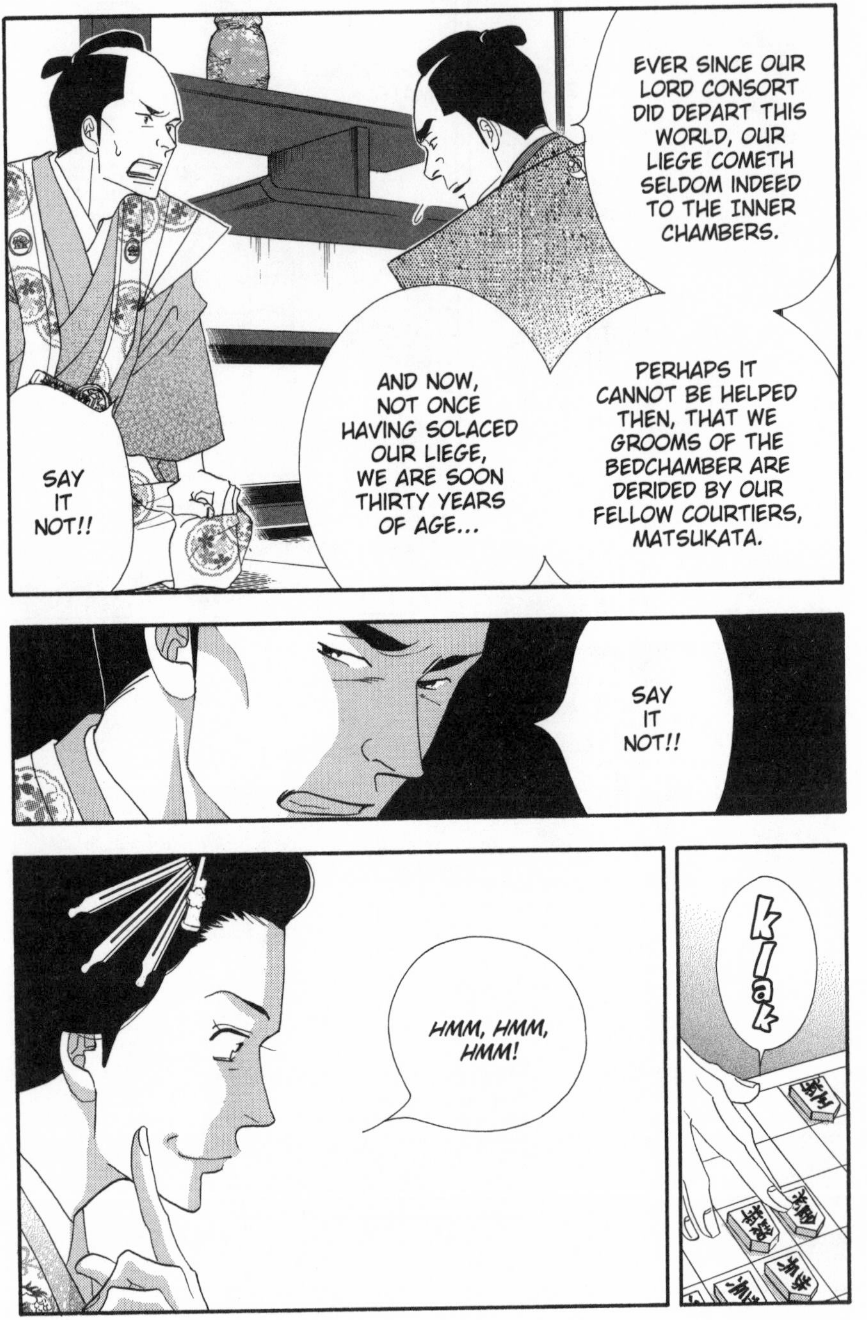
EVER SINCE OUR LORD CONSORT DID DEPART THIS WORLD, OUR LIEGE COMETH SELDOM INDEED TO THE INNER CHAMBERS.
PERHAPS IT CANNOT BE HELPED THEN, THAT WE GROOMS OF THE BEDCHAMBER ARE DERIDED BY OUR FELLOW COURTIERS, MATSUKATA.
AND NOW, NOT ONCE HAVING SOLACED OUR LIEGE, WE ARE SOON THIRTY YEARS OF AGE...
SAY IT NOT!!
SAY IT NOT!!
klak
HMM, HMM, HMM!

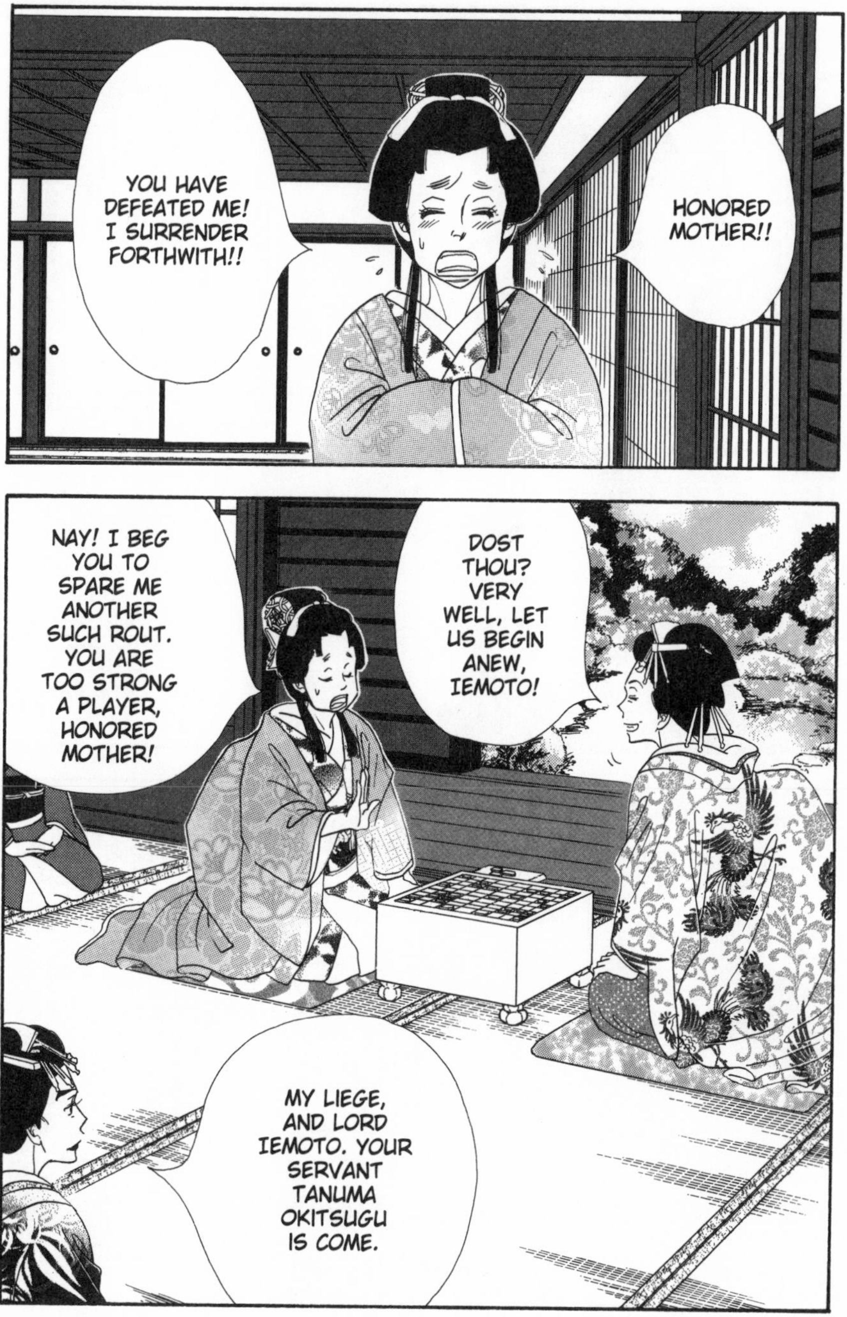
HONORED MOTHER!!
YOU HAVE DEFEATED ME! I SURRENDER FORTHWITH!!
DOST THOU? VERY WELL, LET US BEGIN ANEW, IEMOTO!
NAY! I BEG YOU TO SPARE ME ANOTHER SUCH ROUT. YOU ARE TOO STRONG A PLAYER, HONORED MOTHER!
MY LIEGE, AND LORD IEMOTO. YOUR SERVANT TANUMA OKITSUGU IS COME.

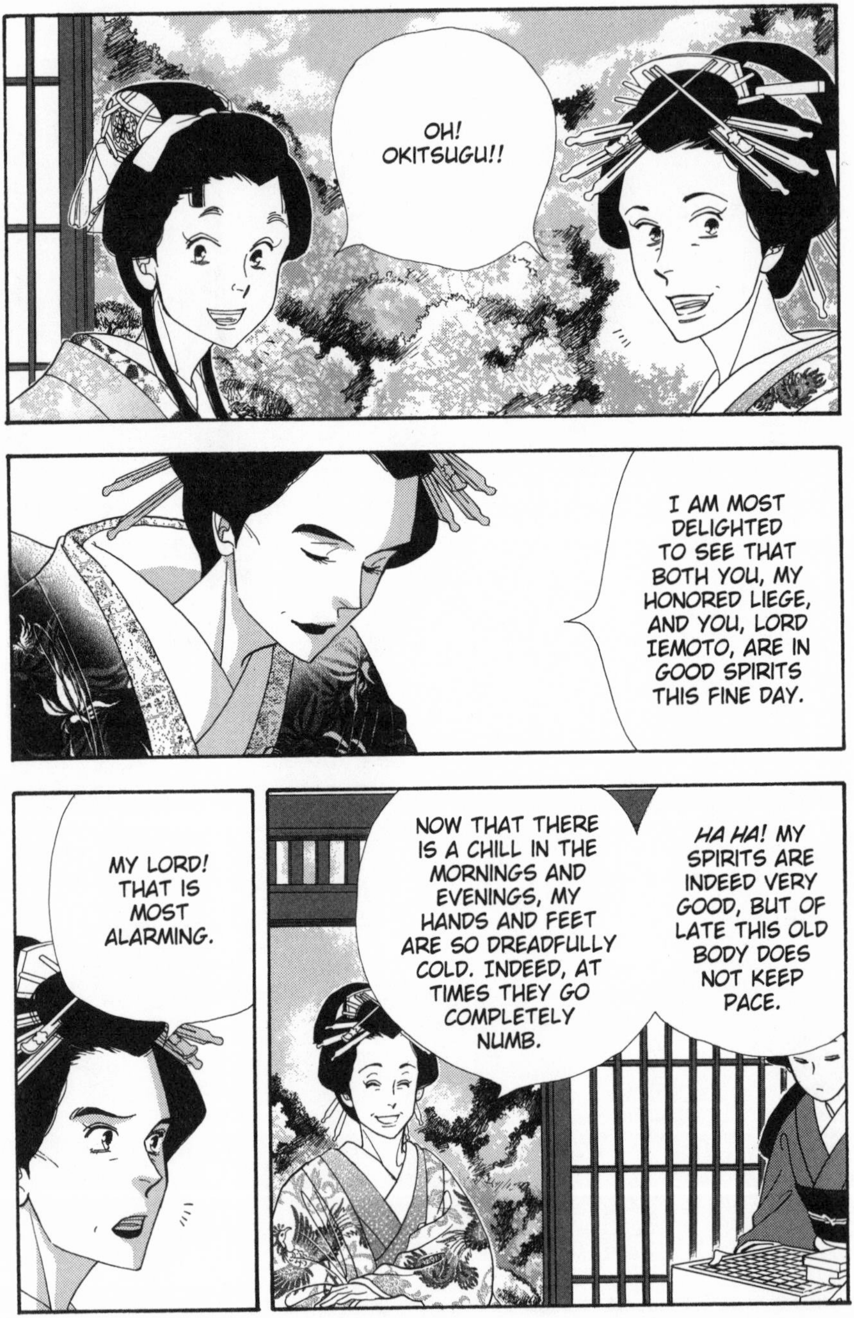
OH! OKITSUGU!!
I AM MOST DELIGHTED TO SEE THAT BOTH YOU, MY HONORED LIEGE, AND YOU, LORD IEMOTO, ARE IN GOOD SPIRITS THIS FINE DAY.
HA HA! MY SPIRITS ARE INDEED VERY GOOD, BUT OF LATE THIS OLD BODY DOES NOT KEEP PACE.
NOW THAT THERE IS A CHILL IN THE MORNINGS AND EVENINGS, MY HANDS AND FEET ARE SO DREADFULLY COLD. INDEED, AT TIMES THEY GO COMPLETELY NUMB.
MY LORD! THAT IS MOST ALARMING.

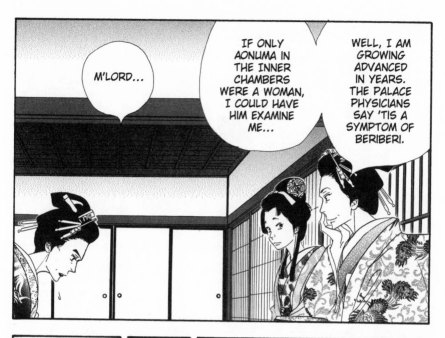

WELL, I AM GROWING ADVANCED IN YEARS. THE PALACE PHYSICIANS SAY 'TIS A SYMPTOM OF BERIBERI.
IF ONLY AONUMA IN THE INNER CHAMBERS WERE A WOMAN, I COULD HAVE HIM EXAMINE ME...
M'LORD...
I OUGHT TO VISIT THE INNER CHAMBERS ONCE IN A WHILE, I KNOW, BUT NOW THAT ISONOMIYA IS GONE, 'TIS TOO DOLEFUL.
IT MAY SEEM LAUGHABLE, THAT A SHOGUN PINES SO AFTER THE LOSS OF HER CONSORT, BUT TO ME HE WAS A PRECIOUS AND IRREPLACEABLE COMPANION...
'TIS ONLY NATURAL THAT YOU MISS MY HONORED FATHER SO, DEAR MOTHER, WHEN THE TWO OF YOU WERE SO DEVOTED AND HARMONIOUS A COUPLE.

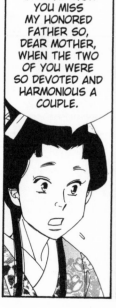

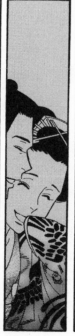

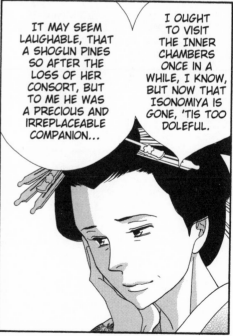

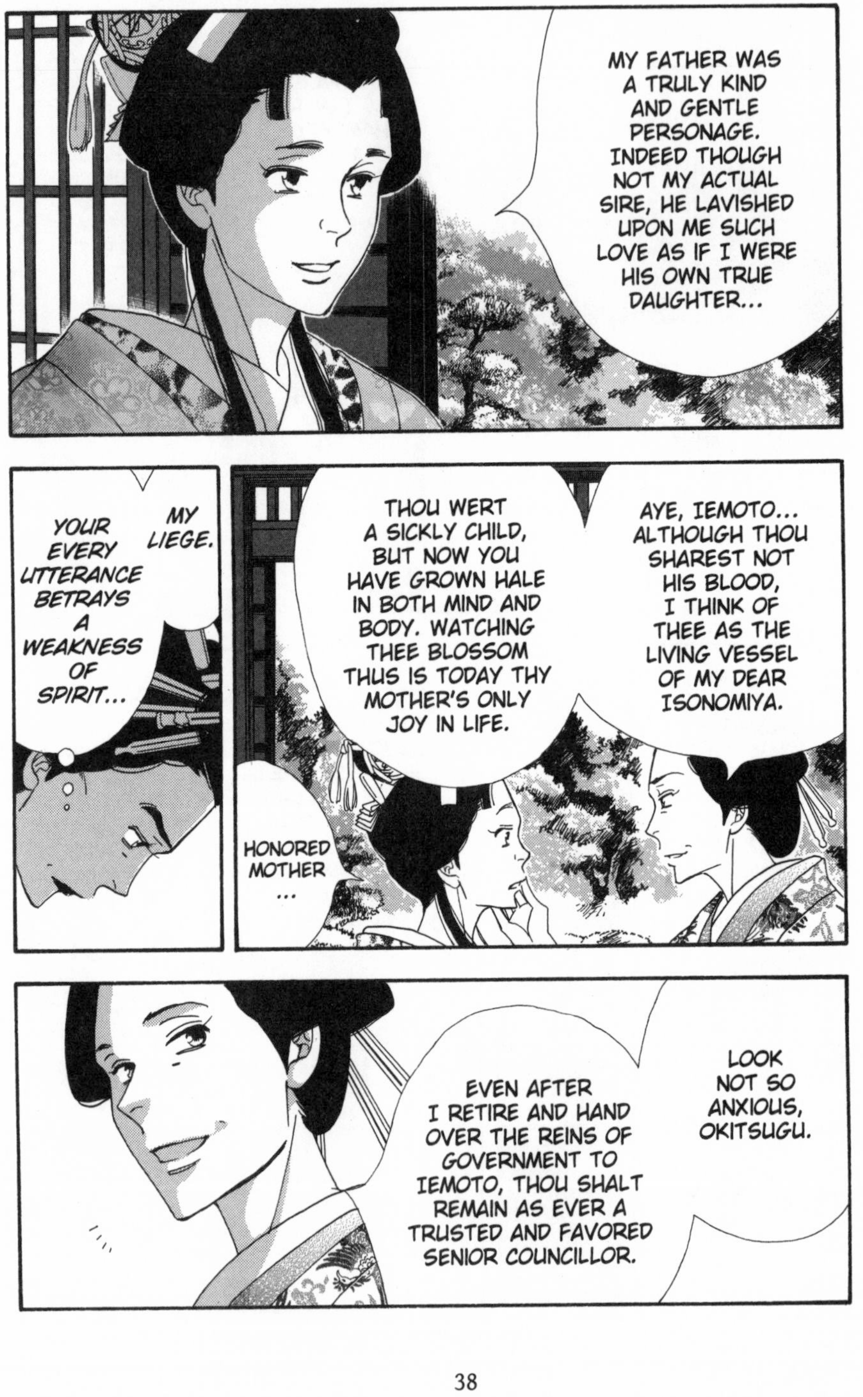
MY FATHER WAS A TRULY KIND AND GENTLE PERSONAGE. INDEED THOUGH NOT MY ACTUAL SIRE, HE LAVISHED UPON ME SUCH LOVE AS IF I WERE HIS OWN TRUE DAUGHTER...
AYE, IEMOTO... ALTHOUGH THOU SHAREST NOT HIS BLOOD, I THINK OF THEE AS THE LIVING VESSEL OF MY DEAR ISONOMIYA.
THOU WERT A SICKLY CHILD, BUT NOW YOU HAVE GROWN HALE IN BOTH MIND AND BODY. WATCHING THEE BLOSSOM THUS IS TODAY THY MOTHER'S ONLY JOY IN LIFE.
HONORED MOTHER ...
MY LIEGE.
YOUR EVERY UTTERANCE BETRAYS A WEAKNESS OF SPIRIT...
LOOK NOT SO ANXIOUS, OKITSUGU.
EVEN AFTER I RETIRE AND HAND OVER THE REINS OF GOVERNMENT TO IEMOTO, THOU SHALT REMAIN AS EVER A TRUSTED AND FAVORED SENIOR COUNCILLOR.

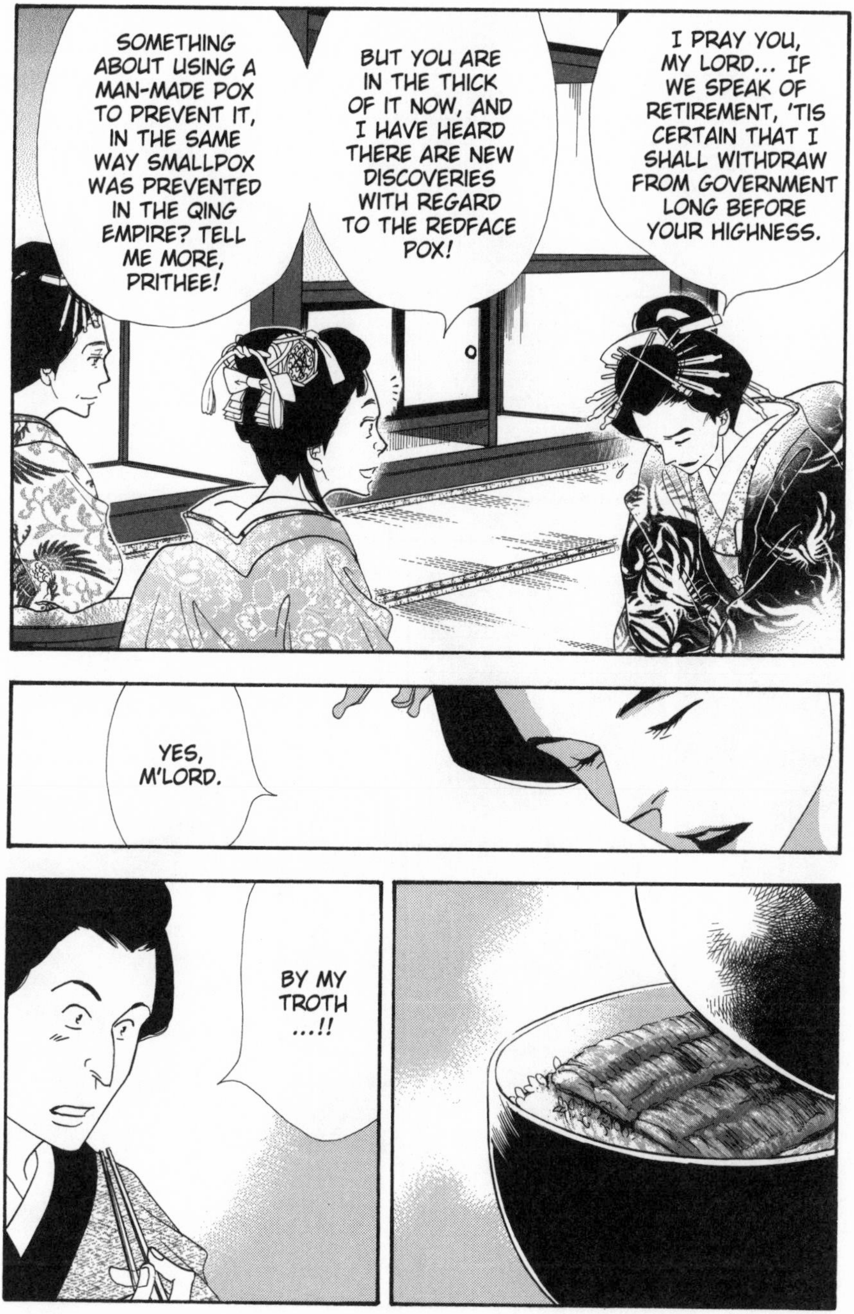
I PRAY YOU, MY LORD... IF WE SPEAK OF RETIREMENT, 'TIS CERTAIN THAT I SHALL WITHDRAW FROM GOVERNMENT LONG BEFORE YOUR HIGHNESS.
BUT YOU ARE IN THE THICK OF IT NOW, AND I HAVE HEARD THERE ARE NEW DISCOVERIES WITH REGARD TO THE REDFACE POX!
SOMETHING ABOUT USING A MAN-MADE POX TO PREVENT IT, IN THE SAME WAY SMALLPOX WAS PREVENTED IN THE QING EMPIRE? TELL ME MORE, PRITHEE!
YES, M'LORD.
BY MY TROTH ...!!

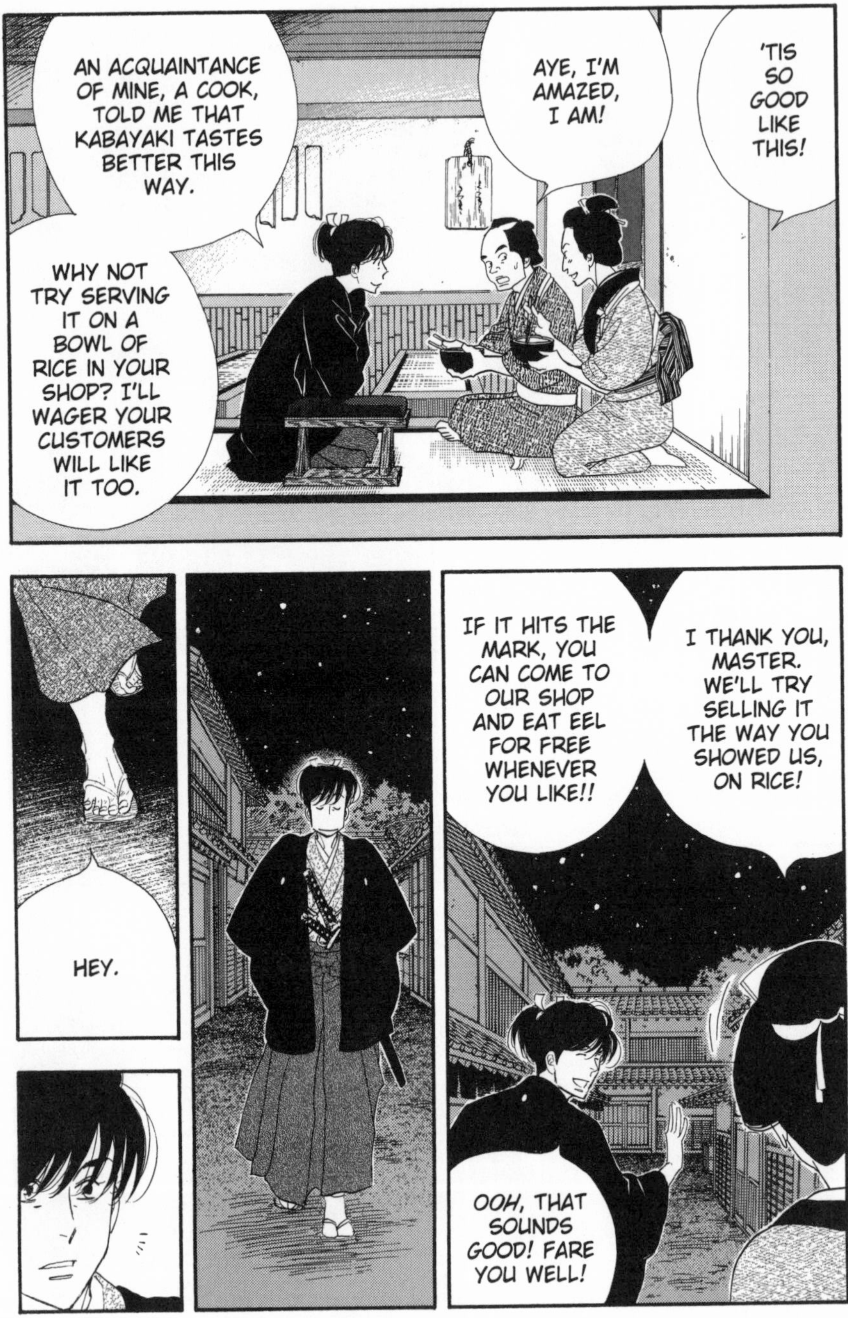
'TIS SO GOOD LIKE THIS!
AYE, I'M AMAZED, I AM!
AN ACQUAINTANCE OF MINE, A COOK, TOLD ME THAT KABAYAKI TASTES BETTER THIS WAY.
WHY NOT TRY SERVING IT ON A BOWL OF RICE IN YOUR SHOP? I'LL WAGER YOUR CUSTOMERS WILL LIKE IT TOO.
I THANK YOU, MASTER. WE'LL TRY SELLING IT THE WAY YOU SHOWED US, ON RICE!
IF IT HITS THE MARK, YOU CAN COME TO OUR SHOP AND EAT EEL FOR FREE WHENEVER YOU LIKE!!
OOH, THAT SOUNDS GOOD! FARE YOU WELL!
HEY.

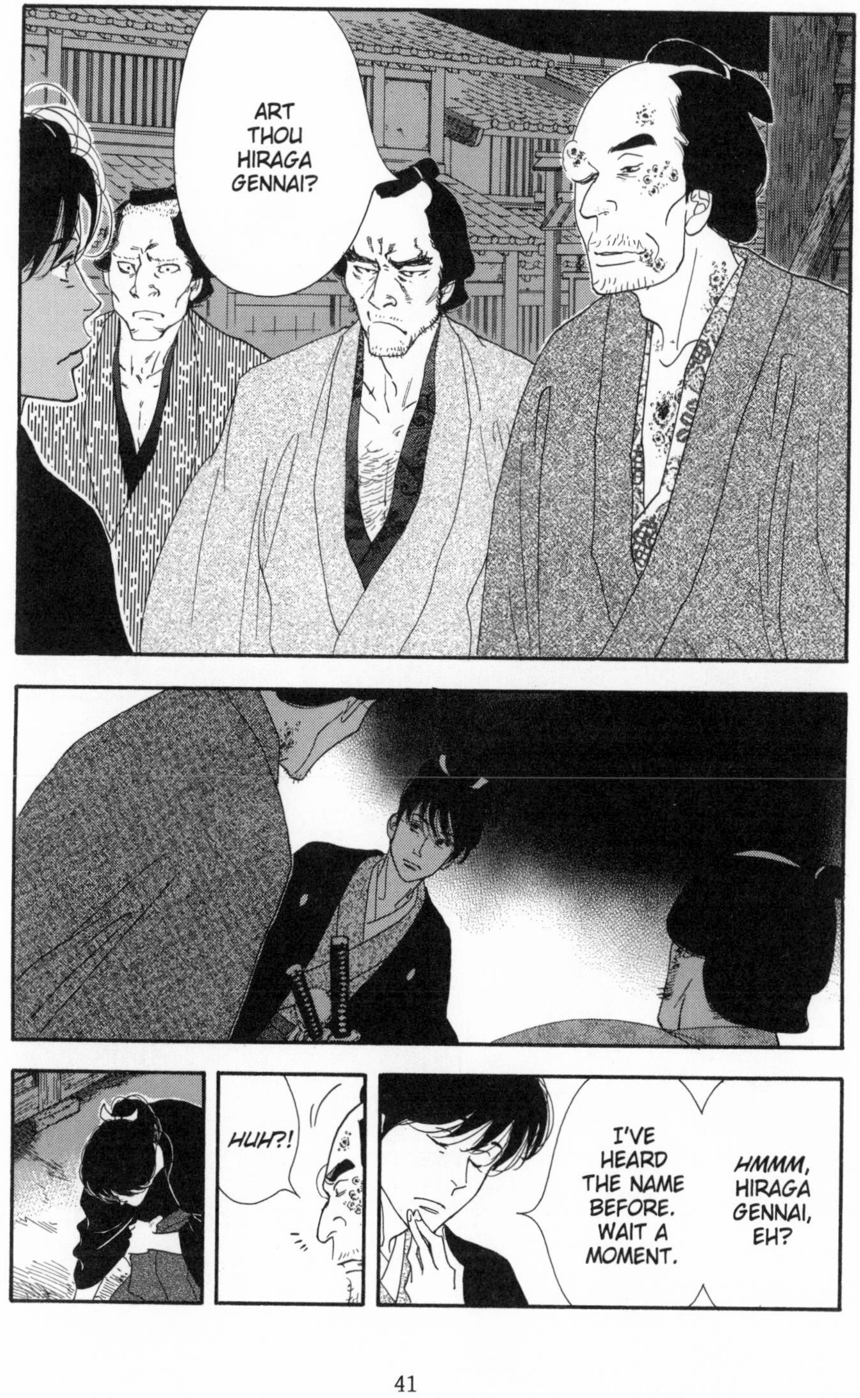
ART THOU HIRAGA GENNAI?
HMMM, HIRAGA GENNAI, EH?
I'VE HEARD THE NAME BEFORE. WAIT A MOMENT.
HUH?!

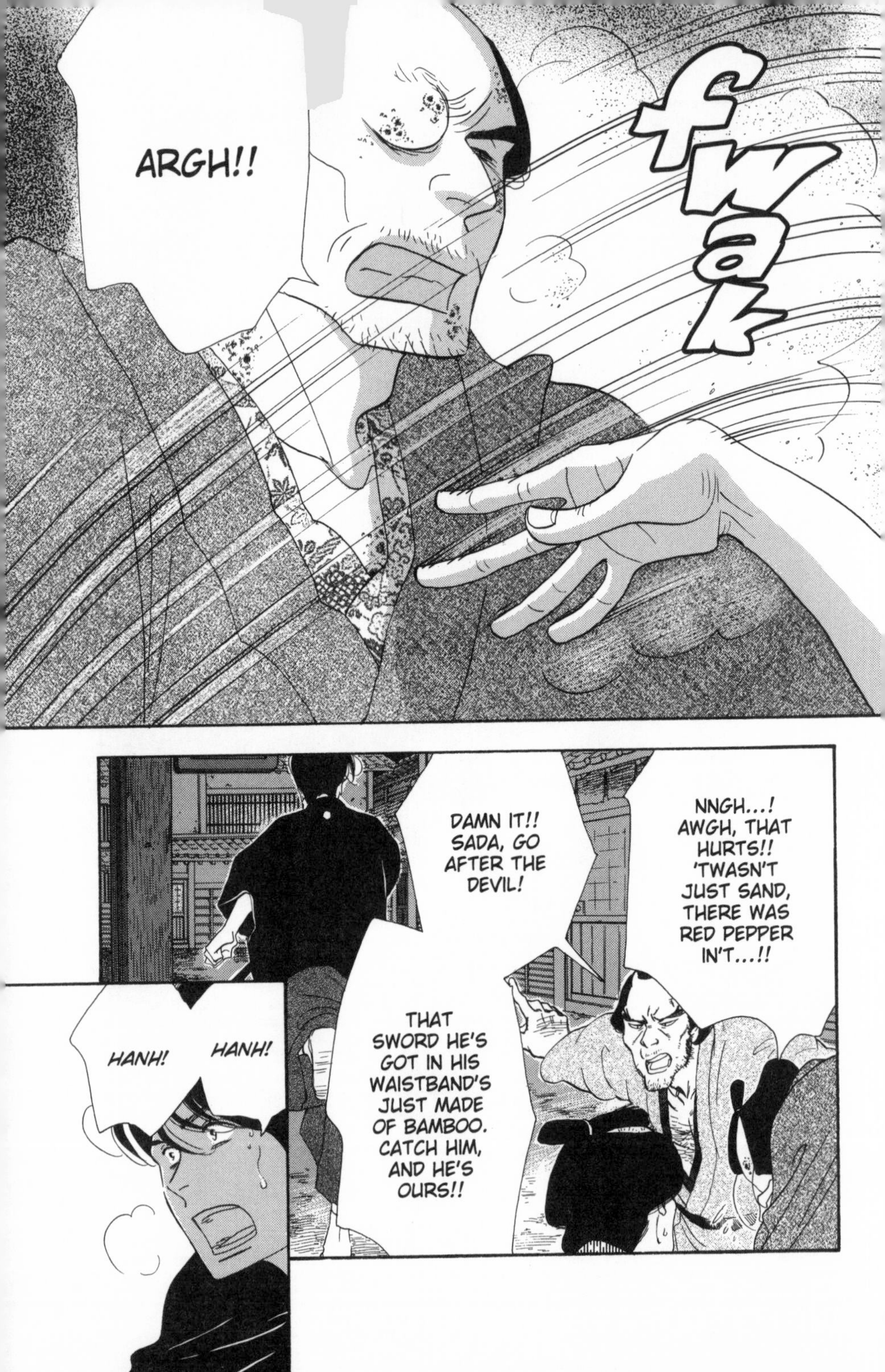
fwak
ARGH!!
NNGH...! AWGH, THAT HURTS!! 'TWASN'T JUST SAND, THERE WAS RED PEPPER IN'T...!!
DAMN IT!! SADA, GO AFTER THE DEVIL!
THAT SWORD HE'S GOT IN HIS WAISTBAND'S JUST MADE OF BAMBOO. CATCH HIM, AND HE'S OURS!!
HANH! HANH!

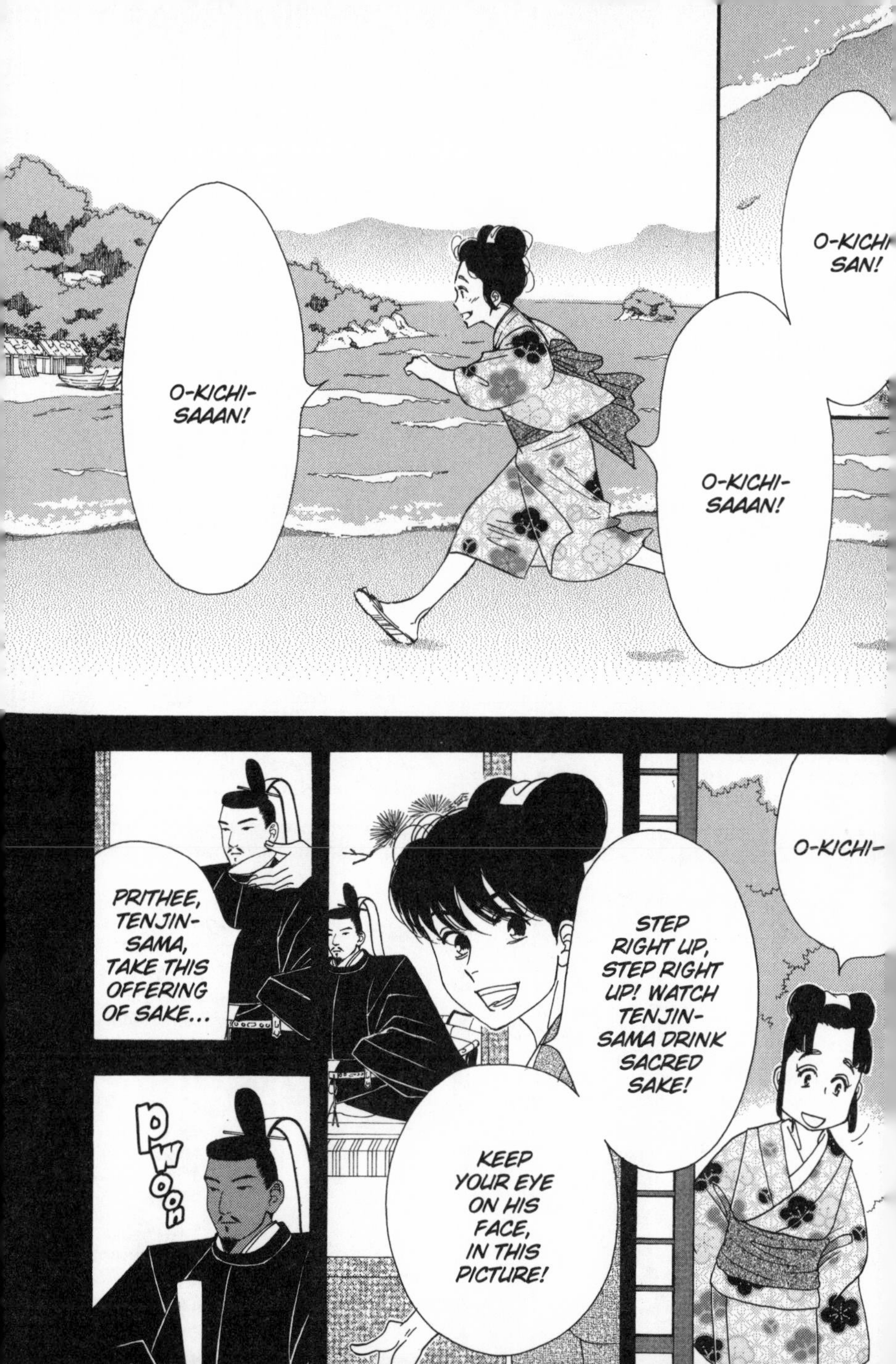
O-KICHI-
SAN!
O-KICHI-SAAAN!
O-KICHI-SAAAN!
O-KICHI-
STEP RIGHT UP, STEP RIGHT UP! WATCH TENJIN-SAMA DRINK SACRED SAKE!
KEEP YOUR EYE ON HIS FACE, IN THIS PICTURE!
PRITHEE, TENJIN-SAMA, TAKE THIS OFFERING OF SAKE...
pwoon

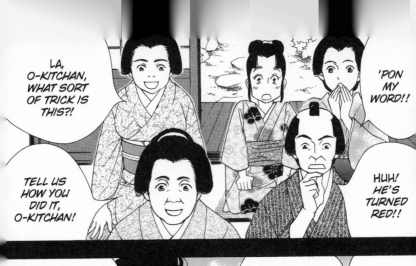

'PON MY WORD!!
HUH! HE'S TURNED RED!!
LA, O-KITCHAN, WHAT SORT OF TRICK IS THIS?!
TELL US HOW YOU DID IT, O-KITCHAN!
HA HA! 'TIS AN EASY TRICK INDEED.
I JUST CUT OUT THE PAPER WHERE TENJIN-SAMA'S FACE WAS, PASTED SOME THIN TRANSLUCENT PAPER OVER IT, AND DREW HIS FACE AGAIN.
THEN I SET SOME RED PAPER BEHIND THE PAINTING, PLACED SO THAT WHEN I PULL A STRING, THE RED PAPER COMES BEHIND THE TRANSLUCENT FACE AND MAKES IT APPEAR FLUSHED.
DOST THOU KNOW WHAT EVERYONE CALLS THEE, O-KICHI-SAN?
SURE, I DO. TENGU URCHIN, RIGHT?
AH, HOW I WISH I REALLY WERE A TENGU! FOR ONE THING THEY'RE MALE, SO I WOULDN'T HAVE TO TAKE AFTER MY MOTHER AND BECOME A KEEPER OF THE DOMAIN WAREHOUSES!
AND SCHOLARS TEND TO BE MEN, DON'T THEY? AFTER ALL, MEN HAVE TIME ON THEIR HANDS. NO FAMILY BUSINESS TO RUN, NO COOKING OR SEWING, NO HEIRS TO BEAR... PLENTY OF TIME TO STUDY!

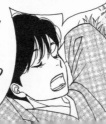

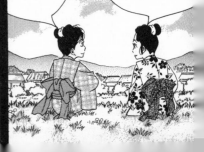

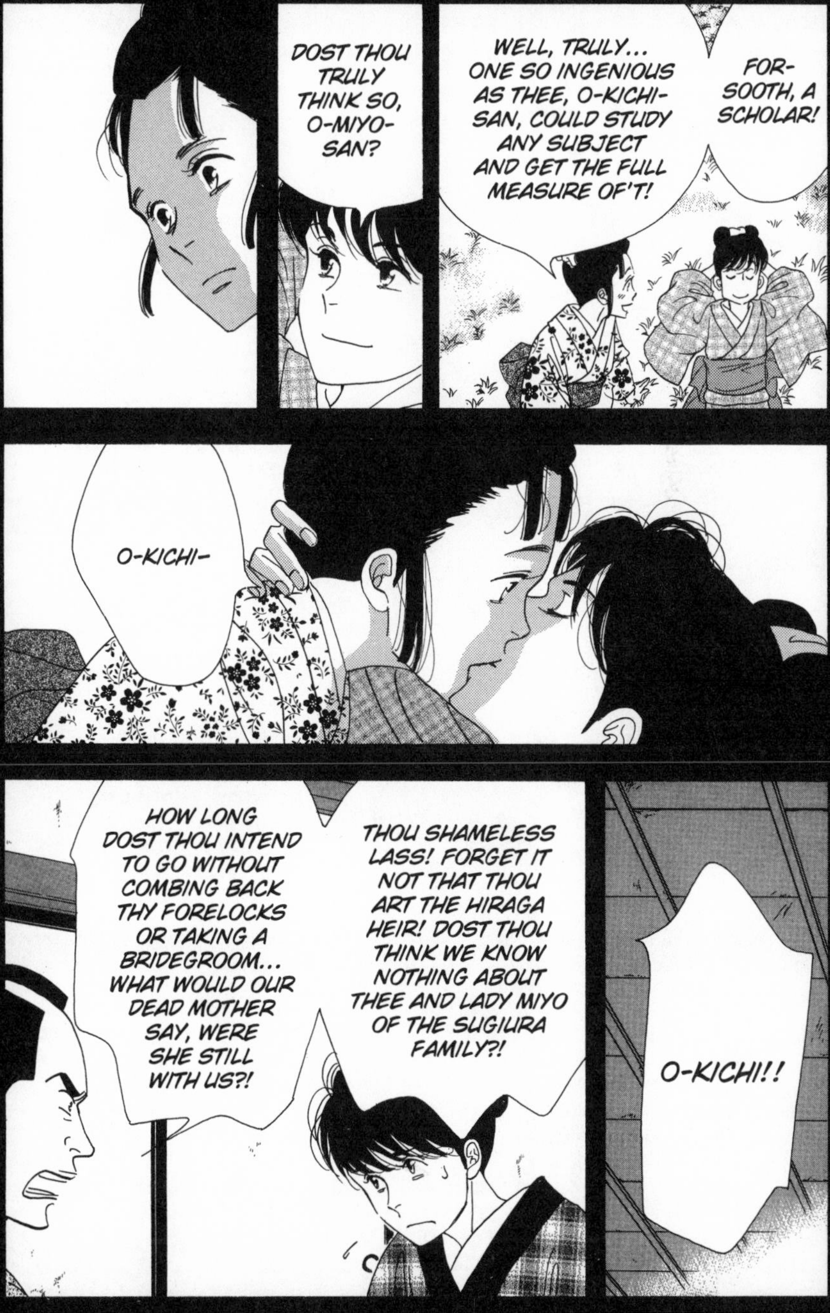
FOR-SOOTH, A SCHOLAR!
WELL, TRULY... ONE SO INGENIOUS AS THEE, O-KICHI-SAN, COULD STUDY ANY SUBJECT AND GET THE FULL MEASURE OF'T!
DOST THOU TRULY THINK SO, O-MIYO-SAN?
O-KICHI-
O-KICHI!!
THOU SHAMELESS LASS! FORGET IT NOT THAT THOU ART THE HIRAGA HEIR! DOST THOU THINK WE KNOW NOTHING ABOUT THEE AND LADY MIYO OF THE SUGIURA FAMILY?!
HOW LONG DOST THOU INTEND TO GO WITHOUT COMBING BACK THY FORELOCKS OR TAKING A BRIDEGROOM... WHAT WOULD OUR DEAD MOTHER SAY, WERE SHE STILL WITH US?!

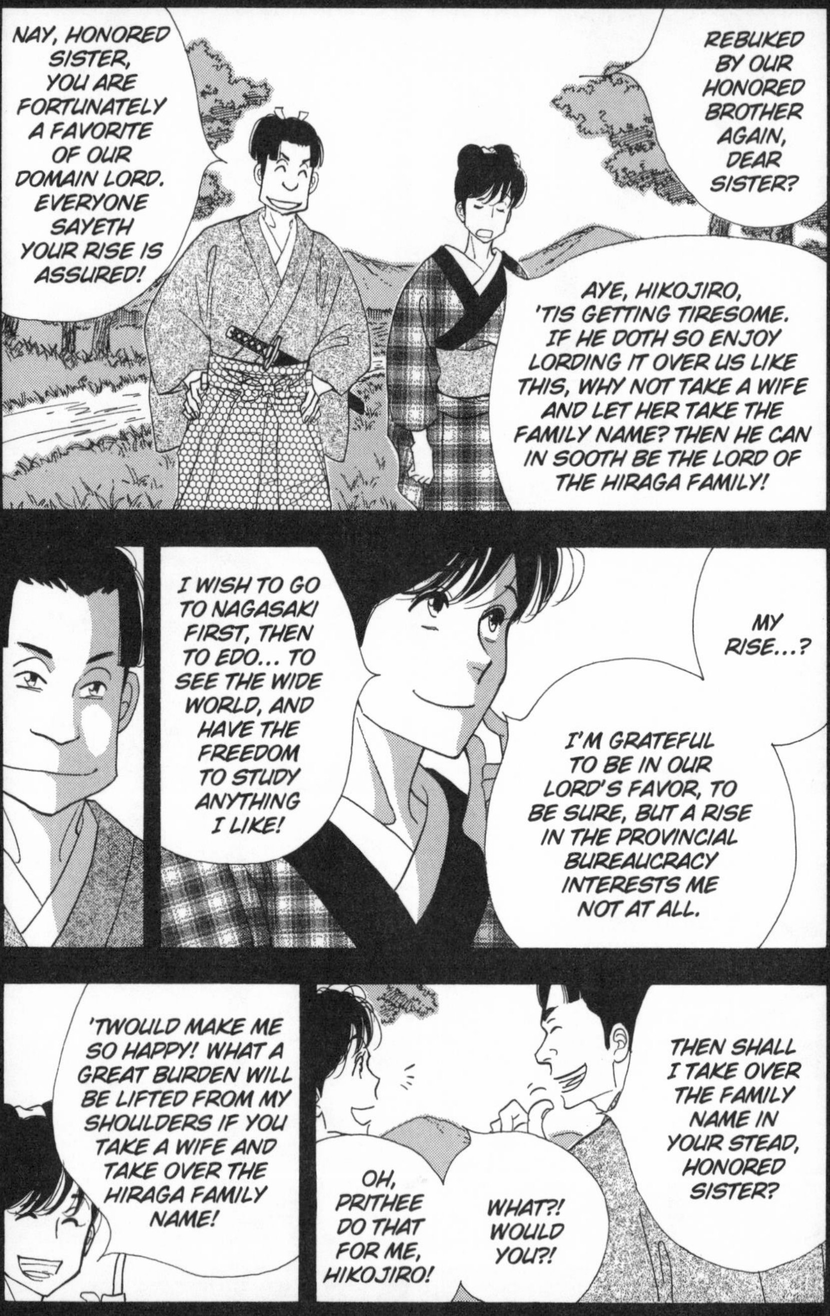
REBUKED BY OUR HONORED BROTHER AGAIN, DEAR SISTER?
AYE, HIKOJIRO, 'TIS GETTING TIRESOME. IF HE DOTH SO ENJOY LORDING IT OVER US LIKE THIS, WHY NOT TAKE A WIFE AND LET HER TAKE THE FAMILY NAME? THEN HE CAN IN SOOTH BE THE LORD OF THE HIRAGA FAMILY!
NAY, HONORED SISTER, YOU ARE FORTUNATELY A FAVORITE OF OUR DOMAIN LORD. EVERYONE SAYETH YOUR RISE IS ASSURED!
MY RISE...?
I'M GRATEFUL TO BE IN OUR LORD'S FAVOR, TO BE SURE, BUT A RISE IN THE PROVINCIAL BUREAUCRACY INTERESTS ME NOT AT ALL.
I WISH TO GO TO NAGASAKI FIRST, THEN TO EDO... TO SEE THE WIDE WORLD, AND HAVE THE FREEDOM TO STUDY ANYTHING I LIKE!
THEN SHALL I TAKE OVER THE FAMILY NAME IN YOUR STEAD, HONORED SISTER?
OH, PRITHEE DO THAT FOR ME, HIKOJIRO!
WHAT?! WOULD YOU?!
'TWOULD MAKE ME SO HAPPY! WHAT A GREAT BURDEN WILL BE LIFTED FROM MY SHOULDERS IF YOU TAKE A WIFE AND TAKE OVER THE HIRAGA FAMILY NAME!

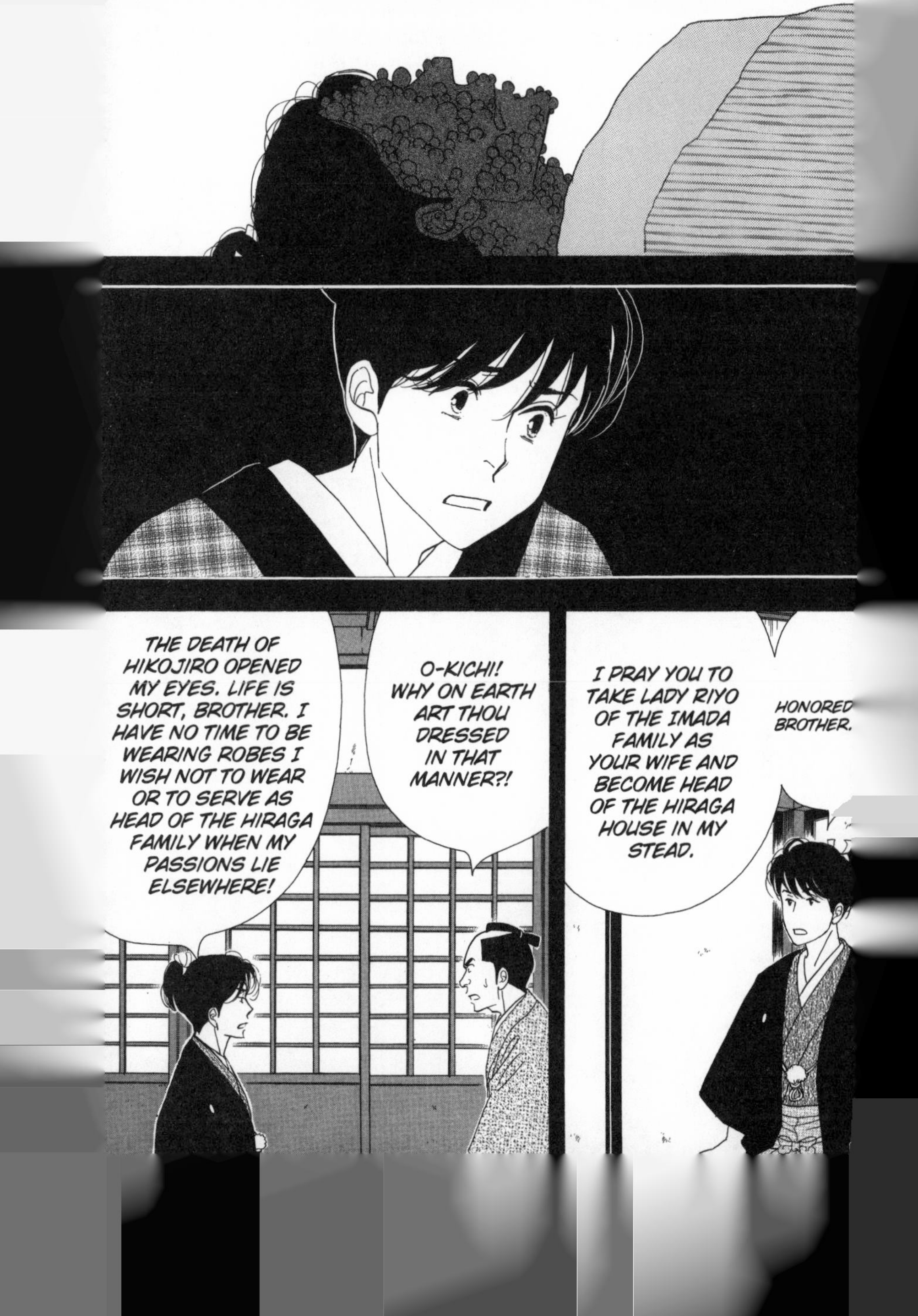
HONORED BROTHER.
I PRAY YOU TO TAKE LADY RIYO OF THE IMADA FAMILY AS YOUR WIFE AND BECOME HEAD OF THE HIRAGA HOUSE IN MY STEAD.
O-KICHI! WHY ON EARTH ART THOU DRESSED IN THAT MANNER?!
THE DEATH OF HIKOJIRO OPENED MY EYES. LIFE IS SHORT, BROTHER. I HAVE NO TIME TO BE WEARING ROBES I WISH NOT TO WEAR OR TO SERVE AS HEAD OF THE HIRAGA FAMILY WHEN MY PASSIONS LIE ELSEWHERE!

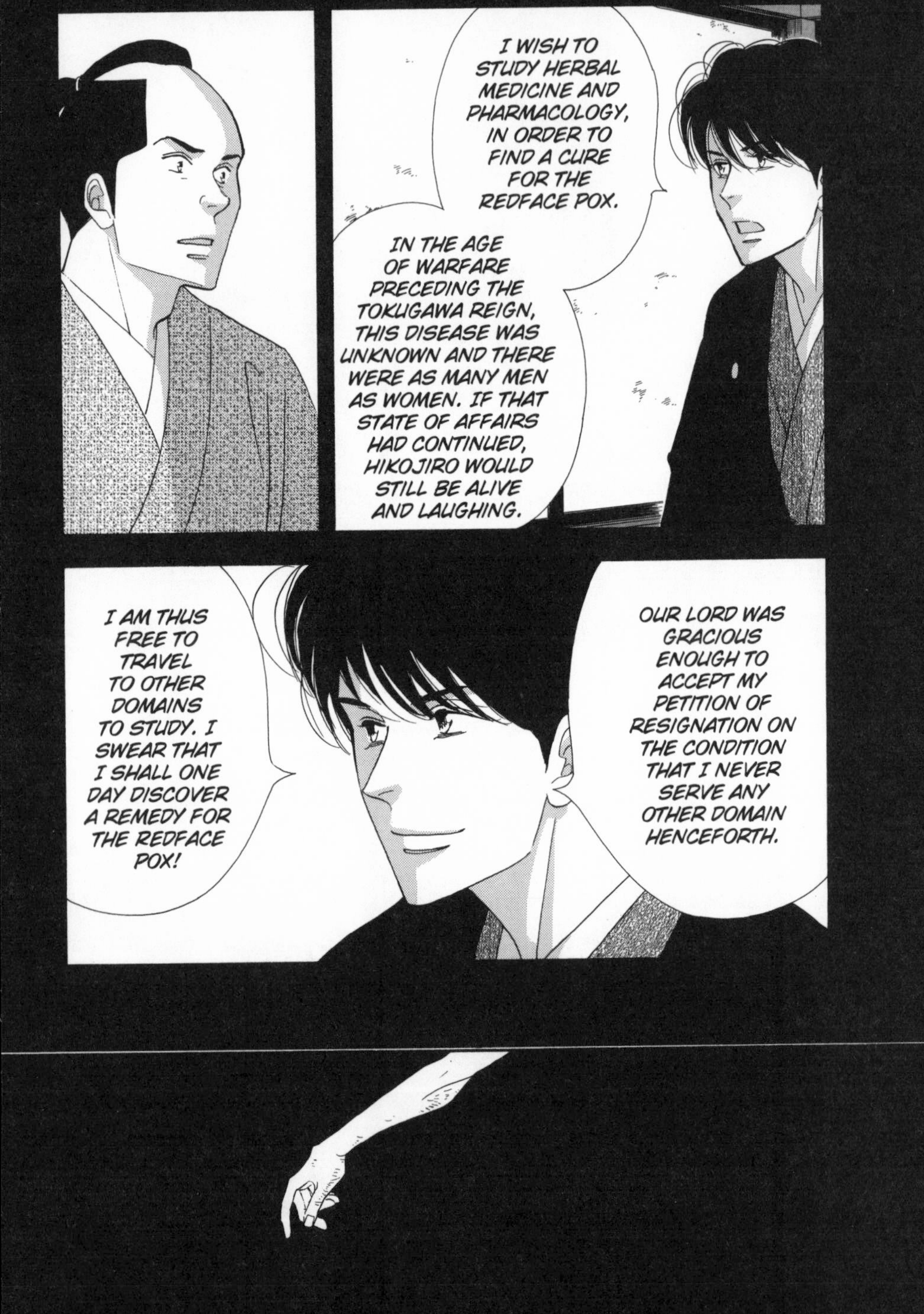
I WISH TO STUDY HERBAL MEDICINE AND PHARMACOLOGY, IN ORDER TO FIND A CURE FOR THE REDFACE POX.
IN THE AGE OF WARFARE PRECEDING THE TOKUGAWA REIGN, THIS DISEASE WAS UNKNOWN AND THERE WERE AS MANY MEN AS WOMEN. IF THAT STATE OF AFFAIRS HAD CONTINUED, HIKOJIRO WOULD STILL BE ALIVE AND LAUGHING.
OUR LORD WAS GRACIOUS ENOUGH TO ACCEPT MY PETITION OF RESIGNATION ON THE CONDITION THAT I NEVER SERVE ANY OTHER DOMAIN HENCEFORTH.
I AM THUS FREE TO TRAVEL TO OTHER DOMAINS TO STUDY. I SWEAR THAT I SHALL ONE DAY DISCOVER A REMEDY FOR THE REDFACE POX!

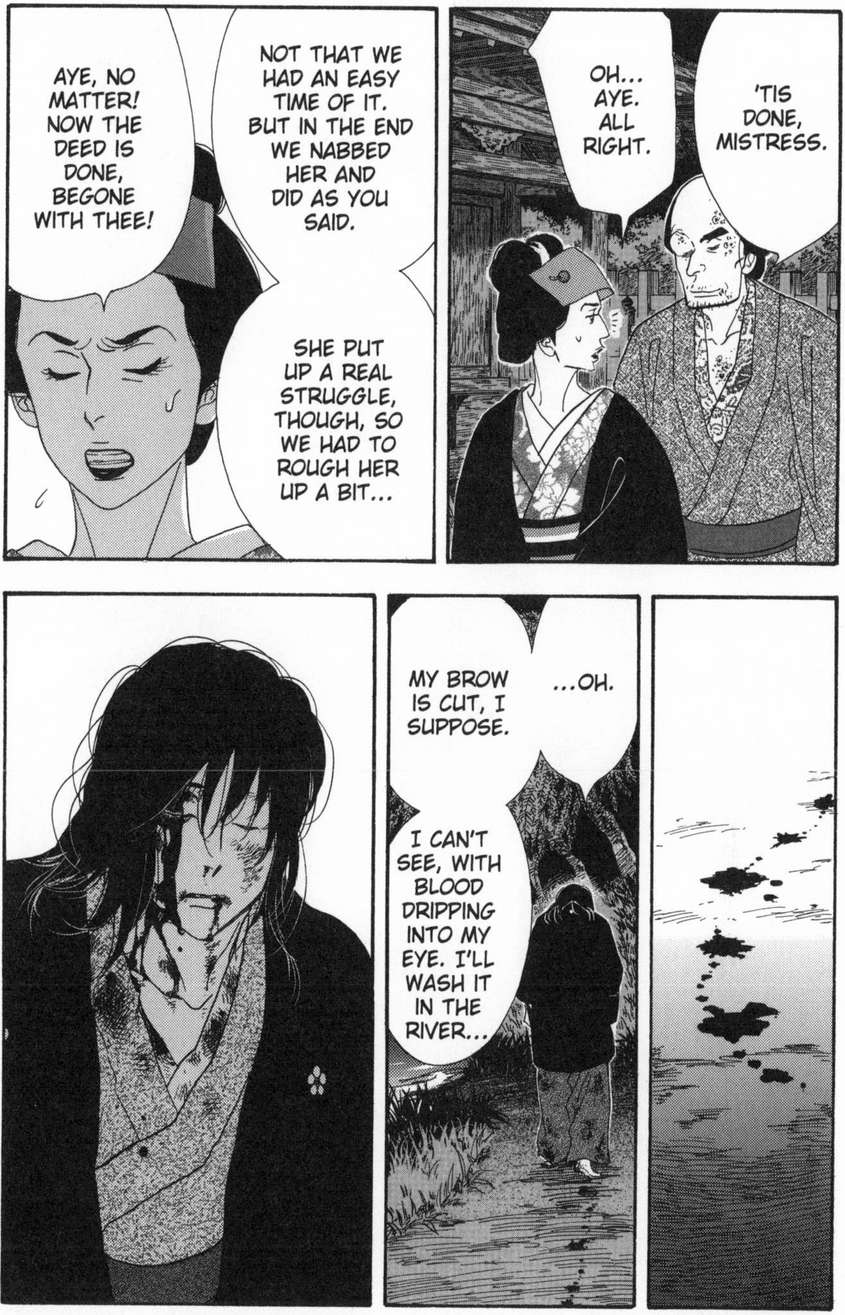
'TIS DONE, MISTRESS.
OH... AYE. ALL RIGHT.
NOT THAT WE HAD AN EASY TIME OF IT. BUT IN THE END WE NABBED HER AND DID AS YOU SAID.
SHE PUT UP A REAL STRUGGLE, THOUGH, SO WE HAD TO ROUGH HER UP A BIT...
AYE, NO MATTER! NOW THE DEED IS DONE, BEGONE WITH THEE!
...OH.
MY BROW IS CUT, I SUPPOSE.
I CAN'T SEE, WITH BLOOD DRIPPING INTO MY EYE. I'LL WASH IT IN THE RIVER...

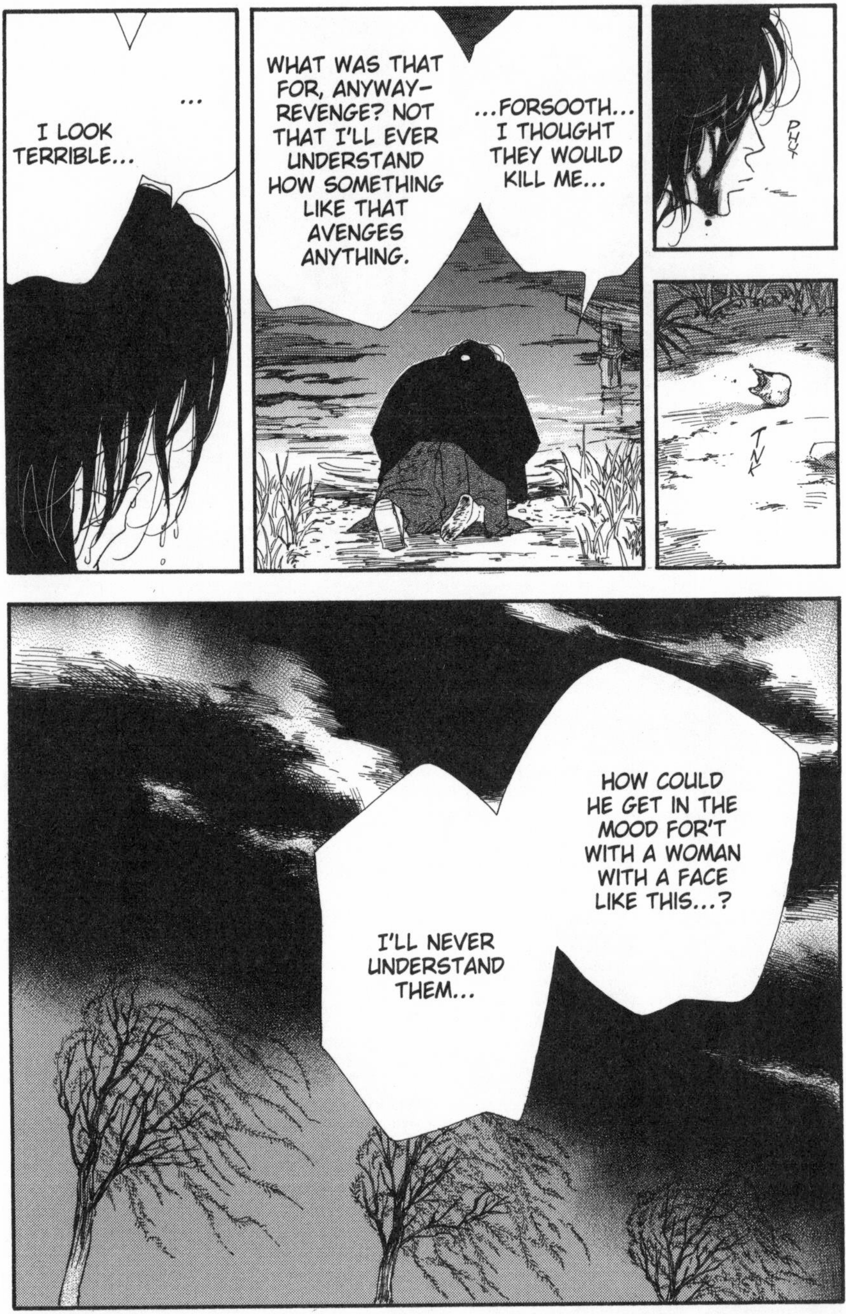
PHUT
TNK
...FORSOOTH... I THOUGHT THEY WOULD KILL ME...
WHAT WAS THAT FOR, ANYWAY—REVENGE? NOT THAT I'LL EVER UNDERSTAND HOW SOMETHING LIKE THAT AVENGES ANYTHING.
...
I LOOK TERRIBLE...
HOW COULD HE GET IN THE MOOD FOR'T WITH A WOMAN WITH A FACE LIKE THIS...?
I'LL NEVER UNDERSTAND THEM...

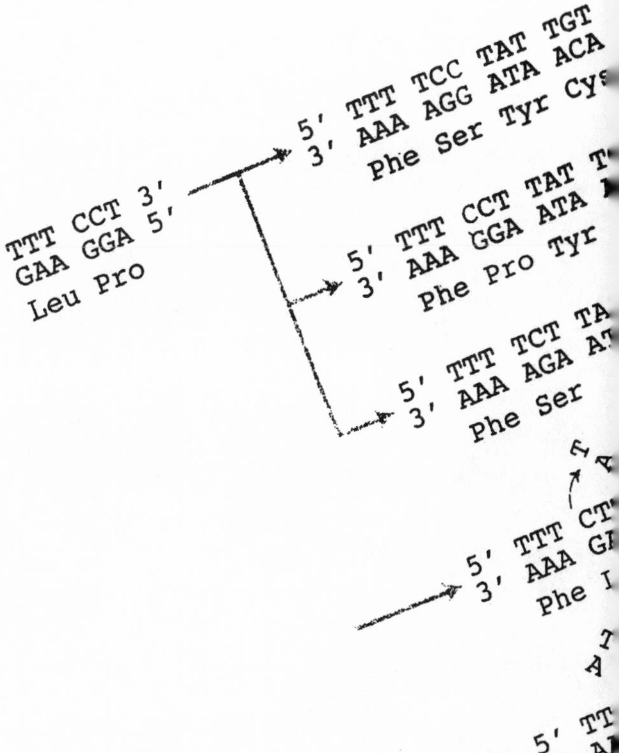
TTT CCT 3′
GAA GGA 5′
Leu Pro
5′ TTT TCC TAT TGT
3′ AAA AGG ATA ACA
Phe Ser Tyr Cys
5′ TTT CCT TAT
3′ AAA GGA ATA
Phe Pro Tyr
5′ TTT TCT TA
3′ AAA AGA AT
Phe Ser
5′ TTT CT
3′ AAA GA
Phe
5′ TT
3′ AA

Ōoku

THE INNER CHAMBERS

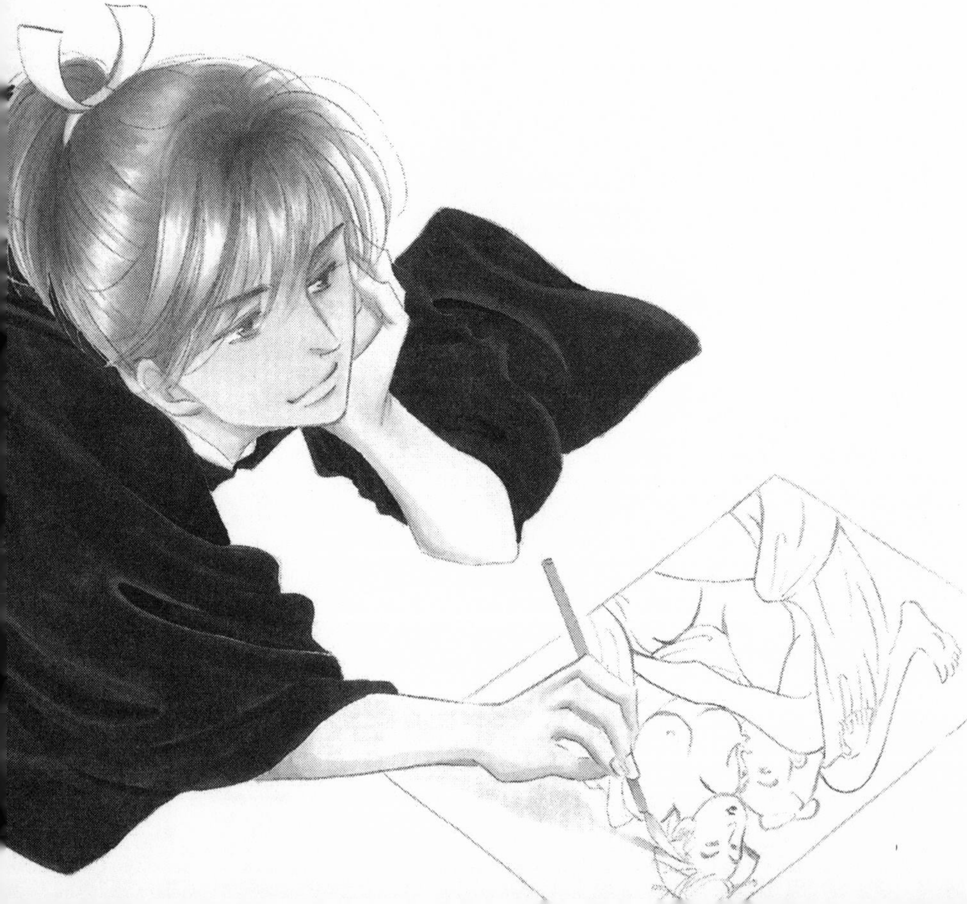

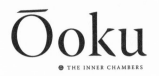

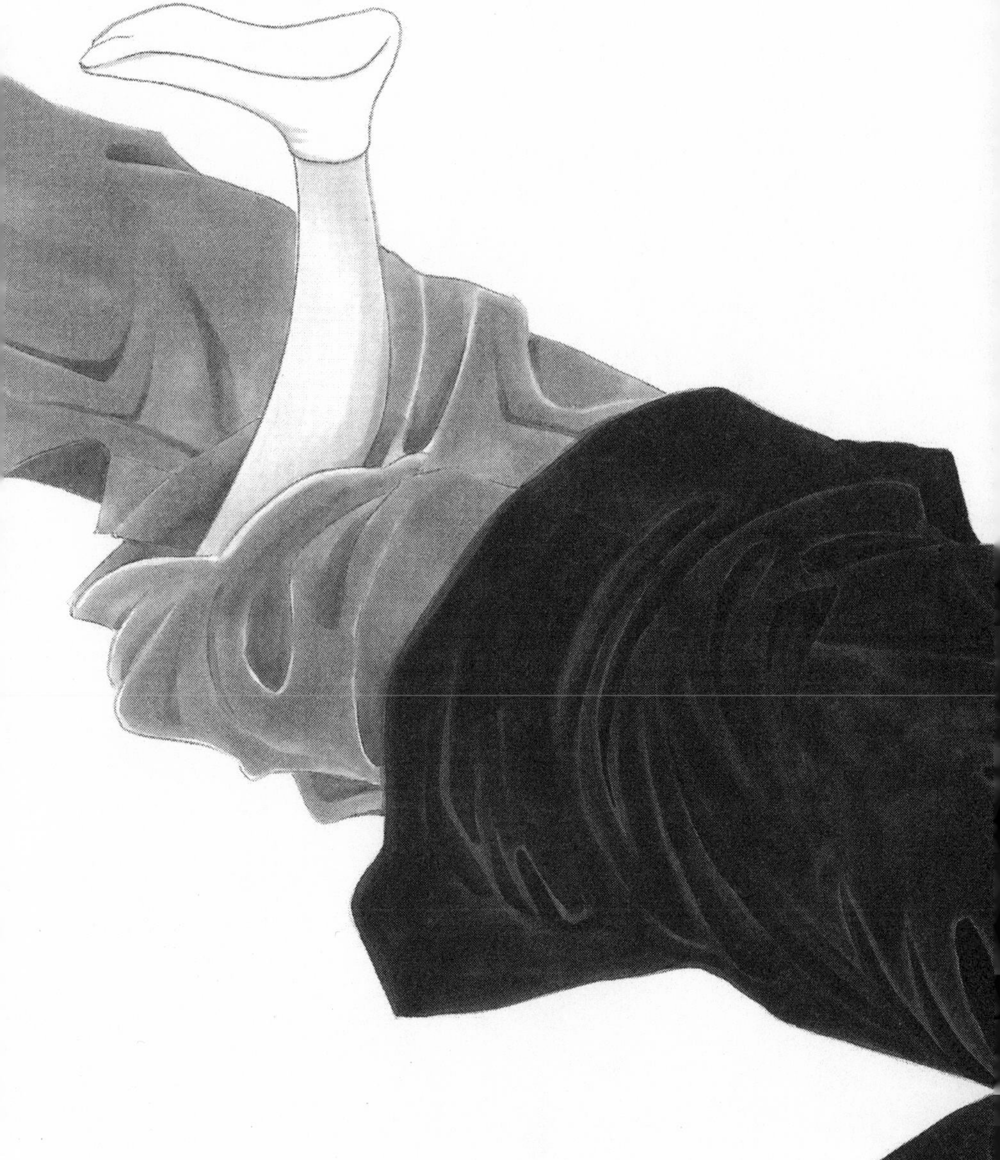

Ōoku

THE INNER CHAMBERS

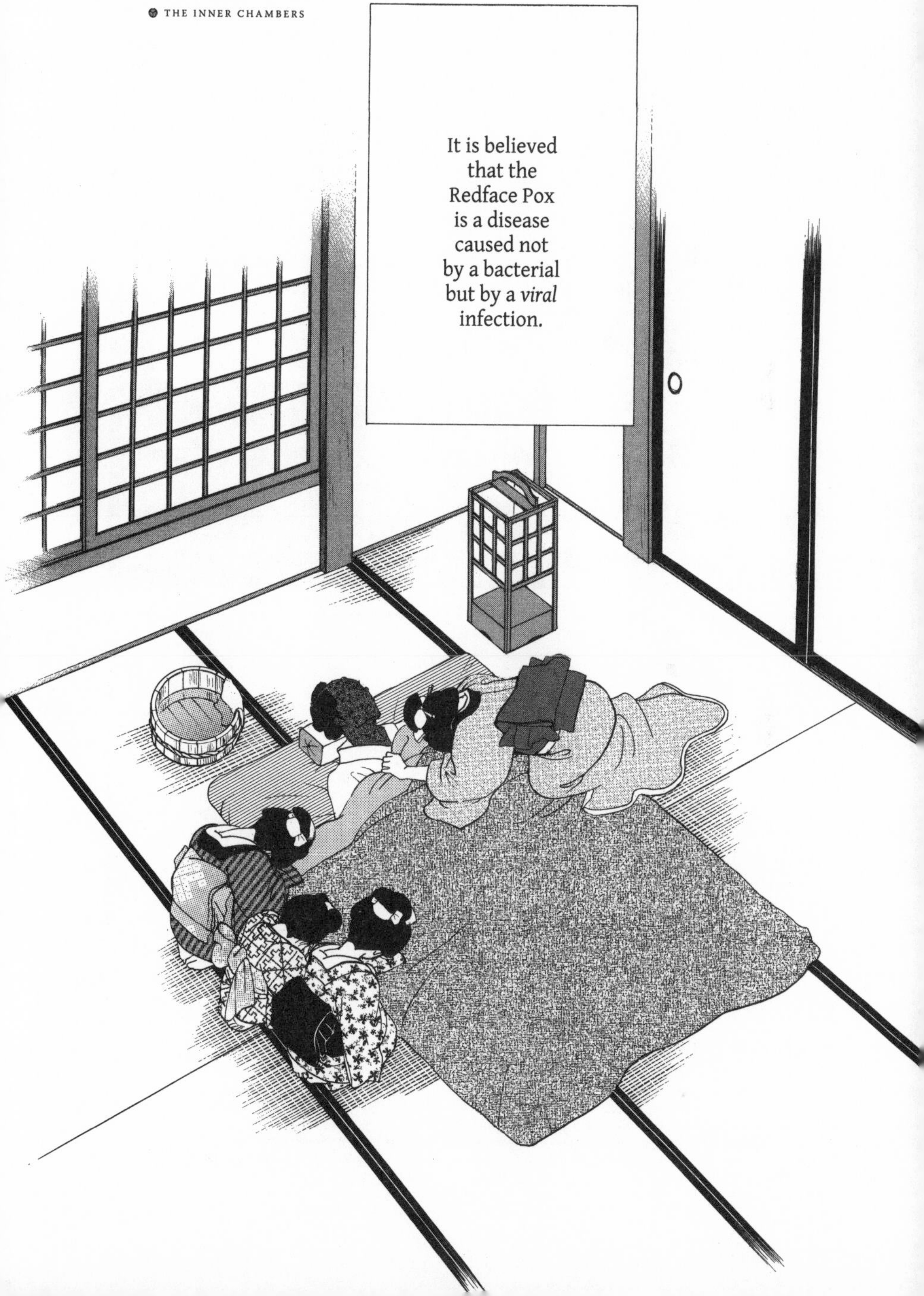
It is believed that the Redface Pox is a disease caused not by a bacterial but by a *viral* infection.

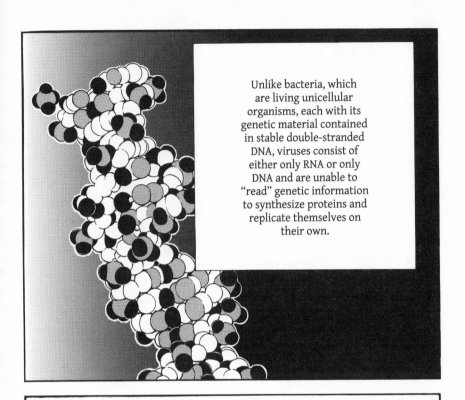

Unlike bacteria, which are living unicellular organisms, each with its genetic material contained in stable double-stranded DNA, viruses consist of either only RNA or only DNA and are unable to "read" genetic information to synthesize proteins and replicate themselves on their own.

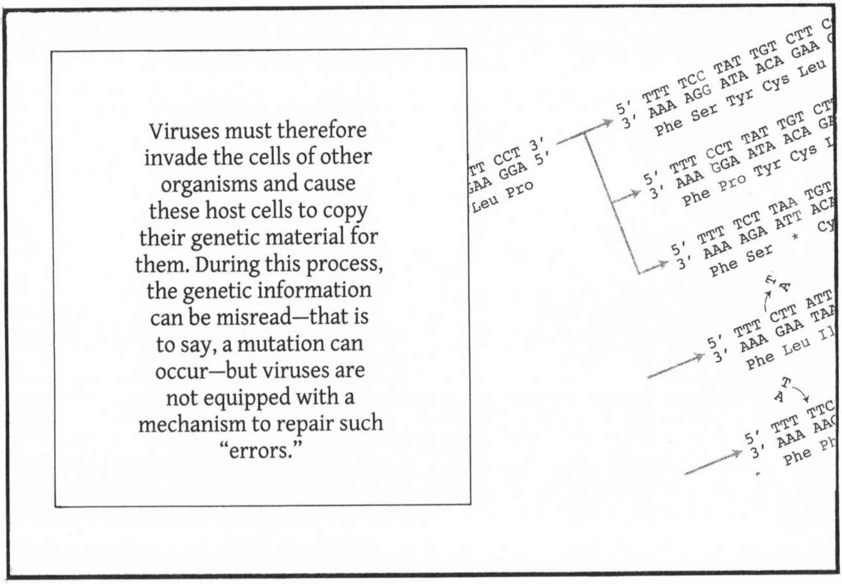

Viruses must therefore invade the cells of other organisms and cause these host cells to copy their genetic material for them. During this process, the genetic information can be misread—that is to say, a mutation can occur—but viruses are not equipped with a mechanism to repair such "errors."

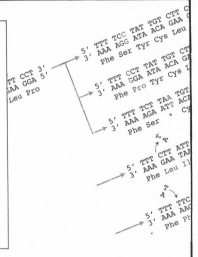

One type of mutation that occurs results in a weakened form of the virus.

If people are infected in advance with this weakened form of the virus, their bodies are able to fight it off, and retain a memory of this resistance.

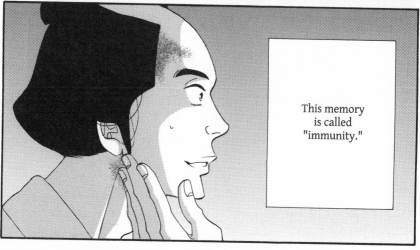

This memory is called "immunity."

The weakened
form of a virus
that is deliberately
inoculated into
people as a
defense against
the original
stronger form is
called a vaccine.

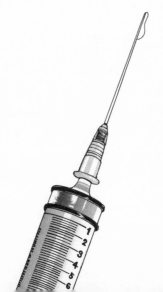

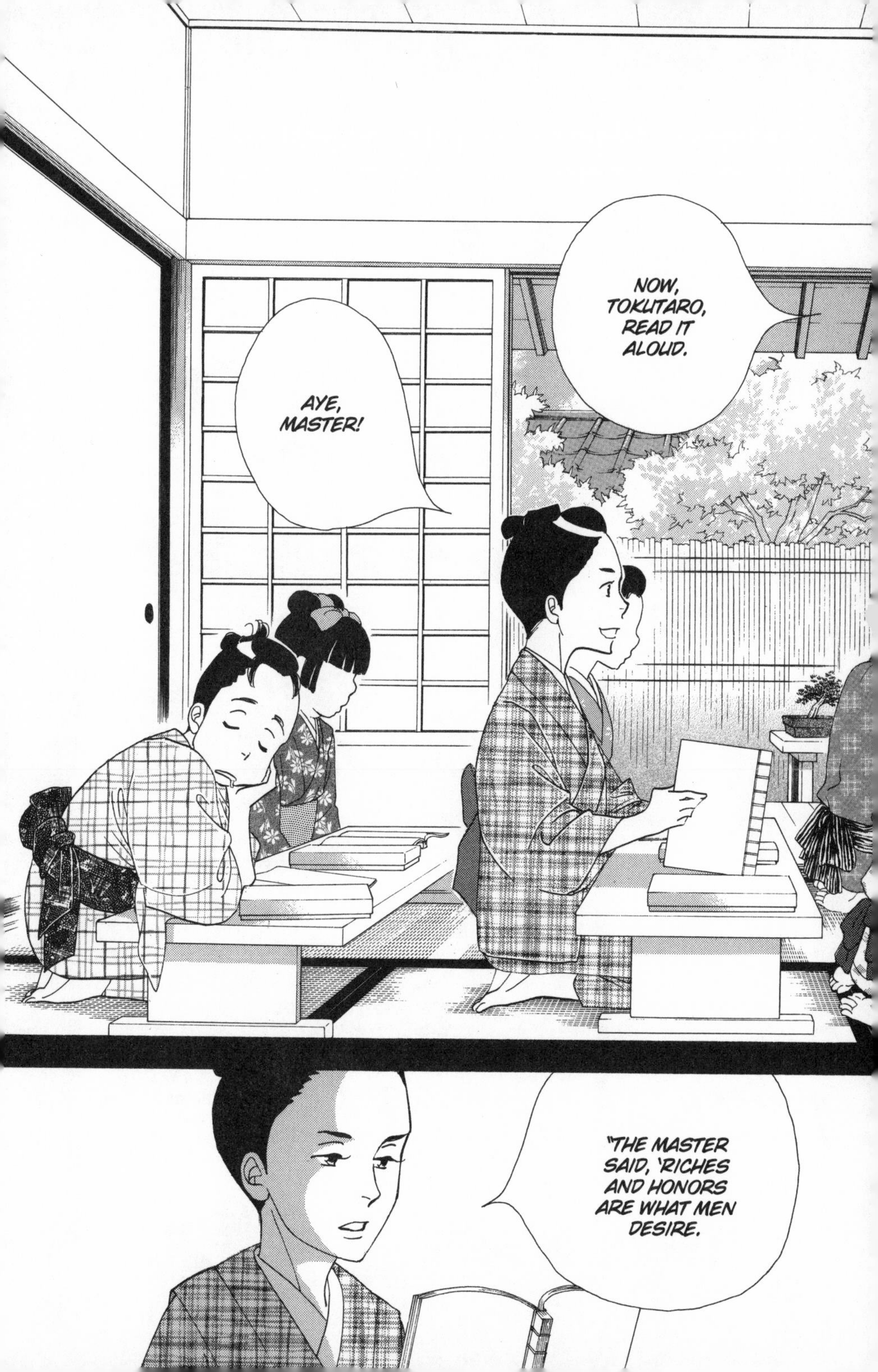
NOW, TOKUTARO, READ IT ALOUD.
AYE, MASTER!
"THE MASTER SAID, 'RICHES AND HONORS ARE WHAT MEN DESIRE.

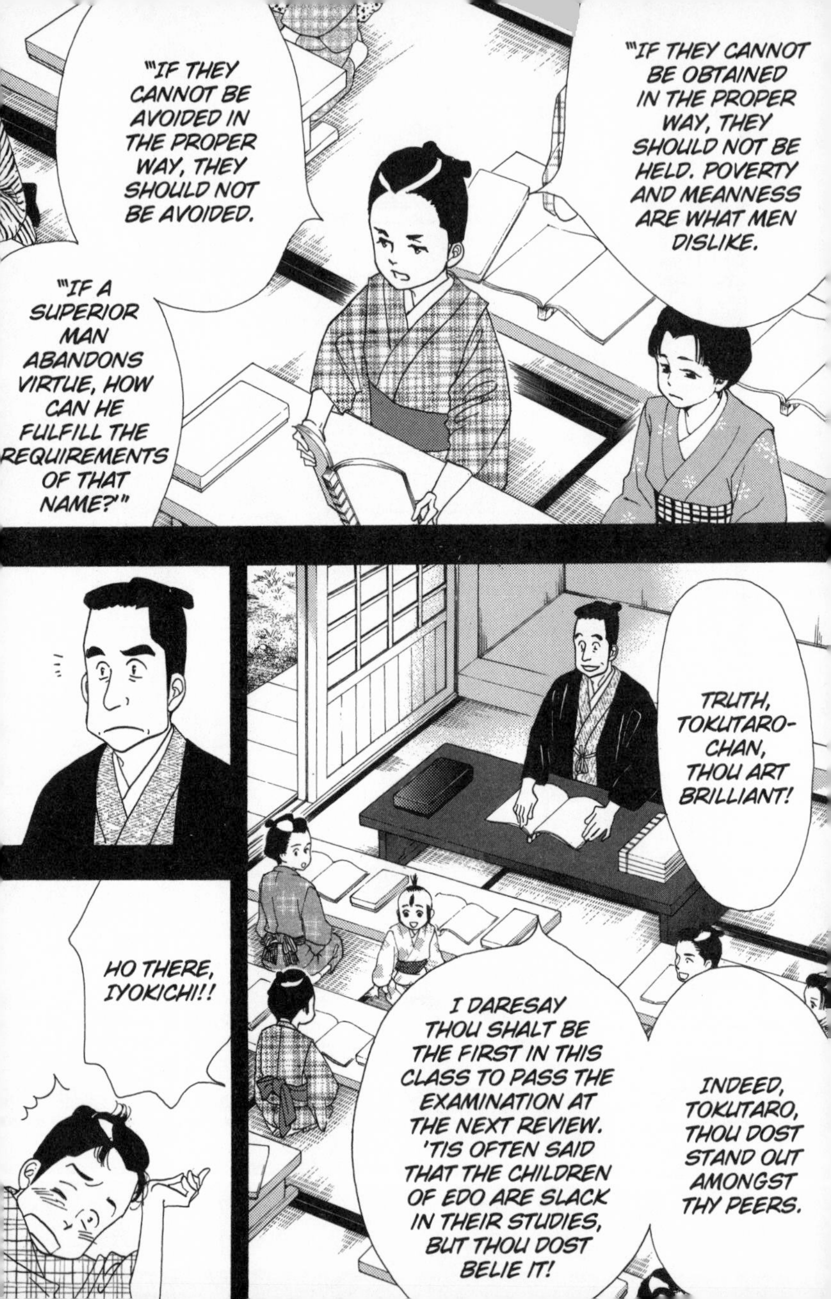
"'IF THEY CANNOT BE OBTAINED IN THE PROPER WAY, THEY SHOULD NOT BE HELD. POVERTY AND MEANNESS ARE WHAT MEN DISLIKE.
"'IF THEY CANNOT BE AVOIDED IN THE PROPER WAY, THEY SHOULD NOT BE AVOIDED.
"'IF A SUPERIOR MAN ABANDONS VIRTUE, HOW CAN HE FULFILL THE REQUIREMENTS OF THAT NAME?'"
TRUTH, TOKUTARO-CHAN, THOU ART BRILLIANT!
INDEED, TOKUTARO, THOU DOST STAND OUT AMONGST THY PEERS.
I DARESAY THOU SHALT BE THE FIRST IN THIS CLASS TO PASS THE EXAMINATION AT THE NEXT REVIEW. 'TIS OFTEN SAID THAT THE CHILDREN OF EDO ARE SLACK IN THEIR STUDIES, BUT THOU DOST BELIE IT!
HO THERE, IYOKICHI!!

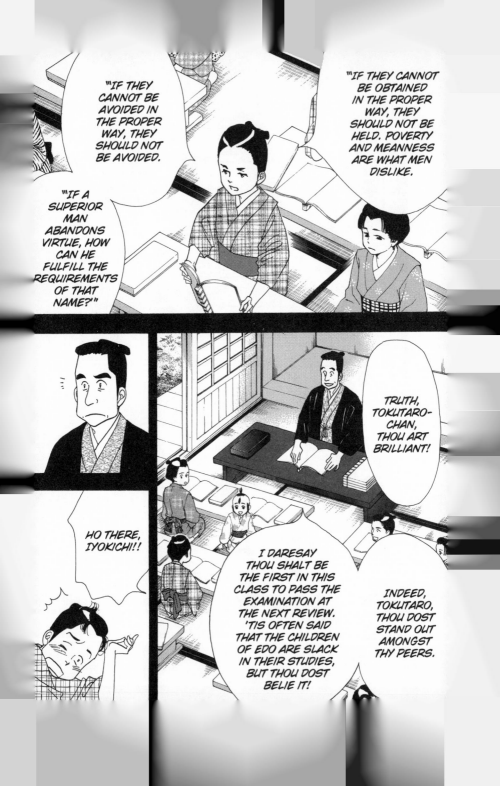

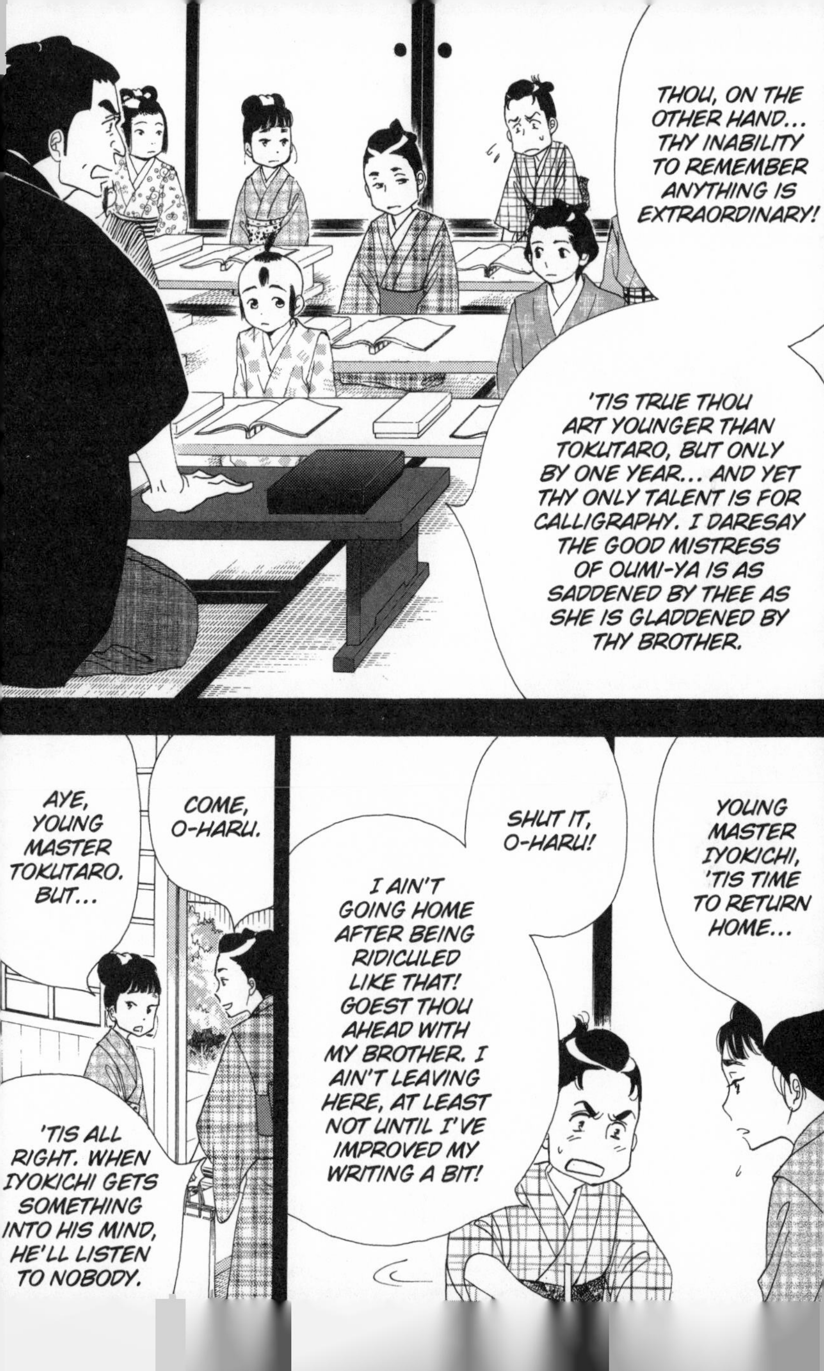
THOU, ON THE OTHER HAND... THY INABILITY TO REMEMBER ANYTHING IS EXTRAORDINARY!
'TIS TRUE THOU ART YOUNGER THAN TOKUTARO, BUT ONLY BY ONE YEAR... AND YET THY ONLY TALENT IS FOR CALLIGRAPHY. I DARESAY THE GOOD MISTRESS OF OUMI-YA IS AS SADDENED BY THEE AS SHE IS GLADDENED BY THY BROTHER.
YOUNG MASTER IYOKICHI, 'TIS TIME TO RETURN HOME...
SHUT IT, O-HARU!
I AIN'T GOING HOME AFTER BEING RIDICULED LIKE THAT! GOEST THOU AHEAD WITH MY BROTHER. I AIN'T LEAVING HERE, AT LEAST NOT UNTIL I'VE IMPROVED MY WRITING A BIT!
COME, O-HARU.
AYE, YOUNG MASTER TOKUTARO. BUT...
'TIS ALL RIGHT. WHEN IYOKICHI GETS SOMETHING INTO HIS MIND, HE'LL LISTEN TO NOBODY.

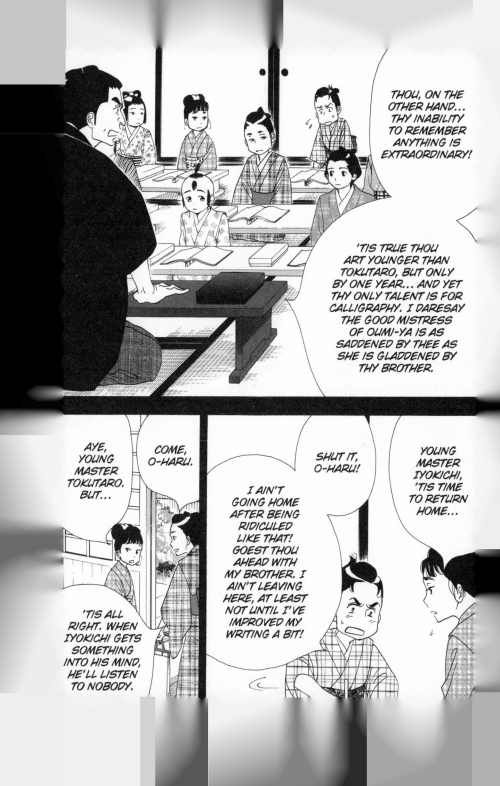

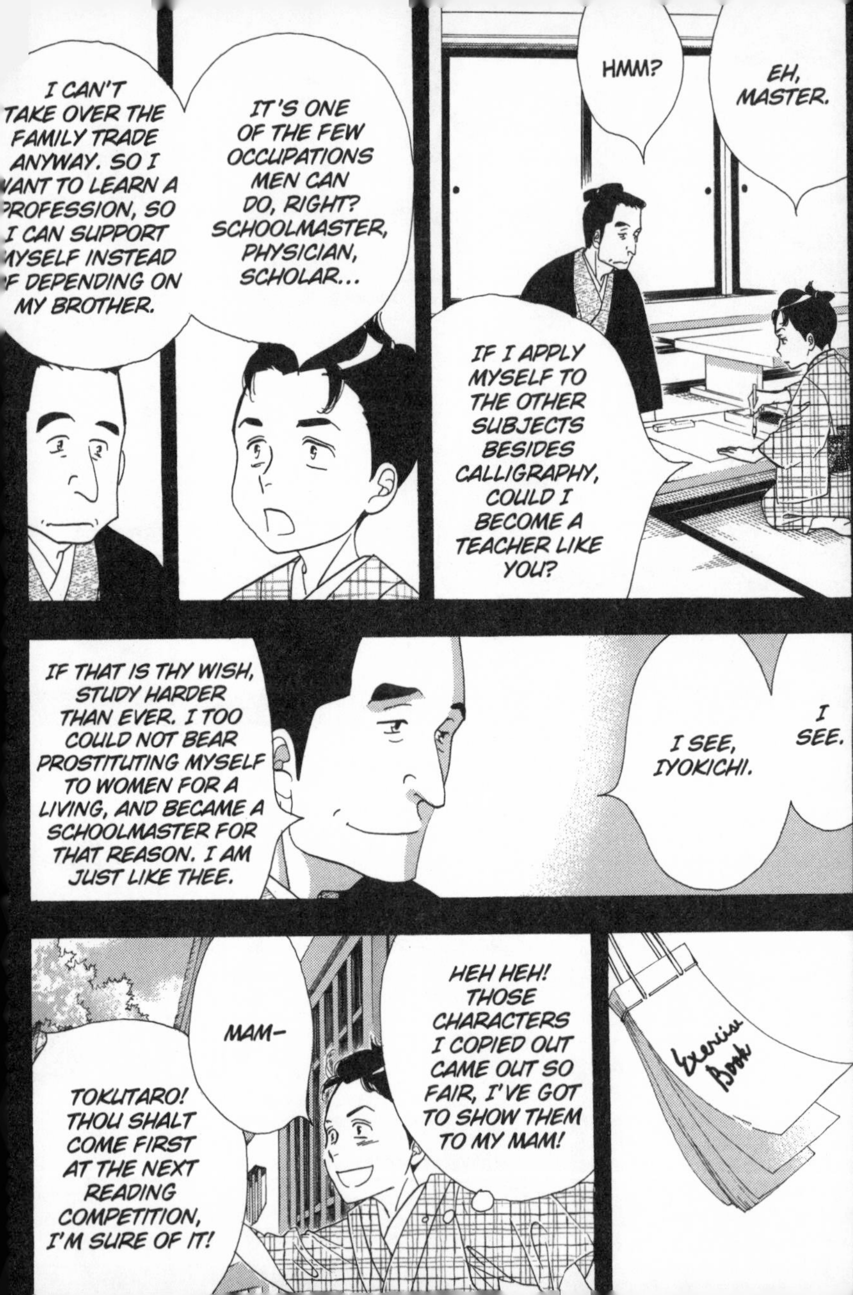
EH, MASTER.
HMM?
IF I APPLY MYSELF TO THE OTHER SUBJECTS BESIDES CALLIGRAPHY, COULD I BECOME A TEACHER LIKE YOU?
IT'S ONE OF THE FEW OCCUPATIONS MEN CAN DO, RIGHT? SCHOOLMASTER, PHYSICIAN, SCHOLAR...
I CAN'T TAKE OVER THE FAMILY TRADE ANYWAY. SO I WANT TO LEARN A PROFESSION, SO I CAN SUPPORT MYSELF INSTEAD OF DEPENDING ON MY BROTHER.
I SEE.
I SEE, IYOKICHI.
IF THAT IS THY WISH, STUDY HARDER THAN EVER. I TOO COULD NOT BEAR PROSTITUTING MYSELF TO WOMEN FOR A LIVING, AND BECAME A SCHOOLMASTER FOR THAT REASON. I AM JUST LIKE THEE.
Exercise Book
HEH HEH! THOSE CHARACTERS I COPIED OUT CAME OUT SO FAIR, I'VE GOT TO SHOW THEM TO MY MAM!
MAM-
TOKUTARO! THOU SHALT COME FIRST AT THE NEXT READING COMPETITION, I'M SURE OF IT!

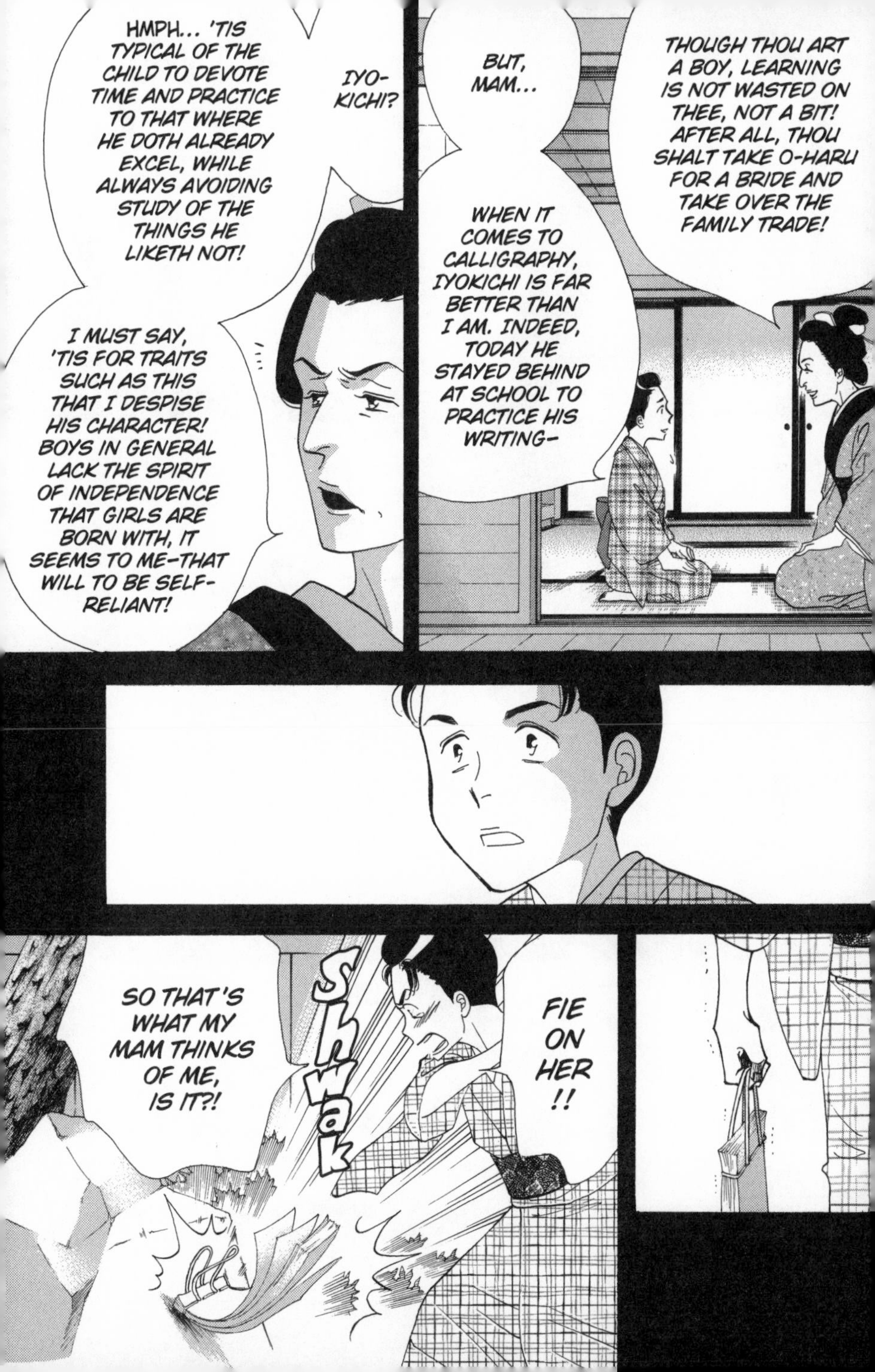
THOUGH THOU ART A BOY, LEARNING IS NOT WASTED ON THEE, NOT A BIT! AFTER ALL, THOU SHALT TAKE O-HARU FOR A BRIDE AND TAKE OVER THE FAMILY TRADE!
BUT, MAM...
WHEN IT COMES TO CALLIGRAPHY, IYOKICHI IS FAR BETTER THAN I AM. INDEED, TODAY HE STAYED BEHIND AT SCHOOL TO PRACTICE HIS WRITING-
IYO-KICHI?
HMPH... 'TIS TYPICAL OF THE CHILD TO DEVOTE TIME AND PRACTICE TO THAT WHERE HE DOTH ALREADY EXCEL, WHILE ALWAYS AVOIDING STUDY OF THE THINGS HE LIKETH NOT!
I MUST SAY, 'TIS FOR TRAITS SUCH AS THIS THAT I DESPISE HIS CHARACTER! BOYS IN GENERAL LACK THE SPIRIT OF INDEPENDENCE THAT GIRLS ARE BORN WITH, IT SEEMS TO ME-THAT WILL TO BE SELF-RELIANT!
FIE ON HER !!
Shwak
SO THAT'S WHAT MY MAM THINKS OF ME, IS IT?!

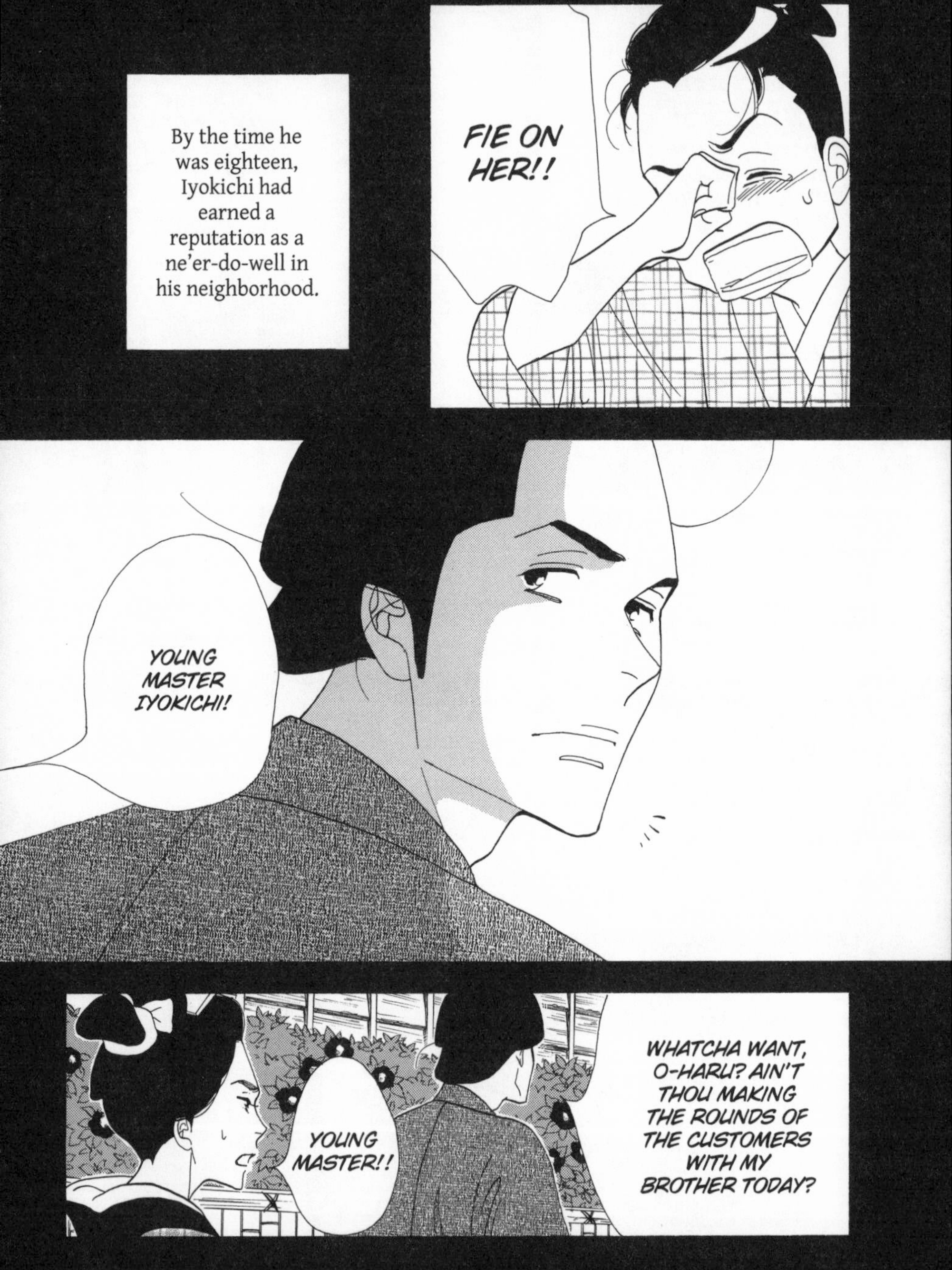
FIE ON HER!!
By the time he was eighteen, Iyokichi had earned a reputation as a ne'er-do-well in his neighborhood.
YOUNG MASTER IYOKICHI!
WHATCHA WANT, O-HARU? AIN'T THOU MAKING THE ROUNDS OF THE CUSTOMERS WITH MY BROTHER TODAY?
YOUNG MASTER!!

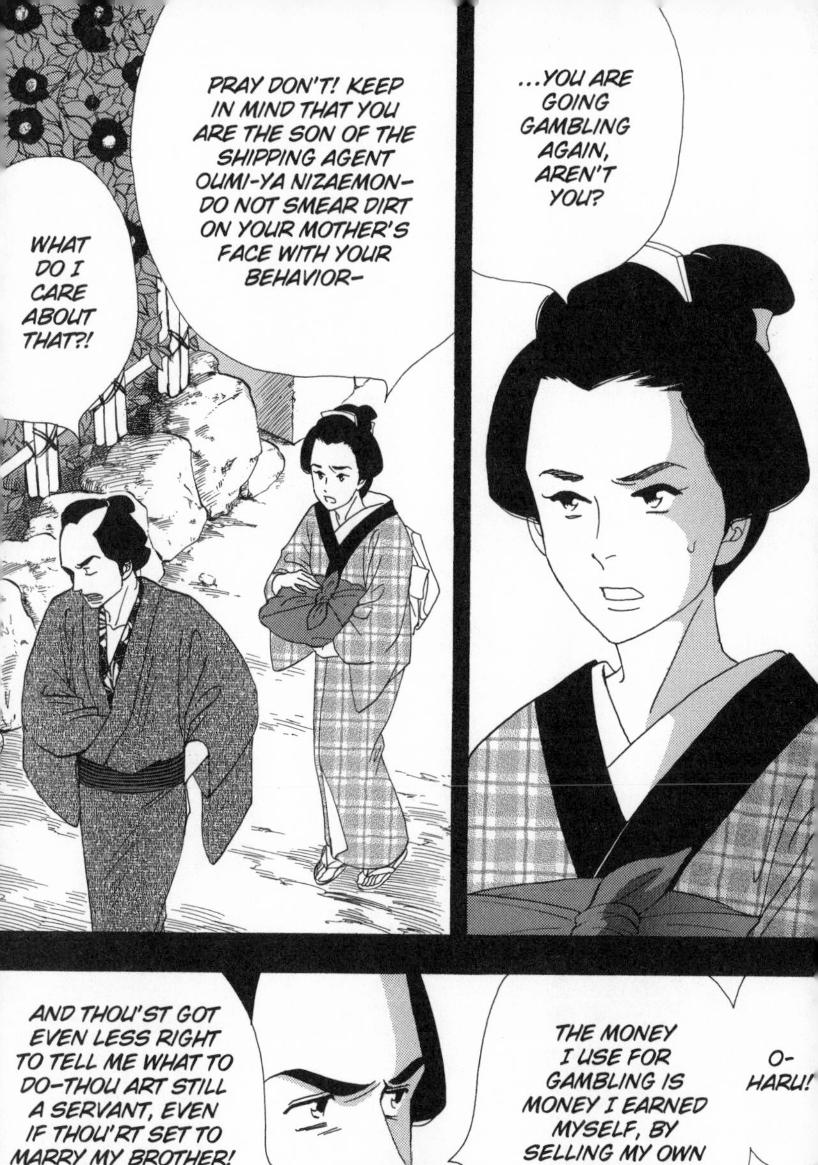
...YOU ARE GOING GAMBLING AGAIN, AREN'T YOU?
PRAY DON'T! KEEP IN MIND THAT YOU ARE THE SON OF THE SHIPPING AGENT OUMI-YA NIZAEMON- DO NOT SMEAR DIRT ON YOUR MOTHER'S FACE WITH YOUR BEHAVIOR-
WHAT DO I CARE ABOUT THAT?!
O-HARU!
THE MONEY I USE FOR GAMBLING IS MONEY I EARNED MYSELF, BY SELLING MY OWN BODY-MY MAM'S GOT NO RIGHT TO SAY ANYTHING ABOUT IT!
AND THOU'ST GOT EVEN LESS RIGHT TO TELL ME WHAT TO DO-THOU ART STILL A SERVANT, EVEN IF THOU'RT SET TO MARRY MY BROTHER! THOU NE'ER SPAKEST TO ME LIKE THIS BEFORE, EH, SISTER O-HARU?!

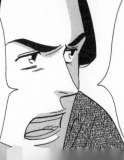

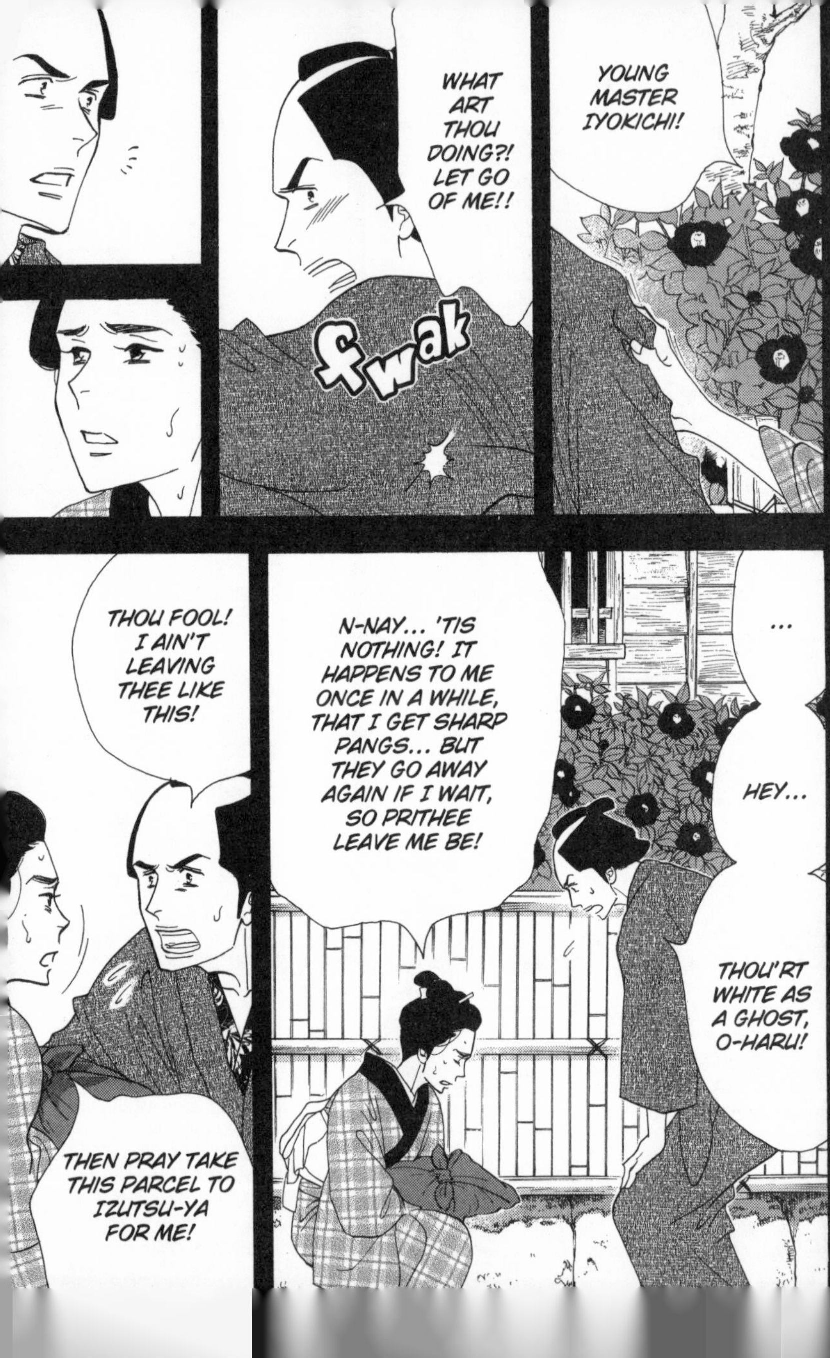
YOUNG MASTER IYOKICHI!
WHAT ART THOU DOING?! LET GO OF ME!!
fwak
...
HEY...
THOU'RT WHITE AS A GHOST, O-HARU!
N-NAY... 'TIS NOTHING! IT HAPPENS TO ME ONCE IN A WHILE, THAT I GET SHARP PANGS... BUT THEY GO AWAY AGAIN IF I WAIT, SO PRITHEE LEAVE ME BE!
THOU FOOL! I AIN'T LEAVING THEE LIKE THIS!
THEN PRAY TAKE THIS PARCEL TO IZUTSU-YA FOR ME!

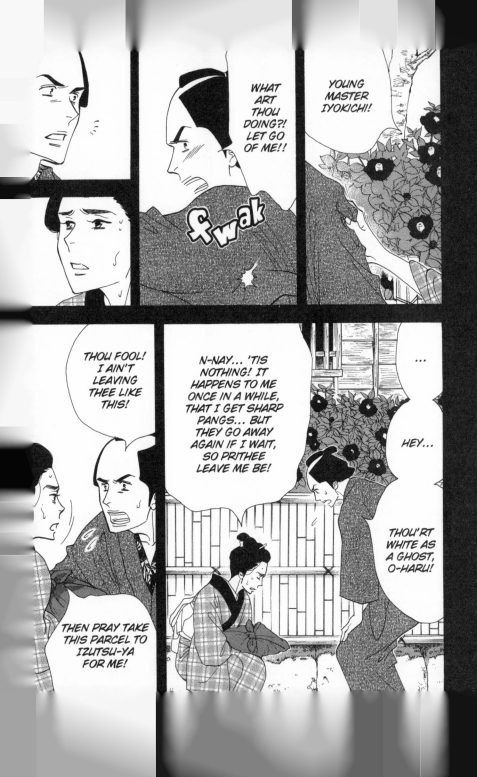

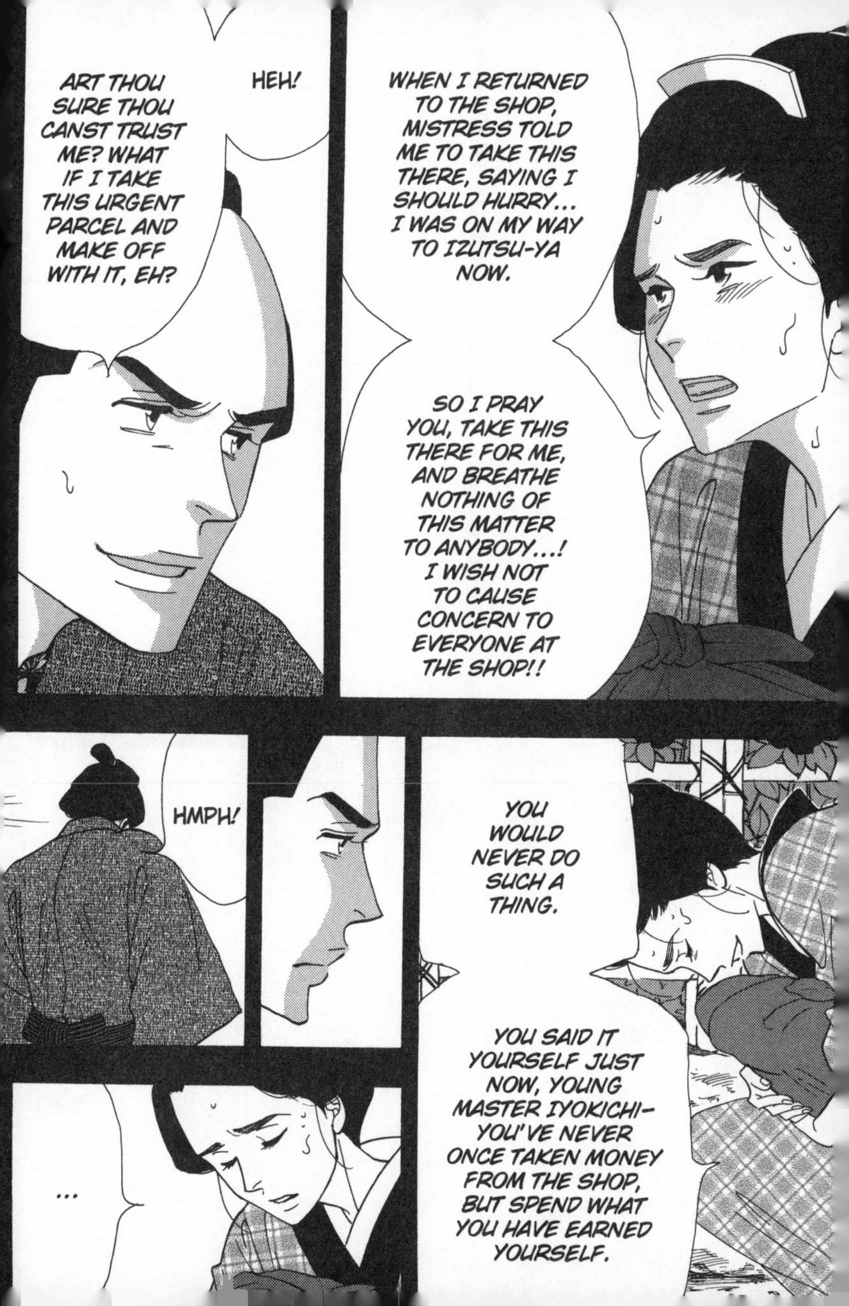
WHEN I RETURNED TO THE SHOP, MISTRESS TOLD ME TO TAKE THIS THERE, SAYING I SHOULD HURRY... I WAS ON MY WAY TO IZUTSU-YA NOW.
SO I PRAY YOU, TAKE THIS THERE FOR ME, AND BREATHE NOTHING OF THIS MATTER TO ANYBODY...! I WISH NOT TO CAUSE CONCERN TO EVERYONE AT THE SHOP!!
HEH!
ART THOU SURE THOU CANST TRUST ME? WHAT IF I TAKE THIS URGENT PARCEL AND MAKE OFF WITH IT, EH?
YOU WOULD NEVER DO SUCH A THING.
YOU SAID IT YOURSELF JUST NOW, YOUNG MASTER IYOKICHI-YOU'VE NEVER ONCE TAKEN MONEY FROM THE SHOP, BUT SPEND WHAT YOU HAVE EARNED YOURSELF.
HMPH!
...

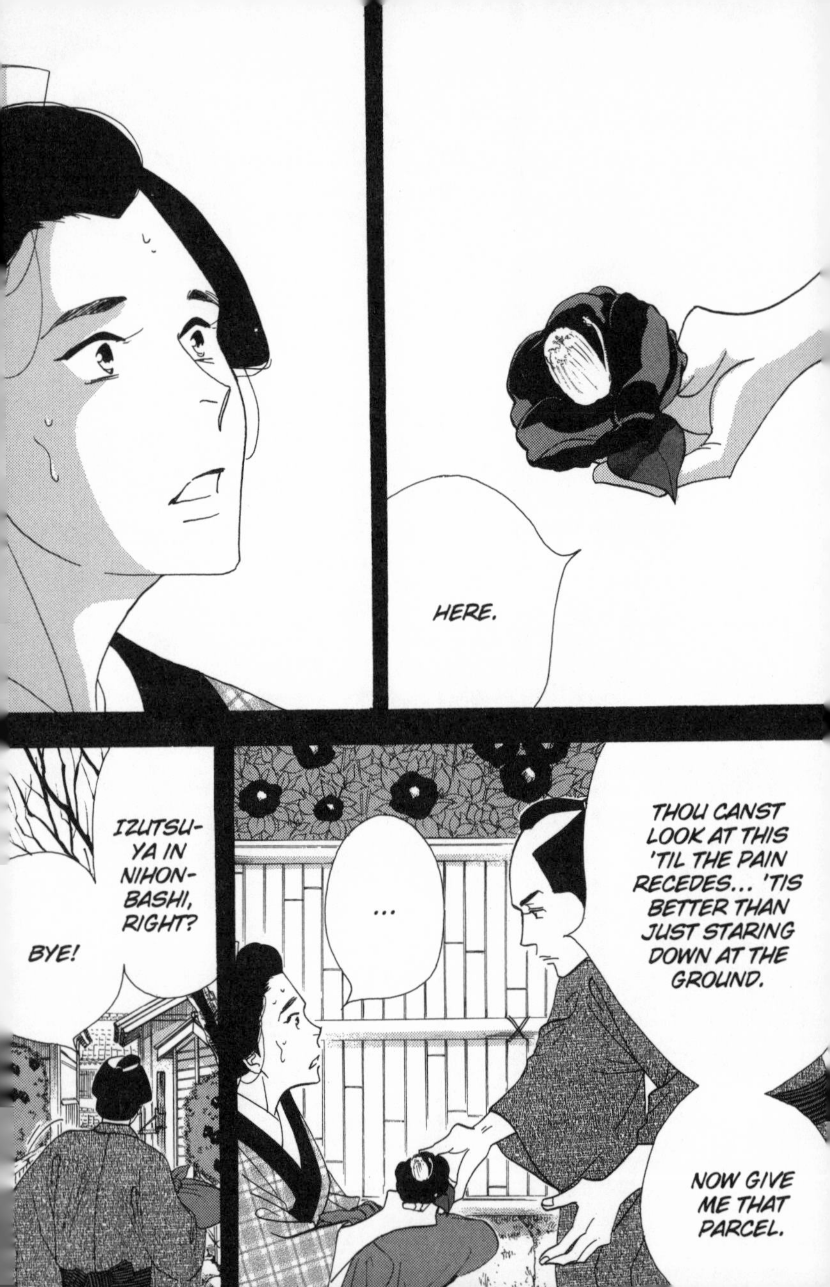
HERE.
THOU CANST LOOK AT THIS 'TIL THE PAIN RECEDES... 'TIS BETTER THAN JUST STARING DOWN AT THE GROUND.
...
NOW GIVE ME THAT PARCEL.
IZUTSU-YA IN NIHON-BASHI, RIGHT?
BYE!

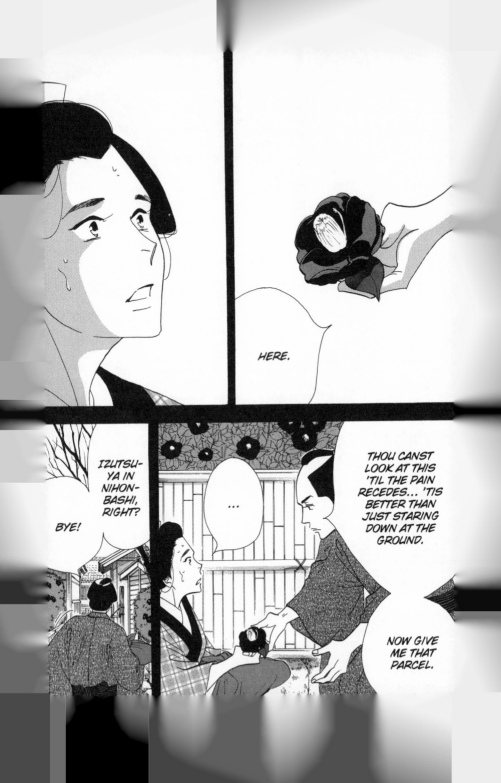

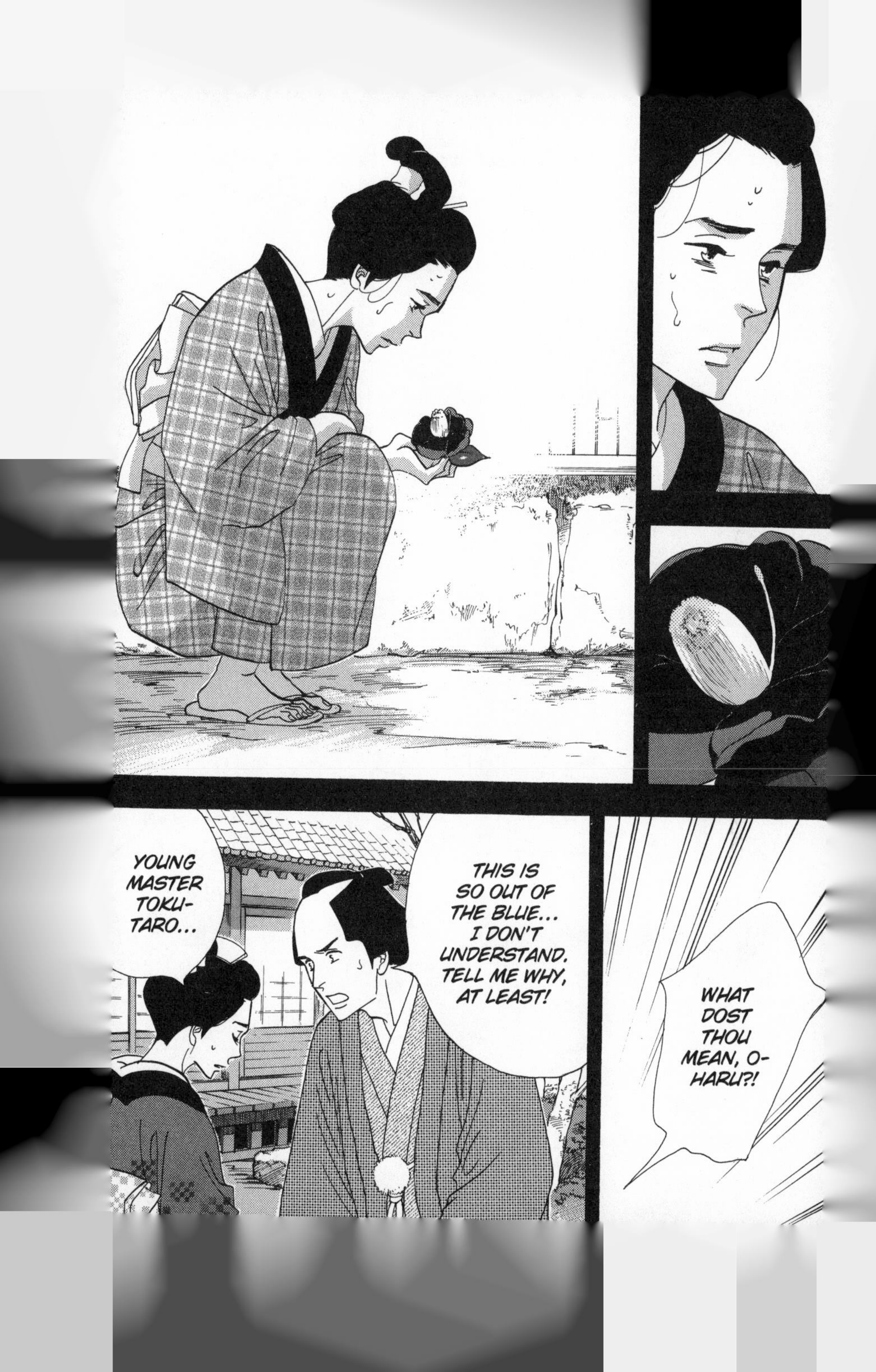
WHAT DOST THOU MEAN, O-HARU?!
THIS IS SO OUT OF THE BLUE... I DON'T UNDERSTAND. TELL ME WHY, AT LEAST!
YOUNG MASTER TOKU-TARO...

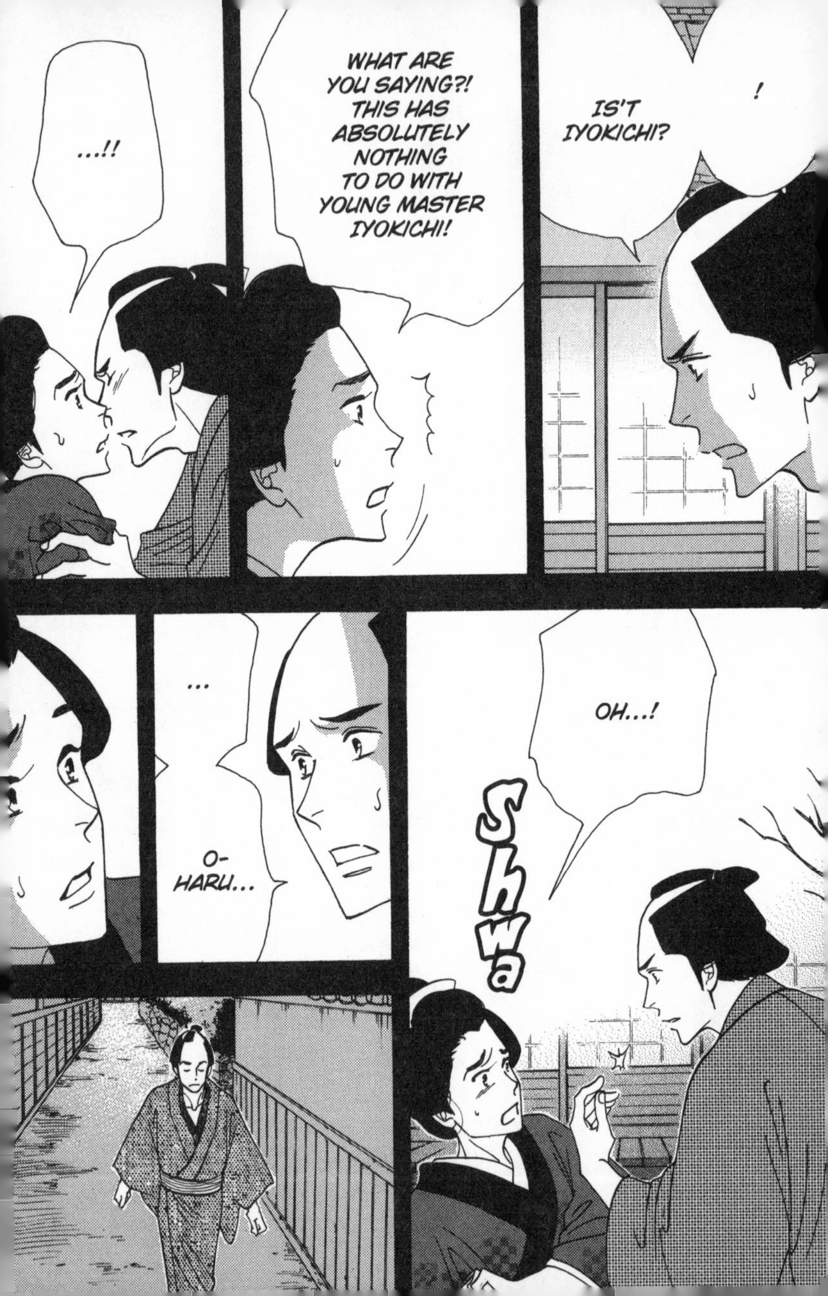
!
IS'T IYOKICHI?
WHAT ARE YOU SAYING?! THIS HAS ABSOLUTELY NOTHING TO DO WITH YOUNG MASTER IYOKICHI!
...!!
OH...!
Shwa
...
O-HARU...

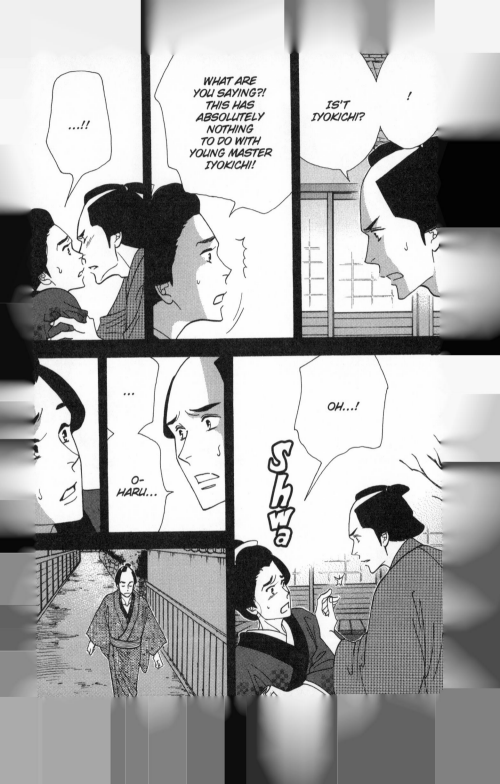

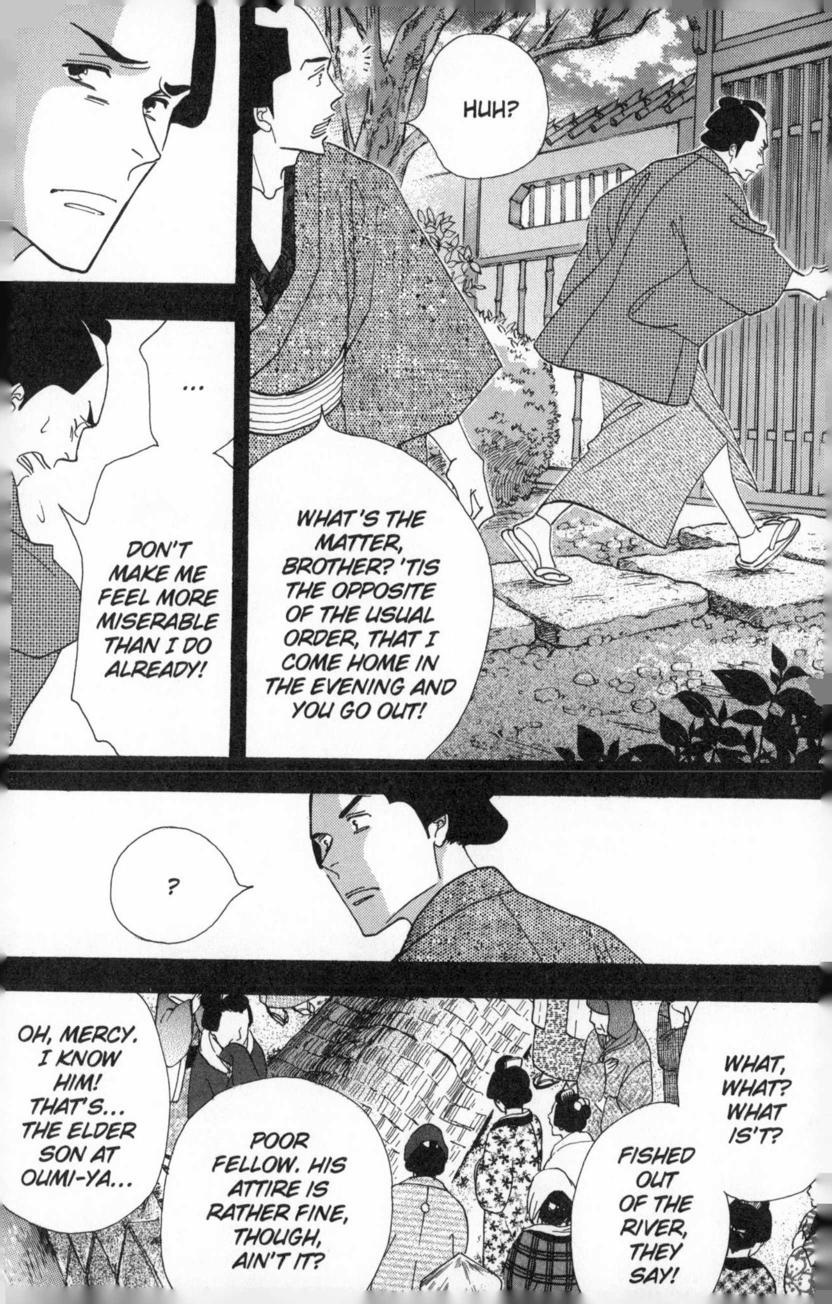
HUH?
WHAT'S THE MATTER, BROTHER? 'TIS THE OPPOSITE OF THE USUAL ORDER, THAT I COME HOME IN THE EVENING AND YOU GO OUT!
...
DON'T MAKE ME FEEL MORE MISERABLE THAN I DO ALREADY!
?
WHAT, WHAT? WHAT IS'T?
FISHED OUT OF THE RIVER, THEY SAY!
POOR FELLOW. HIS ATTIRE IS RATHER FINE, THOUGH, AIN'T IT?
OH, MERCY. I KNOW HIM! THAT'S... THE ELDER SON AT OUMI-YA...

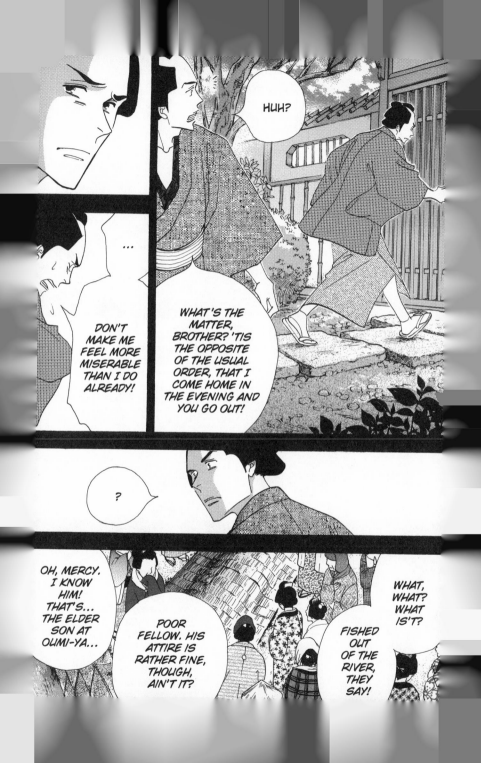

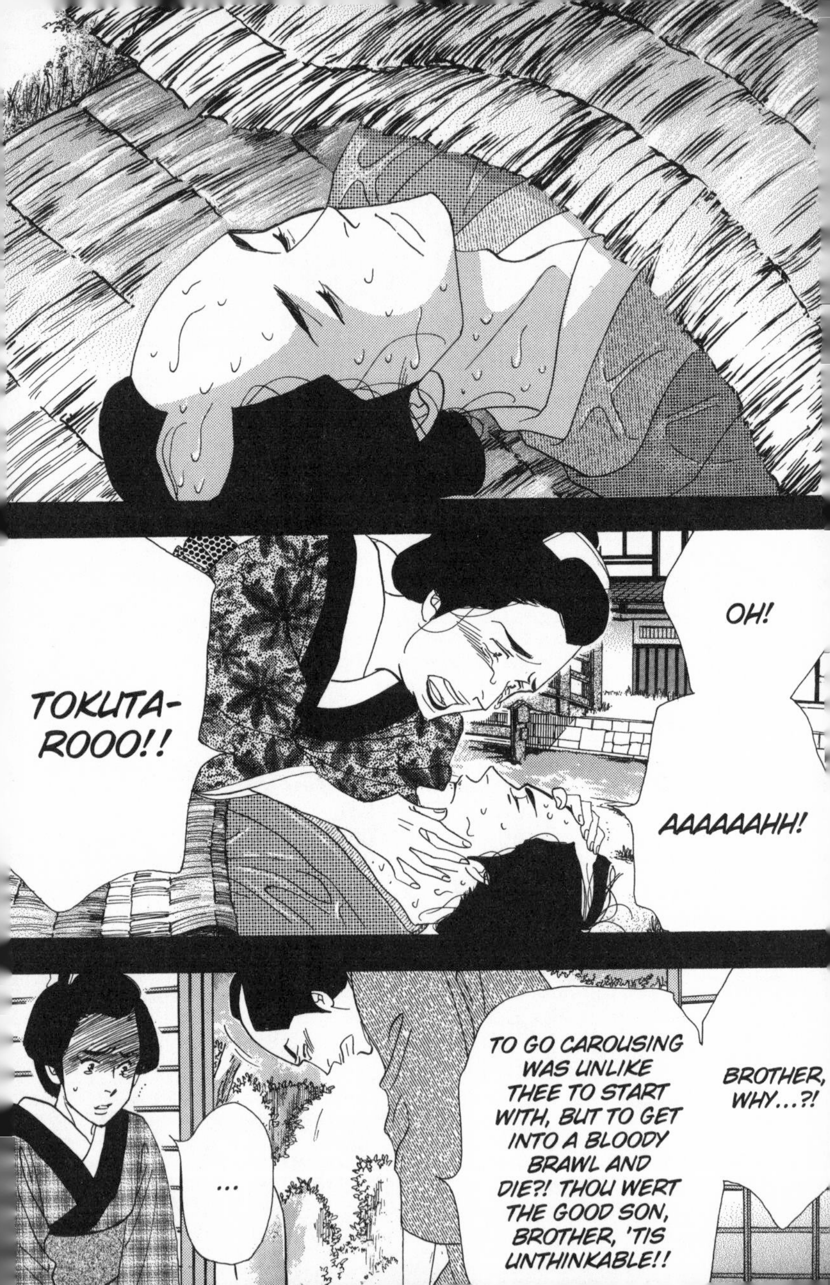
OH!
AAAAAAHH!
TOKUTA-ROOO!!
BROTHER, WHY...?!
TO GO CAROUSING WAS UNLIKE THEE TO START WITH, BUT TO GET INTO A BLOODY BRAWL AND DIE?! THOU WERT THE GOOD SON, BROTHER, 'TIS UNTHINKABLE!!
...

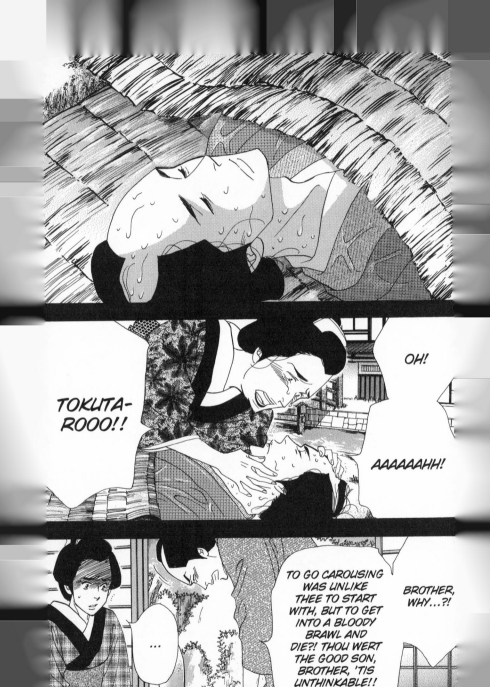

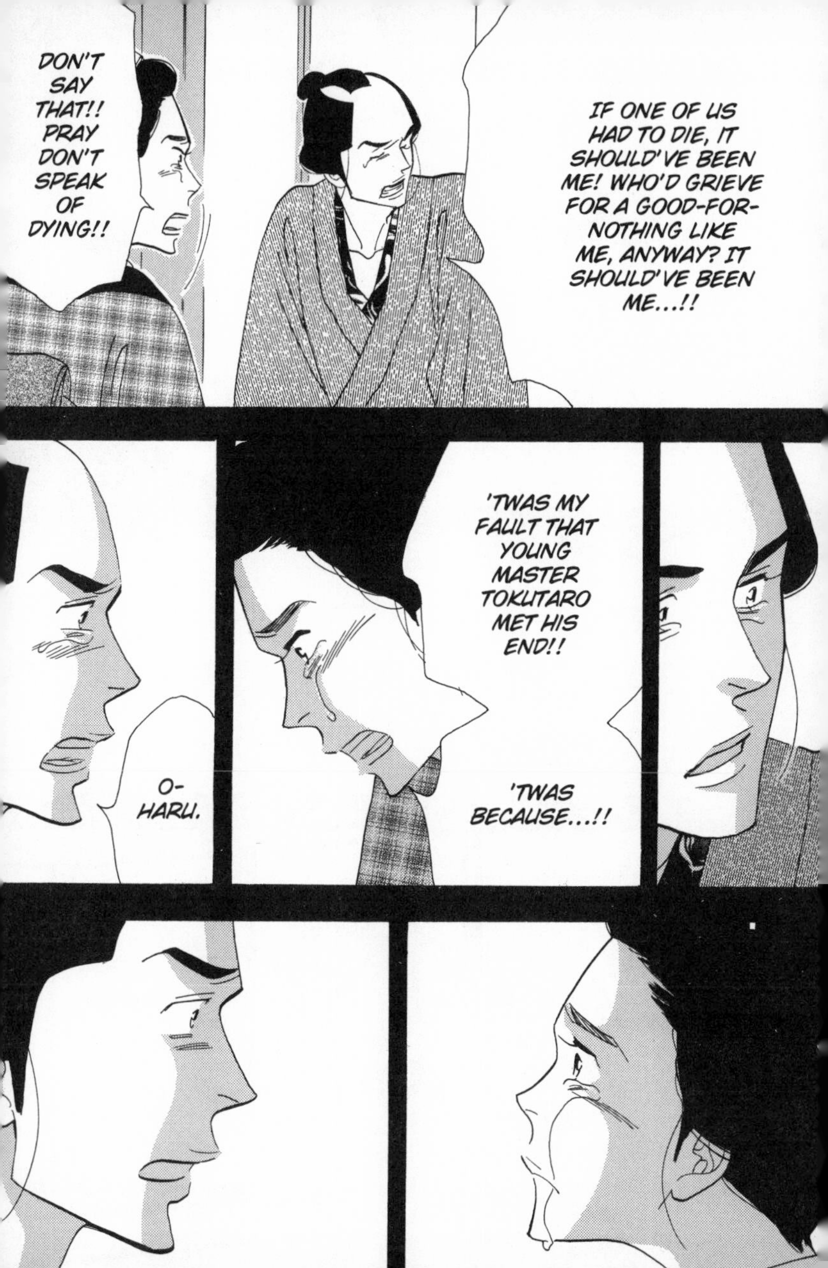
IF ONE OF US HAD TO DIE, IT SHOULD'VE BEEN ME! WHO'D GRIEVE FOR A GOOD-FOR-NOTHING LIKE ME, ANYWAY? IT SHOULD'VE BEEN ME...!!
DON'T SAY THAT!! PRAY DON'T SPEAK OF DYING!!
'TWAS MY FAULT THAT YOUNG MASTER TOKUTARO MET HIS END!!
'TWAS BECAUSE...!!
O-HARU.

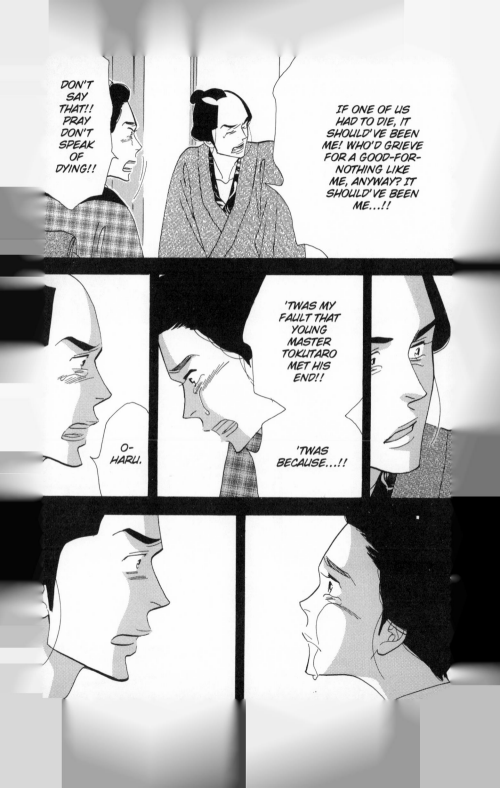

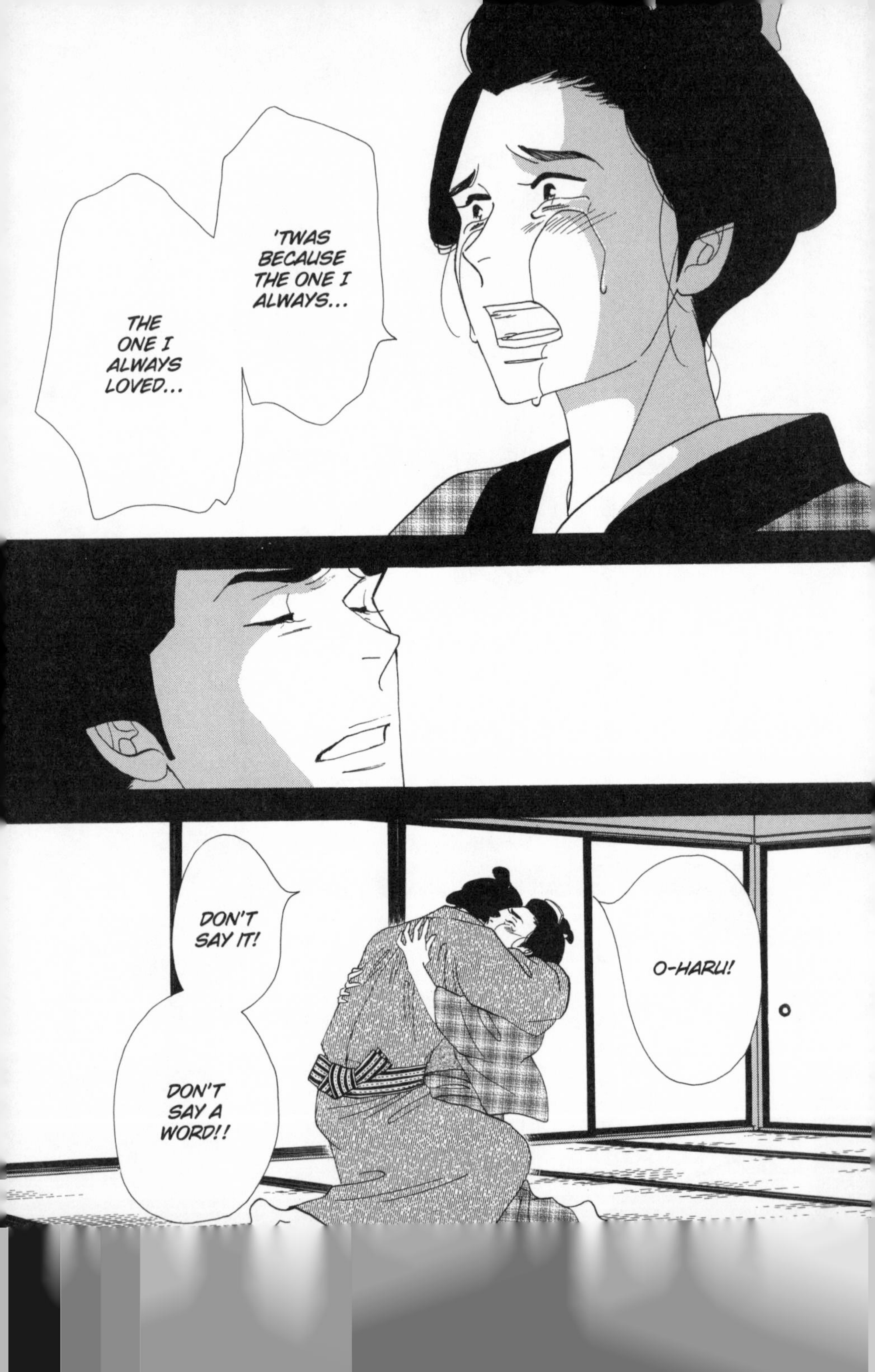
'TWAS BECAUSE THE ONE I ALWAYS...
THE ONE I ALWAYS LOVED...
O-HARU!
DON'T SAY IT!
DON'T SAY A WORD!!

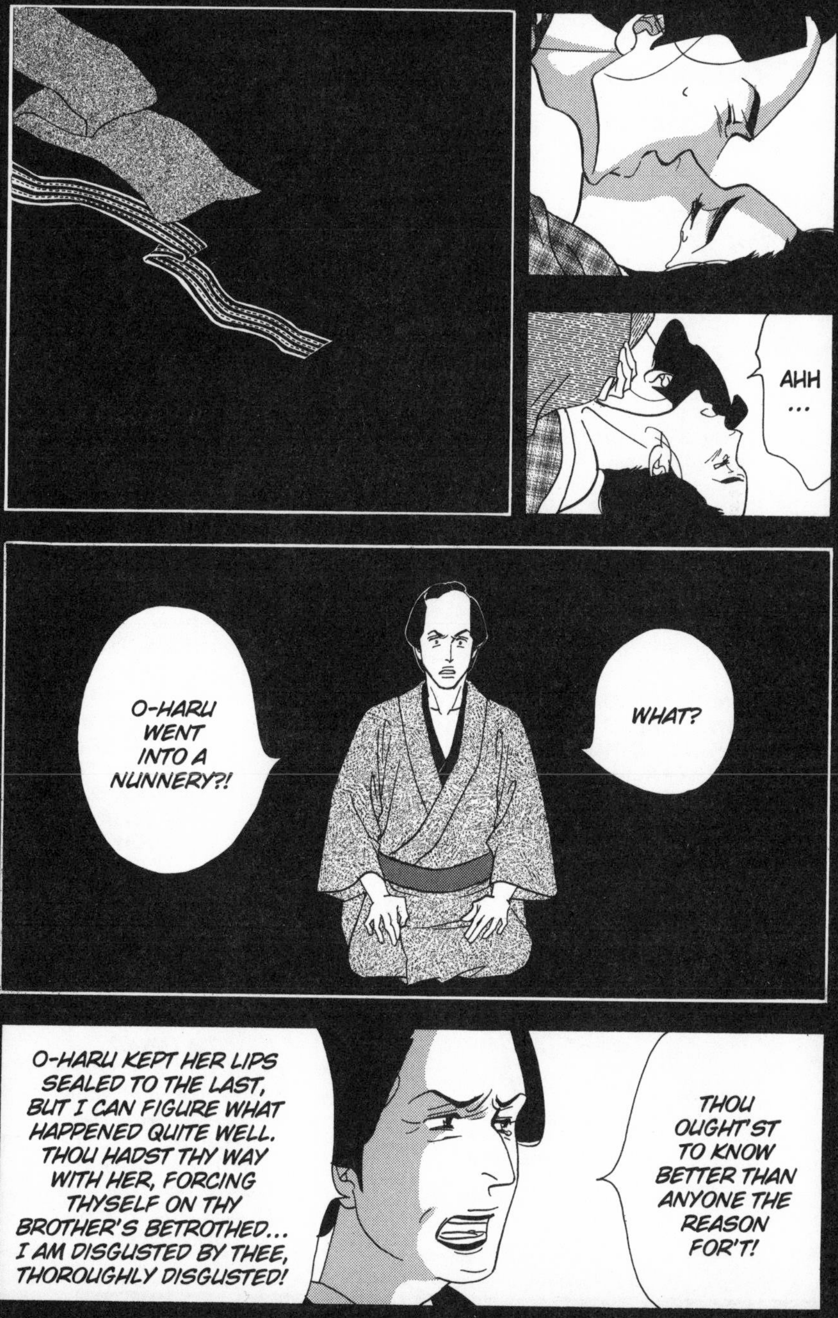
AHH ...
WHAT?
O-HARU WENT INTO A NUNNERY?!
THOU OUGHT'ST TO KNOW BETTER THAN ANYONE THE REASON FOR'T!
O-HARU KEPT HER LIPS SEALED TO THE LAST, BUT I CAN FIGURE WHAT HAPPENED QUITE WELL. THOU HADST THY WAY WITH HER, FORCING THYSELF ON THY BROTHER'S BETROTHED... I AM DISGUSTED BY THEE, THOROUGHLY DISGUSTED!

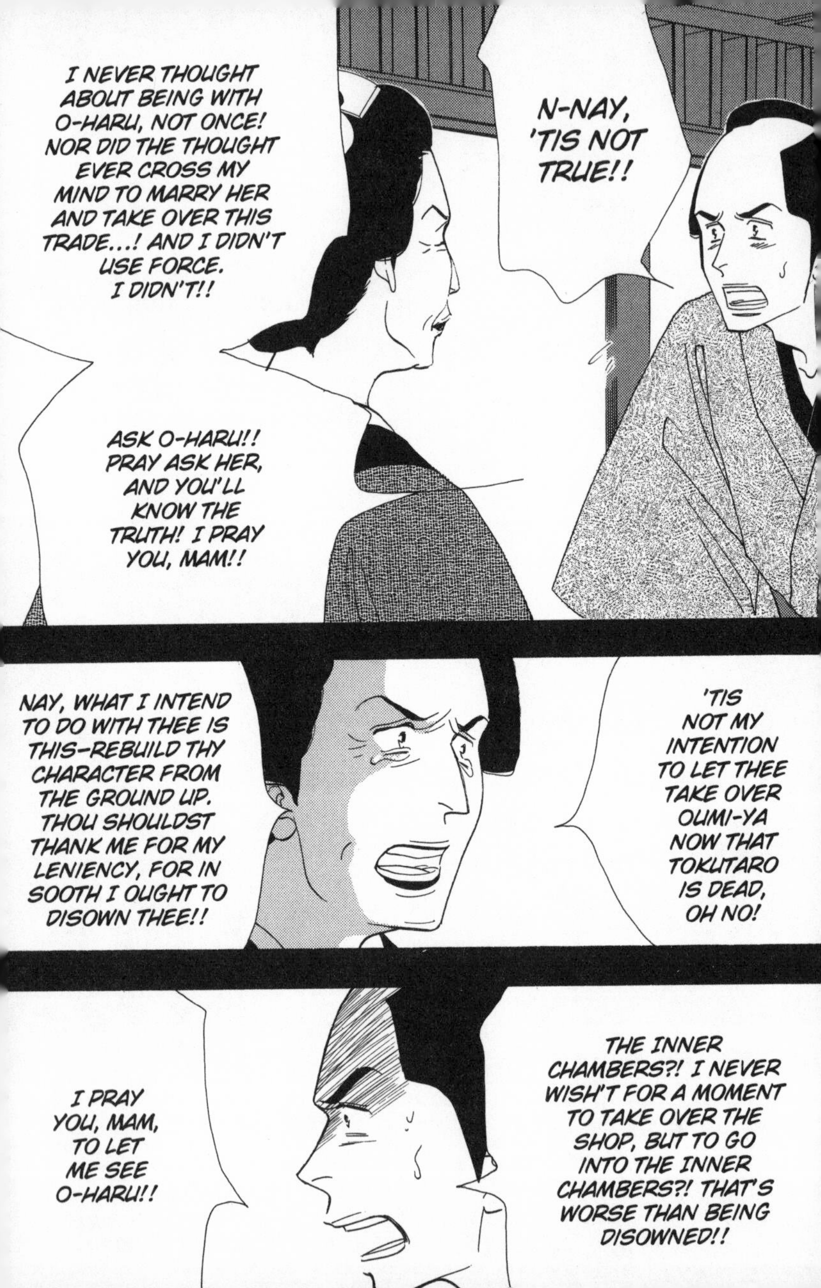
N-NAY, 'TIS NOT TRUE!!
I NEVER THOUGHT ABOUT BEING WITH O-HARU, NOT ONCE! NOR DID THE THOUGHT EVER CROSS MY MIND TO MARRY HER AND TAKE OVER THIS TRADE...! AND I DIDN'T USE FORCE. I DIDN'T!!
ASK O-HARU!! PRAY ASK HER, AND YOU'LL KNOW THE TRUTH! I PRAY YOU, MAM!!
'TIS NOT MY INTENTION TO LET THEE TAKE OVER OUMI-YA NOW THAT TOKUTARO IS DEAD, OH NO!
NAY, WHAT I INTEND TO DO WITH THEE IS THIS—REBUILD THY CHARACTER FROM THE GROUND UP. THOU SHOULDST THANK ME FOR MY LENIENCY, FOR IN SOOTH I OUGHT TO DISOWN THEE!!
THE INNER CHAMBERS?! I NEVER WISH'T FOR A MOMENT TO TAKE OVER THE SHOP, BUT TO GO INTO THE INNER CHAMBERS?! THAT'S WORSE THAN BEING DISOWNED!!
I PRAY YOU, MAM, TO LET ME SEE O-HARU!!

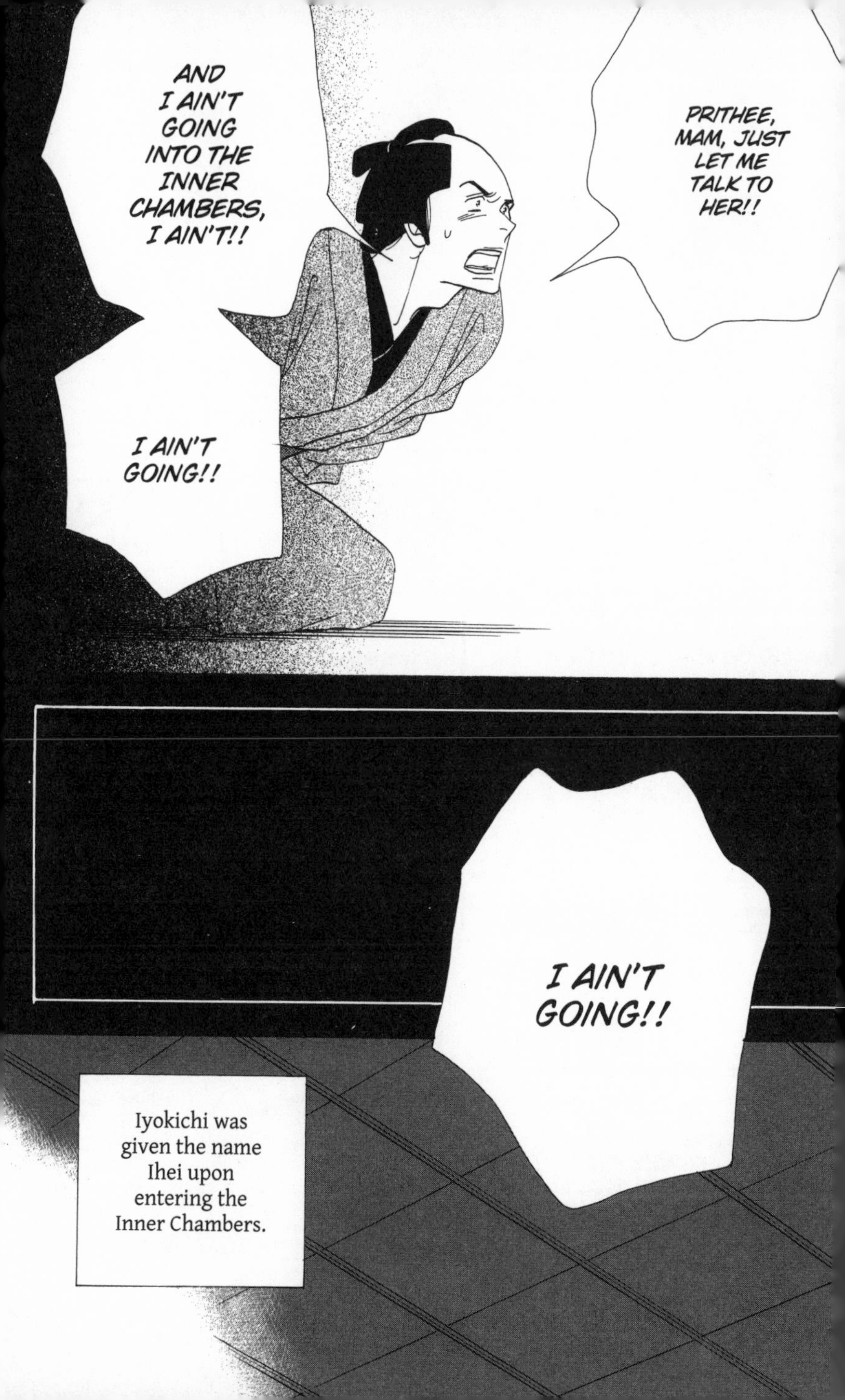
PRITHEE, MAM, JUST LET ME TALK TO HER!!
AND I AIN'T GOING INTO THE INNER CHAMBERS, I AIN'T!!
I AIN'T GOING!!
I AIN'T GOING!!
Iyokichi was given the name Ihei upon entering the Inner Chambers.

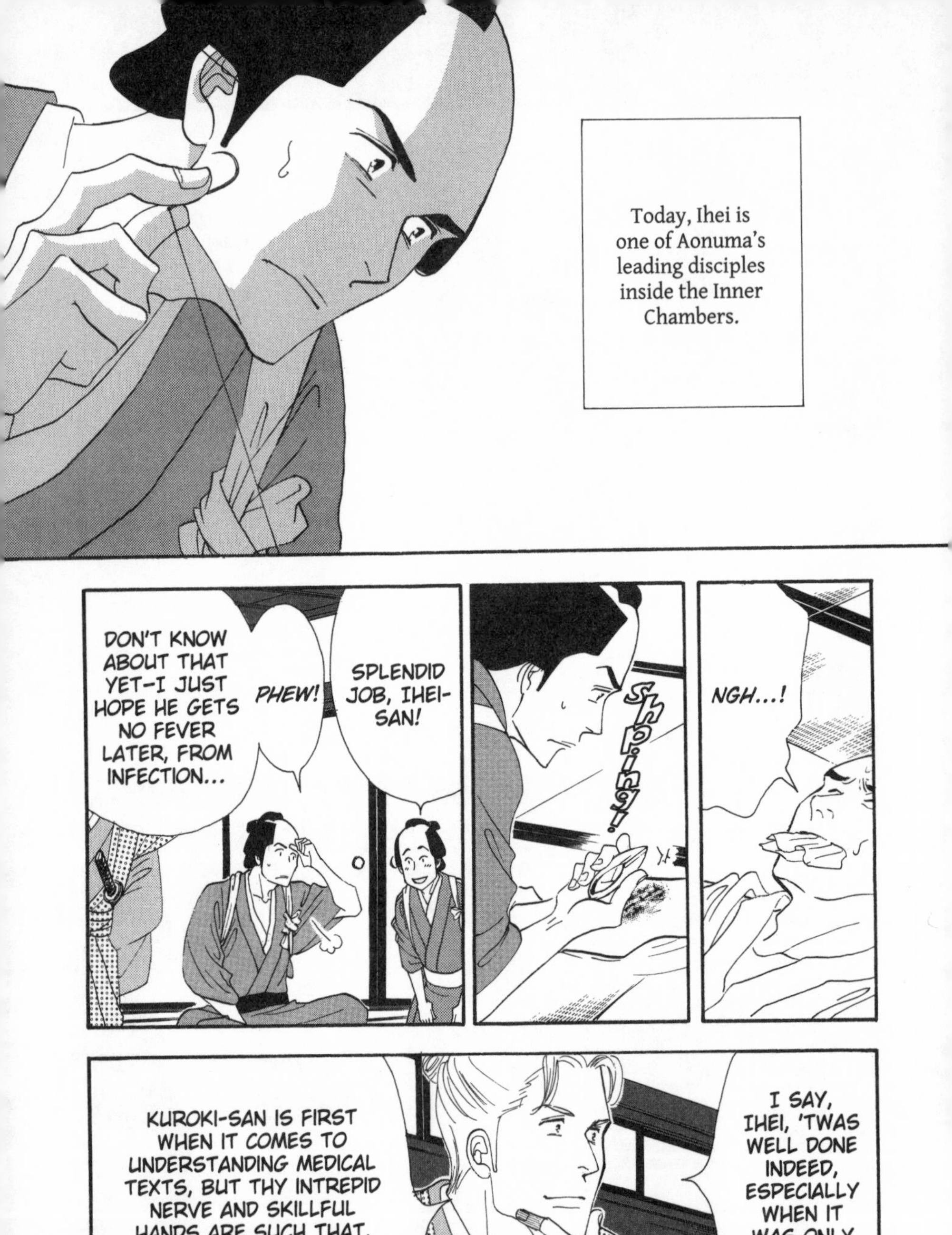
Today, Ihei is one of Aonuma's leading disciples inside the Inner Chambers.
NGH...!
Shping!
SPLENDID JOB, IHEI-SAN!
PHEW!
DON'T KNOW ABOUT THAT YET—I JUST HOPE HE GETS NO FEVER LATER, FROM INFECTION...
I SAY, IHEI, 'TWAS WELL DONE INDEED, ESPECIALLY WHEN IT WAS ONLY THY SECOND TIME!
KUROKI-SAN IS FIRST WHEN IT COMES TO UNDERSTANDING MEDICAL TEXTS, BUT THY INTREPID NERVE AND SKILLFUL HANDS ARE SUCH THAT, AS A SURGEON, I DARESAY THOU SHALT OUTSTRIP ME ONE DAY.

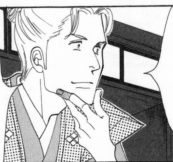

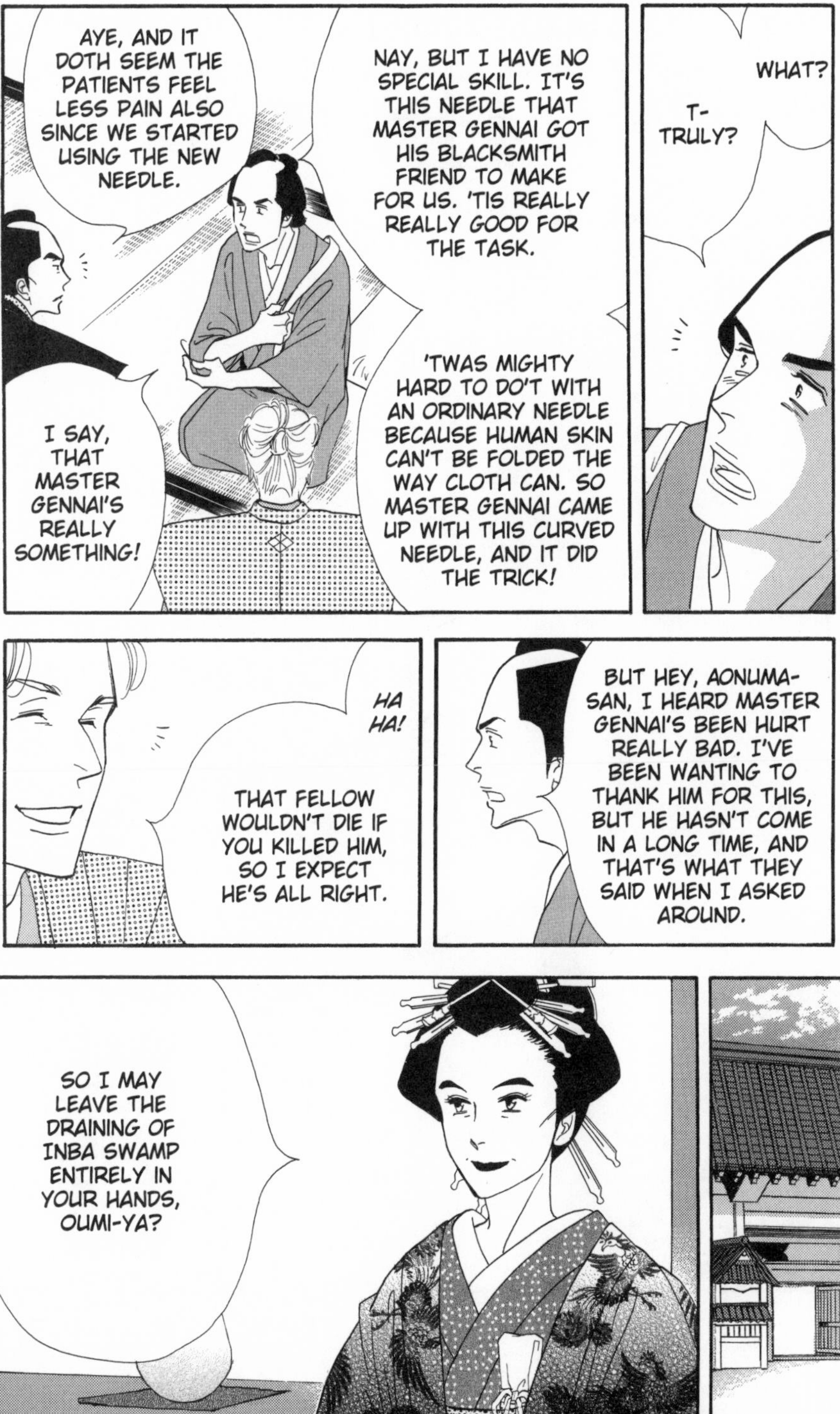
WHAT?
T-TRULY?
NAY, BUT I HAVE NO SPECIAL SKILL. IT'S THIS NEEDLE THAT MASTER GENNAI GOT HIS BLACKSMITH FRIEND TO MAKE FOR US. 'TIS REALLY REALLY GOOD FOR THE TASK.
AYE, AND IT DOTH SEEM THE PATIENTS FEEL LESS PAIN ALSO SINCE WE STARTED USING THE NEW NEEDLE.
'TWAS MIGHTY HARD TO DO'T WITH AN ORDINARY NEEDLE BECAUSE HUMAN SKIN CAN'T BE FOLDED THE WAY CLOTH CAN. SO MASTER GENNAI CAME UP WITH THIS CURVED NEEDLE, AND IT DID THE TRICK!
I SAY, THAT MASTER GENNAI'S REALLY SOMETHING!
BUT HEY, AONUMA-SAN, I HEARD MASTER GENNAI'S BEEN HURT REALLY BAD. I'VE BEEN WANTING TO THANK HIM FOR THIS, BUT HE HASN'T COME IN A LONG TIME, AND THAT'S WHAT THEY SAID WHEN I ASKED AROUND.
HA HA!
THAT FELLOW WOULDN'T DIE IF YOU KILLED HIM, SO I EXPECT HE'S ALL RIGHT.
SO I MAY LEAVE THE DRAINING OF INBA SWAMP ENTIRELY IN YOUR HANDS, OUMI-YA?

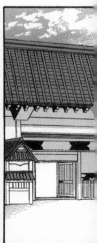

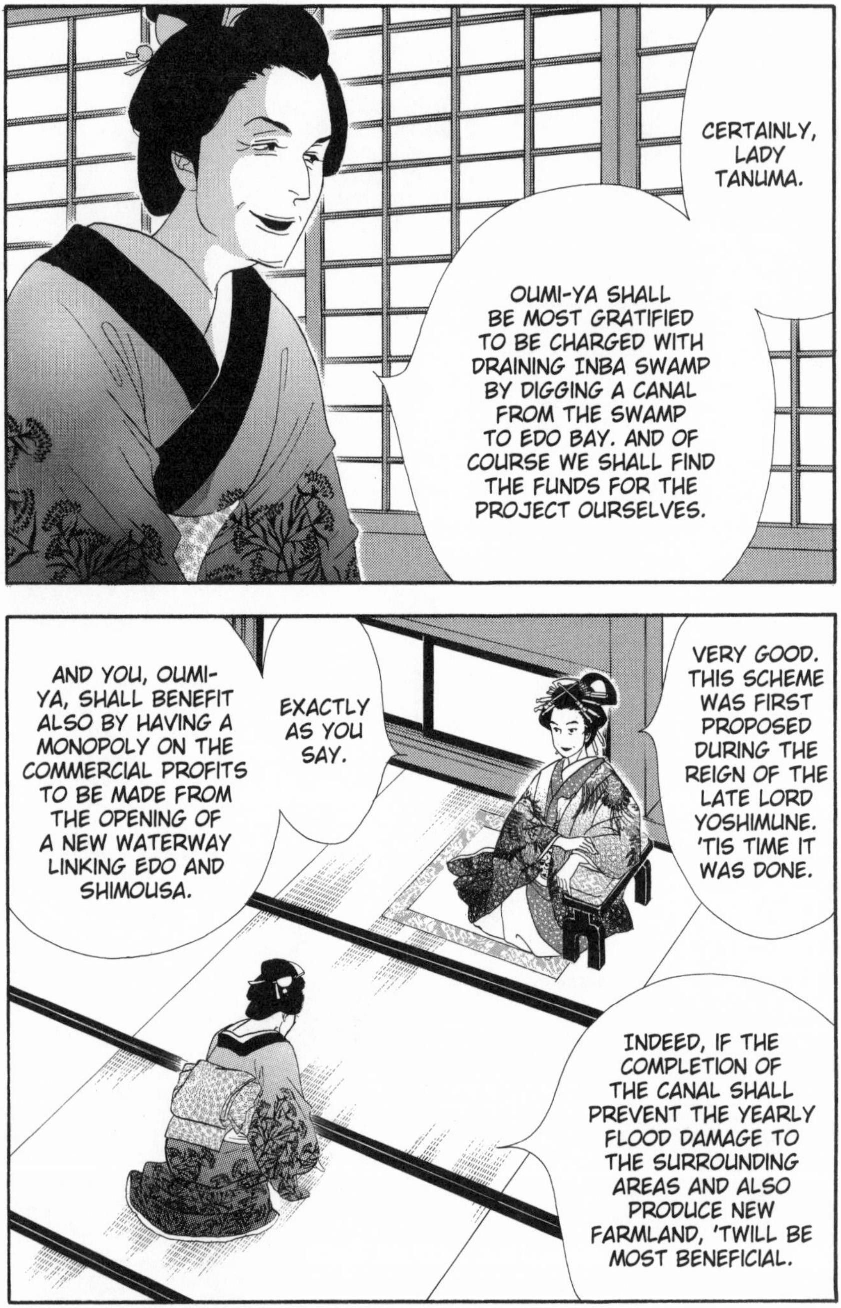
CERTAINLY, LADY TANUMA.
OUMI-YA SHALL BE MOST GRATIFIED TO BE CHARGED WITH DRAINING INBA SWAMP BY DIGGING A CANAL FROM THE SWAMP TO EDO BAY. AND OF COURSE WE SHALL FIND THE FUNDS FOR THE PROJECT OURSELVES.
VERY GOOD. THIS SCHEME WAS FIRST PROPOSED DURING THE REIGN OF THE LATE LORD YOSHIMUNE. 'TIS TIME IT WAS DONE.
EXACTLY AS YOU SAY.
AND YOU, OUMI-YA, SHALL BENEFIT ALSO BY HAVING A MONOPOLY ON THE COMMERCIAL PROFITS TO BE MADE FROM THE OPENING OF A NEW WATERWAY LINKING EDO AND SHIMOUSA.
INDEED, IF THE COMPLETION OF THE CANAL SHALL PREVENT THE YEARLY FLOOD DAMAGE TO THE SURROUNDING AREAS AND ALSO PRODUCE NEW FARMLAND, 'TWILL BE MOST BENEFICIAL.

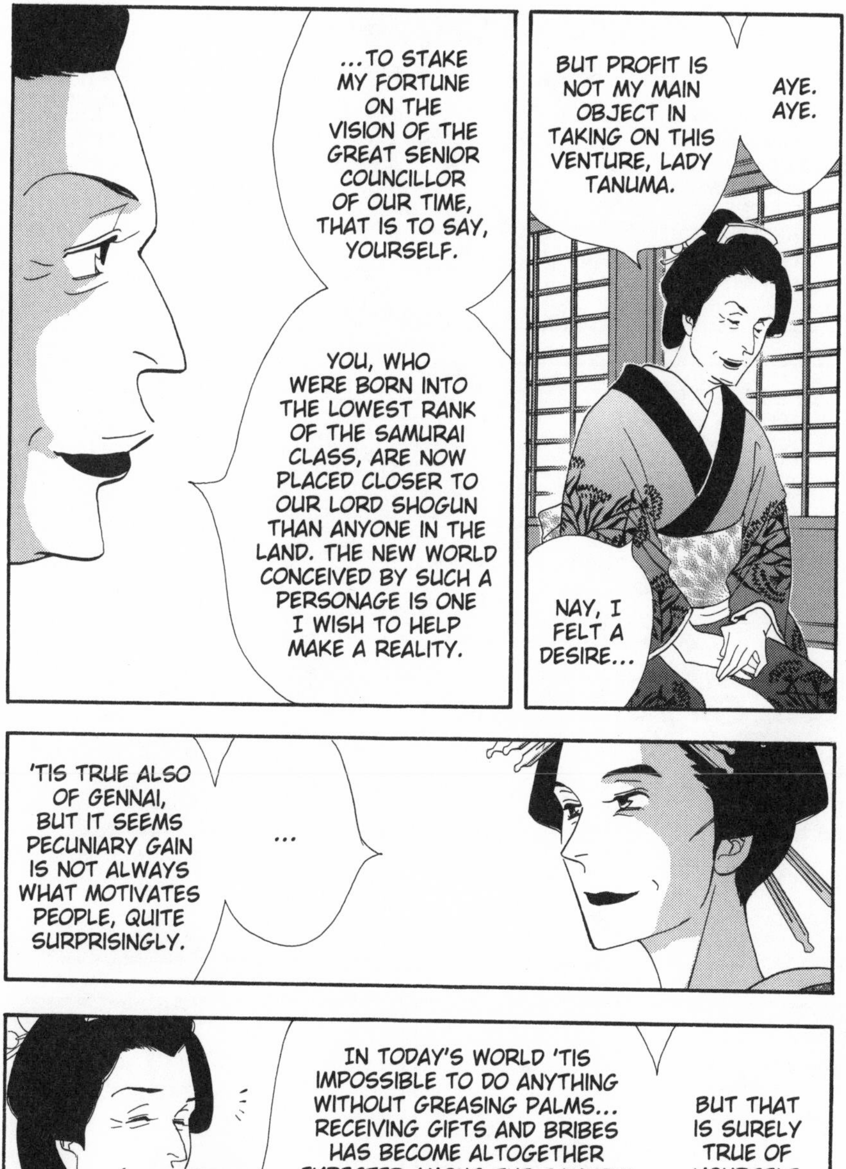
BUT PROFIT IS NOT MY MAIN OBJECT IN TAKING ON THIS VENTURE, LADY TANUMA.
AYE. AYE.
NAY, I FELT A DESIRE...
...TO STAKE MY FORTUNE ON THE VISION OF THE GREAT SENIOR COUNCILLOR OF OUR TIME, THAT IS TO SAY, YOURSELF.
YOU, WHO WERE BORN INTO THE LOWEST RANK OF THE SAMURAI CLASS, ARE NOW PLACED CLOSER TO OUR LORD SHOGUN THAN ANYONE IN THE LAND. THE NEW WORLD CONCEIVED BY SUCH A PERSONAGE IS ONE I WISH TO HELP MAKE A REALITY.
...
'TIS TRUE ALSO OF GENNAI, BUT IT SEEMS PECUNIARY GAIN IS NOT ALWAYS WHAT MOTIVATES PEOPLE, QUITE SURPRISINGLY.
IN TODAY'S WORLD 'TIS IMPOSSIBLE TO DO ANYTHING WITHOUT GREASING PALMS... RECEIVING GIFTS AND BRIBES HAS BECOME ALTOGETHER EXPECTED AMONG THE SAMURAI CLASS, AND YET I KNOW THAT YOU, LADY TANUMA, IN FACT ACCEPT VERY FEW SUCH GRATUITIES.
BUT THAT IS SURELY TRUE OF YOURSELF ALSO, LADY TANUMA.

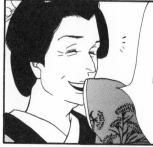

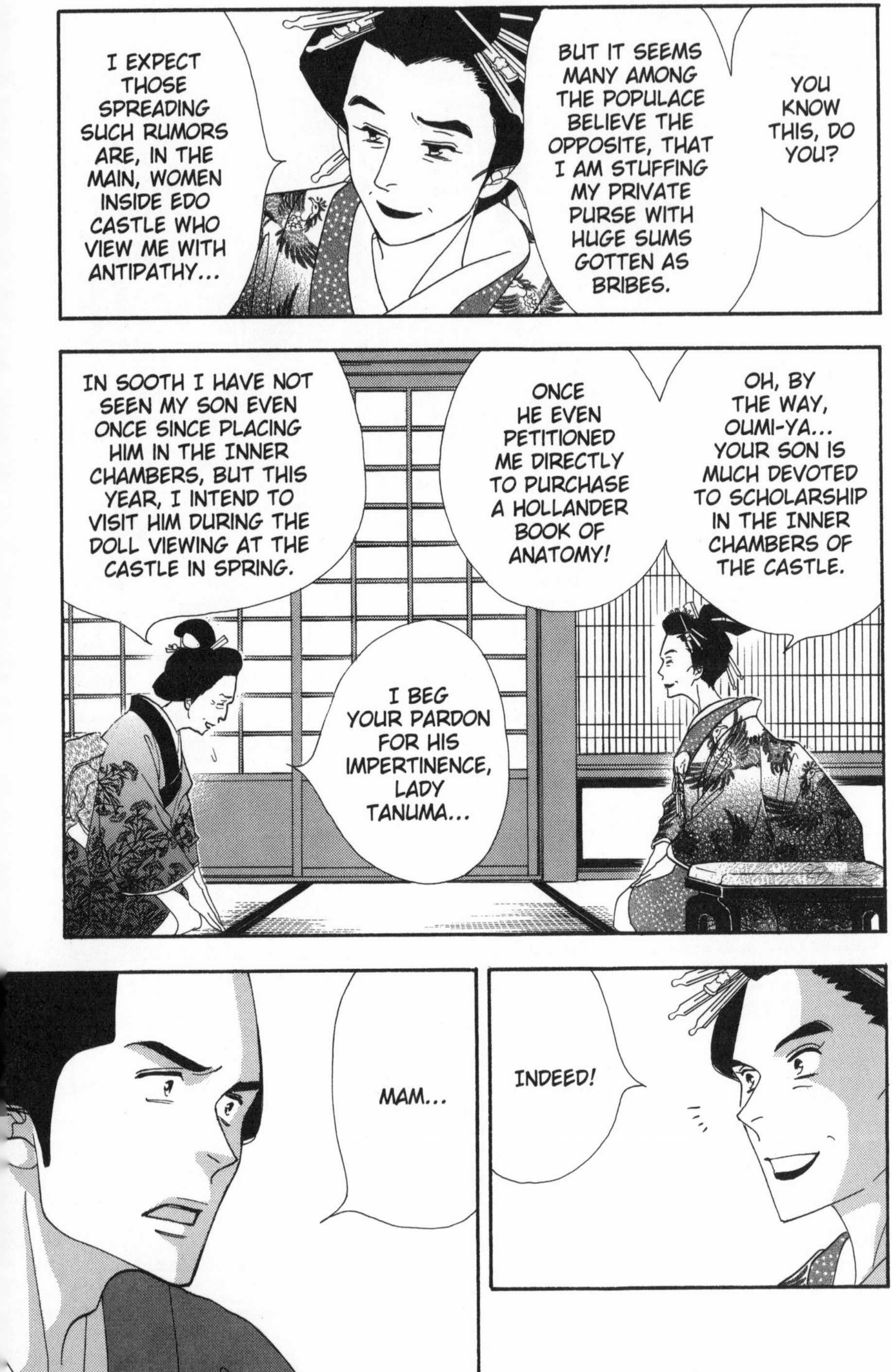
YOU KNOW THIS, DO YOU?
BUT IT SEEMS MANY AMONG THE POPULACE BELIEVE THE OPPOSITE, THAT I AM STUFFING MY PRIVATE PURSE WITH HUGE SUMS GOTTEN AS BRIBES.
I EXPECT THOSE SPREADING SUCH RUMORS ARE, IN THE MAIN, WOMEN INSIDE EDO CASTLE WHO VIEW ME WITH ANTIPATHY...
OH, BY THE WAY, OUMI-YA... YOUR SON IS MUCH DEVOTED TO SCHOLARSHIP IN THE INNER CHAMBERS OF THE CASTLE.
ONCE HE EVEN PETITIONED ME DIRECTLY TO PURCHASE A HOLLANDER BOOK OF ANATOMY!
IN SOOTH I HAVE NOT SEEN MY SON EVEN ONCE SINCE PLACING HIM IN THE INNER CHAMBERS, BUT THIS YEAR, I INTEND TO VISIT HIM DURING THE DOLL VIEWING AT THE CASTLE IN SPRING.
I BEG YOUR PARDON FOR HIS IMPERTINENCE, LADY TANUMA...
INDEED!
MAM...

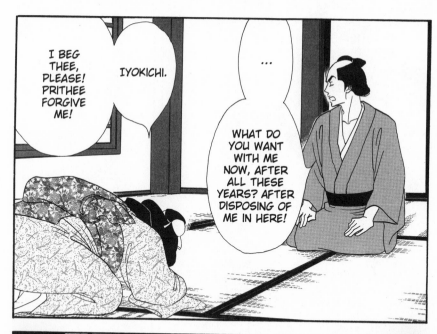

...
IYOKICHI.
I BEG THEE, PLEASE! PRITHEE FORGIVE ME!
WHAT DO YOU WANT WITH ME NOW, AFTER ALL THESE YEARS? AFTER DISPOSING OF ME IN HERE!
A LETTER CAME FROM O-HARU A MONTH AGO, AND I WENT TO SEE HER.
YOU SAW O-HARU?!
WHAT DID SHE TELL YOU, MAM?! DID SHE SAY WHY SHE WENT INTO THAT NUNNERY...?!
O-HARU IS NO LONGER WITH US, IYOKICHI!

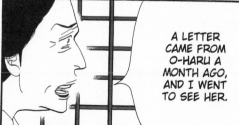

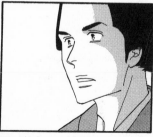

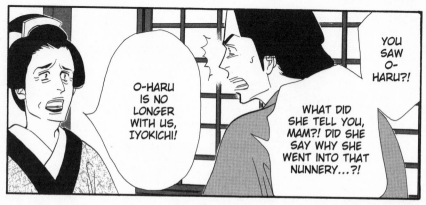

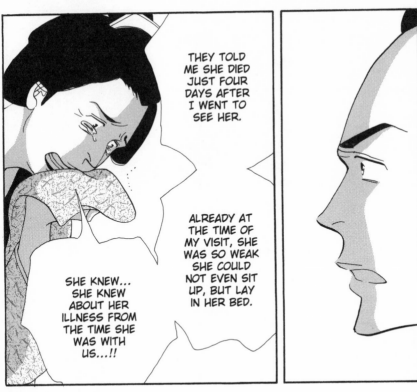

THEY TOLD ME SHE DIED JUST FOUR DAYS AFTER I WENT TO SEE HER.
ALREADY AT THE TIME OF MY VISIT, SHE WAS SO WEAK SHE COULD NOT EVEN SIT UP, BUT LAY IN HER BED.
SHE KNEW... SHE KNEW ABOUT HER ILLNESS FROM THE TIME SHE WAS WITH US...!!
FORGIVE ME, MISTRESS, I PRAY YOU.
'TWAS MY FAULT THAT YOUNG MASTER TOKUTARO LOST HIS LIFE... I NEVER TOLD HIM ABOUT MY MALADY, AND I FEAR MY SILENCE MADE HIM BLAME HIMSELF FOR MY BEHAVIOR. HE MIGHT NEVER HAVE GONE OUT THAT NIGHT, HAD I BEEN OPEN WITH HIM...
'TWAS MY FAULT HE DIED ...!!

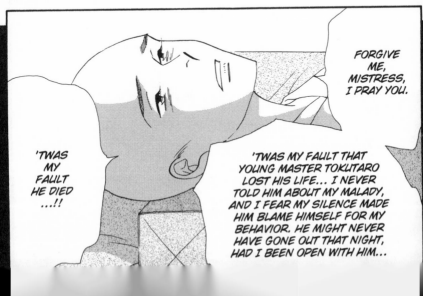

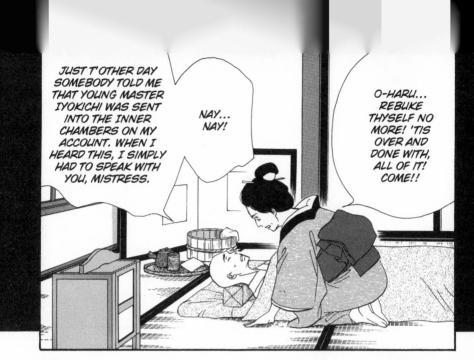

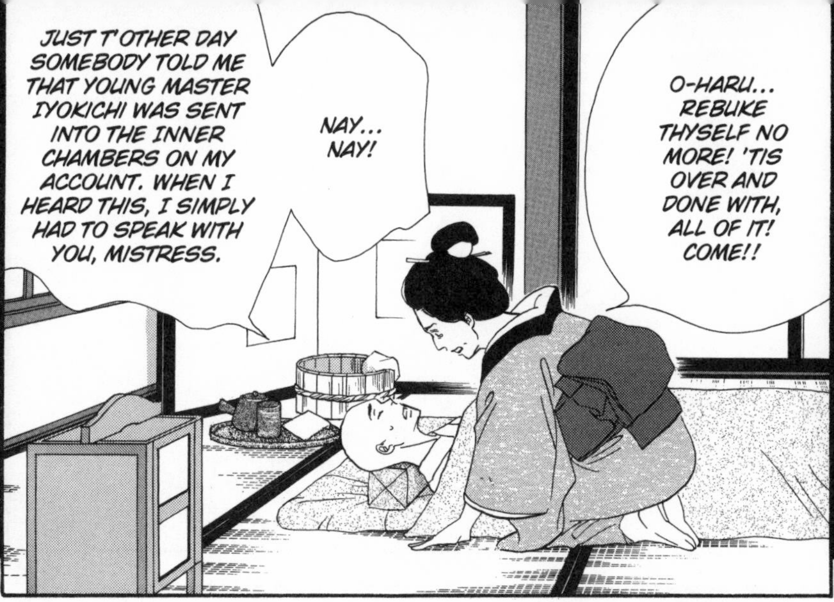
O-HARU... REBUKE THYSELF NO MORE! 'TIS OVER AND DONE WITH, ALL OF IT! COME!!
NAY... NAY!
JUST T'OTHER DAY SOMEBODY TOLD ME THAT YOUNG MASTER IYOKICHI WAS SENT INTO THE INNER CHAMBERS ON MY ACCOUNT. WHEN I HEARD THIS, I SIMPLY HAD TO SPEAK WITH YOU, MISTRESS.

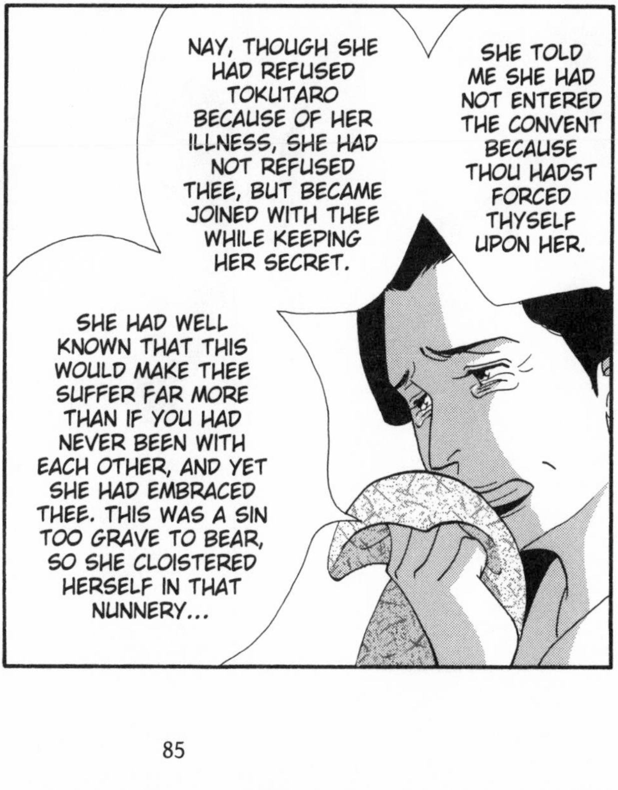
SHE TOLD ME SHE HAD NOT ENTERED THE CONVENT BECAUSE THOU HADST FORCED THYSELF UPON HER.
NAY, THOUGH SHE HAD REFUSED TOKUTARO BECAUSE OF HER ILLNESS, SHE HAD NOT REFUSED THEE, BUT BECAME JOINED WITH THEE WHILE KEEPING HER SECRET.
SHE HAD WELL KNOWN THAT THIS WOULD MAKE THEE SUFFER FAR MORE THAN IF YOU HAD NEVER BEEN WITH EACH OTHER, AND YET SHE HAD EMBRACED THEE. THIS WAS A SIN TOO GRAVE TO BEAR, SO SHE CLOISTERED HERSELF IN THAT NUNNERY...

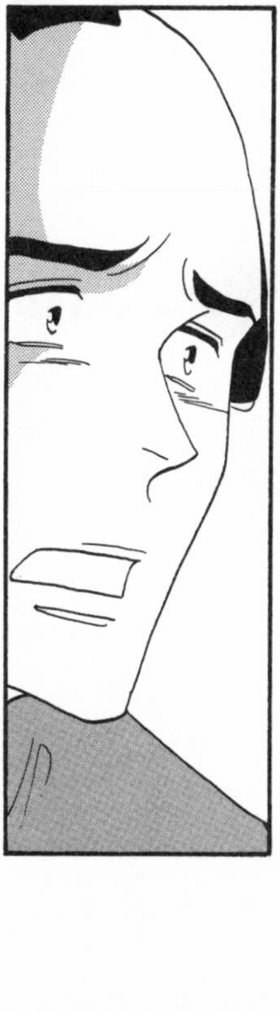

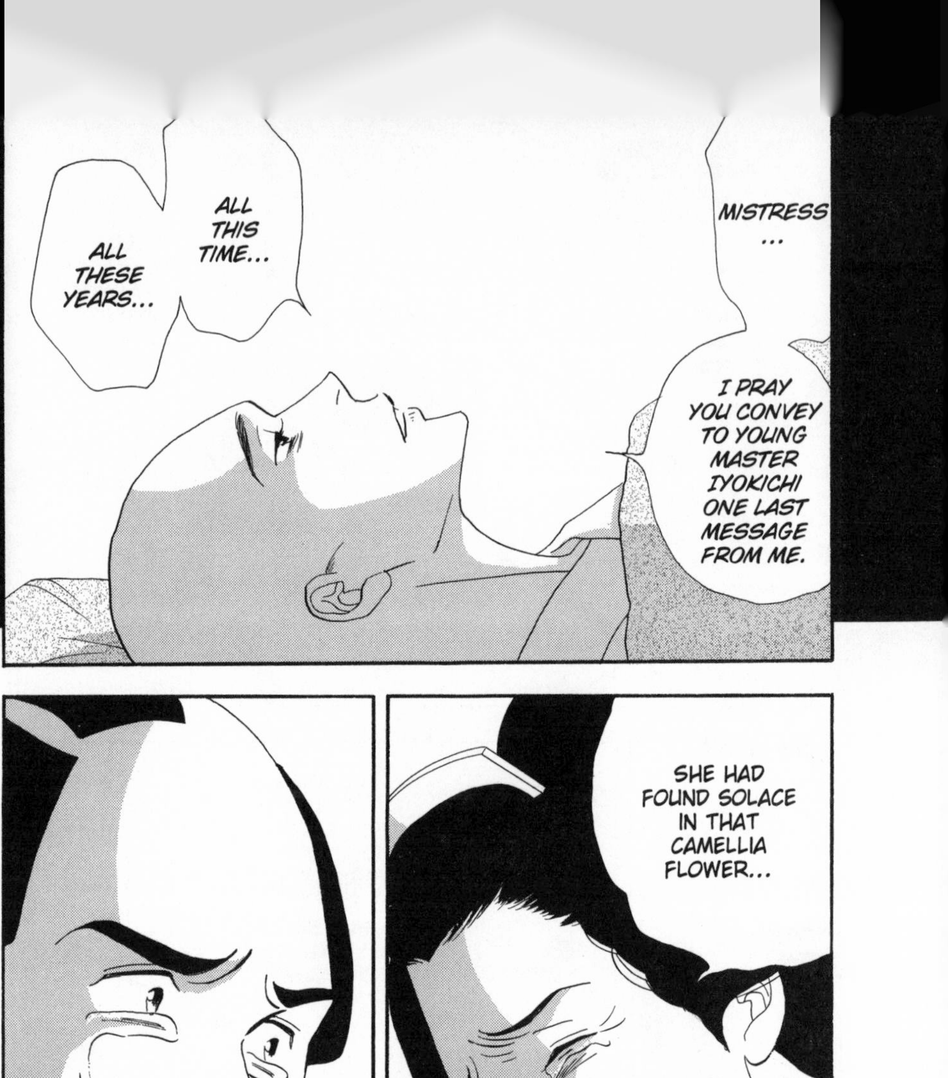
MISTRESS ...
I PRAY YOU CONVEY TO YOUNG MASTER IYOKICHI ONE LAST MESSAGE FROM ME.
ALL THIS TIME...
ALL THESE YEARS...
SHE HAD FOUND SOLACE IN THAT CAMELLIA FLOWER...

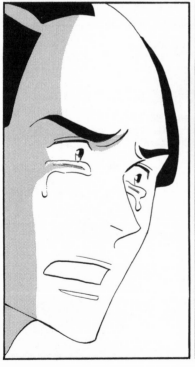

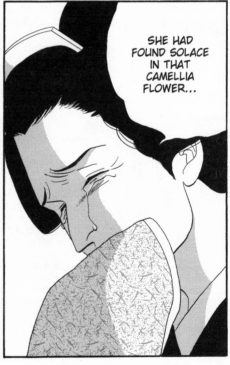

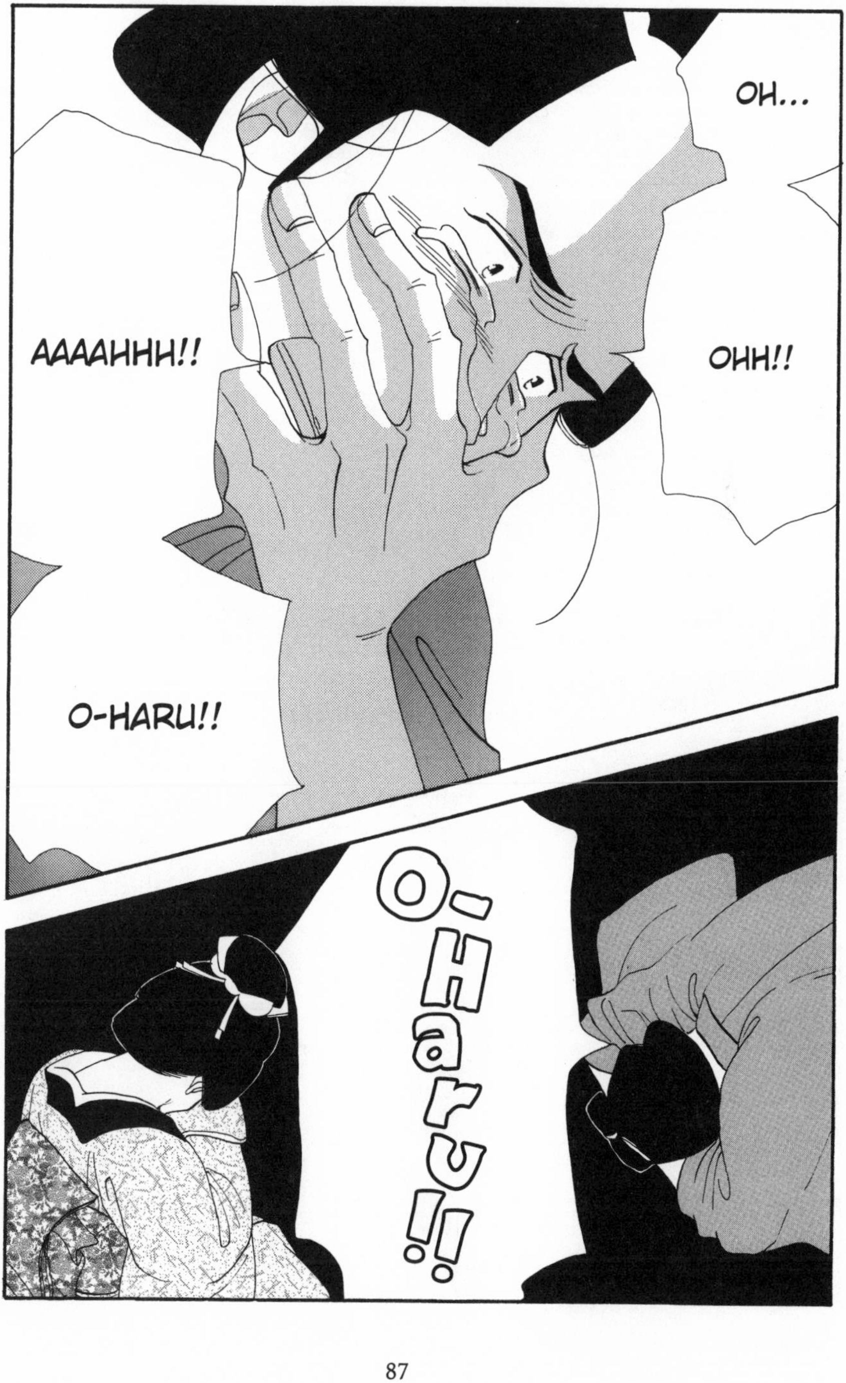
OH...
AAAAHHH!!
OHH!!
O-HARU!!
O-Haru!!

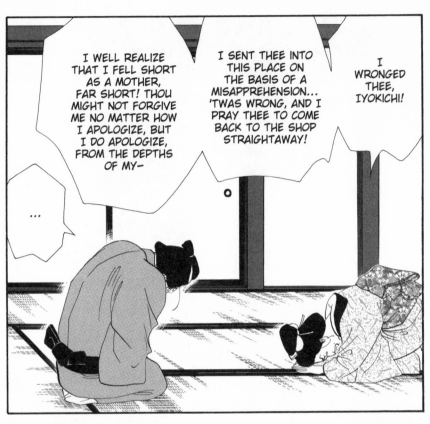

I WRONGED THEE, IYOKICHI!
I SENT THEE INTO THIS PLACE ON THE BASIS OF A MISAPPREHENSION... 'TWAS WRONG, AND I PRAY THEE TO COME BACK TO THE SHOP STRAIGHTAWAY!
I WELL REALIZE THAT I FELL SHORT AS A MOTHER, FAR SHORT! THOU MIGHT NOT FORGIVE ME NO MATTER HOW I APOLOGIZE, BUT I DO APOLOGIZE, FROM THE DEPTHS OF MY—
...
NAY.
I AIN'T GOING BACK TO THE SHOP.
IYO-KICHI!
I AIN'T SAYING IT OUT OF ANGER AT YOU, MAM. AND I AIN'T BEING PIGHEADED, EITHER!
I HOPE YOU FIND A GOOD HEIR TO ADOPT AND HAND OVER THE BUSINESS TO!

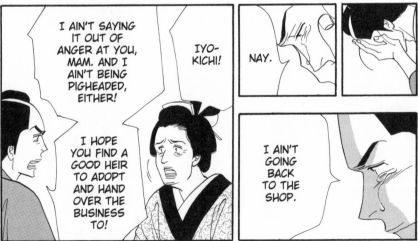

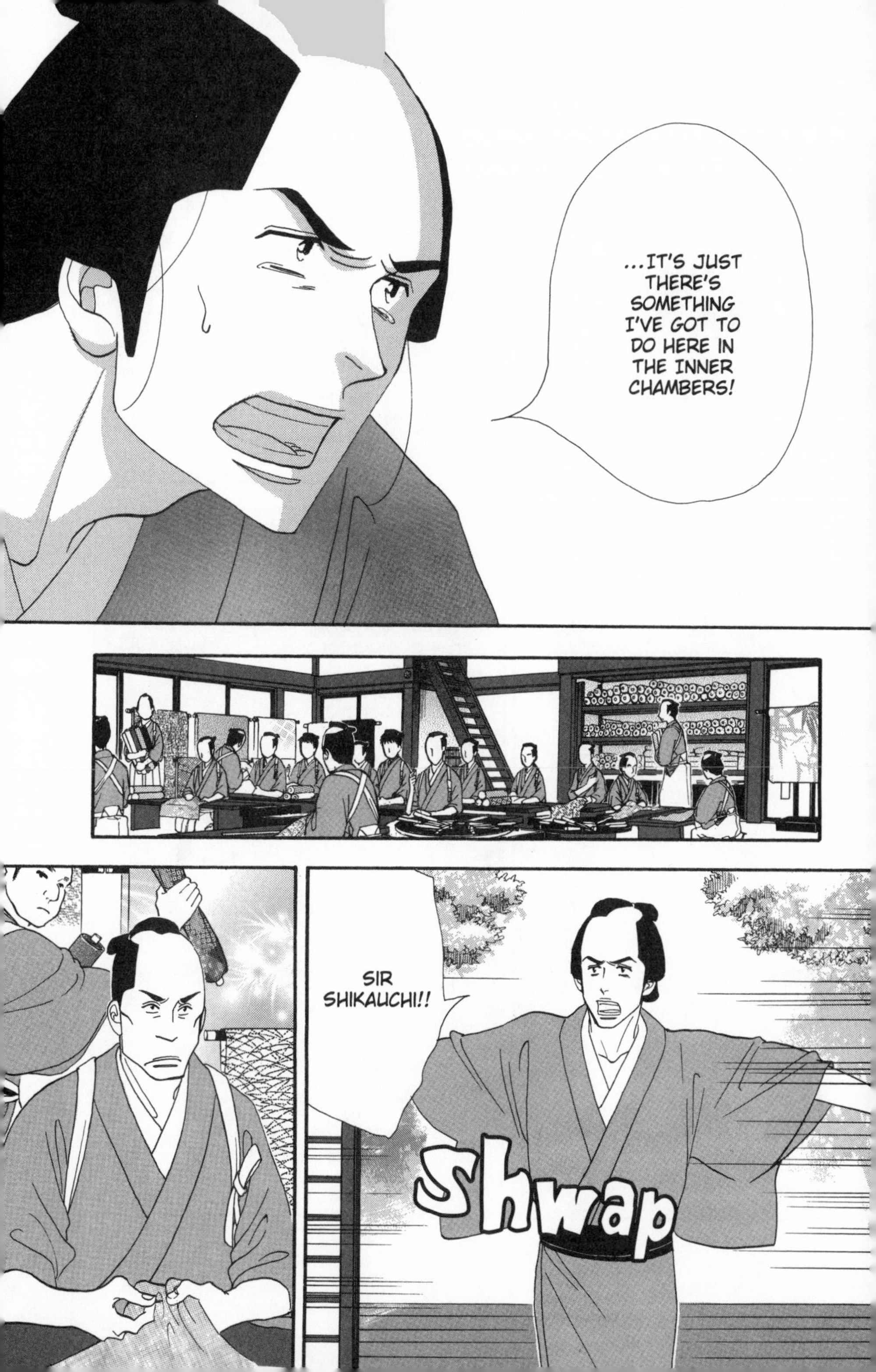
...IT'S JUST THERE'S SOMETHING I'VE GOT TO DO HERE IN THE INNER CHAMBERS!
SIR SHIKAUCHI!!
Shwap

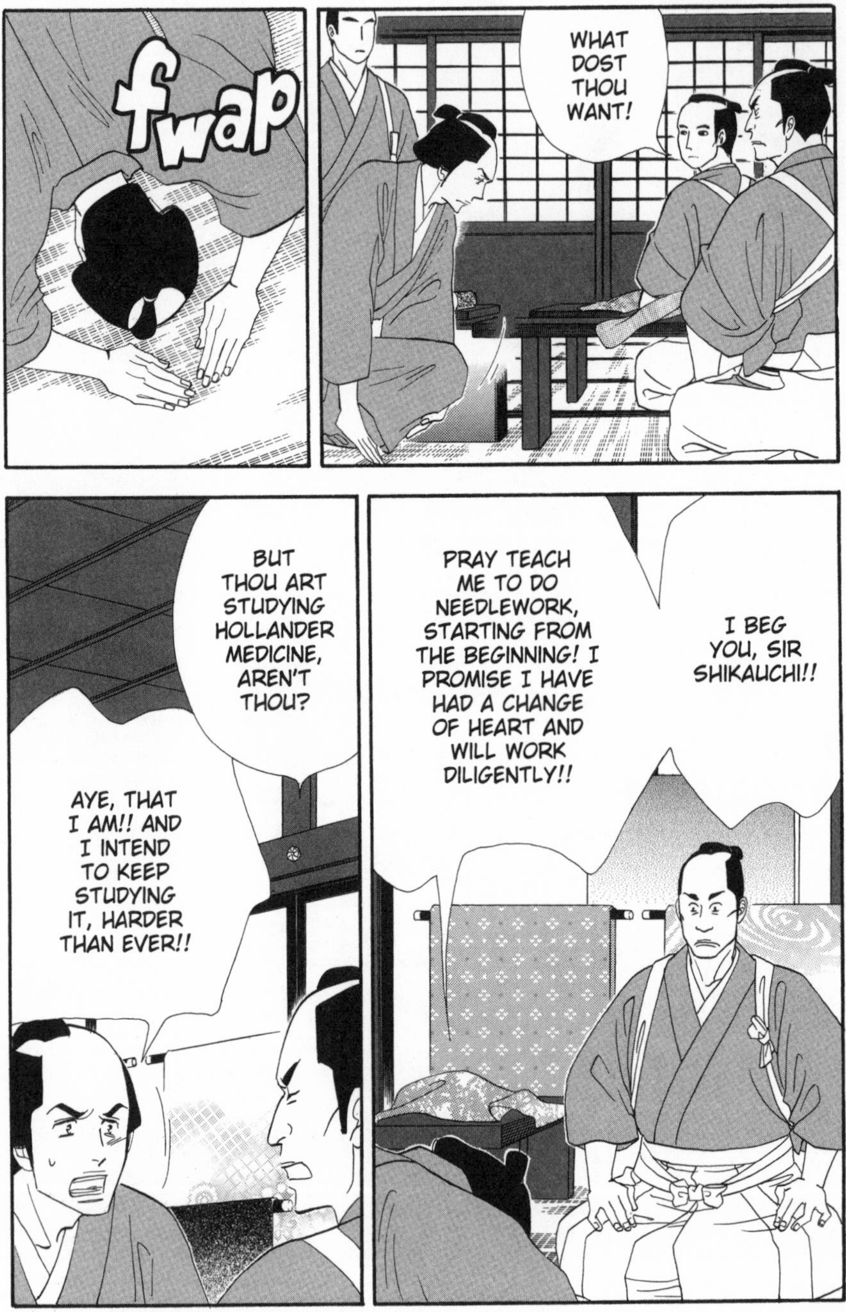
WHAT DOST THOU WANT!
fwap
I BEG YOU, SIR SHIKAUCHI!!
PRAY TEACH ME TO DO NEEDLEWORK, STARTING FROM THE BEGINNING! I PROMISE I HAVE HAD A CHANGE OF HEART AND WILL WORK DILIGENTLY!!
BUT THOU ART STUDYING HOLLANDER MEDICINE, AREN'T THOU?
AYE, THAT I AM!! AND I INTEND TO KEEP STUDYING IT, HARDER THAN EVER!!

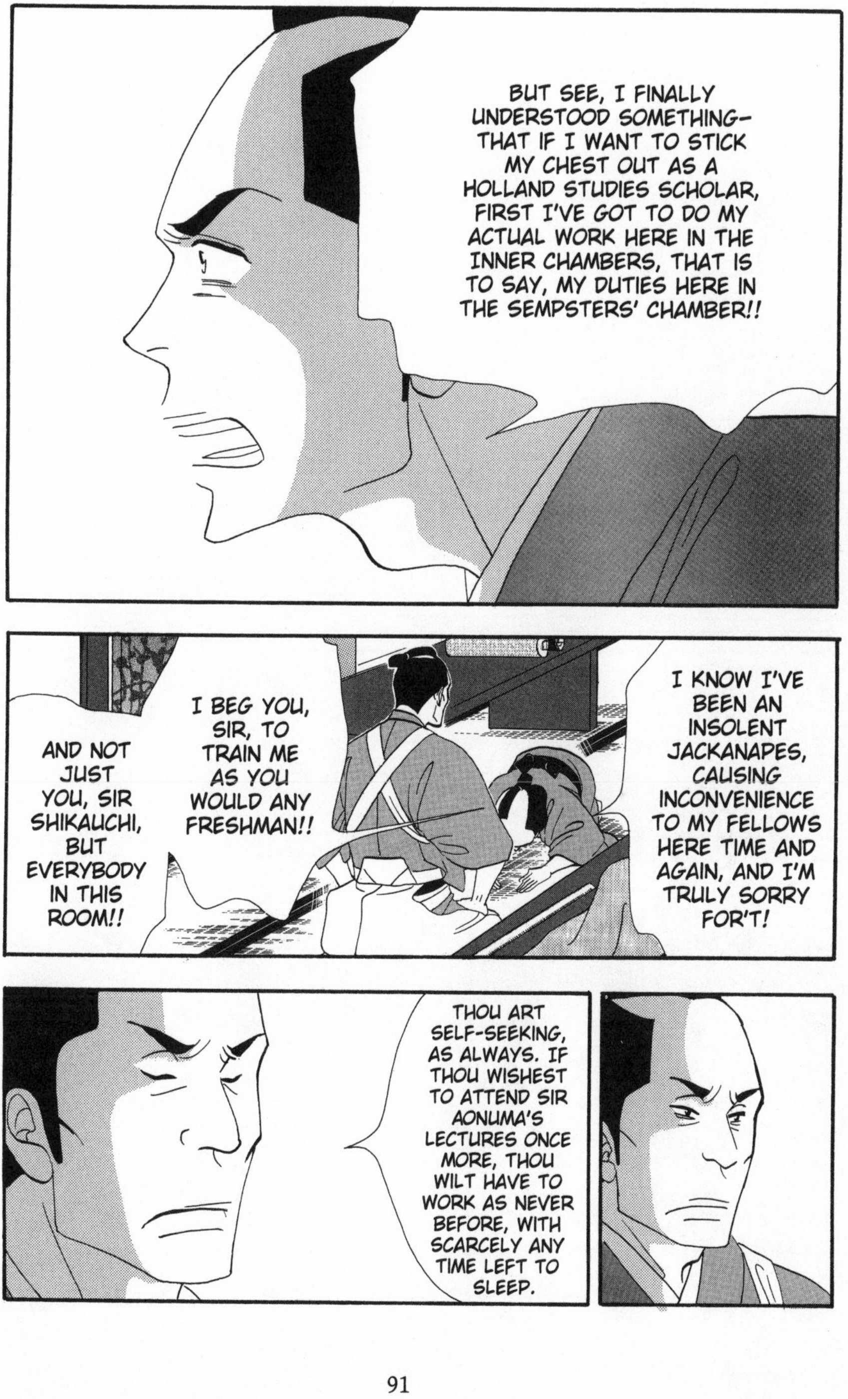
BUT SEE, I FINALLY UNDERSTOOD SOMETHING- THAT IF I WANT TO STICK MY CHEST OUT AS A HOLLAND STUDIES SCHOLAR, FIRST I'VE GOT TO DO MY ACTUAL WORK HERE IN THE INNER CHAMBERS, THAT IS TO SAY, MY DUTIES HERE IN THE SEMPSTERS' CHAMBER!!
I KNOW I'VE BEEN AN INSOLENT JACKANAPES, CAUSING INCONVENIENCE TO MY FELLOWS HERE TIME AND AGAIN, AND I'M TRULY SORRY FOR'T!
I BEG YOU, SIR, TO TRAIN ME AS YOU WOULD ANY FRESHMAN!!
AND NOT JUST YOU, SIR SHIKAUCHI, BUT EVERYBODY IN THIS ROOM!!
THOU ART SELF-SEEKING, AS ALWAYS. IF THOU WISHEST TO ATTEND SIR AONUMA'S LECTURES ONCE MORE, THOU WILT HAVE TO WORK AS NEVER BEFORE, WITH SCARCELY ANY TIME LEFT TO SLEEP.

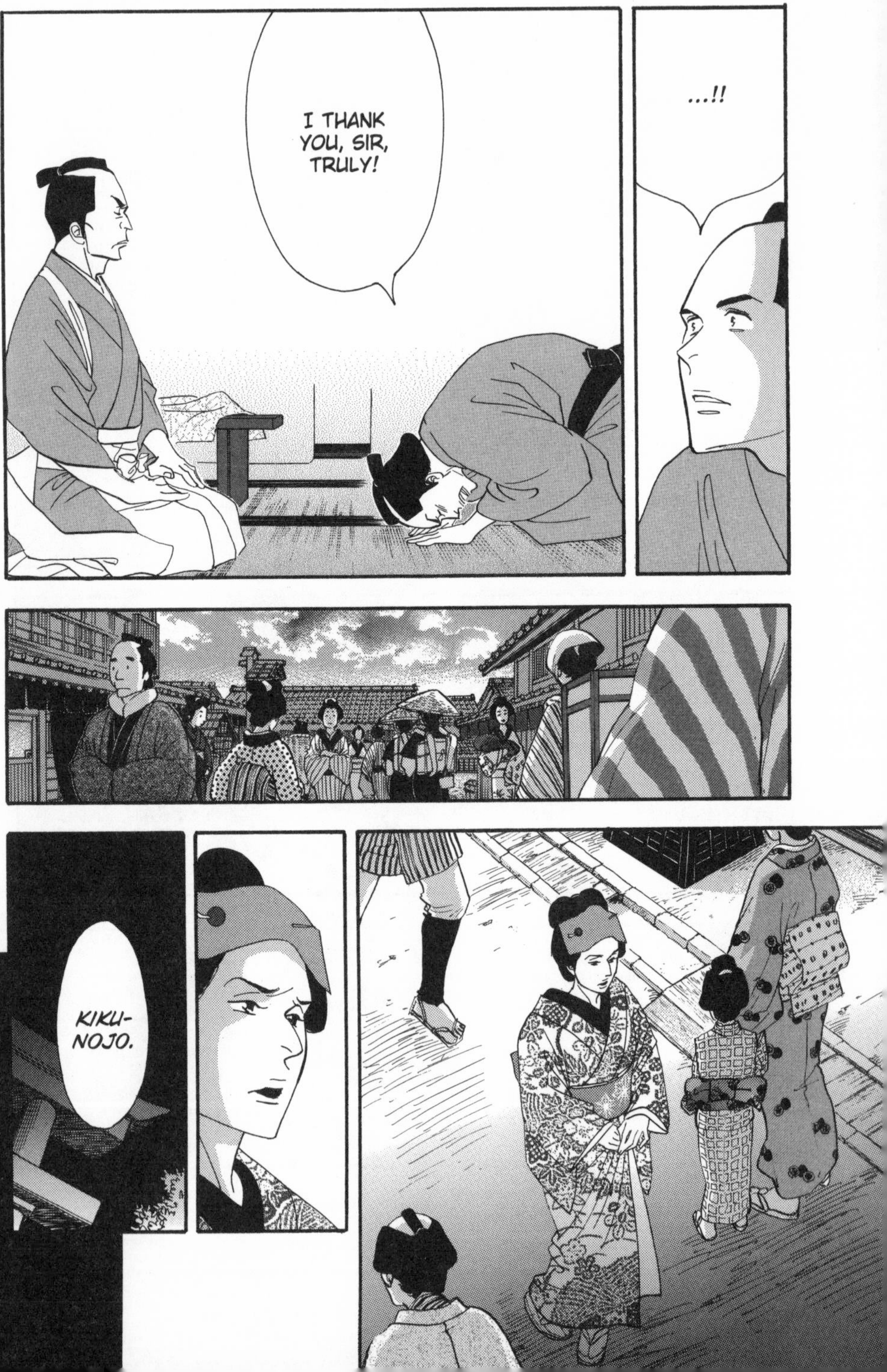
...!!
I THANK YOU, SIR, TRULY!
KIKU-NOJO.

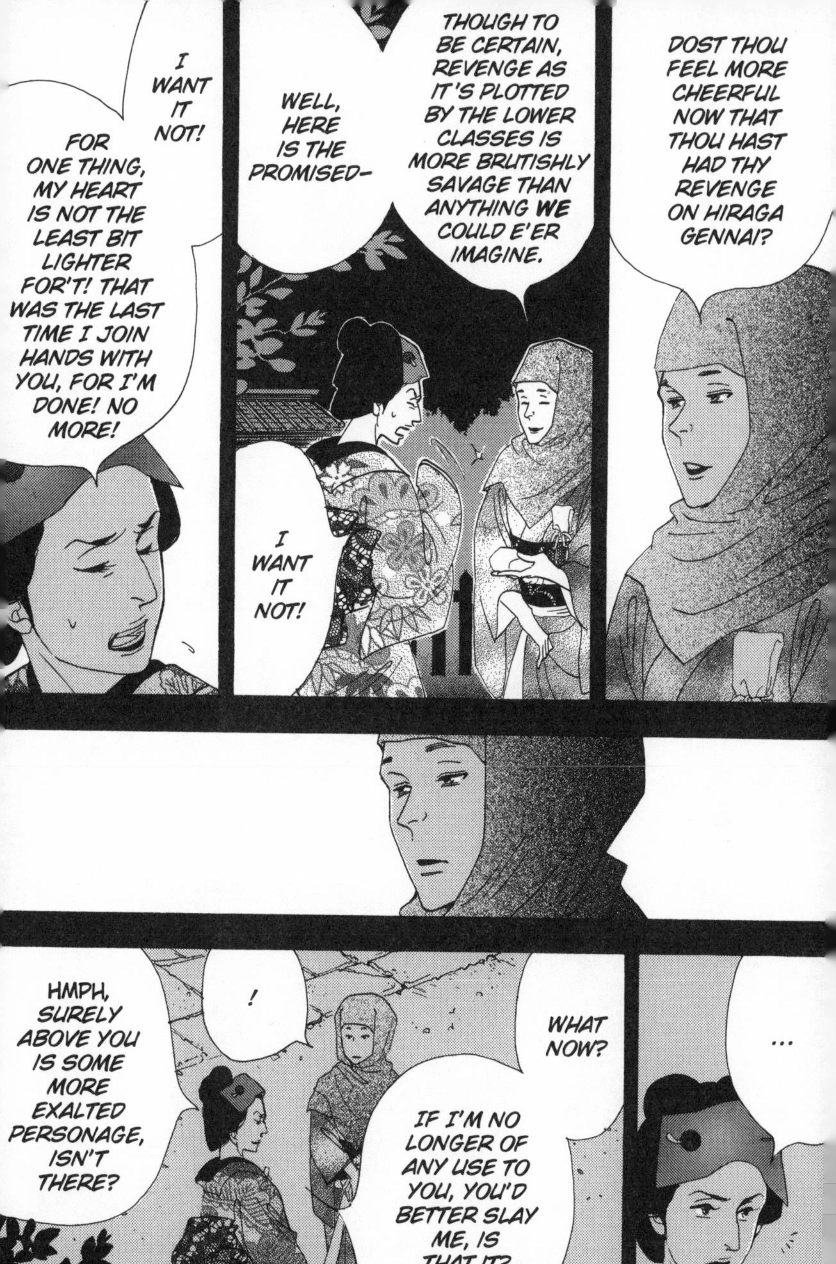
DOST THOU FEEL MORE CHEERFUL NOW THAT THOU HAST HAD THY REVENGE ON HIRAGA GENNAI?
THOUGH TO BE CERTAIN, REVENGE AS IT'S PLOTTED BY THE LOWER CLASSES IS MORE BRUTISHLY SAVAGE THAN ANYTHING **WE** COULD E'ER IMAGINE.
WELL, HERE IS THE PROMISED-
I WANT IT NOT!
I WANT IT NOT!
FOR ONE THING, MY HEART IS NOT THE LEAST BIT LIGHTER FOR'T! THAT WAS THE LAST TIME I JOIN HANDS WITH YOU, FOR I'M DONE! NO MORE!
...
WHAT NOW?
IF I'M NO LONGER OF ANY USE TO YOU, YOU'D BETTER SLAY ME, IS THAT IT?
!
HMPH, SURELY ABOVE YOU IS SOME MORE EXALTED PERSONAGE, ISN'T THERE?

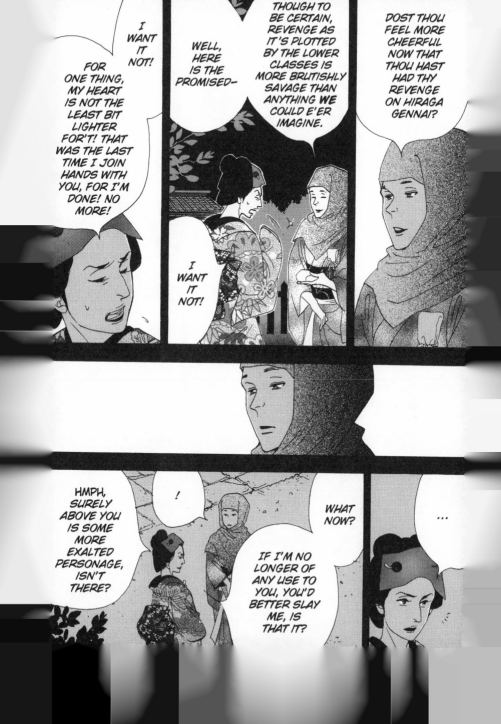

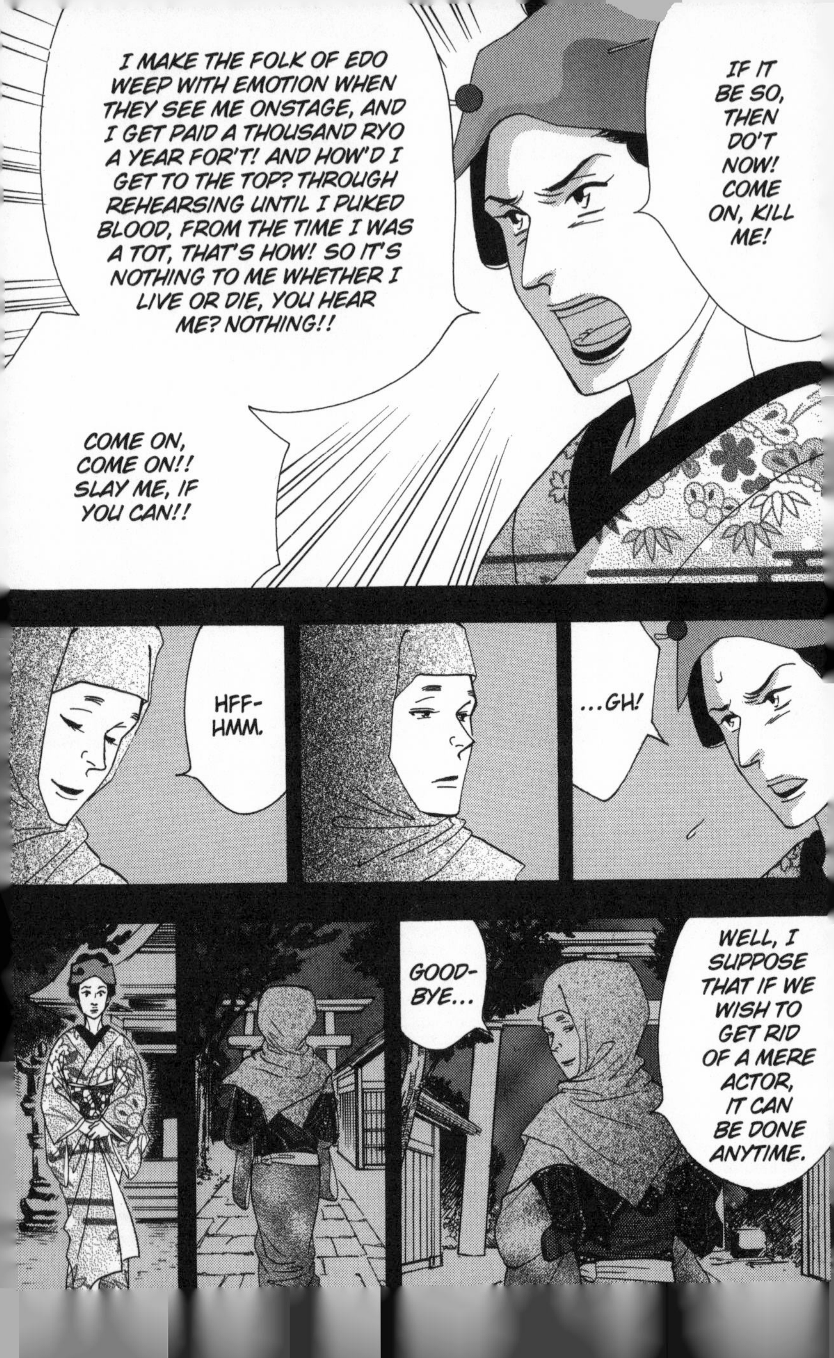
IF IT BE SO, THEN DO'T NOW! COME ON, KILL ME!
I MAKE THE FOLK OF EDO WEEP WITH EMOTION WHEN THEY SEE ME ONSTAGE, AND I GET PAID A THOUSAND RYO A YEAR FOR'T! AND HOW'D I GET TO THE TOP? THROUGH REHEARSING UNTIL I PUKED BLOOD, FROM THE TIME I WAS A TOT, THAT'S HOW! SO IT'S NOTHING TO ME WHETHER I LIVE OR DIE, YOU HEAR ME? NOTHING!!
COME ON, COME ON!! SLAY ME, IF YOU CAN!!
...GH!
HFF-HMM.
WELL, I SUPPOSE THAT IF WE WISH TO GET RID OF A MERE ACTOR, IT CAN BE DONE ANYTIME.
GOOD-BYE...

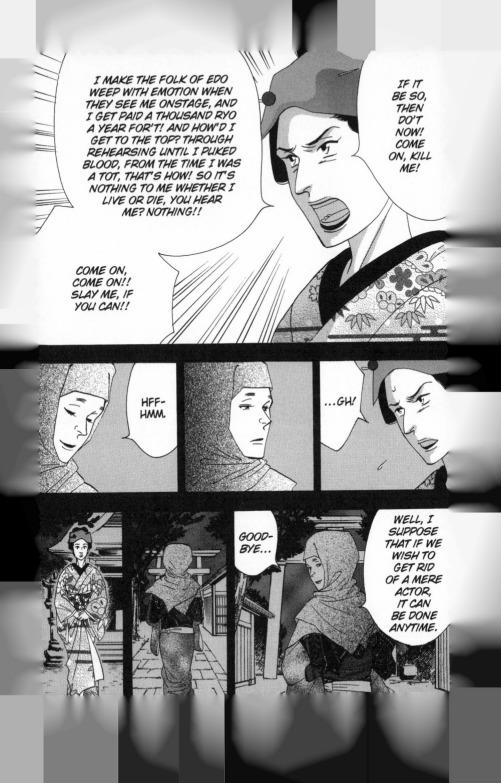

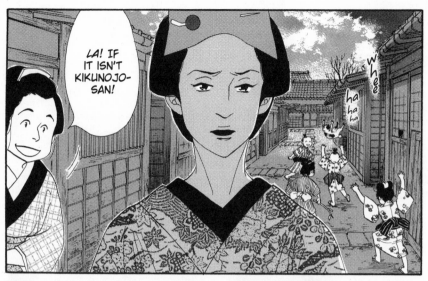

LA! IF IT ISN'T KIKUNOJO-SAN!
whee
ha ha ha
I HEARD YOU'D HAD A FIGHT AND BROKE UP, BUT HERE YOU ARE TO SEE HOW MASTER IS!
I SHOULD WARN YOU, THOUGH, THAT MASTER GENNAI HAS BEEN PACKING THEM IN LATELY. IT'S A FULL HOUSE!
WHAT?
MASTER GENNAAAI! YOU CAN'T BATHE IN YOUR CONDITION, CAN YOU? HERE, LET ME WASH YOU CLEAN WITH THIS DAMP CLOTH!
THINK THOU CANST ELBOW THY WAY IN, HUSSY?! I'M THE ONE WHO'S WASHING MASTER'S BODY, MAKE NO MISTAKE!
OH, MASTER, ARE YOU HUNGRY YET? I'VE BROUGHT SOME FOOD I COOKED, JUST FOR YOU, MASTER! PRAY TRY IT...

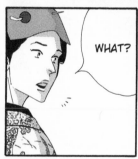

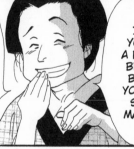

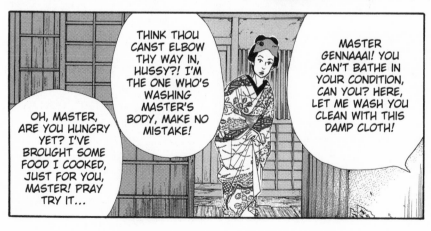

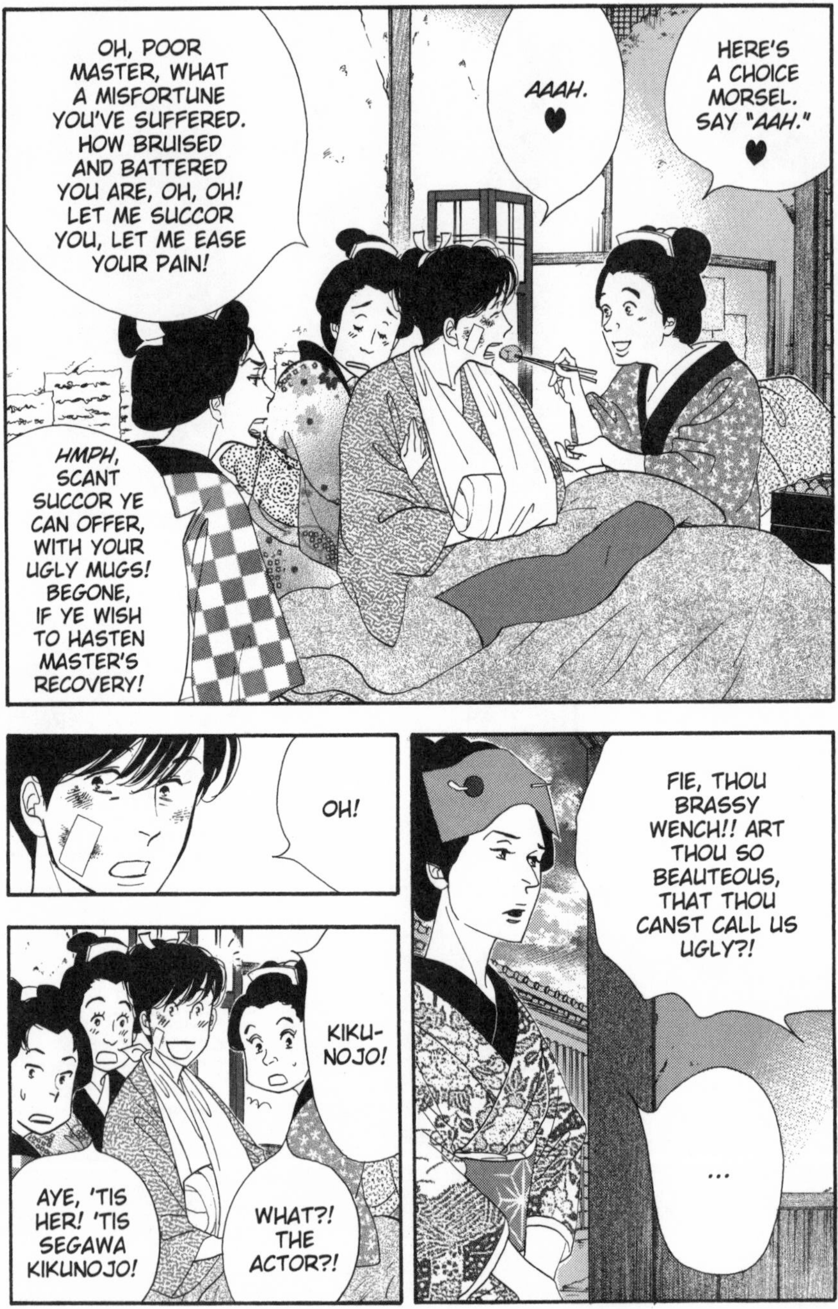
HERE'S A CHOICE MORSEL. SAY "AAH." ♥
AAAH. ♥
OH, POOR MASTER, WHAT A MISFORTUNE YOU'VE SUFFERED. HOW BRUISED AND BATTERED YOU ARE, OH, OH! LET ME SUCCOR YOU, LET ME EASE YOUR PAIN!
HMPH, SCANT SUCCOR YE CAN OFFER, WITH YOUR UGLY MUGS! BEGONE, IF YE WISH TO HASTEN MASTER'S RECOVERY!
FIE, THOU BRASSY WENCH!! ART THOU SO BEAUTEOUS, THAT THOU CANST CALL US UGLY?!
...
OH!
KIKU-NOJO!
WHAT?! THE ACTOR?!
AYE, 'TIS HER! 'TIS SEGAWA KIKUNOJO!

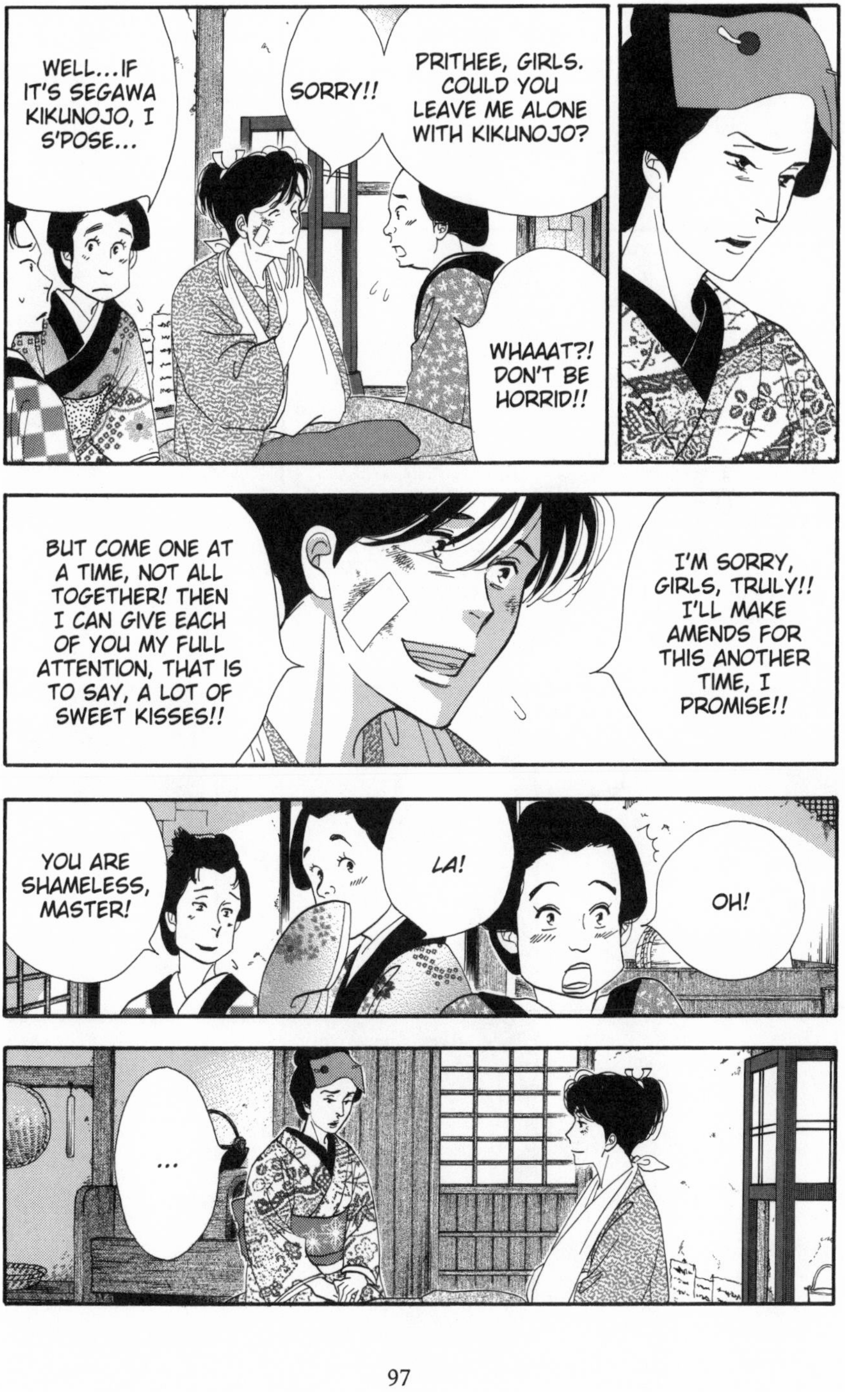
PRITHEE, GIRLS. COULD YOU LEAVE ME ALONE WITH KIKUNOJO?
SORRY!!
WELL...IF IT'S SEGAWA KIKUNOJO, I S'POSE...
WHAAAT?! DON'T BE HORRID!!
I'M SORRY, GIRLS, TRULY!! I'LL MAKE AMENDS FOR THIS ANOTHER TIME, I PROMISE!!
BUT COME ONE AT A TIME, NOT ALL TOGETHER! THEN I CAN GIVE EACH OF YOU MY FULL ATTENTION, THAT IS TO SAY, A LOT OF SWEET KISSES!!
OH!
LA!
YOU ARE SHAMELESS, MASTER!
...

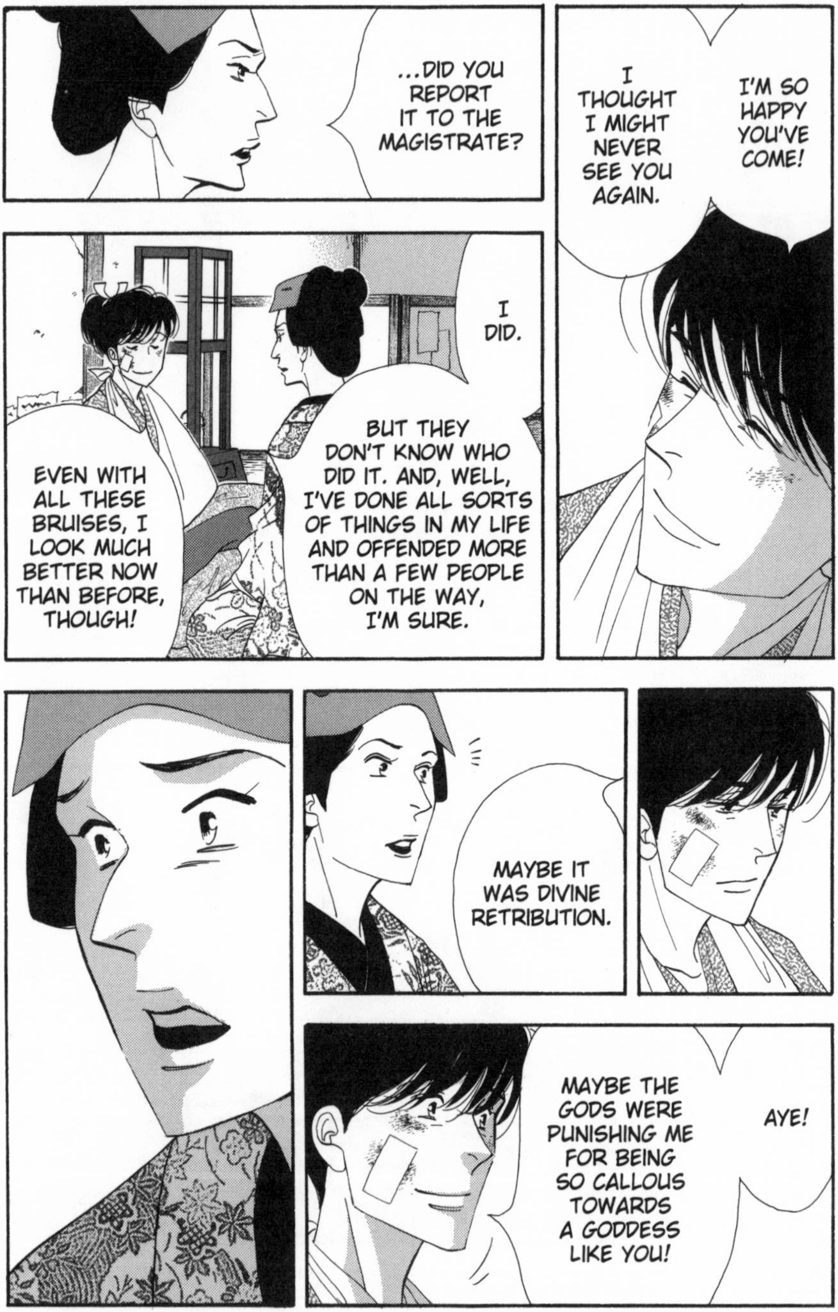
I'M SO HAPPY YOU'VE COME!
I THOUGHT I MIGHT NEVER SEE YOU AGAIN.
...DID YOU REPORT IT TO THE MAGISTRATE?
I DID.
BUT THEY DON'T KNOW WHO DID IT. AND, WELL, I'VE DONE ALL SORTS OF THINGS IN MY LIFE AND OFFENDED MORE THAN A FEW PEOPLE ON THE WAY, I'M SURE.
EVEN WITH ALL THESE BRUISES, I LOOK MUCH BETTER NOW THAN BEFORE, THOUGH!
MAYBE IT WAS DIVINE RETRIBUTION.
AYE!
MAYBE THE GODS WERE PUNISHING ME FOR BEING SO CALLOUS TOWARDS A GODDESS LIKE YOU!

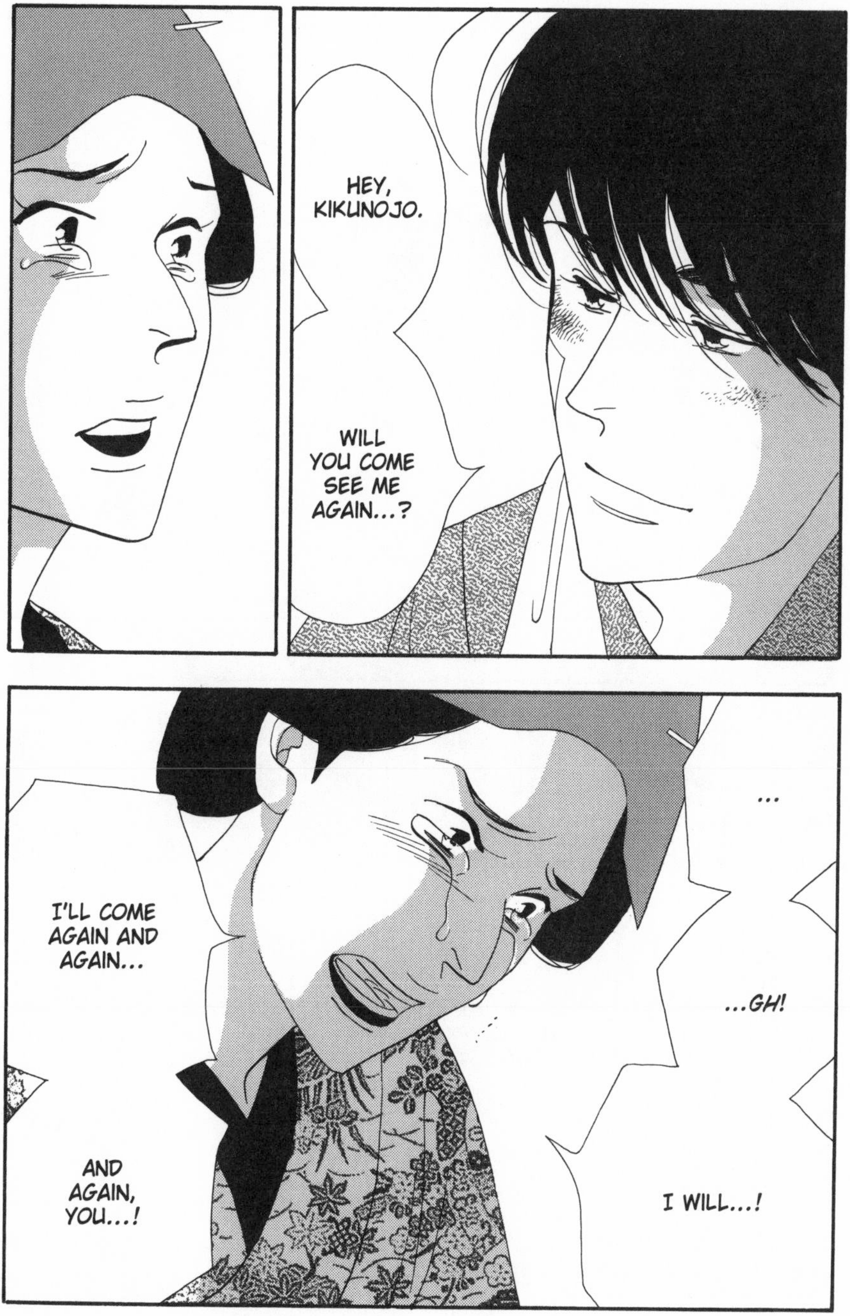
HEY, KIKUNOJO.
WILL YOU COME SEE ME AGAIN...?
...
...GH!
I WILL...!
I'LL COME AGAIN AND AGAIN...
AND AGAIN, YOU...!

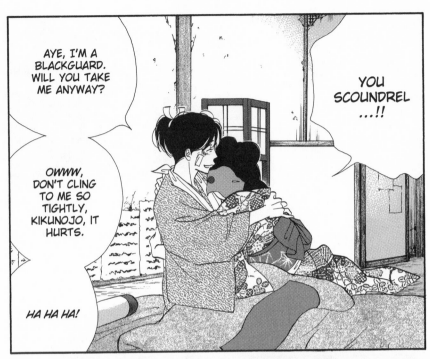

YOU SCOUNDREL ...!!
AYE, I'M A BLACKGUARD. WILL YOU TAKE ME ANYWAY?
OWWW, DON'T CLING TO ME SO TIGHTLY, KIKUNOJO, IT HURTS.
HA HA HA!
PRAY, COULD YOU EXPLICATE THE MEANING OF THIS?
ERM...
LET ME SEE.
HMM... WAIT A MOMENT. I BELIEVE I REMEMBER SEEING THIS WORD AMONG SIR AONUMA'S NOTES.
SIR KUROKI, THAT'S THE WORD FOR PARTY. AND THIS WORD... "POKKEN"... HUH?

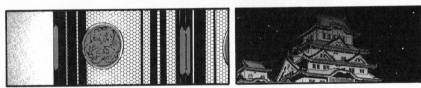

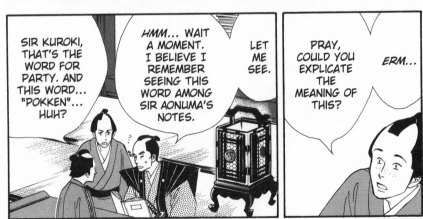

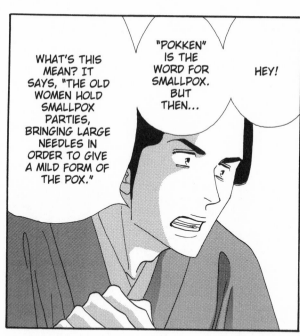

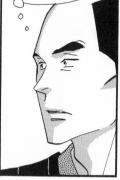

NOW THAT HE'S BACK IN THE SEMPSTERS' CHAMBER, IHEI OUGHT TO HAVE FAR LESS TIME THAN BEFORE FOR HIS STUDIES. AND YET...
HEY!
"POKKEN" IS THE WORD FOR SMALLPOX. BUT THEN...
WHAT'S THIS MEAN? IT SAYS, "THE OLD WOMEN HOLD SMALLPOX PARTIES, BRINGING LARGE NEEDLES IN ORDER TO GIVE A MILD FORM OF THE POX."
WHAT?!
NEEDLES?!
I'VE NEVER HEARD OF AN INOCULATION METHOD USING NEEDLES BEFORE!
WELL, IT SOUNDS LIKE THE HOLLANDERS HADN'T, EITHER. THIS PASSAGE IS RECOUNTING WHAT'S DONE IN A DISTANT COUNTRY, NOT ENGLAND, BUT SOMEPLACE EVEN MORE REMOTE!

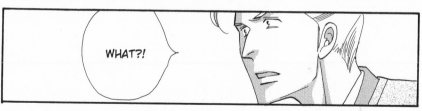

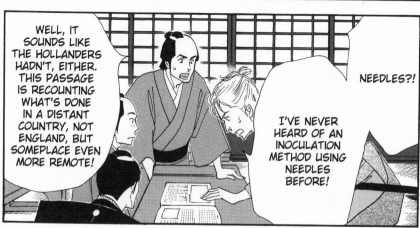

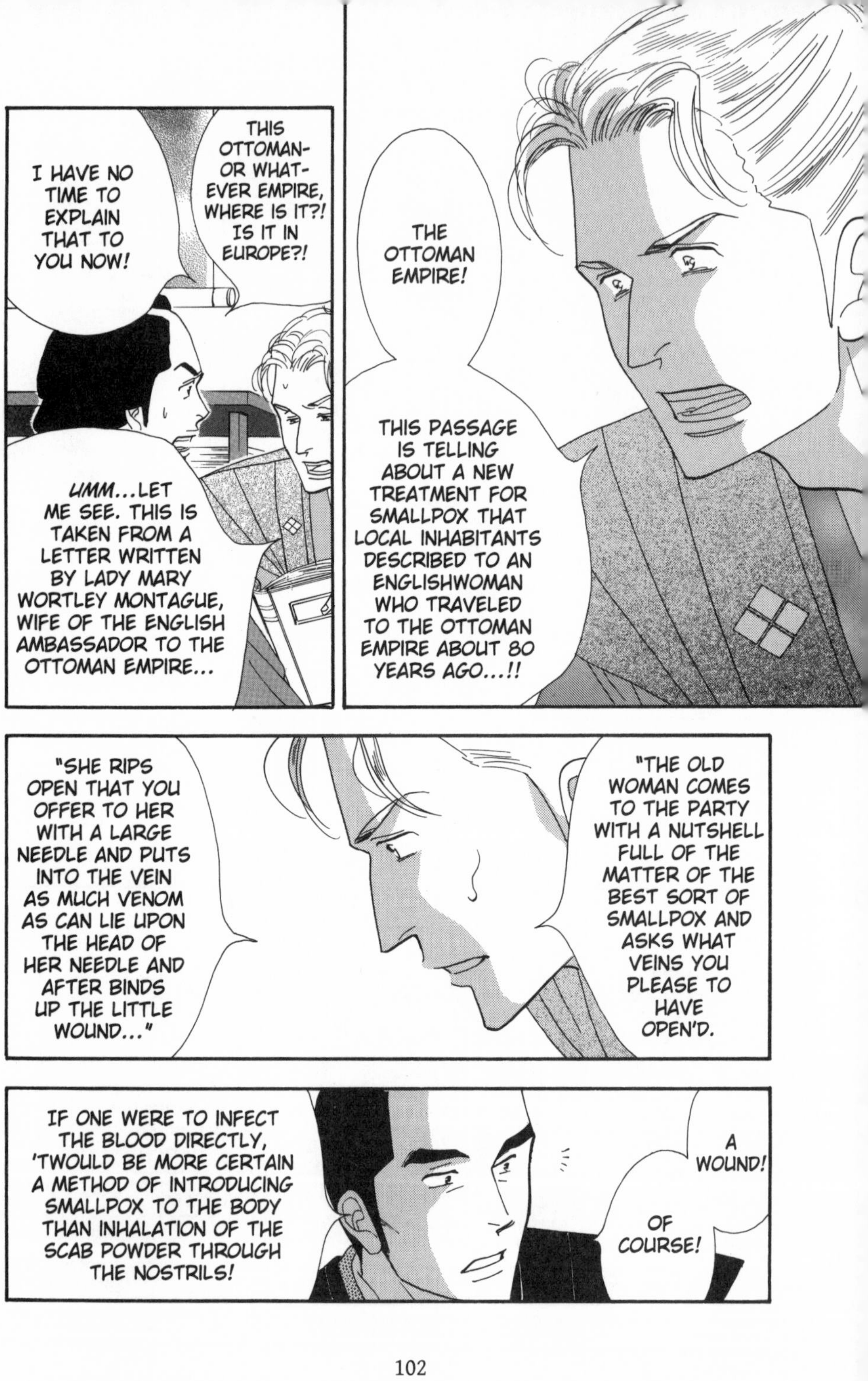
THE OTTOMAN EMPIRE!
THIS PASSAGE IS TELLING ABOUT A NEW TREATMENT FOR SMALLPOX THAT LOCAL INHABITANTS DESCRIBED TO AN ENGLISHWOMAN WHO TRAVELED TO THE OTTOMAN EMPIRE ABOUT 80 YEARS AGO...!!
THIS OTTOMAN-OR WHATEVER EMPIRE, WHERE IS IT?! IS IT IN EUROPE?!
I HAVE NO TIME TO EXPLAIN THAT TO YOU NOW!
UMM...LET ME SEE. THIS IS TAKEN FROM A LETTER WRITTEN BY LADY MARY WORTLEY MONTAGUE, WIFE OF THE ENGLISH AMBASSADOR TO THE OTTOMAN EMPIRE...
"THE OLD WOMAN COMES TO THE PARTY WITH A NUTSHELL FULL OF THE MATTER OF THE BEST SORT OF SMALLPOX AND ASKS WHAT VEINS YOU PLEASE TO HAVE OPEN'D.
"SHE RIPS OPEN THAT YOU OFFER TO HER WITH A LARGE NEEDLE AND PUTS INTO THE VEIN AS MUCH VENOM AS CAN LIE UPON THE HEAD OF HER NEEDLE AND AFTER BINDS UP THE LITTLE WOUND..."
A WOUND!
OF COURSE!
IF ONE WERE TO INFECT THE BLOOD DIRECTLY, 'TWOULD BE MORE CERTAIN A METHOD OF INTRODUCING SMALLPOX TO THE BODY THAN INHALATION OF THE SCAB POWDER THROUGH THE NOSTRILS!

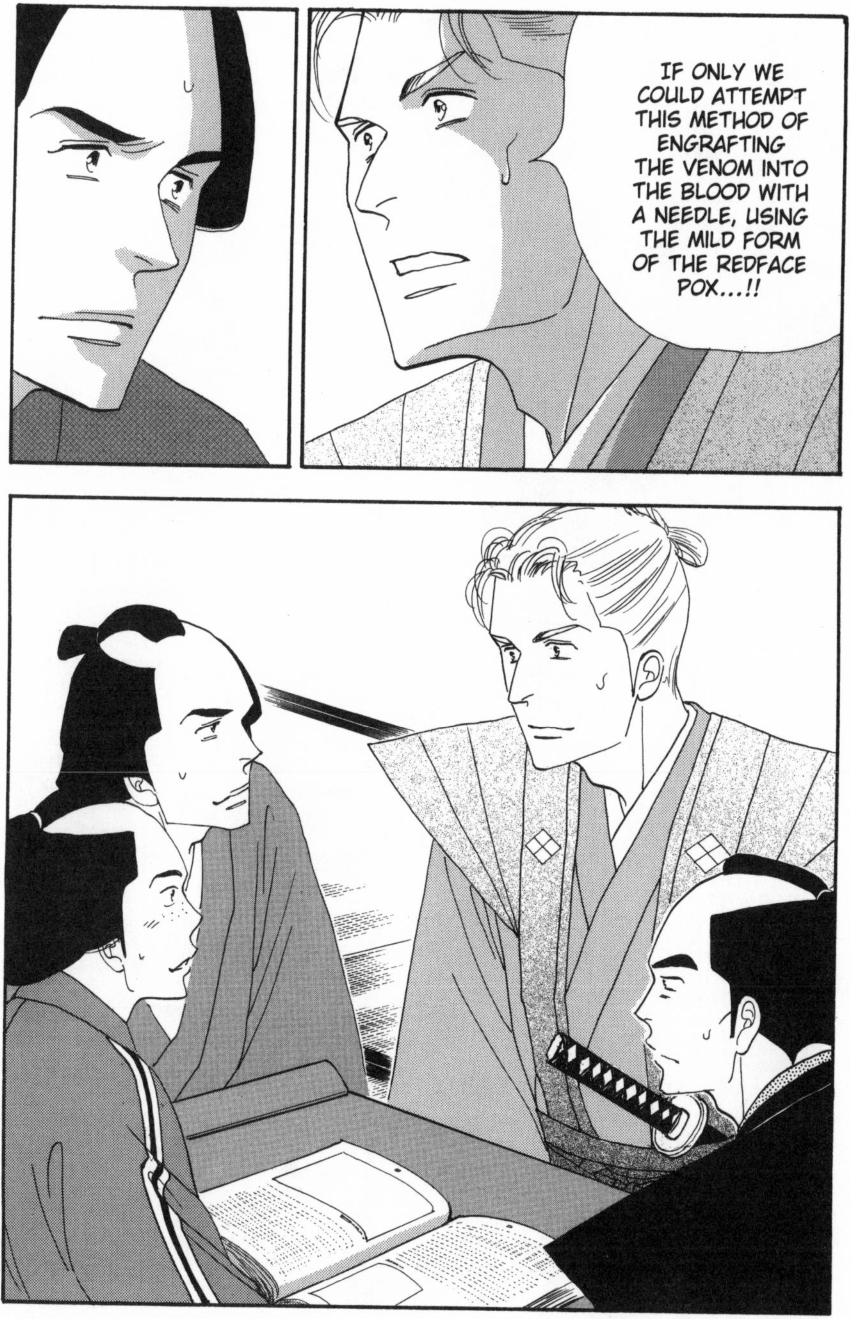
IF ONLY WE COULD ATTEMPT THIS METHOD OF ENGRAFTING THE VENOM INTO THE BLOOD WITH A NEEDLE, USING THE MILD FORM OF THE REDFACE POX...!!

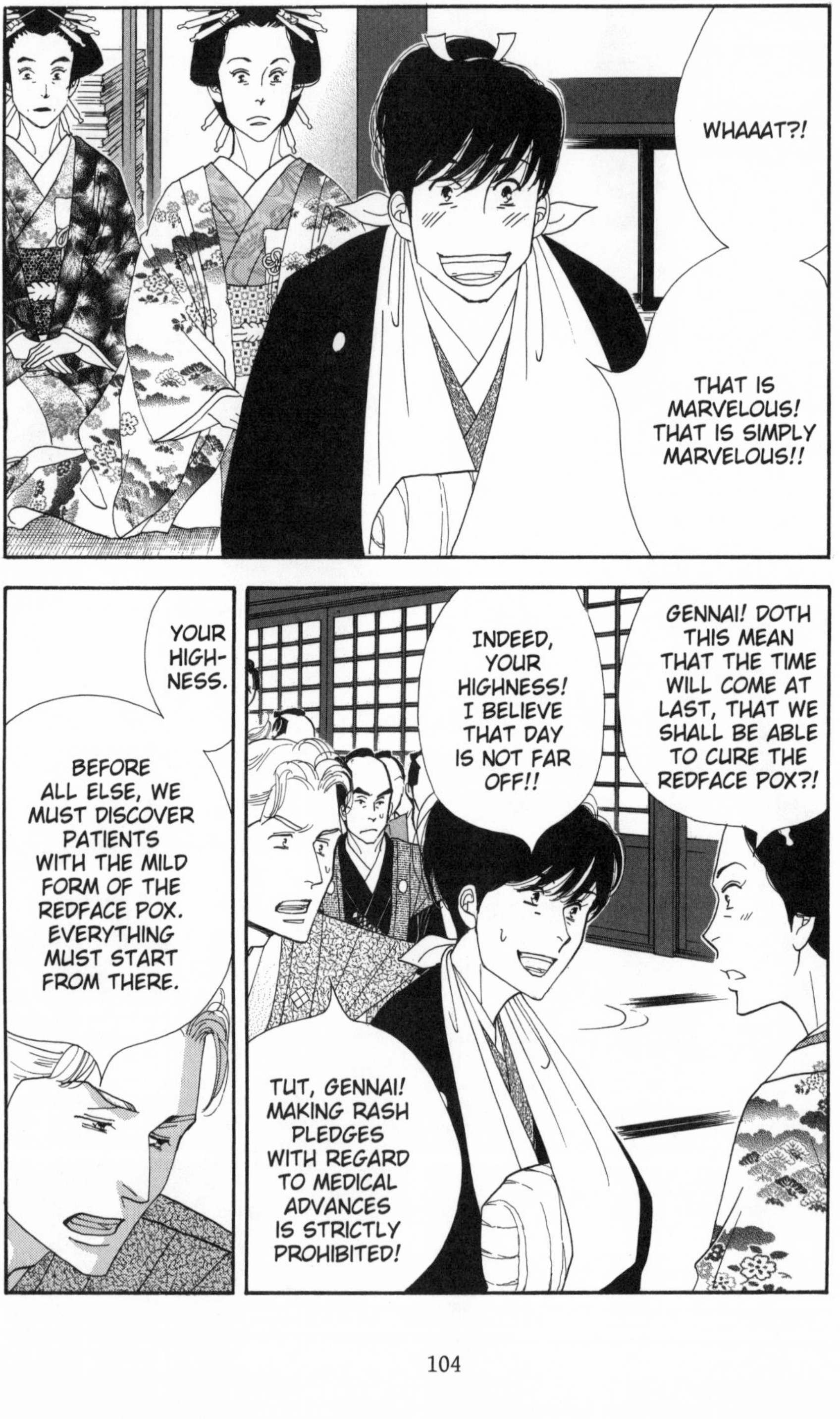
WHAAAT?!
THAT IS MARVELOUS! THAT IS SIMPLY MARVELOUS!!
GENNAI! DOTH THIS MEAN THAT THE TIME WILL COME AT LAST, THAT WE SHALL BE ABLE TO CURE THE REDFACE POX?!
INDEED, YOUR HIGHNESS! I BELIEVE THAT DAY IS NOT FAR OFF!!
TUT, GENNAI! MAKING RASH PLEDGES WITH REGARD TO MEDICAL ADVANCES IS STRICTLY PROHIBITED!
YOUR HIGH-NESS.
BEFORE ALL ELSE, WE MUST DISCOVER PATIENTS WITH THE MILD FORM OF THE REDFACE POX. EVERYTHING MUST START FROM THERE.

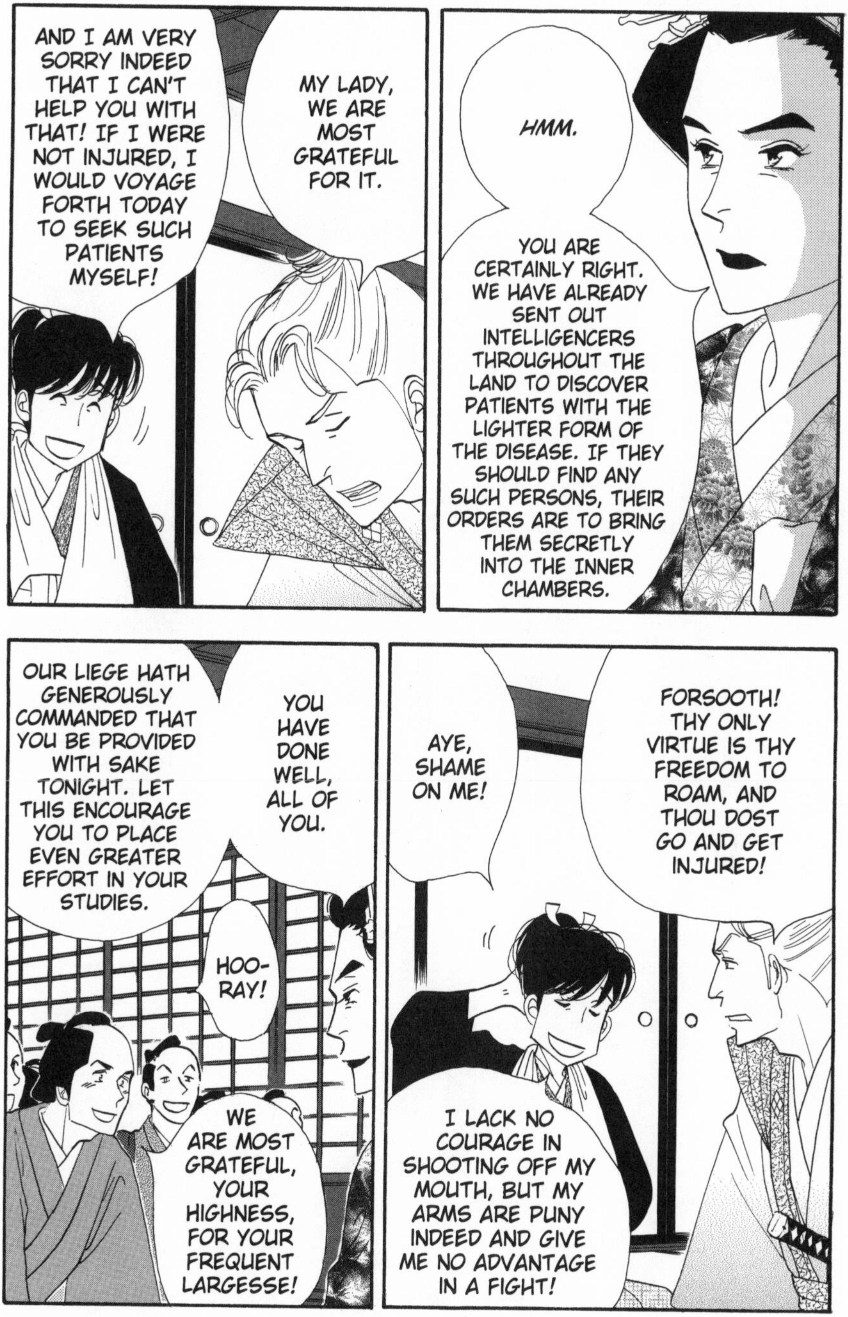
HMM.
YOU ARE CERTAINLY RIGHT. WE HAVE ALREADY SENT OUT INTELLIGENCERS THROUGHOUT THE LAND TO DISCOVER PATIENTS WITH THE LIGHTER FORM OF THE DISEASE. IF THEY SHOULD FIND ANY SUCH PERSONS, THEIR ORDERS ARE TO BRING THEM SECRETLY INTO THE INNER CHAMBERS.
MY LADY, WE ARE MOST GRATEFUL FOR IT.
AND I AM VERY SORRY INDEED THAT I CAN'T HELP YOU WITH THAT! IF I WERE NOT INJURED, I WOULD VOYAGE FORTH TODAY TO SEEK SUCH PATIENTS MYSELF!
FORSOOTH! THY ONLY VIRTUE IS THY FREEDOM TO ROAM, AND THOU DOST GO AND GET INJURED!
AYE, SHAME ON ME!
I LACK NO COURAGE IN SHOOTING OFF MY MOUTH, BUT MY ARMS ARE PUNY INDEED AND GIVE ME NO ADVANTAGE IN A FIGHT!
YOU HAVE DONE WELL, ALL OF YOU.
OUR LIEGE HATH GENEROUSLY COMMANDED THAT YOU BE PROVIDED WITH SAKE TONIGHT. LET THIS ENCOURAGE YOU TO PLACE EVEN GREATER EFFORT IN YOUR STUDIES.
HOO-RAY!
WE ARE MOST GRATEFUL, YOUR HIGHNESS, FOR YOUR FREQUENT LARGESSE!

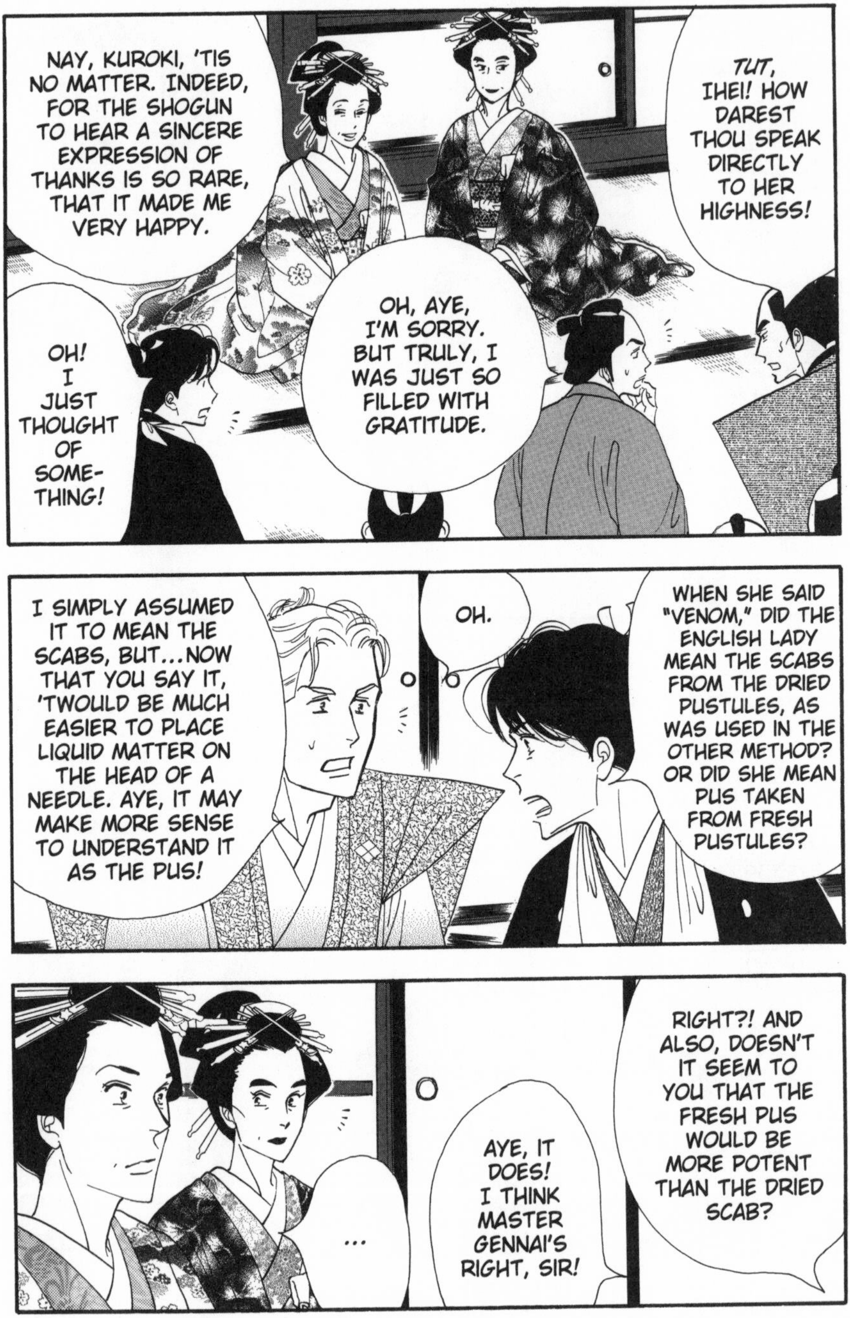
TUT, IHEI! HOW DAREST THOU SPEAK DIRECTLY TO HER HIGHNESS!
NAY, KUROKI, 'TIS NO MATTER. INDEED, FOR THE SHOGUN TO HEAR A SINCERE EXPRESSION OF THANKS IS SO RARE, THAT IT MADE ME VERY HAPPY.
OH, AYE, I'M SORRY. BUT TRULY, I WAS JUST SO FILLED WITH GRATITUDE.
OH! I JUST THOUGHT OF SOME-THING!
WHEN SHE SAID "VENOM," DID THE ENGLISH LADY MEAN THE SCABS FROM THE DRIED PUSTULES, AS WAS USED IN THE OTHER METHOD? OR DID SHE MEAN PUS TAKEN FROM FRESH PUSTULES?
OH.
I SIMPLY ASSUMED IT TO MEAN THE SCABS, BUT...NOW THAT YOU SAY IT, 'TWOULD BE MUCH EASIER TO PLACE LIQUID MATTER ON THE HEAD OF A NEEDLE. AYE, IT MAY MAKE MORE SENSE TO UNDERSTAND IT AS THE PUS!
RIGHT?! AND ALSO, DOESN'T IT SEEM TO YOU THAT THE FRESH PUS WOULD BE MORE POTENT THAN THE DRIED SCAB?
AYE, IT DOES! I THINK MASTER GENNAI'S RIGHT, SIR!
...

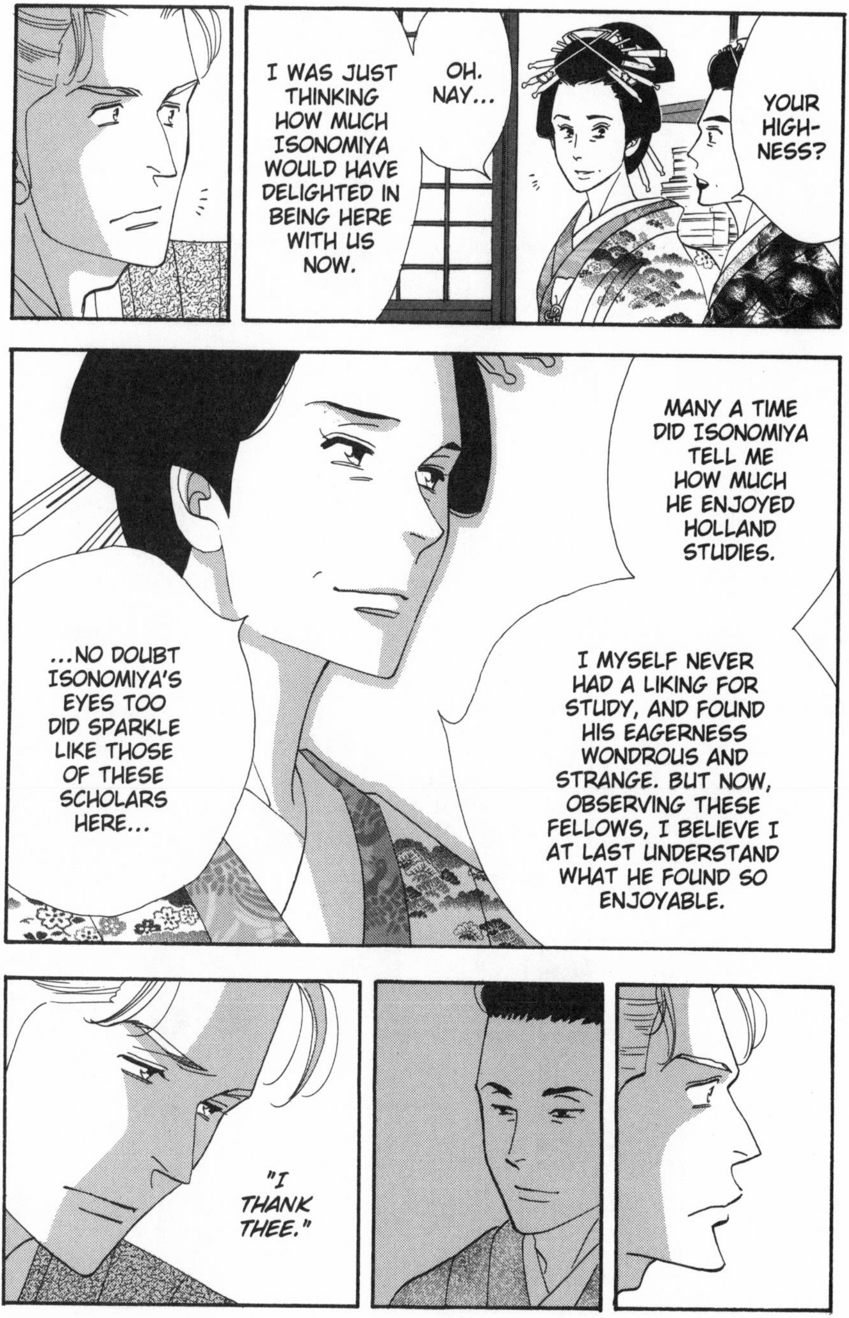
YOUR HIGHNESS?
OH. NAY...
I WAS JUST THINKING HOW MUCH ISONOMIYA WOULD HAVE DELIGHTED IN BEING HERE WITH US NOW.
MANY A TIME DID ISONOMIYA TELL ME HOW MUCH HE ENJOYED HOLLAND STUDIES.
I MYSELF NEVER HAD A LIKING FOR STUDY, AND FOUND HIS EAGERNESS WONDROUS AND STRANGE. BUT NOW, OBSERVING THESE FELLOWS, I BELIEVE I AT LAST UNDERSTAND WHAT HE FOUND SO ENJOYABLE.
...NO DOUBT ISONOMIYA'S EYES TOO DID SPARKLE LIKE THOSE OF THESE SCHOLARS HERE...
"I THANK THEE."

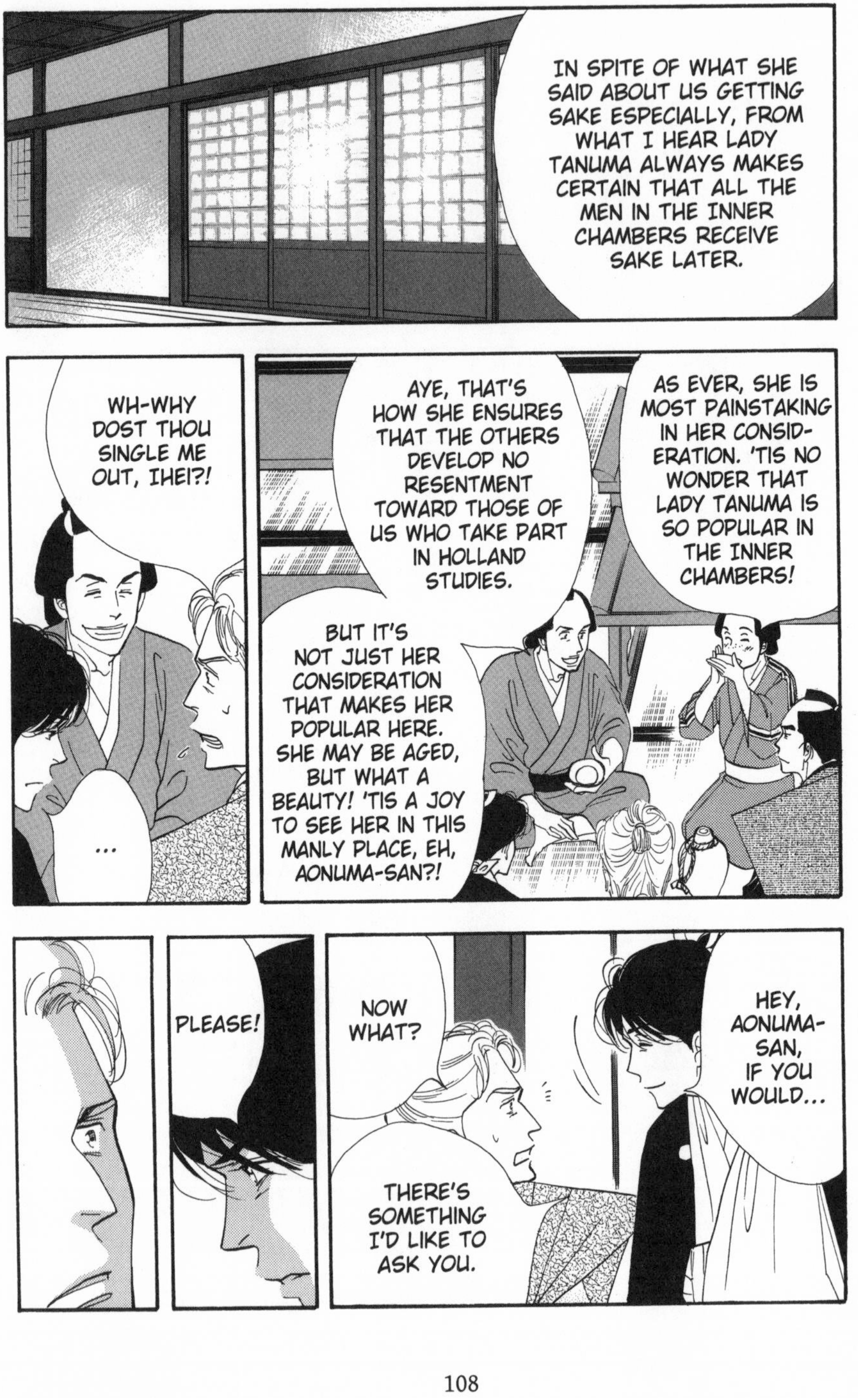
IN SPITE OF WHAT SHE SAID ABOUT US GETTING SAKE ESPECIALLY, FROM WHAT I HEAR LADY TANUMA ALWAYS MAKES CERTAIN THAT ALL THE MEN IN THE INNER CHAMBERS RECEIVE SAKE LATER.
AS EVER, SHE IS MOST PAINSTAKING IN HER CONSID-ERATION. 'TIS NO WONDER THAT LADY TANUMA IS SO POPULAR IN THE INNER CHAMBERS!
AYE, THAT'S HOW SHE ENSURES THAT THE OTHERS DEVELOP NO RESENTMENT TOWARD THOSE OF US WHO TAKE PART IN HOLLAND STUDIES.
BUT IT'S NOT JUST HER CONSIDERATION THAT MAKES HER POPULAR HERE. SHE MAY BE AGED, BUT WHAT A BEAUTY! 'TIS A JOY TO SEE HER IN THIS MANLY PLACE, EH, AONUMA-SAN?!
WH-WHY DOST THOU SINGLE ME OUT, IHEI?!
...
HEY, AONUMA-SAN, IF YOU WOULD...
NOW WHAT?
THERE'S SOMETHING I'D LIKE TO ASK YOU.
PLEASE!

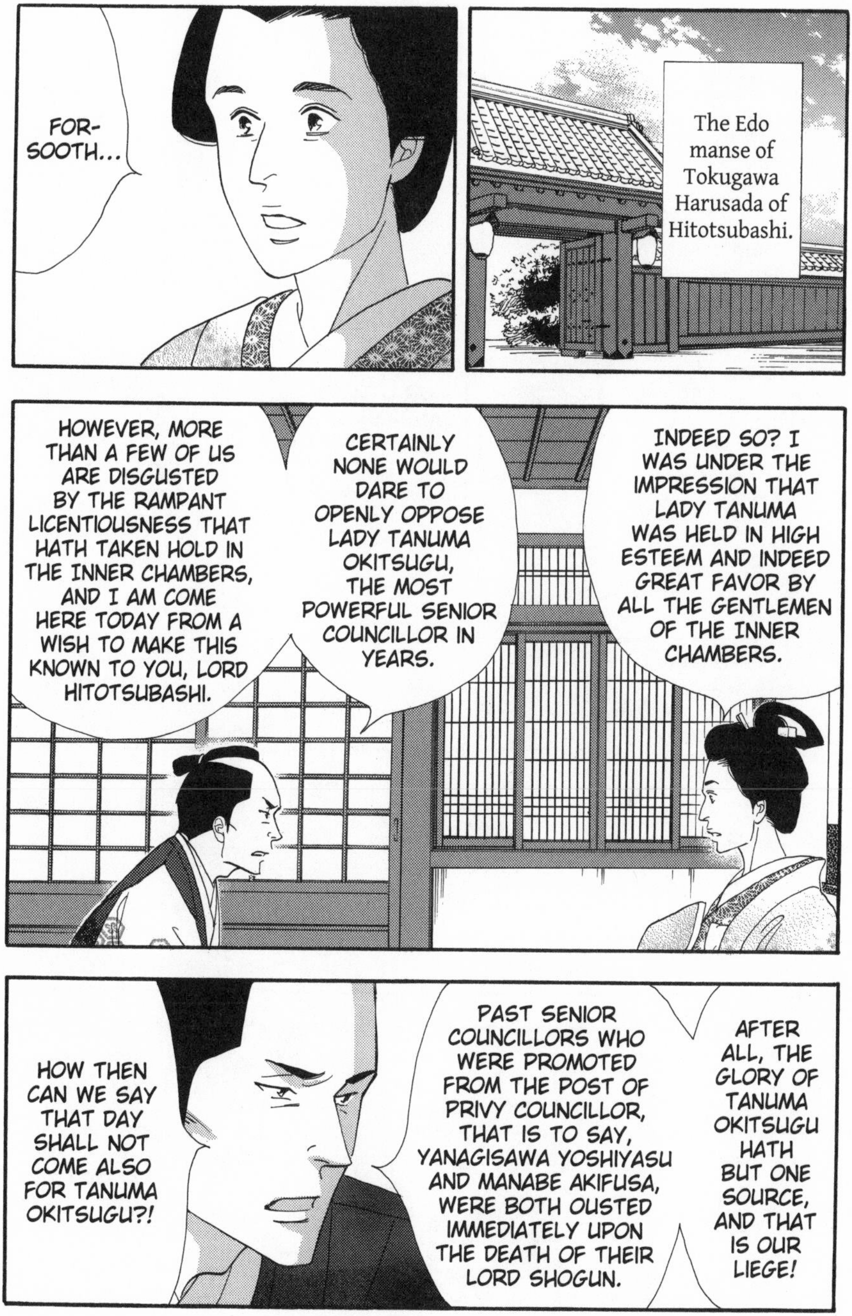
The Edo manse of Tokugawa Harusada of Hitotsubashi.
FOR-SOOTH...
INDEED SO? I WAS UNDER THE IMPRESSION THAT LADY TANUMA WAS HELD IN HIGH ESTEEM AND INDEED GREAT FAVOR BY ALL THE GENTLEMEN OF THE INNER CHAMBERS.
CERTAINLY NONE WOULD DARE TO OPENLY OPPOSE LADY TANUMA OKITSUGU, THE MOST POWERFUL SENIOR COUNCILLOR IN YEARS.
HOWEVER, MORE THAN A FEW OF US ARE DISGUSTED BY THE RAMPANT LICENTIOUSNESS THAT HATH TAKEN HOLD IN THE INNER CHAMBERS, AND I AM COME HERE TODAY FROM A WISH TO MAKE THIS KNOWN TO YOU, LORD HITOTSUBASHI.
AFTER ALL, THE GLORY OF TANUMA OKITSUGU HATH BUT ONE SOURCE, AND THAT IS OUR LIEGE!
PAST SENIOR COUNCILLORS WHO WERE PROMOTED FROM THE POST OF PRIVY COUNCILLOR, THAT IS TO SAY, YANAGISAWA YOSHIYASU AND MANABE AKIFUSA, WERE BOTH OUSTED IMMEDIATELY UPON THE DEATH OF THEIR LORD SHOGUN.
HOW THEN CAN WE SAY THAT DAY SHALL NOT COME ALSO FOR TANUMA OKITSUGU?!

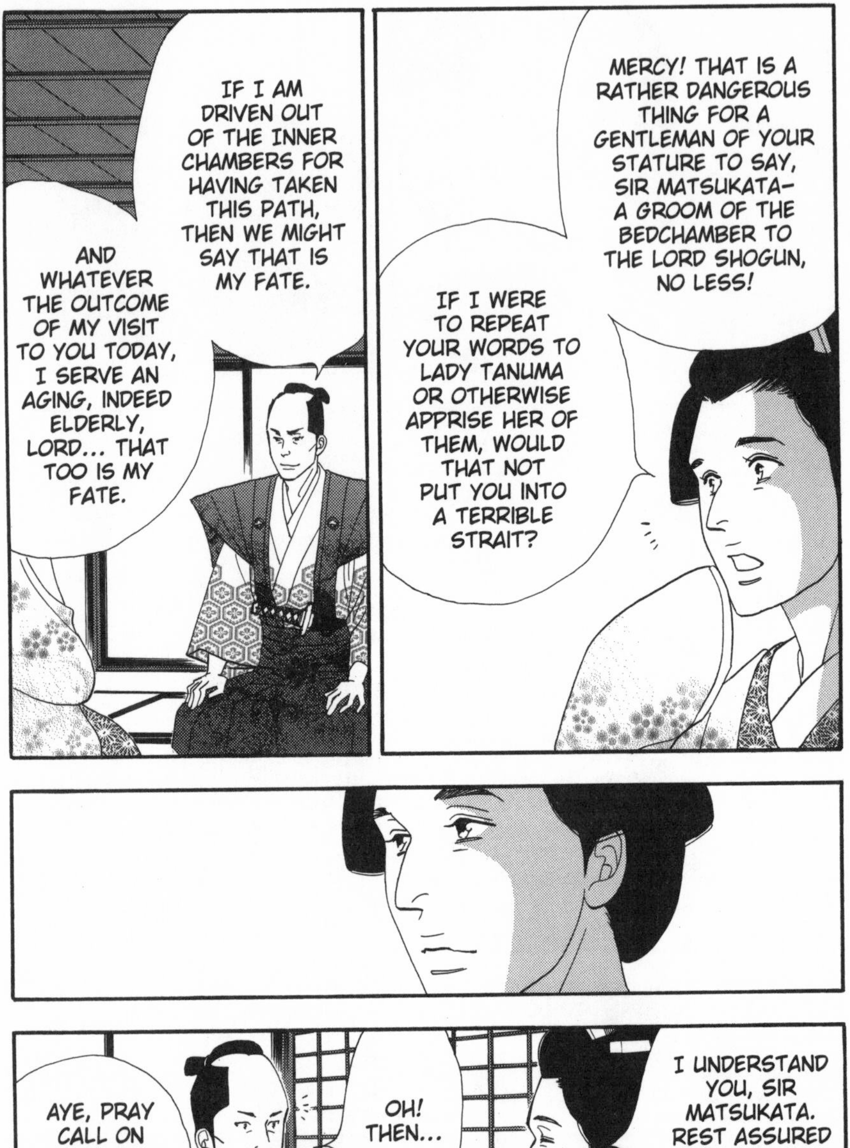
MERCY! THAT IS A RATHER DANGEROUS THING FOR A GENTLEMAN OF YOUR STATURE TO SAY, SIR MATSUKATA– A GROOM OF THE BEDCHAMBER TO THE LORD SHOGUN, NO LESS!
IF I WERE TO REPEAT YOUR WORDS TO LADY TANUMA OR OTHERWISE APPRISE HER OF THEM, WOULD THAT NOT PUT YOU INTO A TERRIBLE STRAIT?
IF I AM DRIVEN OUT OF THE INNER CHAMBERS FOR HAVING TAKEN THIS PATH, THEN WE MIGHT SAY THAT IS MY FATE.
AND WHATEVER THE OUTCOME OF MY VISIT TO YOU TODAY, I SERVE AN AGING, INDEED ELDERLY, LORD... THAT TOO IS MY FATE.
I UNDERSTAND YOU, SIR MATSUKATA. REST ASSURED YOU SHALL NOT BE SORRY FOR HAVING COME TO SEE ME.
OH! THEN...
AYE, PRAY CALL ON ME AGAIN WHENEVER YOU LEAVE THE CASTLE FOR TEMPLE PRAYERS.

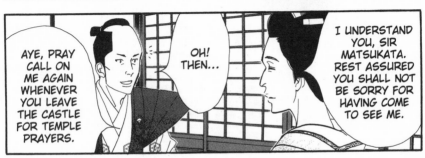

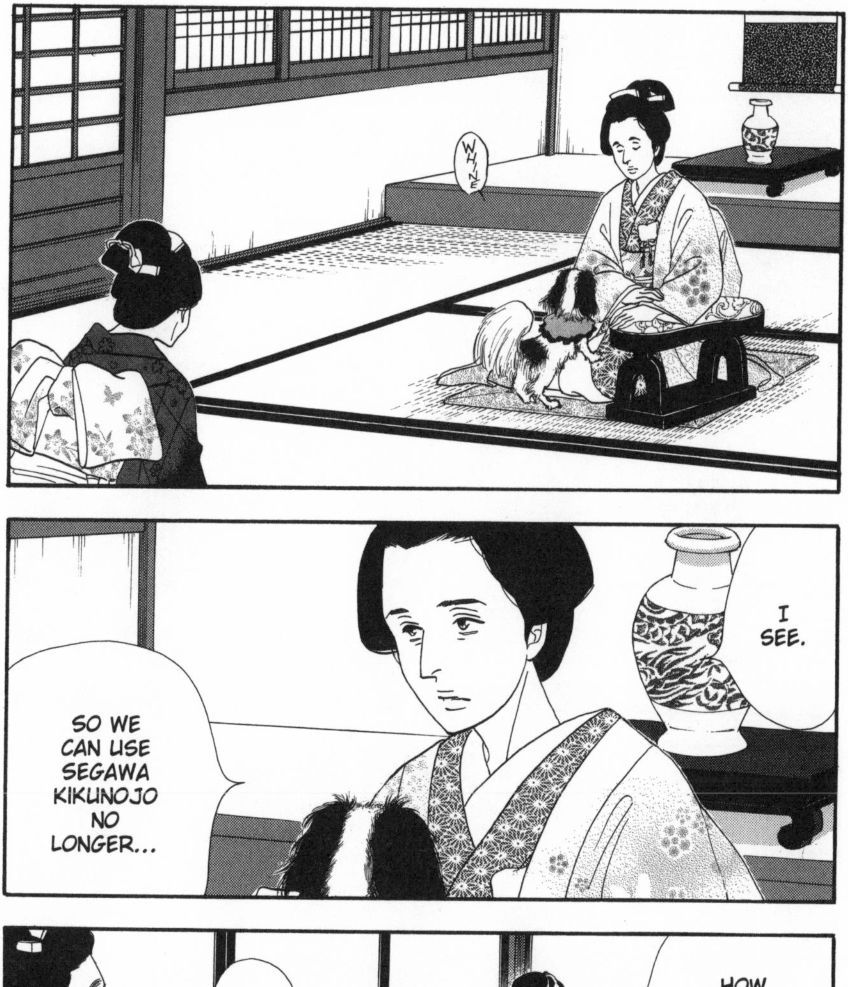
WHINE
I SEE.
SO WE CAN USE SEGAWA KIKUNOJO NO LONGER...
HOW SHALL WE PROCEED, LORD HARUSADA? SHALL WE GET RID OF HER?
HMMM...
YIP

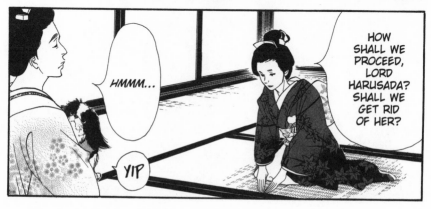

NAY.

NOT AS YET. FROM WHAT I HEAR, THEY ARE CLOSE TO DISCOVERING A CURE FOR THE REDFACE POX IN THE INNER CHAMBERS.

IF HIRAGA GENNAI IS INDEED ABLE TO ACCOMPLISH THAT, IT WILL BE USEFUL TO LET HER LIVE UNTIL SHE DOES.

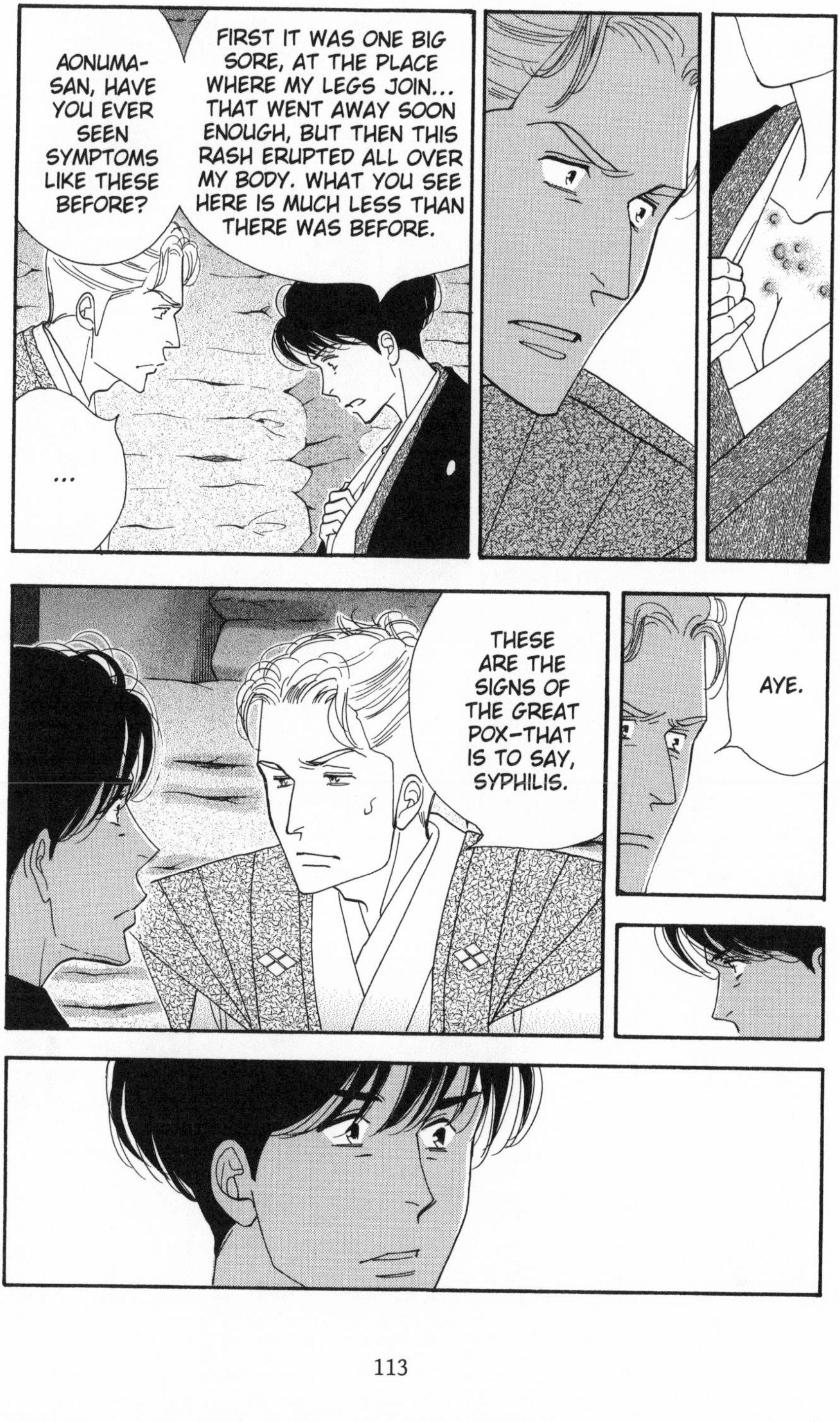
FIRST IT WAS ONE BIG SORE, AT THE PLACE WHERE MY LEGS JOIN... THAT WENT AWAY SOON ENOUGH, BUT THEN THIS RASH ERUPTED ALL OVER MY BODY. WHAT YOU SEE HERE IS MUCH LESS THAN THERE WAS BEFORE.
AONUMA-SAN, HAVE YOU EVER SEEN SYMPTOMS LIKE THESE BEFORE?
...
AYE.
THESE ARE THE SIGNS OF THE GREAT POX—THAT IS TO SAY, SYPHILIS.

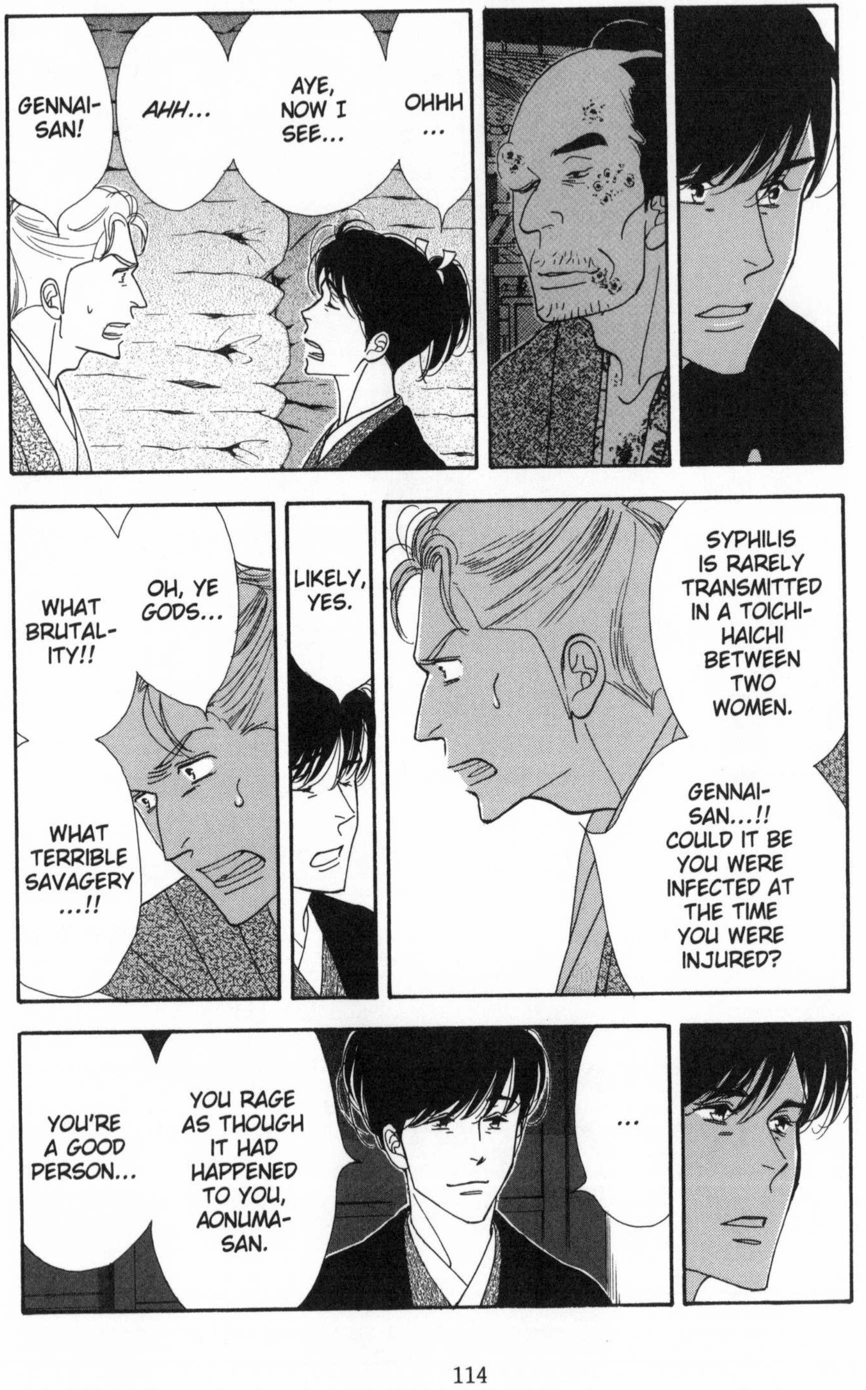
OHHH ...
AYE, NOW I SEE...
AHH...
GENNAI-SAN!
SYPHILIS IS RARELY TRANSMITTED IN A TOICHI-HAICHI BETWEEN TWO WOMEN.
GENNAI-SAN...!! COULD IT BE YOU WERE INFECTED AT THE TIME YOU WERE INJURED?
LIKELY, YES.
OH, YE GODS...
WHAT BRUTAL-ITY!!
WHAT TERRIBLE SAVAGERY ...!!
...
YOU RAGE AS THOUGH IT HAD HAPPENED TO YOU, AONUMA-SAN.
YOU'RE A GOOD PERSON...

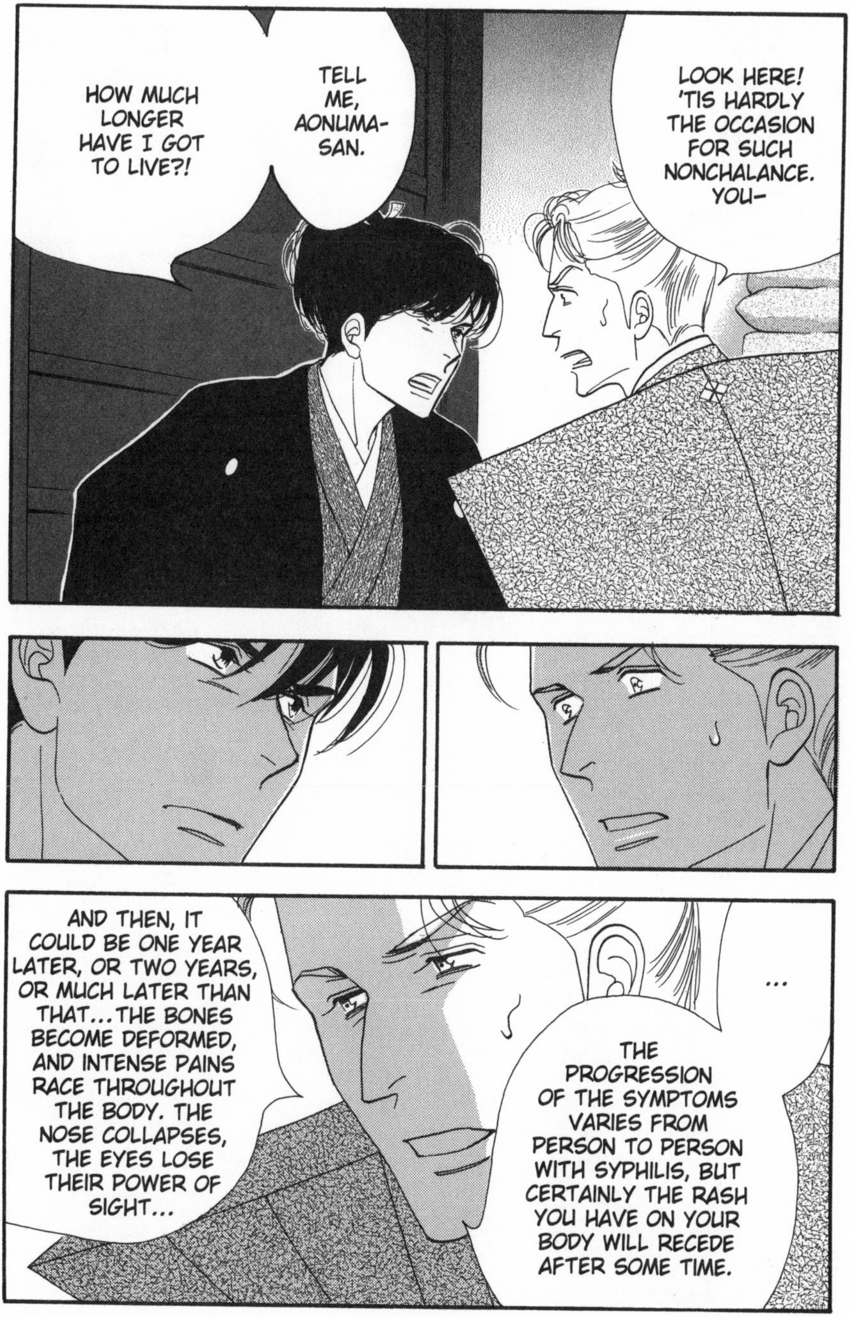
LOOK HERE! 'TIS HARDLY THE OCCASION FOR SUCH NONCHALANCE. YOU–
TELL ME, AONUMA-SAN.
HOW MUCH LONGER HAVE I GOT TO LIVE?!
...
THE PROGRESSION OF THE SYMPTOMS VARIES FROM PERSON TO PERSON WITH SYPHILIS, BUT CERTAINLY THE RASH YOU HAVE ON YOUR BODY WILL RECEDE AFTER SOME TIME.
AND THEN, IT COULD BE ONE YEAR LATER, OR TWO YEARS, OR MUCH LATER THAN THAT...THE BONES BECOME DEFORMED, AND INTENSE PAINS RACE THROUGHOUT THE BODY. THE NOSE COLLAPSES, THE EYES LOSE THEIR POWER OF SIGHT...

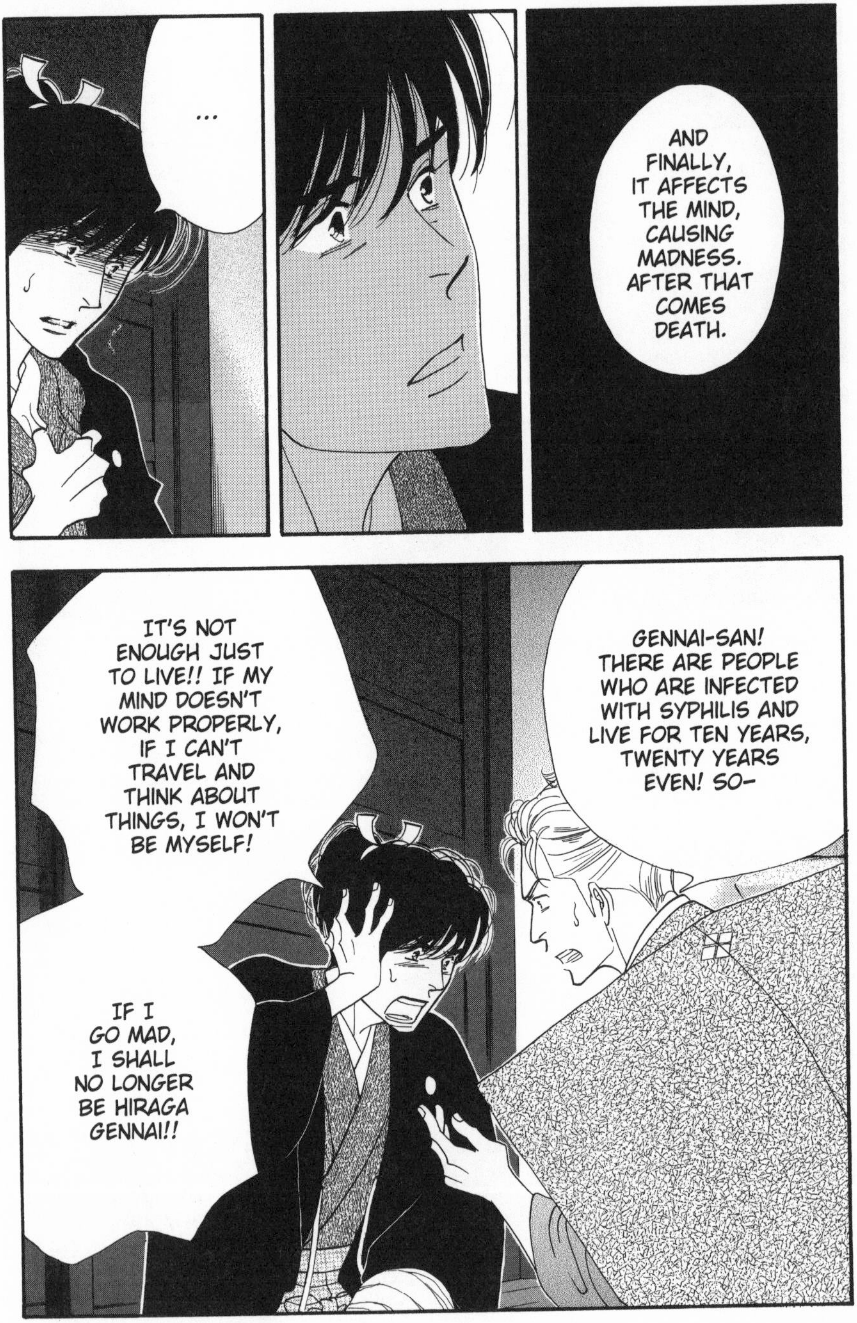
AND FINALLY, IT AFFECTS THE MIND, CAUSING MADNESS. AFTER THAT COMES DEATH.
...
GENNAI-SAN! THERE ARE PEOPLE WHO ARE INFECTED WITH SYPHILIS AND LIVE FOR TEN YEARS, TWENTY YEARS EVEN! SO–
IT'S NOT ENOUGH JUST TO LIVE!! IF MY MIND DOESN'T WORK PROPERLY, IF I CAN'T TRAVEL AND THINK ABOUT THINGS, I WON'T BE MYSELF!
IF I GO MAD, I SHALL NO LONGER BE HIRAGA GENNAI!!

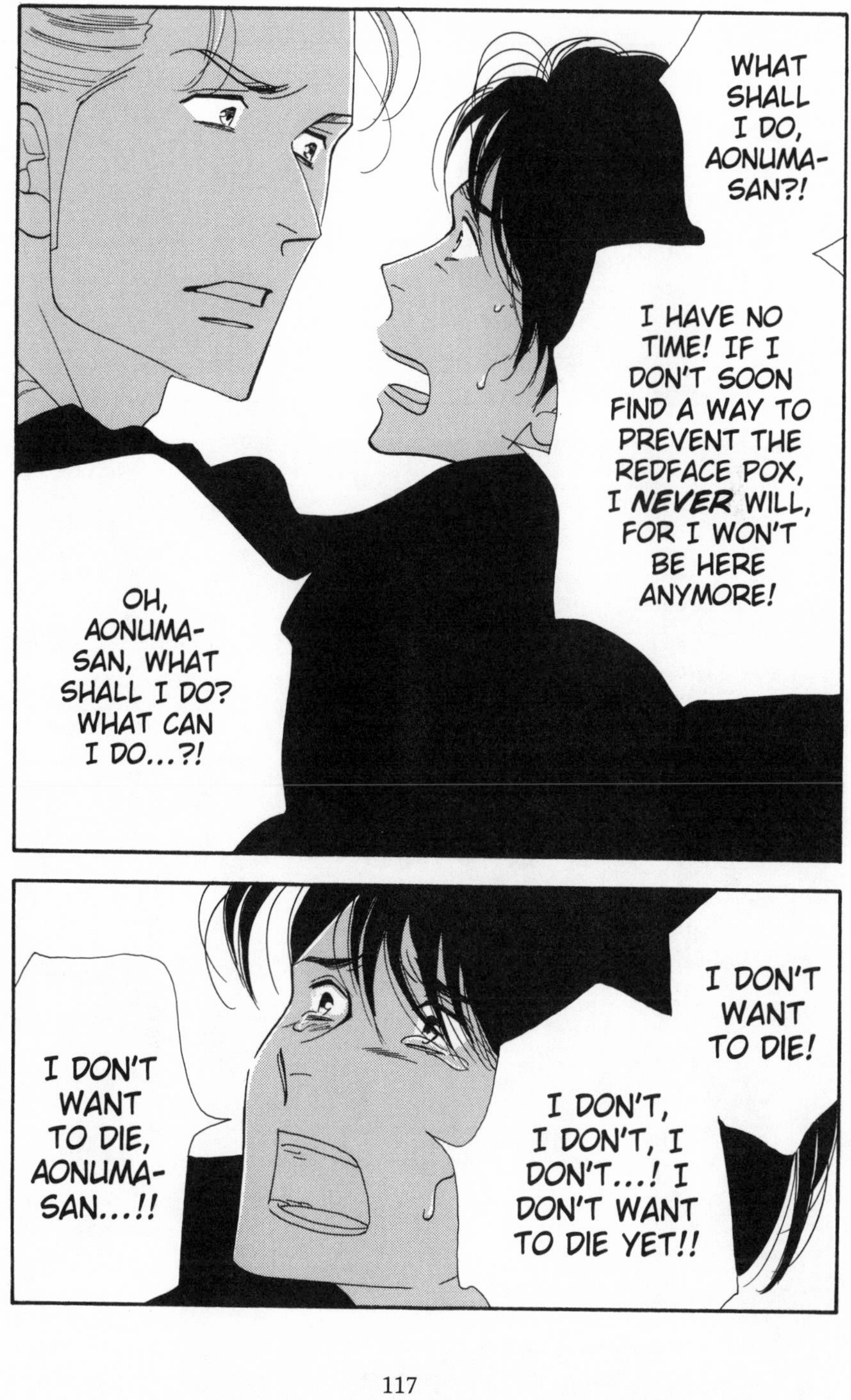
WHAT SHALL I DO, AONUMA-SAN?!
I HAVE NO TIME! IF I DON'T SOON FIND A WAY TO PREVENT THE REDFACE POX, I **NEVER** WILL, FOR I WON'T BE HERE ANYMORE!
OH, AONUMA-SAN, WHAT SHALL I DO? WHAT CAN I DO...?!
I DON'T WANT TO DIE!
I DON'T, I DON'T, I DON'T...! I DON'T WANT TO DIE YET!!
I DON'T WANT TO DIE, AONUMA-SAN...!!

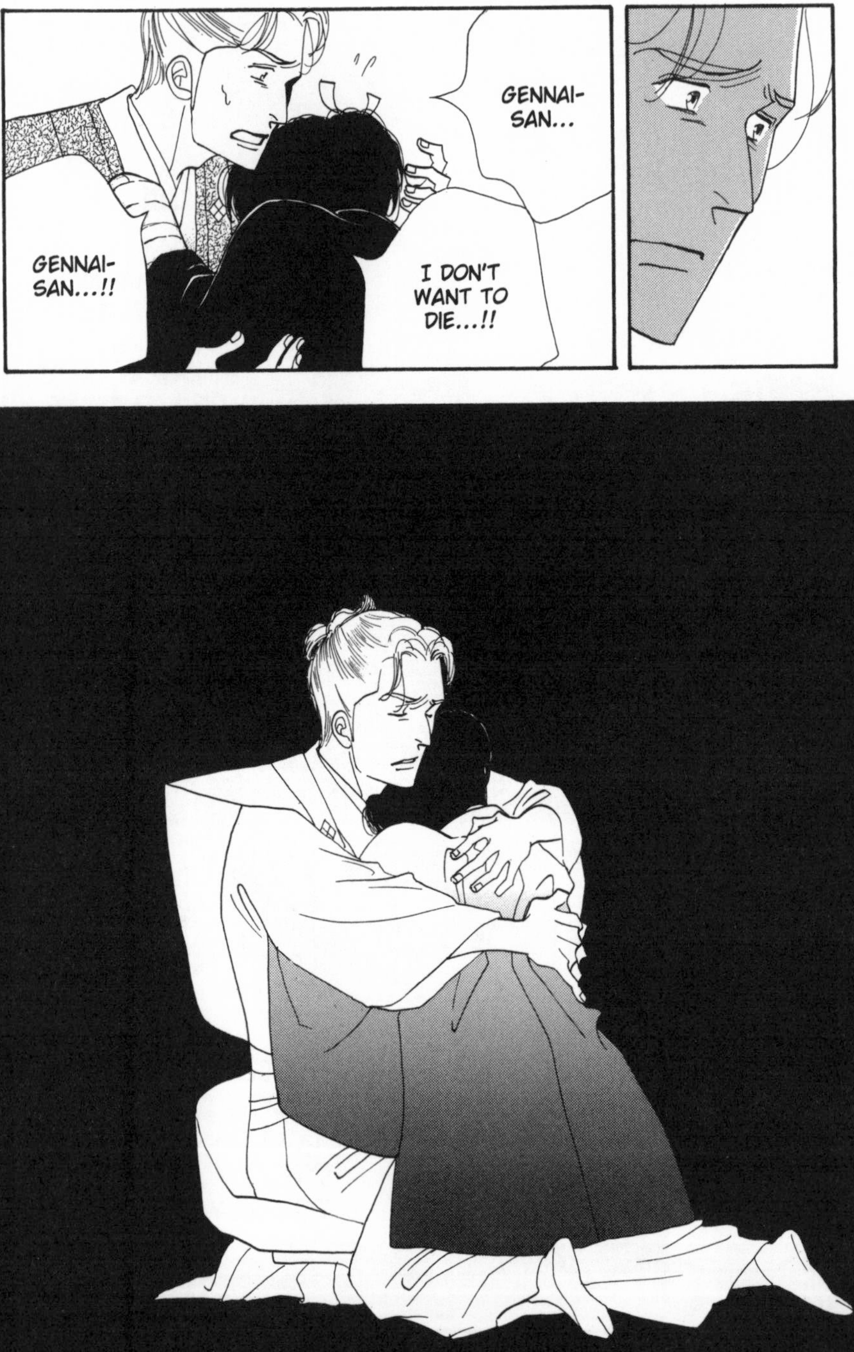
GENNAI-SAN...
I DON'T WANT TO DIE...!!
GENNAI-SAN...!!

Ōoku

THE INNER CHAMBERS

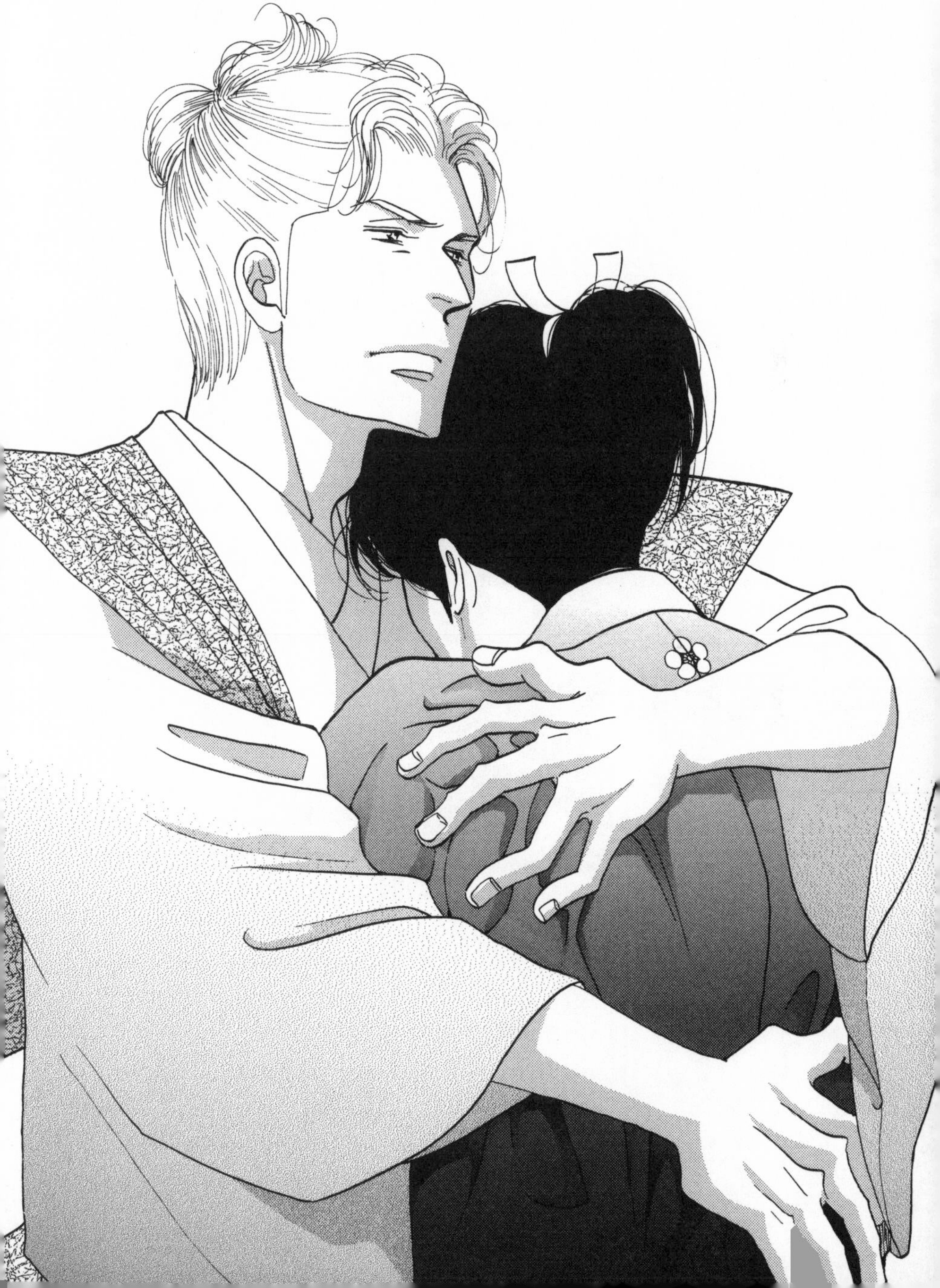

IEMOTO.

A MAIDEN OF JUST EIGHTEEN SHOULD BE IN THE FULL BLOOM OF HER YOUTH, NOT LYING PALE AND GAUNT IN HER BED...

IEMOTO!!

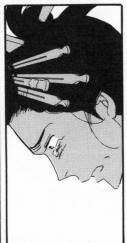

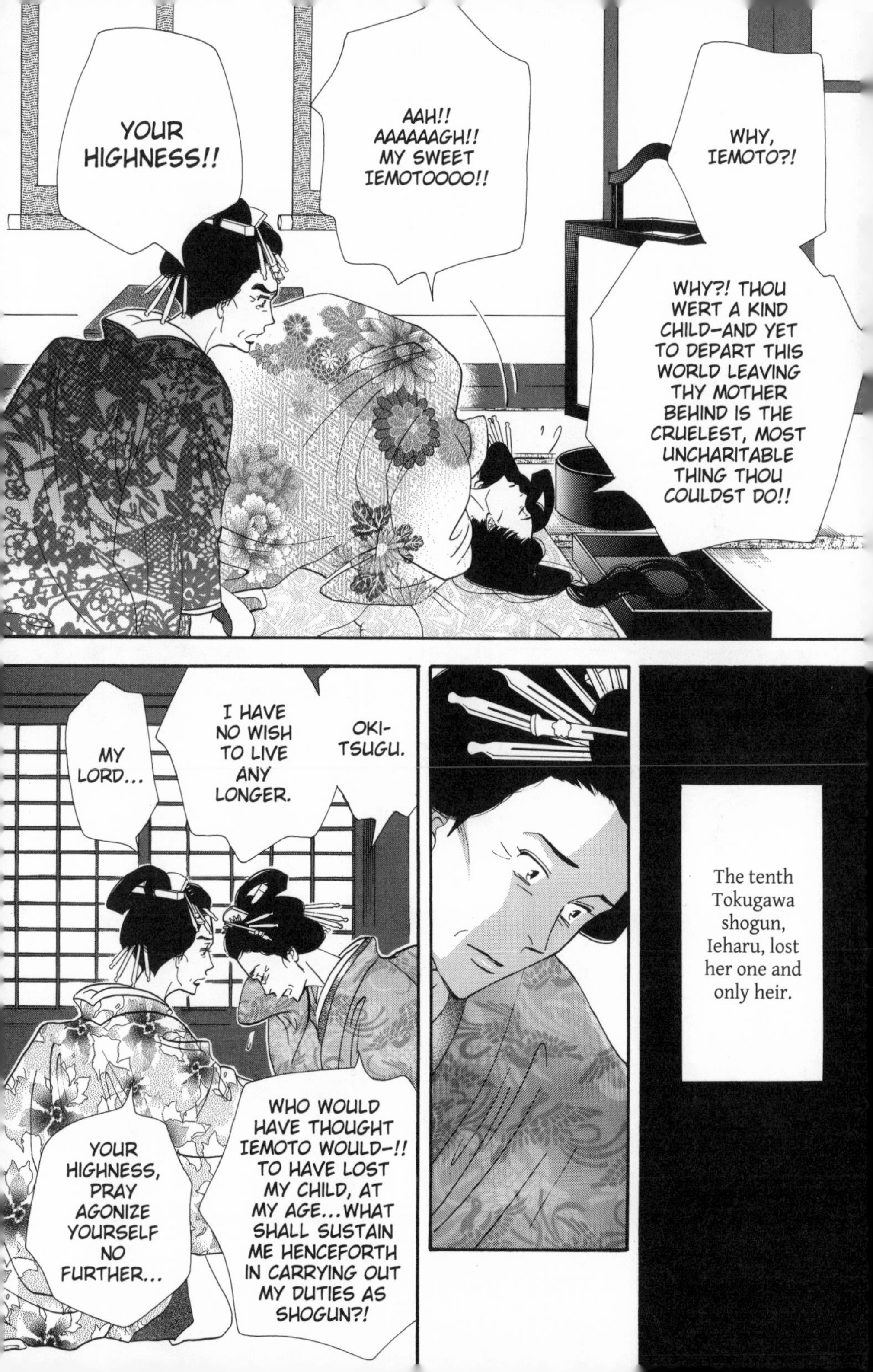
WHY, IEMOTO?!
WHY?! THOU WERT A KIND CHILD—AND YET TO DEPART THIS WORLD LEAVING THY MOTHER BEHIND IS THE CRUELEST, MOST UNCHARITABLE THING THOU COULDST DO!!
AAH!! AAAAAAGH!! MY SWEET IEMOTOOOO!!
YOUR HIGHNESS!!
The tenth Tokugawa shogun, Ieharu, lost her one and only heir.
OKI-TSUGU.
I HAVE NO WISH TO LIVE ANY LONGER.
MY LORD...
WHO WOULD HAVE THOUGHT IEMOTO WOULD—!! TO HAVE LOST MY CHILD, AT MY AGE...WHAT SHALL SUSTAIN ME HENCEFORTH IN CARRYING OUT MY DUTIES AS SHOGUN?!
YOUR HIGHNESS, PRAY AGONIZE YOURSELF NO FURTHER...

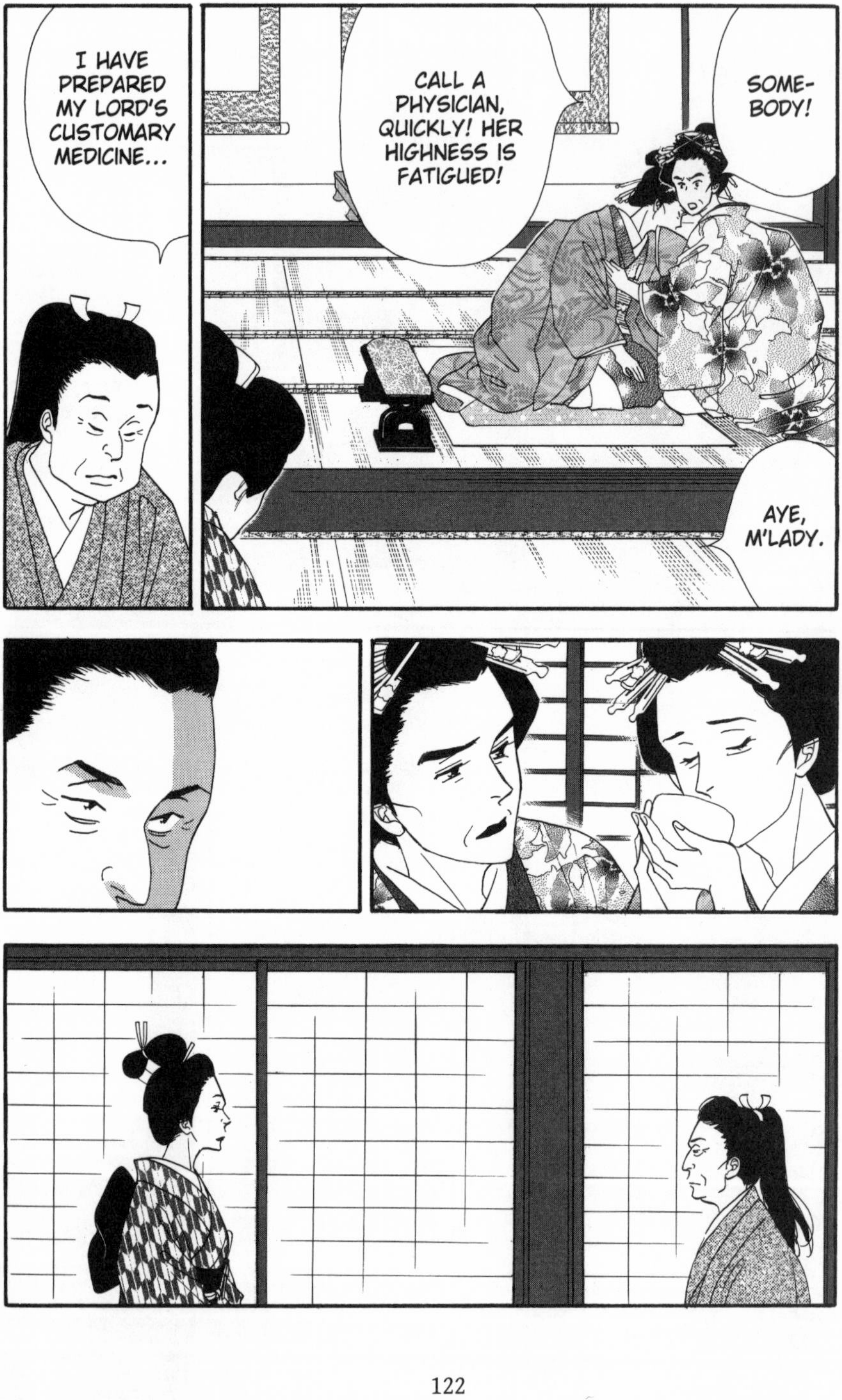
SOME-BODY!
CALL A PHYSICIAN, QUICKLY! HER HIGHNESS IS FATIGUED!
AYE, M'LADY.
I HAVE PREPARED MY LORD'S CUSTOMARY MEDICINE...

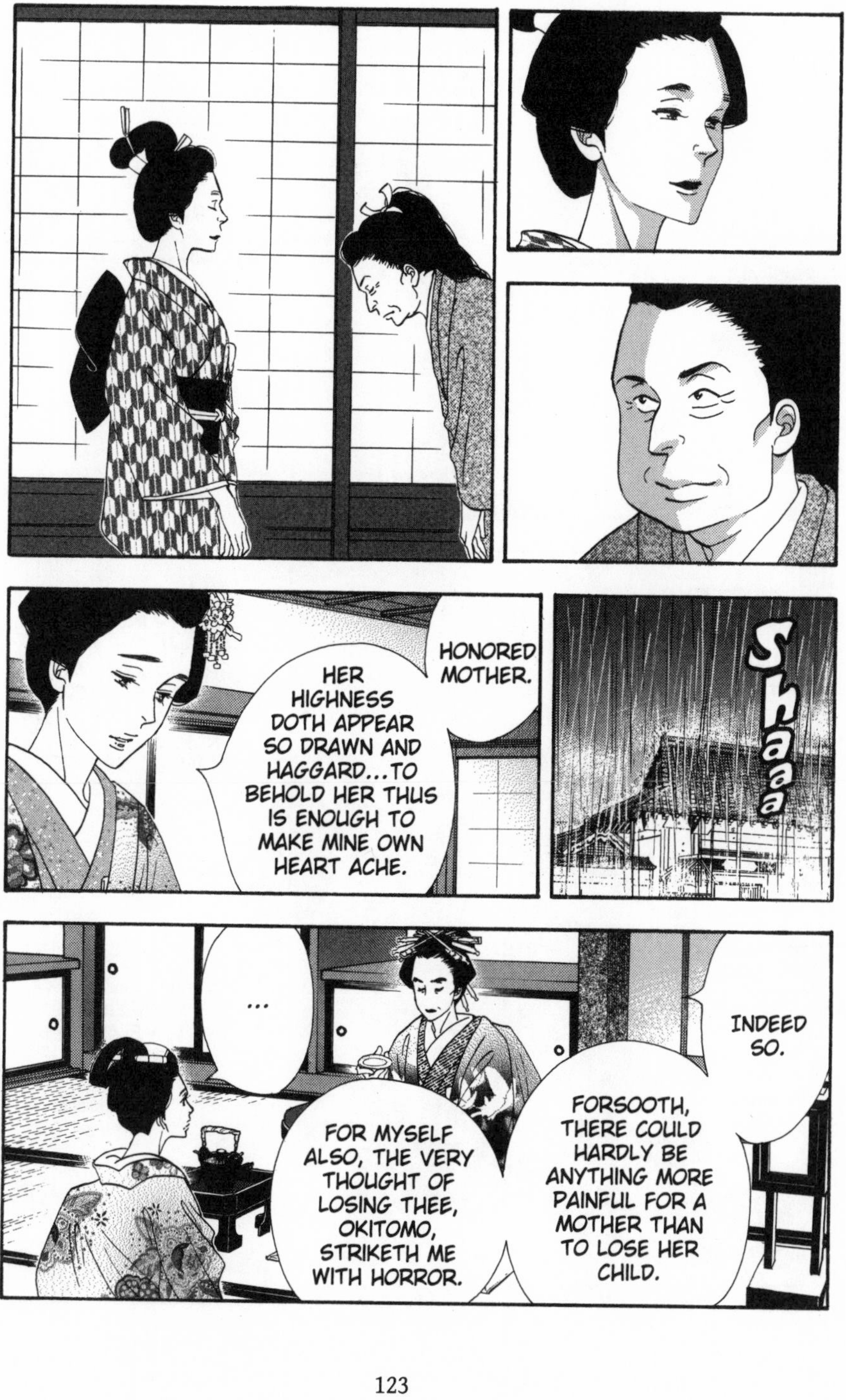
Shaaa
HONORED MOTHER.
HER HIGHNESS DOTH APPEAR SO DRAWN AND HAGGARD...TO BEHOLD HER THUS IS ENOUGH TO MAKE MINE OWN HEART ACHE.
INDEED SO.
FORSOOTH, THERE COULD HARDLY BE ANYTHING MORE PAINFUL FOR A MOTHER THAN TO LOSE HER CHILD.
FOR MYSELF ALSO, THE VERY THOUGHT OF LOSING THEE, OKITOMO, STRIKETH ME WITH HORROR.
...

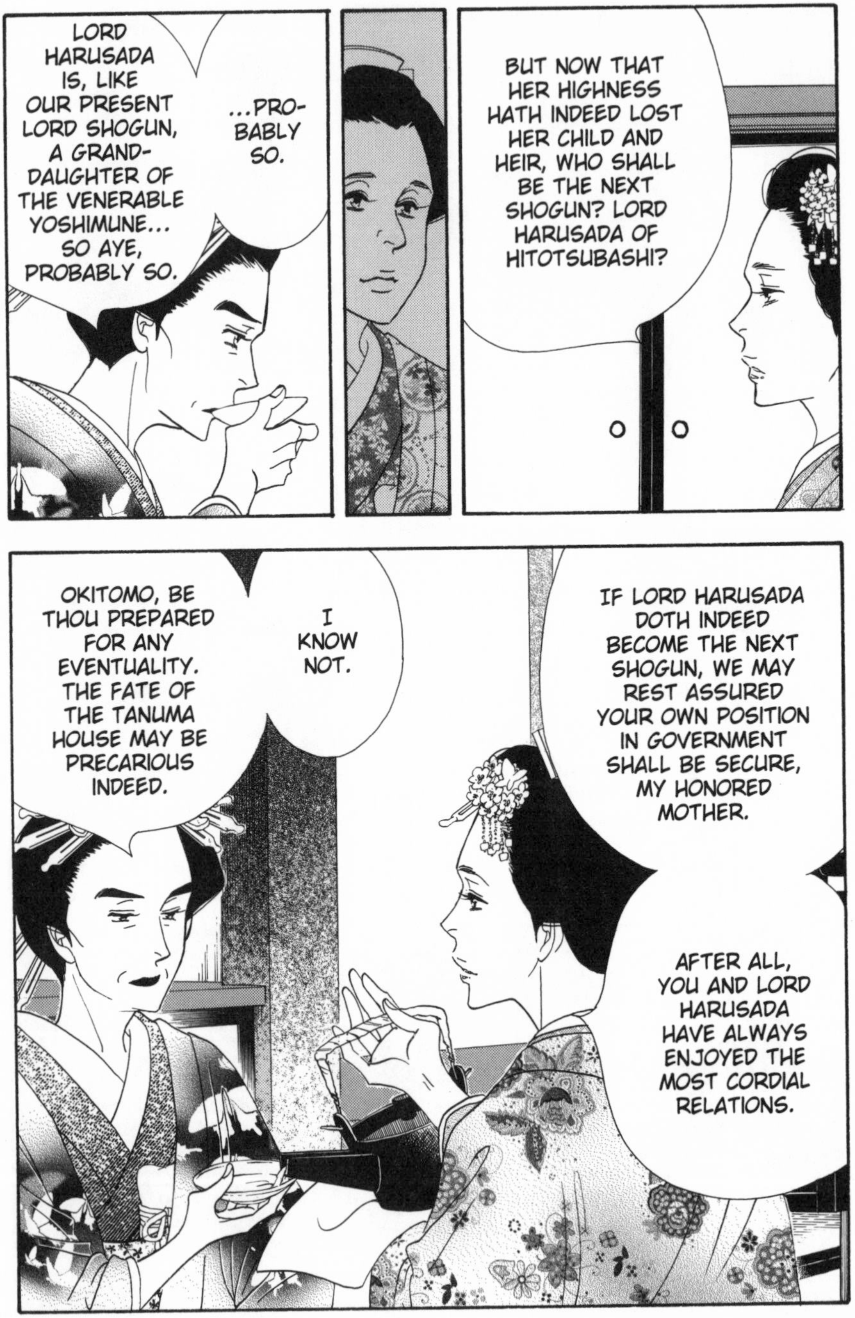
BUT NOW THAT HER HIGHNESS HATH INDEED LOST HER CHILD AND HEIR, WHO SHALL BE THE NEXT SHOGUN? LORD HARUSADA OF HITOTSUBASHI?
...PRO-BABLY SO.
LORD HARUSADA IS, LIKE OUR PRESENT LORD SHOGUN, A GRAND-DAUGHTER OF THE VENERABLE YOSHIMUNE... SO AYE, PROBABLY SO.
IF LORD HARUSADA DOTH INDEED BECOME THE NEXT SHOGUN, WE MAY REST ASSURED YOUR OWN POSITION IN GOVERNMENT SHALL BE SECURE, MY HONORED MOTHER.
AFTER ALL, YOU AND LORD HARUSADA HAVE ALWAYS ENJOYED THE MOST CORDIAL RELATIONS.
I KNOW NOT.
OKITOMO, BE THOU PREPARED FOR ANY EVENTUALITY. THE FATE OF THE TANUMA HOUSE MAY BE PRECARIOUS INDEED.

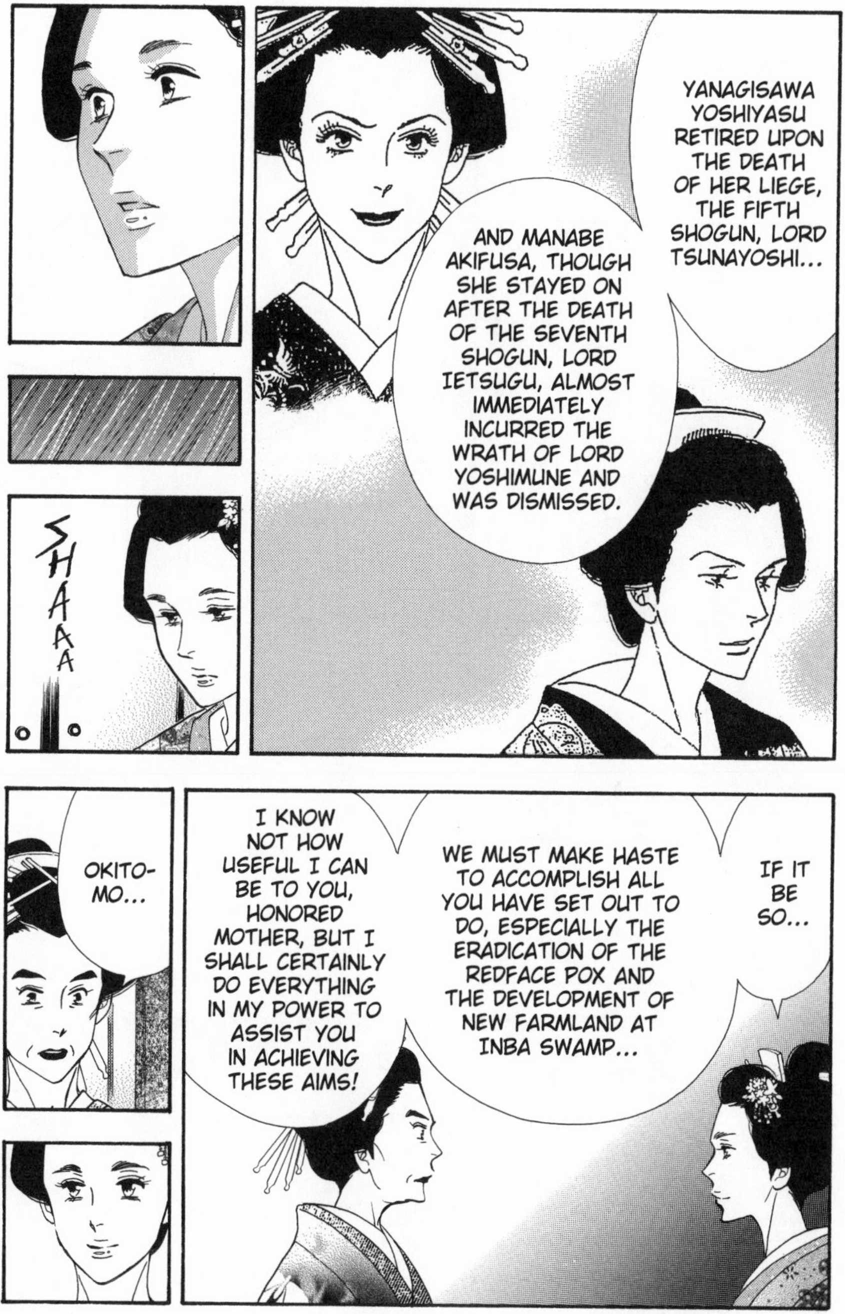
YANAGISAWA YOSHIYASU RETIRED UPON THE DEATH OF HER LIEGE, THE FIFTH SHOGUN, LORD TSUNAYOSHI...
AND MANABE AKIFUSA, THOUGH SHE STAYED ON AFTER THE DEATH OF THE SEVENTH SHOGUN, LORD IETSUGU, ALMOST IMMEDIATELY INCURRED THE WRATH OF LORD YOSHIMUNE AND WAS DISMISSED.
SHAAA
IF IT BE SO...
WE MUST MAKE HASTE TO ACCOMPLISH ALL YOU HAVE SET OUT TO DO, ESPECIALLY THE ERADICATION OF THE REDFACE POX AND THE DEVELOPMENT OF NEW FARMLAND AT INBA SWAMP...
I KNOW NOT HOW USEFUL I CAN BE TO YOU, HONORED MOTHER, BUT I SHALL CERTAINLY DO EVERYTHING IN MY POWER TO ASSIST YOU IN ACHIEVING THESE AIMS!
OKITO-MO...

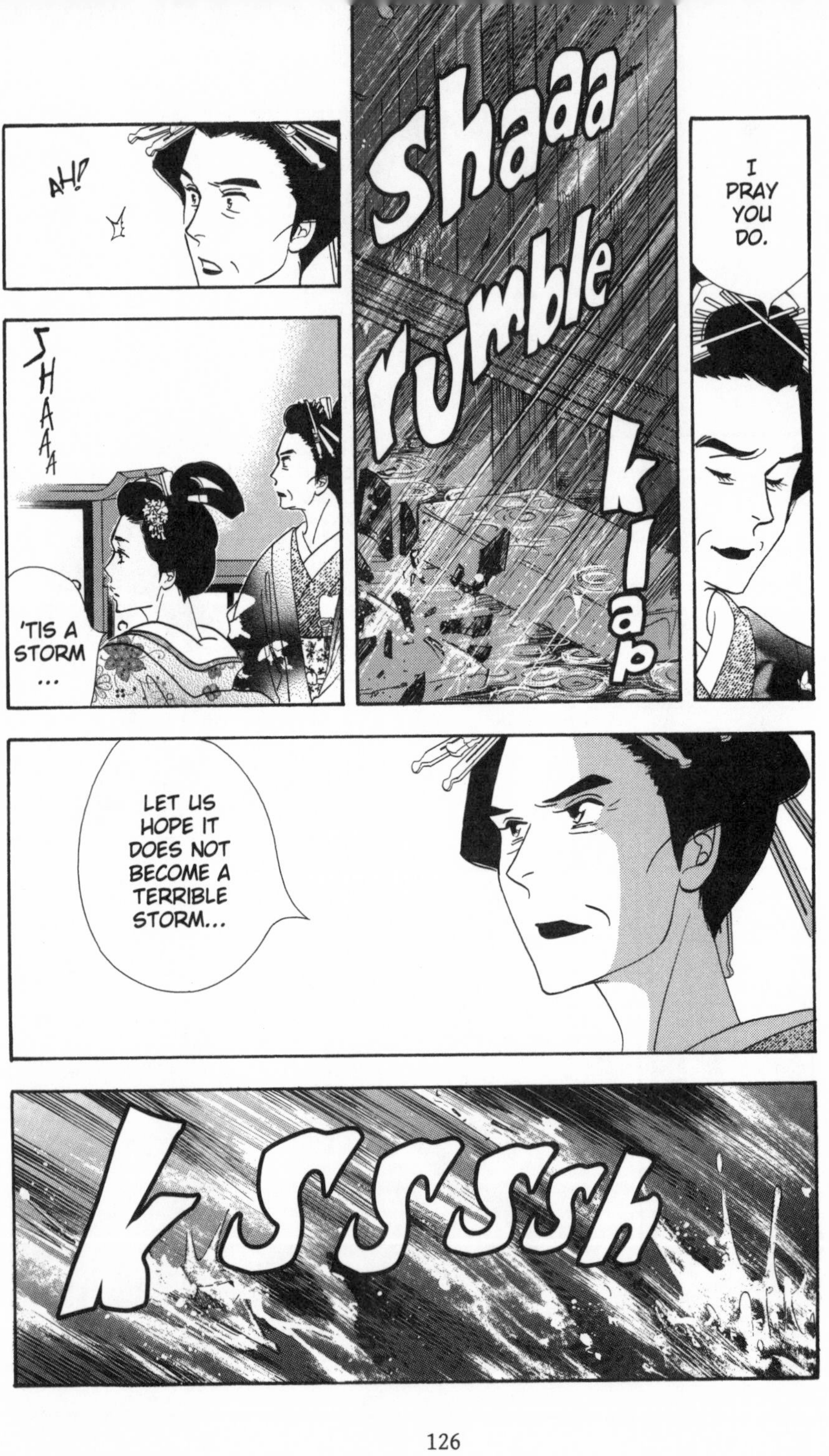
I PRAY YOU DO.
Shaaa
rumble
klap
AH!?
SHAAAA
'TIS A STORM...
LET US HOPE IT DOES NOT BECOME A TERRIBLE STORM...
KSSSSH

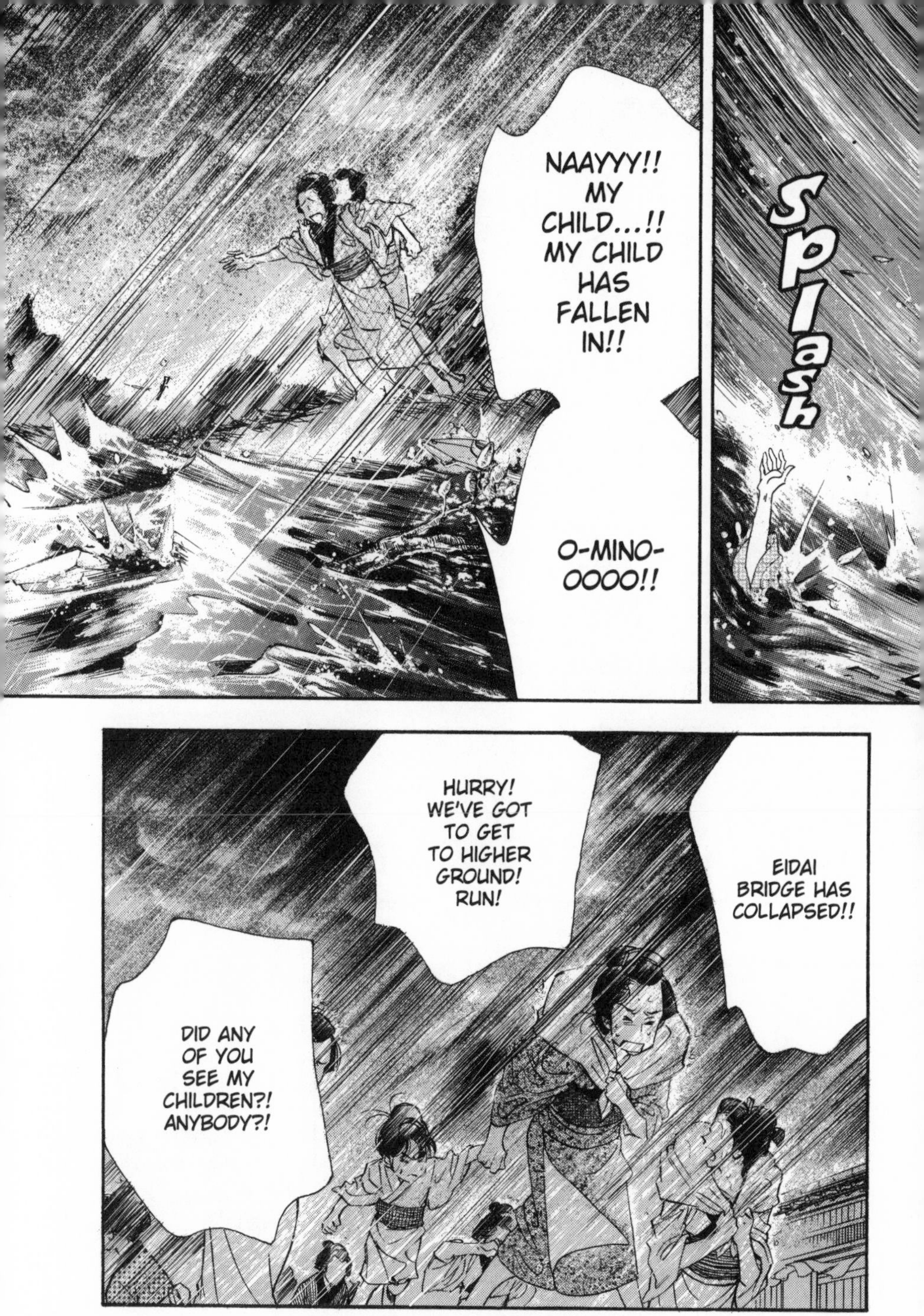
Splash
NAAYYY!! MY CHILD...!! MY CHILD HAS FALLEN IN!!
O-MINO-OOOO!!
EIDAI BRIDGE HAS COLLAPSED!!
HURRY! WE'VE GOT TO GET TO HIGHER GROUND! RUN!
DID ANY OF YOU SEE MY CHILDREN?! ANYBODY?!

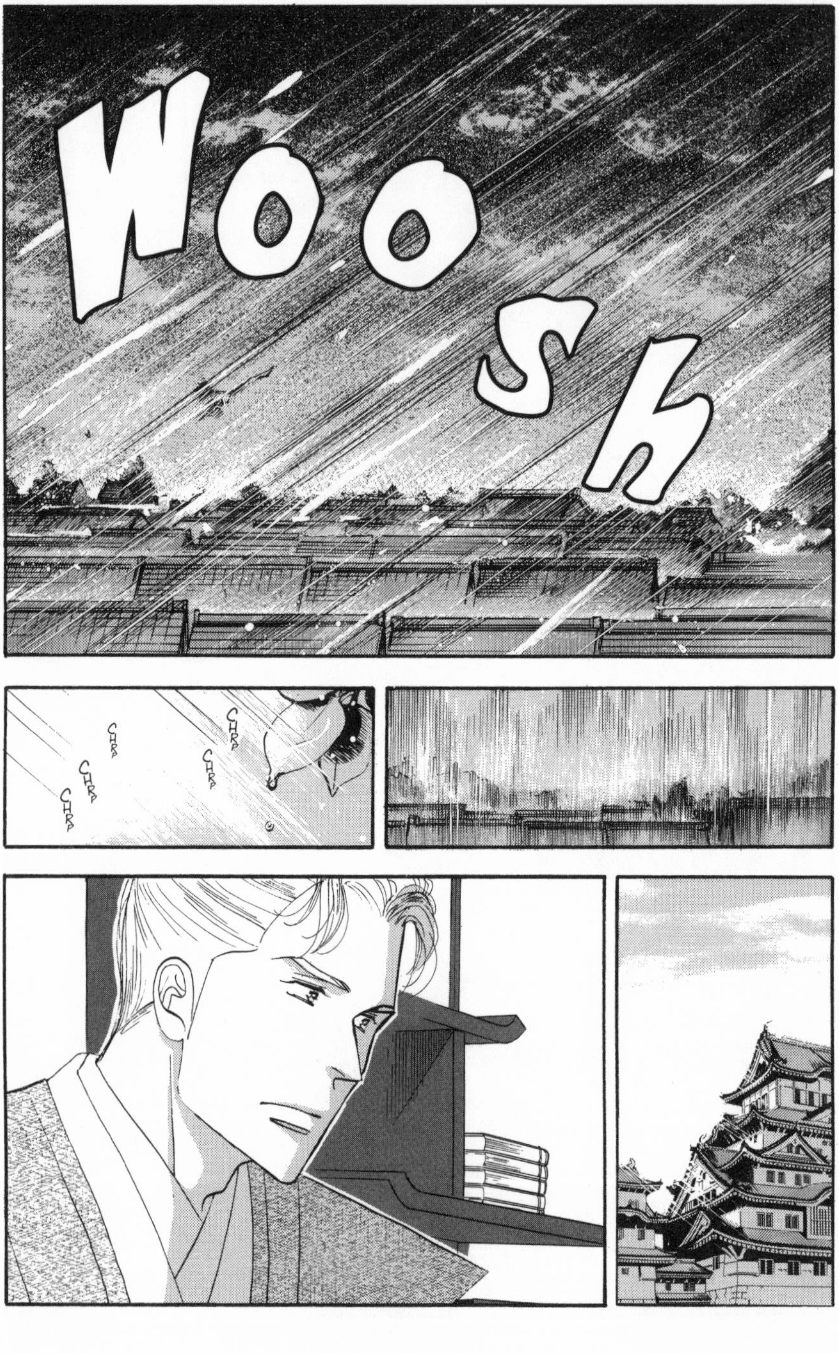
WOOSH
CHRP
CHRP
CHRP
CHRP
CHRP

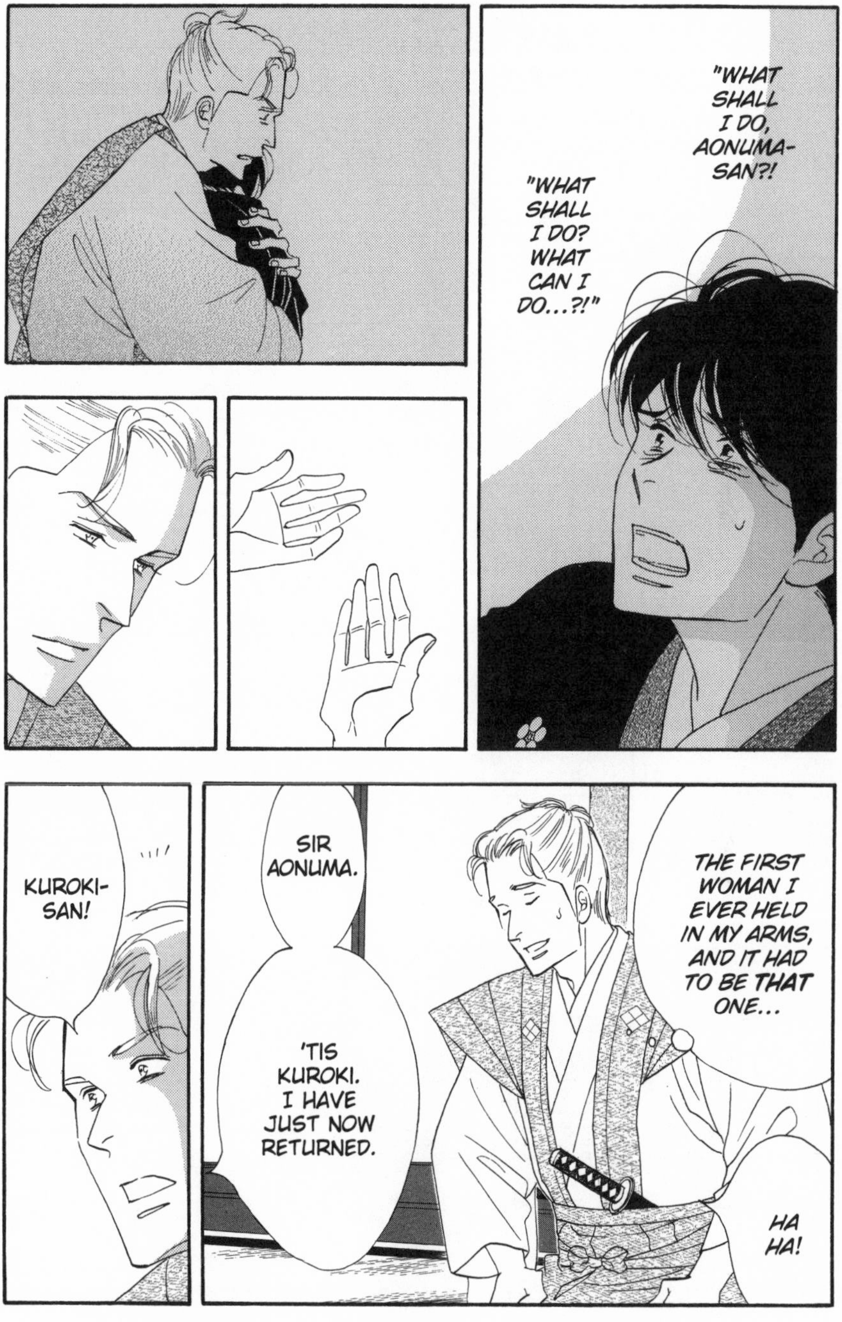
"WHAT SHALL I DO, AONUMA-SAN?!
"WHAT SHALL I DO? WHAT CAN I DO...?!"
THE FIRST WOMAN I EVER HELD IN MY ARMS, AND IT HAD TO BE THAT ONE...
HA HA!
SIR AONUMA.
'TIS KUROKI. I HAVE JUST NOW RETURNED.
KUROKI-SAN!

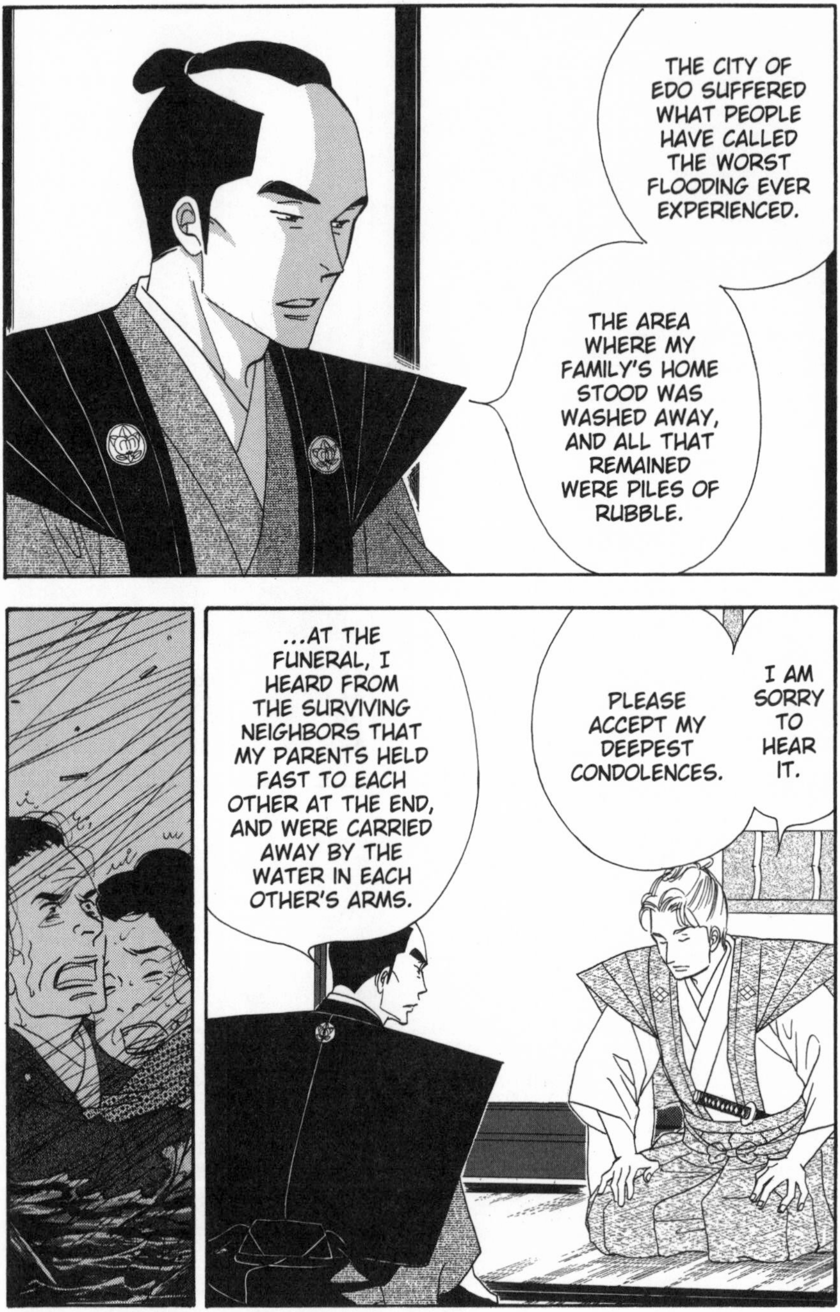
THE CITY OF EDO SUFFERED WHAT PEOPLE HAVE CALLED THE WORST FLOODING EVER EXPERIENCED.
THE AREA WHERE MY FAMILY'S HOME STOOD WAS WASHED AWAY, AND ALL THAT REMAINED WERE PILES OF RUBBLE.
I AM SORRY TO HEAR IT.
PLEASE ACCEPT MY DEEPEST CONDOLENCES.
...AT THE FUNERAL, I HEARD FROM THE SURVIVING NEIGHBORS THAT MY PARENTS HELD FAST TO EACH OTHER AT THE END, AND WERE CARRIED AWAY BY THE WATER IN EACH OTHER'S ARMS.

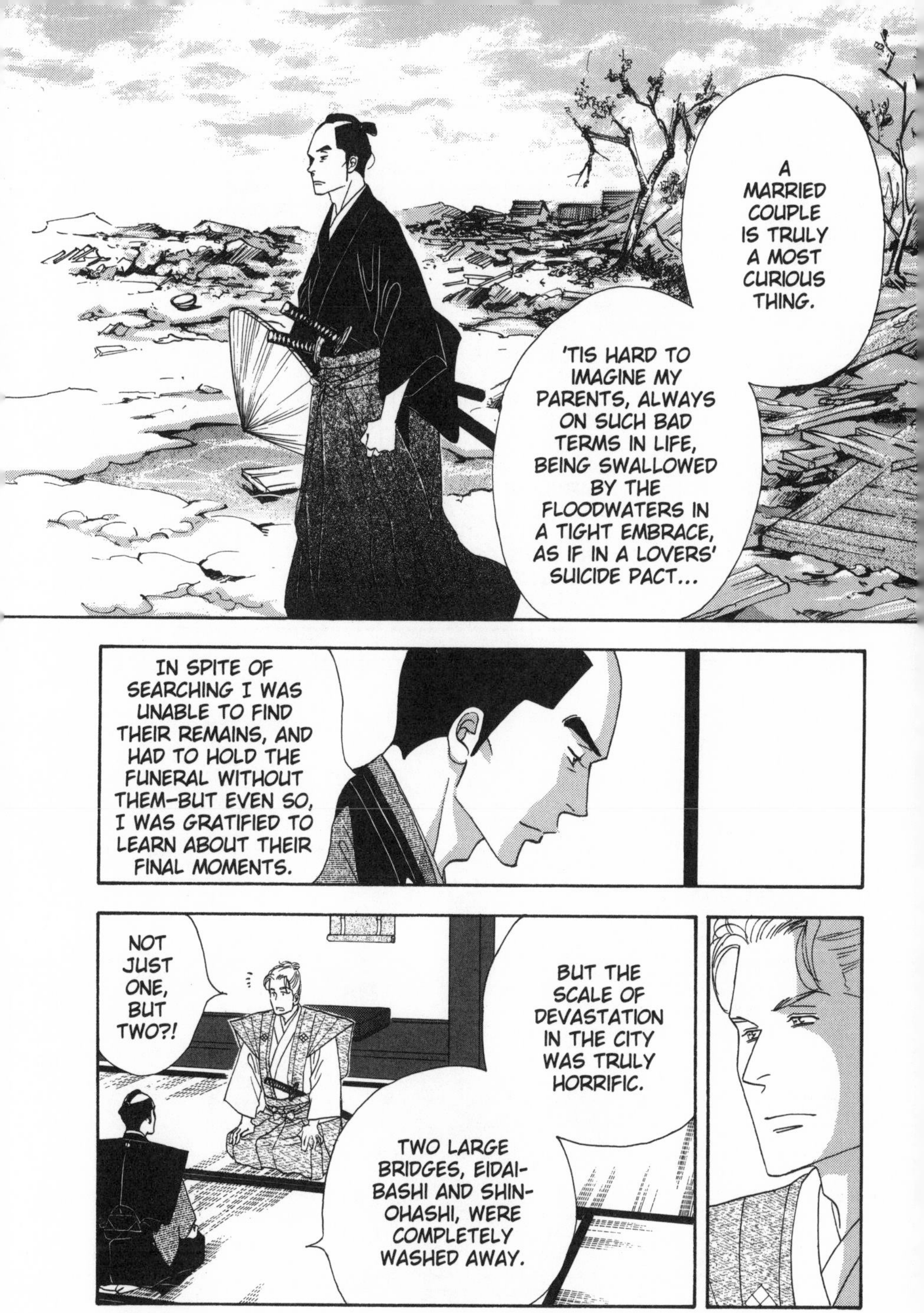
A MARRIED COUPLE IS TRULY A MOST CURIOUS THING.
'TIS HARD TO IMAGINE MY PARENTS, ALWAYS ON SUCH BAD TERMS IN LIFE, BEING SWALLOWED BY THE FLOODWATERS IN A TIGHT EMBRACE, AS IF IN A LOVERS' SUICIDE PACT...
IN SPITE OF SEARCHING I WAS UNABLE TO FIND THEIR REMAINS, AND HAD TO HOLD THE FUNERAL WITHOUT THEM—BUT EVEN SO, I WAS GRATIFIED TO LEARN ABOUT THEIR FINAL MOMENTS.
BUT THE SCALE OF DEVASTATION IN THE CITY WAS TRULY HORRIFIC.
TWO LARGE BRIDGES, EIDAI-BASHI AND SHIN-OHASHI, WERE COMPLETELY WASHED AWAY.
NOT JUST ONE, BUT TWO?!

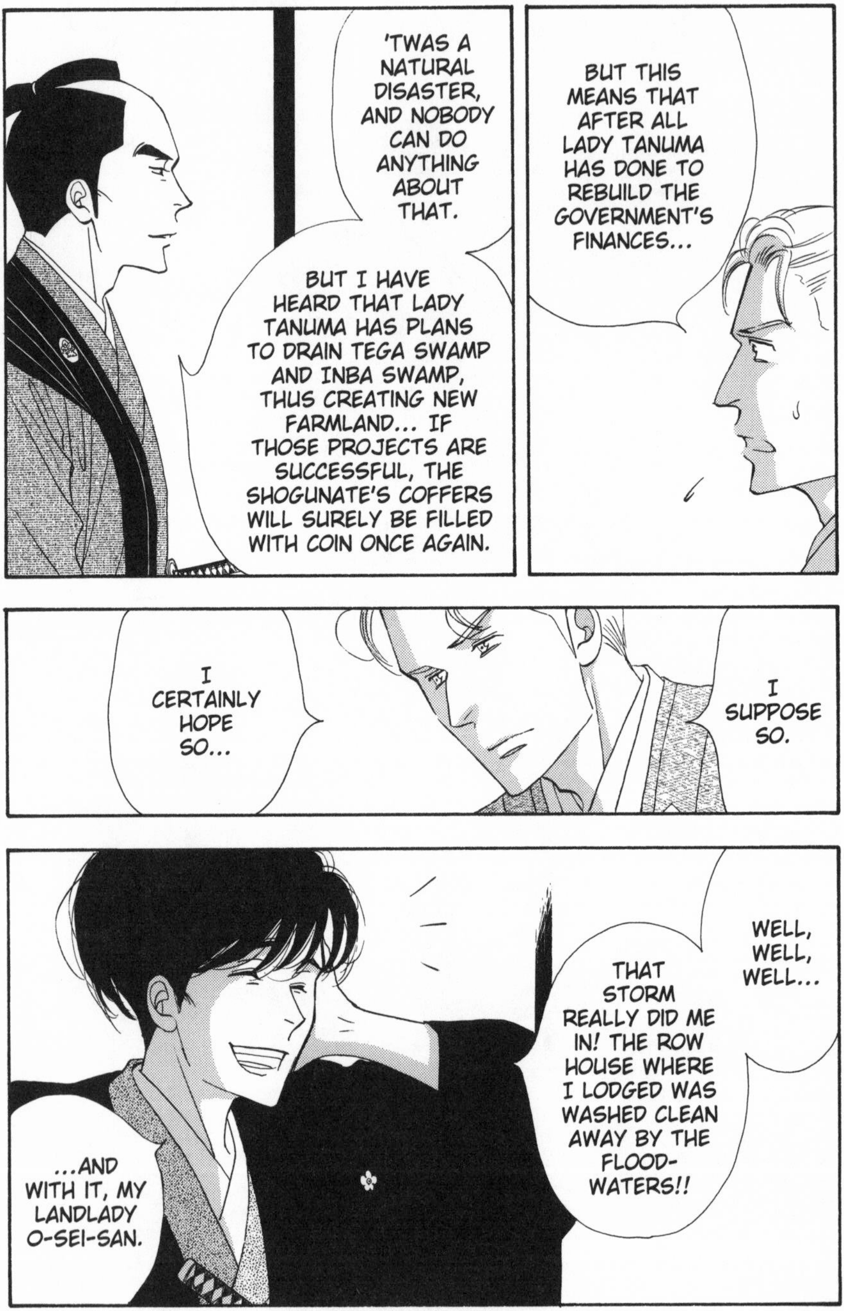
BUT THIS MEANS THAT AFTER ALL LADY TANUMA HAS DONE TO REBUILD THE GOVERNMENT'S FINANCES...
'TWAS A NATURAL DISASTER, AND NOBODY CAN DO ANYTHING ABOUT THAT.
BUT I HAVE HEARD THAT LADY TANUMA HAS PLANS TO DRAIN TEGA SWAMP AND INBA SWAMP, THUS CREATING NEW FARMLAND... IF THOSE PROJECTS ARE SUCCESSFUL, THE SHOGUNATE'S COFFERS WILL SURELY BE FILLED WITH COIN ONCE AGAIN.
I SUPPOSE SO.
I CERTAINLY HOPE SO...
WELL, WELL, WELL...
THAT STORM REALLY DID ME IN! THE ROW HOUSE WHERE I LODGED WAS WASHED CLEAN AWAY BY THE FLOOD-WATERS!!
...AND WITH IT, MY LANDLADY O-SEI-SAN.

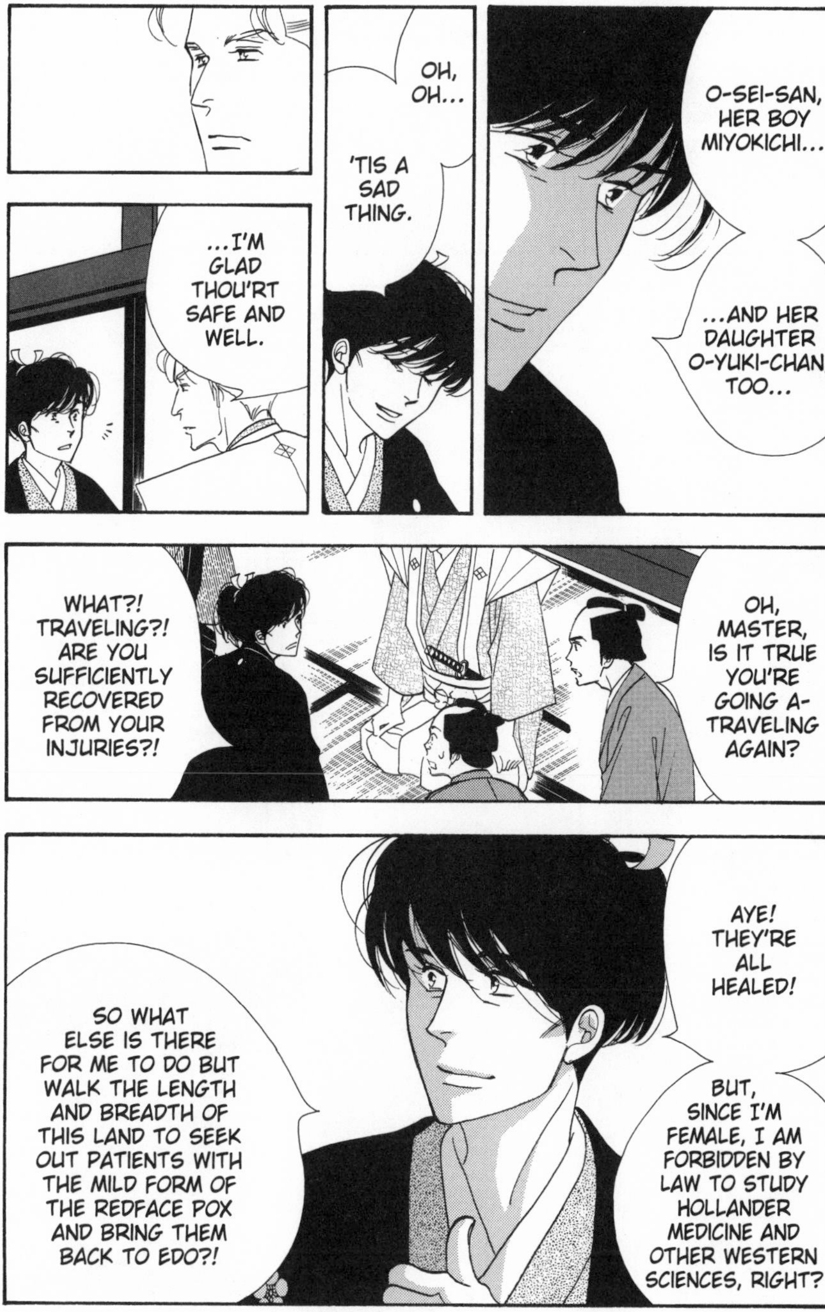
O-SEI-SAN, HER BOY MIYOKICHI...
...AND HER DAUGHTER O-YUKI-CHAN, TOO...
OH, OH...
'TIS A SAD THING.
...I'M GLAD THOU'RT SAFE AND WELL.
OH, MASTER, IS IT TRUE YOU'RE GOING A-TRAVELING AGAIN?
WHAT?! TRAVELING?! ARE YOU SUFFICIENTLY RECOVERED FROM YOUR INJURIES?!
AYE! THEY'RE ALL HEALED!
BUT, SINCE I'M FEMALE, I AM FORBIDDEN BY LAW TO STUDY HOLLANDER MEDICINE AND OTHER WESTERN SCIENCES, RIGHT?
SO WHAT ELSE IS THERE FOR ME TO DO BUT WALK THE LENGTH AND BREADTH OF THIS LAND TO SEEK OUT PATIENTS WITH THE MILD FORM OF THE REDFACE POX AND BRING THEM BACK TO EDO?!

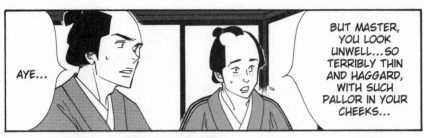

BUT MASTER, YOU LOOK UNWELL...SO TERRIBLY THIN AND HAGGARD, WITH SUCH PALLOR IN YOUR CHEEKS...
AYE...
I SAY YOU SHOULD GO.
SIR AONUMA!
IF THIS FELLOW WISHES TO GO, HE WILL GO, AND NOBODY CAN STOP HIM.
HA HA, AONUMA-SAN, YOU KNOW ME WELL!
I SWEAR I SHALL BE BACK.

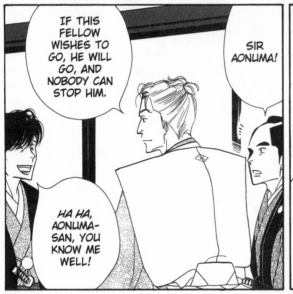

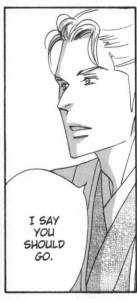

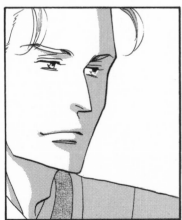

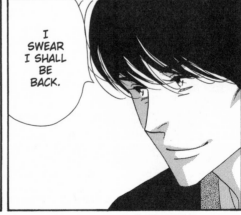

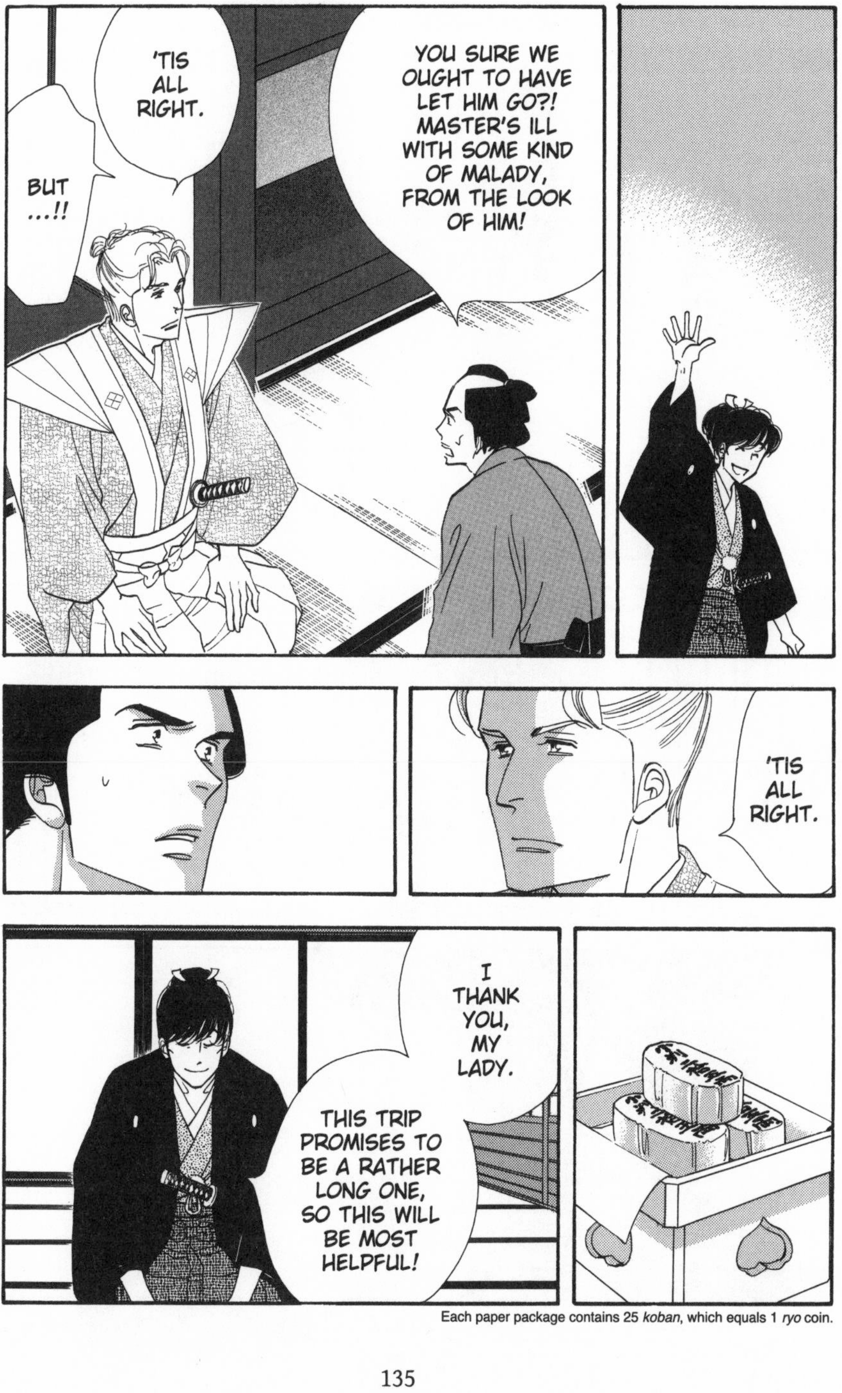
YOU SURE WE OUGHT TO HAVE LET HIM GO?! MASTER'S ILL WITH SOME KIND OF MALADY, FROM THE LOOK OF HIM!
'TIS ALL RIGHT.
BUT ...!!
'TIS ALL RIGHT.
I THANK YOU, MY LADY.
THIS TRIP PROMISES TO BE A RATHER LONG ONE, SO THIS WILL BE MOST HELPFUL!

Each paper package contains 25 *koban*, which equals 1 *ryo* coin.

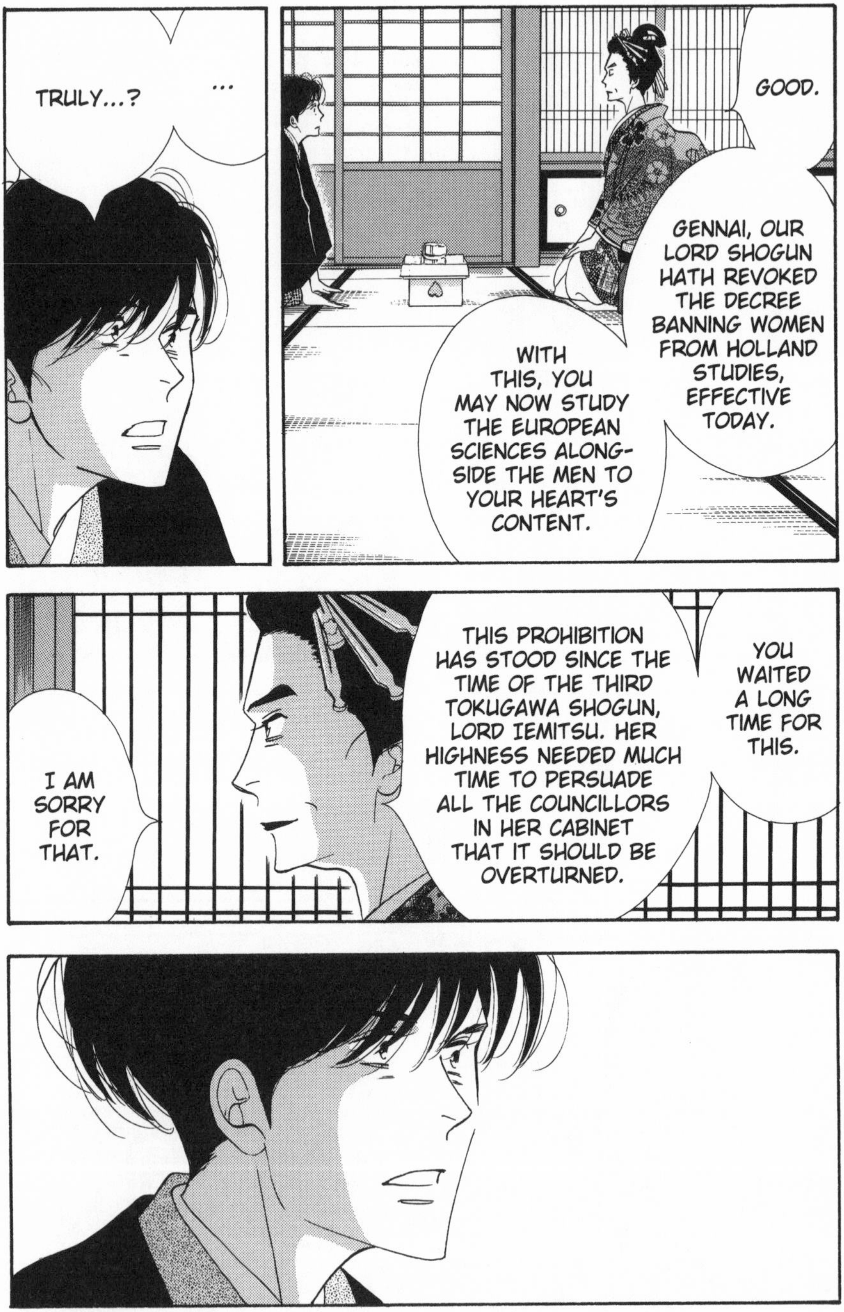
GOOD.
GENNAI, OUR LORD SHOGUN HATH REVOKED THE DECREE BANNING WOMEN FROM HOLLAND STUDIES, EFFECTIVE TODAY.
WITH THIS, YOU MAY NOW STUDY THE EUROPEAN SCIENCES ALONG-SIDE THE MEN TO YOUR HEART'S CONTENT.
...
TRULY...?
YOU WAITED A LONG TIME FOR THIS.
THIS PROHIBITION HAS STOOD SINCE THE TIME OF THE THIRD TOKUGAWA SHOGUN, LORD IEMITSU. HER HIGHNESS NEEDED MUCH TIME TO PERSUADE ALL THE COUNCILLORS IN HER CABINET THAT IT SHOULD BE OVERTURNED.
I AM SORRY FOR THAT.

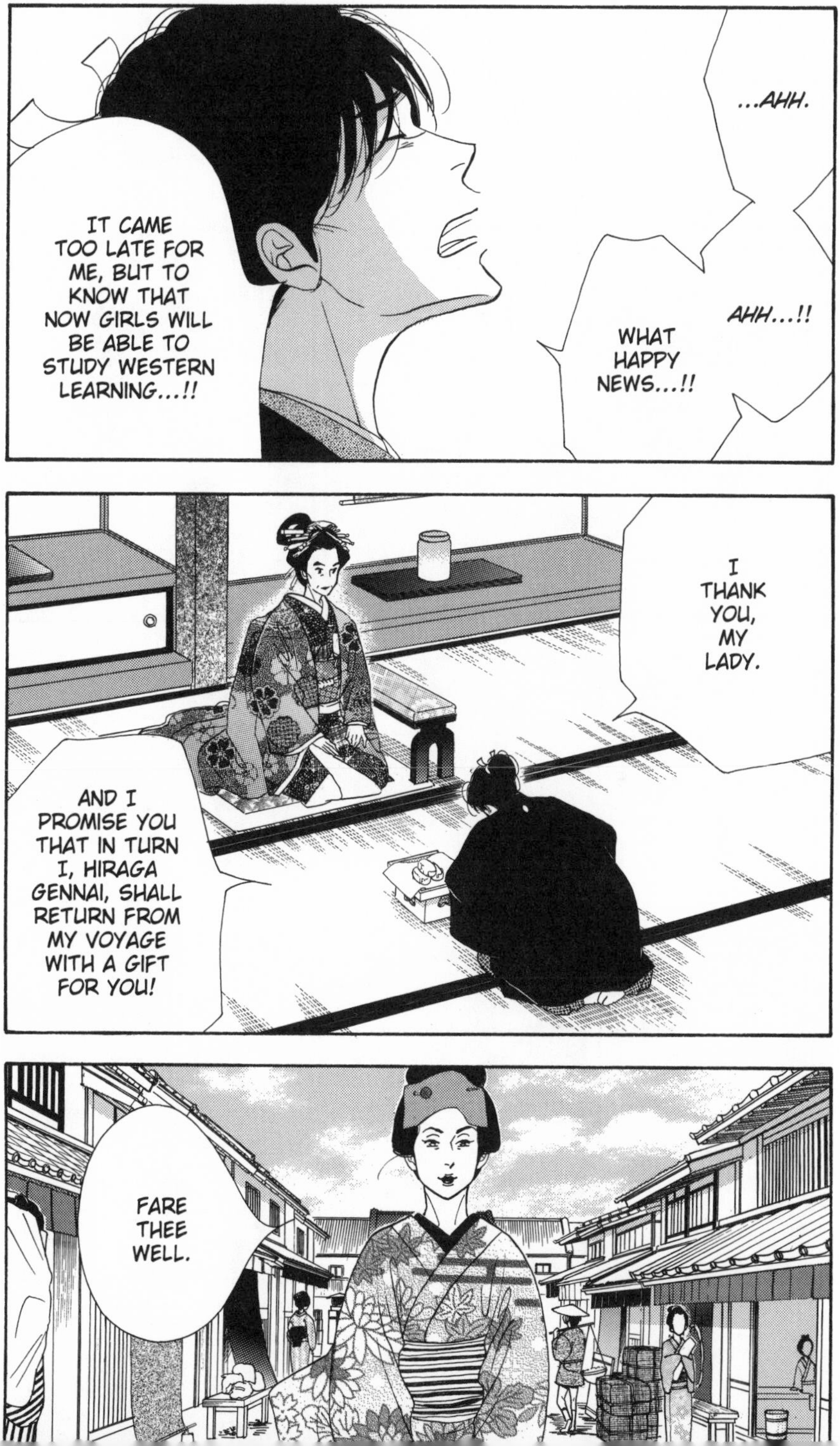
...AHH.
AHH...!!
WHAT HAPPY NEWS...!!
IT CAME TOO LATE FOR ME, BUT TO KNOW THAT NOW GIRLS WILL BE ABLE TO STUDY WESTERN LEARNING...!!
I THANK YOU, MY LADY.
AND I PROMISE YOU THAT IN TURN I, HIRAGA GENNAI, SHALL RETURN FROM MY VOYAGE WITH A GIFT FOR YOU!
FARE THEE WELL.

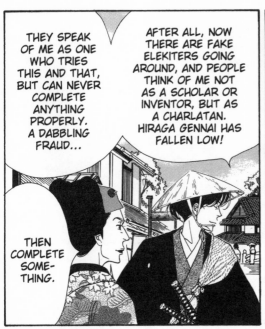

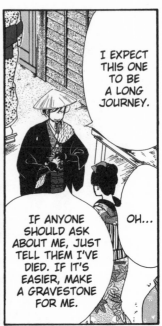

I EXPECT THIS ONE TO BE A LONG JOURNEY.
OH...
IF ANYONE SHOULD ASK ABOUT ME, JUST TELL THEM I'VE DIED. IF IT'S EASIER, MAKE A GRAVESTONE FOR ME.
AFTER ALL, NOW THERE ARE FAKE ELEKITERS GOING AROUND, AND PEOPLE THINK OF ME NOT AS A SCHOLAR OR INVENTOR, BUT AS A CHARLATAN. HIRAGA GENNAI HAS FALLEN LOW!
THEY SPEAK OF ME AS ONE WHO TRIES THIS AND THAT, BUT CAN NEVER COMPLETE ANYTHING PROPERLY. A DABBLING FRAUD...
THEN COMPLETE SOME-THING.
SEE AT LEAST ONE THING THROUGH TO THE END, PROPERLY.
OH!
WHAT A GOOD WOMAN YOU'VE BECOME!
I'LL BE GOING NOW.
FARE THEE WELL ...!!

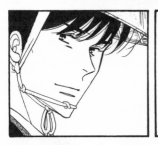

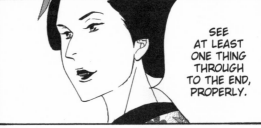

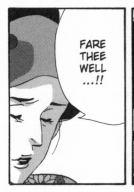

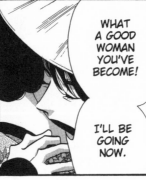

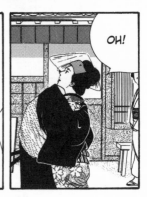

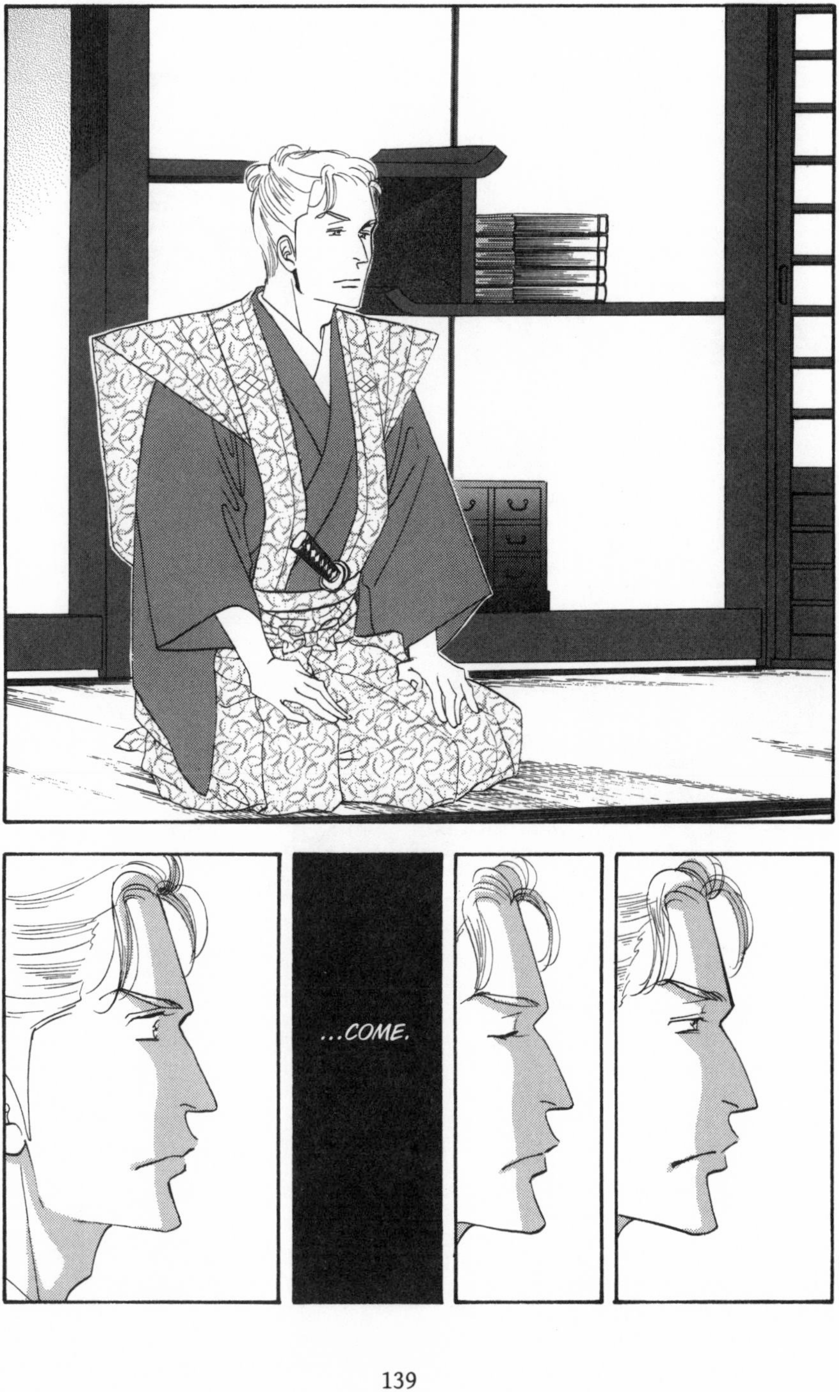
...COME.

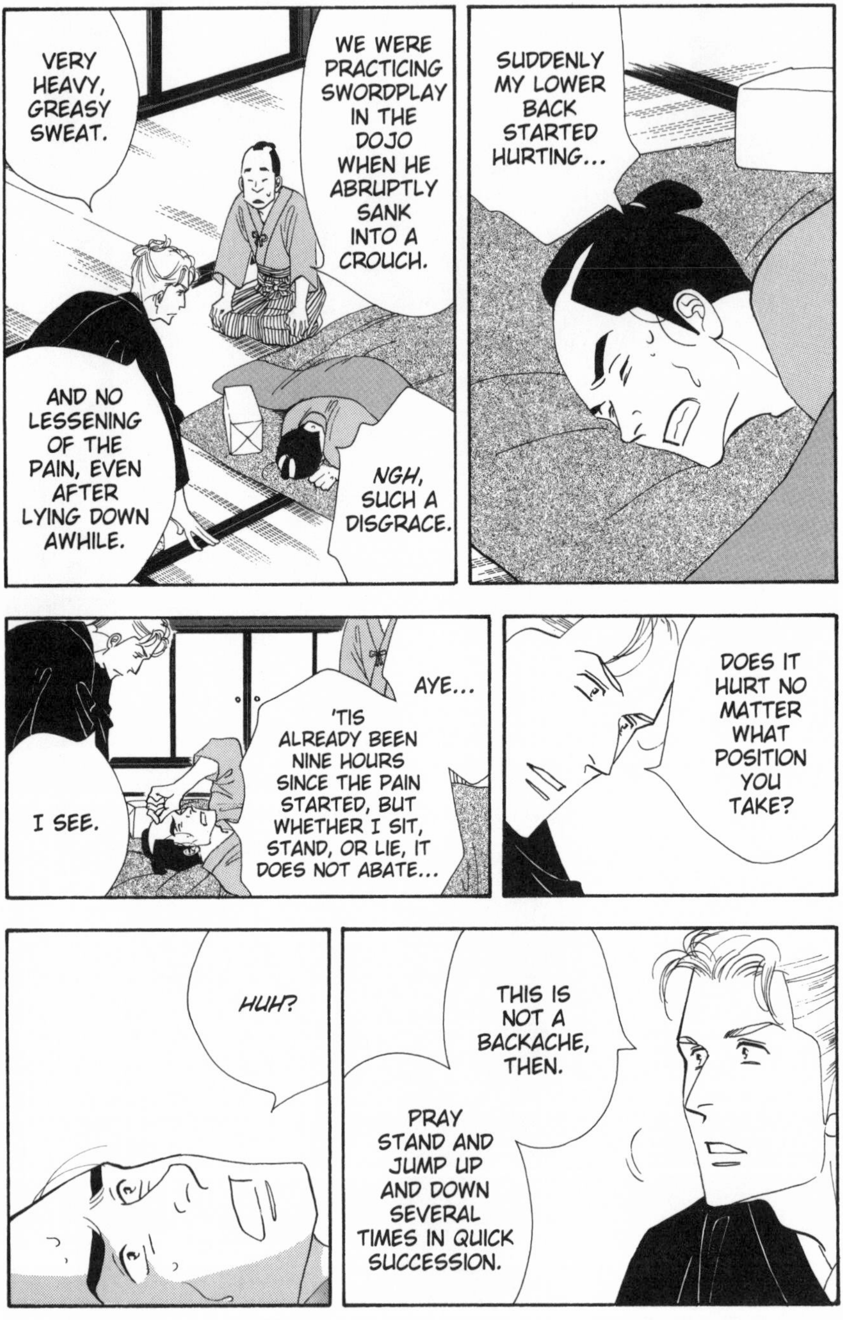
SUDDENLY MY LOWER BACK STARTED HURTING...
WE WERE PRACTICING SWORDPLAY IN THE DOJO WHEN HE ABRUPTLY SANK INTO A CROUCH.
VERY HEAVY, GREASY SWEAT.
NGH, SUCH A DISGRACE.
AND NO LESSENING OF THE PAIN, EVEN AFTER LYING DOWN AWHILE.
DOES IT HURT NO MATTER WHAT POSITION YOU TAKE?
AYE...
'TIS ALREADY BEEN NINE HOURS SINCE THE PAIN STARTED, BUT WHETHER I SIT, STAND, OR LIE, IT DOES NOT ABATE...
I SEE.
THIS IS NOT A BACKACHE, THEN.
PRAY STAND AND JUMP UP AND DOWN SEVERAL TIMES IN QUICK SUCCESSION.
HUH?

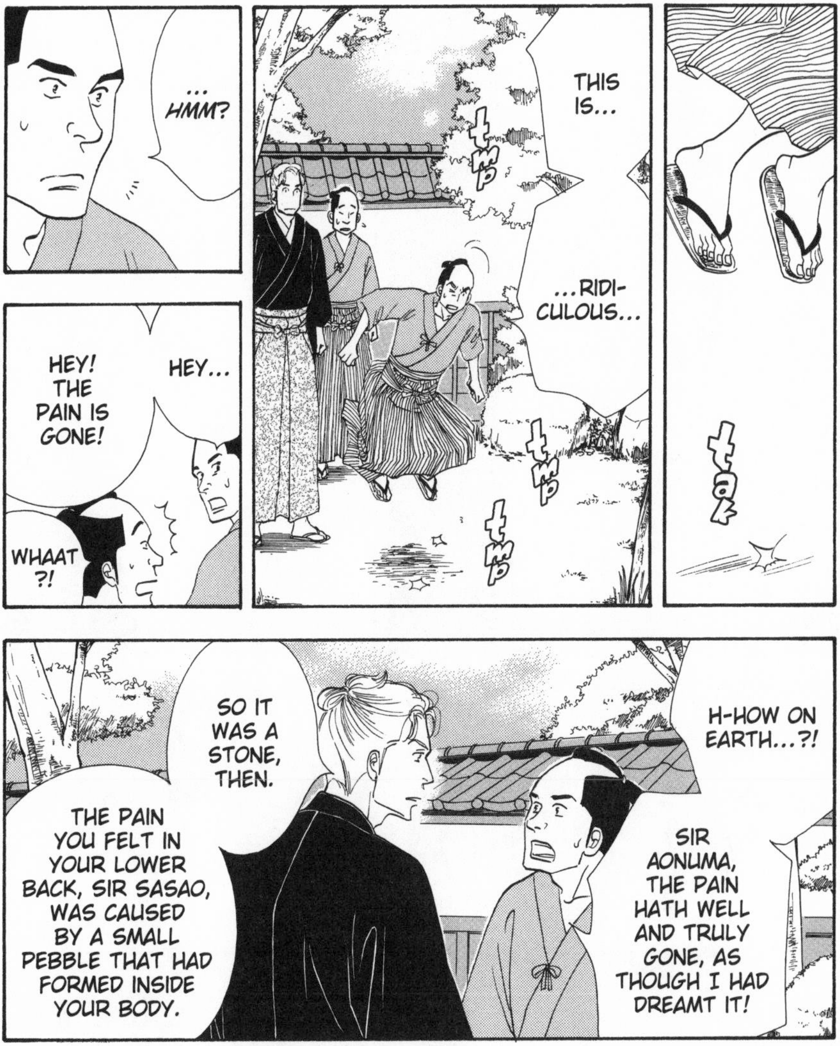
tak
THIS IS...
tmp
...RIDICULOUS...
tmp
tmp
...HMM?
HEY...
HEY! THE PAIN IS GONE!
WHAAT?!
H-HOW ON EARTH...?!
SIR AONUMA, THE PAIN HATH WELL AND TRULY GONE, AS THOUGH I HAD DREAMT IT!
SO IT WAS A STONE, THEN.
THE PAIN YOU FELT IN YOUR LOWER BACK, SIR SASAO, WAS CAUSED BY A SMALL PEBBLE THAT HAD FORMED INSIDE YOUR BODY.
IT IS OFTEN MISTAKEN FOR A BACKACHE, BECAUSE THE LOCATION OF THE PAIN IS SO SIMILAR. THE PEBBLE WILL SOON ENOUGH COME OUT WITH YOUR URINE.
SUCH STONES FORM MORE EASILY WHEN THE BODY LACKS SUFFICIENT FLUIDS, SO PRAY DRINK PLENTY OF WATER WHEN YOU ARE AT THE DOJO.

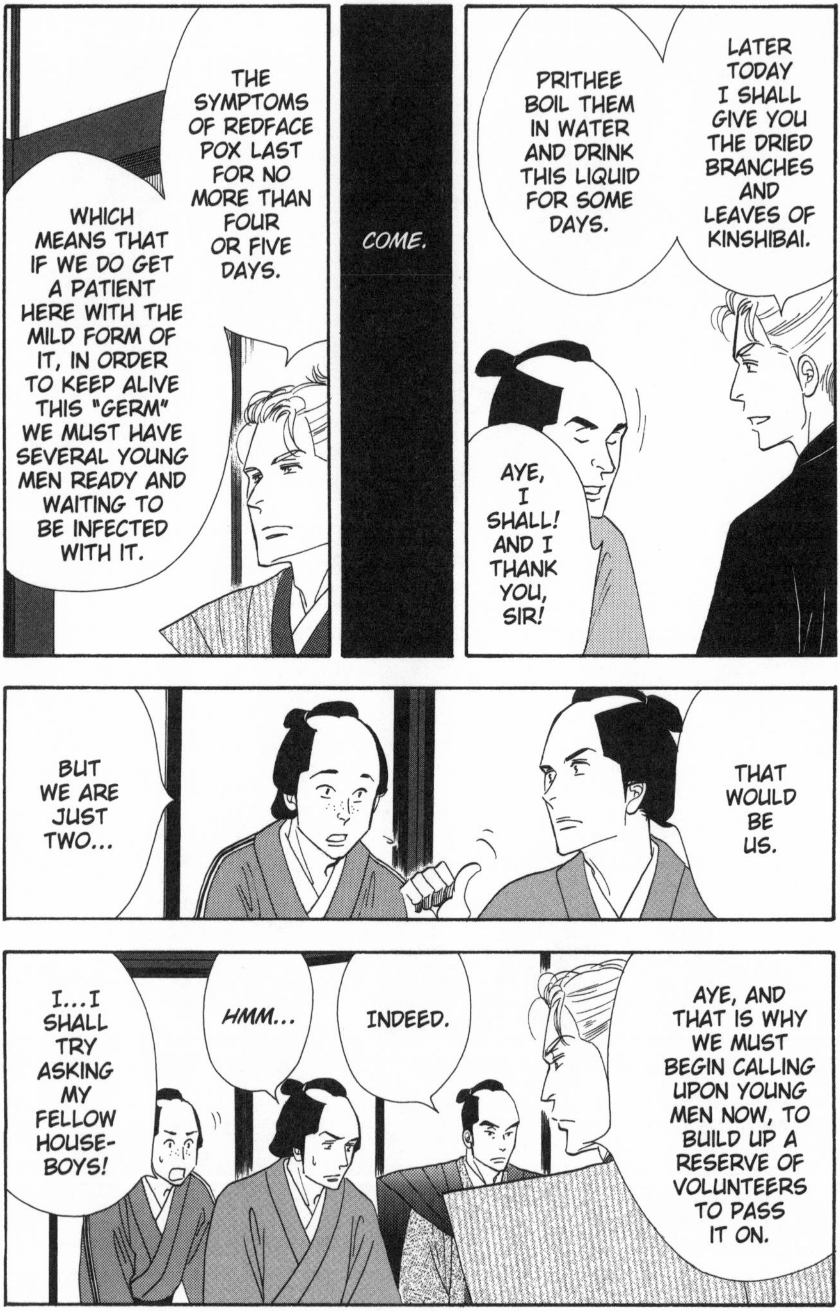
LATER TODAY I SHALL GIVE YOU THE DRIED BRANCHES AND LEAVES OF KINSHIBAI.
PRITHEE BOIL THEM IN WATER AND DRINK THIS LIQUID FOR SOME DAYS.
AYE, I SHALL! AND I THANK YOU, SIR!
COME.
THE SYMPTOMS OF REDFACE POX LAST FOR NO MORE THAN FOUR OR FIVE DAYS.
WHICH MEANS THAT IF WE DO GET A PATIENT HERE WITH THE MILD FORM OF IT, IN ORDER TO KEEP ALIVE THIS "GERM" WE MUST HAVE SEVERAL YOUNG MEN READY AND WAITING TO BE INFECTED WITH IT.
THAT WOULD BE US.
BUT WE ARE JUST TWO...
AYE, AND THAT IS WHY WE MUST BEGIN CALLING UPON YOUNG MEN NOW, TO BUILD UP A RESERVE OF VOLUNTEERS TO PASS IT ON.
INDEED.
HMM...
I...I SHALL TRY ASKING MY FELLOW HOUSE-BOYS!

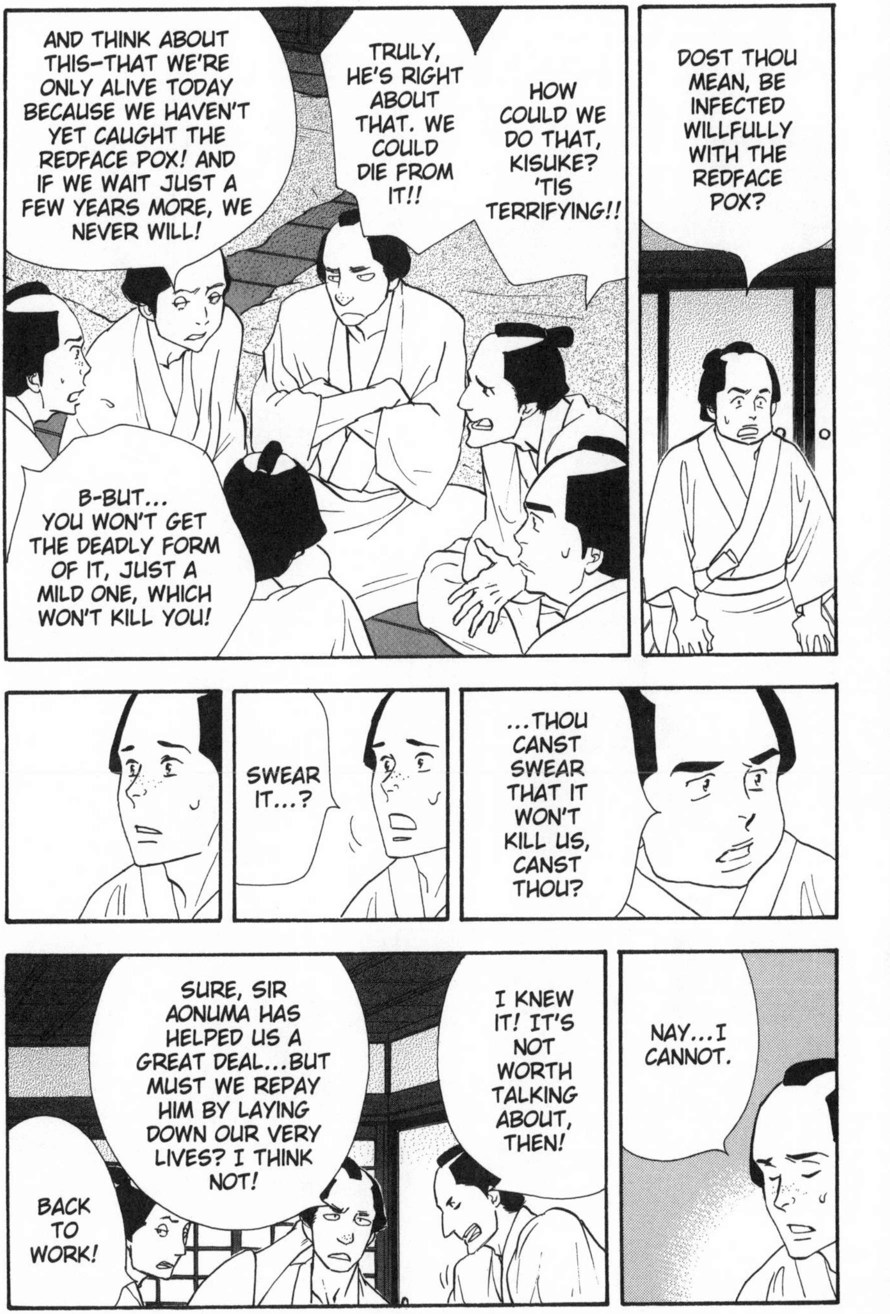
DOST THOU MEAN, BE INFECTED WILLFULLY WITH THE REDFACE POX?
HOW COULD WE DO THAT, KISUKE? 'TIS TERRIFYING!!
TRULY, HE'S RIGHT ABOUT THAT. WE COULD DIE FROM IT!!
AND THINK ABOUT THIS—THAT WE'RE ONLY ALIVE TODAY BECAUSE WE HAVEN'T YET CAUGHT THE REDFACE POX! AND IF WE WAIT JUST A FEW YEARS MORE, WE NEVER WILL!
B-BUT... YOU WON'T GET THE DEADLY FORM OF IT, JUST A MILD ONE, WHICH WON'T KILL YOU!
...THOU CANST SWEAR THAT IT WON'T KILL US, CANST THOU?
SWEAR IT...?
NAY...I CANNOT.
I KNEW IT! IT'S NOT WORTH TALKING ABOUT, THEN!
SURE, SIR AONUMA HAS HELPED US A GREAT DEAL...BUT MUST WE REPAY HIM BY LAYING DOWN OUR VERY LIVES? I THINK NOT!
BACK TO WORK!

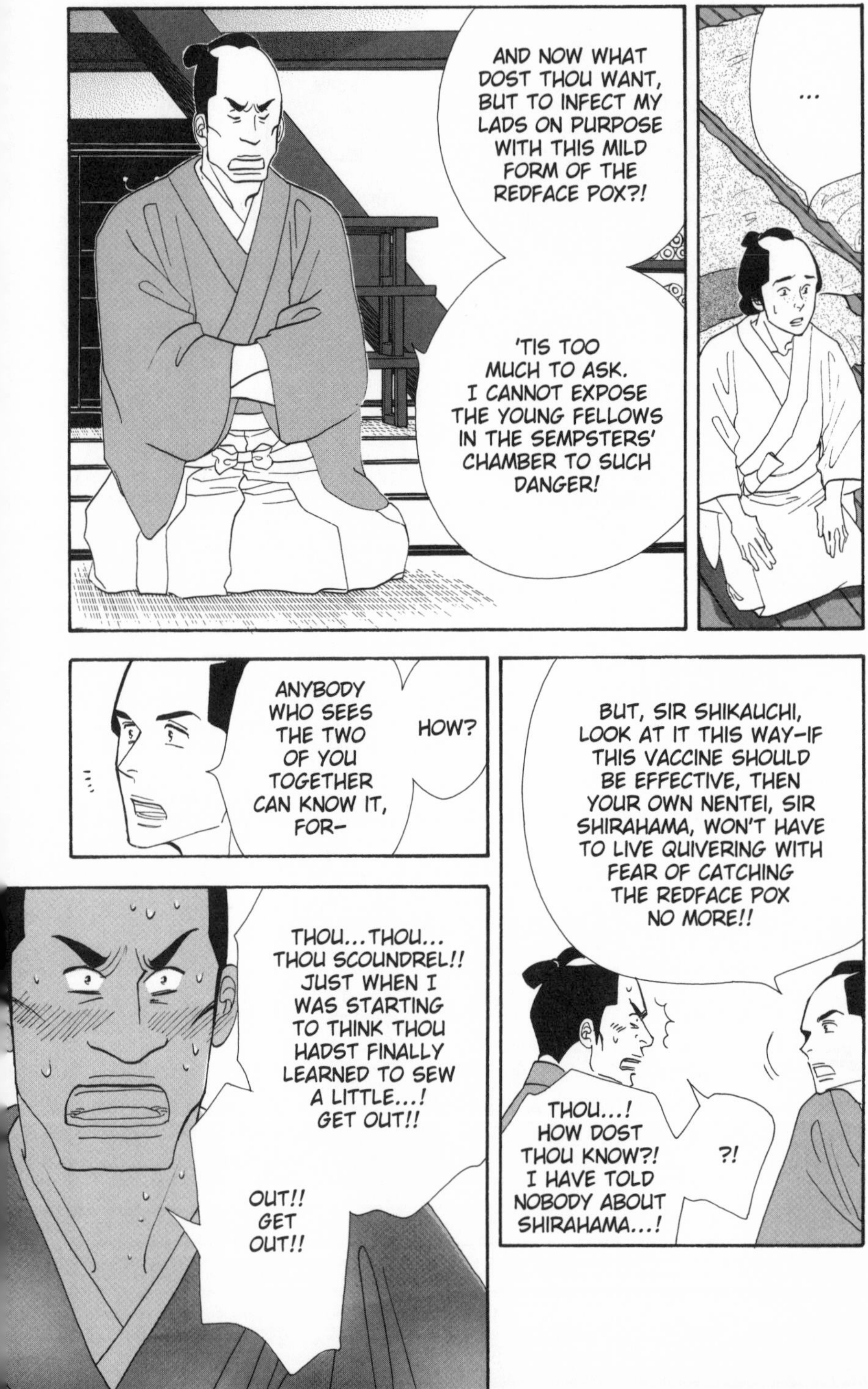
...
AND NOW WHAT DOST THOU WANT, BUT TO INFECT MY LADS ON PURPOSE WITH THIS MILD FORM OF THE REDFACE POX?!
'TIS TOO MUCH TO ASK. I CANNOT EXPOSE THE YOUNG FELLOWS IN THE SEMPSTERS' CHAMBER TO SUCH DANGER!
BUT, SIR SHIKAUCHI, LOOK AT IT THIS WAY–IF THIS VACCINE SHOULD BE EFFECTIVE, THEN YOUR OWN NENTEI, SIR SHIRAHAMA, WON'T HAVE TO LIVE QUIVERING WITH FEAR OF CATCHING THE REDFACE POX NO MORE!!
THOU...! HOW DOST THOU KNOW?! I HAVE TOLD NOBODY ABOUT SHIRAHAMA...!
?!
HOW?
ANYBODY WHO SEES THE TWO OF YOU TOGETHER CAN KNOW IT, FOR–
THOU...THOU... THOU SCOUNDREL!! JUST WHEN I WAS STARTING TO THINK THOU HADST FINALLY LEARNED TO SEW A LITTLE...! GET OUT!!
OUT!! GET OUT!!

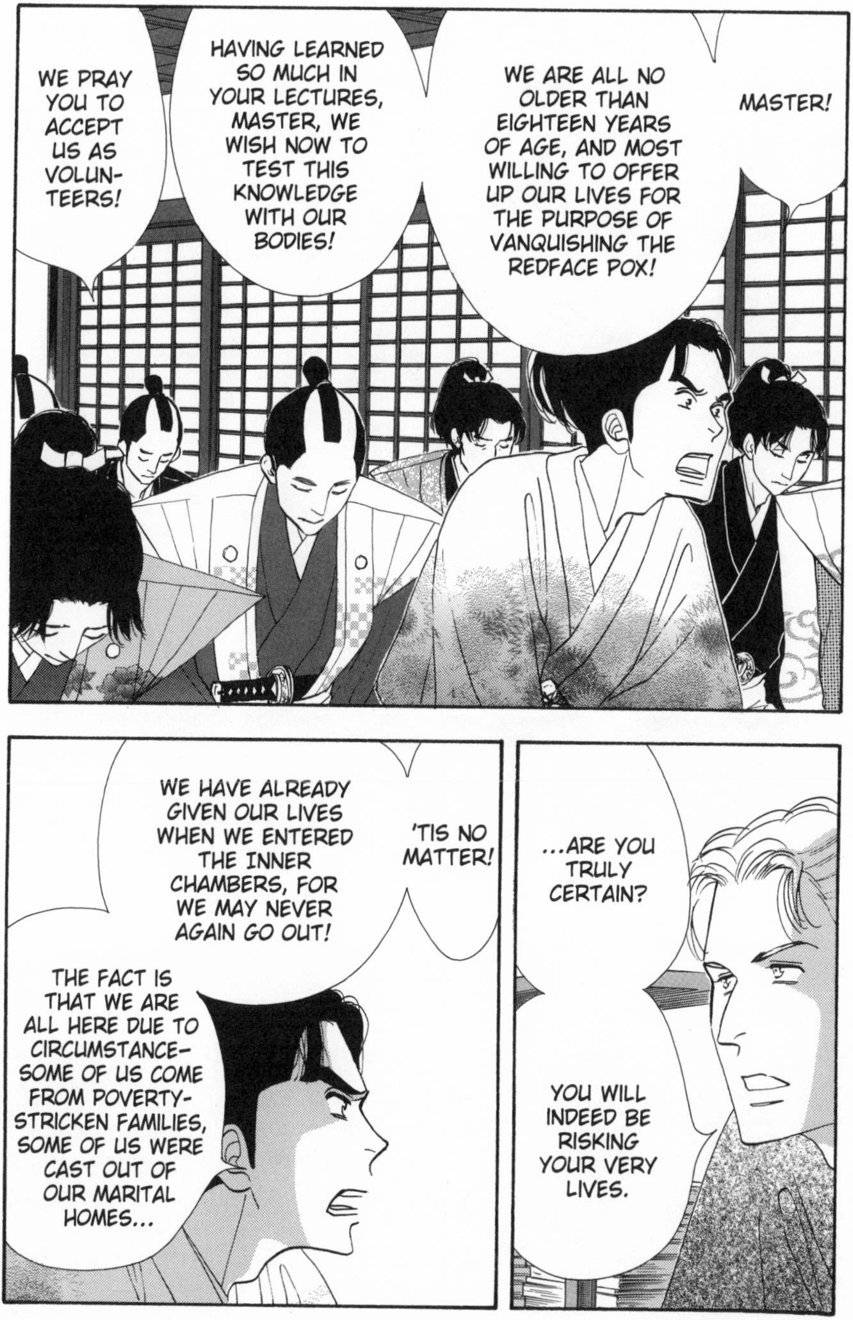
MASTER!
WE ARE ALL NO OLDER THAN EIGHTEEN YEARS OF AGE, AND MOST WILLING TO OFFER UP OUR LIVES FOR THE PURPOSE OF VANQUISHING THE REDFACE POX!
HAVING LEARNED SO MUCH IN YOUR LECTURES, MASTER, WE WISH NOW TO TEST THIS KNOWLEDGE WITH OUR BODIES!
WE PRAY YOU TO ACCEPT US AS VOLUN-TEERS!
...ARE YOU TRULY CERTAIN?
YOU WILL INDEED BE RISKING YOUR VERY LIVES.
'TIS NO MATTER!
WE HAVE ALREADY GIVEN OUR LIVES WHEN WE ENTERED THE INNER CHAMBERS, FOR WE MAY NEVER AGAIN GO OUT!
THE FACT IS THAT WE ARE ALL HERE DUE TO CIRCUMSTANCE-SOME OF US COME FROM POVERTY-STRICKEN FAMILIES, SOME OF US WERE CAST OUT OF OUR MARITAL HOMES...

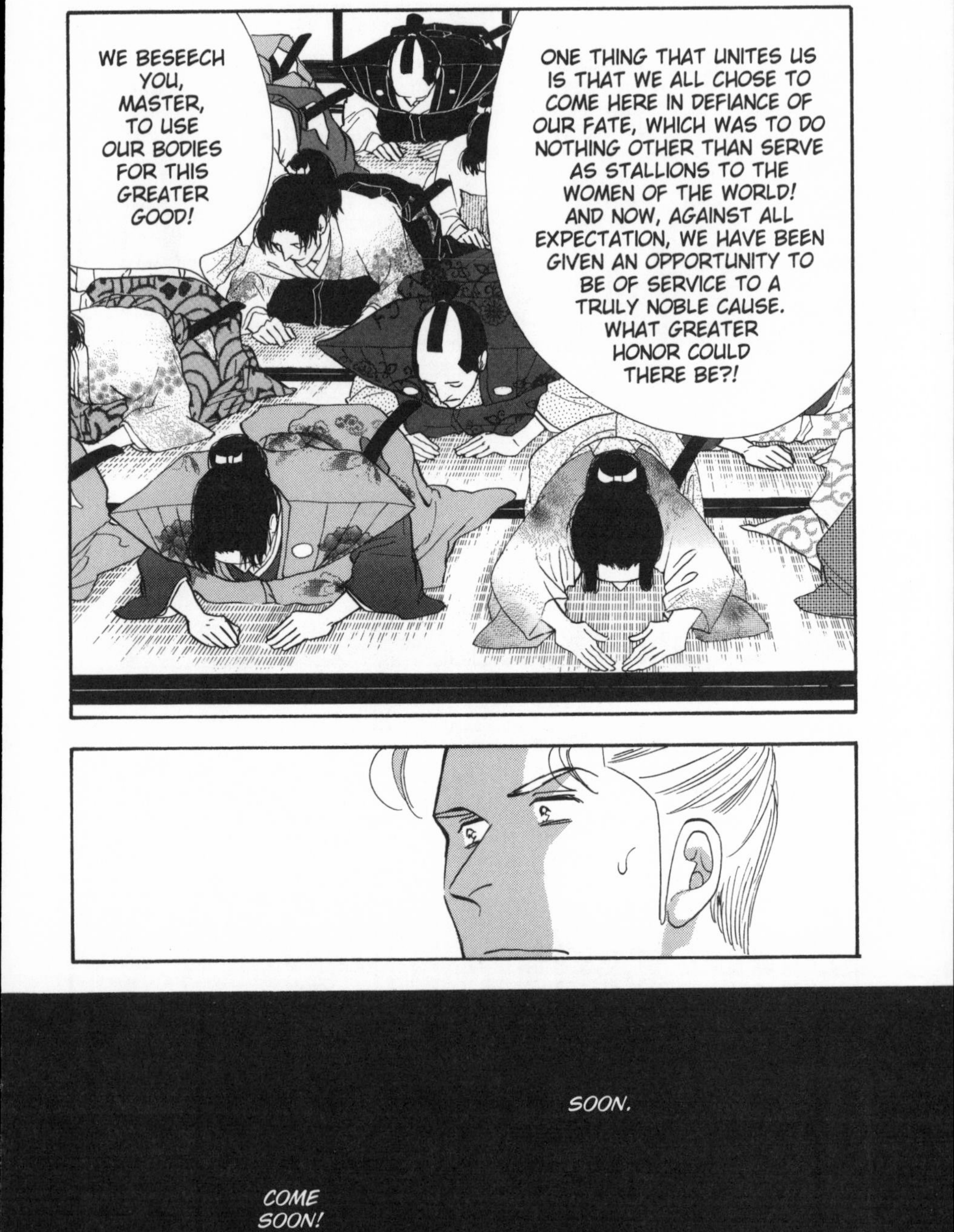
ONE THING THAT UNITES US IS THAT WE ALL CHOSE TO COME HERE IN DEFIANCE OF OUR FATE, WHICH WAS TO DO NOTHING OTHER THAN SERVE AS STALLIONS TO THE WOMEN OF THE WORLD! AND NOW, AGAINST ALL EXPECTATION, WE HAVE BEEN GIVEN AN OPPORTUNITY TO BE OF SERVICE TO A TRULY NOBLE CAUSE. WHAT GREATER HONOR COULD THERE BE?!
WE BESEECH YOU, MASTER, TO USE OUR BODIES FOR THIS GREATER GOOD!
SOON.
COME SOON!

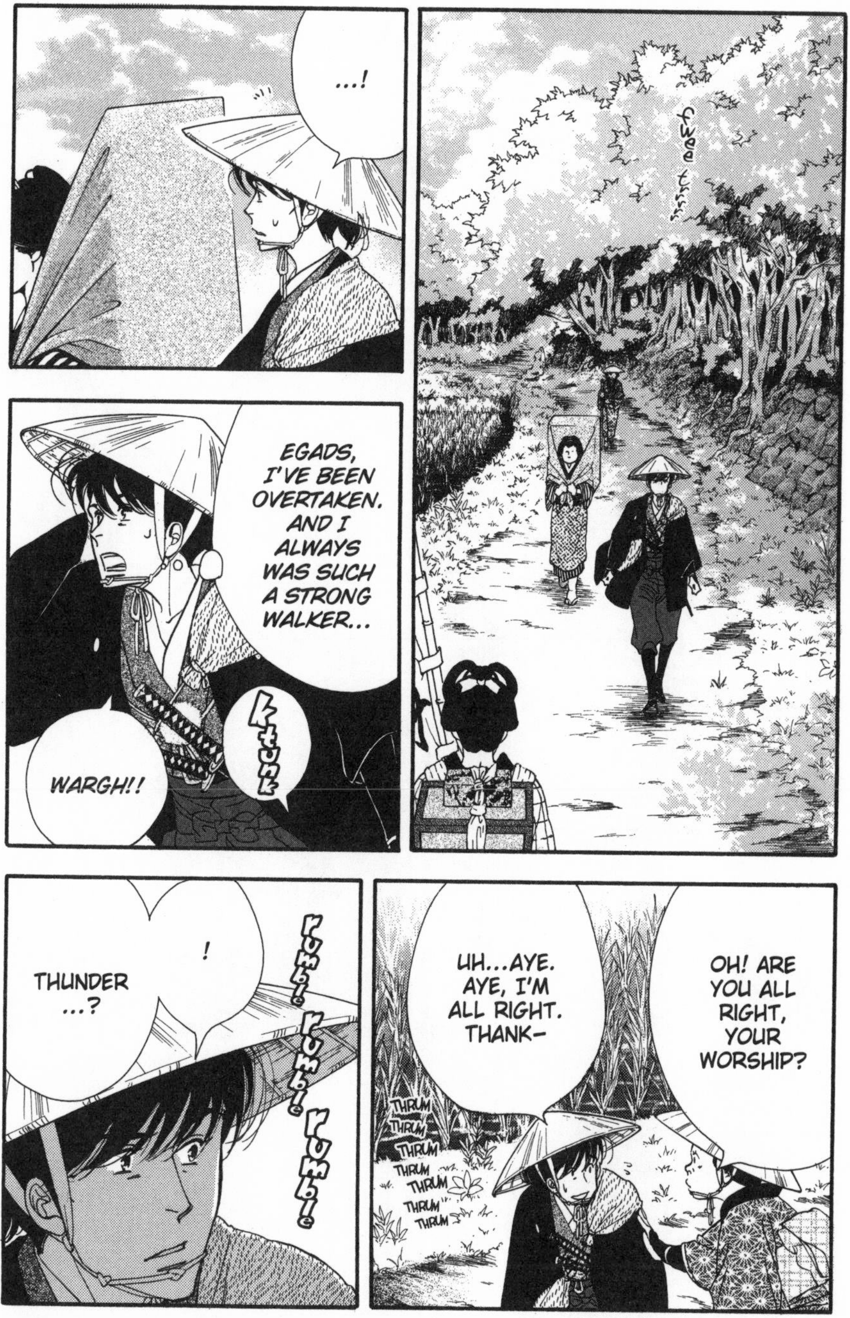
fwee tsssss
...!
EGADS, I'VE BEEN OVERTAKEN. AND I ALWAYS WAS SUCH A STRONG WALKER...
ktunk
WARGH!!
OH! ARE YOU ALL RIGHT, YOUR WORSHIP?
UH...AYE. AYE, I'M ALL RIGHT. THANK-
THRUM THRUM THRUM THRUM THRUM THRUM THRUM
rumble rumble rumble
!
THUNDER ...?

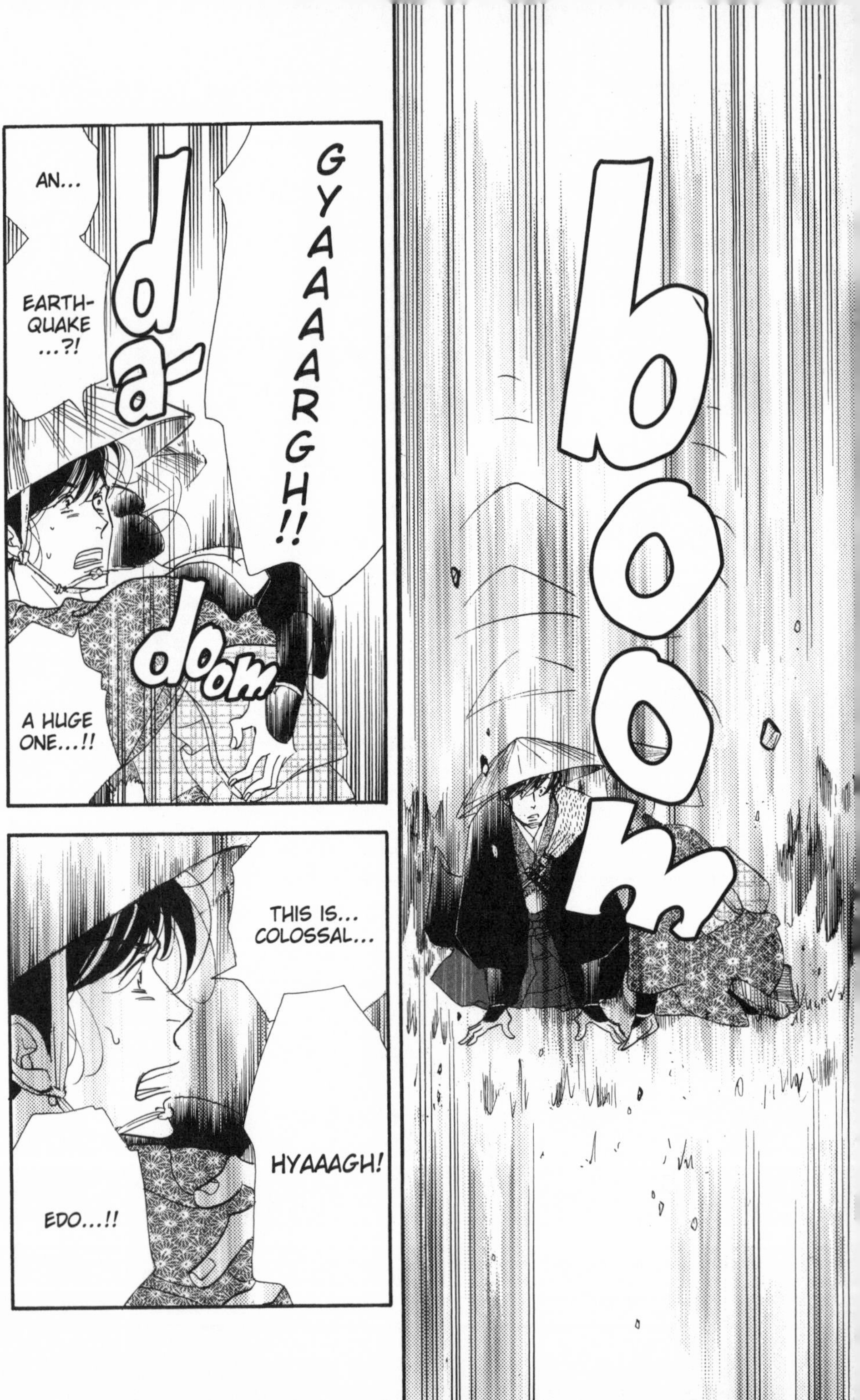
boom
GYAAAAARGH!!
da-
AN...
EARTH-QUAKE...?!
doom
A HUGE ONE...!!
THIS IS... COLOSSAL...
HYAAAGH!
EDO...!!

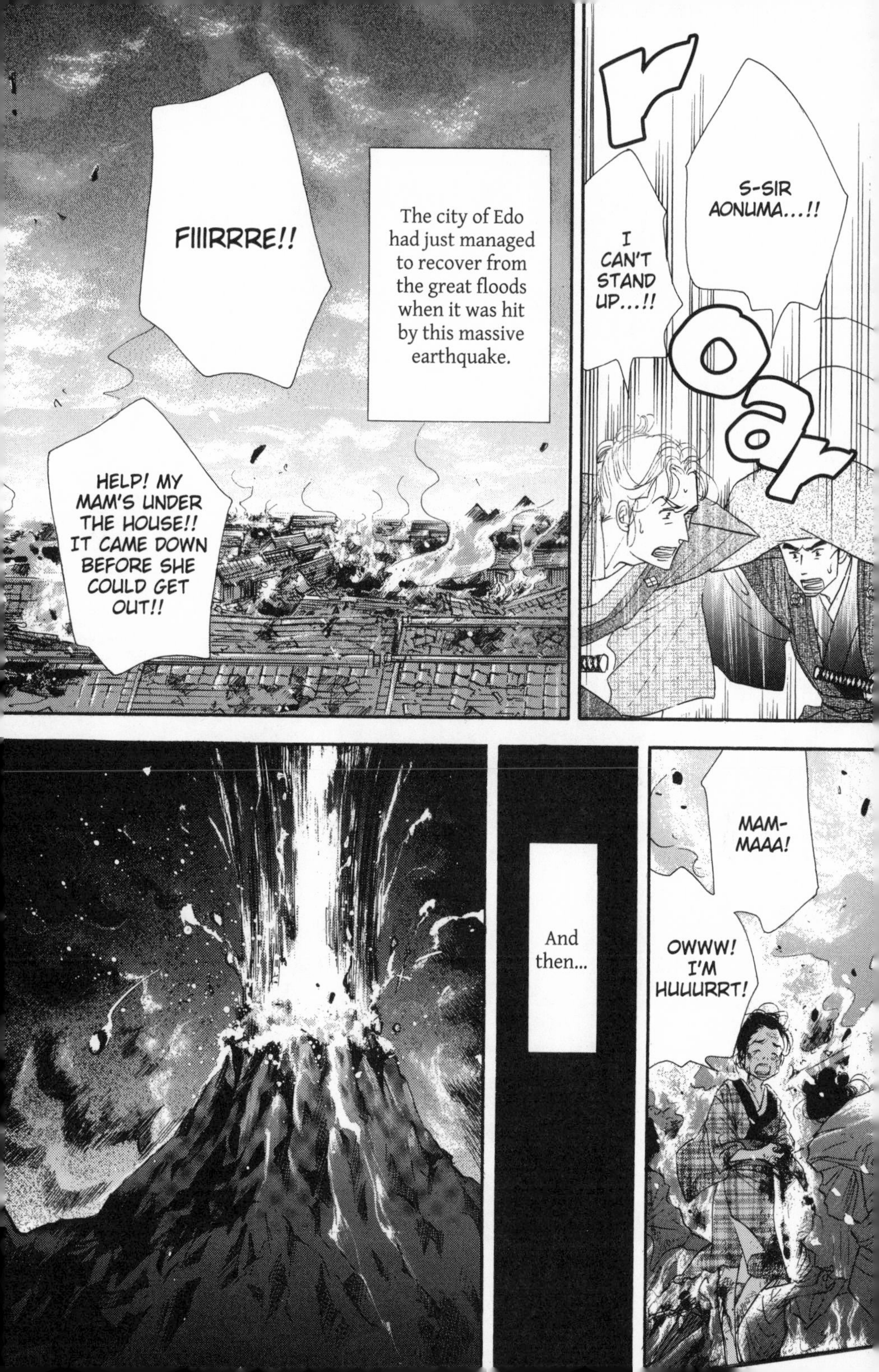

r
S-SIR AONUMA...!!
I CAN'T STAND UP...!!
oar
The city of Edo had just managed to recover from the great floods when it was hit by this massive earthquake.
FIIIRRRE!!
HELP! MY MAM'S UNDER THE HOUSE!! IT CAME DOWN BEFORE SHE COULD GET OUT!!
MAM-MAAA!
OWWW! I'M HUUURRT!
And then...

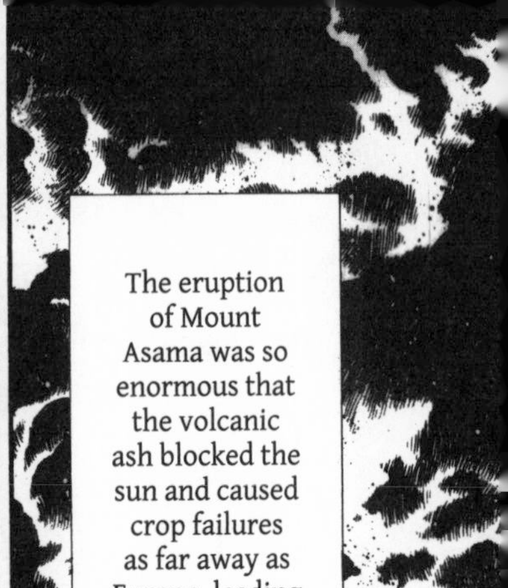
The eruption of Mount Asama was so enormous that the volcanic ash blocked the sun and caused crop failures as far away as Europe, leading to serious famine.

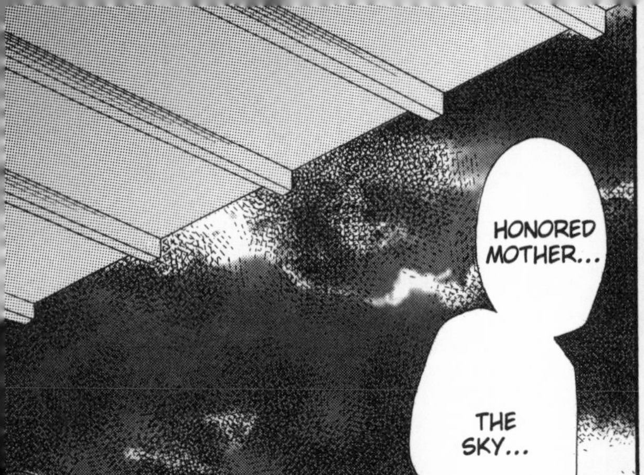
HONORED MOTHER...
THE SKY...
...IS AS BLACK AS NIGHT, THOUGH IT STILL BE DAY...

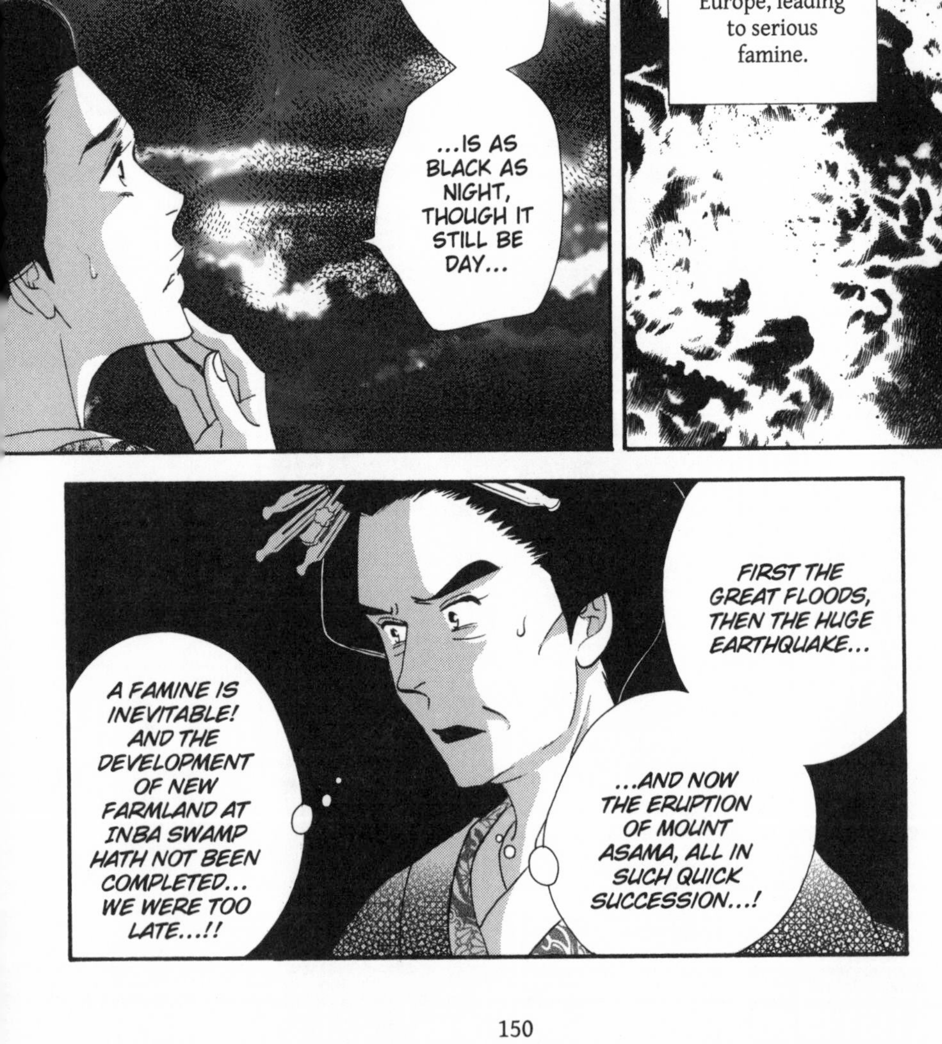
FIRST THE GREAT FLOODS, THEN THE HUGE EARTHQUAKE...
...AND NOW THE ERUPTION OF MOUNT ASAMA, ALL IN SUCH QUICK SUCCESSION...!
A FAMINE IS INEVITABLE! AND THE DEVELOPMENT OF NEW FARMLAND AT INBA SWAMP HATH NOT BEEN COMPLETED... WE WERE TOO LATE...!!

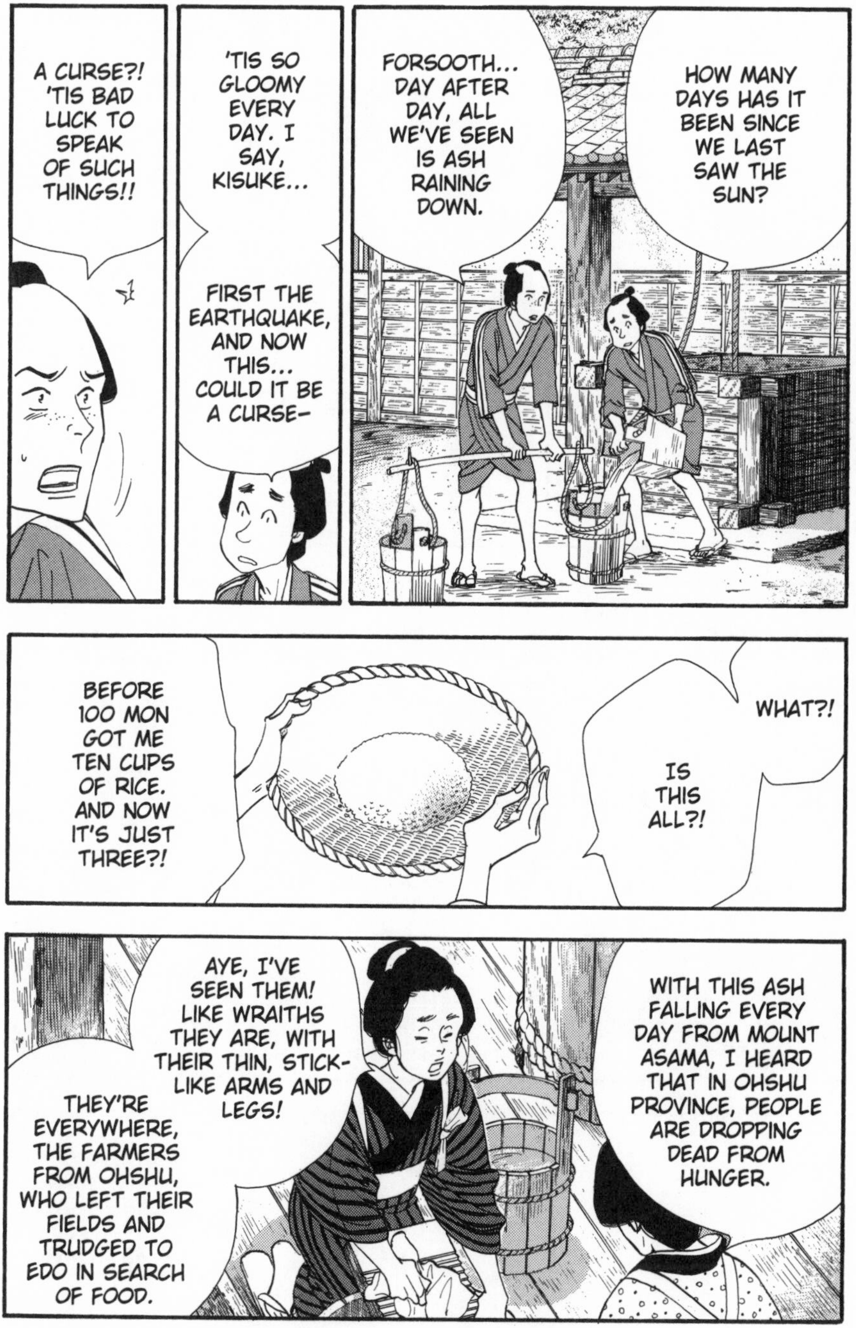
HOW MANY DAYS HAS IT BEEN SINCE WE LAST SAW THE SUN?
FORSOOTH... DAY AFTER DAY, ALL WE'VE SEEN IS ASH RAINING DOWN.
'TIS SO GLOOMY EVERY DAY. I SAY, KISUKE...
FIRST THE EARTHQUAKE, AND NOW THIS... COULD IT BE A CURSE-
A CURSE?! 'TIS BAD LUCK TO SPEAK OF SUCH THINGS!!
WHAT?!
IS THIS ALL?!
BEFORE 100 MON GOT ME TEN CUPS OF RICE. AND NOW IT'S JUST THREE?!
WITH THIS ASH FALLING EVERY DAY FROM MOUNT ASAMA, I HEARD THAT IN OHSHU PROVINCE, PEOPLE ARE DROPPING DEAD FROM HUNGER.
AYE, I'VE SEEN THEM! LIKE WRAITHS THEY ARE, WITH THEIR THIN, STICK-LIKE ARMS AND LEGS!
THEY'RE EVERYWHERE, THE FARMERS FROM OHSHU, WHO LEFT THEIR FIELDS AND TRUDGED TO EDO IN SEARCH OF FOOD.

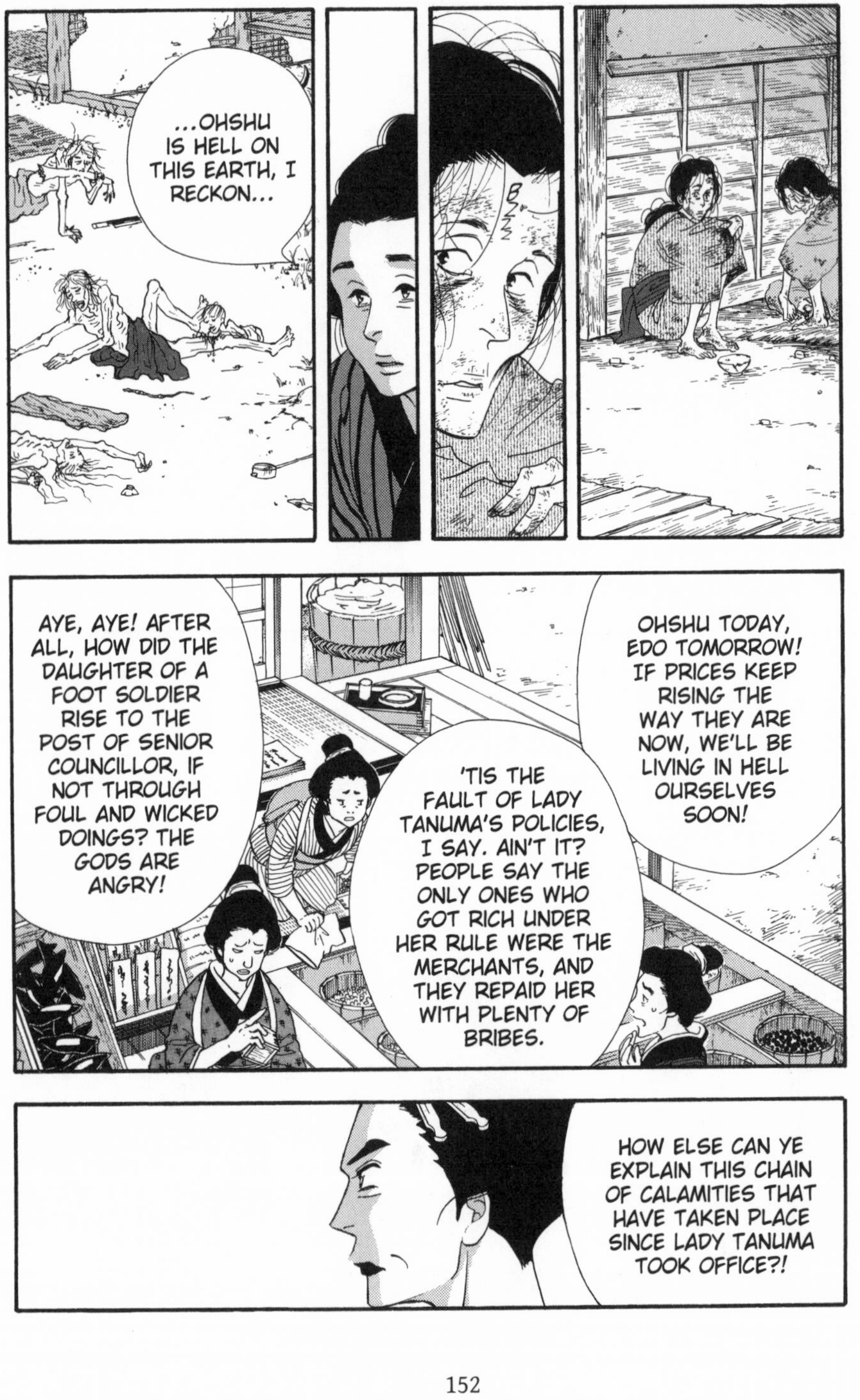
BZZZ
...OHSHU IS HELL ON THIS EARTH, I RECKON...
OHSHU TODAY, EDO TOMORROW! IF PRICES KEEP RISING THE WAY THEY ARE NOW, WE'LL BE LIVING IN HELL OURSELVES SOON!
'TIS THE FAULT OF LADY TANUMA'S POLICIES, I SAY. AIN'T IT? PEOPLE SAY THE ONLY ONES WHO GOT RICH UNDER HER RULE WERE THE MERCHANTS, AND THEY REPAID HER WITH PLENTY OF BRIBES.
AYE, AYE! AFTER ALL, HOW DID THE DAUGHTER OF A FOOT SOLDIER RISE TO THE POST OF SENIOR COUNCILLOR, IF NOT THROUGH FOUL AND WICKED DOINGS? THE GODS ARE ANGRY!
HOW ELSE CAN YE EXPLAIN THIS CHAIN OF CALAMITIES THAT HAVE TAKEN PLACE SINCE LADY TANUMA TOOK OFFICE?!

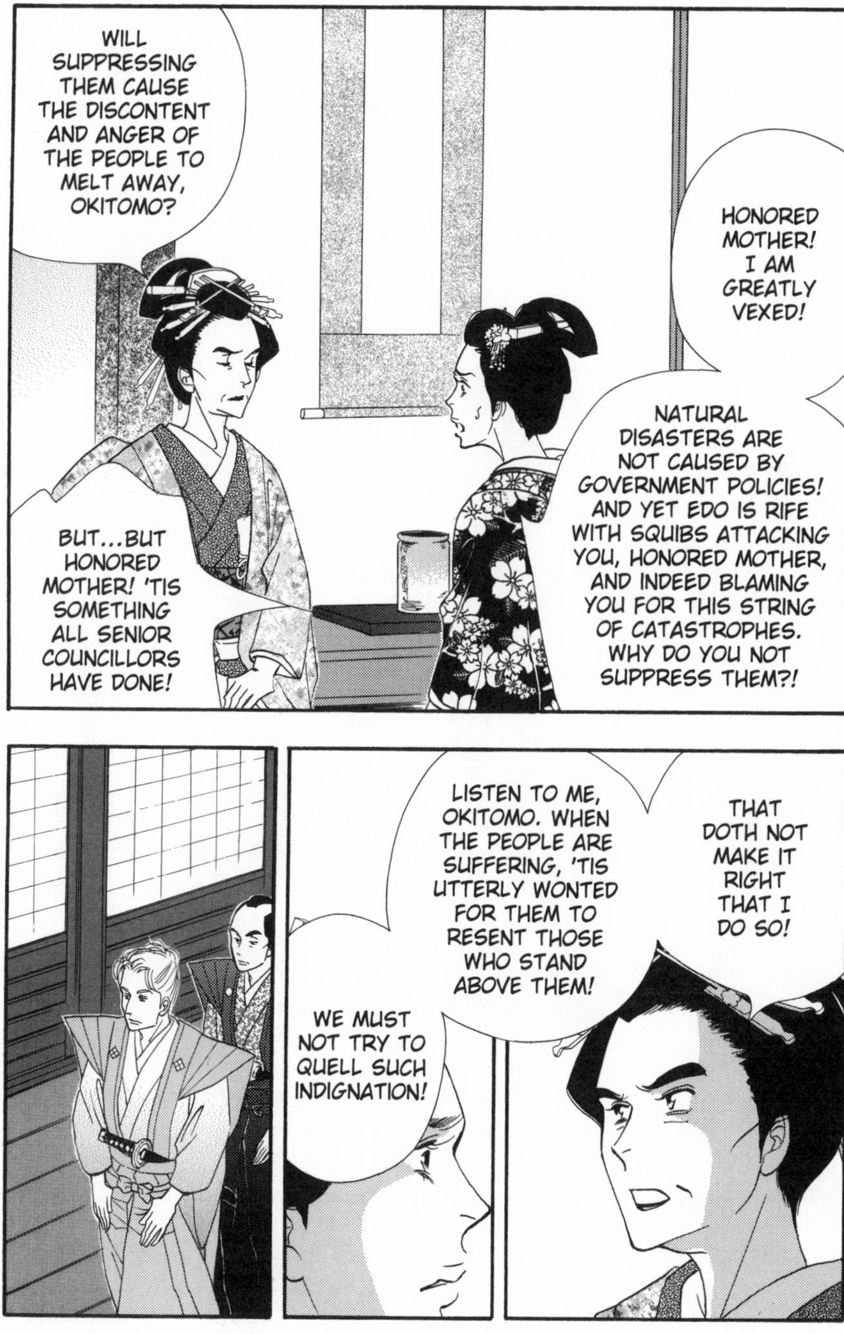
HONORED MOTHER! I AM GREATLY VEXED!
NATURAL DISASTERS ARE NOT CAUSED BY GOVERNMENT POLICIES! AND YET EDO IS RIFE WITH SQUIBS ATTACKING YOU, HONORED MOTHER, AND INDEED BLAMING YOU FOR THIS STRING OF CATASTROPHES. WHY DO YOU NOT SUPPRESS THEM?!
WILL SUPPRESSING THEM CAUSE THE DISCONTENT AND ANGER OF THE PEOPLE TO MELT AWAY, OKITOMO?
BUT...BUT HONORED MOTHER! 'TIS SOMETHING ALL SENIOR COUNCILLORS HAVE DONE!
THAT DOTH NOT MAKE IT RIGHT THAT I DO SO!
LISTEN TO ME, OKITOMO. WHEN THE PEOPLE ARE SUFFERING, 'TIS UTTERLY WONTED FOR THEM TO RESENT THOSE WHO STAND ABOVE THEM!
WE MUST NOT TRY TO QUELL SUCH INDIGNATION!

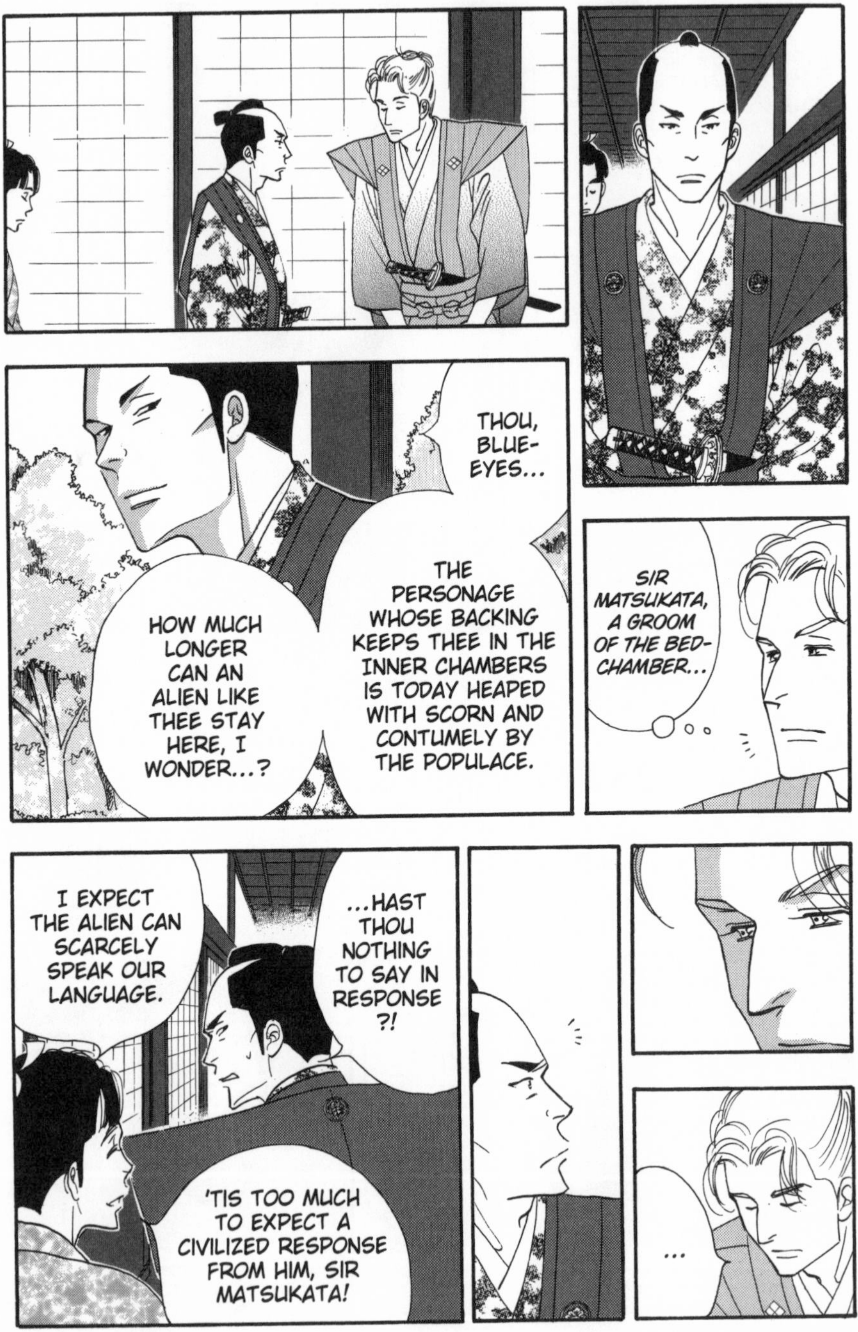
SIR MATSUKATA, A GROOM OF THE BED-CHAMBER...
THOU, BLUE-EYES...
THE PERSONAGE WHOSE BACKING KEEPS THEE IN THE INNER CHAMBERS IS TODAY HEAPED WITH SCORN AND CONTUMELY BY THE POPULACE.
HOW MUCH LONGER CAN AN ALIEN LIKE THEE STAY HERE, I WONDER...?
...
...HAST THOU NOTHING TO SAY IN RESPONSE ?!
I EXPECT THE ALIEN CAN SCARCELY SPEAK OUR LANGUAGE.
'TIS TOO MUCH TO EXPECT A CIVILIZED RESPONSE FROM HIM, SIR MATSUKATA!

...

THE CUR!

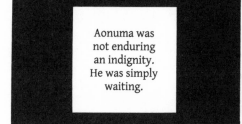

Aonuma was not enduring an indignity. He was simply waiting.

COME! COME.

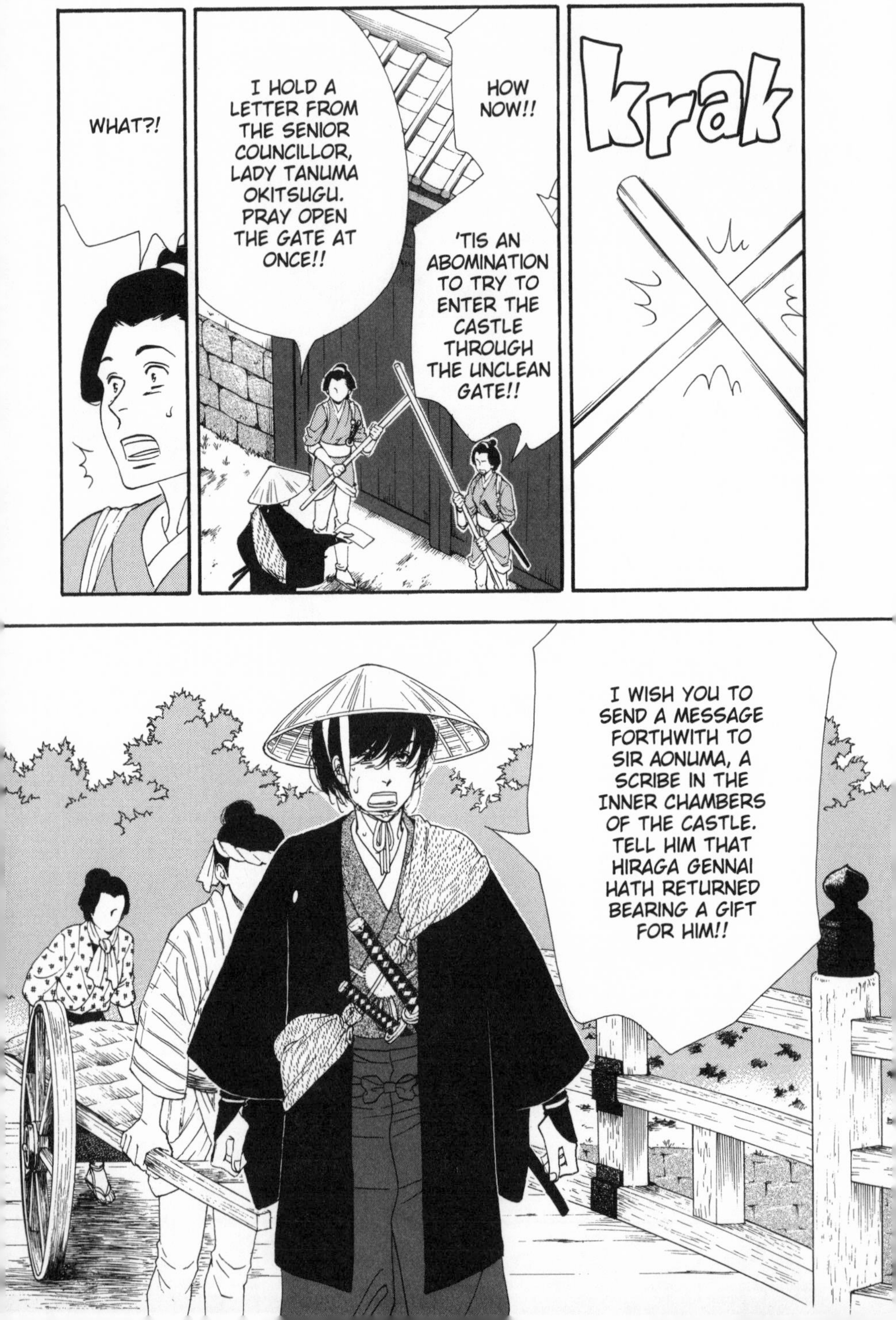
krak
HOW NOW!!
'TIS AN ABOMINATION TO TRY TO ENTER THE CASTLE THROUGH THE UNCLEAN GATE!!
I HOLD A LETTER FROM THE SENIOR COUNCILLOR, LADY TANUMA OKITSUGU. PRAY OPEN THE GATE AT ONCE!!
WHAT?!
I WISH YOU TO SEND A MESSAGE FORTHWITH TO SIR AONUMA, A SCRIBE IN THE INNER CHAMBERS OF THE CASTLE. TELL HIM THAT HIRAGA GENNAI HATH RETURNED BEARING A GIFT FOR HIM!!

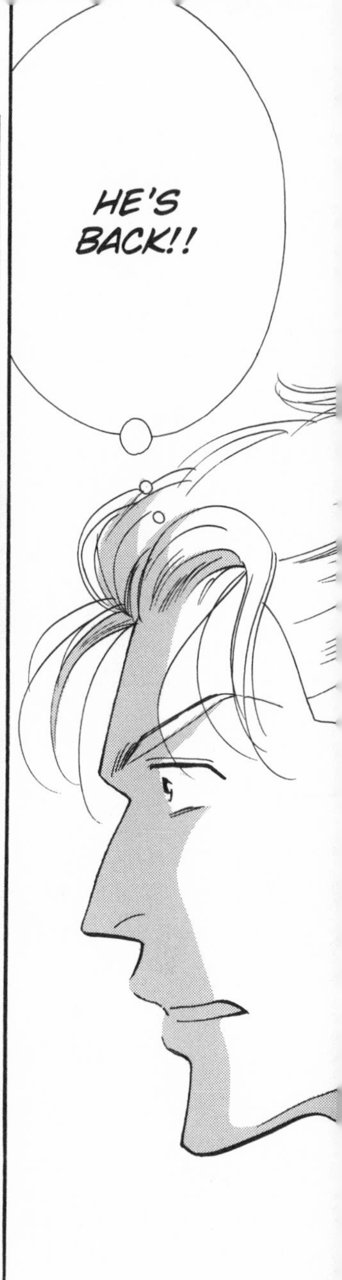
HE'S BACK!!

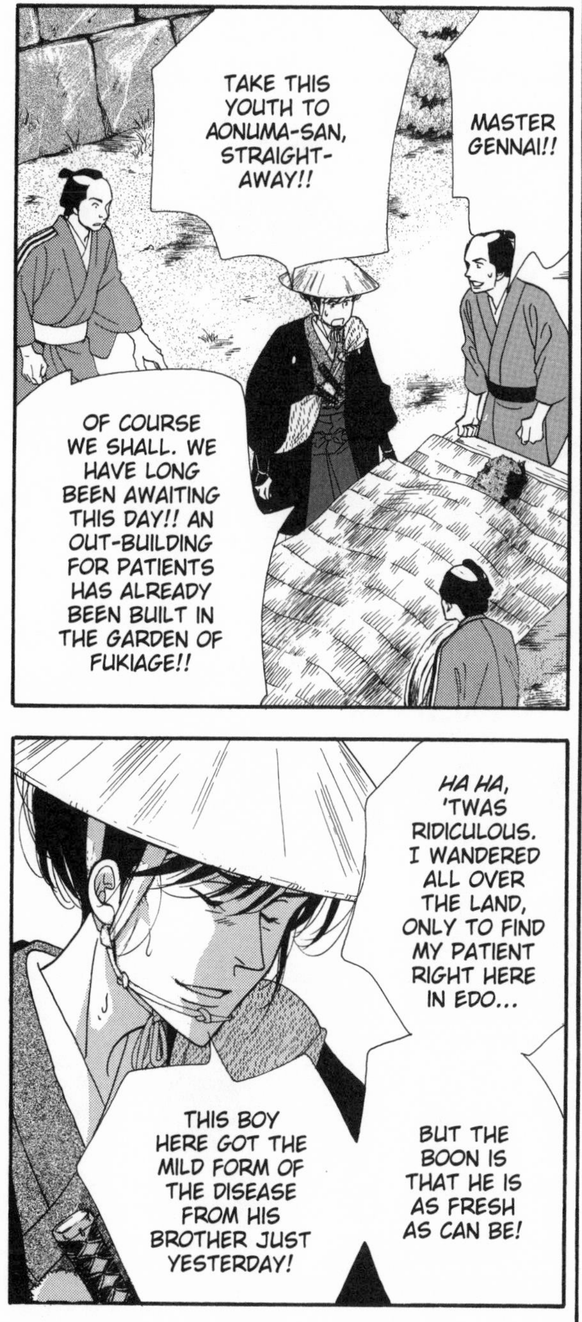
MASTER GENNAI!!
TAKE THIS YOUTH TO AONUMA-SAN, STRAIGHT-AWAY!!
OF COURSE WE SHALL. WE HAVE LONG BEEN AWAITING THIS DAY!! AN OUT-BUILDING FOR PATIENTS HAS ALREADY BEEN BUILT IN THE GARDEN OF FUKIAGE!!
HA HA, 'TWAS RIDICULOUS. I WANDERED ALL OVER THE LAND, ONLY TO FIND MY PATIENT RIGHT HERE IN EDO...
THIS BOY HERE GOT THE MILD FORM OF THE DISEASE FROM HIS BROTHER JUST YESTERDAY!
BUT THE BOON IS THAT HE IS AS FRESH AS CAN BE!

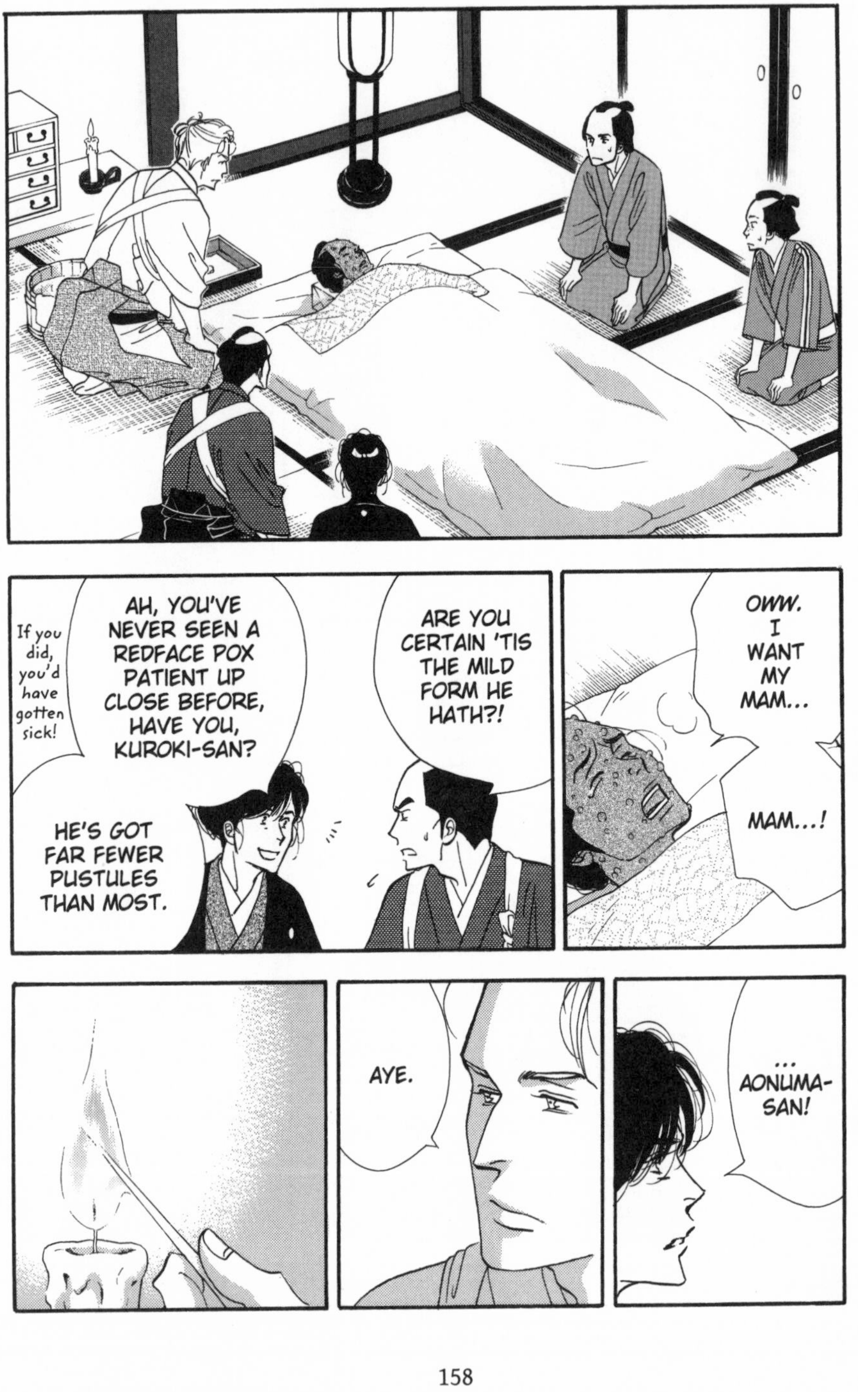
OWW. I WANT MY MAM...
MAM...!
ARE YOU CERTAIN 'TIS THE MILD FORM HE HATH?!
AH, YOU'VE NEVER SEEN A REDFACE POX PATIENT UP CLOSE BEFORE, HAVE YOU, KUROKI-SAN?
If you did, you'd have gotten sick!
HE'S GOT FAR FEWER PUSTULES THAN MOST.
... AONUMA-SAN!
AYE.

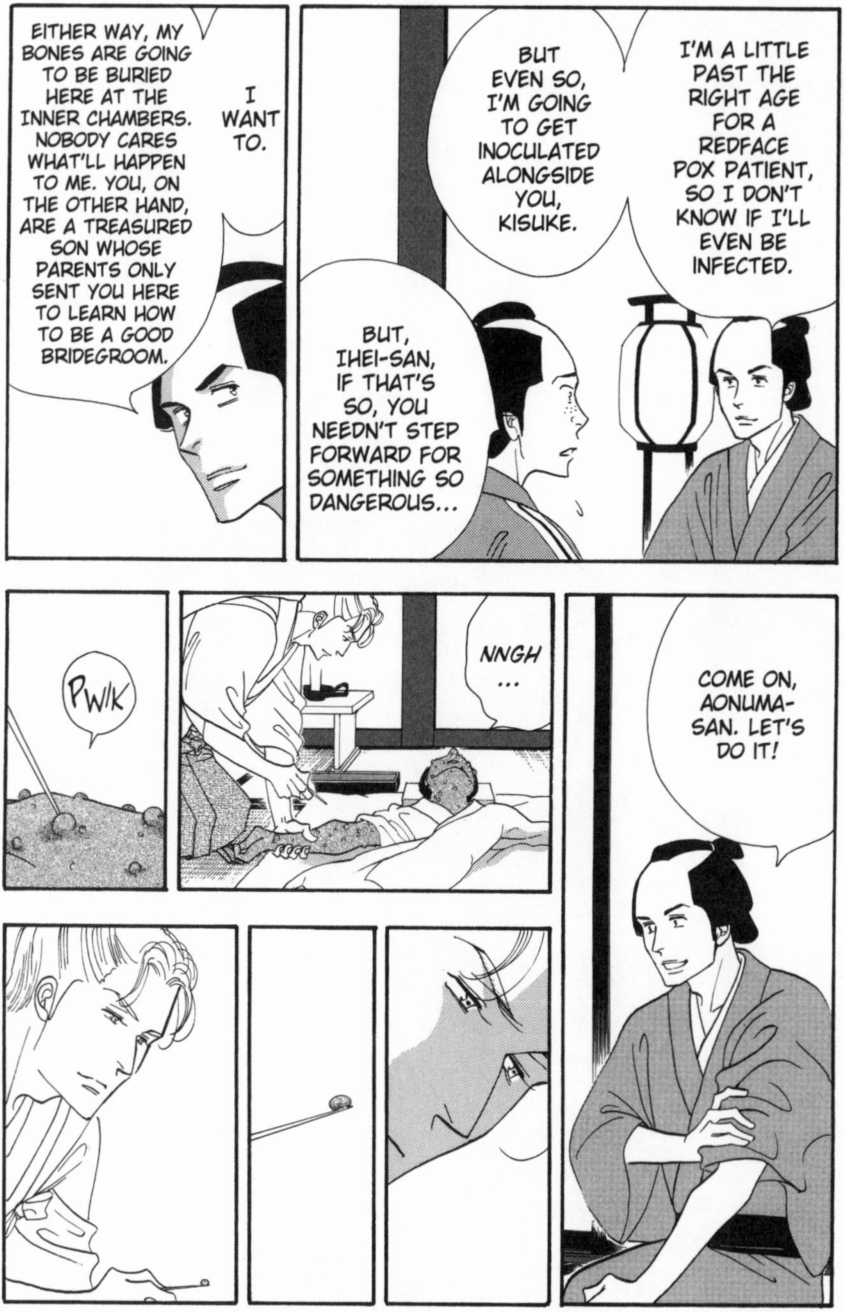
I'M A LITTLE PAST THE RIGHT AGE FOR A REDFACE POX PATIENT, SO I DON'T KNOW IF I'LL EVEN BE INFECTED.
BUT EVEN SO, I'M GOING TO GET INOCULATED ALONGSIDE YOU, KISUKE.
BUT, IHEI-SAN, IF THAT'S SO, YOU NEEDN'T STEP FORWARD FOR SOMETHING SO DANGEROUS...
I WANT TO.
EITHER WAY, MY BONES ARE GOING TO BE BURIED HERE AT THE INNER CHAMBERS. NOBODY CARES WHAT'LL HAPPEN TO ME. YOU, ON THE OTHER HAND, ARE A TREASURED SON WHOSE PARENTS ONLY SENT YOU HERE TO LEARN HOW TO BE A GOOD BRIDEGROOM.
COME ON, AONUMA-SAN. LET'S DO IT!
NNGH ...
PWIK

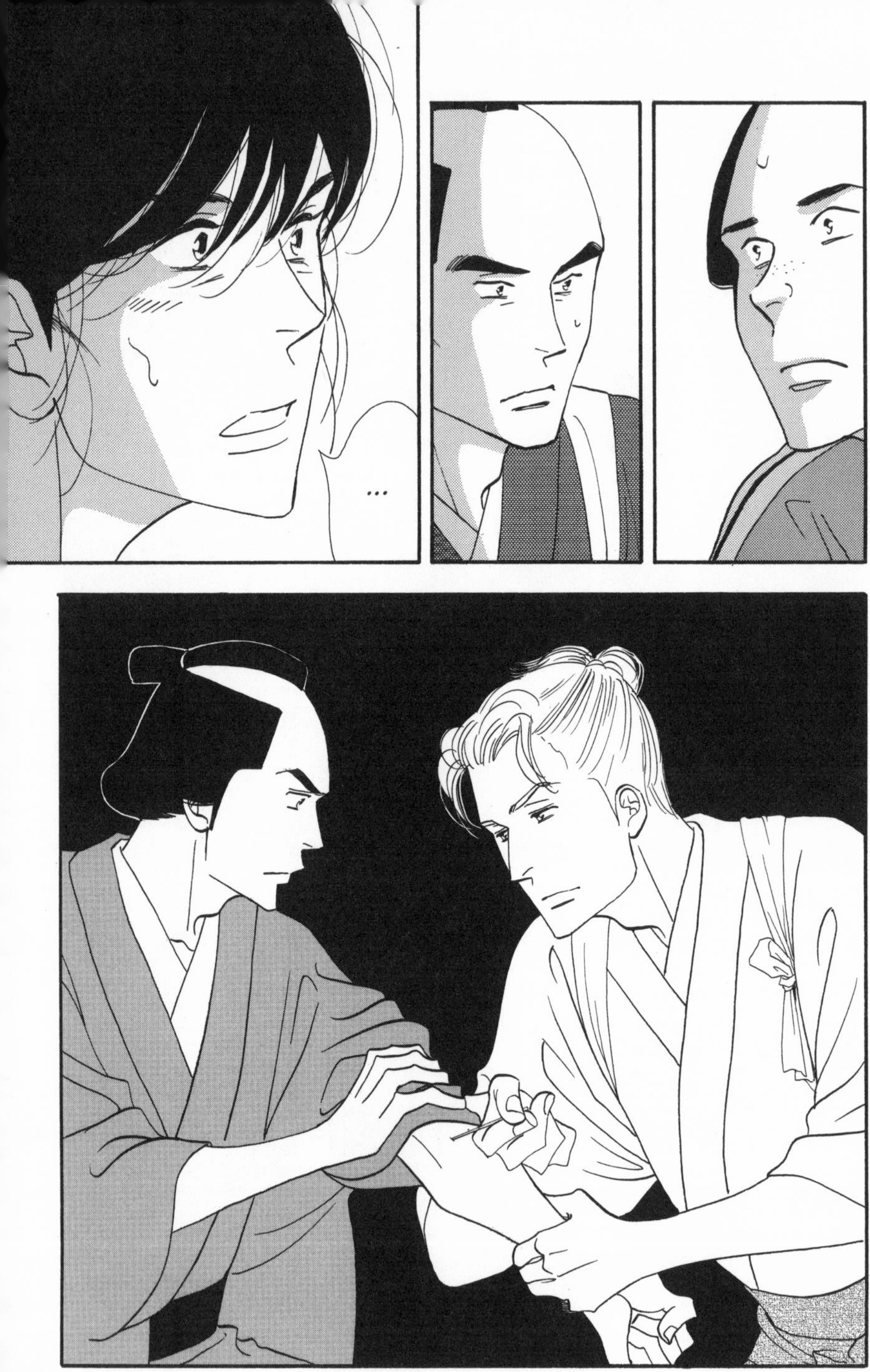
...

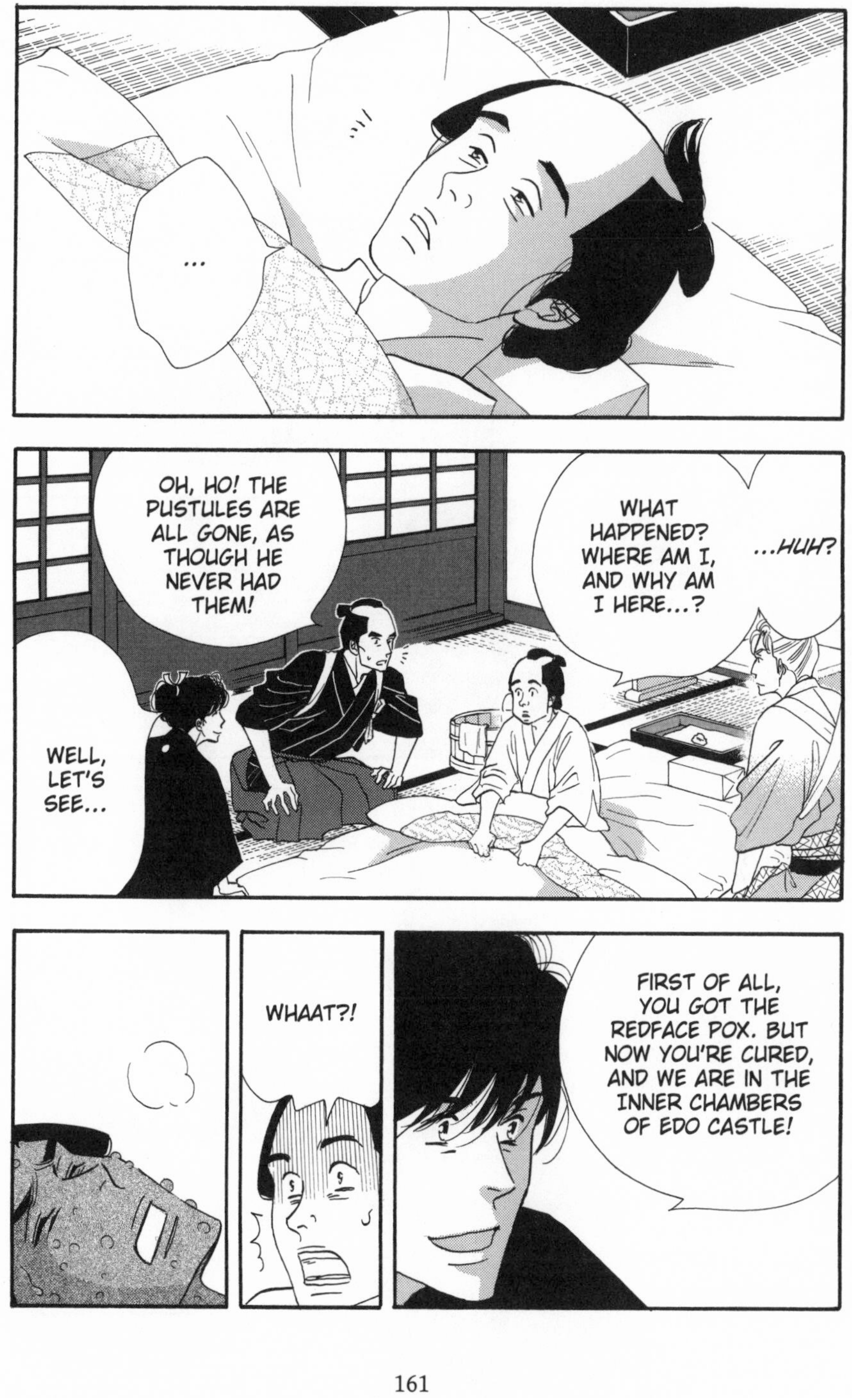
...
...HUH?
WHAT HAPPENED? WHERE AM I, AND WHY AM I HERE...?
OH, HO! THE PUSTULES ARE ALL GONE, AS THOUGH HE NEVER HAD THEM!
WELL, LET'S SEE...
FIRST OF ALL, YOU GOT THE REDFACE POX. BUT NOW YOU'RE CURED, AND WE ARE IN THE INNER CHAMBERS OF EDO CASTLE!
WHAAT?!

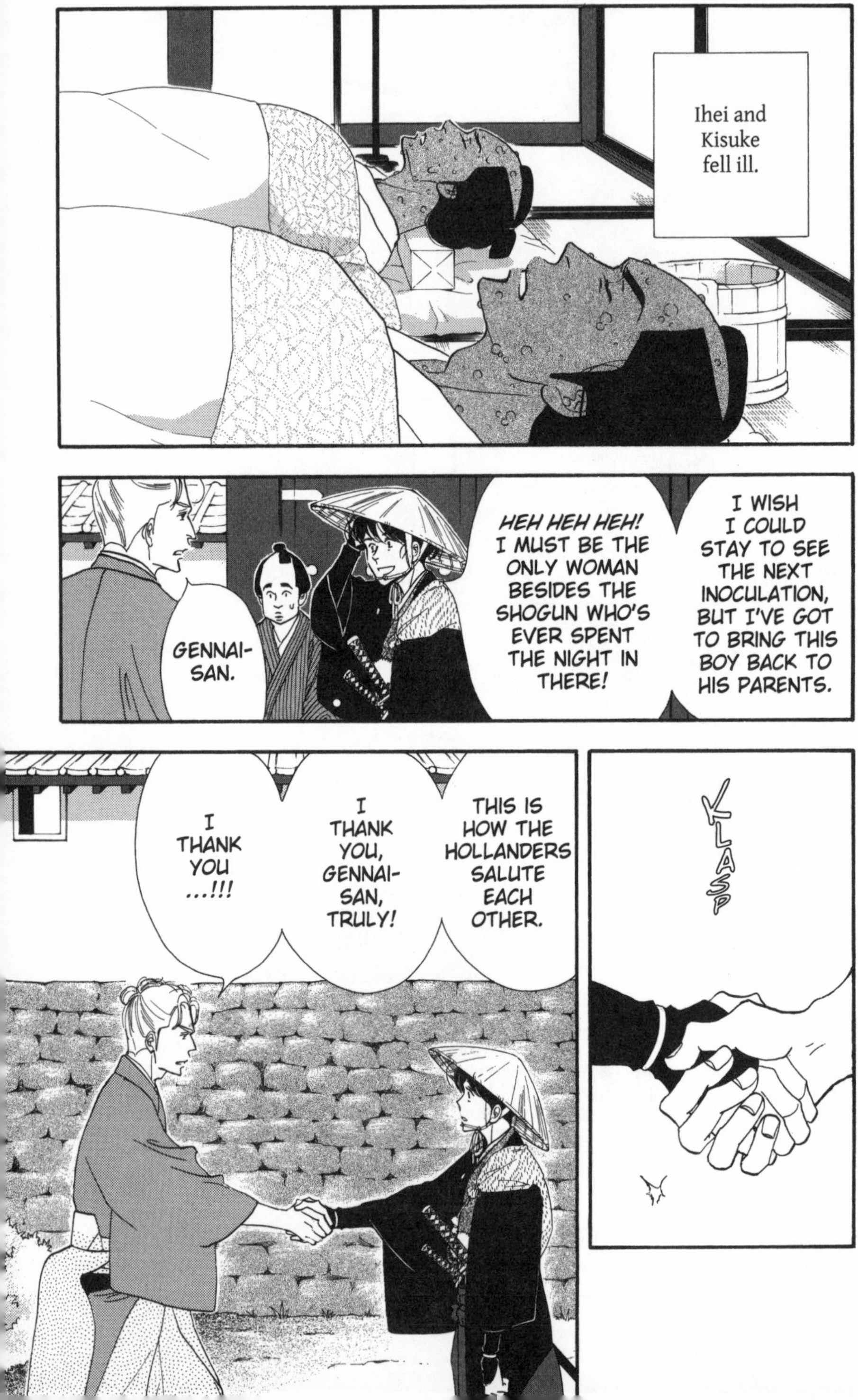
Ihei and Kisuke fell ill.
I WISH I COULD STAY TO SEE THE NEXT INOCULATION, BUT I'VE GOT TO BRING THIS BOY BACK TO HIS PARENTS.
HEH HEH HEH! I MUST BE THE ONLY WOMAN BESIDES THE SHOGUN WHO'S EVER SPENT THE NIGHT IN THERE!
GENNAI-SAN.
KLASP
THIS IS HOW THE HOLLANDERS SALUTE EACH OTHER.
I THANK YOU, GENNAI-SAN, TRULY!
I THANK YOU ...!!!

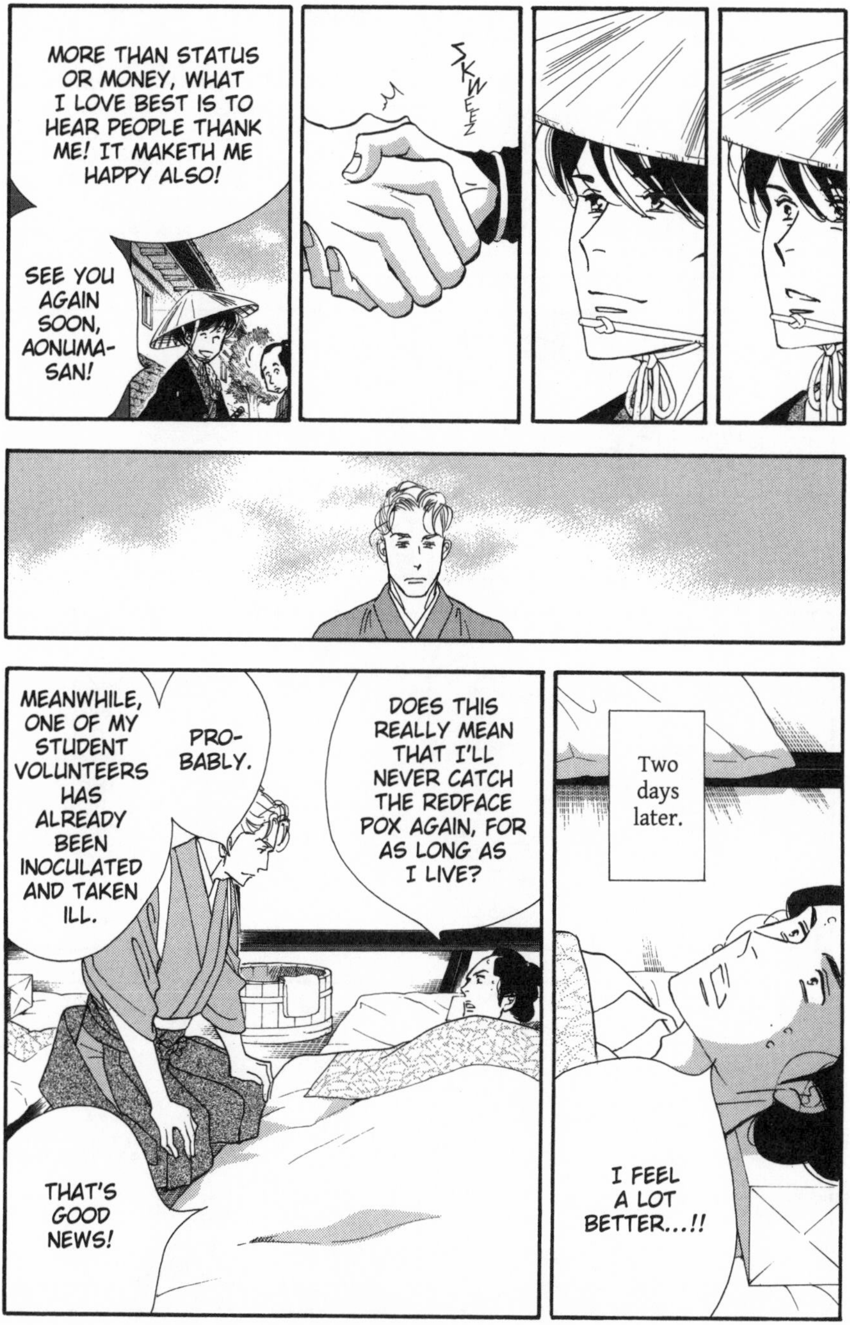
SKWEEZ
MORE THAN STATUS OR MONEY, WHAT I LOVE BEST IS TO HEAR PEOPLE THANK ME! IT MAKETH ME HAPPY ALSO!
SEE YOU AGAIN SOON, AONUMA-SAN!
Two days later.
I FEEL A LOT BETTER...!!
DOES THIS REALLY MEAN THAT I'LL NEVER CATCH THE REDFACE POX AGAIN, FOR AS LONG AS I LIVE?
PRO-BABLY.
MEANWHILE, ONE OF MY STUDENT VOLUNTEERS HAS ALREADY BEEN INOCULATED AND TAKEN ILL.
THAT'S GOOD NEWS!

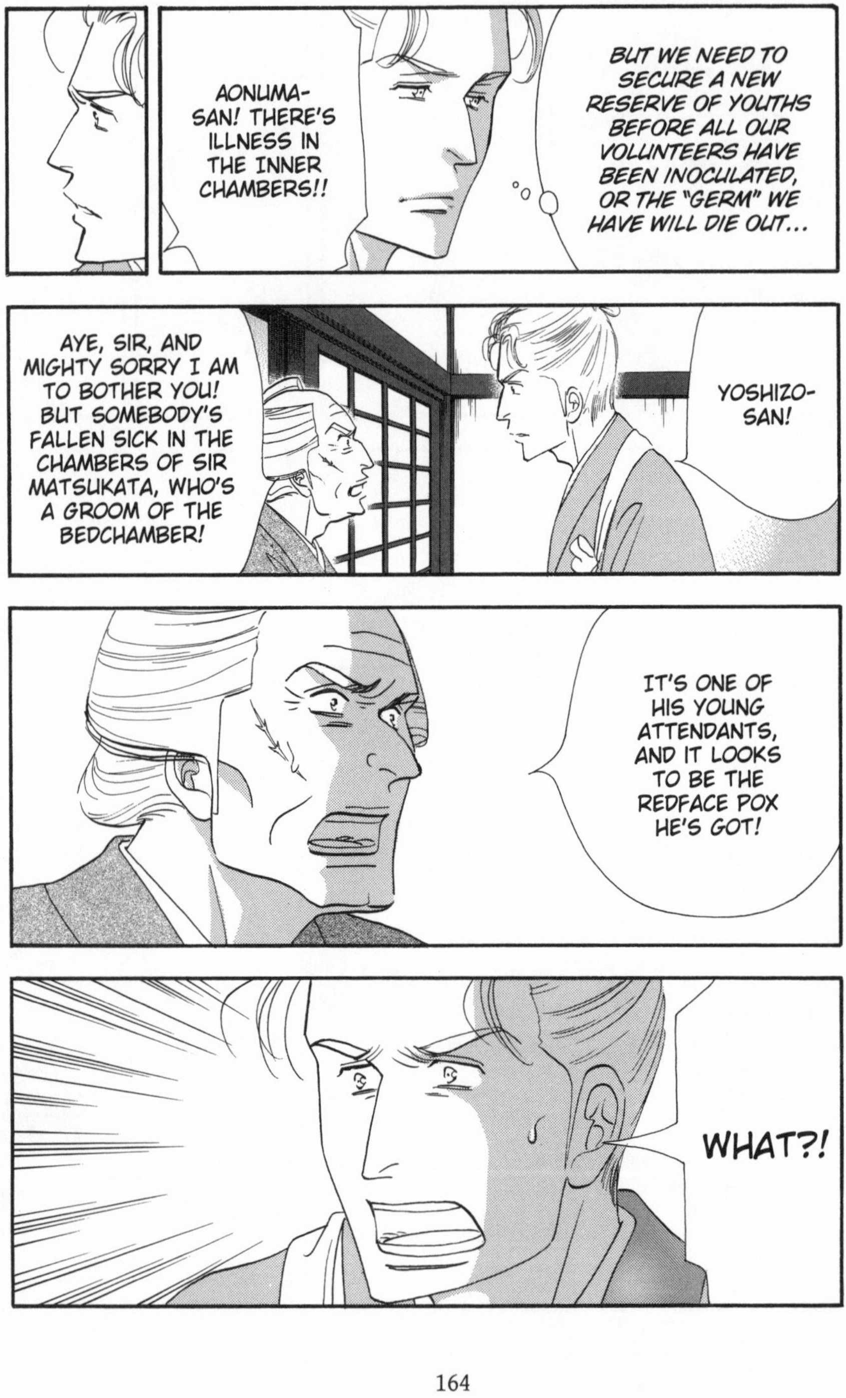
BUT WE NEED TO SECURE A NEW RESERVE OF YOUTHS BEFORE ALL OUR VOLUNTEERS HAVE BEEN INOCULATED, OR THE "GERM" WE HAVE WILL DIE OUT...
AONUMA-SAN! THERE'S ILLNESS IN THE INNER CHAMBERS!!
YOSHIZO-SAN!
AYE, SIR, AND MIGHTY SORRY I AM TO BOTHER YOU! BUT SOMEBODY'S FALLEN SICK IN THE CHAMBERS OF SIR MATSUKATA, WHO'S A GROOM OF THE BEDCHAMBER!
IT'S ONE OF HIS YOUNG ATTENDANTS, AND IT LOOKS TO BE THE REDFACE POX HE'S GOT!
WHAT?!

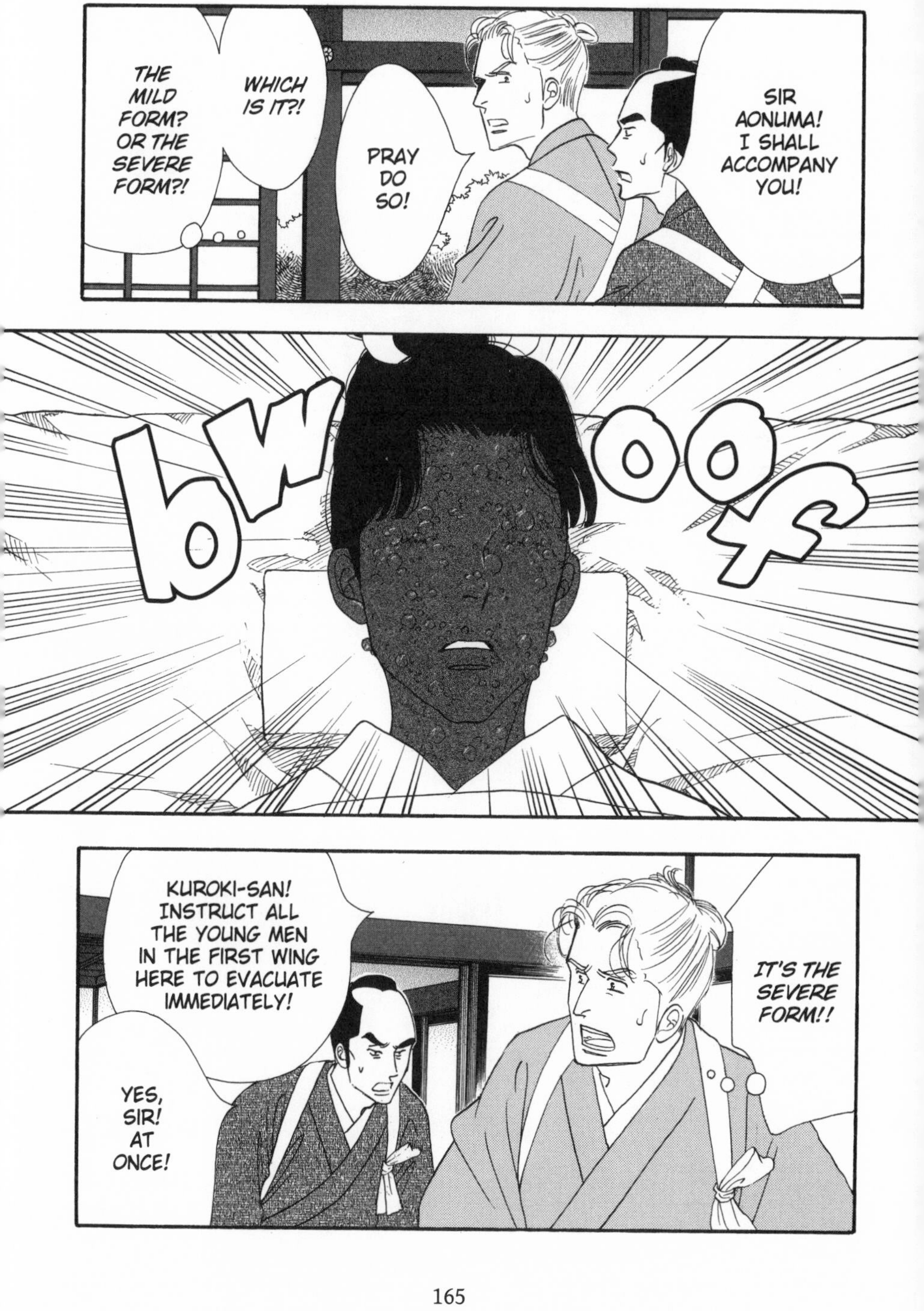
SIR AONUMA! I SHALL ACCOMPANY YOU!
PRAY DO SO!
WHICH IS IT?!
THE MILD FORM? OR THE SEVERE FORM?!
bwoof
IT'S THE SEVERE FORM!!
KUROKI-SAN! INSTRUCT ALL THE YOUNG MEN IN THE FIRST WING HERE TO EVACUATE IMMEDIATELY!
YES, SIR! AT ONCE!

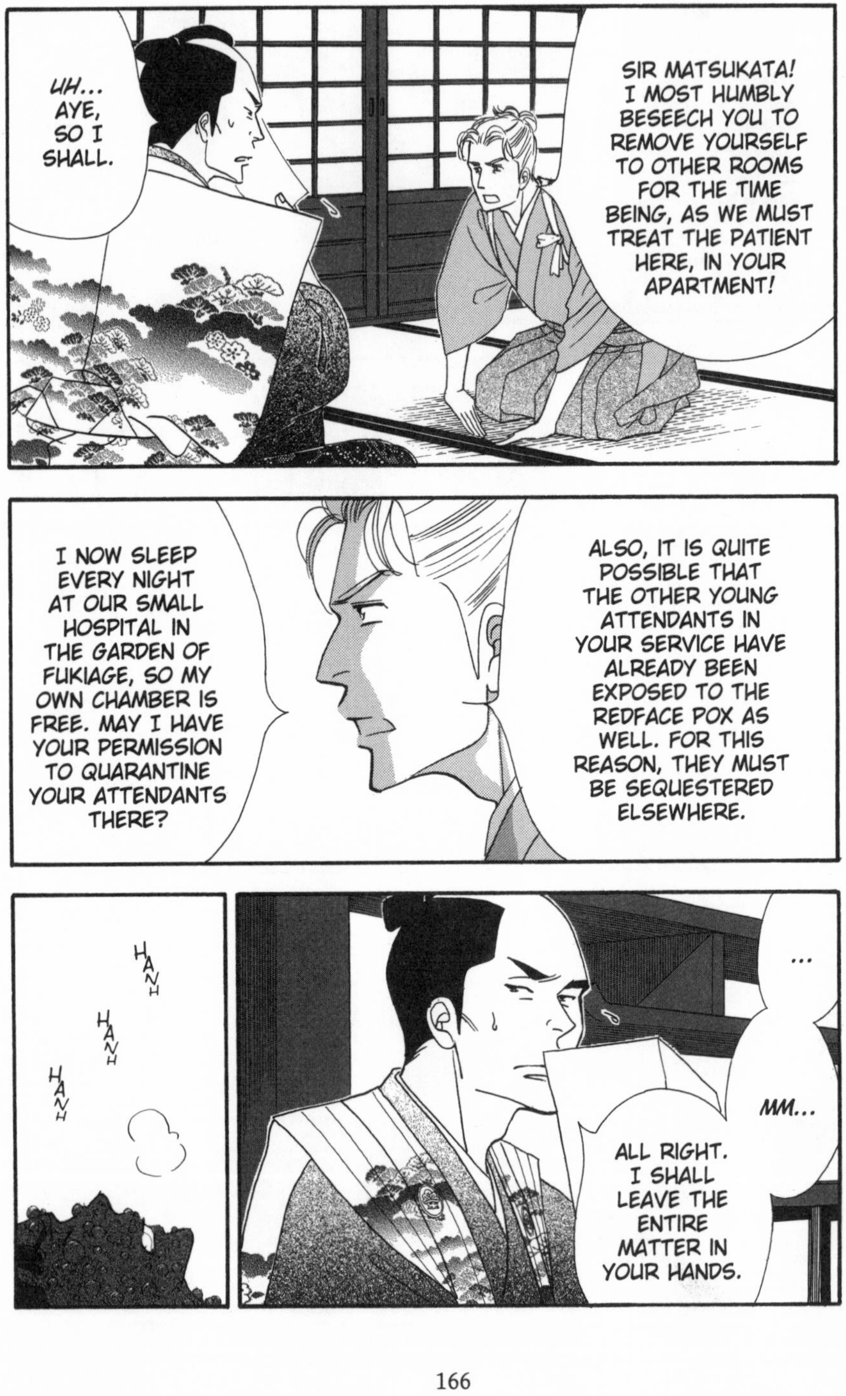
SIR MATSUKATA! I MOST HUMBLY BESEECH YOU TO REMOVE YOURSELF TO OTHER ROOMS FOR THE TIME BEING, AS WE MUST TREAT THE PATIENT HERE, IN YOUR APARTMENT!
UH... AYE, SO I SHALL.
ALSO, IT IS QUITE POSSIBLE THAT THE OTHER YOUNG ATTENDANTS IN YOUR SERVICE HAVE ALREADY BEEN EXPOSED TO THE REDFACE POX AS WELL. FOR THIS REASON, THEY MUST BE SEQUESTERED ELSEWHERE.
I NOW SLEEP EVERY NIGHT AT OUR SMALL HOSPITAL IN THE GARDEN OF FUKIAGE, SO MY OWN CHAMBER IS FREE. MAY I HAVE YOUR PERMISSION TO QUARANTINE YOUR ATTENDANTS THERE?
...
MM...
ALL RIGHT. I SHALL LEAVE THE ENTIRE MATTER IN YOUR HANDS.
HANH
HANH
HANH

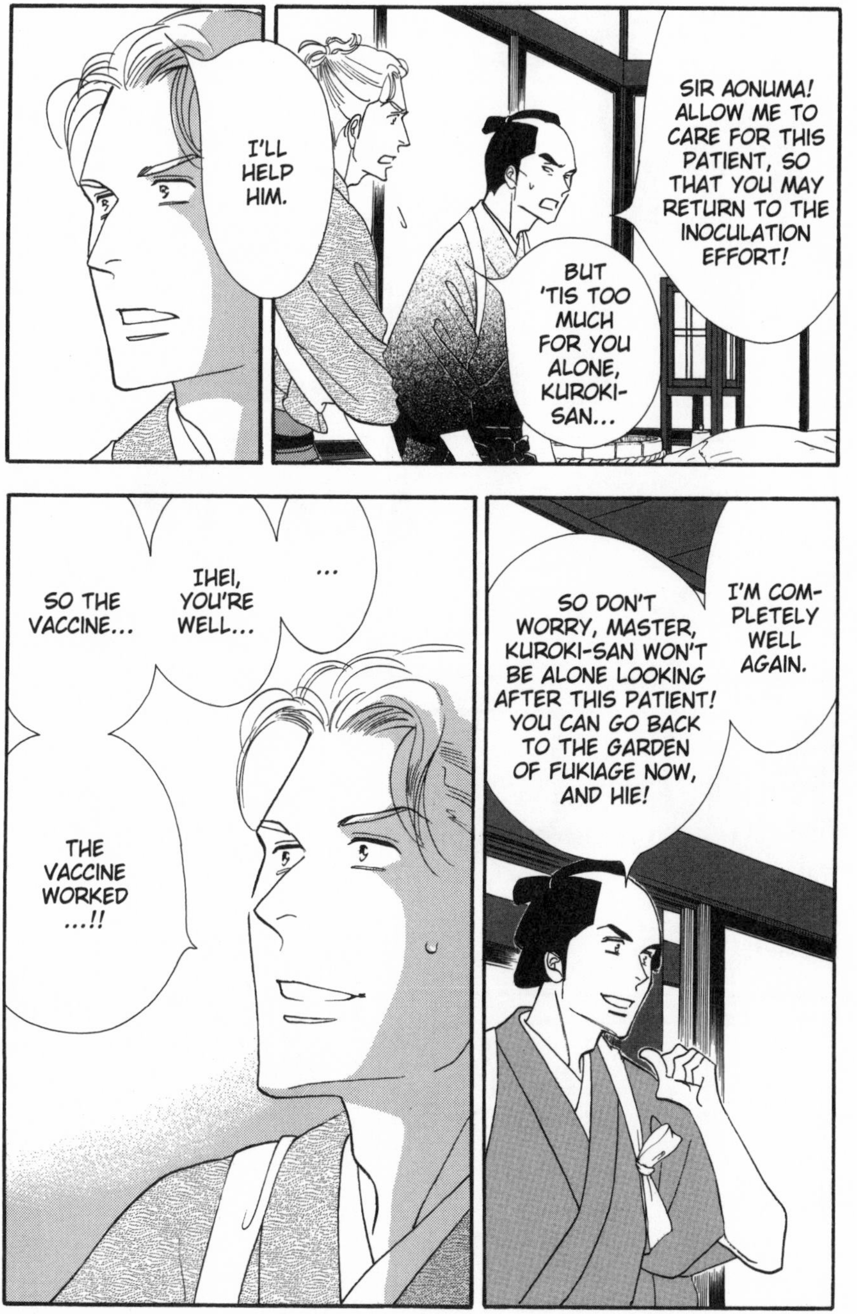
SIR AONUMA! ALLOW ME TO CARE FOR THIS PATIENT, SO THAT YOU MAY RETURN TO THE INOCULATION EFFORT!
BUT 'TIS TOO MUCH FOR YOU ALONE, KUROKI-SAN...
I'LL HELP HIM.
I'M COM-PLETELY WELL AGAIN.
SO DON'T WORRY, MASTER, KUROKI-SAN WON'T BE ALONE LOOKING AFTER THIS PATIENT! YOU CAN GO BACK TO THE GARDEN OF FUKIAGE NOW, AND HIE!
...
IHEI, YOU'RE WELL...
SO THE VACCINE...
THE VACCINE WORKED ...!!

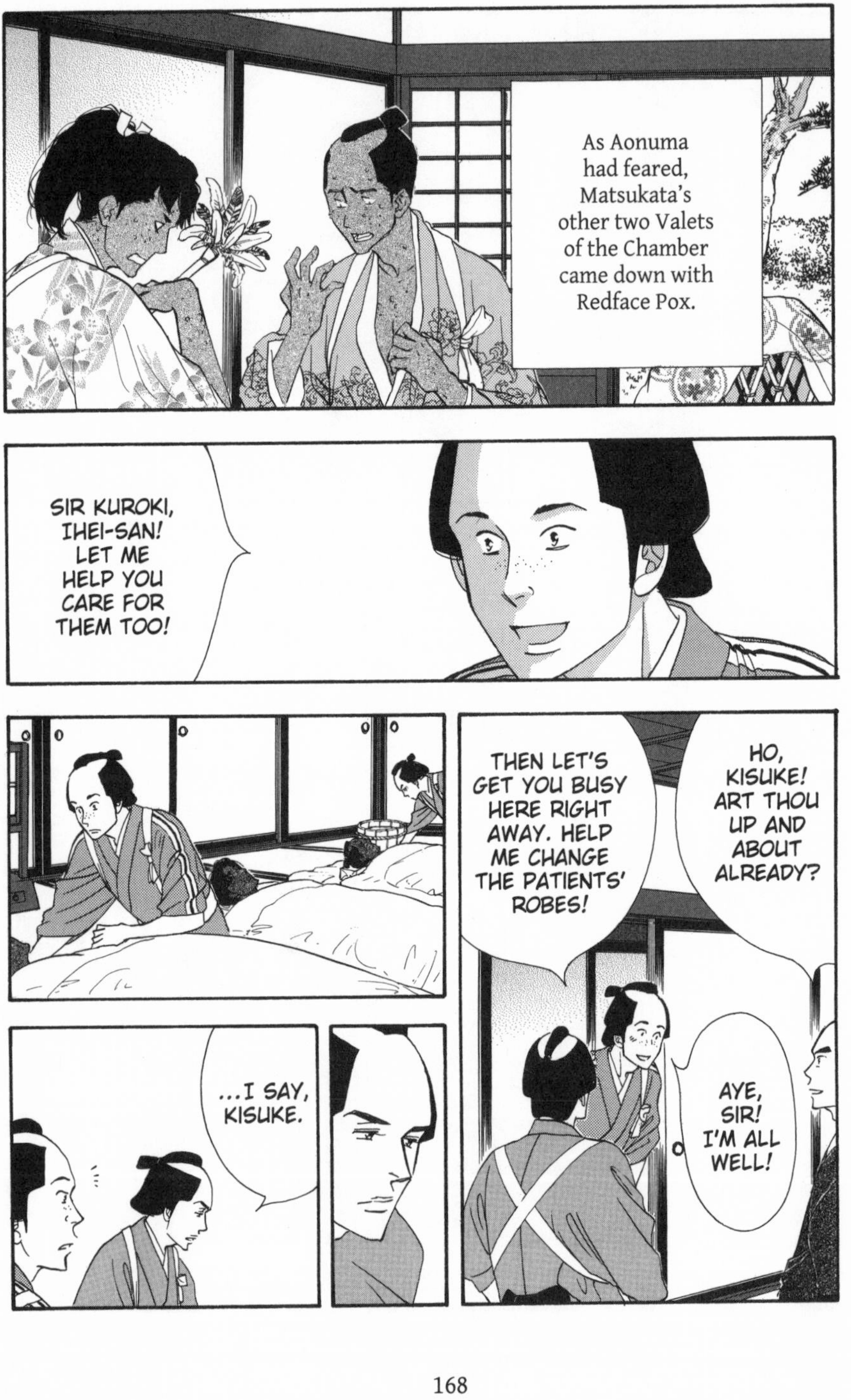
As Aonuma had feared, Matsukata's other two Valets of the Chamber came down with Redface Pox.
SIR KUROKI, IHEI-SAN! LET ME HELP YOU CARE FOR THEM TOO!
HO, KISUKE! ART THOU UP AND ABOUT ALREADY?
AYE, SIR! I'M ALL WELL!
THEN LET'S GET YOU BUSY HERE RIGHT AWAY. HELP ME CHANGE THE PATIENTS' ROBES!
...I SAY, KISUKE.

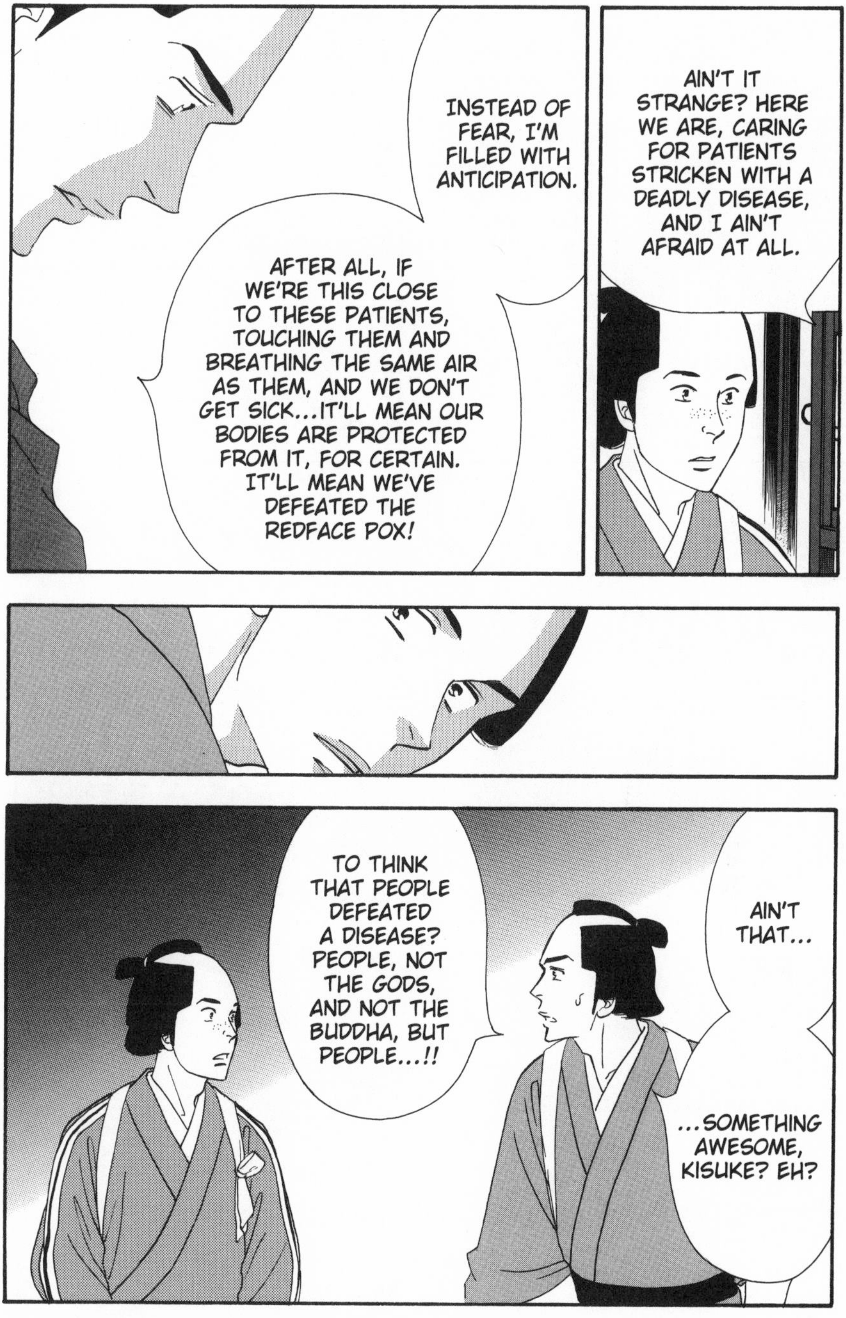
AIN'T IT STRANGE? HERE WE ARE, CARING FOR PATIENTS STRICKEN WITH A DEADLY DISEASE, AND I AIN'T AFRAID AT ALL.
INSTEAD OF FEAR, I'M FILLED WITH ANTICIPATION.
AFTER ALL, IF WE'RE THIS CLOSE TO THESE PATIENTS, TOUCHING THEM AND BREATHING THE SAME AIR AS THEM, AND WE DON'T GET SICK...IT'LL MEAN OUR BODIES ARE PROTECTED FROM IT, FOR CERTAIN. IT'LL MEAN WE'VE DEFEATED THE REDFACE POX!
TO THINK THAT PEOPLE DEFEATED A DISEASE? PEOPLE, NOT THE GODS, AND NOT THE BUDDHA, BUT PEOPLE...!!
AIN'T THAT...
...SOMETHING AWESOME, KISUKE? EH?

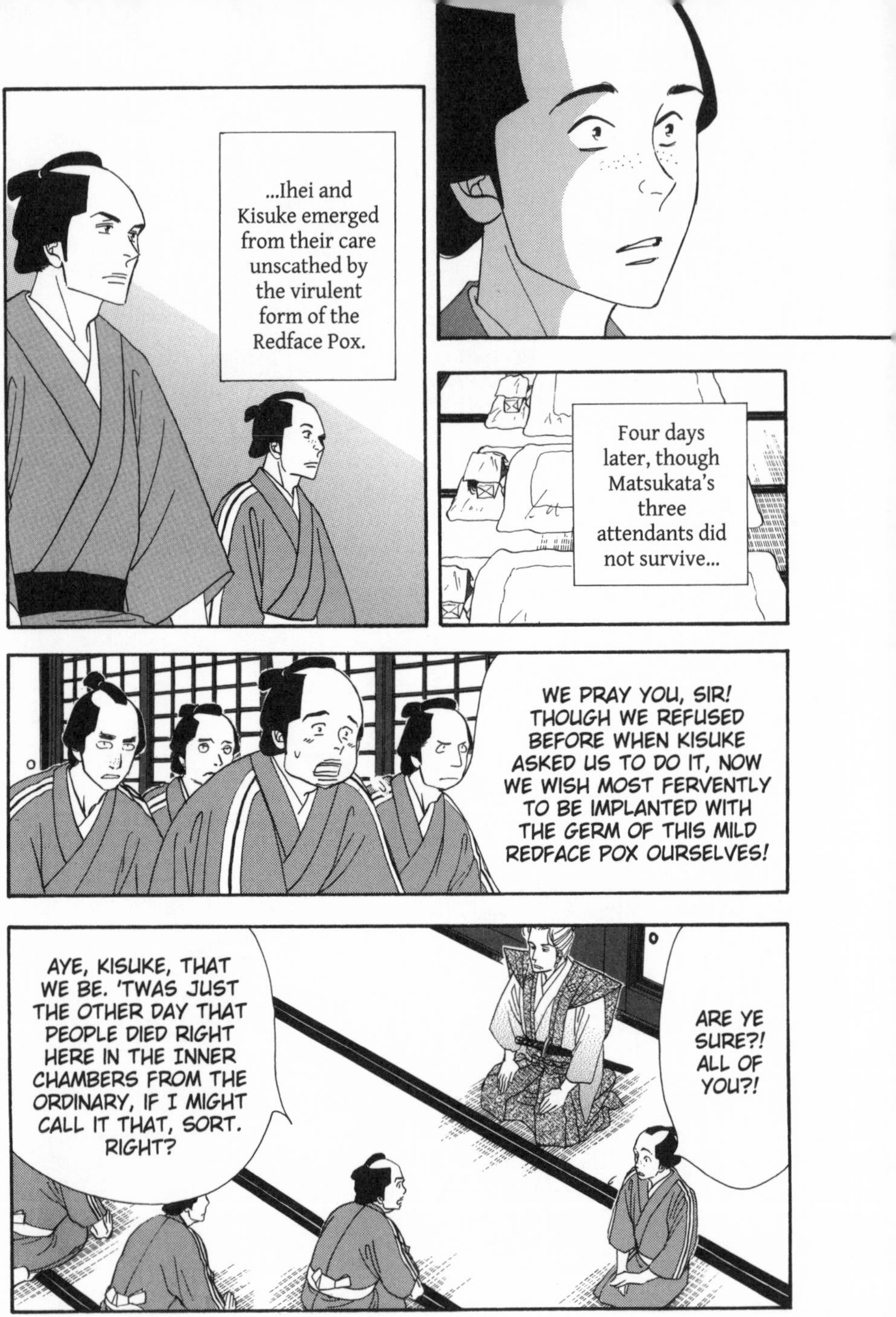
Four days later, though Matsukata's three attendants did not survive...
...Ihei and Kisuke emerged from their care unscathed by the virulent form of the Redface Pox.
WE PRAY YOU, SIR! THOUGH WE REFUSED BEFORE WHEN KISUKE ASKED US TO DO IT, NOW WE WISH MOST FERVENTLY TO BE IMPLANTED WITH THE GERM OF THIS MILD REDFACE POX OURSELVES!
ARE YE SURE?! ALL OF YOU?!
AYE, KISUKE, THAT WE BE. 'TWAS JUST THE OTHER DAY THAT PEOPLE DIED RIGHT HERE IN THE INNER CHAMBERS FROM THE ORDINARY, IF I MIGHT CALL IT THAT, SORT. RIGHT?

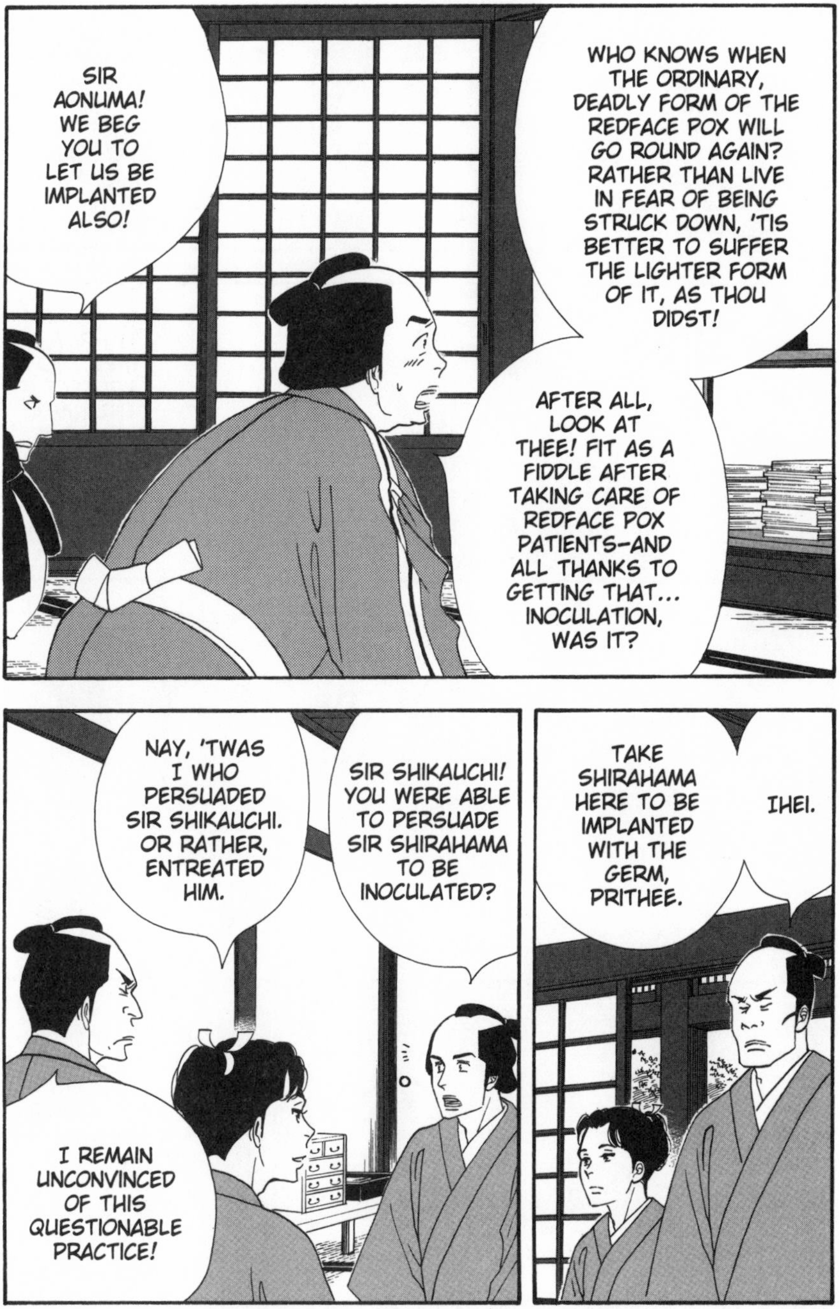
WHO KNOWS WHEN THE ORDINARY, DEADLY FORM OF THE REDFACE POX WILL GO ROUND AGAIN? RATHER THAN LIVE IN FEAR OF BEING STRUCK DOWN, 'TIS BETTER TO SUFFER THE LIGHTER FORM OF IT, AS THOU DIDST!
SIR AONUMA! WE BEG YOU TO LET US BE IMPLANTED ALSO!
AFTER ALL, LOOK AT THEE! FIT AS A FIDDLE AFTER TAKING CARE OF REDFACE POX PATIENTS—AND ALL THANKS TO GETTING THAT... INOCULATION, WAS IT?
IHEI.
TAKE SHIRAHAMA HERE TO BE IMPLANTED WITH THE GERM, PRITHEE.
SIR SHIKAUCHI! YOU WERE ABLE TO PERSUADE SIR SHIRAHAMA TO BE INOCULATED?
NAY, 'TWAS I WHO PERSUADED SIR SHIKAUCHI. OR RATHER, ENTREATED HIM.
I REMAIN UNCONVINCED OF THIS QUESTIONABLE PRACTICE!

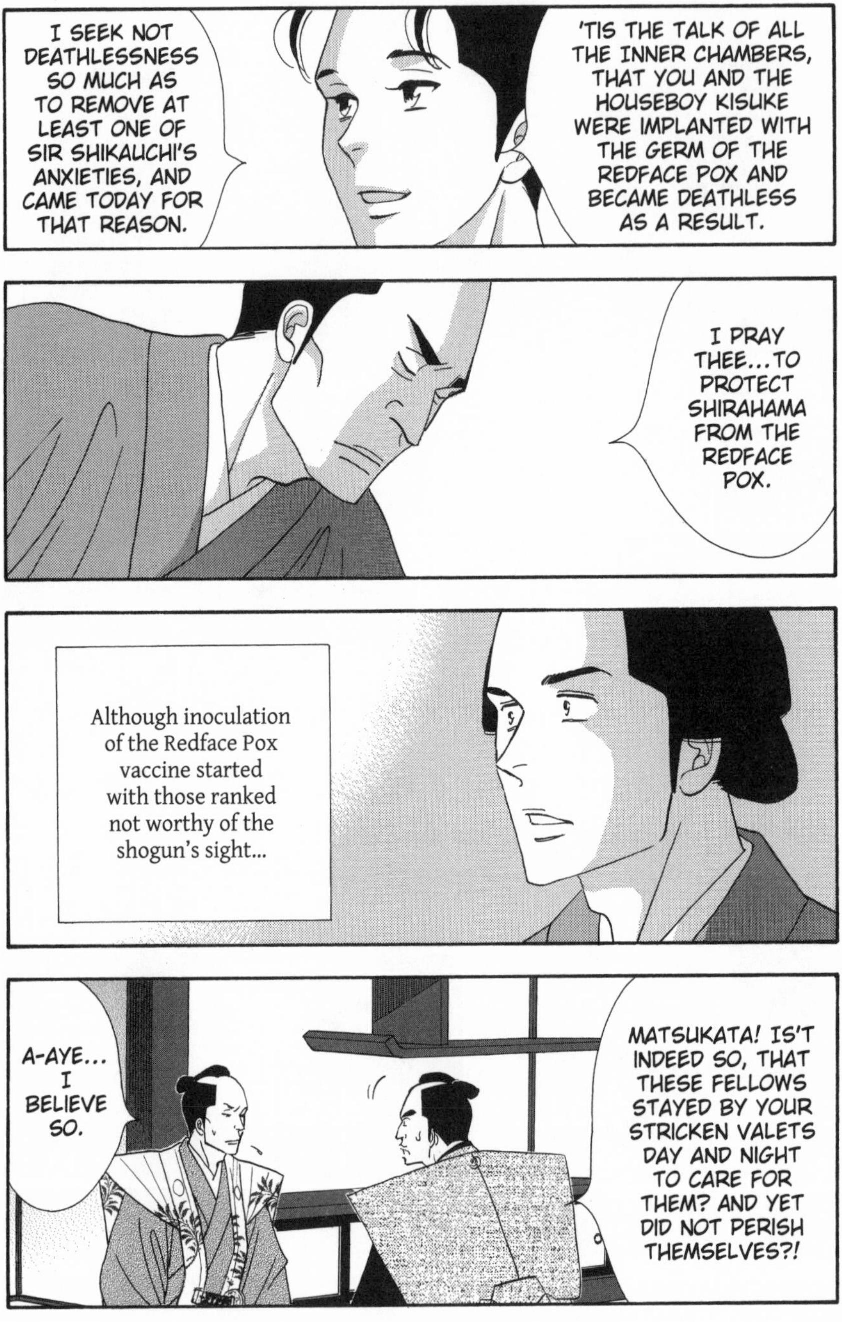
'TIS THE TALK OF ALL THE INNER CHAMBERS, THAT YOU AND THE HOUSEBOY KISUKE WERE IMPLANTED WITH THE GERM OF THE REDFACE POX AND BECAME DEATHLESS AS A RESULT.
I SEEK NOT DEATHLESSNESS SO MUCH AS TO REMOVE AT LEAST ONE OF SIR SHIKAUCHI'S ANXIETIES, AND CAME TODAY FOR THAT REASON.
I PRAY THEE...TO PROTECT SHIRAHAMA FROM THE REDFACE POX.
Although inoculation of the Redface Pox vaccine started with those ranked not worthy of the shogun's sight...
MATSUKATA! IS'T INDEED SO, THAT THESE FELLOWS STAYED BY YOUR STRICKEN VALETS DAY AND NIGHT TO CARE FOR THEM? AND YET DID NOT PERISH THEMSELVES?!
A-AYE... I BELIEVE SO.

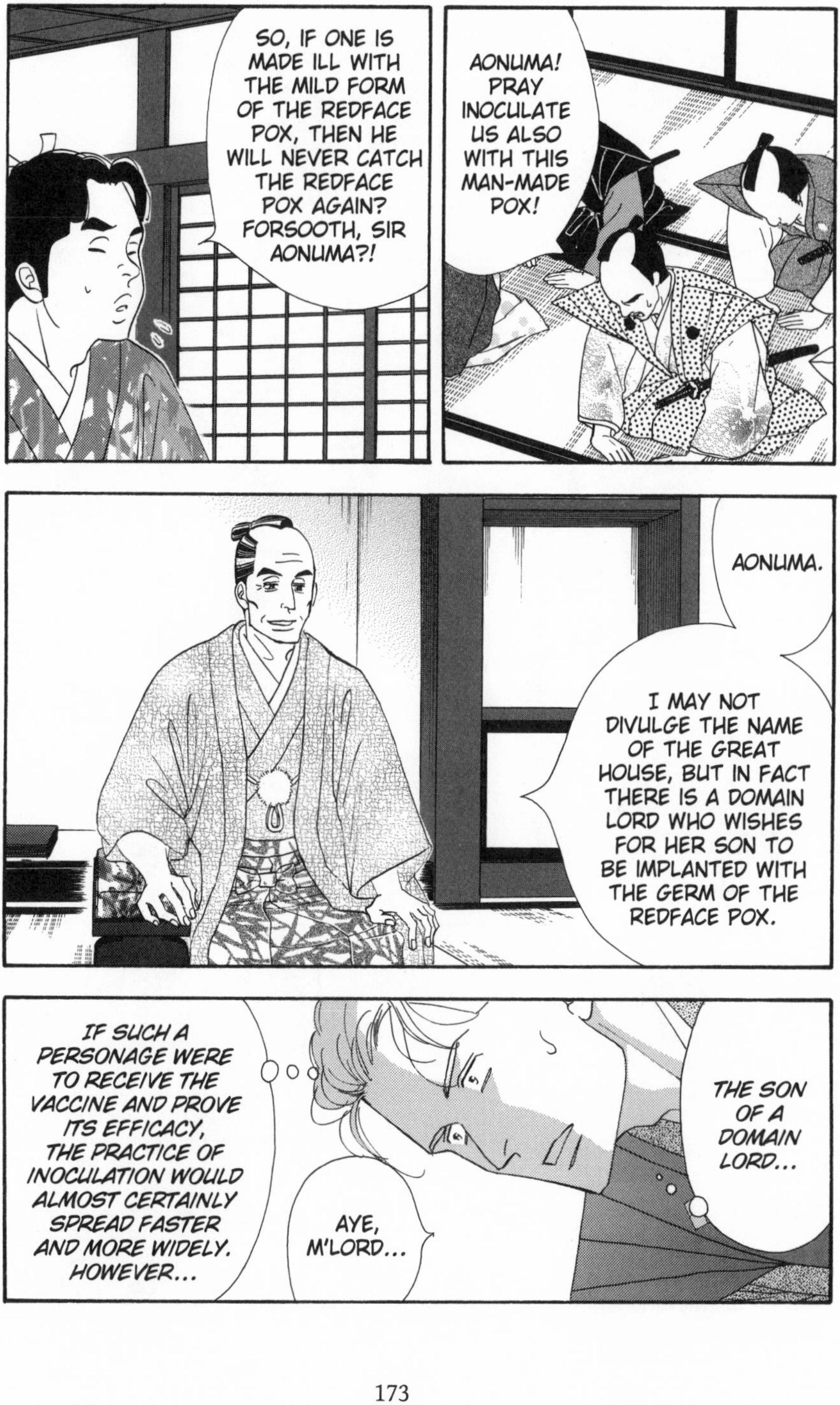
AONUMA! PRAY INOCULATE US ALSO WITH THIS MAN-MADE POX!
SO, IF ONE IS MADE ILL WITH THE MILD FORM OF THE REDFACE POX, THEN HE WILL NEVER CATCH THE REDFACE POX AGAIN? FORSOOTH, SIR AONUMA?!
AONUMA.
I MAY NOT DIVULGE THE NAME OF THE GREAT HOUSE, BUT IN FACT THERE IS A DOMAIN LORD WHO WISHES FOR HER SON TO BE IMPLANTED WITH THE GERM OF THE REDFACE POX.
THE SON OF A DOMAIN LORD...
IF SUCH A PERSONAGE WERE TO RECEIVE THE VACCINE AND PROVE ITS EFFICACY, THE PRACTICE OF INOCULATION WOULD ALMOST CERTAINLY SPREAD FASTER AND MORE WIDELY. HOWEVER...
AYE, M'LORD...

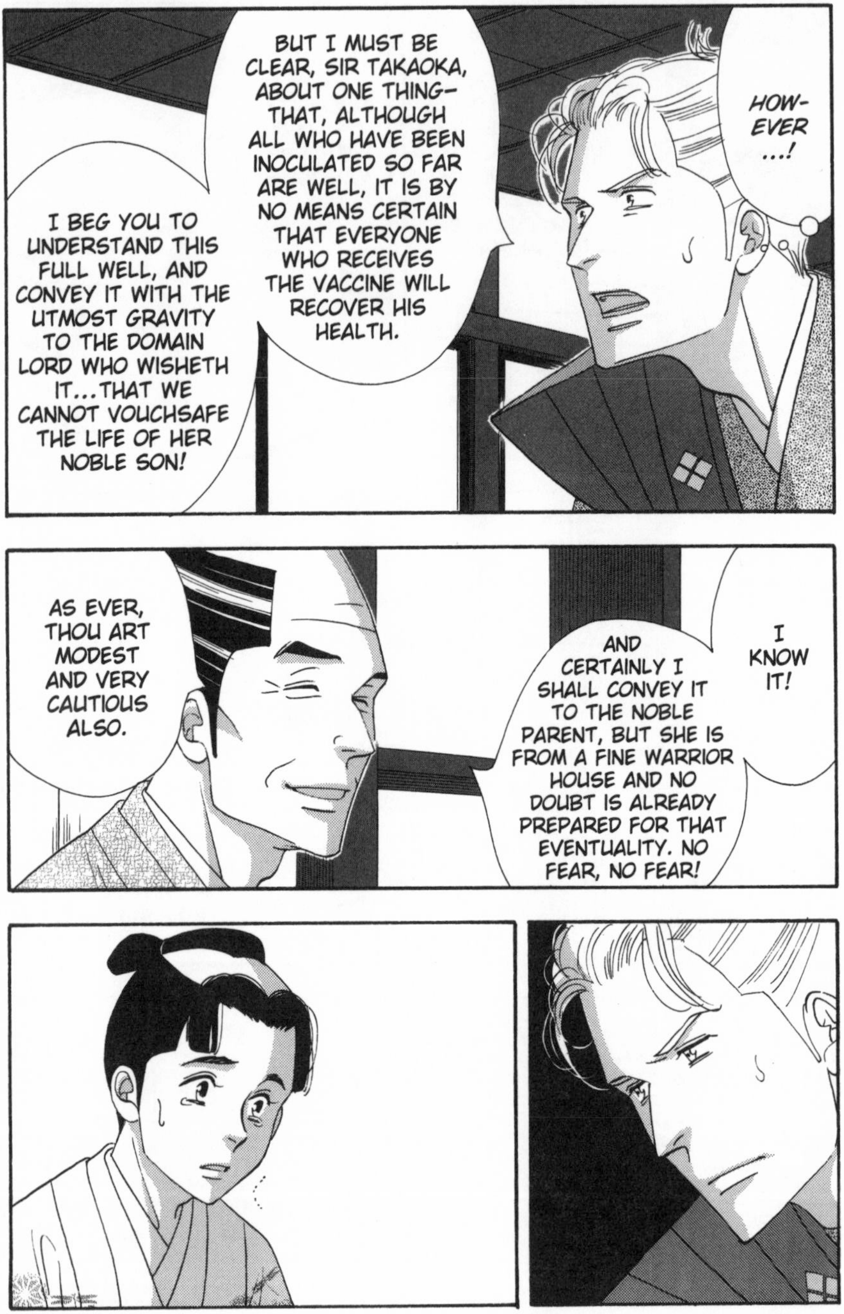
HOW-EVER...!
BUT I MUST BE CLEAR, SIR TAKAOKA, ABOUT ONE THING—THAT, ALTHOUGH ALL WHO HAVE BEEN INOCULATED SO FAR ARE WELL, IT IS BY NO MEANS CERTAIN THAT EVERYONE WHO RECEIVES THE VACCINE WILL RECOVER HIS HEALTH.
I BEG YOU TO UNDERSTAND THIS FULL WELL, AND CONVEY IT WITH THE UTMOST GRAVITY TO THE DOMAIN LORD WHO WISHETH IT...THAT WE CANNOT VOUCHSAFE THE LIFE OF HER NOBLE SON!
I KNOW IT!
AND CERTAINLY I SHALL CONVEY IT TO THE NOBLE PARENT, BUT SHE IS FROM A FINE WARRIOR HOUSE AND NO DOUBT IS ALREADY PREPARED FOR THAT EVENTUALITY. NO FEAR, NO FEAR!
AS EVER, THOU ART MODEST AND VERY CAUTIOUS ALSO.

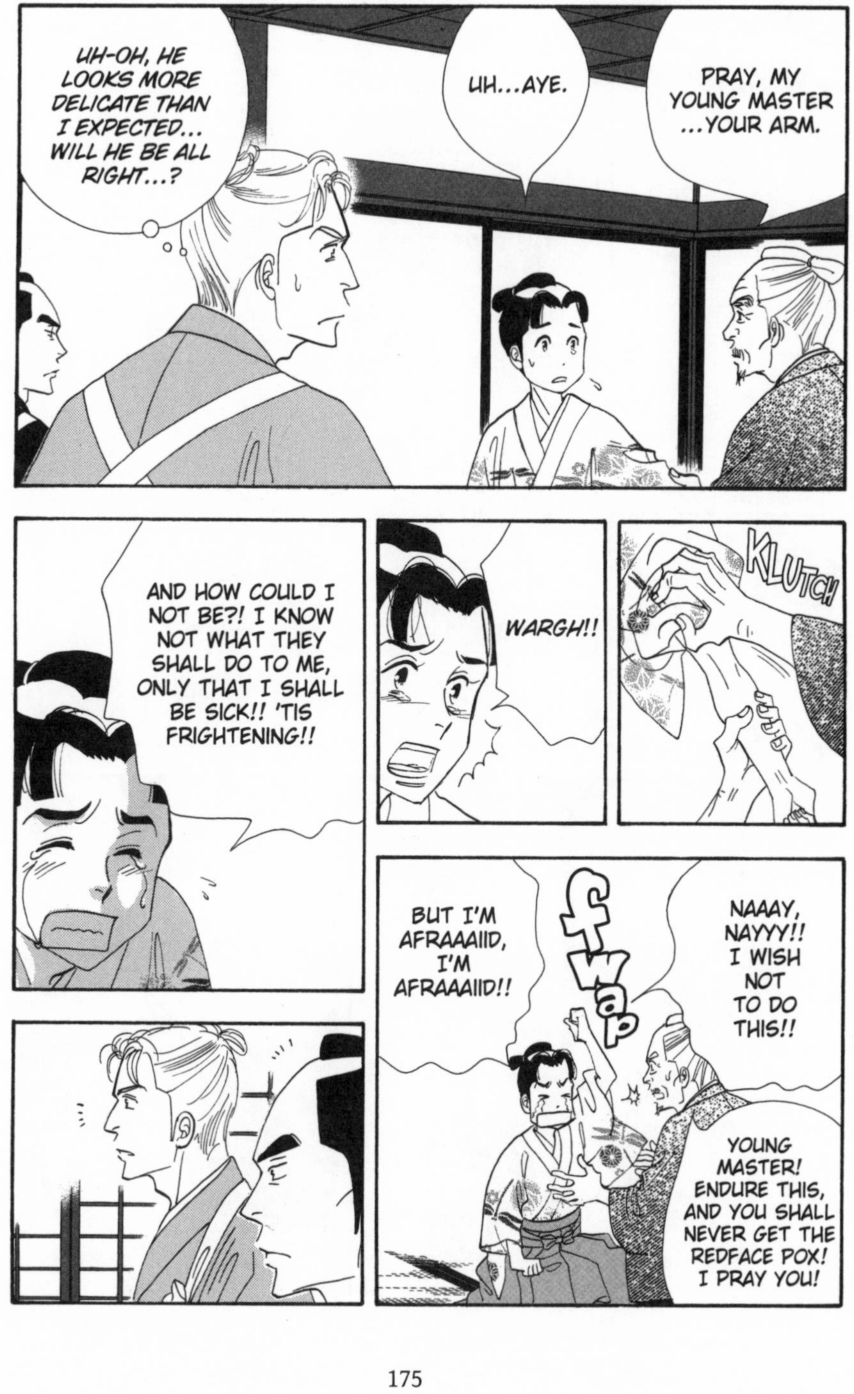
PRAY, MY YOUNG MASTER ...YOUR ARM.
UH...AYE.
UH-OH, HE LOOKS MORE DELICATE THAN I EXPECTED... WILL HE BE ALL RIGHT...?
KLUTCH
WARGH!!
AND HOW COULD I NOT BE?! I KNOW NOT WHAT THEY SHALL DO TO ME, ONLY THAT I SHALL BE SICK!! 'TIS FRIGHTENING!!
NAAAY, NAYYY!! I WISH NOT TO DO THIS!!
fwap
BUT I'M AFRAAAIID, I'M AFRAAAIID!!
YOUNG MASTER! ENDURE THIS, AND YOU SHALL NEVER GET THE REDFACE POX! I PRAY YOU!

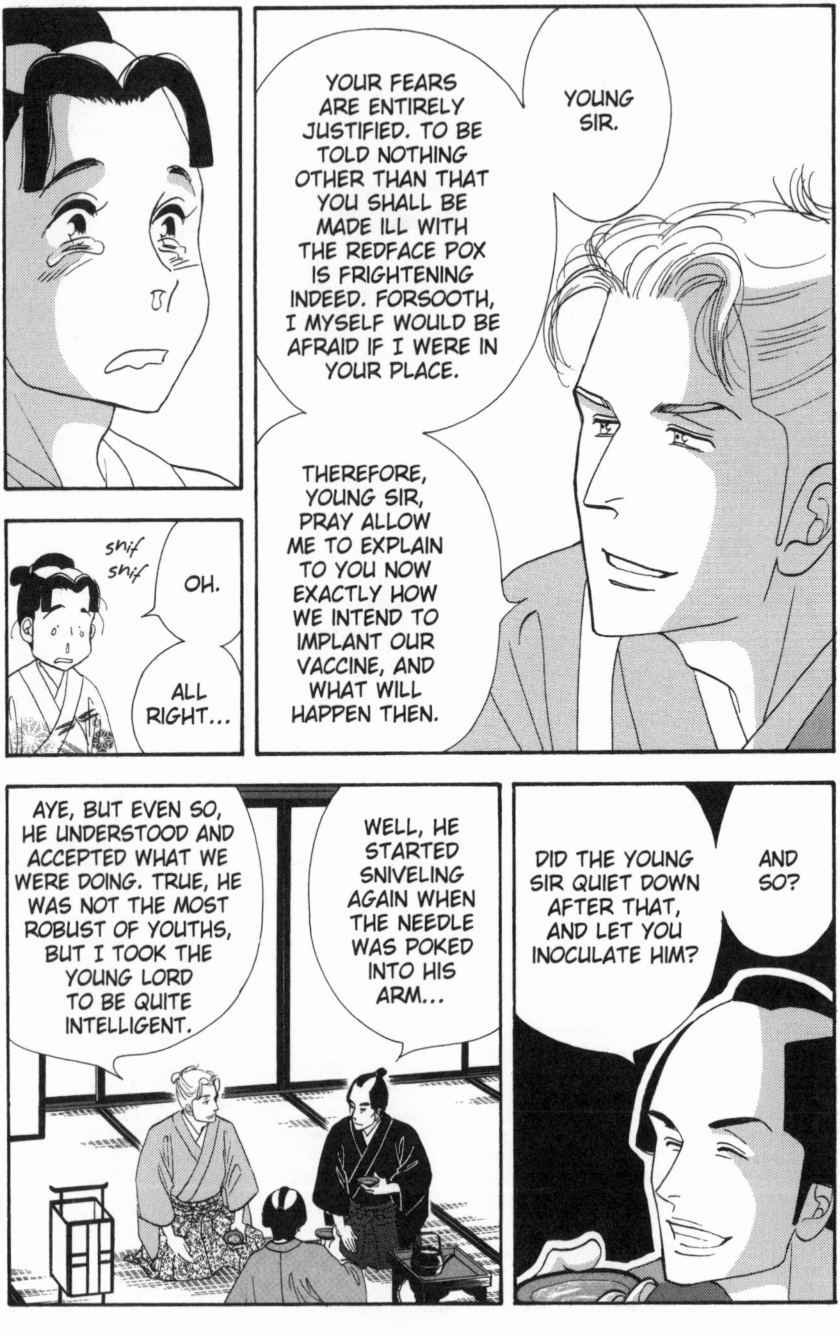
YOUNG SIR.
YOUR FEARS ARE ENTIRELY JUSTIFIED. TO BE TOLD NOTHING OTHER THAN THAT YOU SHALL BE MADE ILL WITH THE REDFACE POX IS FRIGHTENING INDEED. FORSOOTH, I MYSELF WOULD BE AFRAID IF I WERE IN YOUR PLACE.
THEREFORE, YOUNG SIR, PRAY ALLOW ME TO EXPLAIN TO YOU NOW EXACTLY HOW WE INTEND TO IMPLANT OUR VACCINE, AND WHAT WILL HAPPEN THEN.
snif snif
OH.
ALL RIGHT...
AND SO?
DID THE YOUNG SIR QUIET DOWN AFTER THAT, AND LET YOU INOCULATE HIM?
WELL, HE STARTED SNIVELING AGAIN WHEN THE NEEDLE WAS POKED INTO HIS ARM...
AYE, BUT EVEN SO, HE UNDERSTOOD AND ACCEPTED WHAT WE WERE DOING. TRUE, HE WAS NOT THE MOST ROBUST OF YOUTHS, BUT I TOOK THE YOUNG LORD TO BE QUITE INTELLIGENT.

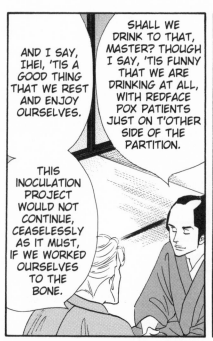

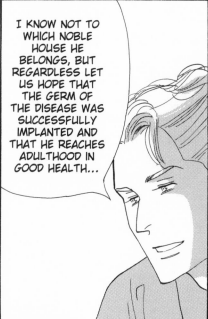

I KNOW NOT TO WHICH NOBLE HOUSE HE BELONGS, BUT REGARDLESS LET US HOPE THAT THE GERM OF THE DISEASE WAS SUCCESSFULLY IMPLANTED AND THAT HE REACHES ADULTHOOD IN GOOD HEALTH...
SHALL WE DRINK TO THAT, MASTER? THOUGH I SAY, 'TIS FUNNY THAT WE ARE DRINKING AT ALL, WITH REDFACE POX PATIENTS JUST ON T'OTHER SIDE OF THE PARTITION.
AND I SAY, IHEI, 'TIS A GOOD THING THAT WE REST AND ENJOY OURSELVES.
THIS INOCULATION PROJECT WOULD NOT CONTINUE, CEASELESSLY AS IT MUST, IF WE WORKED OURSELVES TO THE BONE.
WE ARE DOING JUST AS 'TWAS WRITTEN BY LADY MARY—WE ARE HAVING A "POX PARTY."
YOUNG SIR TAKE-CHIYO.
HOW DOTH THE YOUNG SIR FEEL TODAY?
...

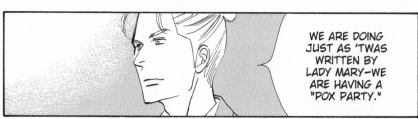

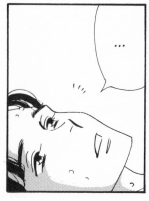

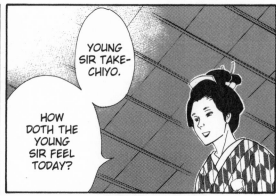

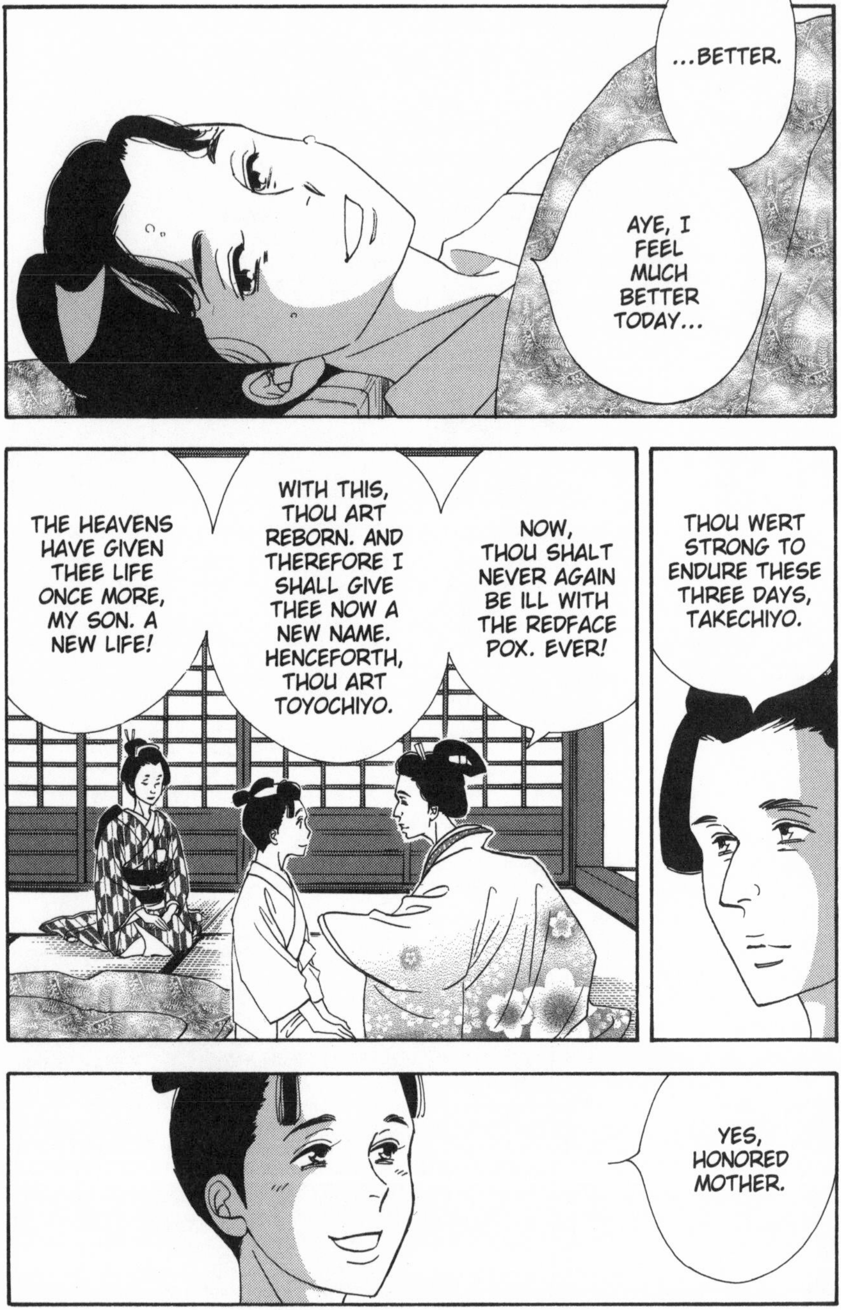
...BETTER.
AYE, I FEEL MUCH BETTER TODAY...
THOU WERT STRONG TO ENDURE THESE THREE DAYS, TAKECHIYO.
NOW, THOU SHALT NEVER AGAIN BE ILL WITH THE REDFACE POX. EVER!
WITH THIS, THOU ART REBORN. AND THEREFORE I SHALL GIVE THEE NOW A NEW NAME. HENCEFORTH, THOU ART TOYOCHIYO.
THE HEAVENS HAVE GIVEN THEE LIFE ONCE MORE, MY SON. A NEW LIFE!
YES, HONORED MOTHER.

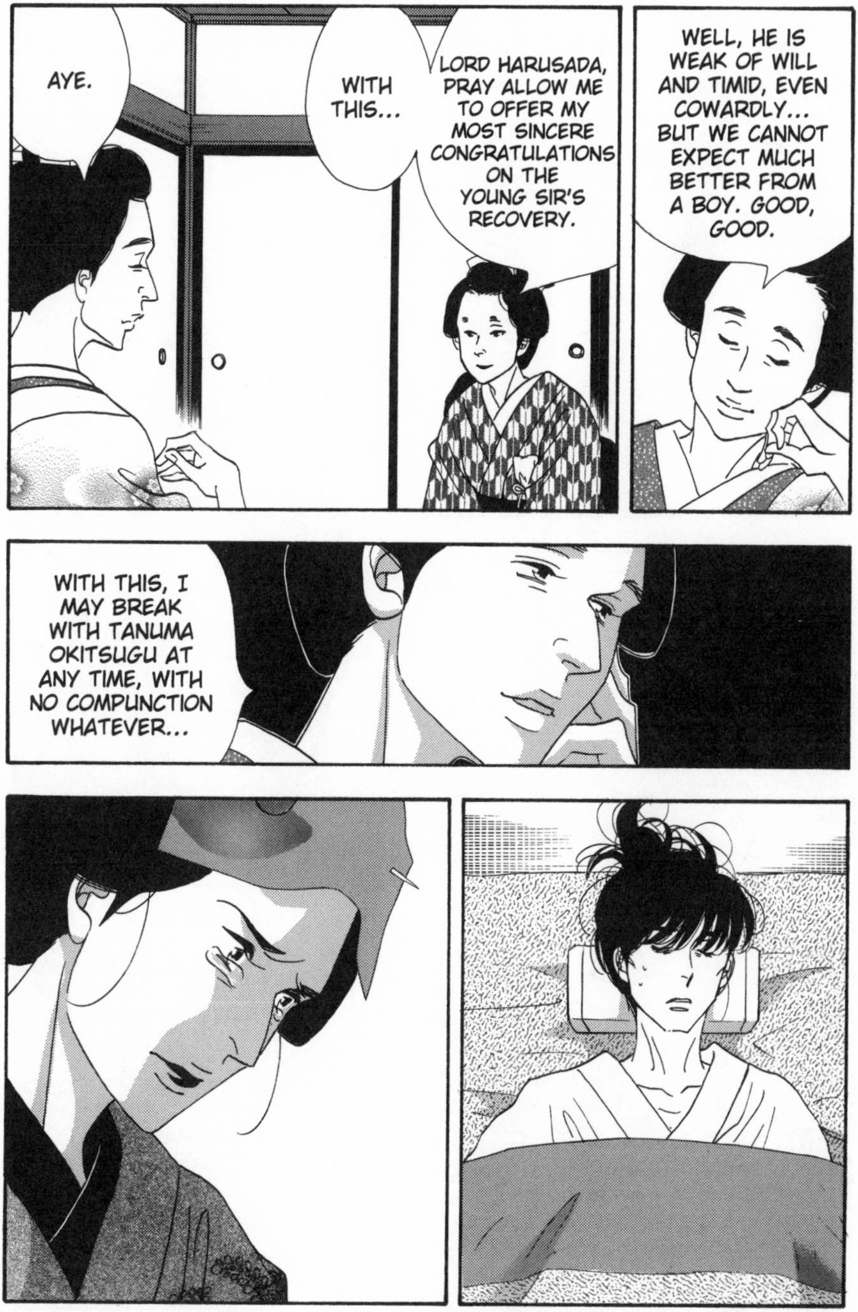
WELL, HE IS WEAK OF WILL AND TIMID, EVEN COWARDLY... BUT WE CANNOT EXPECT MUCH BETTER FROM A BOY. GOOD, GOOD.
LORD HARUSADA, PRAY ALLOW ME TO OFFER MY MOST SINCERE CONGRATULATIONS ON THE YOUNG SIR'S RECOVERY.
WITH THIS...
AYE.
WITH THIS, I MAY BREAK WITH TANUMA OKITSUGU AT ANY TIME, WITH NO COMPUNCTION WHATEVER...

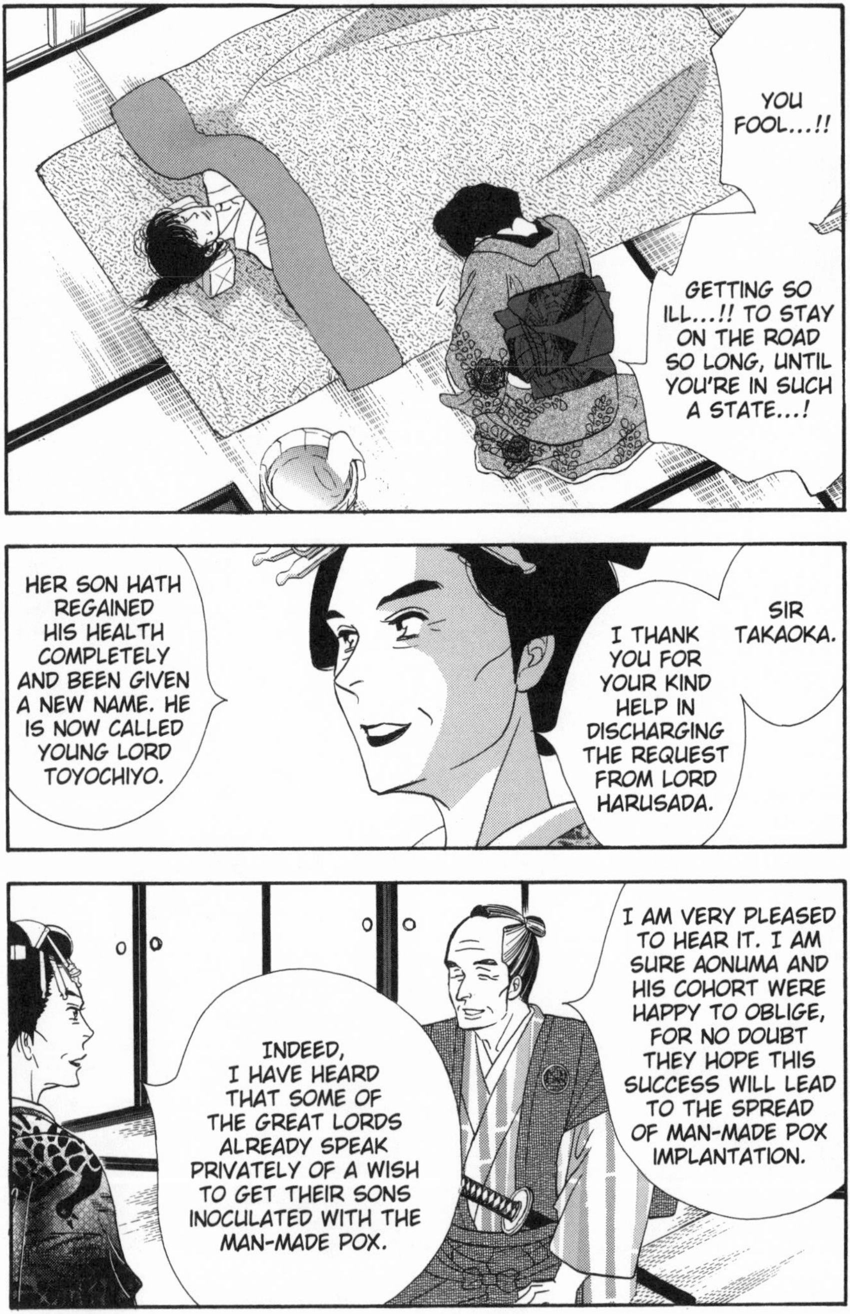
YOU FOOL...!!
GETTING SO ILL...!! TO STAY ON THE ROAD SO LONG, UNTIL YOU'RE IN SUCH A STATE...!
SIR TAKAOKA.
I THANK YOU FOR YOUR KIND HELP IN DISCHARGING THE REQUEST FROM LORD HARUSADA.
HER SON HATH REGAINED HIS HEALTH COMPLETELY AND BEEN GIVEN A NEW NAME. HE IS NOW CALLED YOUNG LORD TOYOCHIYO.
I AM VERY PLEASED TO HEAR IT. I AM SURE AONUMA AND HIS COHORT WERE HAPPY TO OBLIGE, FOR NO DOUBT THEY HOPE THIS SUCCESS WILL LEAD TO THE SPREAD OF MAN-MADE POX IMPLANTATION.
INDEED, I HAVE HEARD THAT SOME OF THE GREAT LORDS ALREADY SPEAK PRIVATELY OF A WISH TO GET THEIR SONS INOCULATED WITH THE MAN-MADE POX.

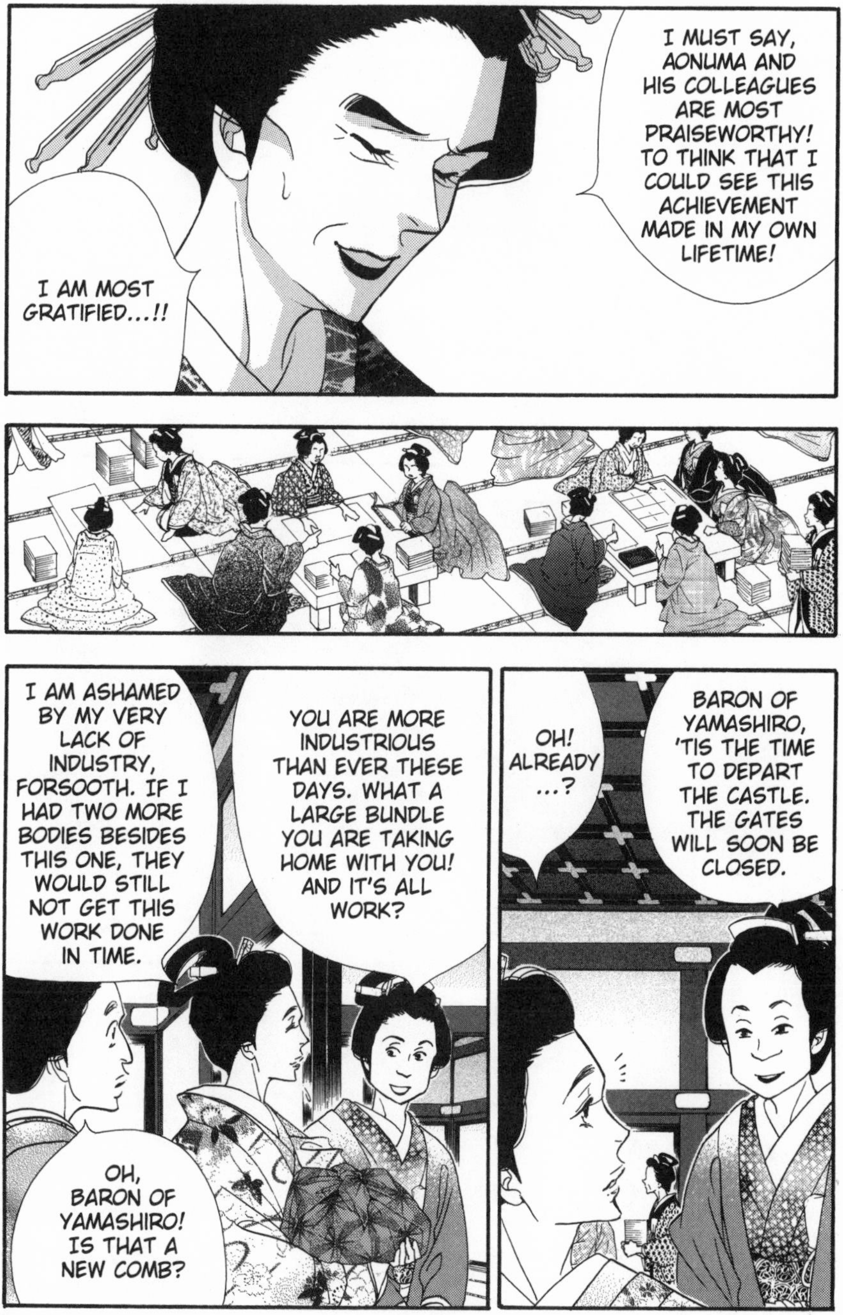
I MUST SAY, AONUMA AND HIS COLLEAGUES ARE MOST PRAISEWORTHY! TO THINK THAT I COULD SEE THIS ACHIEVEMENT MADE IN MY OWN LIFETIME!
I AM MOST GRATIFIED...!!
BARON OF YAMASHIRO, 'TIS THE TIME TO DEPART THE CASTLE. THE GATES WILL SOON BE CLOSED.
OH! ALREADY ...?
YOU ARE MORE INDUSTRIOUS THAN EVER THESE DAYS. WHAT A LARGE BUNDLE YOU ARE TAKING HOME WITH YOU! AND IT'S ALL WORK?
I AM ASHAMED BY MY VERY LACK OF INDUSTRY, FORSOOTH. IF I HAD TWO MORE BODIES BESIDES THIS ONE, THEY WOULD STILL NOT GET THIS WORK DONE IN TIME.
OH, BARON OF YAMASHIRO! IS THAT A NEW COMB?

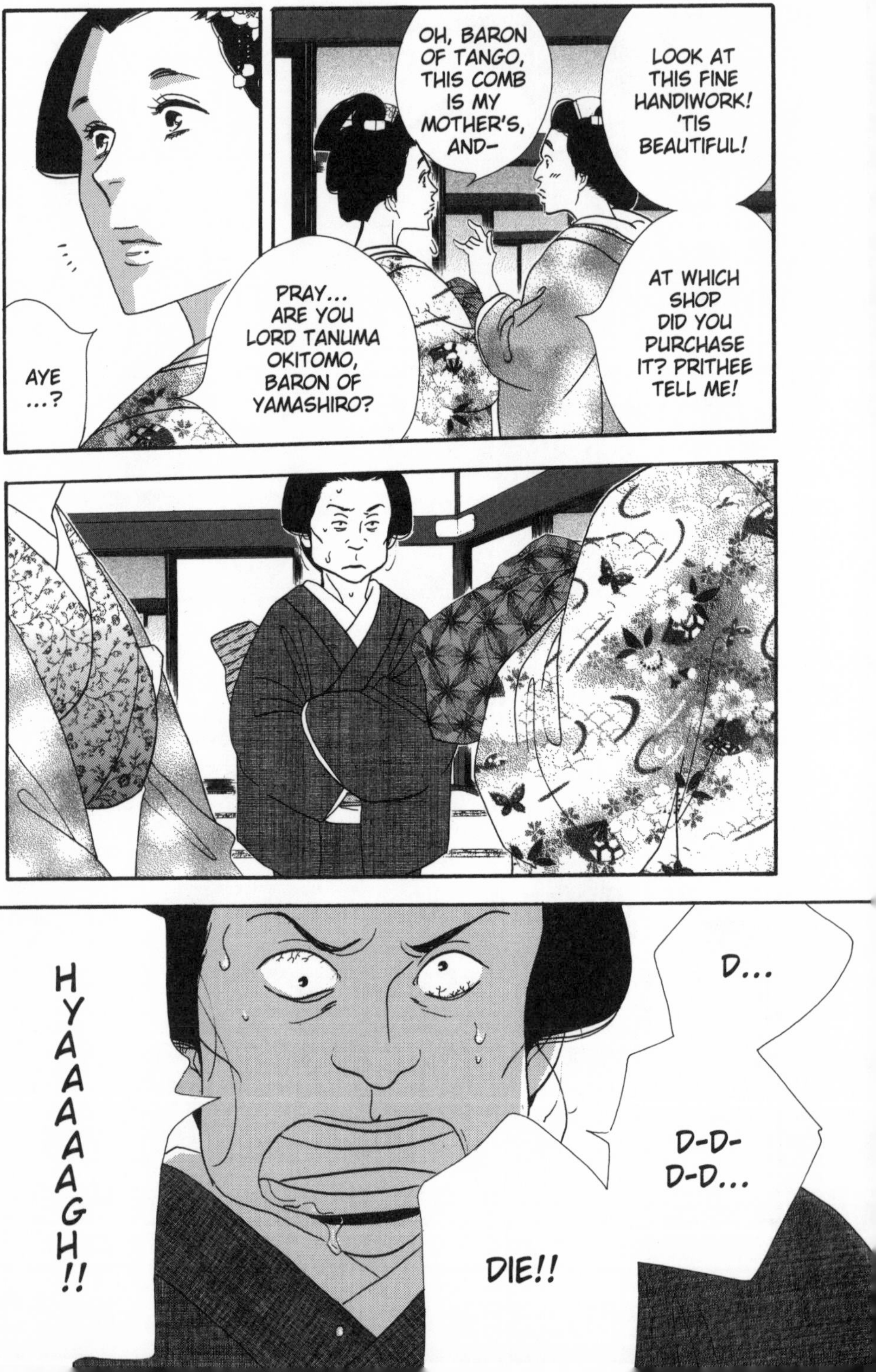
LOOK AT THIS FINE HANDIWORK! 'TIS BEAUTIFUL!
OH, BARON OF TANGO, THIS COMB IS MY MOTHER'S, AND–
AT WHICH SHOP DID YOU PURCHASE IT? PRITHEE TELL ME!
PRAY... ARE YOU LORD TANUMA OKITOMO, BARON OF YAMASHIRO?
AYE ...?
D...
D-D- D-D...
DIE!!
HYAAAAAAAGH!!

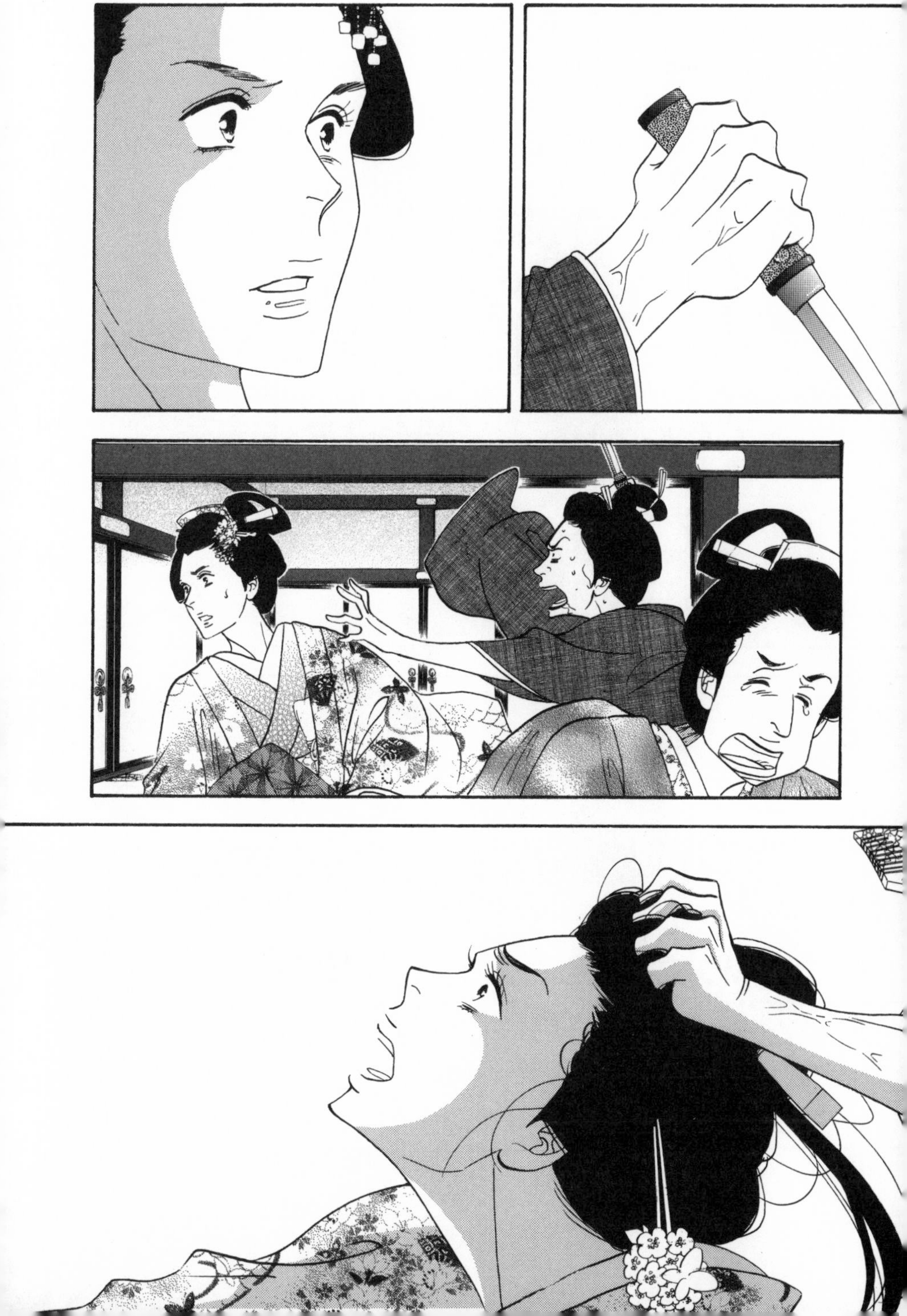

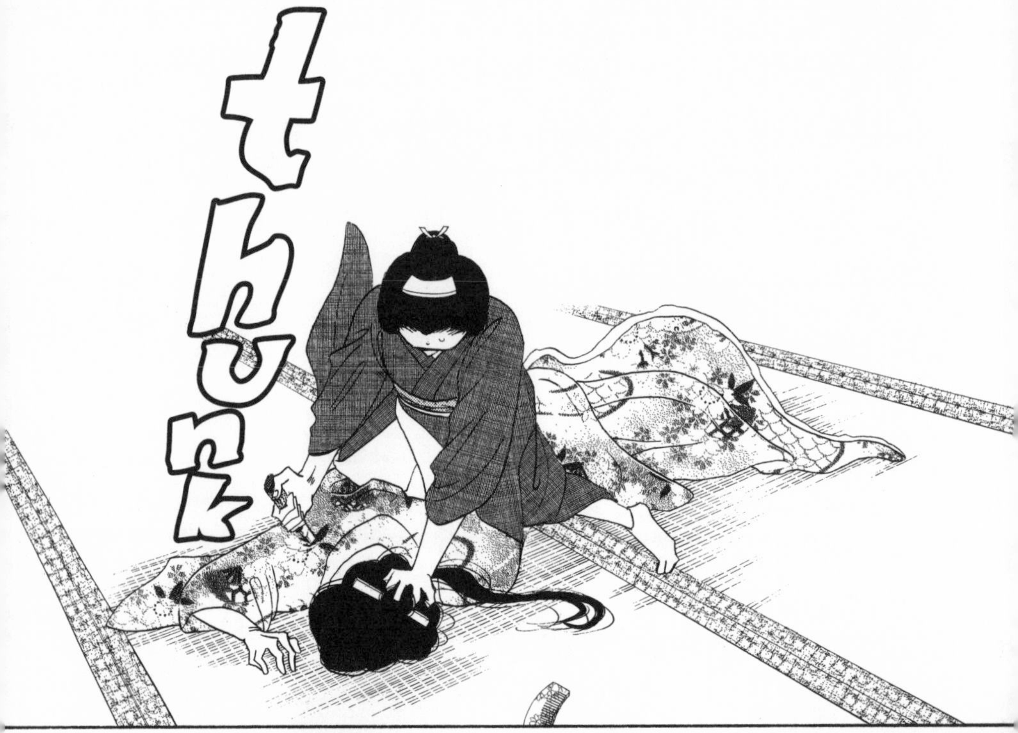
thunk
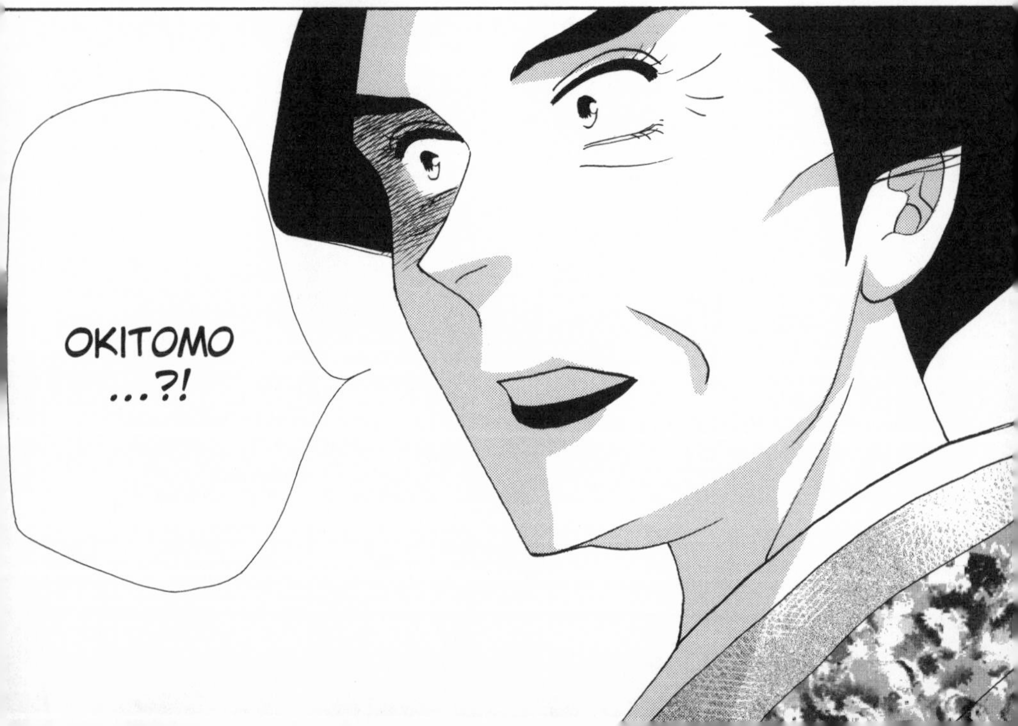
OKITOMO ...?!

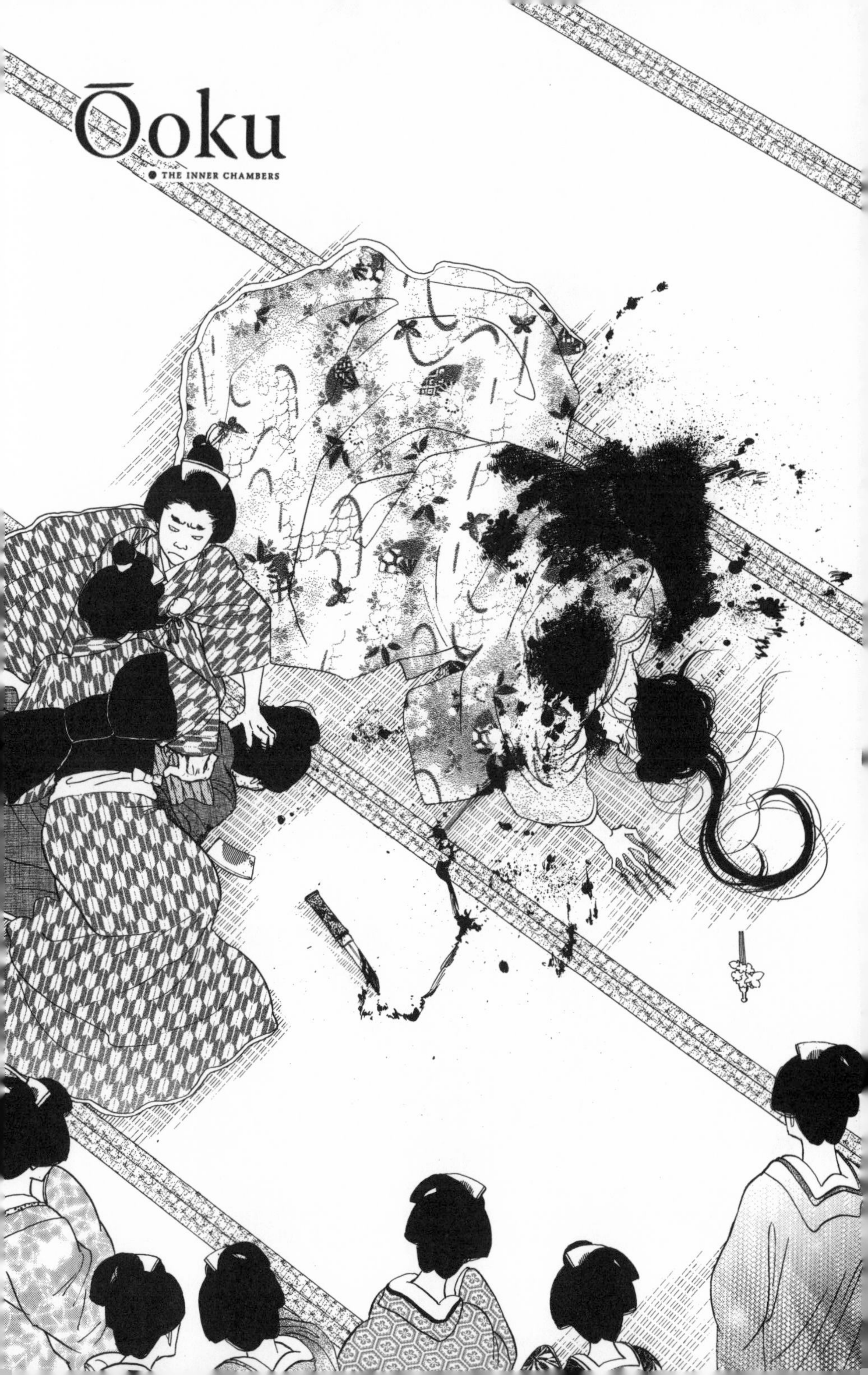
Ōoku
THE INNER CHAMBERS

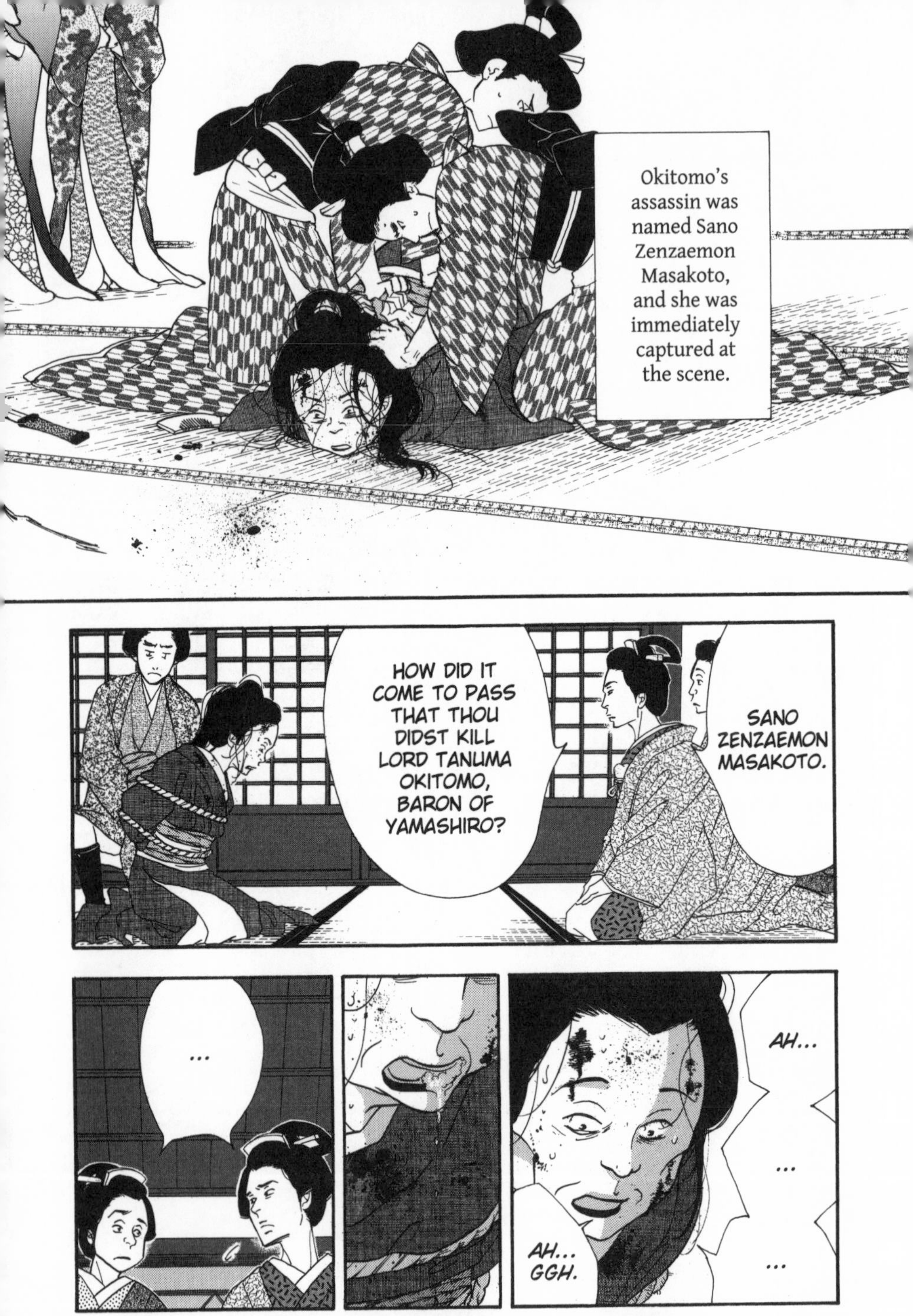
Okitomo's assassin was named Sano Zenzaemon Masakoto, and she was immediately captured at the scene.
SANO ZENZAEMON MASAKOTO.
HOW DID IT COME TO PASS THAT THOU DIDST KILL LORD TANUMA OKITOMO, BARON OF YAMASHIRO?
AH...
...
...
AH... GGH.
...

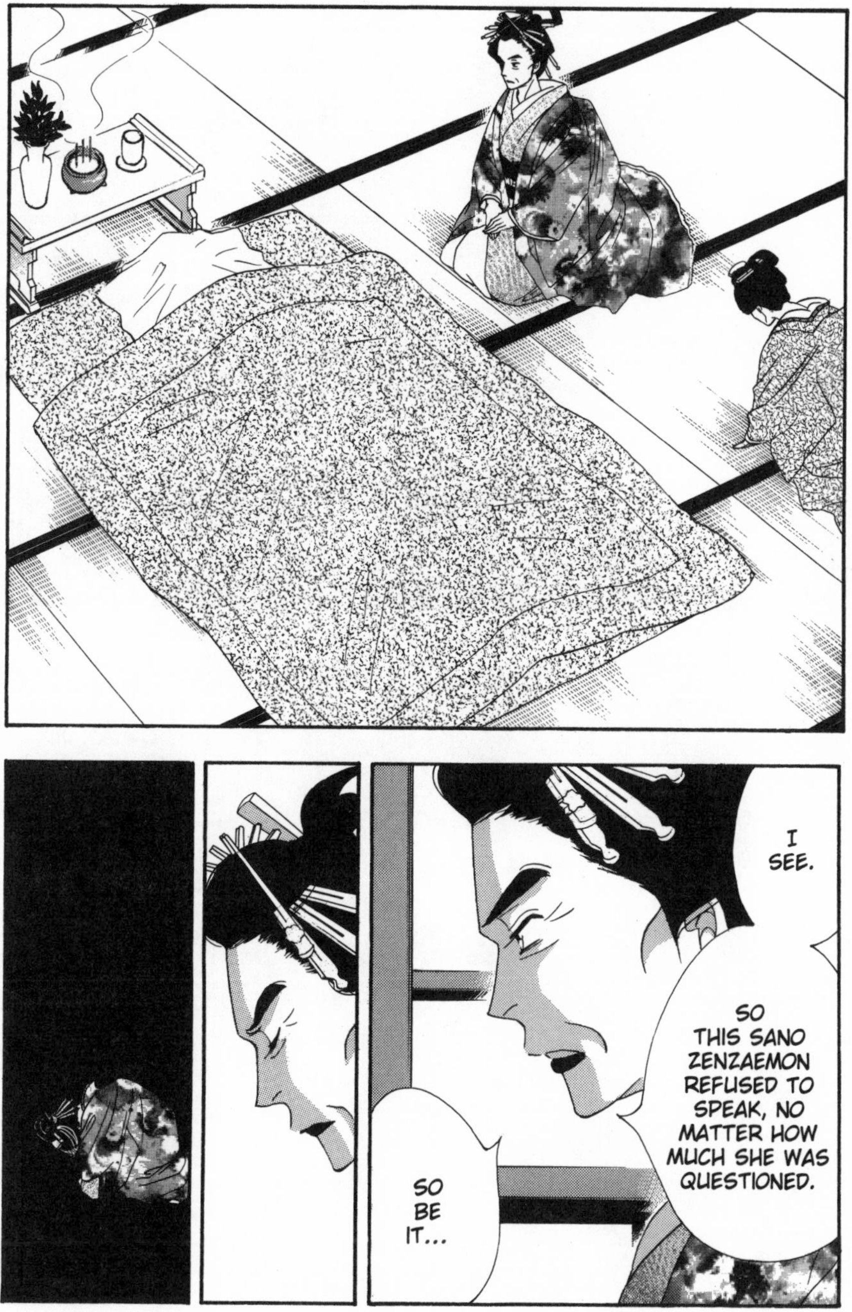
I SEE.
SO THIS SANO ZENZAEMON REFUSED TO SPEAK, NO MATTER HOW MUCH SHE WAS QUESTIONED.
SO BE IT...

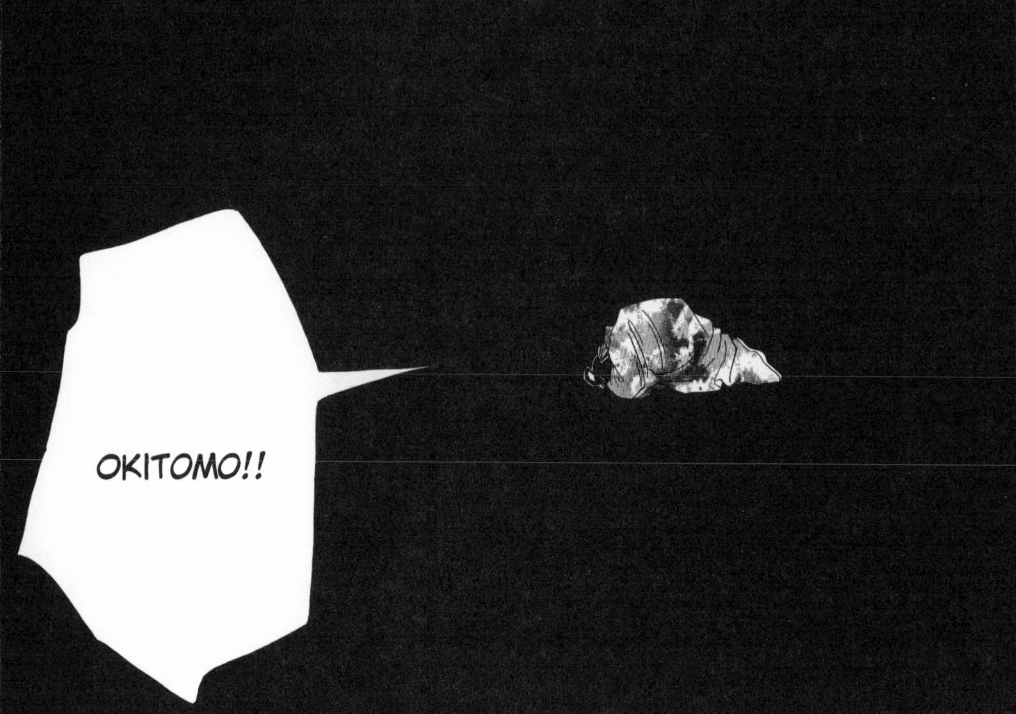
OKITOMO!!

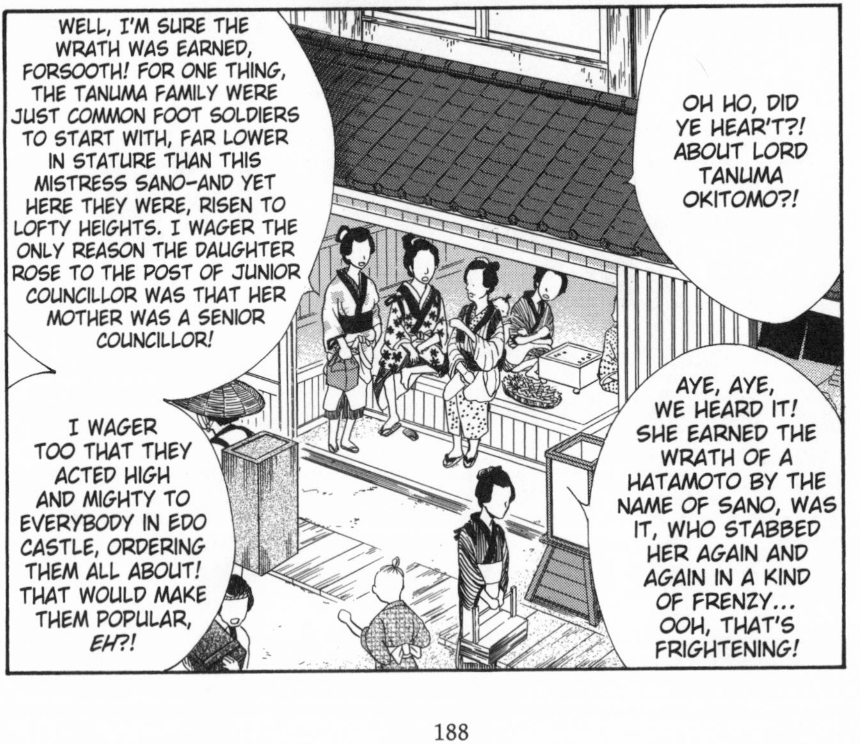
OH HO, DID YE HEAR'T?! ABOUT LORD TANUMA OKITOMO?!
AYE, AYE, WE HEARD IT! SHE EARNED THE WRATH OF A HATAMOTO BY THE NAME OF SANO, WAS IT, WHO STABBED HER AGAIN AND AGAIN IN A KIND OF FRENZY... OOH, THAT'S FRIGHTENING!
WELL, I'M SURE THE WRATH WAS EARNED, FORSOOTH! FOR ONE THING, THE TANUMA FAMILY WERE JUST COMMON FOOT SOLDIERS TO START WITH, FAR LOWER IN STATURE THAN THIS MISTRESS SANO—AND YET HERE THEY WERE, RISEN TO LOFTY HEIGHTS. I WAGER THE ONLY REASON THE DAUGHTER ROSE TO THE POST OF JUNIOR COUNCILLOR WAS THAT HER MOTHER WAS A SENIOR COUNCILLOR!
I WAGER TOO THAT THEY ACTED HIGH AND MIGHTY TO EVERYBODY IN EDO CASTLE, ORDERING THEM ALL ABOUT! THAT WOULD MAKE THEM POPULAR, *EH?!*

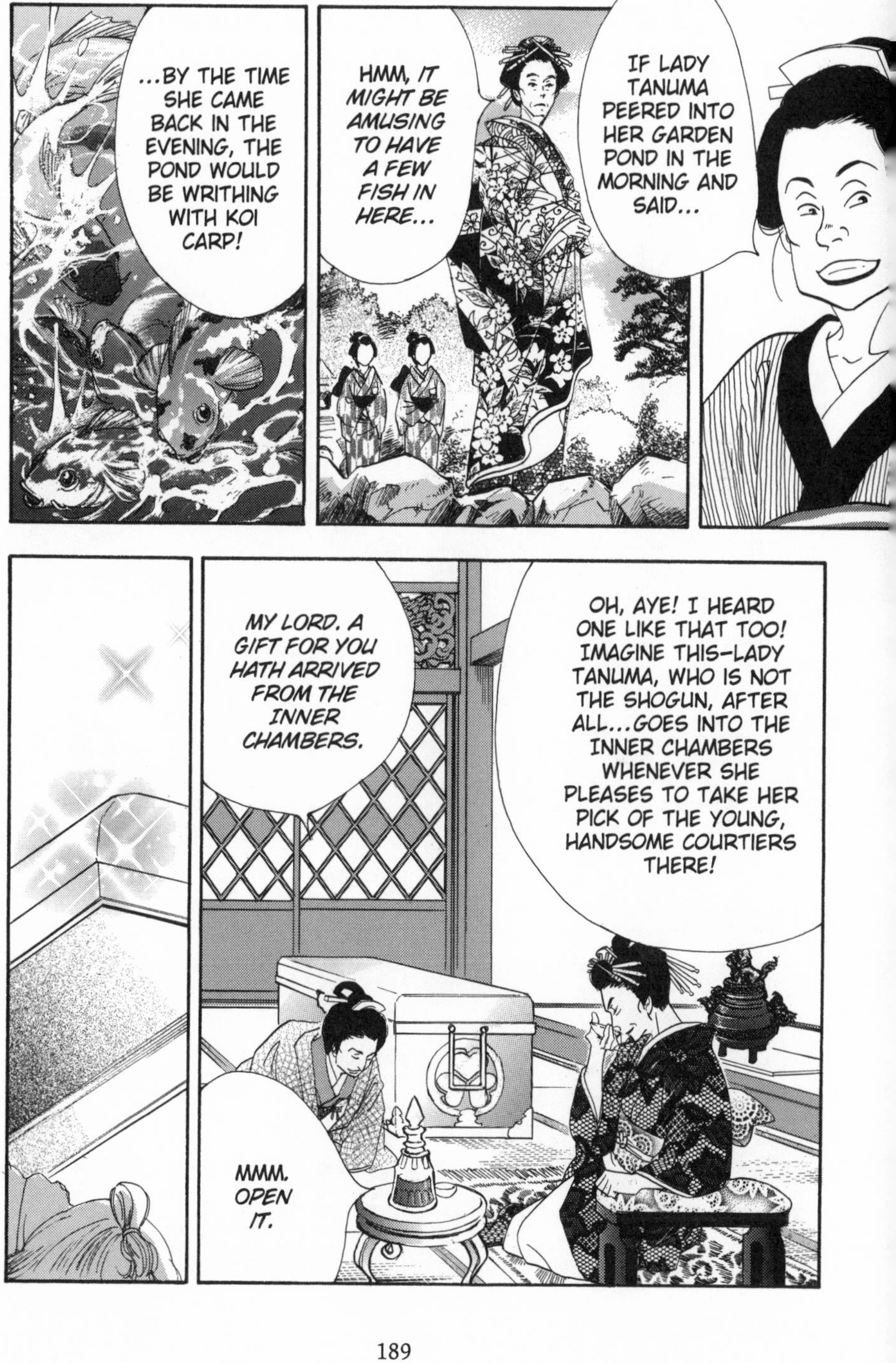
IF LADY TANUMA PEERED INTO HER GARDEN POND IN THE MORNING AND SAID...
HMM, IT MIGHT BE AMUSING TO HAVE A FEW FISH IN HERE...
...BY THE TIME SHE CAME BACK IN THE EVENING, THE POND WOULD BE WRITHING WITH KOI CARP!
OH, AYE! I HEARD ONE LIKE THAT TOO! IMAGINE THIS–LADY TANUMA, WHO IS NOT THE SHOGUN, AFTER ALL...GOES INTO THE INNER CHAMBERS WHENEVER SHE PLEASES TO TAKE HER PICK OF THE YOUNG, HANDSOME COURTIERS THERE!
MY LORD. A GIFT FOR YOU HATH ARRIVED FROM THE INNER CHAMBERS.
MMM. OPEN IT.

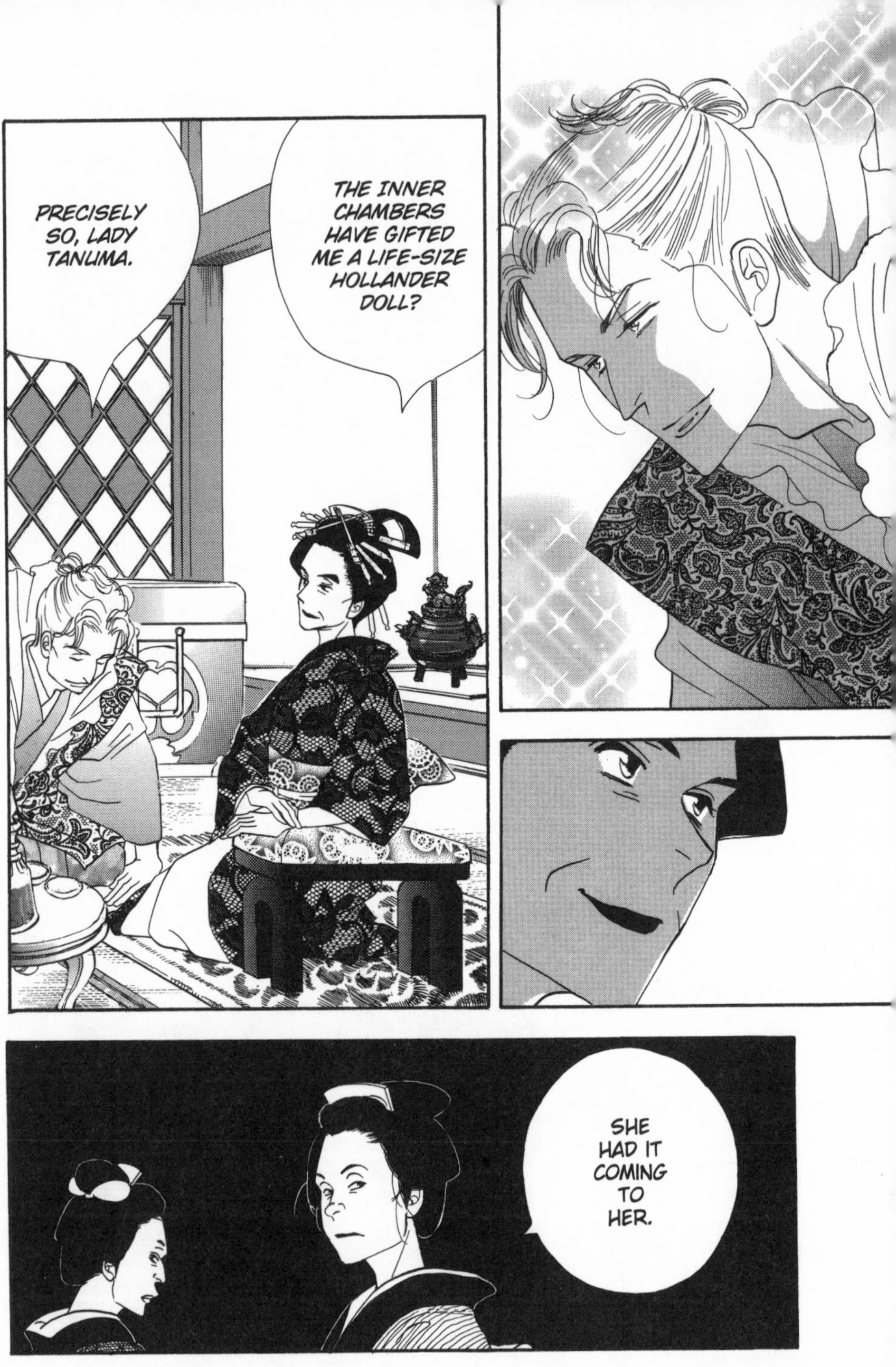
THE INNER CHAMBERS HAVE GIFTED ME A LIFE-SIZE HOLLANDER DOLL?
PRECISELY SO, LADY TANUMA.
SHE HAD IT COMING TO HER.

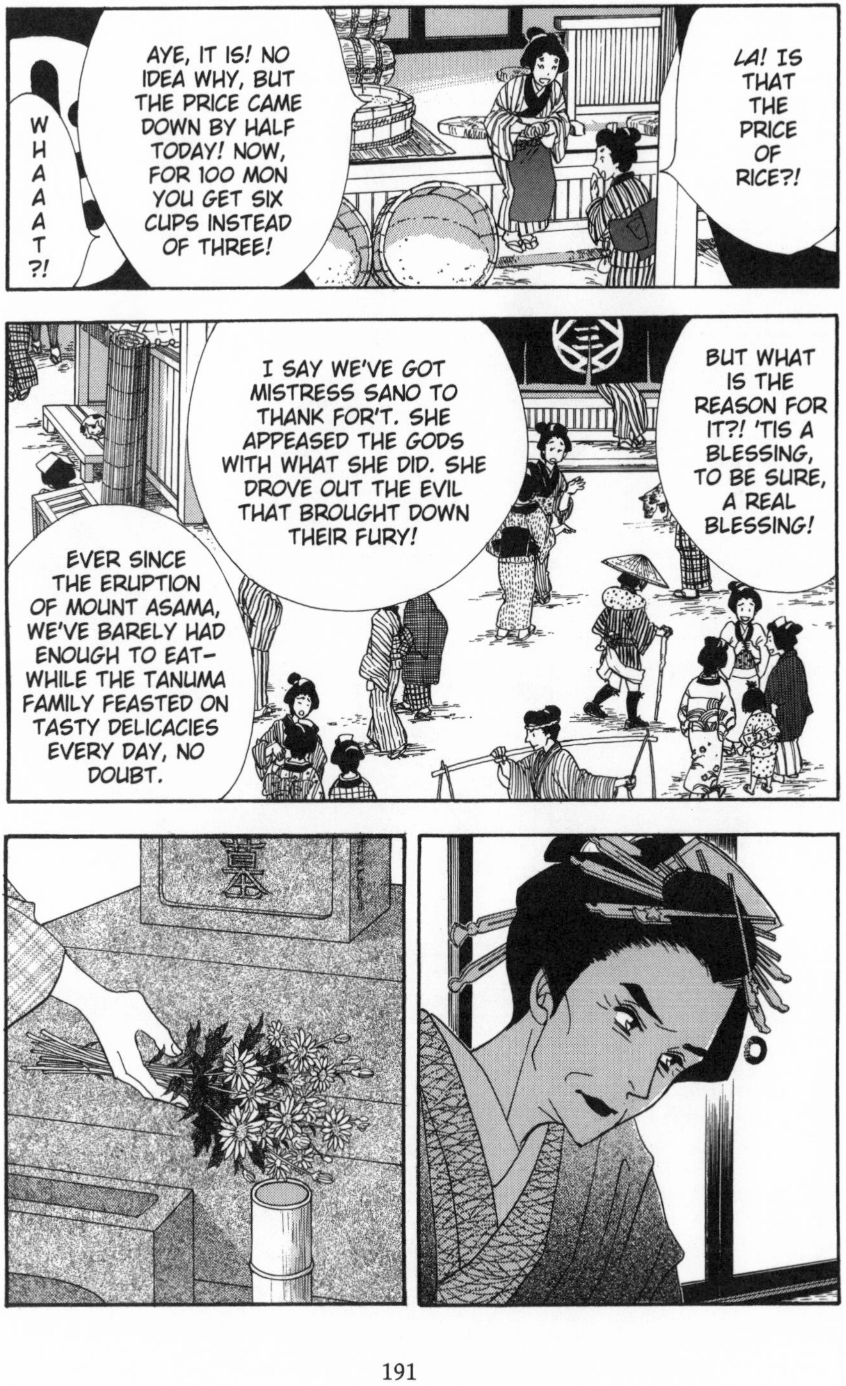
LA! IS THAT THE PRICE OF RICE?!
AYE, IT IS! NO IDEA WHY, BUT THE PRICE CAME DOWN BY HALF TODAY! NOW, FOR 100 MON YOU GET SIX CUPS INSTEAD OF THREE!
WHAAAAT?!
BUT WHAT IS THE REASON FOR IT?! 'TIS A BLESSING, TO BE SURE, A REAL BLESSING!
I SAY WE'VE GOT MISTRESS SANO TO THANK FOR'T. SHE APPEASED THE GODS WITH WHAT SHE DID. SHE DROVE OUT THE EVIL THAT BROUGHT DOWN THEIR FURY!
EVER SINCE THE ERUPTION OF MOUNT ASAMA, WE'VE BARELY HAD ENOUGH TO EAT-WHILE THE TANUMA FAMILY FEASTED ON TASTY DELICACIES EVERY DAY, NO DOUBT.

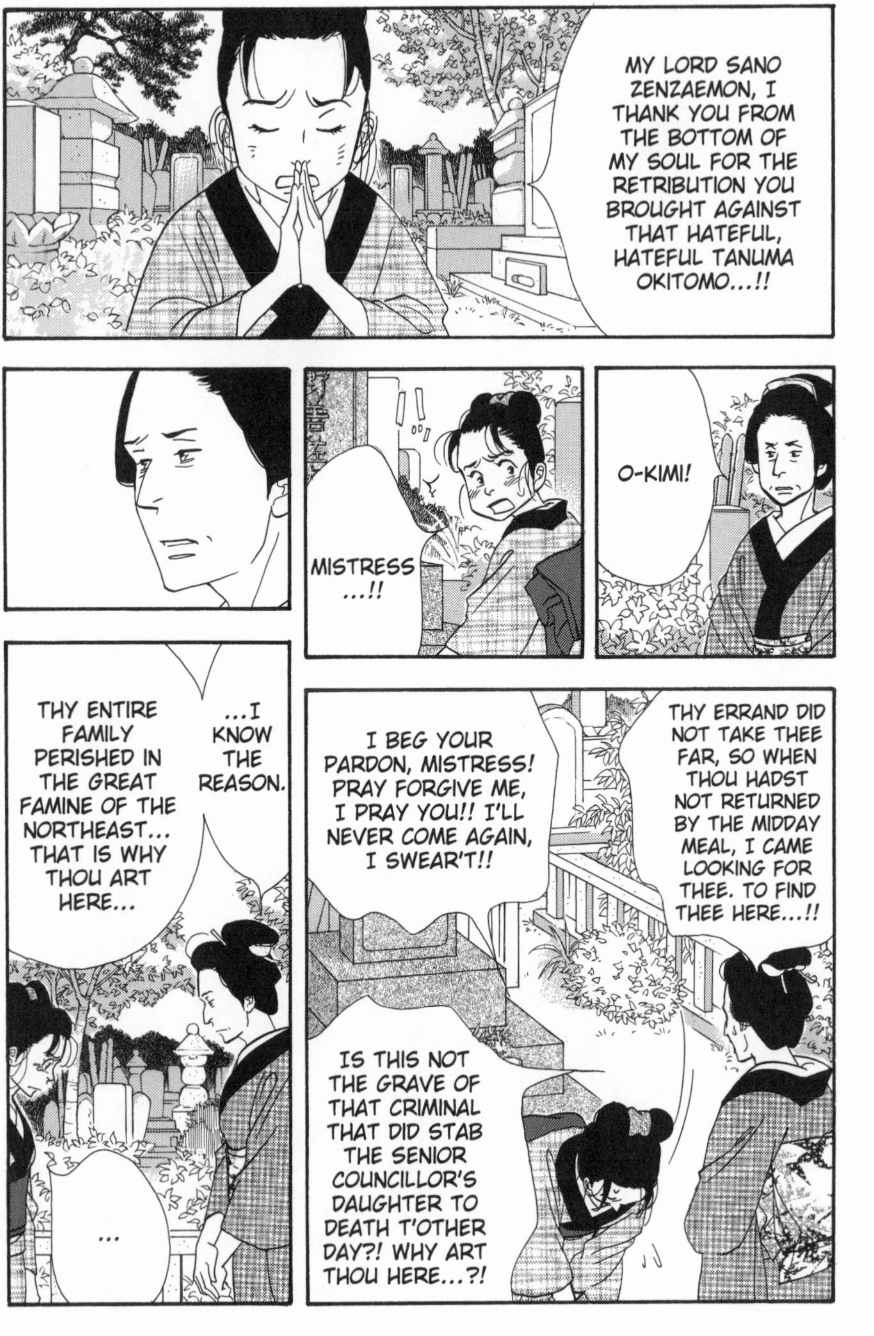
MY LORD SANO ZENZAEMON, I THANK YOU FROM THE BOTTOM OF MY SOUL FOR THE RETRIBUTION YOU BROUGHT AGAINST THAT HATEFUL, HATEFUL TANUMA OKITOMO...!!
O-KIMI!
MISTRESS ...!!
THY ERRAND DID NOT TAKE THEE FAR, SO WHEN THOU HADST NOT RETURNED BY THE MIDDAY MEAL, I CAME LOOKING FOR THEE. TO FIND THEE HERE...!!
I BEG YOUR PARDON, MISTRESS! PRAY FORGIVE ME, I PRAY YOU!! I'LL NEVER COME AGAIN, I SWEAR'T!!
IS THIS NOT THE GRAVE OF THAT CRIMINAL THAT DID STAB THE SENIOR COUNCILLOR'S DAUGHTER TO DEATH T'OTHER DAY?! WHY ART THOU HERE...?!
...I KNOW THE REASON.
THY ENTIRE FAMILY PERISHED IN THE GREAT FAMINE OF THE NORTHEAST... THAT IS WHY THOU ART HERE...
...

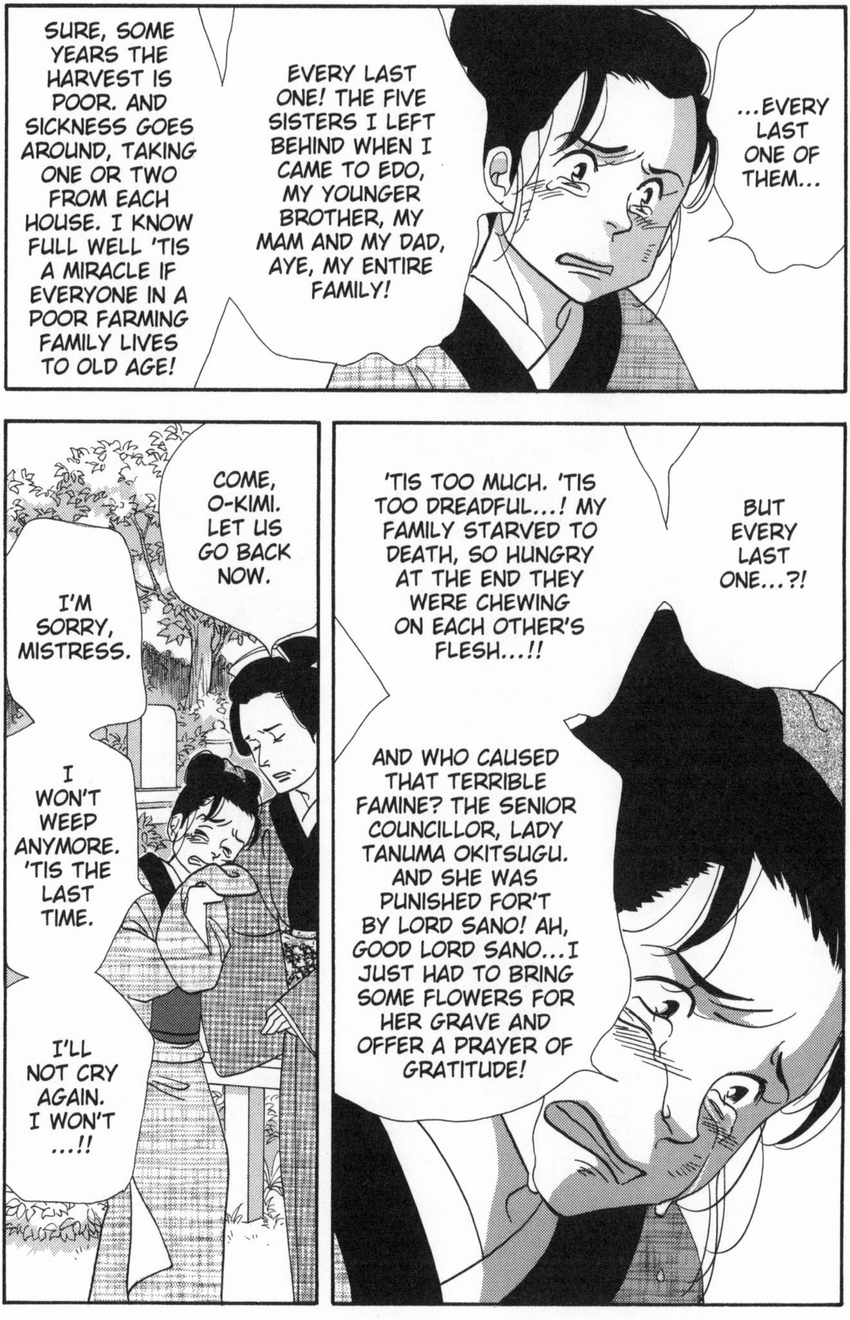
...EVERY LAST ONE OF THEM...
EVERY LAST ONE! THE FIVE SISTERS I LEFT BEHIND WHEN I CAME TO EDO, MY YOUNGER BROTHER, MY MAM AND MY DAD, AYE, MY ENTIRE FAMILY!
SURE, SOME YEARS THE HARVEST IS POOR. AND SICKNESS GOES AROUND, TAKING ONE OR TWO FROM EACH HOUSE. I KNOW FULL WELL 'TIS A MIRACLE IF EVERYONE IN A POOR FARMING FAMILY LIVES TO OLD AGE!
BUT EVERY LAST ONE...?!
'TIS TOO MUCH. 'TIS TOO DREADFUL...! MY FAMILY STARVED TO DEATH, SO HUNGRY AT THE END THEY WERE CHEWING ON EACH OTHER'S FLESH...!!
AND WHO CAUSED THAT TERRIBLE FAMINE? THE SENIOR COUNCILLOR, LADY TANUMA OKITSUGU. AND SHE WAS PUNISHED FOR'T BY LORD SANO! AH, GOOD LORD SANO...I JUST HAD TO BRING SOME FLOWERS FOR HER GRAVE AND OFFER A PRAYER OF GRATITUDE!
COME, O-KIMI. LET US GO BACK NOW.
I'M SORRY, MISTRESS.
I WON'T WEEP ANYMORE. 'TIS THE LAST TIME.
I'LL NOT CRY AGAIN. I WON'T ...!!

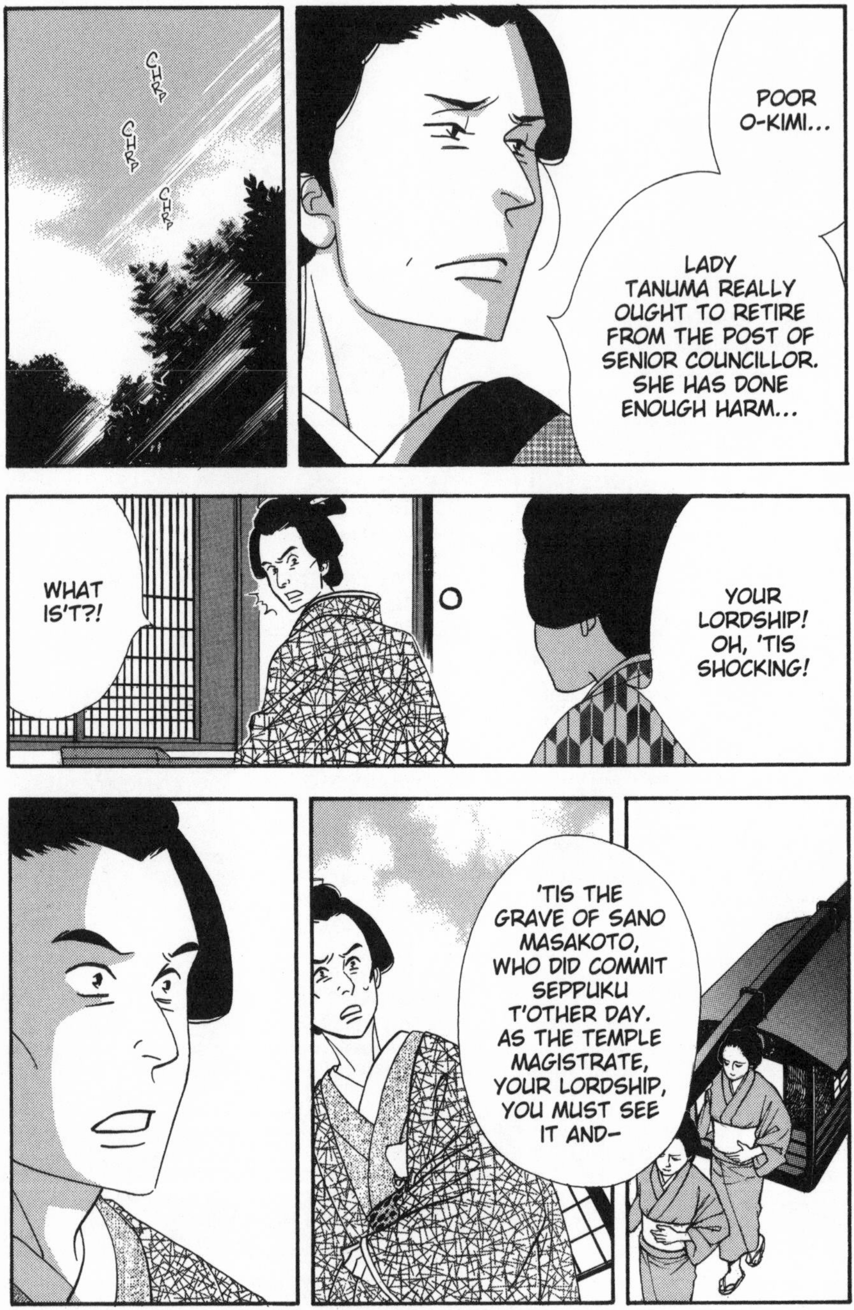
POOR O-KIMI...
LADY TANUMA REALLY OUGHT TO RETIRE FROM THE POST OF SENIOR COUNCILLOR. SHE HAS DONE ENOUGH HARM...
CHRP
CHRP
CHRP
YOUR LORDSHIP! OH, 'TIS SHOCKING!
WHAT IS'T?!
'TIS THE GRAVE OF SANO MASAKOTO, WHO DID COMMIT SEPPUKU T'OTHER DAY. AS THE TEMPLE MAGISTRATE, YOUR LORDSHIP, YOU MUST SEE IT AND–

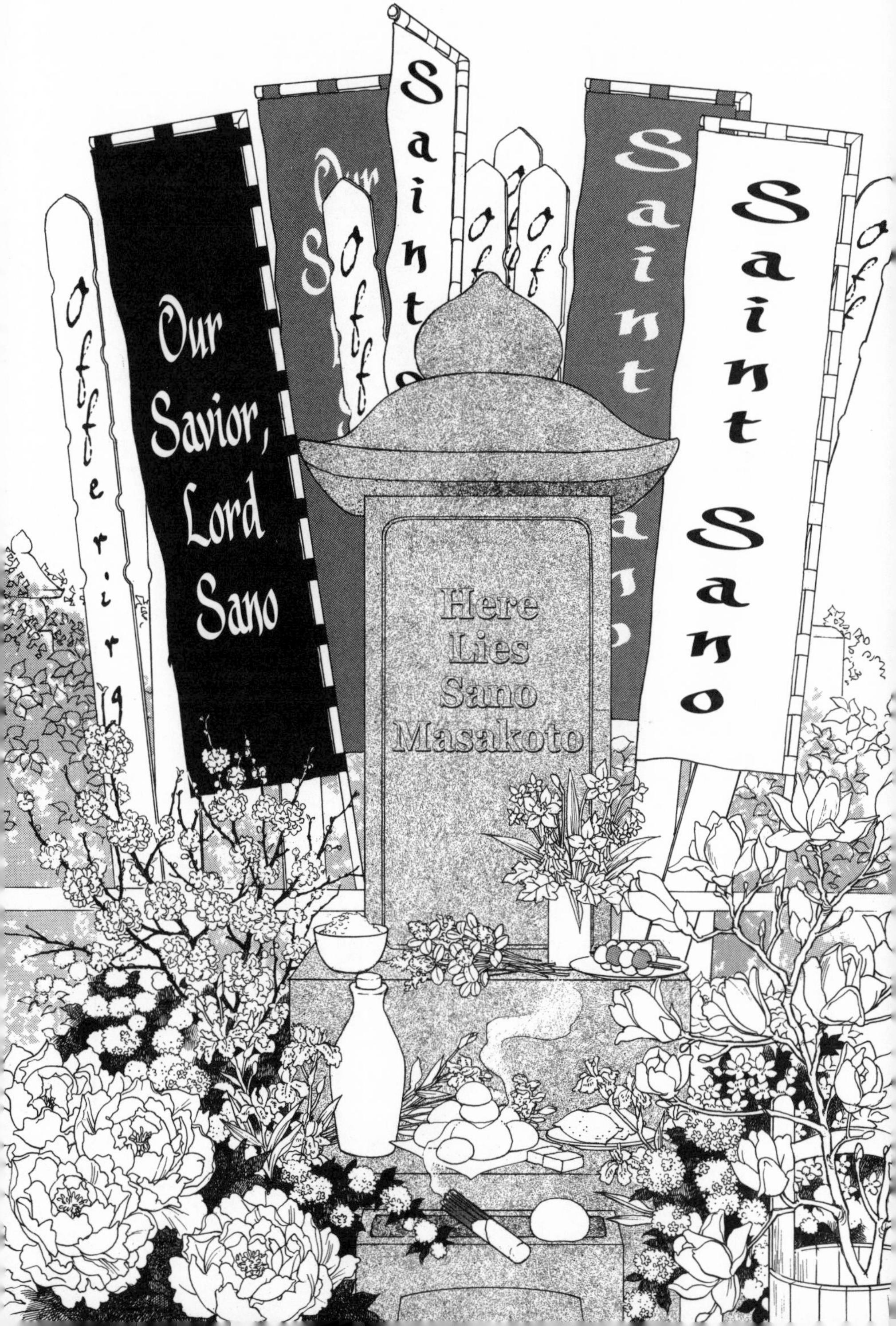

Our Savior, Lord Sano
Saint Sano
Here Lies Sano Masakoto

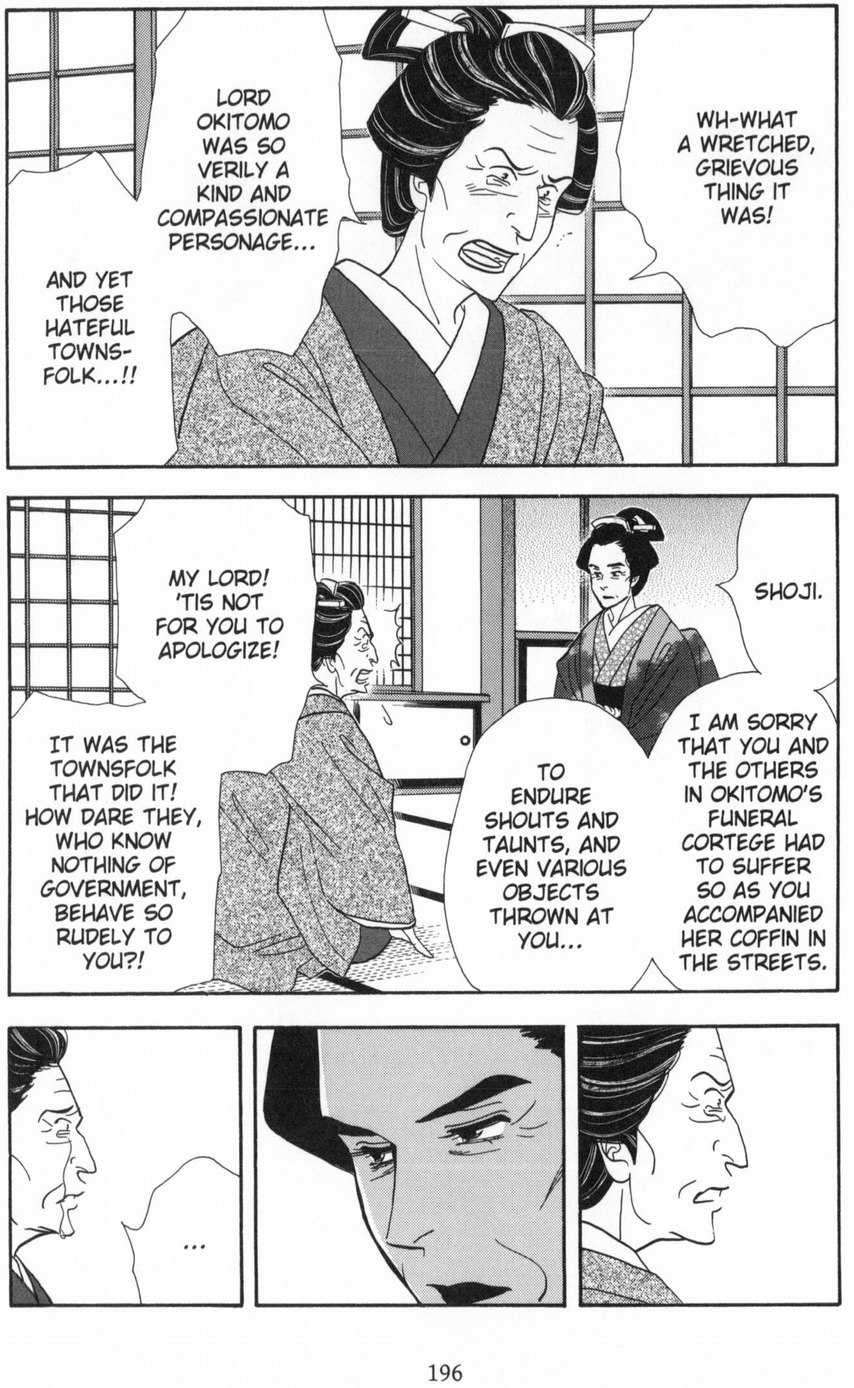
WH-WHAT A WRETCHED, GRIEVOUS THING IT WAS!
LORD OKITOMO WAS SO VERILY A KIND AND COMPASSIONATE PERSONAGE...
AND YET THOSE HATEFUL TOWNS-FOLK...!!
SHOJI.
I AM SORRY THAT YOU AND THE OTHERS IN OKITOMO'S FUNERAL CORTEGE HAD TO SUFFER SO AS YOU ACCOMPANIED HER COFFIN IN THE STREETS.
TO ENDURE SHOUTS AND TAUNTS, AND EVEN VARIOUS OBJECTS THROWN AT YOU...
MY LORD! 'TIS NOT FOR YOU TO APOLOGIZE!
IT WAS THE TOWNSFOLK THAT DID IT! HOW DARE THEY, WHO KNOW NOTHING OF GOVERNMENT, BEHAVE SO RUDELY TO YOU?!
...

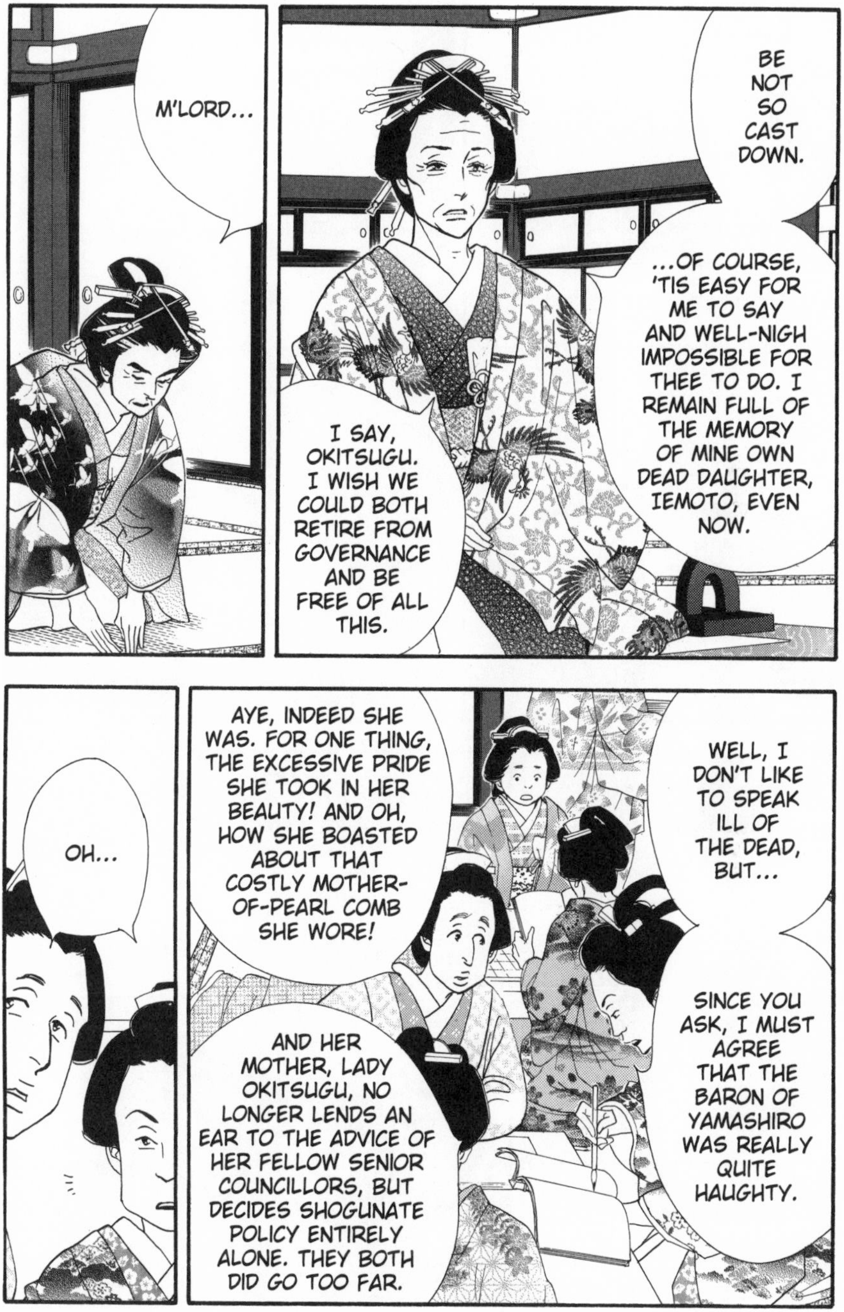
BE NOT SO CAST DOWN.
...OF COURSE, 'TIS EASY FOR ME TO SAY AND WELL-NIGH IMPOSSIBLE FOR THEE TO DO. I REMAIN FULL OF THE MEMORY OF MINE OWN DEAD DAUGHTER, IEMOTO, EVEN NOW.
I SAY, OKITSUGU. I WISH WE COULD BOTH RETIRE FROM GOVERNANCE AND BE FREE OF ALL THIS.
M'LORD...
WELL, I DON'T LIKE TO SPEAK ILL OF THE DEAD, BUT...
SINCE YOU ASK, I MUST AGREE THAT THE BARON OF YAMASHIRO WAS REALLY QUITE HAUGHTY.
AYE, INDEED SHE WAS. FOR ONE THING, THE EXCESSIVE PRIDE SHE TOOK IN HER BEAUTY! AND OH, HOW SHE BOASTED ABOUT THAT COSTLY MOTHER-OF-PEARL COMB SHE WORE!
AND HER MOTHER, LADY OKITSUGU, NO LONGER LENDS AN EAR TO THE ADVICE OF HER FELLOW SENIOR COUNCILLORS, BUT DECIDES SHOGUNATE POLICY ENTIRELY ALONE. THEY BOTH DID GO TOO FAR.
OH...

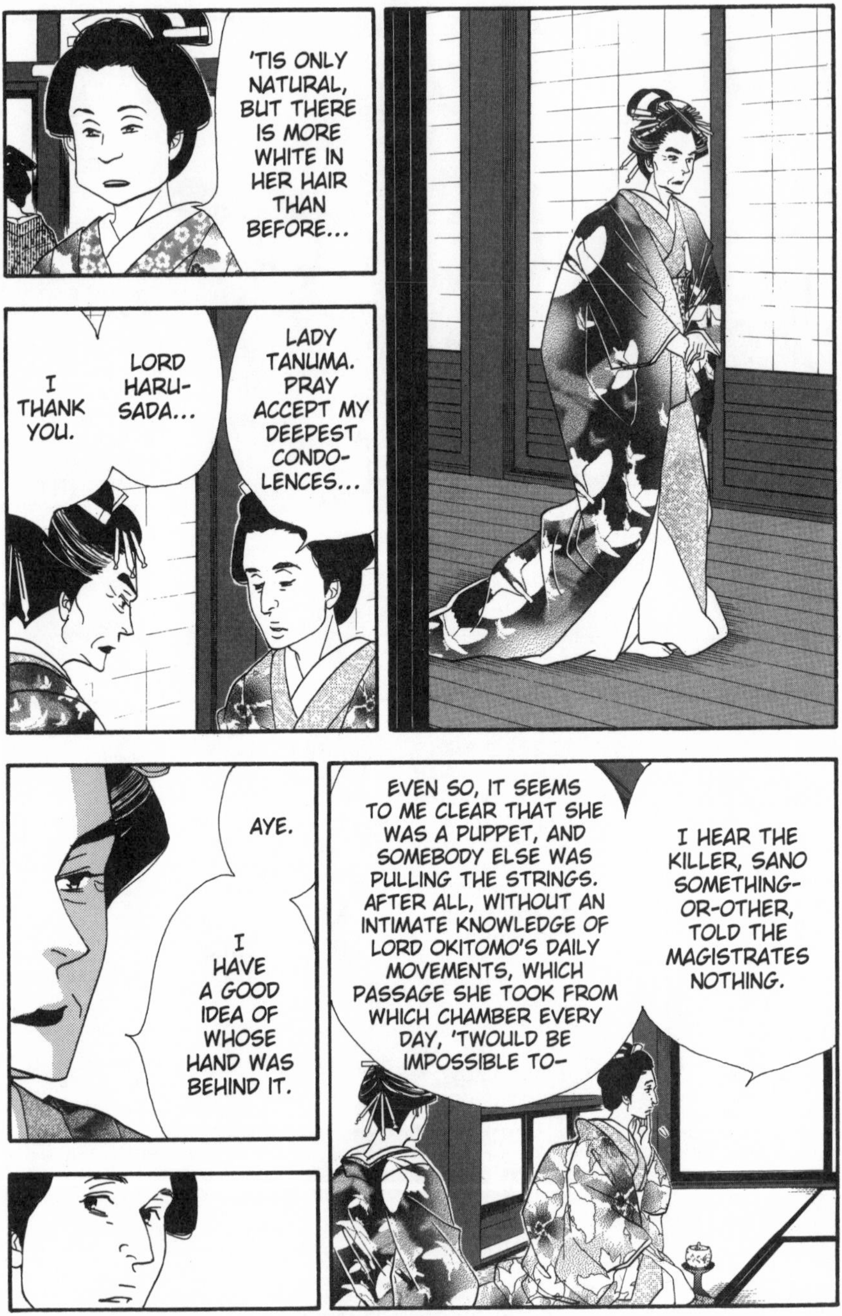
'TIS ONLY NATURAL, BUT THERE IS MORE WHITE IN HER HAIR THAN BEFORE...
LADY TANUMA. PRAY ACCEPT MY DEEPEST CONDO-LENCES...
LORD HARU-SADA...
I THANK YOU.
I HEAR THE KILLER, SANO SOMETHING-OR-OTHER, TOLD THE MAGISTRATES NOTHING.
EVEN SO, IT SEEMS TO ME CLEAR THAT SHE WAS A PUPPET, AND SOMEBODY ELSE WAS PULLING THE STRINGS. AFTER ALL, WITHOUT AN INTIMATE KNOWLEDGE OF LORD OKITOMO'S DAILY MOVEMENTS, WHICH PASSAGE SHE TOOK FROM WHICH CHAMBER EVERY DAY, 'TWOULD BE IMPOSSIBLE TO–
AYE.
I HAVE A GOOD IDEA OF WHOSE HAND WAS BEHIND IT.

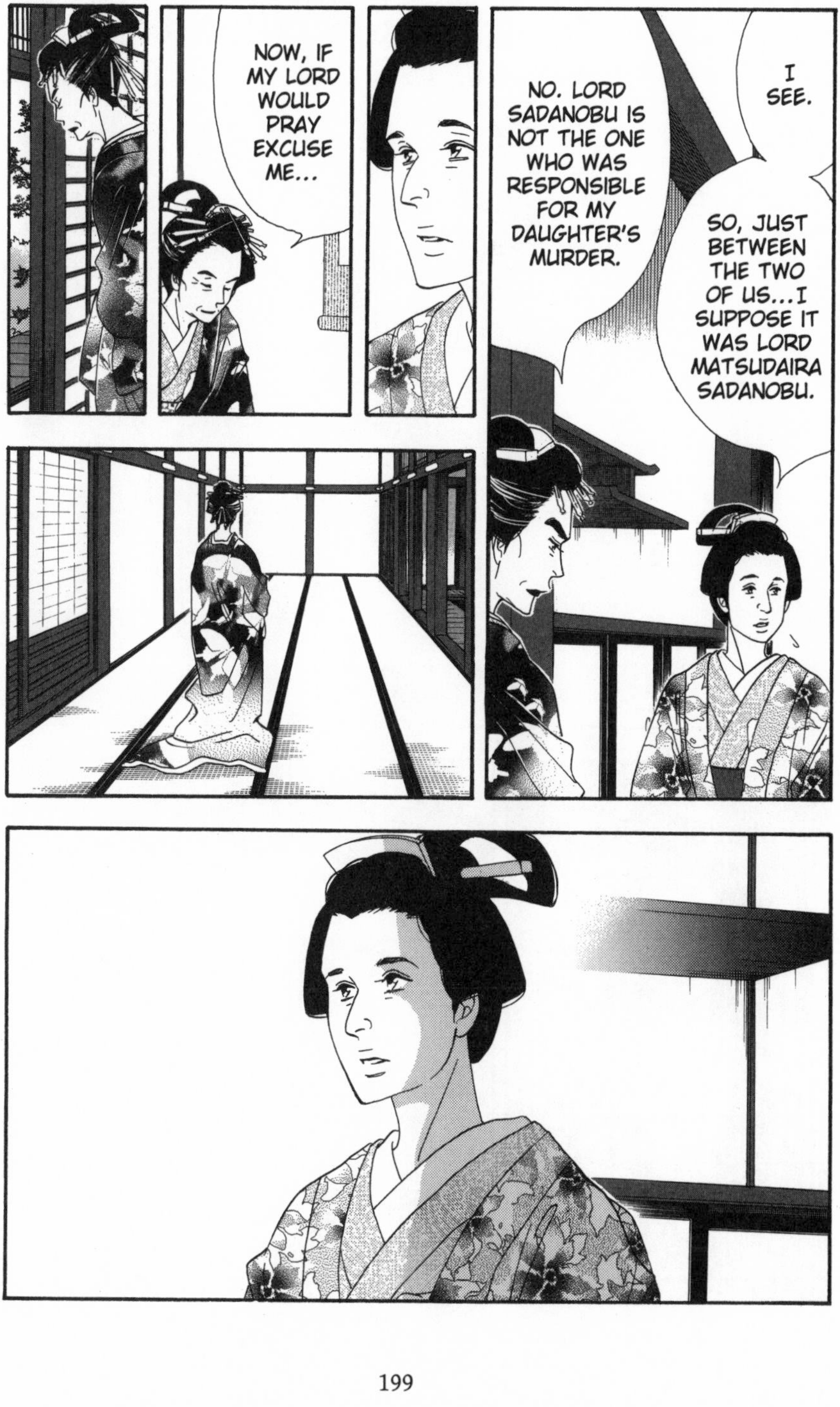
I SEE.
SO, JUST BETWEEN THE TWO OF US...I SUPPOSE IT WAS LORD MATSUDAIRA SADANOBU.
NO. LORD SADANOBU IS NOT THE ONE WHO WAS RESPONSIBLE FOR MY DAUGHTER'S MURDER.
NOW, IF MY LORD WOULD PRAY EXCUSE ME...

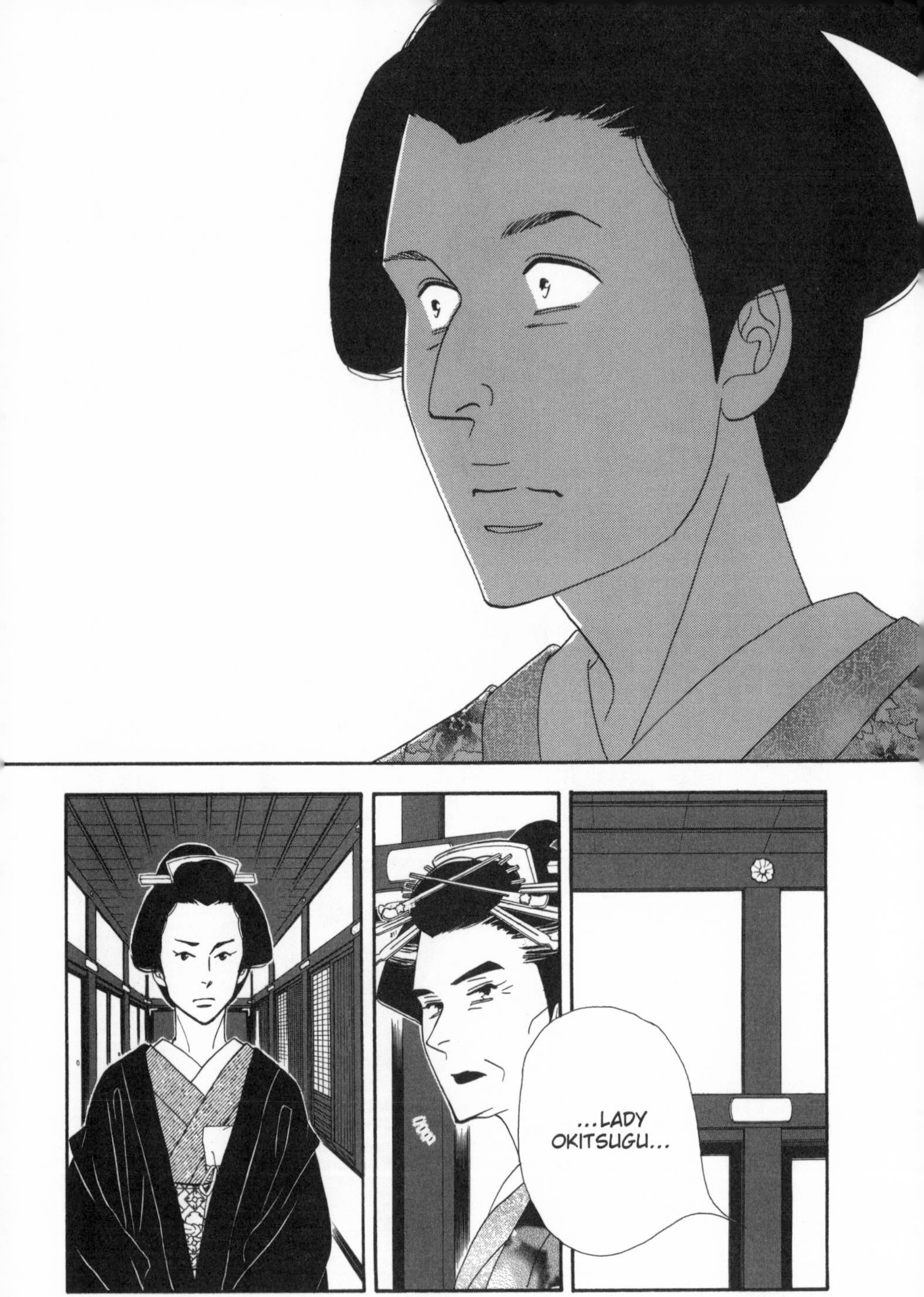
...LADY
OKITSUGU...

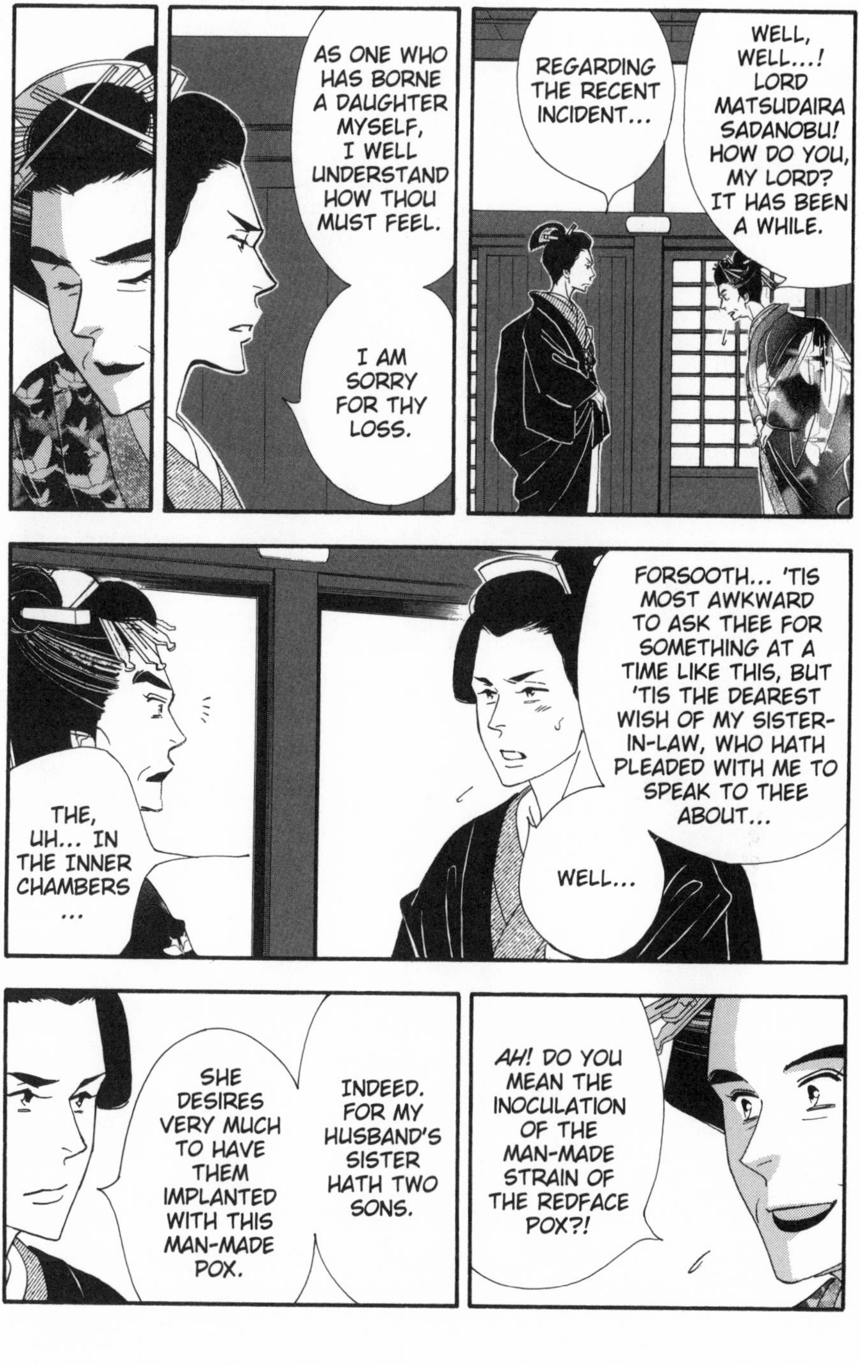
WELL, WELL...! LORD MATSUDAIRA SADANOBU! HOW DO YOU, MY LORD? IT HAS BEEN A WHILE.
REGARDING THE RECENT INCIDENT...
AS ONE WHO HAS BORNE A DAUGHTER MYSELF, I WELL UNDERSTAND HOW THOU MUST FEEL.
I AM SORRY FOR THY LOSS.
FORSOOTH... 'TIS MOST AWKWARD TO ASK THEE FOR SOMETHING AT A TIME LIKE THIS, BUT 'TIS THE DEAREST WISH OF MY SISTER-IN-LAW, WHO HATH PLEADED WITH ME TO SPEAK TO THEE ABOUT...
WELL...
THE, UH... IN THE INNER CHAMBERS ...
AH! DO YOU MEAN THE INOCULATION OF THE MAN-MADE STRAIN OF THE REDFACE POX?!
INDEED. FOR MY HUSBAND'S SISTER HATH TWO SONS.
SHE DESIRES VERY MUCH TO HAVE THEM IMPLANTED WITH THIS MAN-MADE POX.

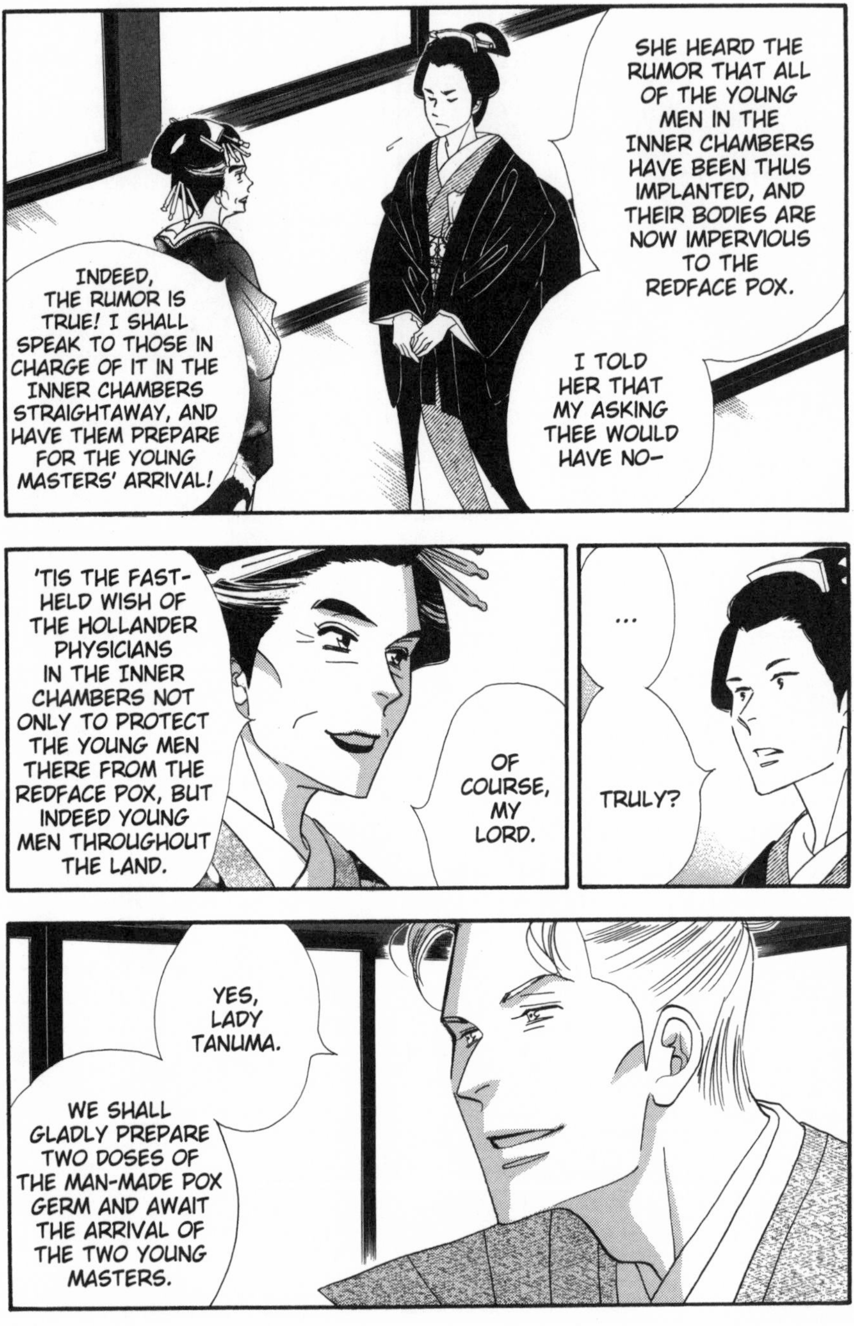
SHE HEARD THE RUMOR THAT ALL OF THE YOUNG MEN IN THE INNER CHAMBERS HAVE BEEN THUS IMPLANTED, AND THEIR BODIES ARE NOW IMPERVIOUS TO THE REDFACE POX.
I TOLD HER THAT MY ASKING THEE WOULD HAVE NO–
INDEED, THE RUMOR IS TRUE! I SHALL SPEAK TO THOSE IN CHARGE OF IT IN THE INNER CHAMBERS STRAIGHTAWAY, AND HAVE THEM PREPARE FOR THE YOUNG MASTERS' ARRIVAL!
...
TRULY?
OF COURSE, MY LORD.
'TIS THE FAST-HELD WISH OF THE HOLLANDER PHYSICIANS IN THE INNER CHAMBERS NOT ONLY TO PROTECT THE YOUNG MEN THERE FROM THE REDFACE POX, BUT INDEED YOUNG MEN THROUGHOUT THE LAND.
YES, LADY TANUMA.
WE SHALL GLADLY PREPARE TWO DOSES OF THE MAN-MADE POX GERM AND AWAIT THE ARRIVAL OF THE TWO YOUNG MASTERS.

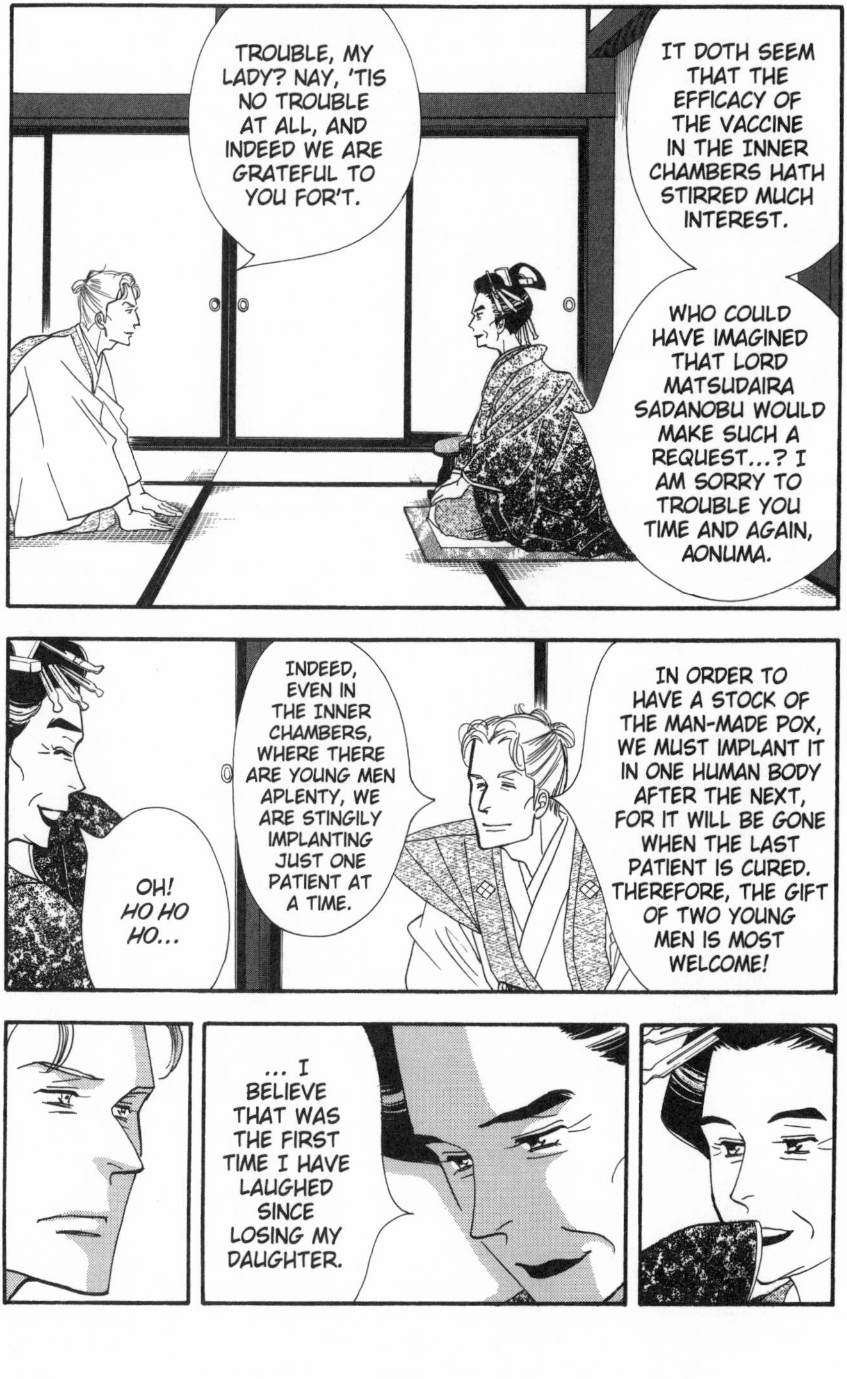
IT DOTH SEEM THAT THE EFFICACY OF THE VACCINE IN THE INNER CHAMBERS HATH STIRRED MUCH INTEREST.
WHO COULD HAVE IMAGINED THAT LORD MATSUDAIRA SADANOBU WOULD MAKE SUCH A REQUEST...? I AM SORRY TO TROUBLE YOU TIME AND AGAIN, AONUMA.
TROUBLE, MY LADY? NAY, 'TIS NO TROUBLE AT ALL, AND INDEED WE ARE GRATEFUL TO YOU FOR'T.
IN ORDER TO HAVE A STOCK OF THE MAN-MADE POX, WE MUST IMPLANT IT IN ONE HUMAN BODY AFTER THE NEXT, FOR IT WILL BE GONE WHEN THE LAST PATIENT IS CURED. THEREFORE, THE GIFT OF TWO YOUNG MEN IS MOST WELCOME!
INDEED, EVEN IN THE INNER CHAMBERS, WHERE THERE ARE YOUNG MEN APLENTY, WE ARE STINGILY IMPLANTING JUST ONE PATIENT AT A TIME.
OH! HO HO HO...
... I BELIEVE THAT WAS THE FIRST TIME I HAVE LAUGHED SINCE LOSING MY DAUGHTER.

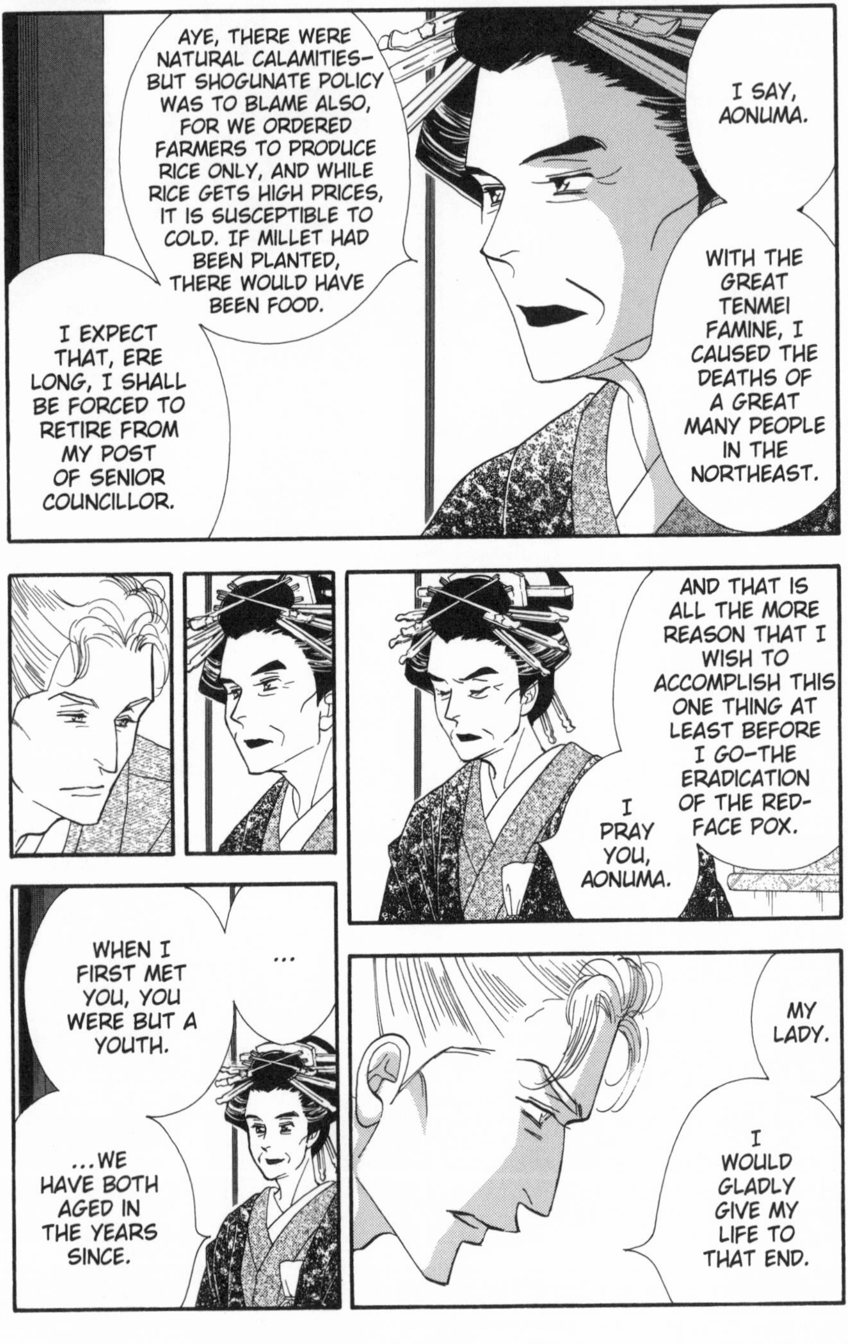
I SAY, AONUMA.
WITH THE GREAT TENMEI FAMINE, I CAUSED THE DEATHS OF A GREAT MANY PEOPLE IN THE NORTHEAST.
AYE, THERE WERE NATURAL CALAMITIES--BUT SHOGUNATE POLICY WAS TO BLAME ALSO, FOR WE ORDERED FARMERS TO PRODUCE RICE ONLY, AND WHILE RICE GETS HIGH PRICES, IT IS SUSCEPTIBLE TO COLD. IF MILLET HAD BEEN PLANTED, THERE WOULD HAVE BEEN FOOD.
I EXPECT THAT, ERE LONG, I SHALL BE FORCED TO RETIRE FROM MY POST OF SENIOR COUNCILLOR.
AND THAT IS ALL THE MORE REASON THAT I WISH TO ACCOMPLISH THIS ONE THING AT LEAST BEFORE I GO--THE ERADICATION OF THE RED-FACE POX.
I PRAY YOU, AONUMA.
MY LADY.
I WOULD GLADLY GIVE MY LIFE TO THAT END.
...
WHEN I FIRST MET YOU, YOU WERE BUT A YOUTH.
...WE HAVE BOTH AGED IN THE YEARS SINCE.

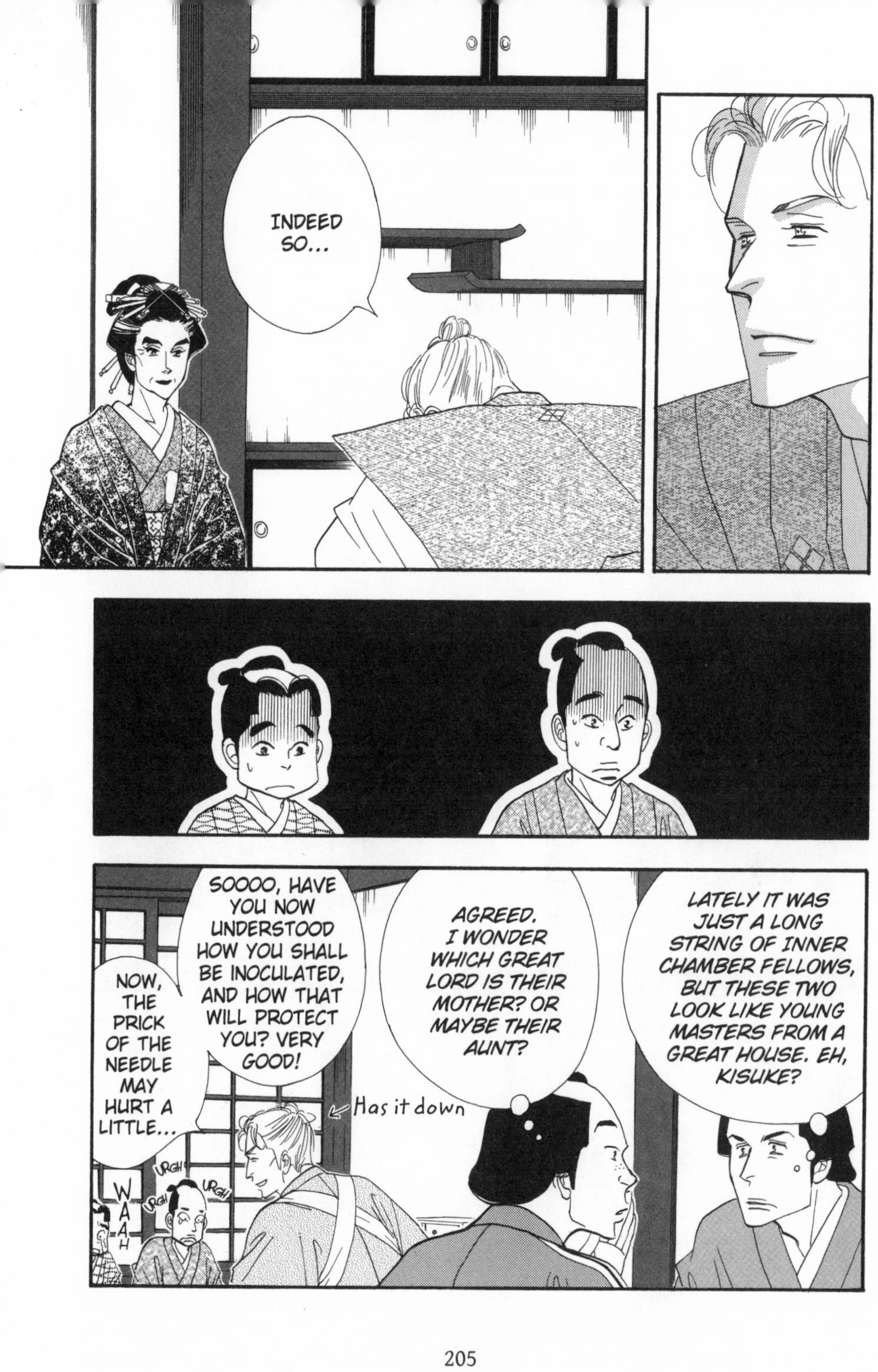
INDEED SO...
LATELY IT WAS JUST A LONG STRING OF INNER CHAMBER FELLOWS, BUT THESE TWO LOOK LIKE YOUNG MASTERS FROM A GREAT HOUSE. EH, KISUKE?
AGREED. I WONDER WHICH GREAT LORD IS THEIR MOTHER? OR MAYBE THEIR AUNT?
Has it down
SOOOO, HAVE YOU NOW UNDERSTOOD HOW YOU SHALL BE INOCULATED, AND HOW THAT WILL PROTECT YOU? VERY GOOD!
NOW, THE PRICK OF THE NEEDLE MAY HURT A LITTLE...
URGH
URGH
URGH
WAAAH

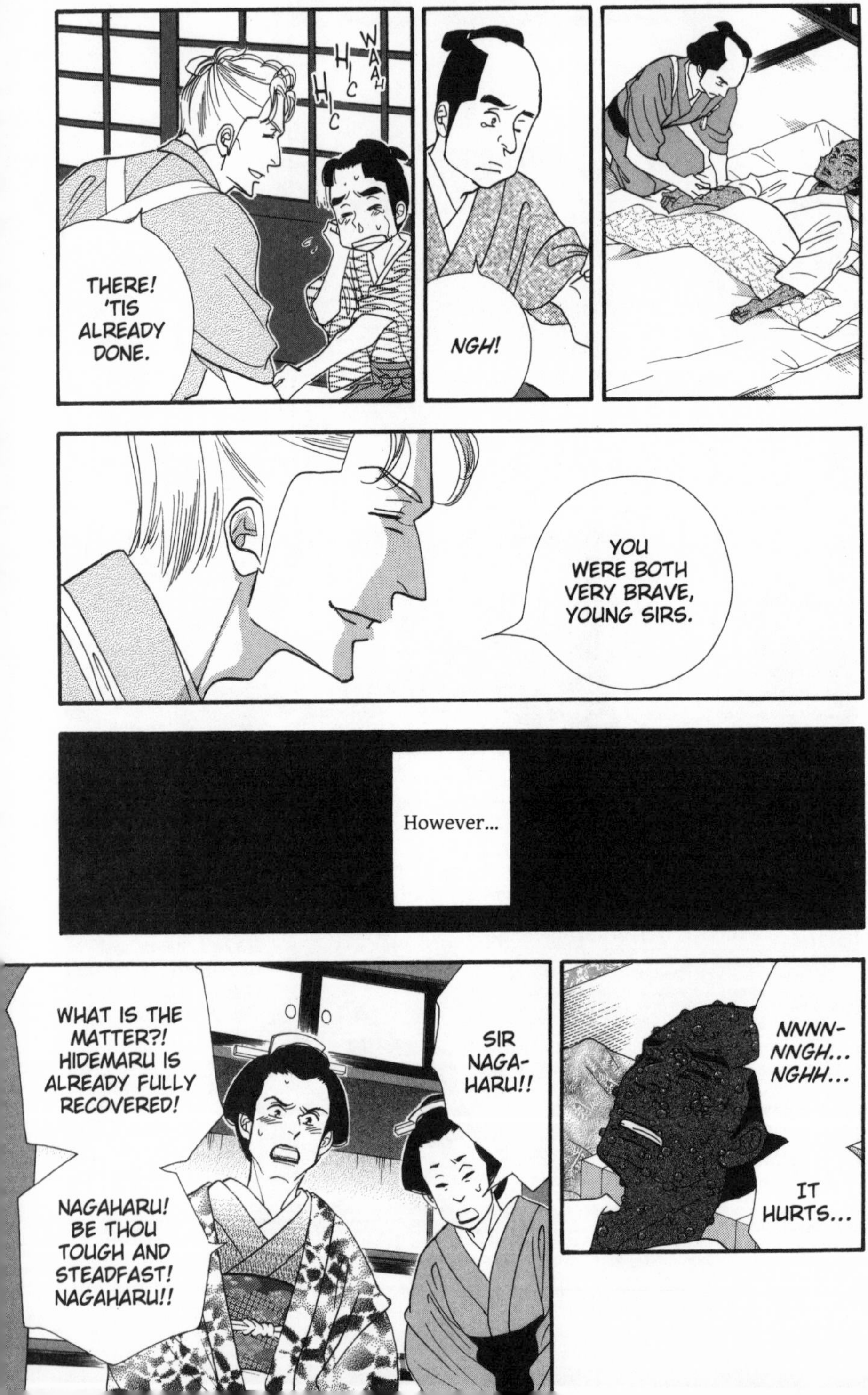
NGH!
WAAH
HIC HIC
THERE! 'TIS ALREADY DONE.
YOU WERE BOTH VERY BRAVE, YOUNG SIRS.
However...
NNNN-NNGH... NGHH...
IT HURTS...
SIR NAGA-HARU!!
WHAT IS THE MATTER?! HIDEMARU IS ALREADY FULLY RECOVERED!
NAGAHARU! BE THOU TOUGH AND STEADFAST! NAGAHARU!!

HONORED MOTHER...
!!
NAGA...
NAGAHARU!!
NAGAHARU IS DEAD...?

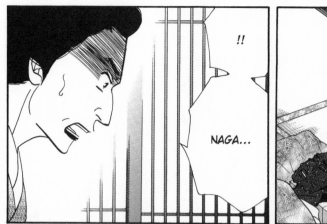

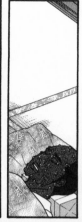

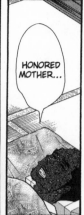

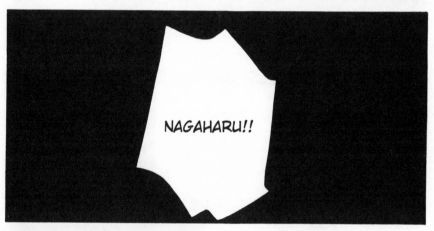

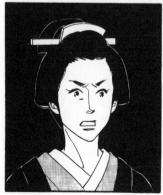

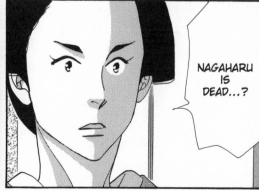

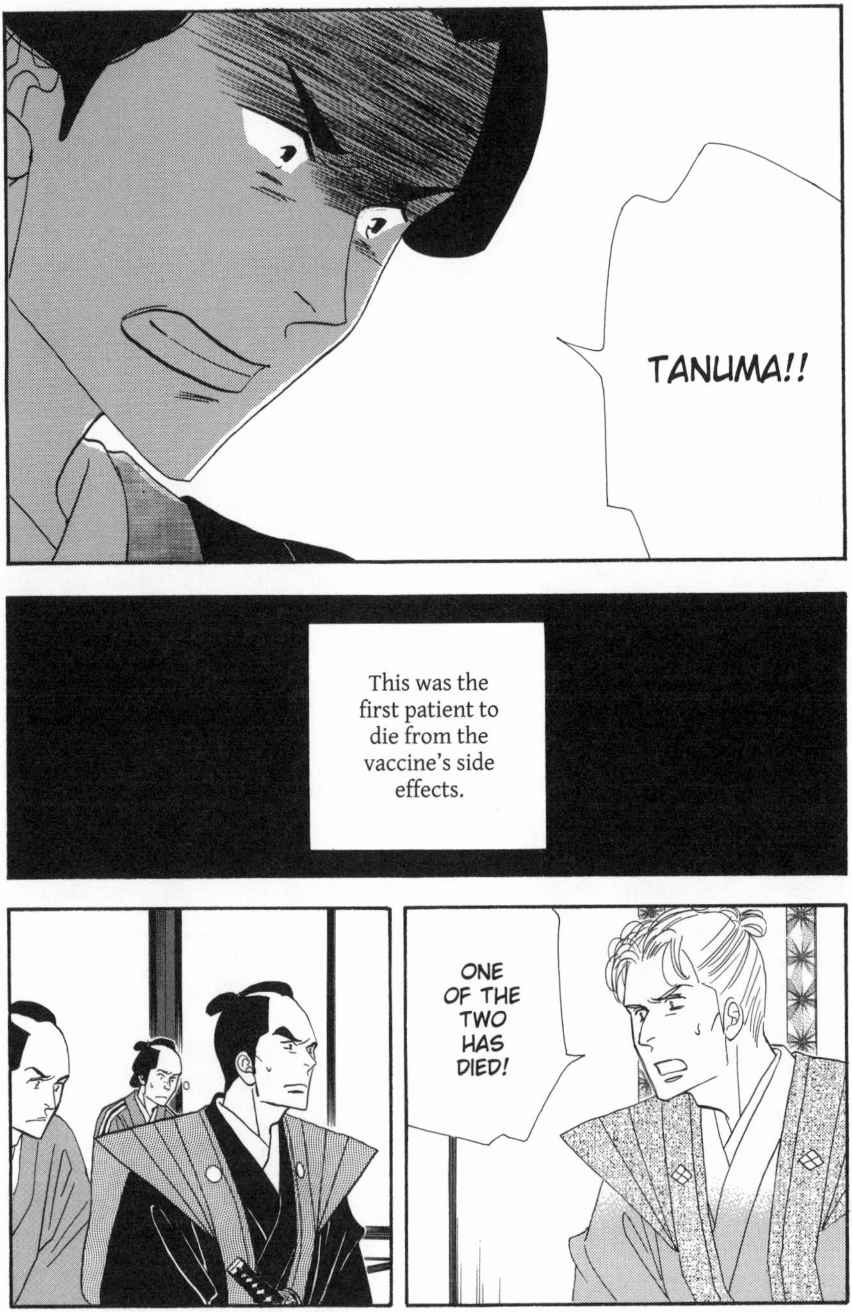
TANUMA!!
This was the first patient to die from the vaccine's side effects.
ONE OF THE TWO HAS DIED!

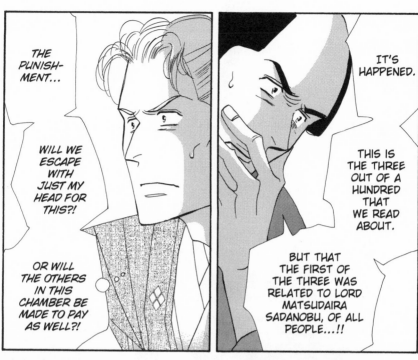

IT'S HAPPENED.
THIS IS THE THREE OUT OF A HUNDRED THAT WE READ ABOUT.
BUT THAT THE FIRST OF THE THREE WAS RELATED TO LORD MATSUDAIRA SADANOBU, OF ALL PEOPLE...!!
THE PUNISHMENT...
WILL WE ESCAPE WITH JUST MY HEAD FOR THIS?!
OR WILL THE OTHERS IN THIS CHAMBER BE MADE TO PAY AS WELL?!
VALET!!
SEND A MESSENGER TO THE MANSE OF TANUMA OKITSUGU, RIGHT AWAY! HO! SERVANTS!
MY LORD!
WHAT IS IT?! I AM DEALING WITH A MATTER OF UTMOST URGENCY!!
AYE, M'LORD!! BUT A MESSENGER HAS JUST ARRIVED FROM EDO CASTLE!!

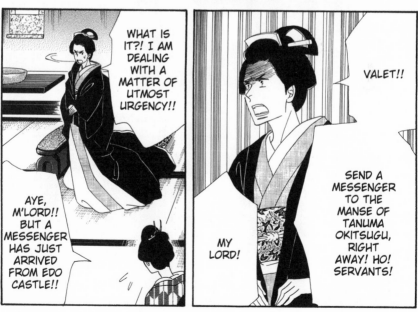

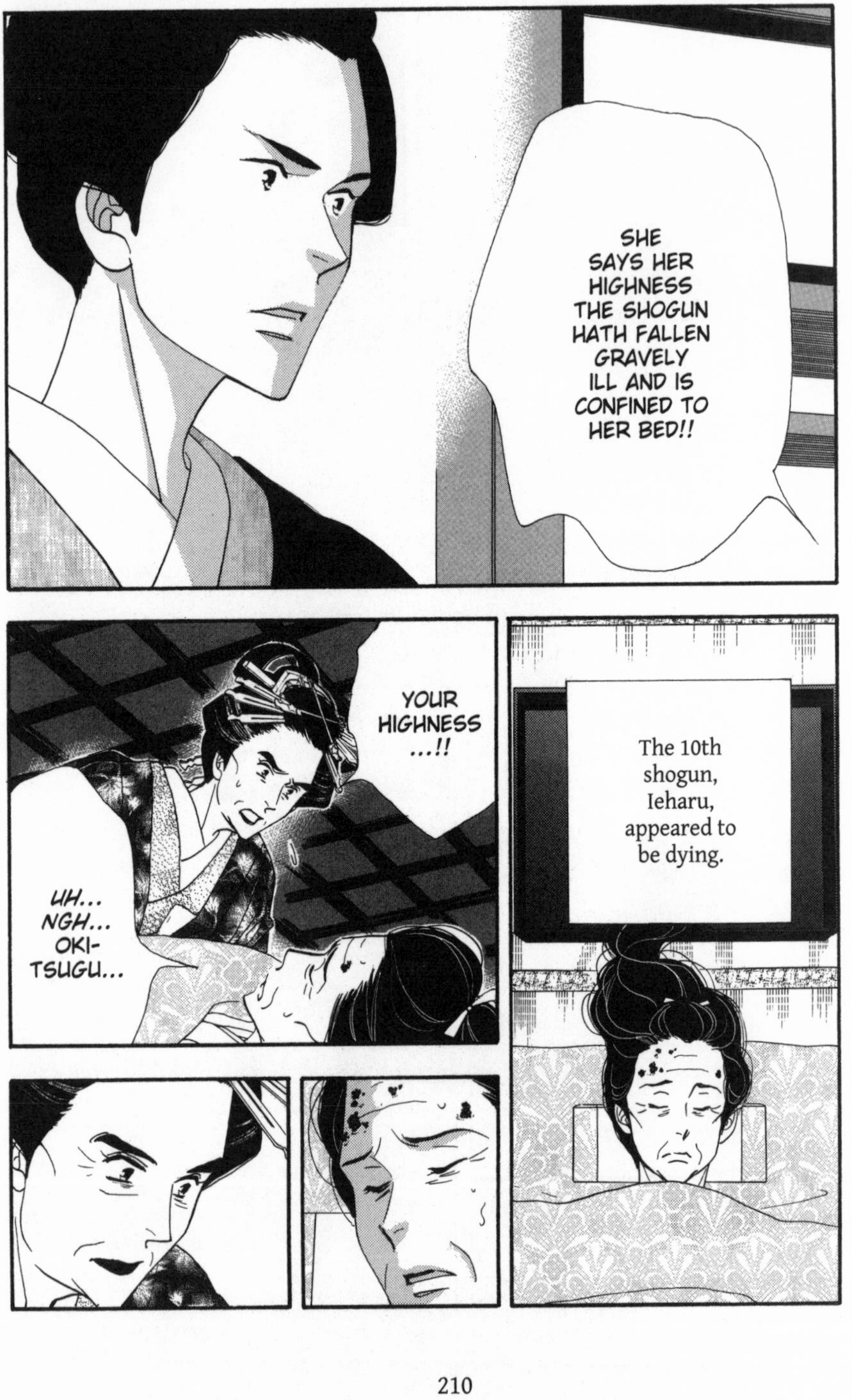
SHE SAYS HER HIGHNESS THE SHOGUN HATH FALLEN GRAVELY ILL AND IS CONFINED TO HER BED!!
The 10th shogun, Ieharu, appeared to be dying.
YOUR HIGHNESS ...!!
UH... NGH... OKI-TSUGU...

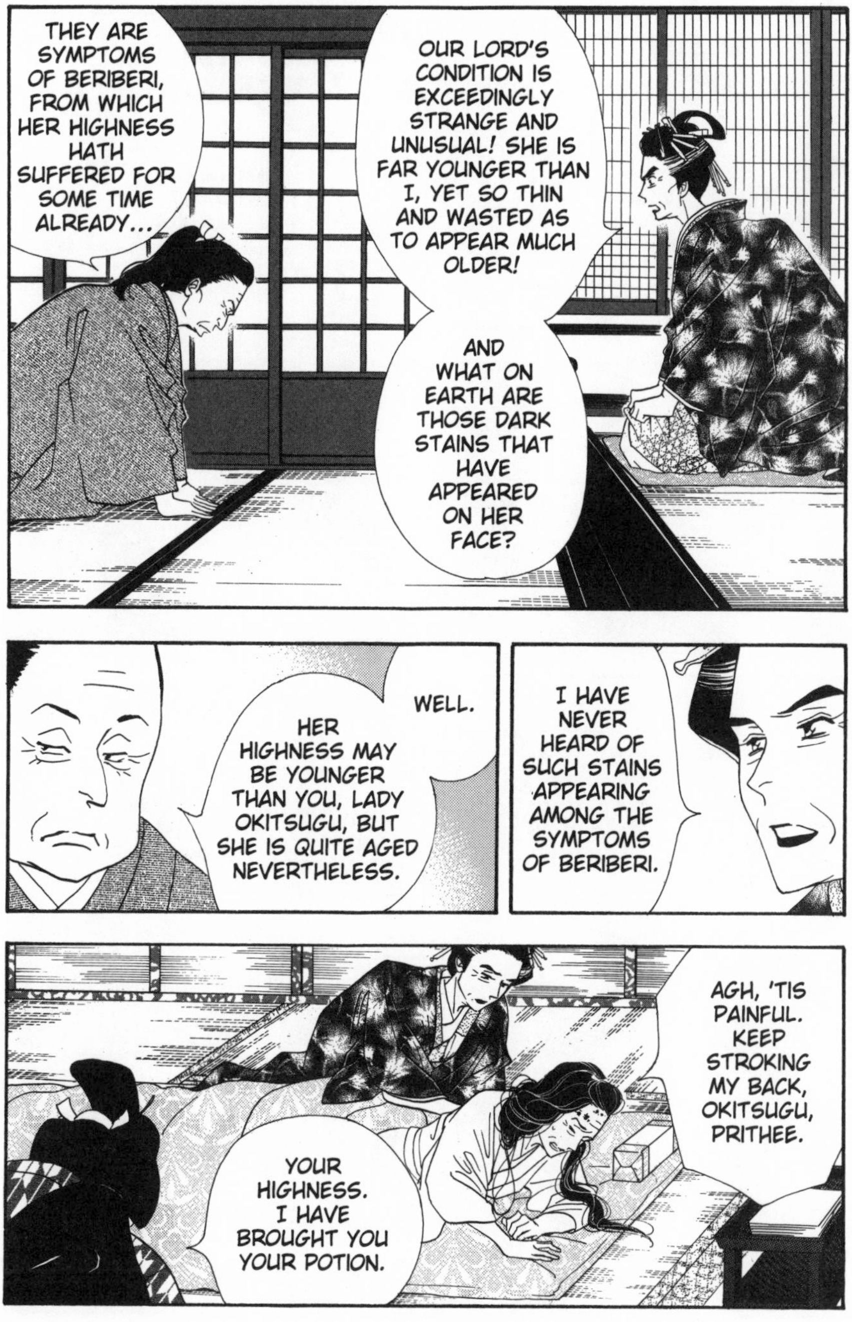
OUR LORD'S CONDITION IS EXCEEDINGLY STRANGE AND UNUSUAL! SHE IS FAR YOUNGER THAN I, YET SO THIN AND WASTED AS TO APPEAR MUCH OLDER!
AND WHAT ON EARTH ARE THOSE DARK STAINS THAT HAVE APPEARED ON HER FACE?
THEY ARE SYMPTOMS OF BERIBERI, FROM WHICH HER HIGHNESS HATH SUFFERED FOR SOME TIME ALREADY...
I HAVE NEVER HEARD OF SUCH STAINS APPEARING AMONG THE SYMPTOMS OF BERIBERI.
WELL.
HER HIGHNESS MAY BE YOUNGER THAN YOU, LADY OKITSUGU, BUT SHE IS QUITE AGED NEVERTHELESS.
AGH, 'TIS PAINFUL. KEEP STROKING MY BACK, OKITSUGU, PRITHEE.
YOUR HIGHNESS. I HAVE BROUGHT YOU YOUR POTION.

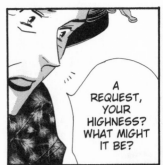

I SHAN'T DRINK IT.
OKITSUGU, LISTEN TO ME. I HAVE A REQUEST TO MAKE OF THEE.
A REQUEST, YOUR HIGHNESS? WHAT MIGHT IT BE?
I WISH TO BE EXAMINED BY THE HOLLANDER PHYSICIAN IN THE INNER CHAMBERS.
WHAT ?!
HAVE A MAN— AND A HOLLANDER PHYSICIAN AT THAT— EXAMINE HER HIGHNESS?!
NAY!! MOST CERTAINLY NOT, LADY TANUMA!
BUT THAT IS THE EXPRESS BEHEST OF OUR LIEGE HERSELF.
BUT ...!!
OH, I DON'T SEE WHY NOT, BARON OF SADO.

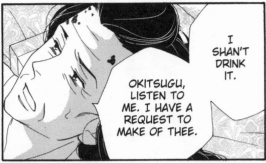

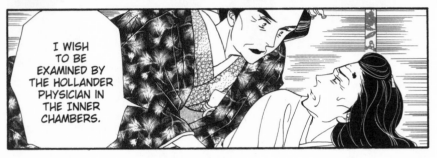

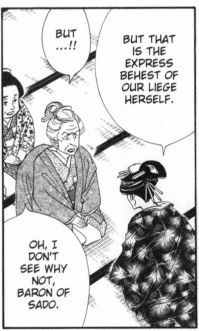

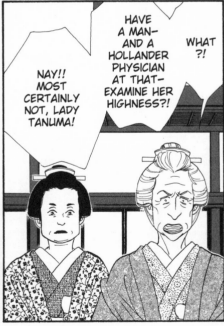

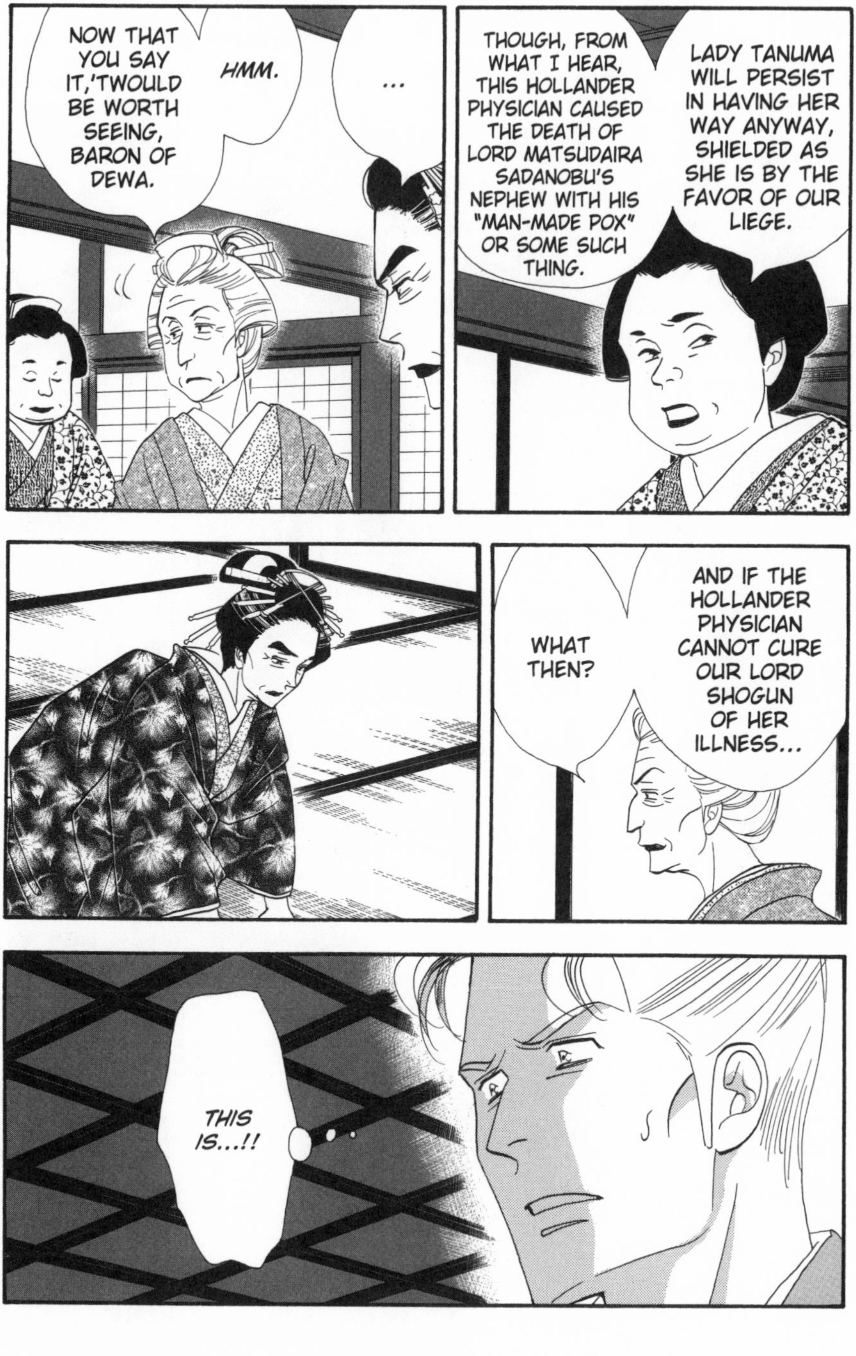
LADY TANUMA WILL PERSIST IN HAVING HER WAY ANYWAY, SHIELDED AS SHE IS BY THE FAVOR OF OUR LIEGE.
THOUGH, FROM WHAT I HEAR, THIS HOLLANDER PHYSICIAN CAUSED THE DEATH OF LORD MATSUDAIRA SADANOBU'S NEPHEW WITH HIS "MAN-MADE POX" OR SOME SUCH THING.
...
HMM.
NOW THAT YOU SAY IT,'TWOULD BE WORTH SEEING, BARON OF DEWA.
AND IF THE HOLLANDER PHYSICIAN CANNOT CURE OUR LORD SHOGUN OF HER ILLNESS...
WHAT THEN?
THIS IS...!!

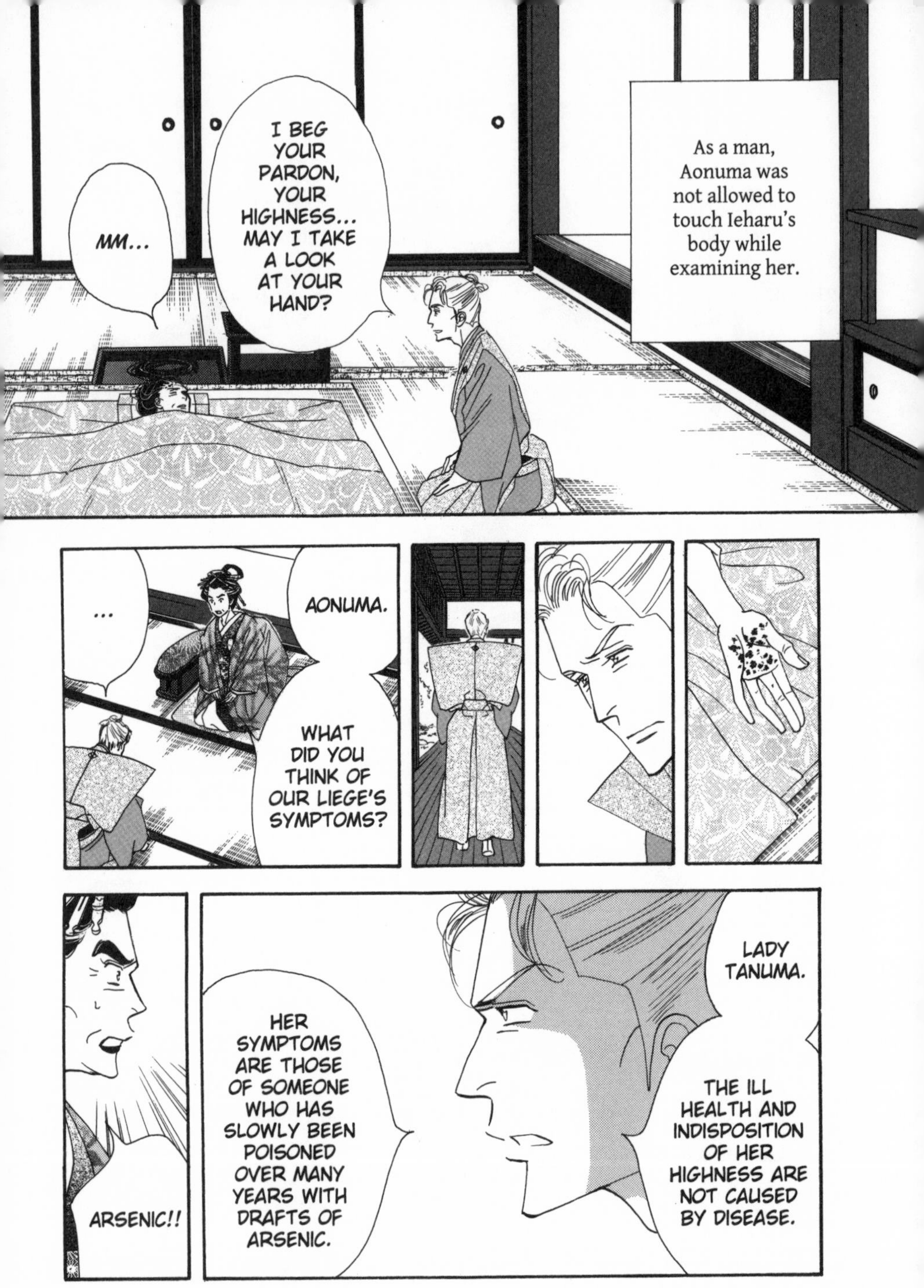
As a man, Aonuma was not allowed to touch Ieharu's body while examining her.
I BEG YOUR PARDON, YOUR HIGHNESS... MAY I TAKE A LOOK AT YOUR HAND?
MM...
AONUMA.
WHAT DID YOU THINK OF OUR LIEGE'S SYMPTOMS?
...
LADY TANUMA.
THE ILL HEALTH AND INDISPOSITION OF HER HIGHNESS ARE NOT CAUSED BY DISEASE.
HER SYMPTOMS ARE THOSE OF SOMEONE WHO HAS SLOWLY BEEN POISONED OVER MANY YEARS WITH DRAFTS OF ARSENIC.
ARSENIC!!

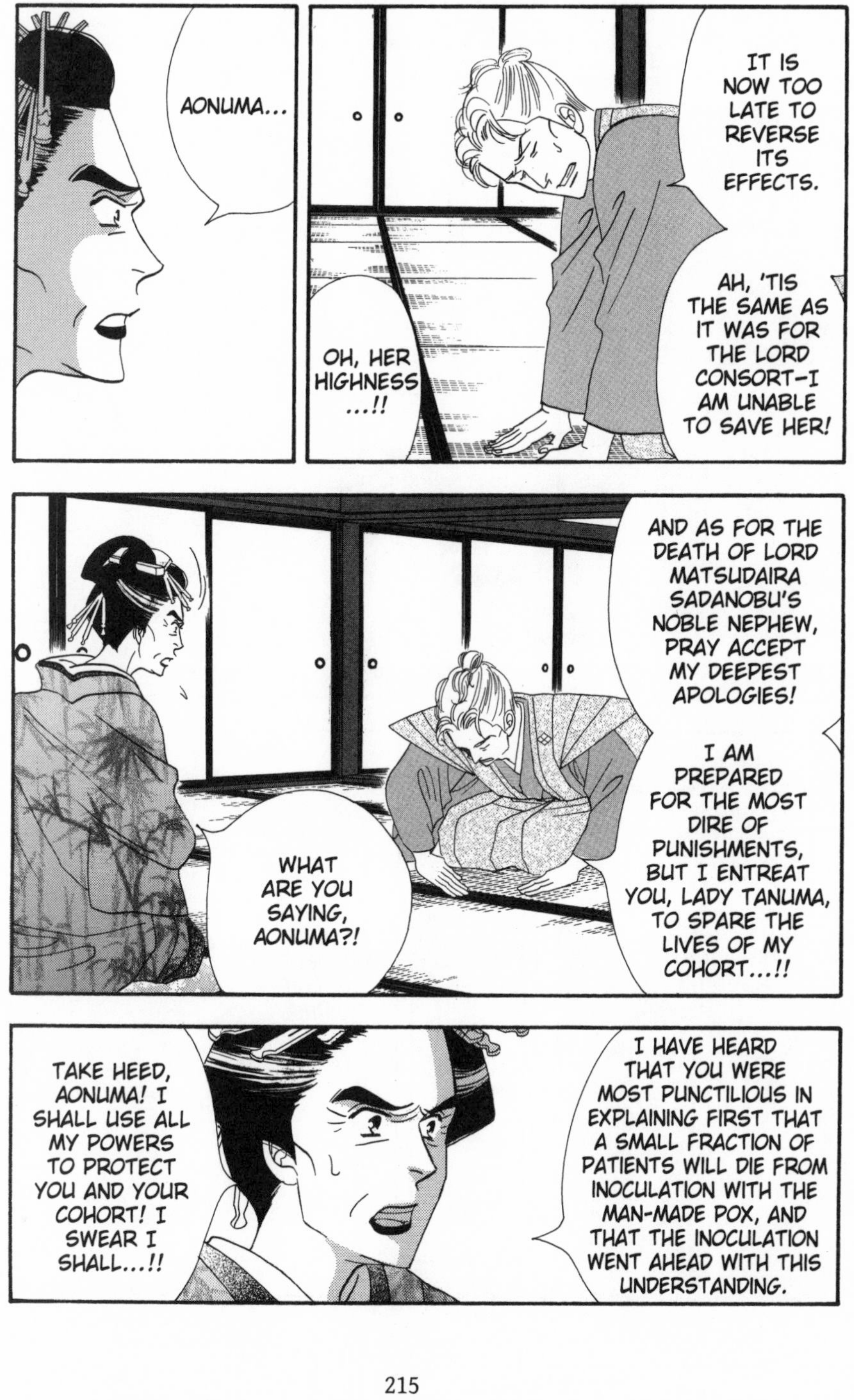
IT IS NOW TOO LATE TO REVERSE ITS EFFECTS.
AH, 'TIS THE SAME AS IT WAS FOR THE LORD CONSORT—I AM UNABLE TO SAVE HER!
OH, HER HIGHNESS ...!!
AONUMA...
AND AS FOR THE DEATH OF LORD MATSUDAIRA SADANOBU'S NOBLE NEPHEW, PRAY ACCEPT MY DEEPEST APOLOGIES!
I AM PREPARED FOR THE MOST DIRE OF PUNISHMENTS, BUT I ENTREAT YOU, LADY TANUMA, TO SPARE THE LIVES OF MY COHORT...!!
WHAT ARE YOU SAYING, AONUMA?!
I HAVE HEARD THAT YOU WERE MOST PUNCTILIOUS IN EXPLAINING FIRST THAT A SMALL FRACTION OF PATIENTS WILL DIE FROM INOCULATION WITH THE MAN-MADE POX, AND THAT THE INOCULATION WENT AHEAD WITH THIS UNDERSTANDING.
TAKE HEED, AONUMA! I SHALL USE ALL MY POWERS TO PROTECT YOU AND YOUR COHORT! I SWEAR I SHALL...!!

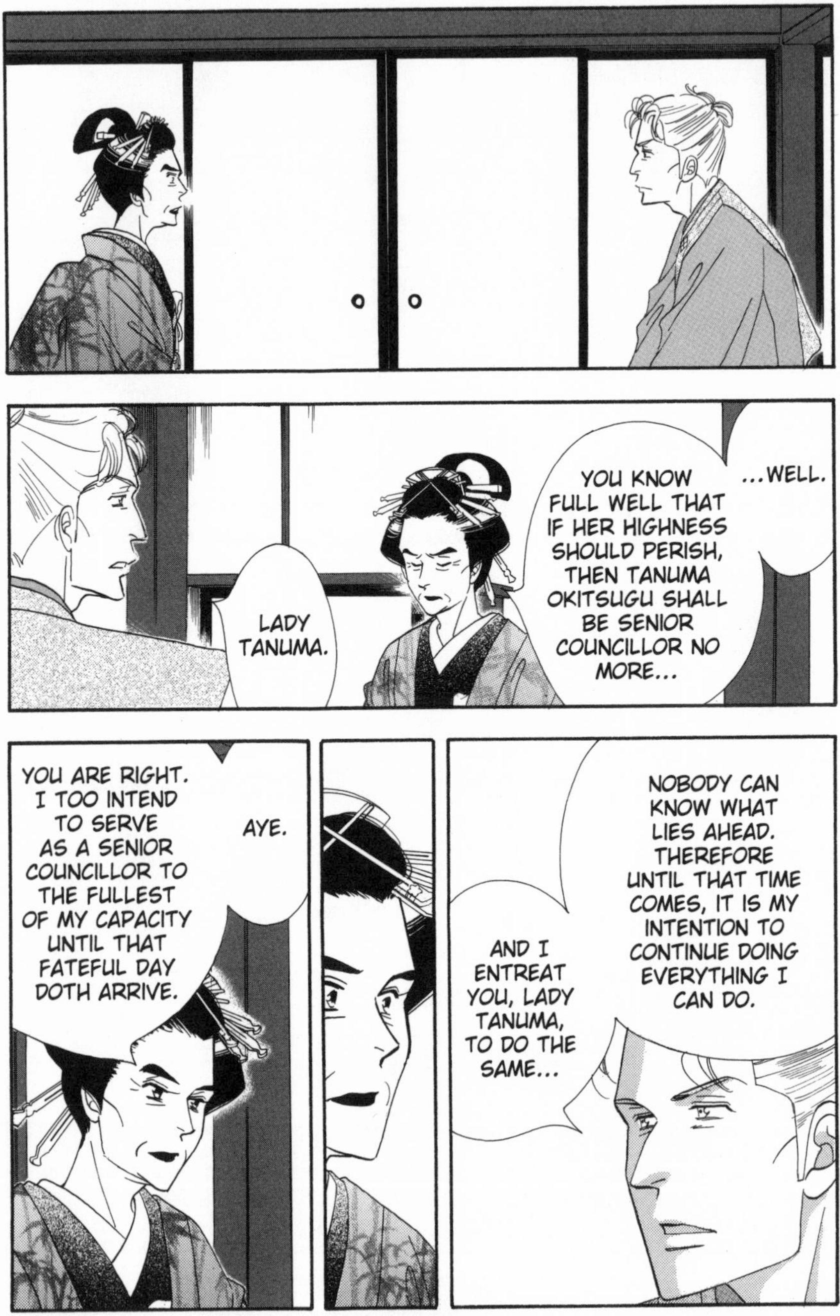
...WELL.
YOU KNOW FULL WELL THAT IF HER HIGHNESS SHOULD PERISH, THEN TANUMA OKITSUGU SHALL BE SENIOR COUNCILLOR NO MORE...
LADY TANUMA.
NOBODY CAN KNOW WHAT LIES AHEAD. THEREFORE UNTIL THAT TIME COMES, IT IS MY INTENTION TO CONTINUE DOING EVERYTHING I CAN DO.
AND I ENTREAT YOU, LADY TANUMA, TO DO THE SAME...
AYE.
YOU ARE RIGHT. I TOO INTEND TO SERVE AS A SENIOR COUNCILLOR TO THE FULLEST OF MY CAPACITY UNTIL THAT FATEFUL DAY DOTH ARRIVE.

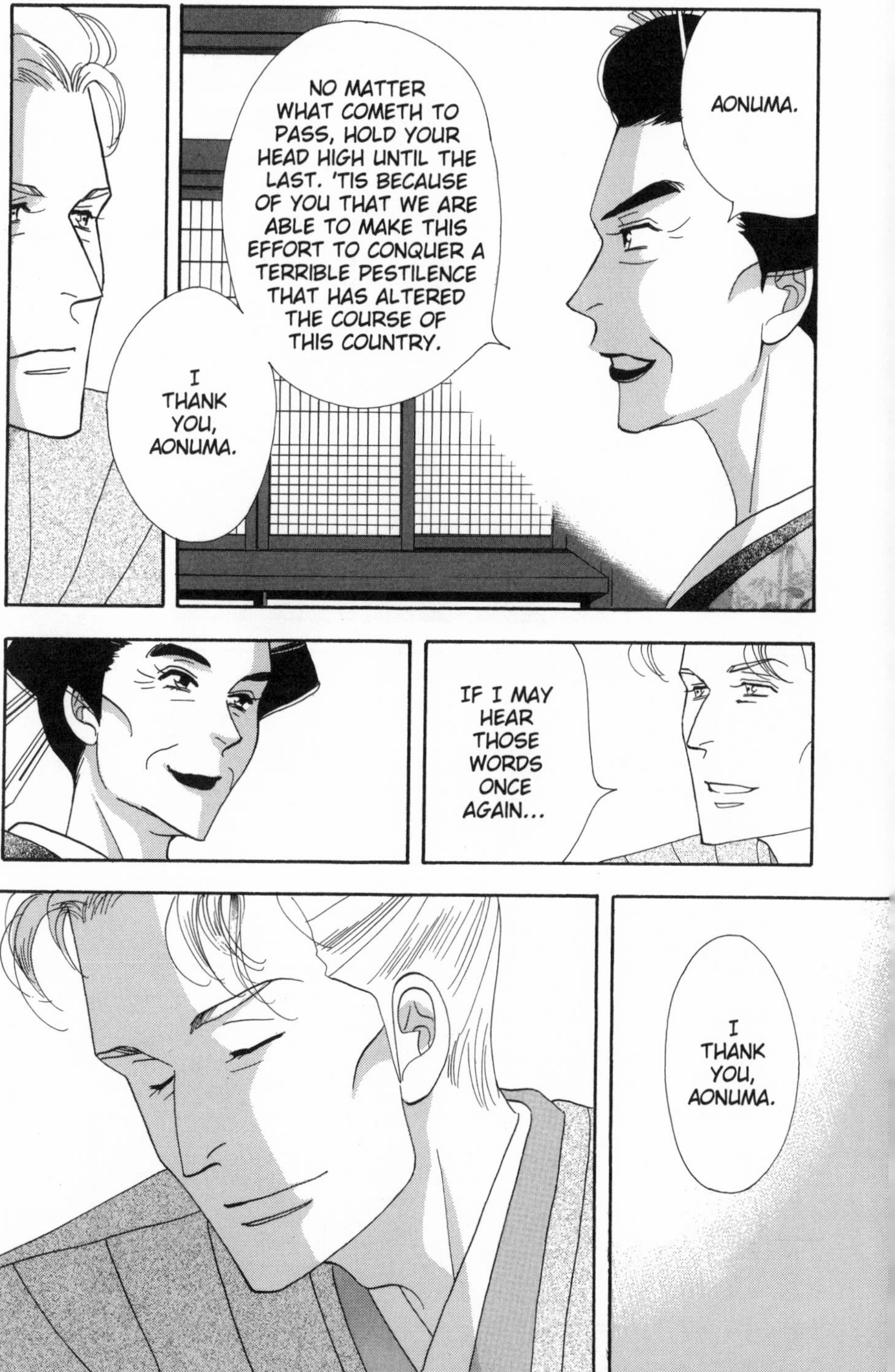
AONUMA.
NO MATTER WHAT COMETH TO PASS, HOLD YOUR HEAD HIGH UNTIL THE LAST. 'TIS BECAUSE OF YOU THAT WE ARE ABLE TO MAKE THIS EFFORT TO CONQUER A TERRIBLE PESTILENCE THAT HAS ALTERED THE COURSE OF THIS COUNTRY.
I THANK YOU, AONUMA.
IF I MAY HEAR THOSE WORDS ONCE AGAIN...
I THANK YOU, AONUMA.

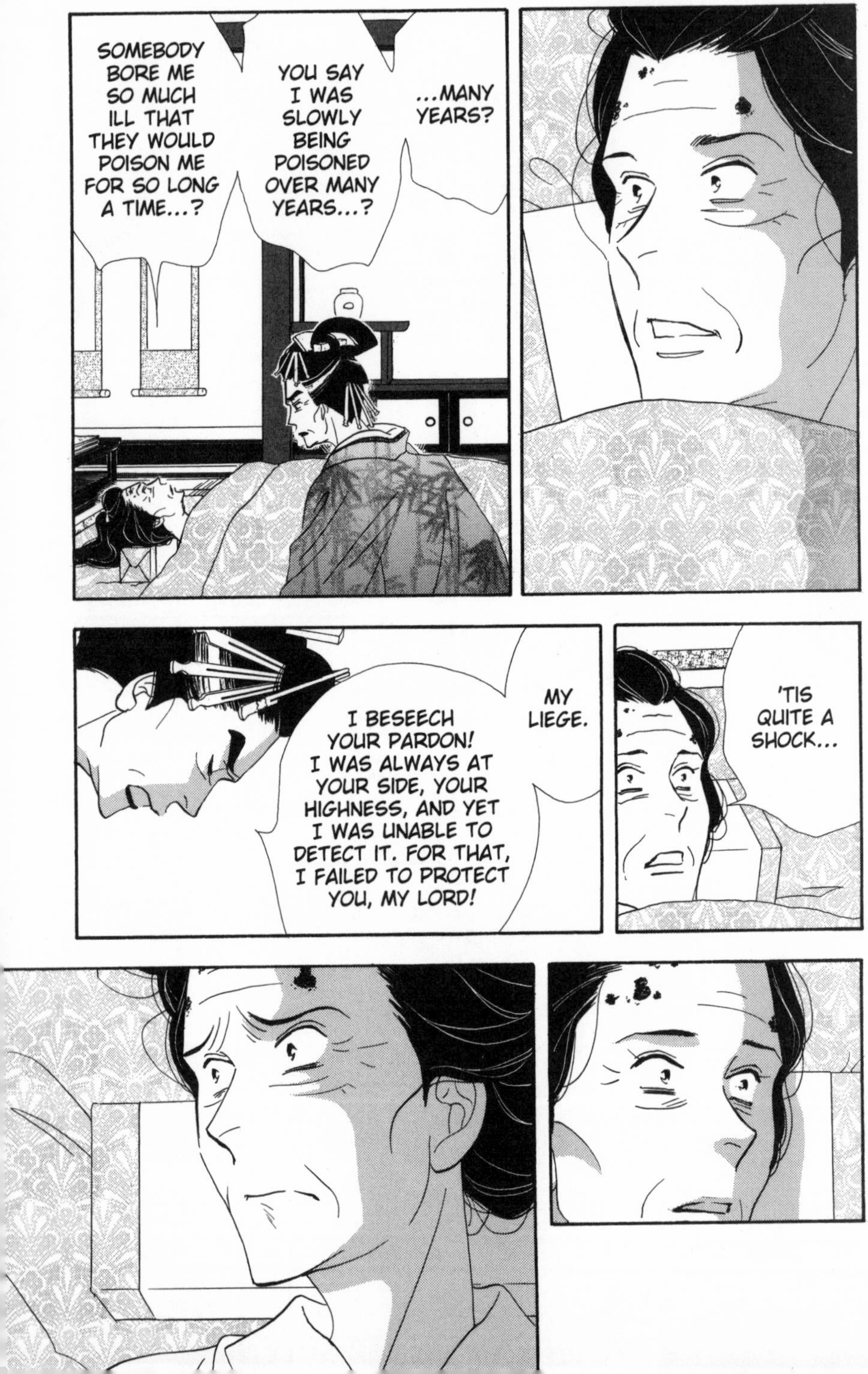
...MANY YEARS?
YOU SAY I WAS SLOWLY BEING POISONED OVER MANY YEARS...?
SOMEBODY BORE ME SO MUCH ILL THAT THEY WOULD POISON ME FOR SO LONG A TIME...?
'TIS QUITE A SHOCK...
MY LIEGE.
I BESEECH YOUR PARDON! I WAS ALWAYS AT YOUR SIDE, YOUR HIGHNESS, AND YET I WAS UNABLE TO DETECT IT. FOR THAT, I FAILED TO PROTECT YOU, MY LORD!

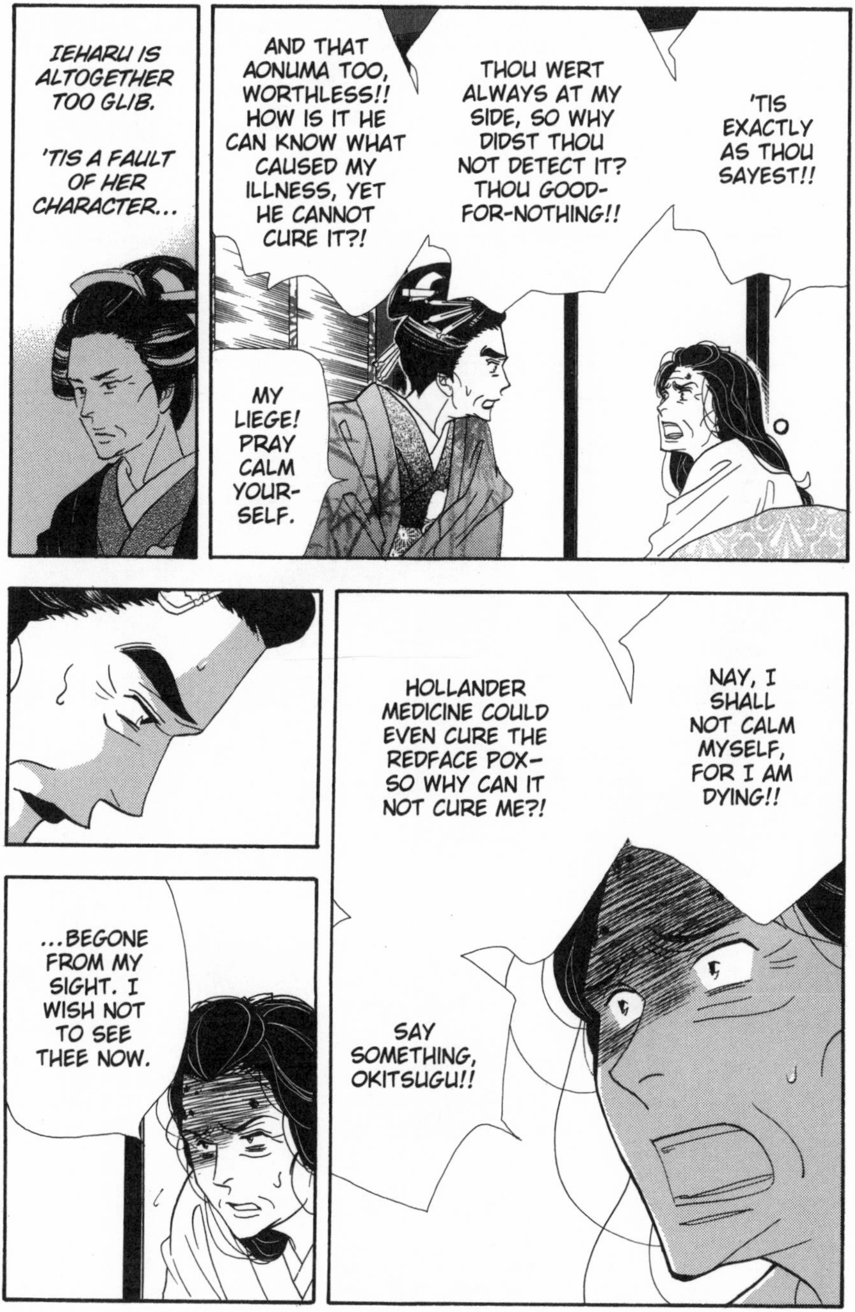
'TIS EXACTLY AS THOU SAYEST!!
THOU WERT ALWAYS AT MY SIDE, SO WHY DIDST THOU NOT DETECT IT? THOU GOOD-FOR-NOTHING!!
AND THAT AONUMA TOO, WORTHLESS!! HOW IS IT HE CAN KNOW WHAT CAUSED MY ILLNESS, YET HE CANNOT CURE IT?!
MY LIEGE! PRAY CALM YOURSELF.
IEHARU IS ALTOGETHER TOO GLIB.
'TIS A FAULT OF HER CHARACTER...
NAY, I SHALL NOT CALM MYSELF, FOR I AM DYING!!
HOLLANDER MEDICINE COULD EVEN CURE THE REDFACE POX–SO WHY CAN IT NOT CURE ME?!
SAY SOMETHING, OKITSUGU!!
...BEGONE FROM MY SIGHT. I WISH NOT TO SEE THEE NOW.

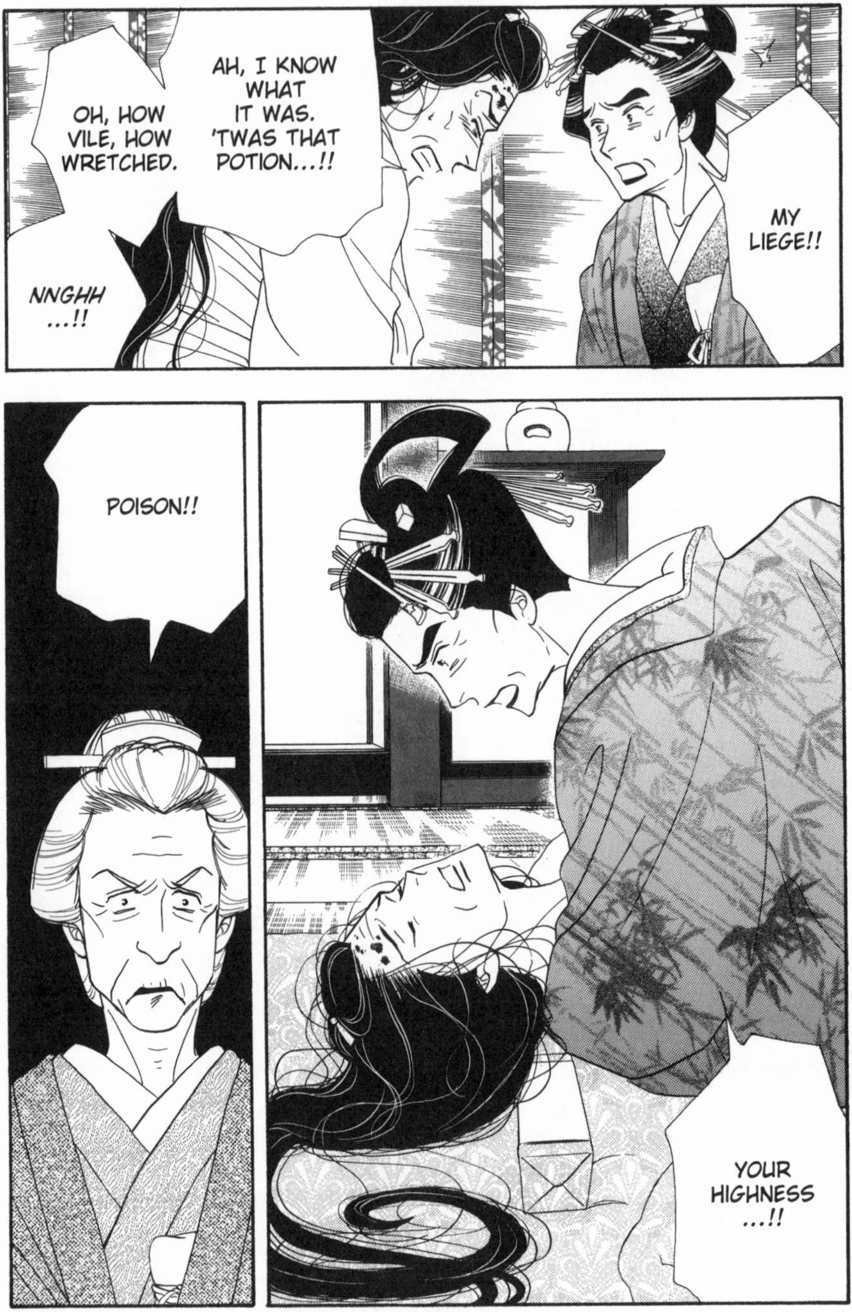
MY LIEGE!!
AH, I KNOW WHAT IT WAS. 'TWAS THAT POTION...!!
OH, HOW VILE, HOW WRETCHED.
NNGHH ...!!
YOUR HIGHNESS ...!!
POISON!!

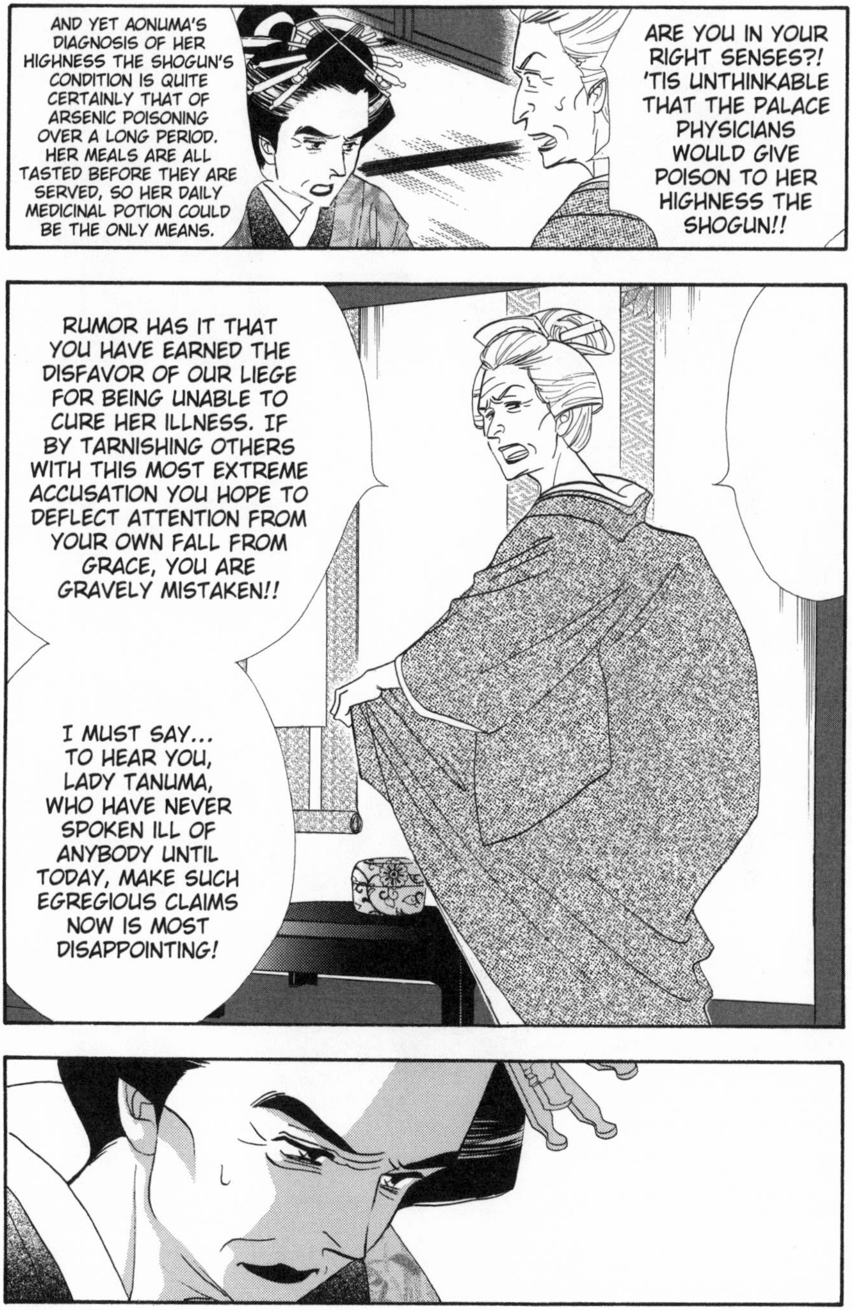
ARE YOU IN YOUR RIGHT SENSES?! 'TIS UNTHINKABLE THAT THE PALACE PHYSICIANS WOULD GIVE POISON TO HER HIGHNESS THE SHOGUN!!
AND YET AONUMA'S DIAGNOSIS OF HER HIGHNESS THE SHOGUN'S CONDITION IS QUITE CERTAINLY THAT OF ARSENIC POISONING OVER A LONG PERIOD. HER MEALS ARE ALL TASTED BEFORE THEY ARE SERVED, SO HER DAILY MEDICINAL POTION COULD BE THE ONLY MEANS.
RUMOR HAS IT THAT YOU HAVE EARNED THE DISFAVOR OF OUR LIEGE FOR BEING UNABLE TO CURE HER ILLNESS. IF BY TARNISHING OTHERS WITH THIS MOST EXTREME ACCUSATION YOU HOPE TO DEFLECT ATTENTION FROM YOUR OWN FALL FROM GRACE, YOU ARE GRAVELY MISTAKEN!!
I MUST SAY... TO HEAR YOU, LADY TANUMA, WHO HAVE NEVER SPOKEN ILL OF ANYBODY UNTIL TODAY, MAKE SUCH EGREGIOUS CLAIMS NOW IS MOST DISAPPOINTING!

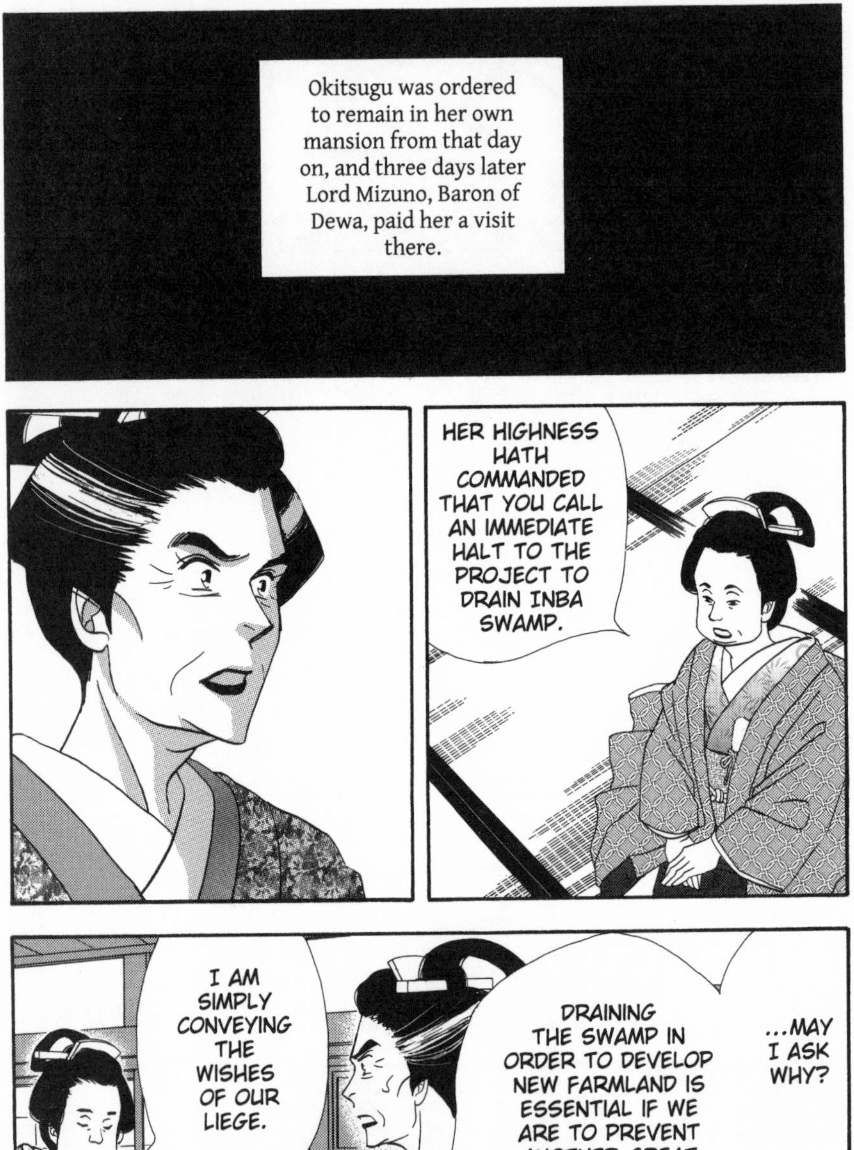
Okitsugu was ordered to remain in her own mansion from that day on, and three days later Lord Mizuno, Baron of Dewa, paid her a visit there.
HER HIGHNESS HATH COMMANDED THAT YOU CALL AN IMMEDIATE HALT TO THE PROJECT TO DRAIN INBA SWAMP.
...MAY I ASK WHY?
DRAINING THE SWAMP IN ORDER TO DEVELOP NEW FARMLAND IS ESSENTIAL IF WE ARE TO PREVENT ANOTHER GREAT FAMINE SUCH AS RECENTLY OCCURRED! ALL OF THE SENIOR COUNCILLORS AGREED–
I AM SIMPLY CONVEYING THE WISHES OF OUR LIEGE.

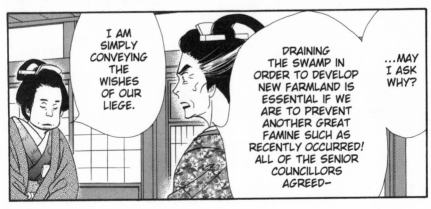

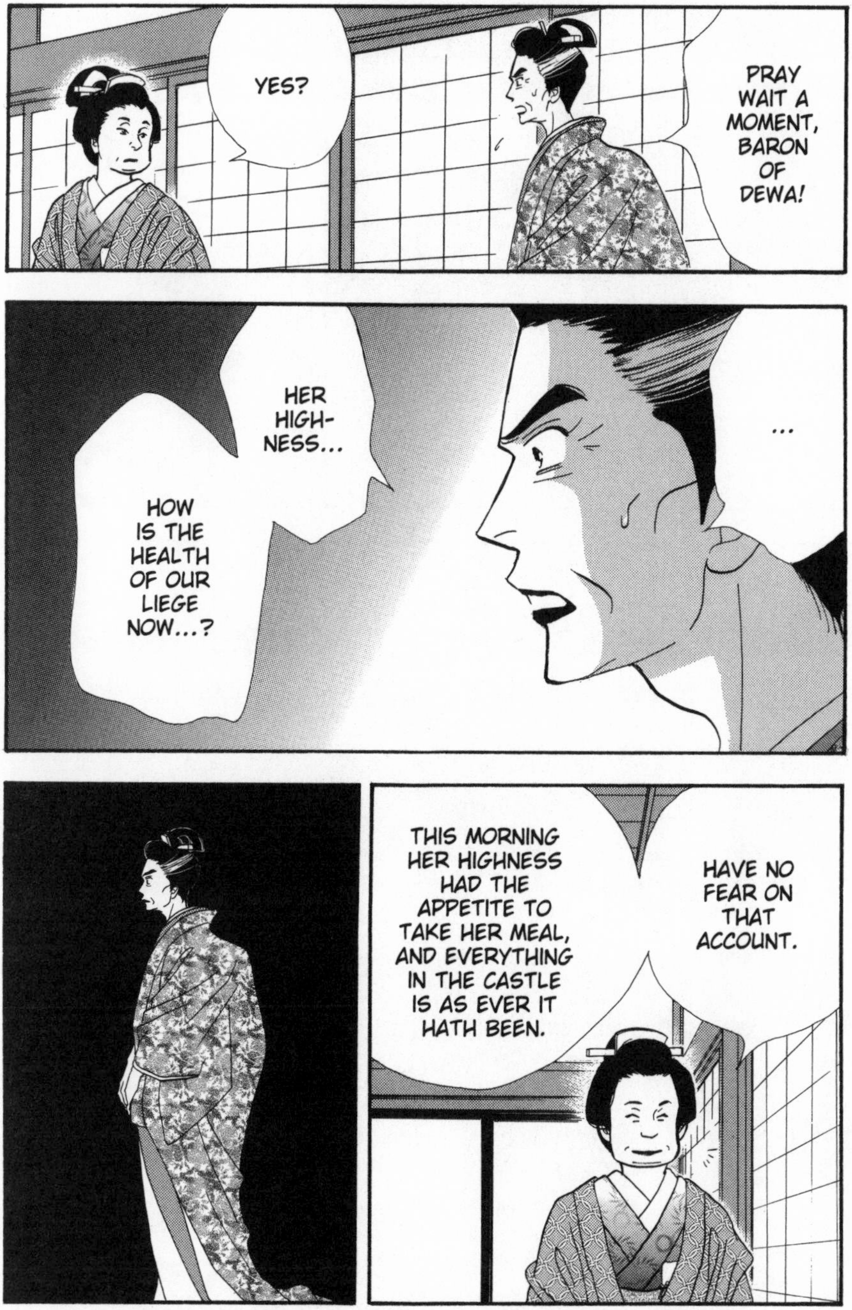
PRAY WAIT A MOMENT, BARON OF DEWA!
YES?
...
HER HIGHNESS...
HOW IS THE HEALTH OF OUR LIEGE NOW...?
HAVE NO FEAR ON THAT ACCOUNT.
THIS MORNING HER HIGHNESS HAD THE APPETITE TO TAKE HER MEAL, AND EVERYTHING IN THE CASTLE IS AS EVER IT HATH BEEN.

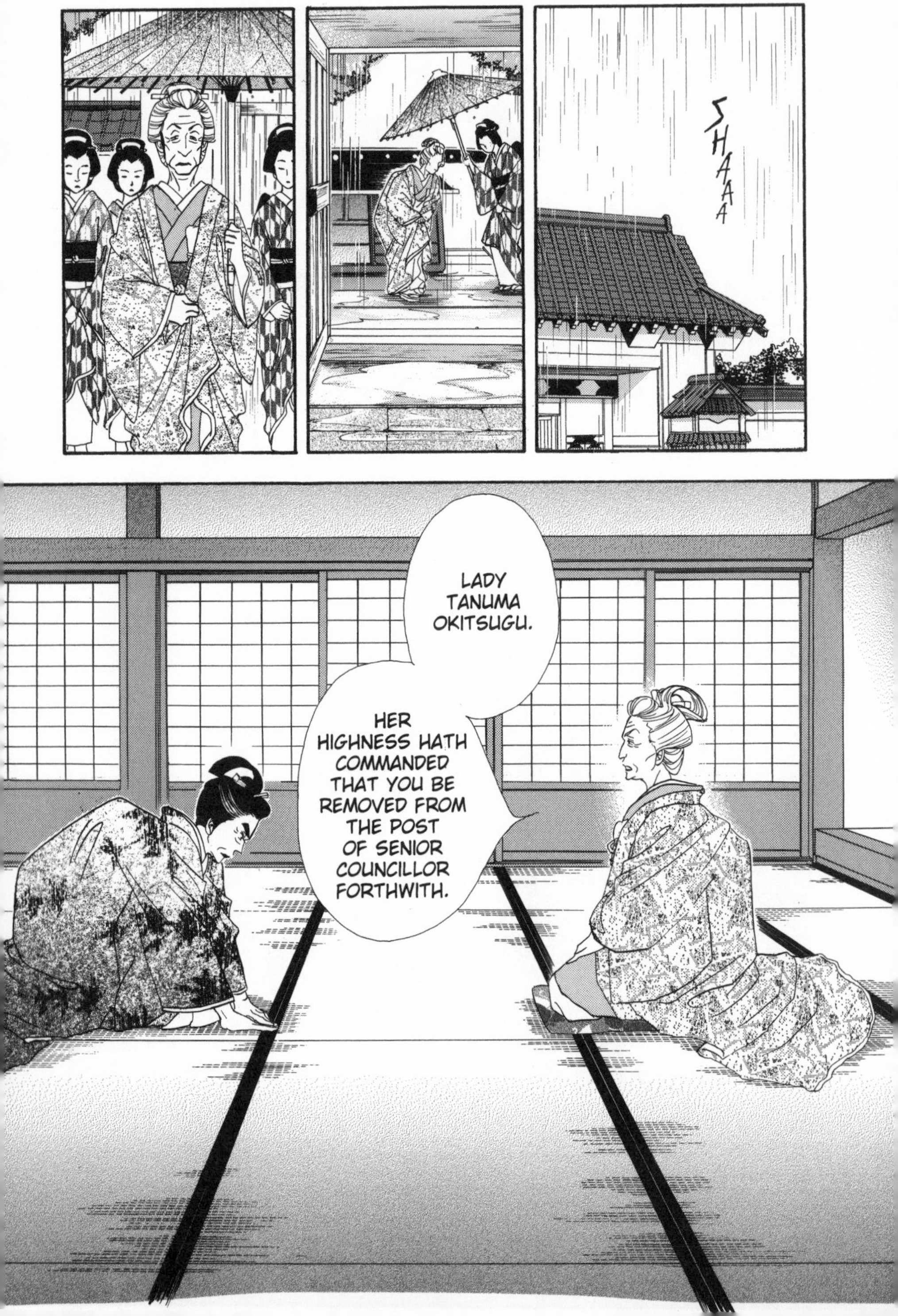
SHAAAA
LADY TANUMA OKITSUGU.
HER HIGHNESS HATH COMMANDED THAT YOU BE REMOVED FROM THE POST OF SENIOR COUNCILLOR FORTHWITH.

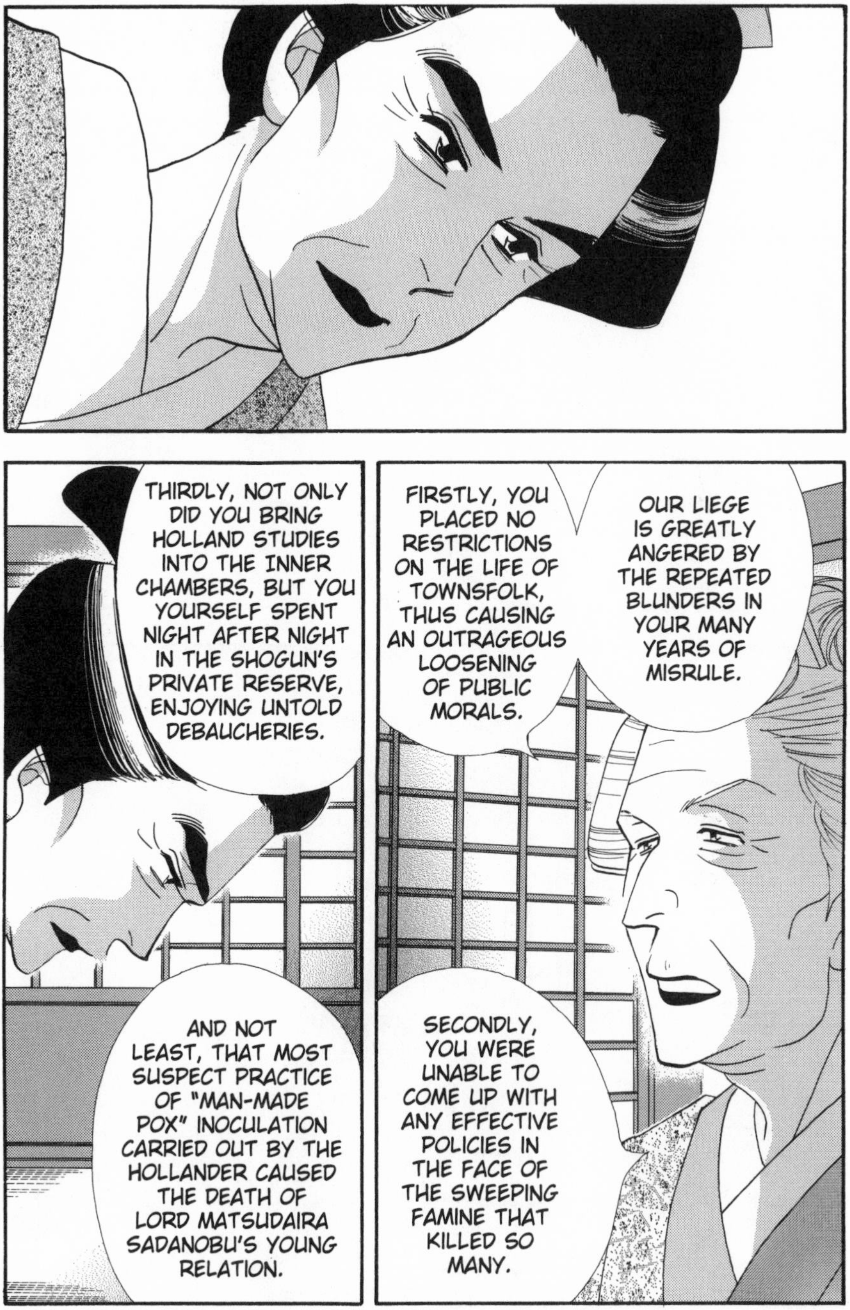
OUR LIEGE IS GREATLY ANGERED BY THE REPEATED BLUNDERS IN YOUR MANY YEARS OF MISRULE.
FIRSTLY, YOU PLACED NO RESTRICTIONS ON THE LIFE OF TOWNSFOLK, THUS CAUSING AN OUTRAGEOUS LOOSENING OF PUBLIC MORALS.
SECONDLY, YOU WERE UNABLE TO COME UP WITH ANY EFFECTIVE POLICIES IN THE FACE OF THE SWEEPING FAMINE THAT KILLED SO MANY.
THIRDLY, NOT ONLY DID YOU BRING HOLLAND STUDIES INTO THE INNER CHAMBERS, BUT YOU YOURSELF SPENT NIGHT AFTER NIGHT IN THE SHOGUN'S PRIVATE RESERVE, ENJOYING UNTOLD DEBAUCHERIES.
AND NOT LEAST, THAT MOST SUSPECT PRACTICE OF "MAN-MADE POX" INOCULATION CARRIED OUT BY THE HOLLANDER CAUSED THE DEATH OF LORD MATSUDAIRA SADANOBU'S YOUNG RELATION.

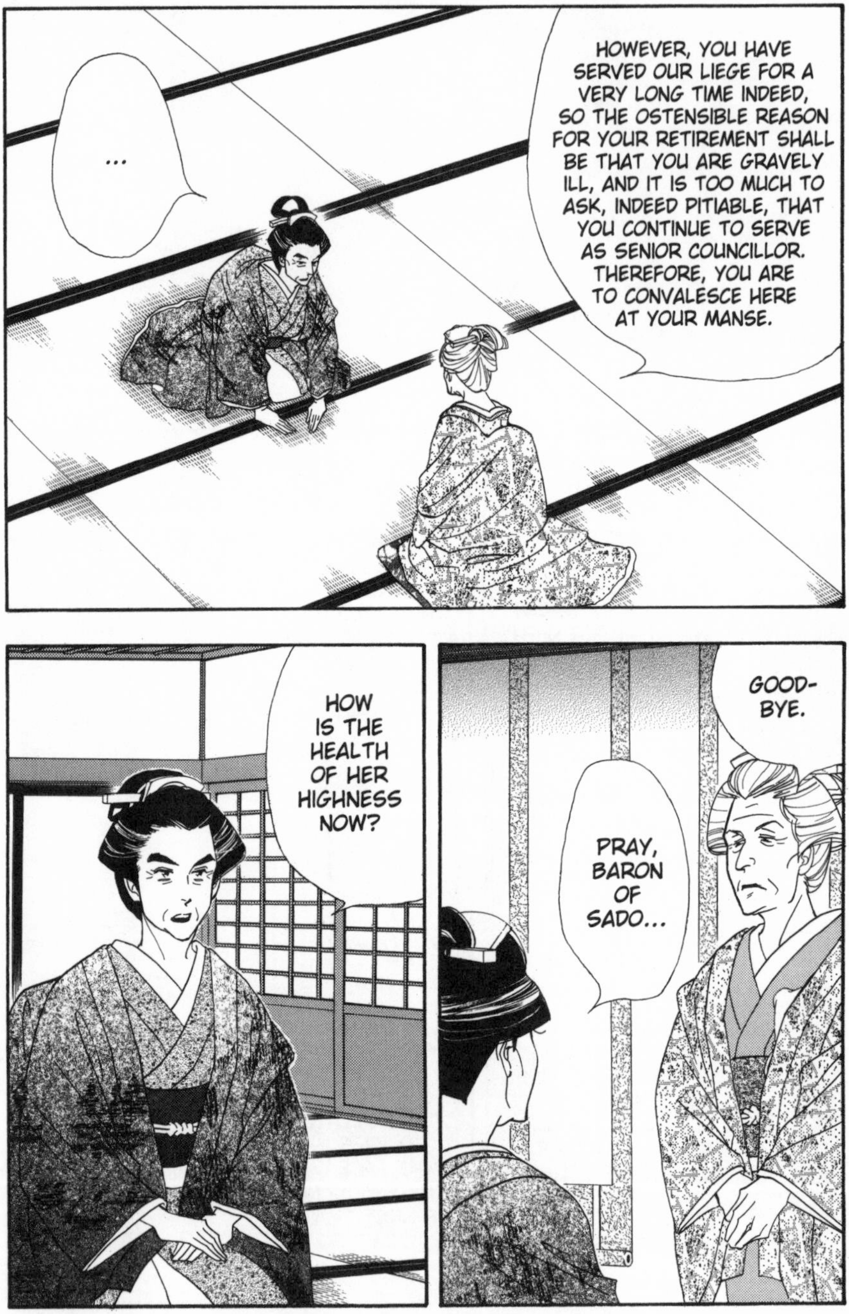
HOWEVER, YOU HAVE SERVED OUR LIEGE FOR A VERY LONG TIME INDEED, SO THE OSTENSIBLE REASON FOR YOUR RETIREMENT SHALL BE THAT YOU ARE GRAVELY ILL, AND IT IS TOO MUCH TO ASK, INDEED PITIABLE, THAT YOU CONTINUE TO SERVE AS SENIOR COUNCILLOR. THEREFORE, YOU ARE TO CONVALESCE HERE AT YOUR MANSE.
...
GOOD-BYE.
PRAY, BARON OF SADO...
HOW IS THE HEALTH OF HER HIGHNESS NOW?

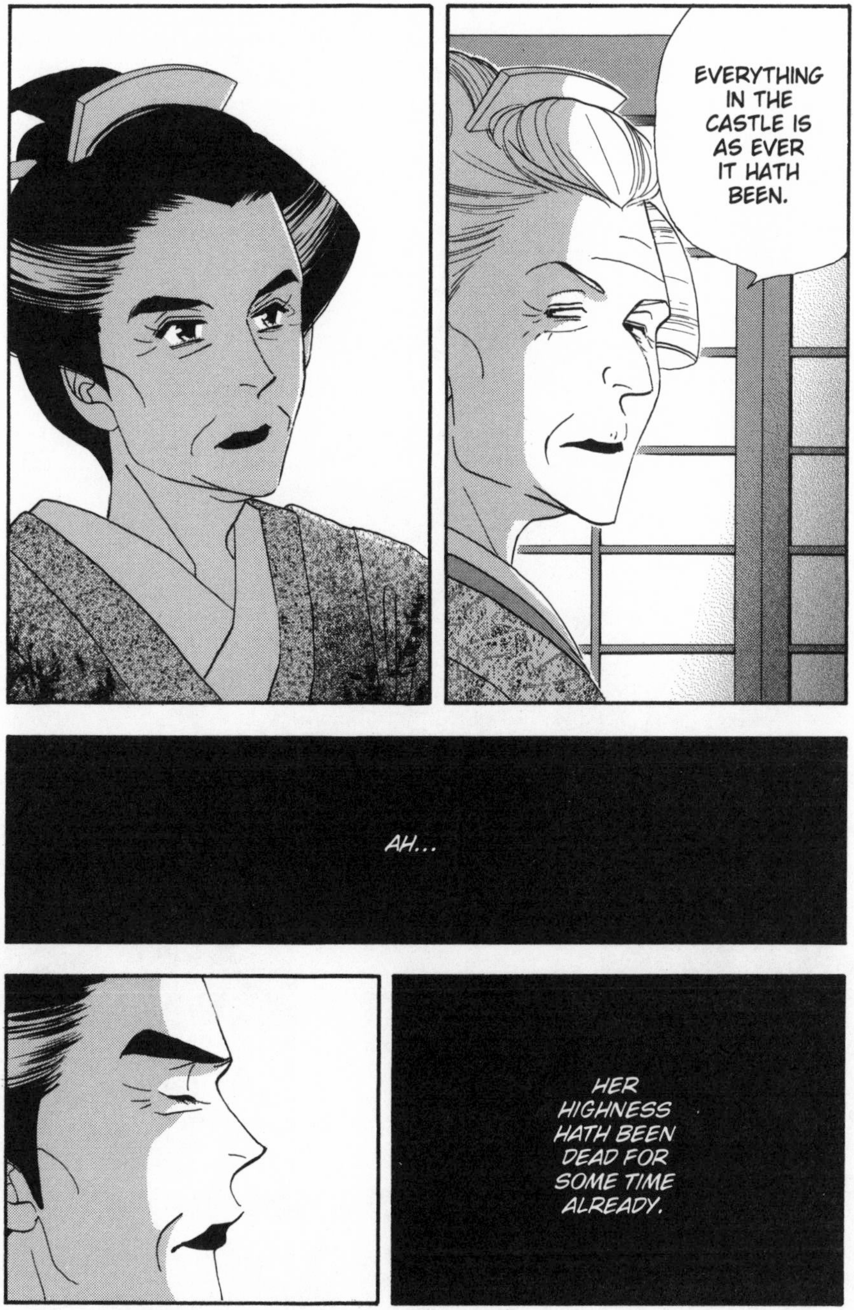
EVERYTHING IN THE CASTLE IS AS EVER IT HATH BEEN.
AH...
HER HIGHNESS HATH BEEN DEAD FOR SOME TIME ALREADY.

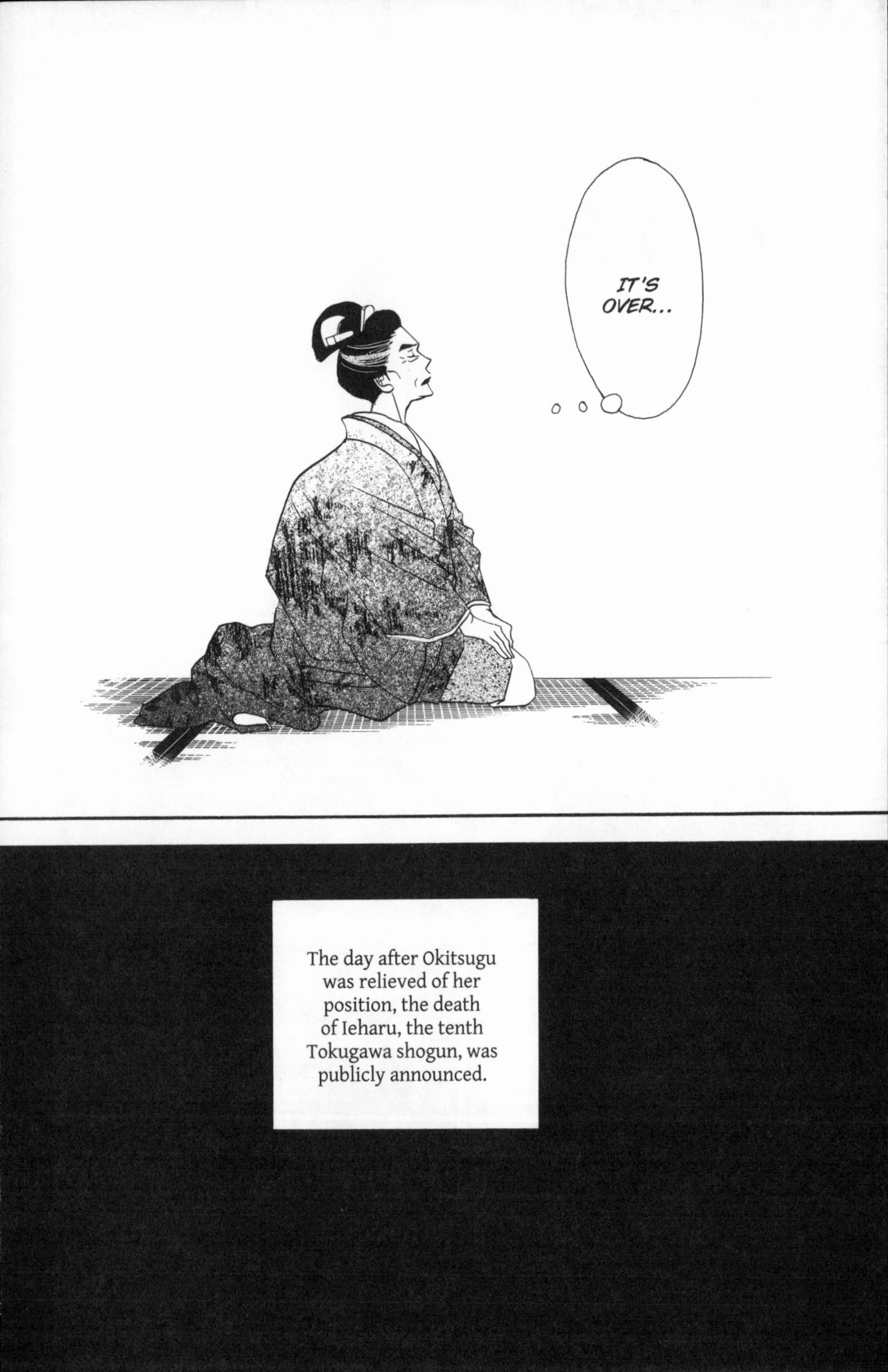
IT'S OVER...
The day after Okitsugu was relieved of her position, the death of Ieharu, the tenth Tokugawa shogun, was publicly announced.

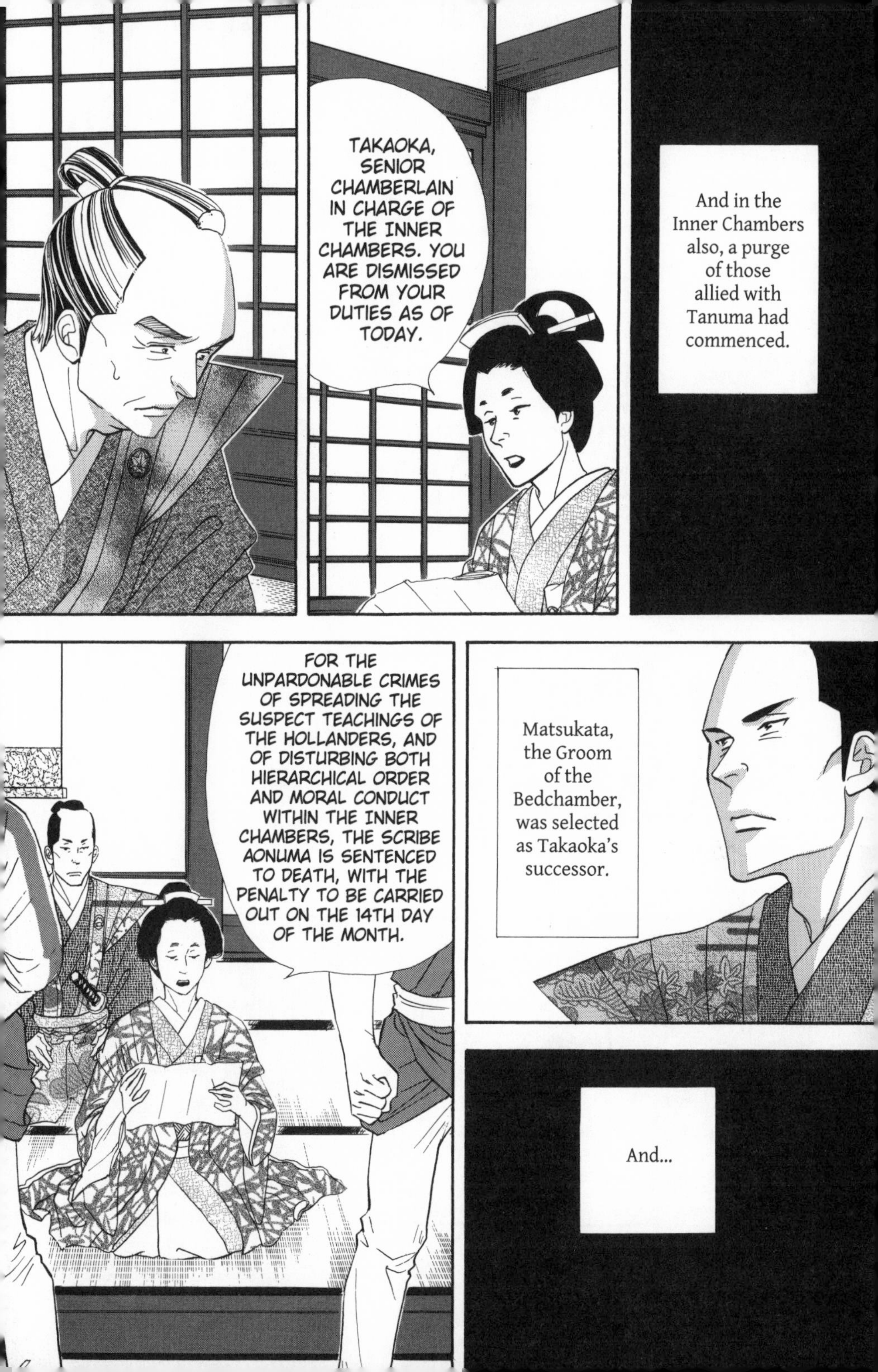
And in the Inner Chambers also, a purge of those allied with Tanuma had commenced.
TAKAOKA, SENIOR CHAMBERLAIN IN CHARGE OF THE INNER CHAMBERS. YOU ARE DISMISSED FROM YOUR DUTIES AS OF TODAY.
Matsukata, the Groom of the Bedchamber, was selected as Takaoka's successor.
And...
FOR THE UNPARDONABLE CRIMES OF SPREADING THE SUSPECT TEACHINGS OF THE HOLLANDERS, AND OF DISTURBING BOTH HIERARCHICAL ORDER AND MORAL CONDUCT WITHIN THE INNER CHAMBERS, THE SCRIBE AONUMA IS SENTENCED TO DEATH, WITH THE PENALTY TO BE CARRIED OUT ON THE 14TH DAY OF THE MONTH.

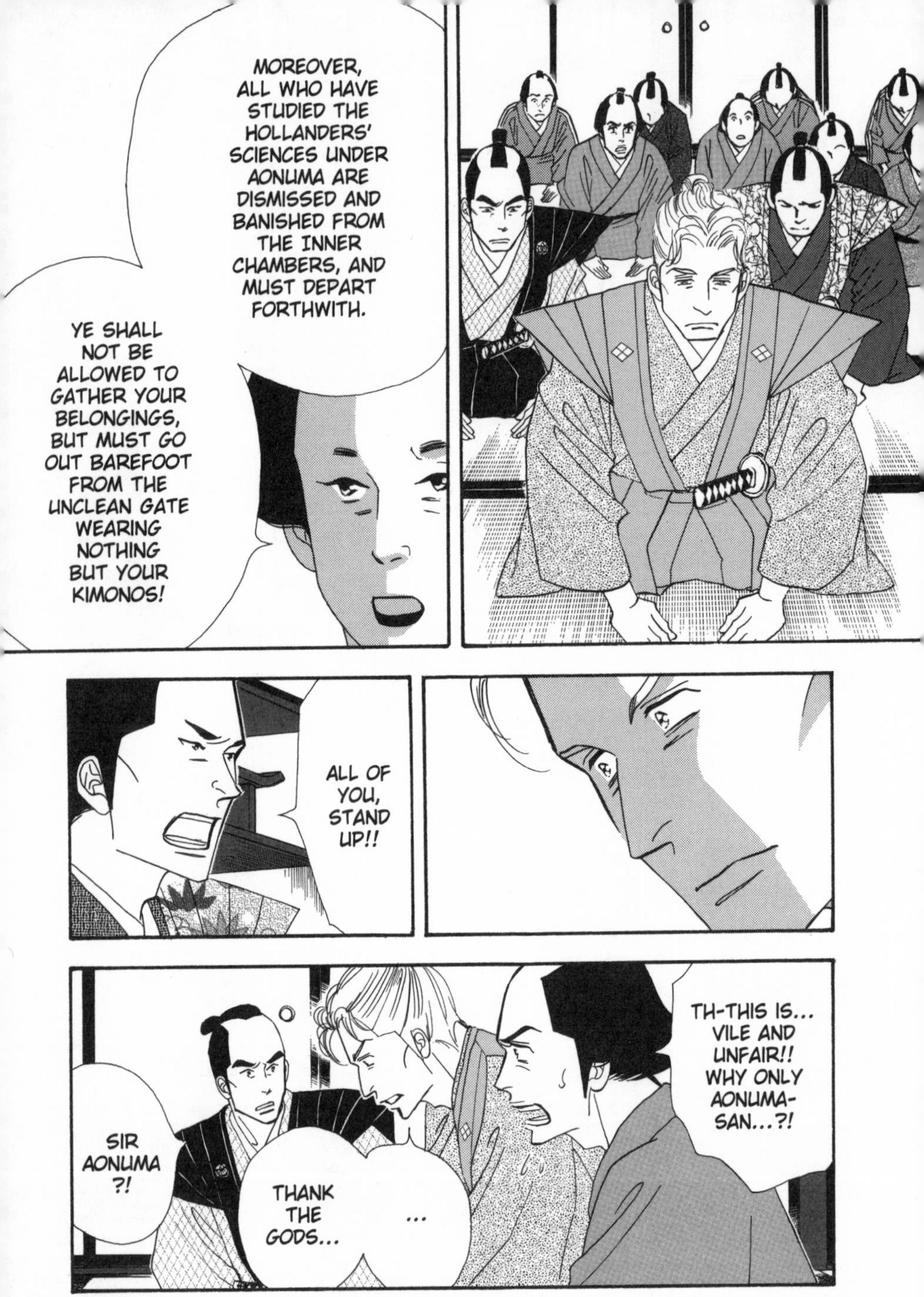
MOREOVER, ALL WHO HAVE STUDIED THE HOLLANDERS' SCIENCES UNDER AONUMA ARE DISMISSED AND BANISHED FROM THE INNER CHAMBERS, AND MUST DEPART FORTHWITH.
YE SHALL NOT BE ALLOWED TO GATHER YOUR BELONGINGS, BUT MUST GO OUT BAREFOOT FROM THE UNCLEAN GATE WEARING NOTHING BUT YOUR KIMONOS!
ALL OF YOU, STAND UP!!
TH-THIS IS... VILE AND UNFAIR!! WHY ONLY AONUMA-SAN...?!
...
THANK THE GODS...
SIR AONUMA?!

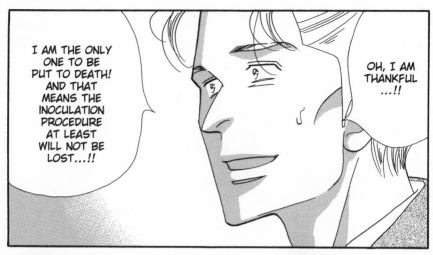

OH, I AM THANKFUL ...!!
I AM THE ONLY ONE TO BE PUT TO DEATH! AND THAT MEANS THE INOCULATION PROCEDURE AT LEAST WILL NOT BE LOST...!!
I SAID, STAND UP, ALL OF YOU! NOW GET UP!!
WHAT ARE YOU SAYING, SIR AONUMA?!
MY FRIENDS!
I HAVE SHARED WITH YOU ALL OF THE KNOWLEDGE I HAD AT MY DISPOSAL.
WHILE THE GERM OF THE MAN-MADE POX THAT WE HAVE KEPT ALIVE MUST ONCE DIE OUT, IF ALL OF YOU KEEP ALIGHT THE FIRE OF RESOLVE, AN OPPORTUNITY WILL ARISE ONCE AGAIN, I AM SURE.
THEREFORE, MY FRIENDS, I PRAY YOU TO STAY ALIVE AND WELL UNTIL THAT DAY ARRIVES!

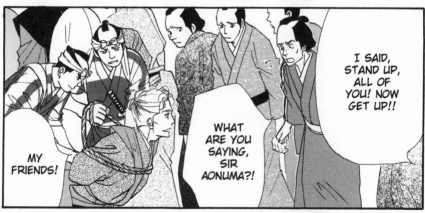

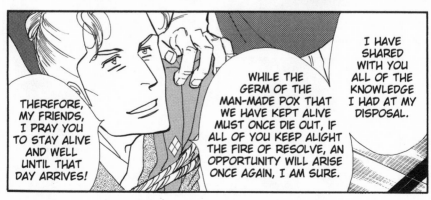

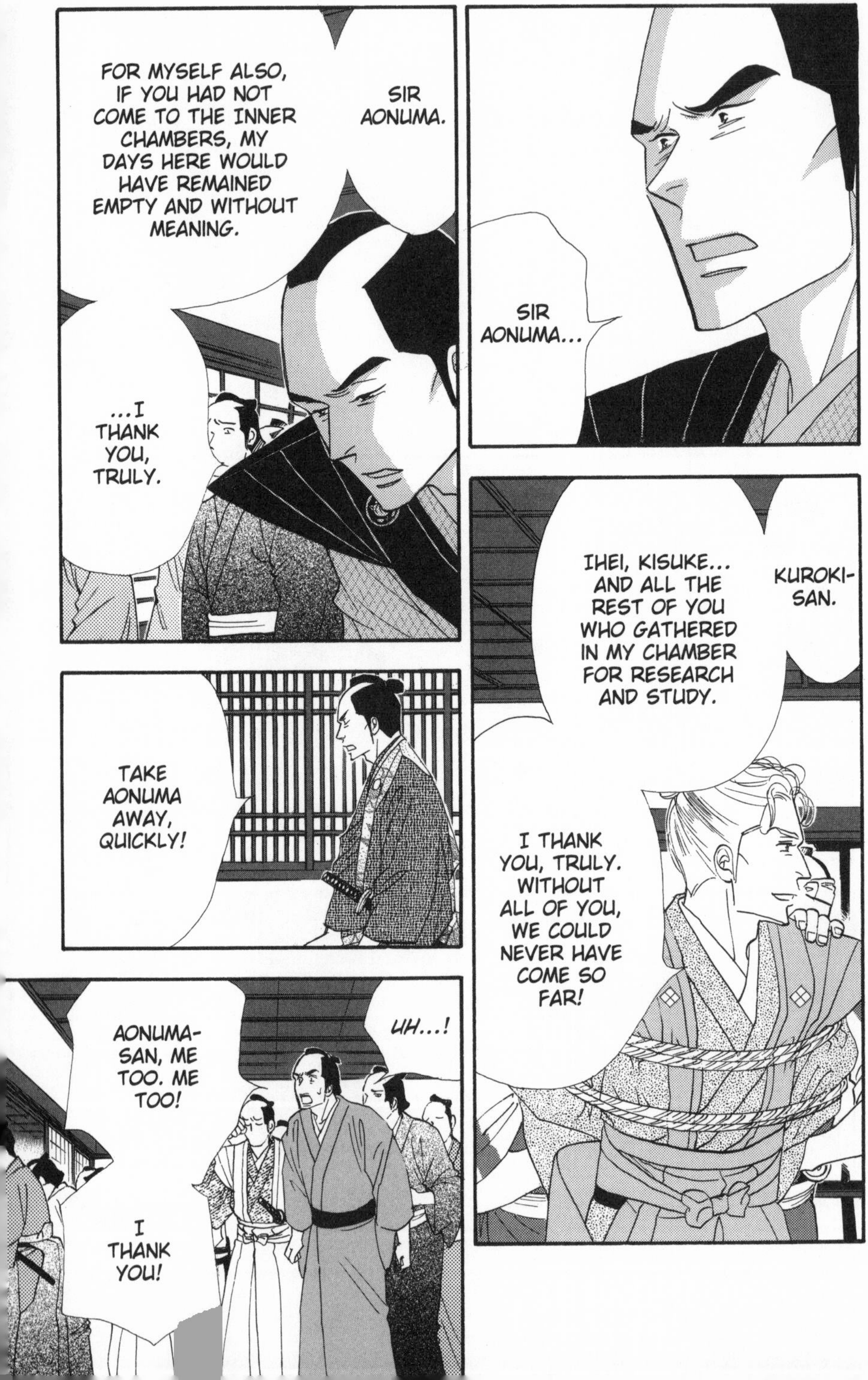
SIR AONUMA...
SIR AONUMA.
FOR MYSELF ALSO, IF YOU HAD NOT COME TO THE INNER CHAMBERS, MY DAYS HERE WOULD HAVE REMAINED EMPTY AND WITHOUT MEANING.
...I THANK YOU, TRULY.
KUROKI-SAN.
IHEI, KISUKE... AND ALL THE REST OF YOU WHO GATHERED IN MY CHAMBER FOR RESEARCH AND STUDY.
I THANK YOU, TRULY. WITHOUT ALL OF YOU, WE COULD NEVER HAVE COME SO FAR!
TAKE AONUMA AWAY, QUICKLY!
UH...!
AONUMA-SAN, ME TOO. ME TOO!
I THANK YOU!

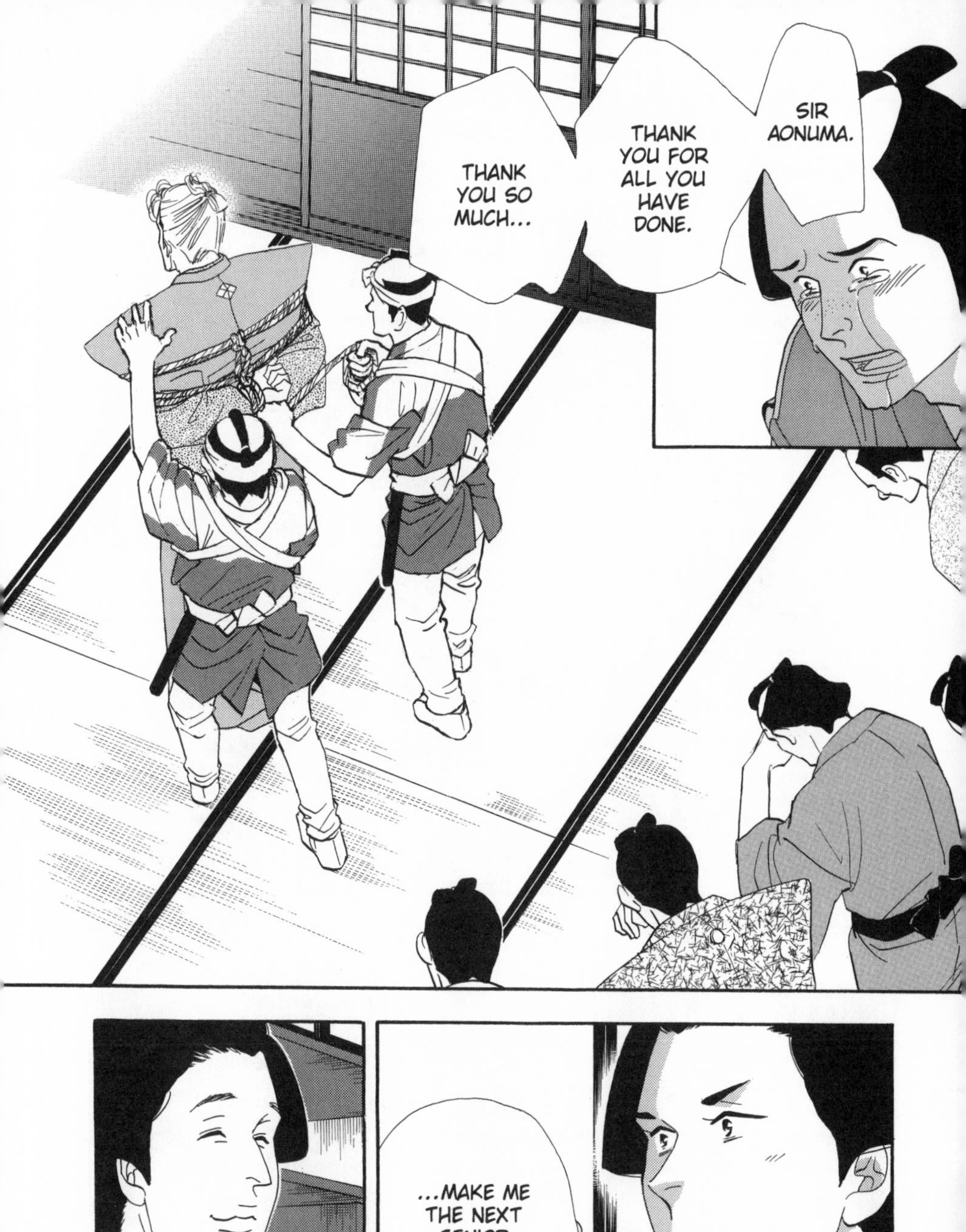
SIR AONUMA.
THANK YOU FOR ALL YOU HAVE DONE.
THANK YOU SO MUCH...
...MAKE ME THE NEXT SENIOR COUNCILLOR?

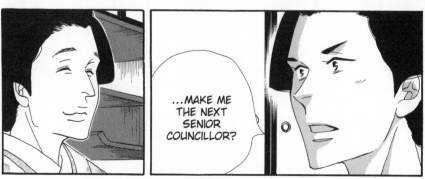

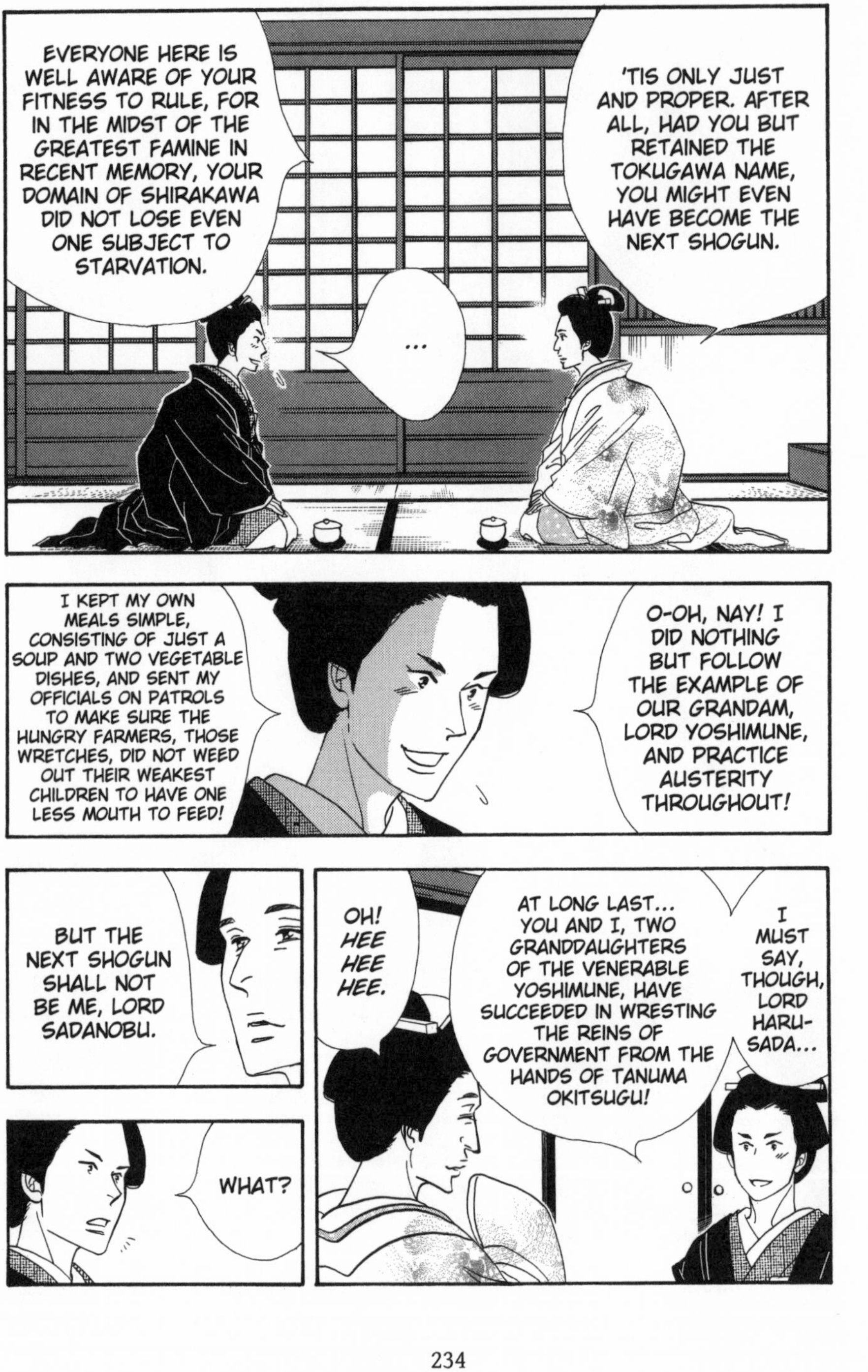
EVERYONE HERE IS WELL AWARE OF YOUR FITNESS TO RULE, FOR IN THE MIDST OF THE GREATEST FAMINE IN RECENT MEMORY, YOUR DOMAIN OF SHIRAKAWA DID NOT LOSE EVEN ONE SUBJECT TO STARVATION.
'TIS ONLY JUST AND PROPER. AFTER ALL, HAD YOU BUT RETAINED THE TOKUGAWA NAME, YOU MIGHT EVEN HAVE BECOME THE NEXT SHOGUN.
...
O-OH, NAY! I DID NOTHING BUT FOLLOW THE EXAMPLE OF OUR GRANDAM, LORD YOSHIMUNE, AND PRACTICE AUSTERITY THROUGHOUT!
I KEPT MY OWN MEALS SIMPLE, CONSISTING OF JUST A SOUP AND TWO VEGETABLE DISHES, AND SENT MY OFFICIALS ON PATROLS TO MAKE SURE THE HUNGRY FARMERS, THOSE WRETCHES, DID NOT WEED OUT THEIR WEAKEST CHILDREN TO HAVE ONE LESS MOUTH TO FEED!
I MUST SAY, THOUGH, LORD HARUSADA...
AT LONG LAST... YOU AND I, TWO GRANDDAUGHTERS OF THE VENERABLE YOSHIMUNE, HAVE SUCCEEDED IN WRESTING THE REINS OF GOVERNMENT FROM THE HANDS OF TANUMA OKITSUGU!
OH! HEE HEE HEE.
BUT THE NEXT SHOGUN SHALL NOT BE ME, LORD SADANOBU.
WHAT?

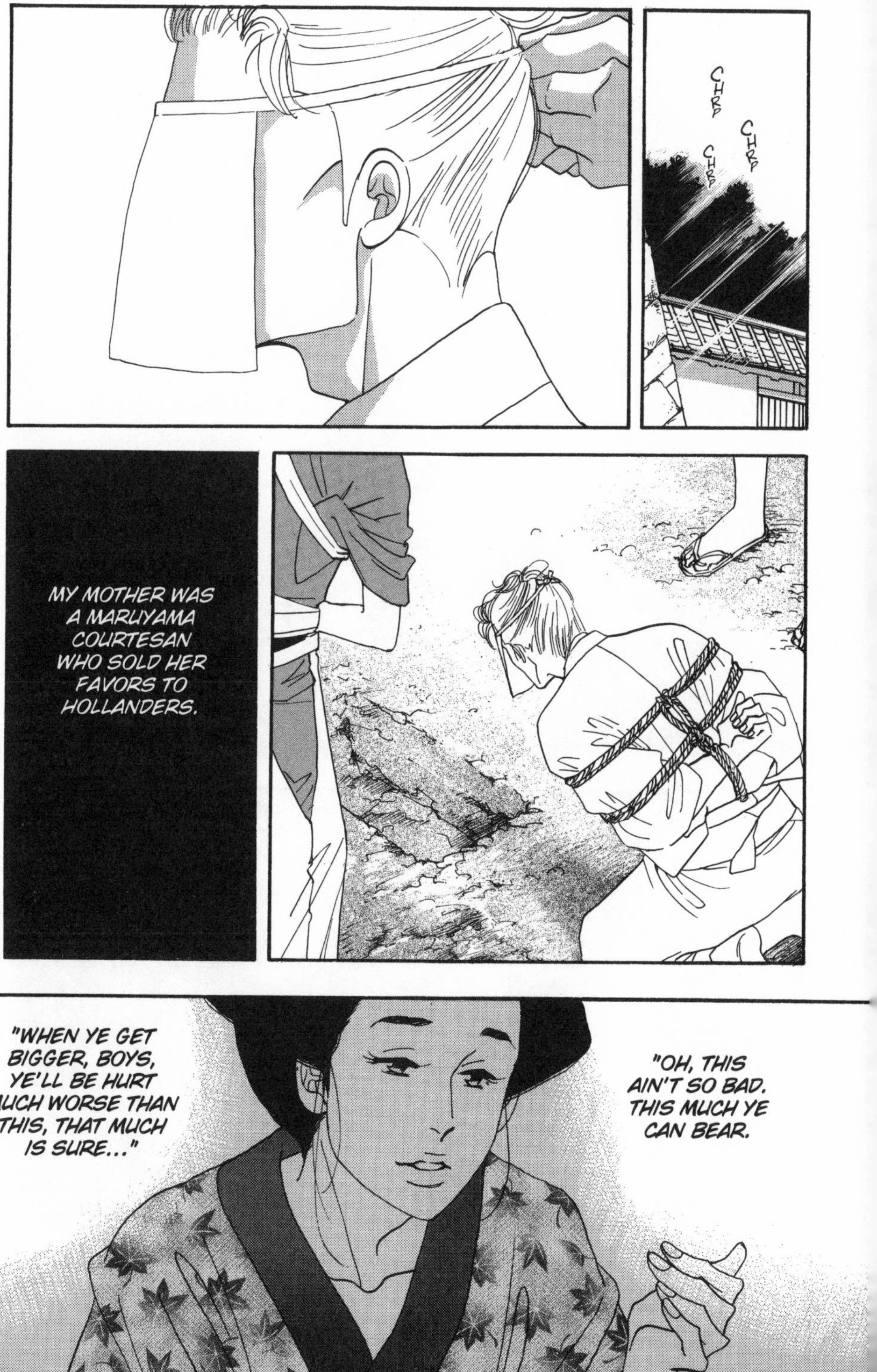
CHRP
CHRP
CHRP
MY MOTHER WAS A MARUYAMA COURTESAN WHO SOLD HER FAVORS TO HOLLANDERS.
"OH, THIS AIN'T SO BAD. THIS MUCH YE CAN BEAR.
"WHEN YE GET BIGGER, BOYS, YE'LL BE HURT MUCH WORSE THAN THIS, THAT MUCH IS SURE..."

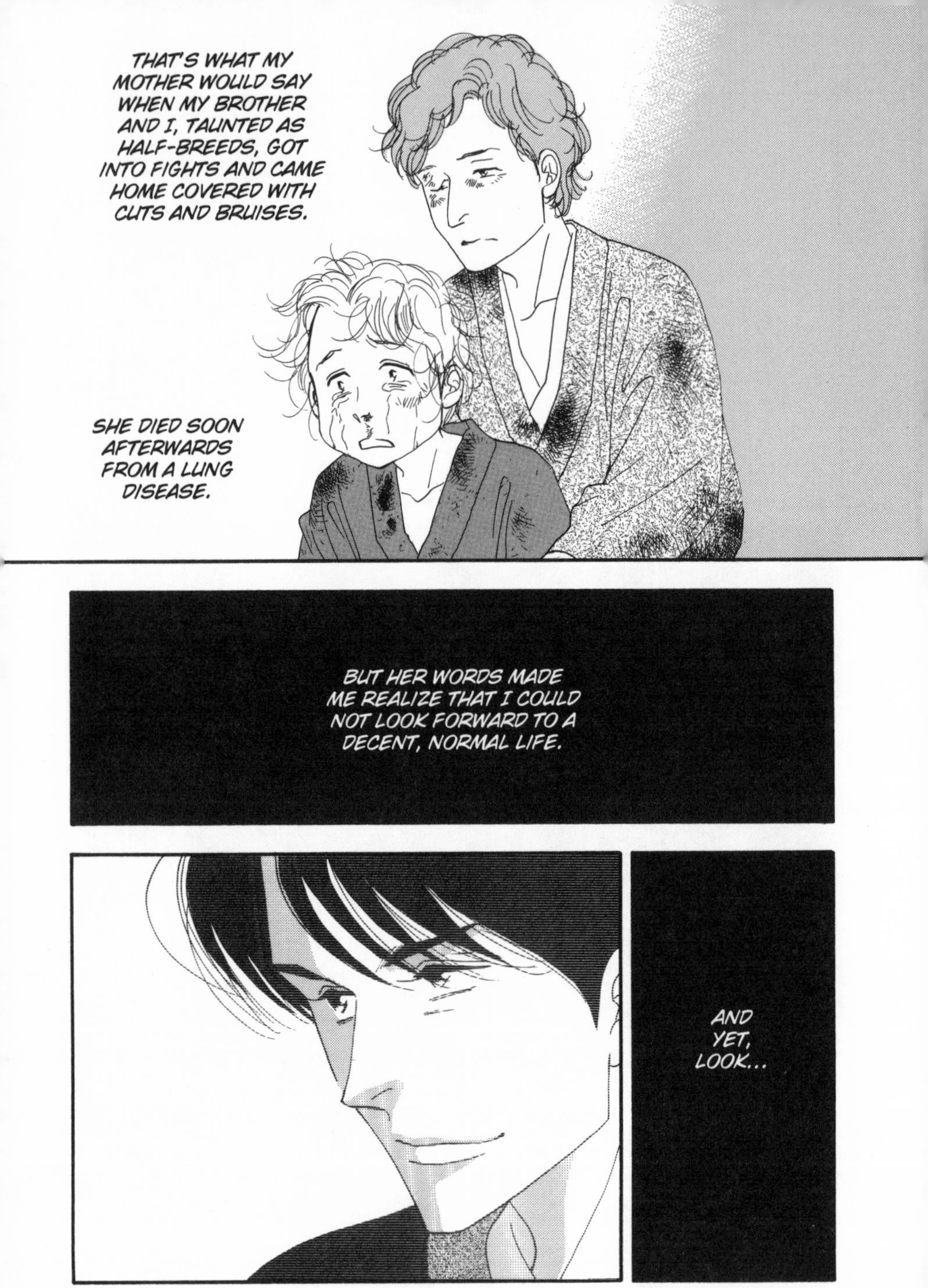
THAT'S WHAT MY MOTHER WOULD SAY WHEN MY BROTHER AND I, TAUNTED AS HALF-BREEDS, GOT INTO FIGHTS AND CAME HOME COVERED WITH CUTS AND BRUISES.
SHE DIED SOON AFTERWARDS FROM A LUNG DISEASE.
BUT HER WORDS MADE ME REALIZE THAT I COULD NOT LOOK FORWARD TO A DECENT, NORMAL LIFE.
AND YET, LOOK...

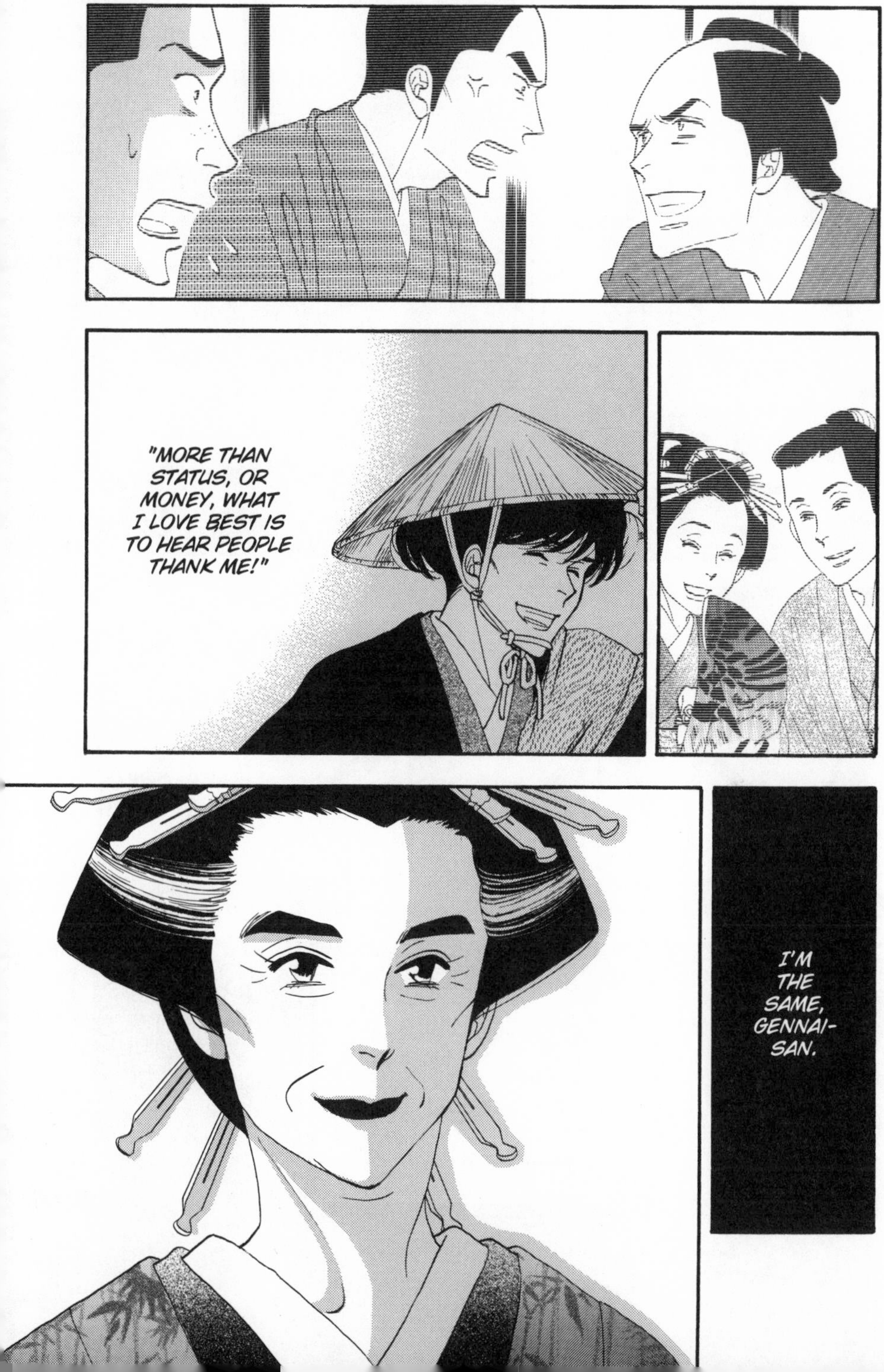
"MORE THAN STATUS, OR MONEY, WHAT I LOVE BEST IS TO HEAR PEOPLE THANK ME!"
I'M THE SAME, GENNAI-SAN.

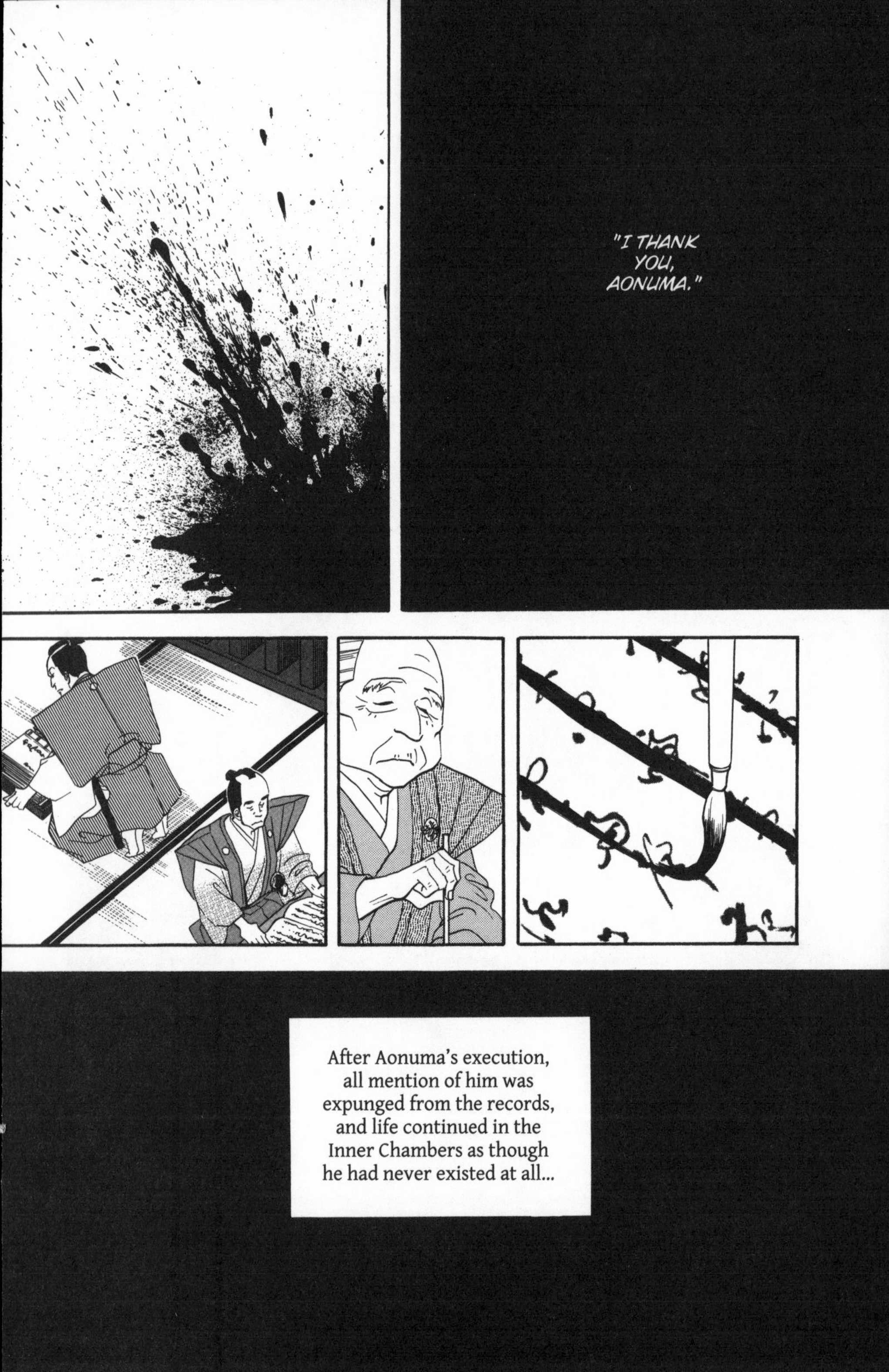
"I THANK YOU, AONUMA."
After Aonuma's execution, all mention of him was expunged from the records, and life continued in the Inner Chambers as though he had never existed at all...

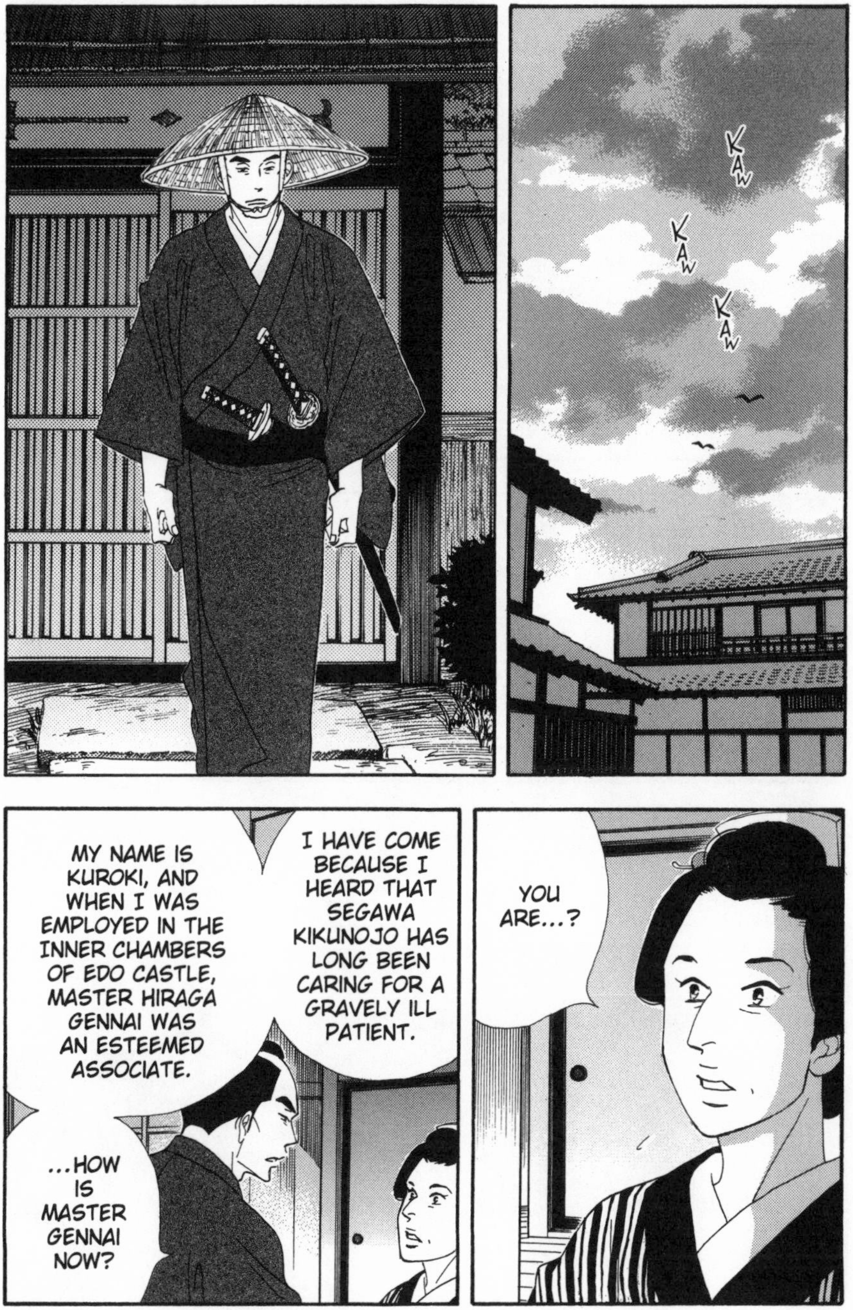
KAW
KAW
KAW
YOU ARE...?
I HAVE COME BECAUSE I HEARD THAT SEGAWA KIKUNOJO HAS LONG BEEN CARING FOR A GRAVELY ILL PATIENT.
MY NAME IS KUROKI, AND WHEN I WAS EMPLOYED IN THE INNER CHAMBERS OF EDO CASTLE, MASTER HIRAGA GENNAI WAS AN ESTEEMED ASSOCIATE.
...HOW IS MASTER GENNAI NOW?

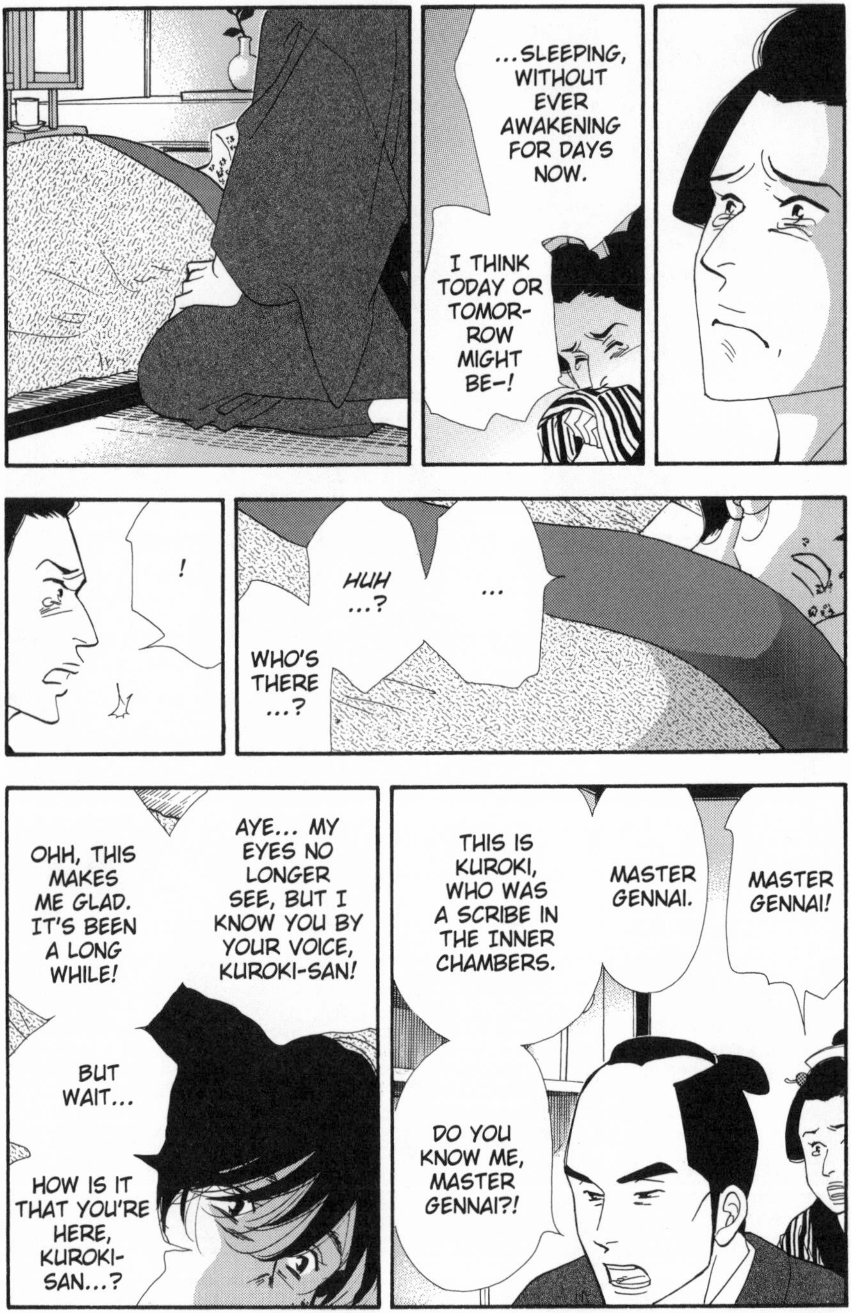
...SLEEPING, WITHOUT EVER AWAKENING FOR DAYS NOW.
I THINK TODAY OR TOMORROW MIGHT BE-!
...
HUH ...?
WHO'S THERE ...?
!
MASTER GENNAI!
MASTER GENNAI.
THIS IS KUROKI, WHO WAS A SCRIBE IN THE INNER CHAMBERS.
DO YOU KNOW ME, MASTER GENNAI?!
AYE... MY EYES NO LONGER SEE, BUT I KNOW YOU BY YOUR VOICE, KUROKI-SAN!
OHH, THIS MAKES ME GLAD. IT'S BEEN A LONG WHILE!
BUT WAIT...
HOW IS IT THAT YOU'RE HERE, KUROKI-SAN...?

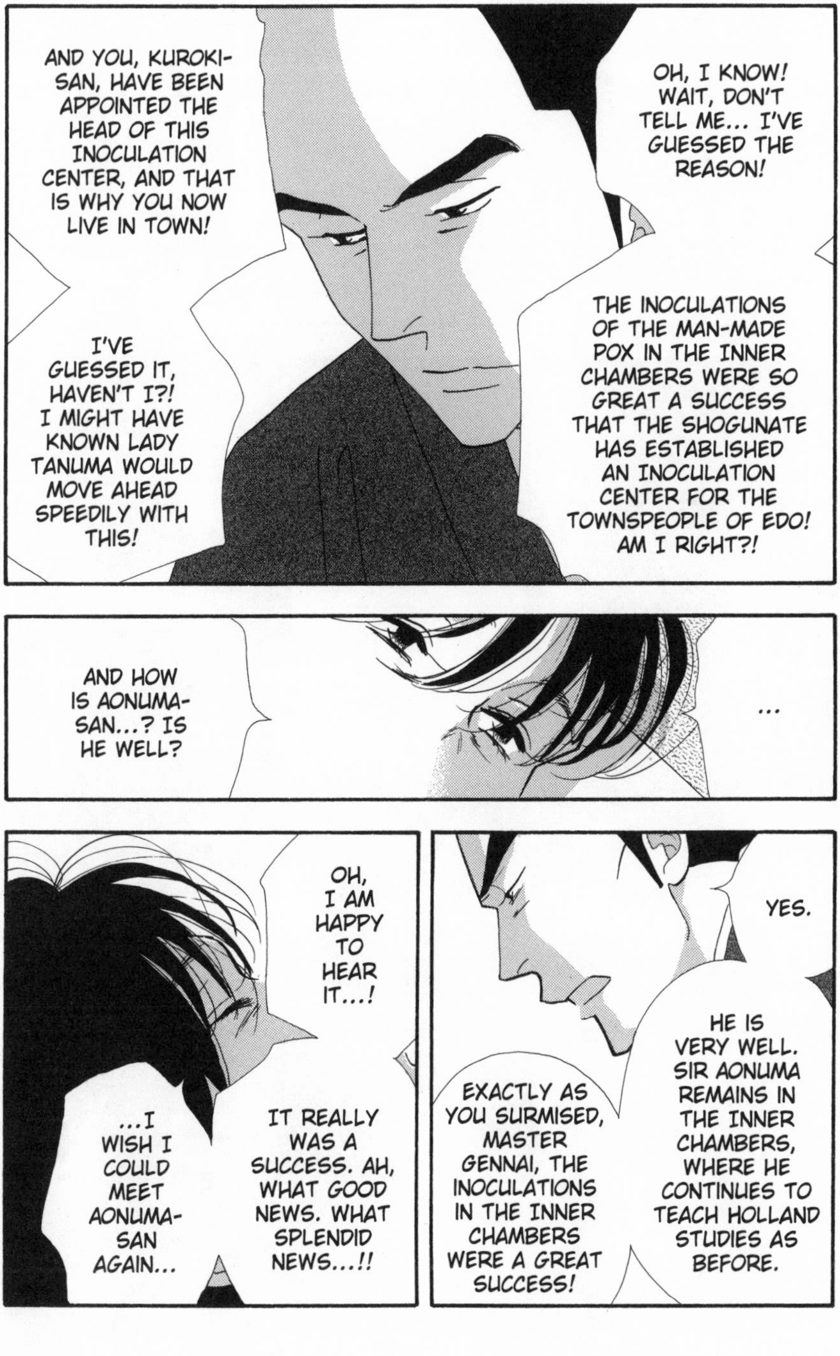
OH, I KNOW! WAIT, DON'T TELL ME... I'VE GUESSED THE REASON!
THE INOCULATIONS OF THE MAN-MADE POX IN THE INNER CHAMBERS WERE SO GREAT A SUCCESS THAT THE SHOGUNATE HAS ESTABLISHED AN INOCULATION CENTER FOR THE TOWNSPEOPLE OF EDO! AM I RIGHT?!
AND YOU, KUROKI-SAN, HAVE BEEN APPOINTED THE HEAD OF THIS INOCULATION CENTER, AND THAT IS WHY YOU NOW LIVE IN TOWN!
I'VE GUESSED IT, HAVEN'T I?! I MIGHT HAVE KNOWN LADY TANUMA WOULD MOVE AHEAD SPEEDILY WITH THIS!
...
AND HOW IS AONUMA-SAN...? IS HE WELL?
YES.
HE IS VERY WELL. SIR AONUMA REMAINS IN THE INNER CHAMBERS, WHERE HE CONTINUES TO TEACH HOLLAND STUDIES AS BEFORE.
EXACTLY AS YOU SURMISED, MASTER GENNAI, THE INOCULATIONS IN THE INNER CHAMBERS WERE A GREAT SUCCESS!
OH, I AM HAPPY TO HEAR IT...!
IT REALLY WAS A SUCCESS. AH, WHAT GOOD NEWS. WHAT SPLENDID NEWS...!!
...I WISH I COULD MEET AONUMA-SAN AGAIN...

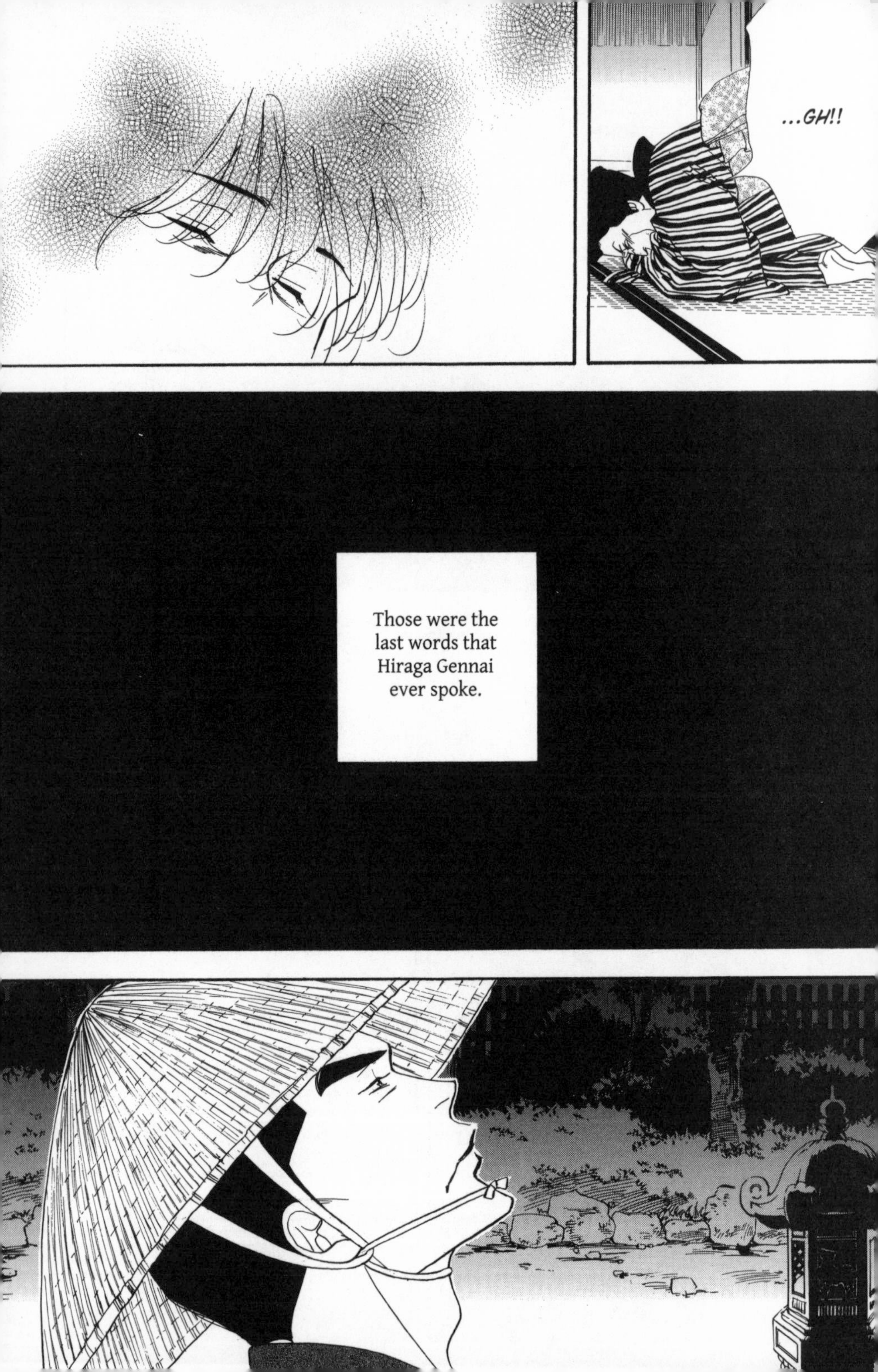
...GH!!
Those were the last words that Hiraga Gennai ever spoke.

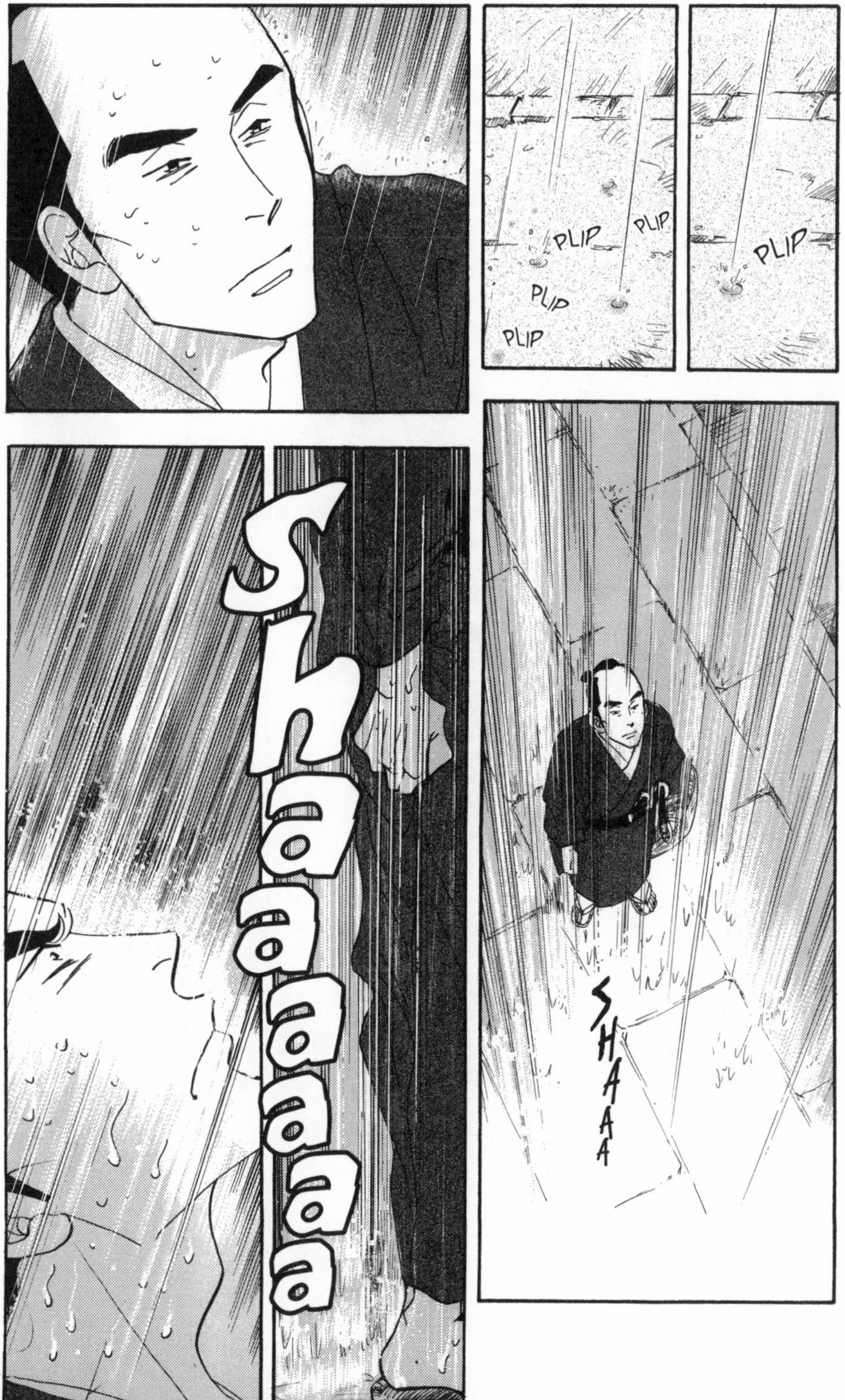
PLIP
PLIP
PLIP
PLIP
PLIP
SHAAAA
Shaaaaaaa

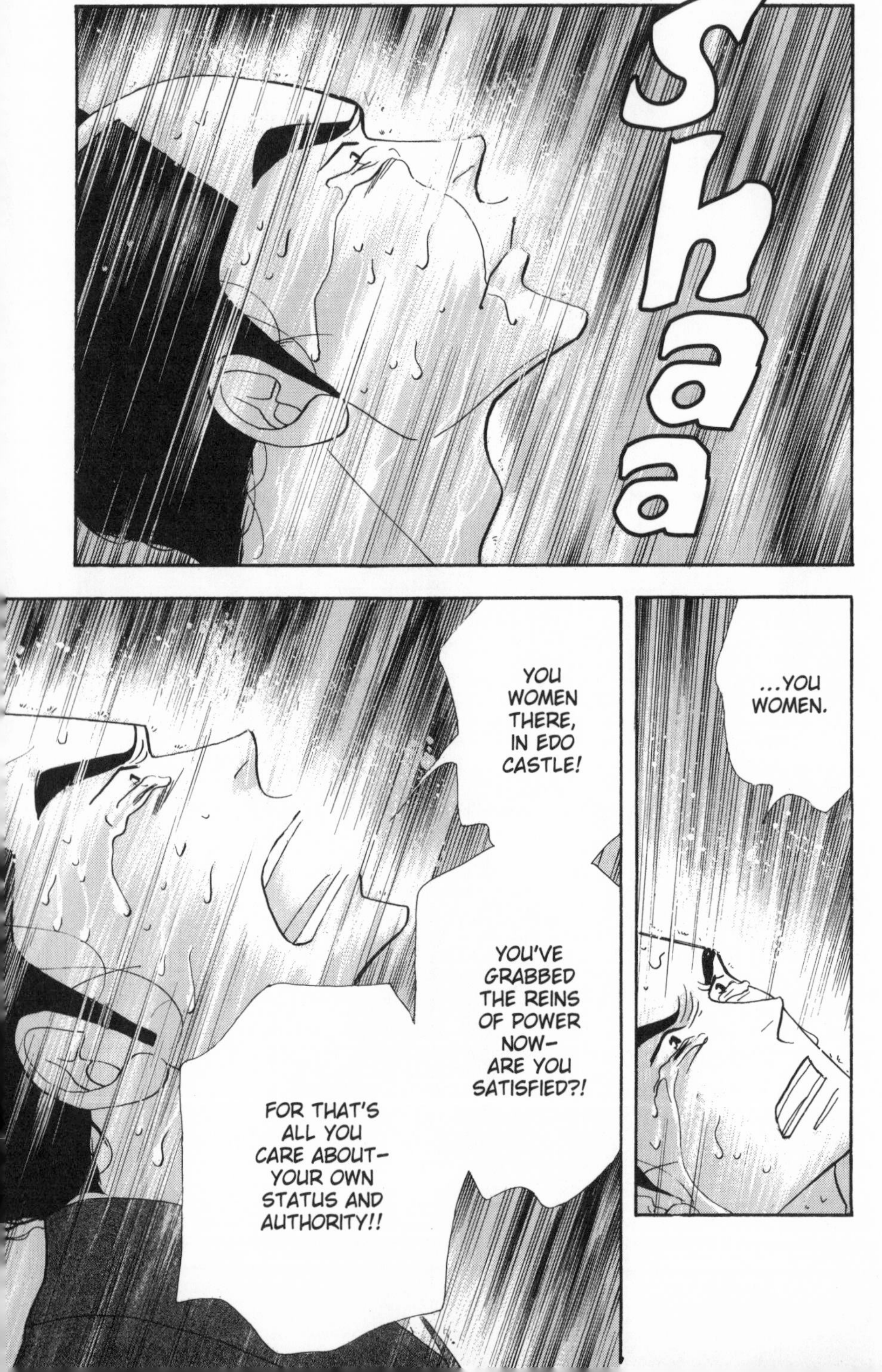
Shaa
...YOU WOMEN.
YOU WOMEN THERE, IN EDO CASTLE!
YOU'VE GRABBED THE REINS OF POWER NOW- ARE YOU SATISFIED?!
FOR THAT'S ALL YOU CARE ABOUT- YOUR OWN STATUS AND AUTHORITY!!

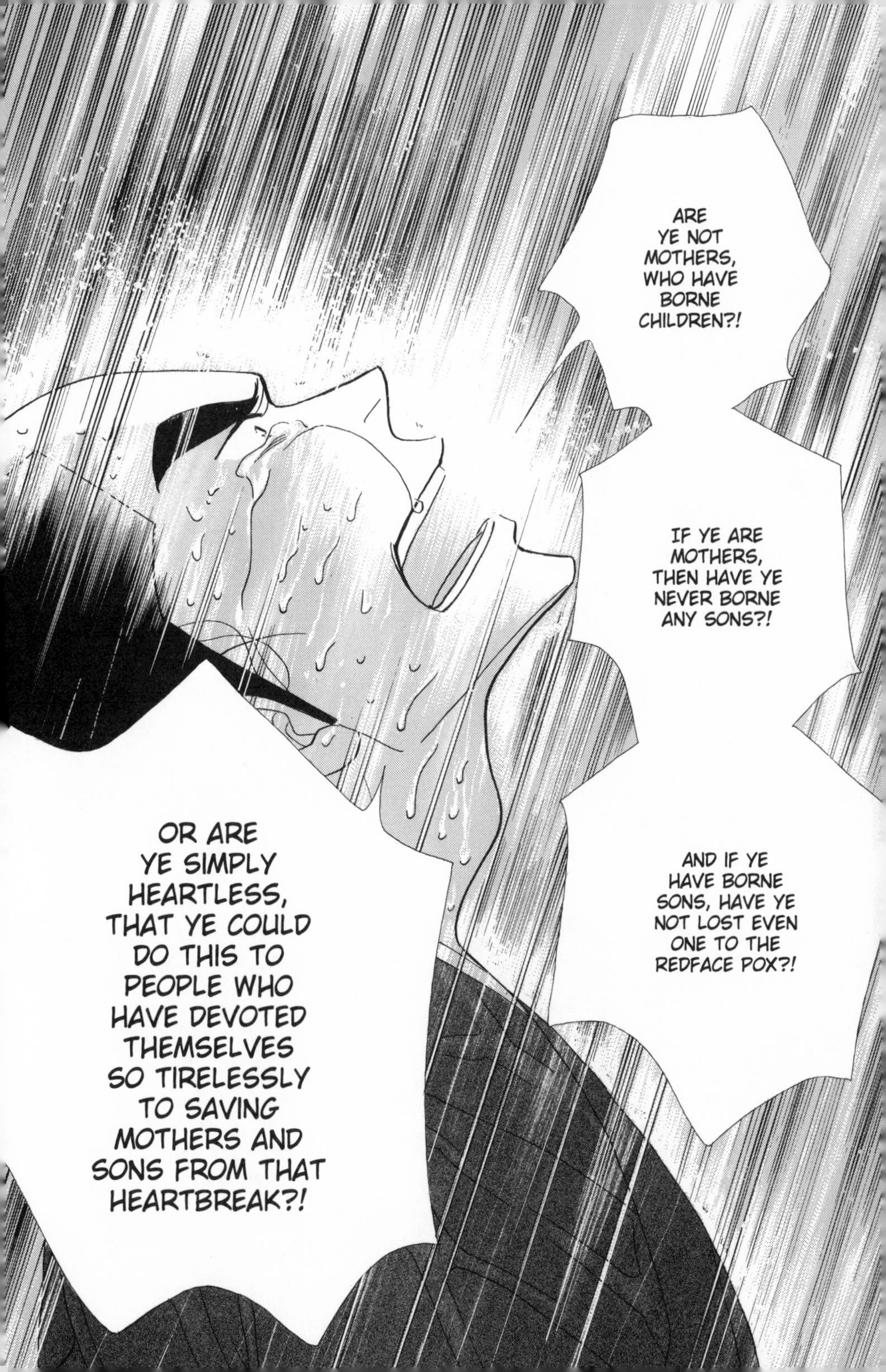
ARE YE NOT MOTHERS, WHO HAVE BORNE CHILDREN?!
IF YE ARE MOTHERS, THEN HAVE YE NEVER BORNE ANY SONS?!
AND IF YE HAVE BORNE SONS, HAVE YE NOT LOST EVEN ONE TO THE REDFACE POX?!
OR ARE YE SIMPLY HEARTLESS, THAT YE COULD DO THIS TO PEOPLE WHO HAVE DEVOTED THEMSELVES SO TIRELESSLY TO SAVING MOTHERS AND SONS FROM THAT HEARTBREAK?!

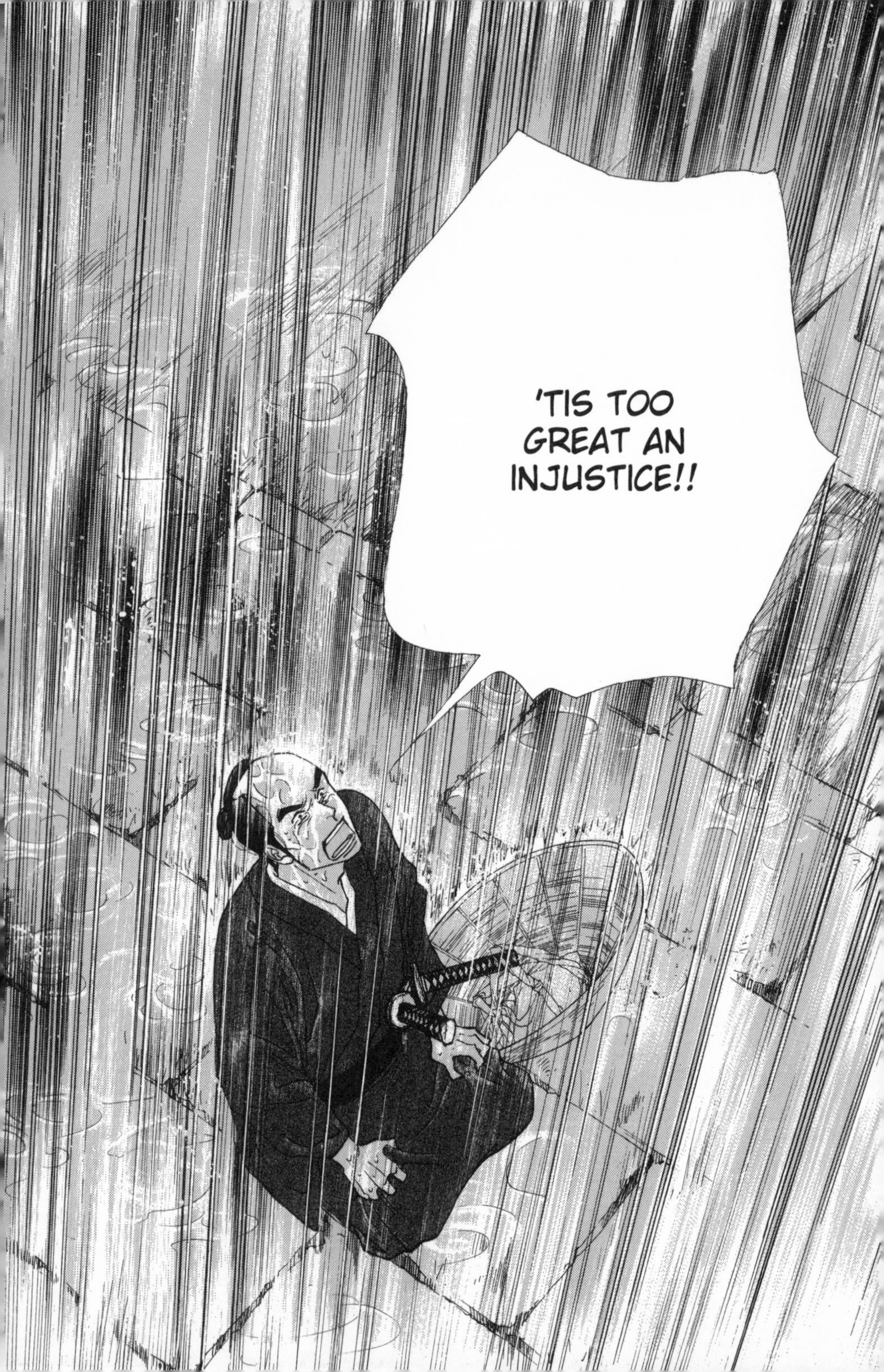
'TIS TOO GREAT AN INJUSTICE!!

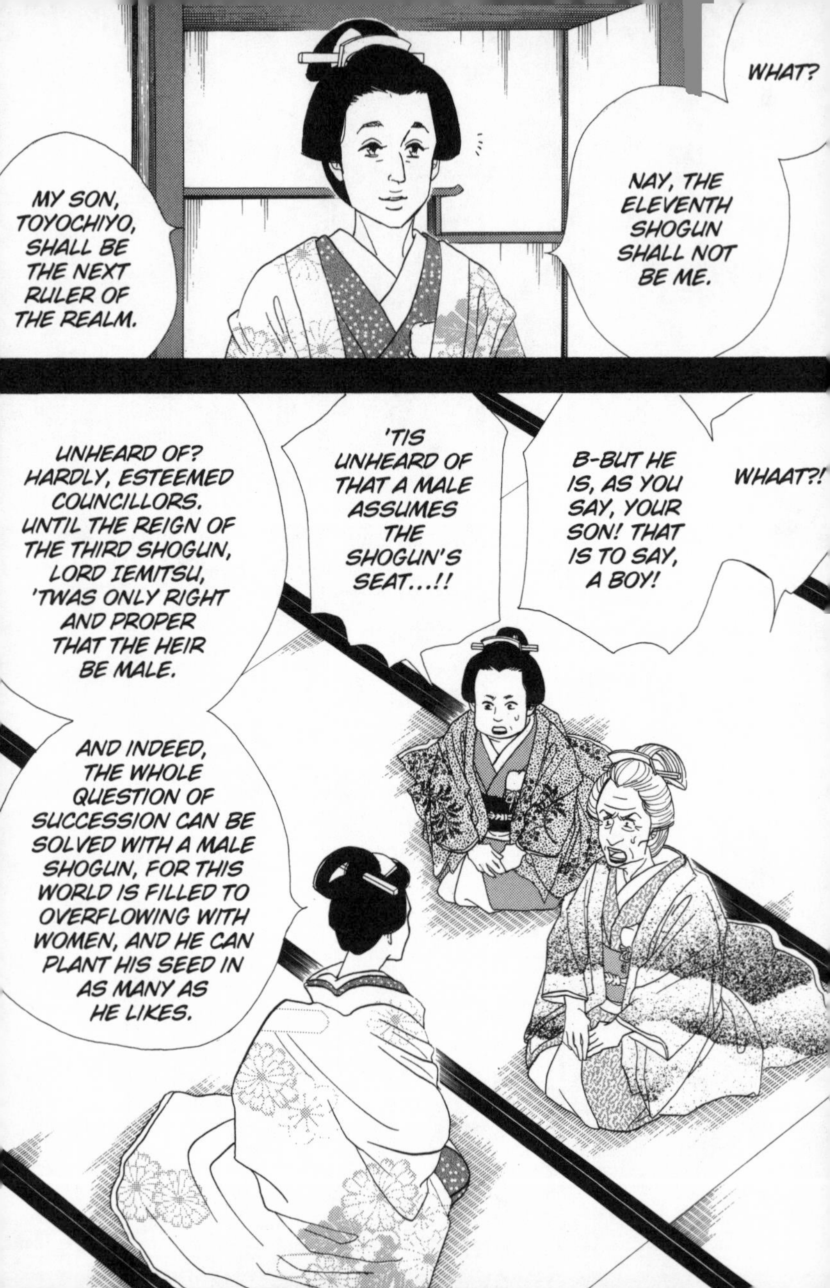
WHAT?
NAY, THE ELEVENTH SHOGUN SHALL NOT BE ME.
MY SON, TOYOCHIYO, SHALL BE THE NEXT RULER OF THE REALM.
WHAAT?!
B-BUT HE IS, AS YOU SAY, YOUR SON! THAT IS TO SAY, A BOY!
'TIS UNHEARD OF THAT A MALE ASSUMES THE SHOGUN'S SEAT...!!
UNHEARD OF? HARDLY, ESTEEMED COUNCILLORS. UNTIL THE REIGN OF THE THIRD SHOGUN, LORD IEMITSU, 'TWAS ONLY RIGHT AND PROPER THAT THE HEIR BE MALE.
AND INDEED, THE WHOLE QUESTION OF SUCCESSION CAN BE SOLVED WITH A MALE SHOGUN, FOR THIS WORLD IS FILLED TO OVERFLOWING WITH WOMEN, AND HE CAN PLANT HIS SEED IN AS MANY AS HE LIKES.

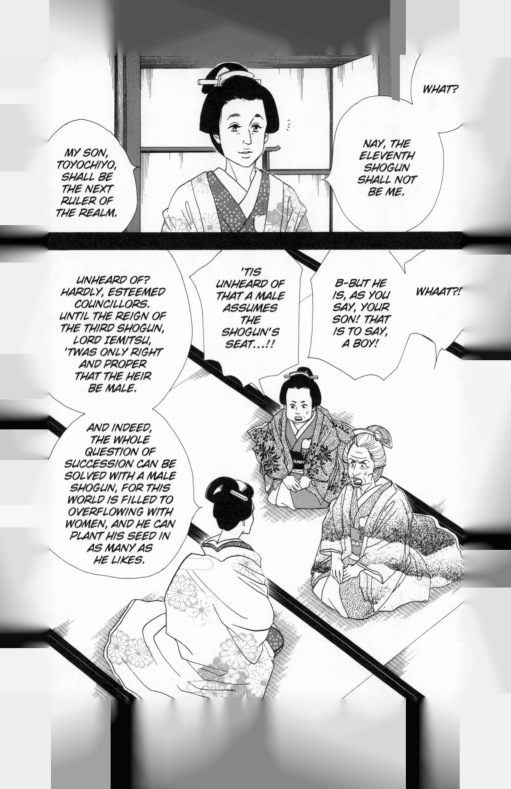

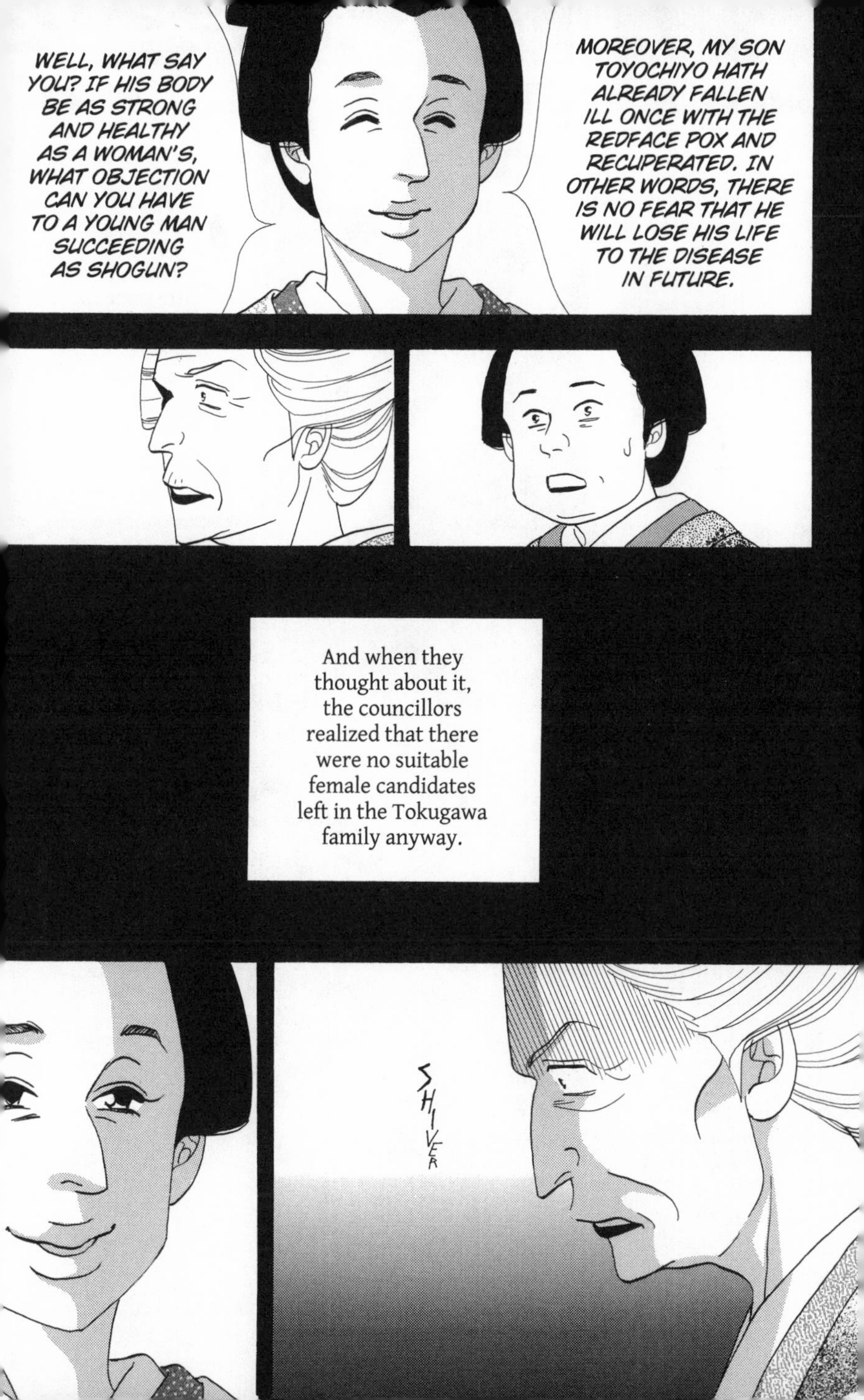
MOREOVER, MY SON TOYOCHIYO HATH ALREADY FALLEN ILL ONCE WITH THE REDFACE POX AND RECUPERATED. IN OTHER WORDS, THERE IS NO FEAR THAT HE WILL LOSE HIS LIFE TO THE DISEASE IN FUTURE.
WELL, WHAT SAY YOU? IF HIS BODY BE AS STRONG AND HEALTHY AS A WOMAN'S, WHAT OBJECTION CAN YOU HAVE TO A YOUNG MAN SUCCEEDING AS SHOGUN?
And when they thought about it, the councillors realized that there were no suitable female candidates left in the Tokugawa family anyway.
SHIVER

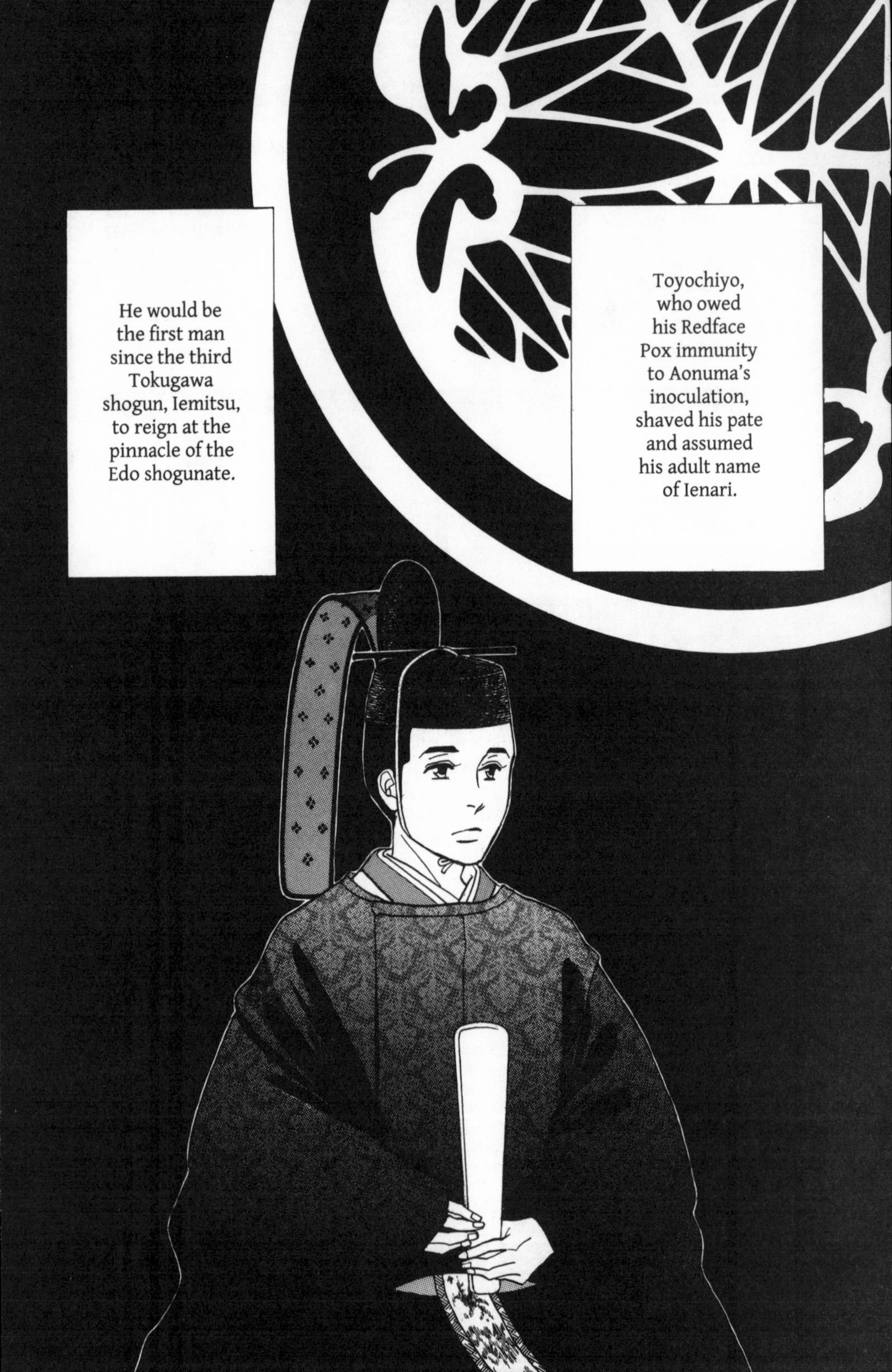
Toyochiyo, who owed his Redface Pox immunity to Aonuma's inoculation, shaved his pate and assumed his adult name of Ienari.
He would be the first man since the third Tokugawa shogun, Iemitsu, to reign at the pinnacle of the Edo shogunate.

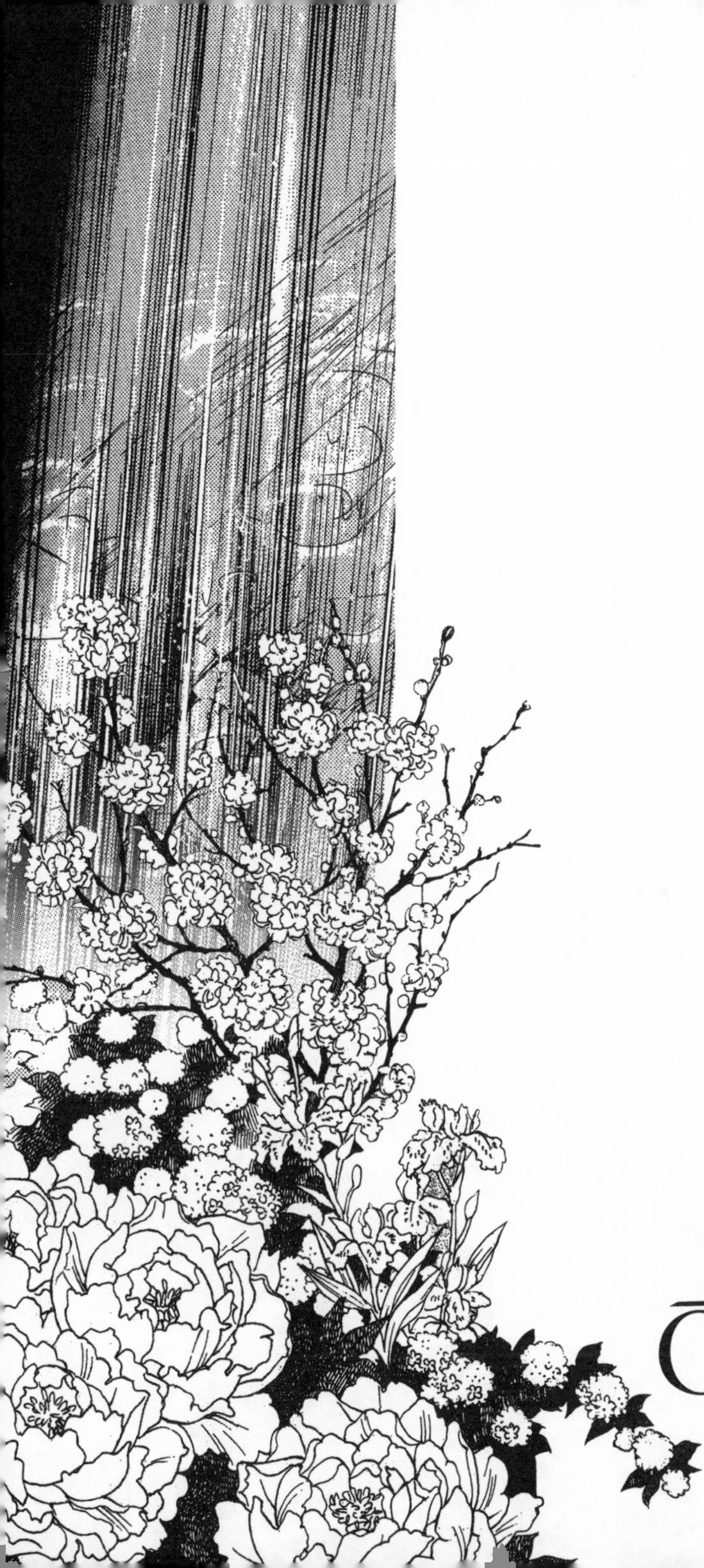

Ōoku

THE INNER CHAMBERS

Ōoku: The Inner Chambers

VOLUME 10 · END NOTES

by Akemi Wegmüller

Panel 9, panel 2 · NATTO
A traditional Japanese staple of fermented soybeans. High in protein and other essential nutrients, *natto* has a rather slimy texture and is an acquired taste. People in Kanto eat it for breakfast.

Panel 11, panel 1 · SHIJIMI, PICKLES
Shijimi are tiny freshwater clams. The pickles are *nukazuke* (salted vegetables that have been fermented in a bed of rice bran).

Page 17, panel 1 · KABAYAKI
Grilled eel such as Zenjiro made in volume 8.

Page 17, panel 1 · DAY OF THE OX
The Ox is the second of the twelve days of the Chinese calendar. This sales pitch for eels actually happened, although the historical Gennai was unlikely to have been involved.

Page 37, panel 1 · BERIBERI
The name given to the effects of a nutritional deficiency of vitamin B1 (thiamine). In Japan, the deficiency was often caused by relying on polished rice, in which the husk and source of thiamine is removed. Among other symptoms, beriberi damages the nervous system, which can cause pain or even paralysis.

Page 43, panel 4 · TENJIN-SAMA
A deification of Sugawara no Michizane (a scholar, poet and politician of the Heian Era) and the god of education in the Shinto pantheon.

Page 44, panel 3 · TENGU
Tengu are long-nosed goblins associated with magic and mischief. The historical Gennai was called *tengu kozo* as a child because of his inventiveness.

Page 59. panel 2 · THE MASTER SAID...
From *Analects of Confucius.*

Page 80, panel 2 · SHIMOUSA
The name of a province roughly equivalent to northern Chiba Prefecture today and site of Inba swamp.

Page 142, panel 1 · KINSHIBAI
A type of St. John's Wort, *hypericum patulum.* St. John's Wort is a traditional treatment for kidney stones and has been shown to improve kidney health and help reduce bleeding from kidney stones.

Page 144, panel 3 · NENTEI
A youth who is the lover of an older man (his *nenja*) who is also his mentor, much like knights and pages in the Western tradition. Although exclusive, the relationship was dissolved when the youth reached adulthood.

Page 151, panel 5 · OHSHU PROVINCE
Ohshu is roughly the area known as the Tohoku region today.

Page 156, panel 2 · UNCLEAN GATE
The Unclean Gate is where dead bodies were carried out. Dismissed or disgraced attendants also exited the castle through this gate.

CREATOR BIOGRAPHY

FUMI YOSHINAGA

Fumi Yoshinaga is a Tokyo-born manga creator who debuted in 1994 with *Tsuki to Sandaru* (*The Moon and the Sandals*). Yoshinaga has won numerous awards, including the 2009 Osamu Tezuka Cultural Prize for *Ōoku*, the 2002 Kodansha Manga Award for her series *Antique Bakery* and the 2006 Japan Media Arts Festival Excellence Award for *Ōoku*. She was also nominated for the 2008 Eisner Award for Best Writer/Artist.